Los Angeles
& Southern California

written and researched by

JD Dickey

www.roughguides.com

CityNational Bank

Contents

Sun, sand and surf colour section following p.112

The Sounds of LA colour section following p.272

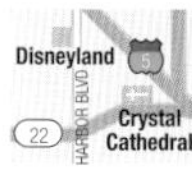

Colour maps following p.400

◀◀ Rodeo Drive ◀ The LA skyline

Introduction to

Los Angeles & Southern California

It's almost impossible not to hold an opinion about Los Angeles, a city loved and scorned in equal measure. Some see it as an environmental and cultural quagmire, its freeways, smog and Hollywood drivel polluting countless bodies and minds. Others consider it the lodestar of urban America, its great diversity of peoples, culture and geography woven into a rich tapestry that's far too complex to describe or dismiss in a few words. Indeed, despite the city's problems, for many residents there's no place in the country or world like it, a veritable crazy quilt of light, colour and energy.

More relaxed altogether than LA itself, the surrounding region of Southern California is well known for its *laissez-faire* lifestyle of suntanning and surfing along endless beaches, posing in the latest fashions along palm-lined boulevards, and skiing and hiking in the mountains above it all. The region's urban nodes of San Diego, Santa Barbara and Palm Springs are among the wealthiest communities in the nation, and flaunt it quite openly. But there's more to the region than the stereotype – the craggy Indian canyons, sun-blasted deserts and ocean coves are a haven from human bustle, and the cities stimulate the eye, mind and palate with good museums, restaurants and cultural treasures.

The region's centrepiece, Los Angeles is a model for modern city development, having traded urban centralization for suburban sprawl, and high-rise corporate towers for strip malls. Although the city had a significant Spanish and Mexican presence through the mid-nineteenth century, it was only after California became an American state in 1850 that LA began to grow into a metropolis, marketing itself as a sunny arcadia full of orange groves, clean, fresh air and wide-open space. When the film and aerospace industries were added to the mix in the early twentieth century, the place truly boomed, eventually displacing Chicago as America's second-largest city. Nowadays, LA's explosive population growth has brought a tumult of peoples and languages from nearly every corner of the earth to a freeway-draped landscape of glaring neon signs and towering palm trees.

The largest port in North America, LA is a burly centre for transpacific trade and a dominant financial hub. It's a magnet for immigrants with newcomers from Armenia, Zimbabwe and everywhere in between. And, the metropolis has slowly accommodated its multicultural character; Mexican-Americans in particular, whether newly arrived or of ancient lineage, are doing much to remind the city of its Hispanic origins, and have discovered the benefits of greater political power in recent years.

Though there's plenty to see here, Los Angeles and Southern California do not reward an attraction-oriented itinerary of dutiful trotting from one museum or exhibit to the next. While there are world-class sights on offer – the Getty Center and San Diego Zoo foremost among them – the big-ticket sights in most of the region's cities tend to be separated by vast distances, and you'll doubtless spend much of your time on the freeway if you try to see them all. Rather, the best approach to the area is to experience those things that really make the area a great place to spend a week – especially the free-spirited bars, upscale restaurants, dynamic clubs, hedonistic beaches, and quirky shopping strips and boardwalks.

Surprisingly, many of these attractions cluster in fairly compact districts, from Venice to Old Pasadena in Los Angeles, or Coronado to La Jolla in San

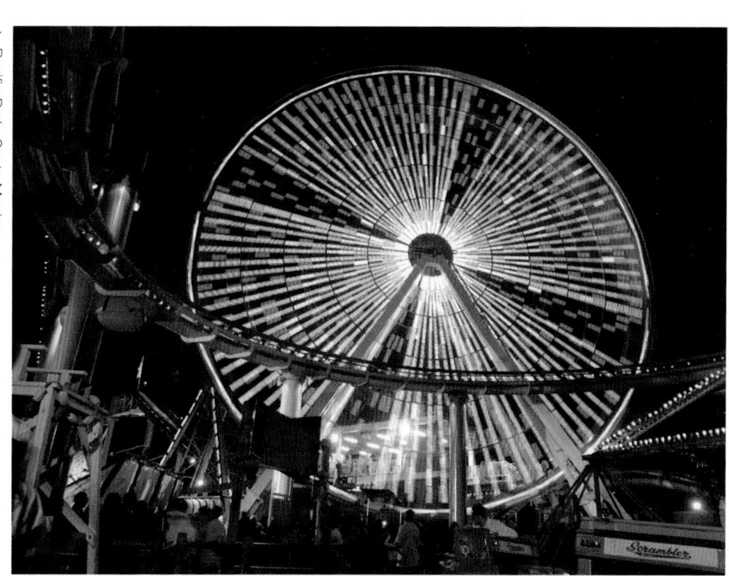

▲ Pacific Park, Santa Monica

Stargazing in LA

If you really want to catch a glimpse of the glitterati in LA, you can do much better than riding around on a tour bus staring at the mansion gates and shrubs of the rich and famous – and paying plenty for the privilege. You can often spot your favourite movie heroes and TV stars, as well as has-beens and pseudo-celebrities, in the city's better bars and clubs (see the LA Weekly for assistance), in the celeb-oriented restaurants listed in the box on p.237, or behind the velvet rope at the various movie premieres taking place around town. You can also sometimes get autographs if you approach the rich and/or famous when they're "performing" for the public – showing off their new duds at a flashy club, doing anything in the company of a publicist or reporter, etc. They're much less likely to blow you off in full public view than they are if you invade their privacy in a secluded beach cabana, back-corner dining booth or on the Stairmaster at an upscale gym, where you can expect the quick embrace of a bodyguard and a curt dismissal before being ushered to the exit.

Diego, so you can leave your car in a car park or just use public transport to get there. To really get into the urban spirit, make sure to try a bit of unstructured wandering around the region's less glitzy zones, where you may stumble upon that perfect diner or funky shoe store, discovering hidden charms away from the theme parks and klieg lights.

What to see

Most of Los Angeles lies in a flat basin, contained within and around the Santa Monica, San Gabriel, Santa Ana and Verdugo mountains, and hemmed in by the Pacific Ocean to the west. From the crest of the Hollywood Hills on any given night you can see the city lights spread out before you in a great illuminated grid. Though etched with a vast network of freeways, the landscape also features undulating hills, coastal bluffs, mountain ranges and rocky canyons – variously home to movie stars, shopping malls and theme attractions, not to mention impressive museums, rugged parks and expansive gardens.

Starting in the centre of the region, at the junction of the Hollywood, Santa Monica, Harbor and Santa Ana freeways, **Downtown** has always been the hub of LA's political and financial

▲ Lifeguard station, Venice Beach

life, a district that has long tried to match the cultural cachet of the Westside and Hollywood. Recent years have brought fresh energy and development to this formerly overlooked area, and there's nowhere else in the city with as much variety of class, culture and design, all within a fairly compact area. Just west, the loosely defined district of **Mid-Wilshire**, built around part of the commercial strip of Wilshire Boulevard, is home to some of LA's best Art Deco architecture and finest residential designs. It's also a good place to take in some culture along "Museum Row" – overlapping the old Miracle Mile commercial zone – where you can find Ice Age-era bones of prehistoric animals in the La Brea Tar Pits and a wide selection of art at the LA County Museum of Art.

◀ The Walk of Fame

Due north is LA's most famous district, **Hollywood**. Despite its well-worn patina of grime, the birthplace of the American movie business is still an essential stop, the site of grand old cinema palaces like the Chinese Theatre and the ever-popular "Walk of Fame" – and like Downtown, the area has experienced something of a minor renaissance in the last decade. Hollywood, Sunset,

Santa Monica and Melrose boulevards are the district's main drags, all of which lead to the chic boutiques and trendy clubs of **West Hollywood**, a centre for gays, seniors and Russian immigrants. In the hills above Hollywood, you can take a break in **Griffith Park**, location of LA's famed observatory, or take in a concert at the fabulous Hollywood Bowl.

West of here, in the heart of the city's Westside, **Beverly Hills** and **West LA** are where visitors often base themselves, keeping close to the all-out glitz of Rodeo Drive or Westwood's movie theatres and affordable shops. In the latter district, there's also the picturesque UCLA campus, and further west, in the Sepulveda corridor, sits LA's showpiece for European art, the colossal Getty Center.

Santa Monica and **Venice** lie at the ocean's edge, sixteen miles from Downtown. These towns give LA its popular beach image (though the waters are cleaner further north), and are highlighted by such favourite attractions as the relaxed Santa Monica Pier, the shopping strips of the Third Street Promenade and Main Street, and the freewheeling Venice Boardwalk and body shrine of Muscle Beach.

Well off the path of most tourists, **South Central** holds a few scattered but notable sights like the Watts Towers, plus a fine array of historic architecture along West Adams and several good cultural institutions in Exposition Park. East of Downtown, **East LA** is the heart of the city's Mexican-American community, with a fairly vibrant street life. To the south, the largely residential **South Bay** features some compelling oceanside scenery and charming

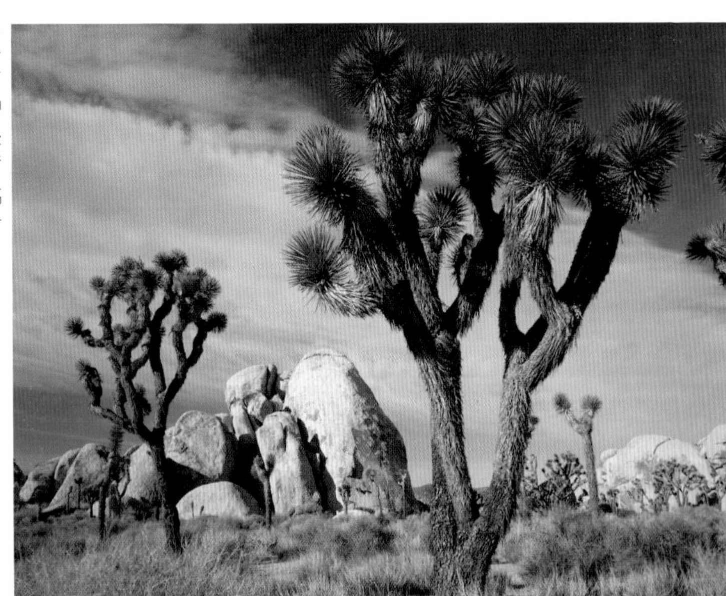

▶ Joshua Tree National Park

Traffic and smog

Among LA's downsides, it's likely you'll only face the typical pitfalls of traffic and smog. The latter, while still virulent, has slowly improved in recent decades. Smog reports, broken down by geographic area, are published daily in the *LA Times*. As for traffic hassles, gridlock can sometimes be avoided if you stick to one place, as many neighbourhoods are surprisingly compact and can be seen on foot. Still, you'll likely need a car to jump around from place to place, or to get a real sense of the city sprawl. Driving on LA's myriad freeways can be a challenge, but as long as you don't try to emulate some of the crazier local motorists, you should have few problems. Whatever your mode of getting around, make sure to budget plenty of time for your travels. While you can theoretically go from Santa Monica to Downtown LA in twenty minutes by freeway, most likely it will take twice that amount of time, or more than seventy-five minutes on side streets. For a heads-up on the latest traffic conditions, visit ⓦwww.sigalert.com.

architecture, and the **Palos Verdes Peninsula** has some of the city's most dramatic ocean vistas. The gritty port cities of San Pedro and Long Beach are the collective home of the LA Harbor – though there's more down here than just that, namely the grand *Queen Mary* ocean liner.

The sprawling suburbs of the **San Gabriel** and **San Fernando valleys**, east and north of the Hollywood Hills, have scattered appeal, from Burbank's working movie studios and Glendale's famed Forest Lawn cemetery to the historic town of Pasadena, site of the Old Pasadena shopping strip and the magnificent Gamble House. The best natural turf in LA is around **Malibu** and the **Santa Monica Mountains**, where the many state and regional parks are ideal for exploring on foot, or by car along the scenic Mulholland Highway. Nearby, the exclusive enclave of Pacific Palisades is home to a handful of architectural highlights, while the city of Malibu to the north is a surfside celebrity enclave whose beaches are famously difficult, though not impossible, to access. More beach options abound in the shoreline communities of **Orange County**, though the area is best known for theme parks like Knott's Berry Farm and **Disneyland**.

Once you've had your fill of LA proper, venture out into greater Southern California. **San Diego** is one of the most populous cities in the US, and renowned for its many fine beaches. It's also terrific for its collection of museums set amid the leafy confines of Balboa Park, for the magisterial ships docked on its harbourfront, and for the Victorian architecture enlivening the nightlife precinct of the Gaslamp District. Two hours east of LA in the desert, **Palm Springs** is best known for the golf and sporting activities that attract the nouveau riche and tourists alike. Also worth a look are its splendid mid-twentieth-century modern architecture and surrounding Indian canyons, and especially the eerie expanse of Joshua trees on the edge of the Mojave desert. Finally, **Santa Barbara** is the old-money redoubt of the Central Coast, gleaming with a grand old mission and handsome Spanish Colonial Revival architecture. Along with an array of fine hotels and dining options, a number of fascinating art and history museums heighten a genteel old-money air that's otherwise absent from Southern California's whiz-bang pop-cultural landscape.

▲ Disney Hall

When to go

Los Angeles holds several types of warm **climate zones**, including desert, semi-arid and Mediterranean areas. Differences between temperatures across the area can be great: for example, Pasadena is ten to fifteen degrees hotter on average than Santa Monica, whose climate can be decidedly maritime. Due to the enclosed topography of the LA basin, high levels of smog can accumulate, worst during the summer months in the eastern parts of the region; torrential rainstorms occur during the winter months. Monthly city temperatures range less than twenty degrees throughout the year, and in general, toasty air and sunny skies reign: summer and autumn months are fairly warm and dry; winter and spring periods are cooler and wetter, but still quite warm. The right time to travel to Los Angeles depends less on the weather than on cultural events – such as parades, festivals, movie previews and surfing tournaments.

Average daytime temperatures

	Jan	Feb	Mar	Apr	May	Jun	Jul	Aug	Sep	Oct	Nov	Dec
Los Angeles and Southern California												
Max/Min °C	18/8	19/9	20/9	22/12	23/13	25/16	28/17	28 17	27/16	25 14	23/12	20/9
Max/Min °F	65/47	66/48	68/49	71/53	73/55	77/60	83/63	82/63	81/60	77/57	73/53	68/49

things not to miss

It's not possible to see everything Los Angeles and Southern California have to offer in one trip – and we don't suggest you try. What follows is a subjective selection of the area's highlights, from sun-soaked beaches to world-class museums, arranged in colour-coded categories. All entries have a page reference to take you straight into the guide, where you can find out more.

01 Cruising the Sunset Strip Page **100** • The essential axis of the California music scene, jammed with groovy bars and clubs as well as swanky hotels, oddball boutiques and towering billboards advertising fashion, spirits and starlets.

02 Watts Towers Page **143** • These spiny towers built from cast-off glass and pottery are a welcome sight in South Central LA, where their graceful silhouettes lend an otherworldly touch to the scruffy neighbourhood.

03 Getty Center Page **115** • This colossal arts centre, looming above West LA and stuffed with the glory of the Old World, has done much to help Los Angeles shake off its reputation as a culture-free zone.

04 Disneyland Page **194** • Much more than a theme park, the "Magic Kingdom" is a carefully planned resort where you can eat, sleep and take a spin on the family-oriented rides without ever leaving its gates.

05 Driving Pacific Coast Highway Page **199** • A favourite setting for biker flicks and road movies, this sinewy stretch of asphalt winds around coastal cliffs and legendary beaches from Malibu to Orange County.

06 Melrose Avenue Page **95** • Vibrant commercial strip that's the best place in LA to pick up the most chic and stylish, as well as most unusual and inexplicable, attire and accessories to show off to (or shock) the folks back home.

07 Amoeba Music Page **303** • The reigning king of California record stores, with acres of space housing thousands of CDs, tapes, DVDs and vinyl records, including a wealth of classics.

08 Strolling the Venice Boardwalk Page **128** • Mix with itinerant artists, rollerbladers, street preachers, T-shirt and trinket vendors and hordes of tourists at this free-spirited beachside strip.

09 Queen Mary Page **156** • Docked in Long Beach, this striking Art Deco-styled ocean liner is open for tours and still retains much of its 1930s luxury.

10 Joshua Tree National Park Page **329** • The personification of desert beauty, these bizarrely gnarled trees are a type of yucca and provide an excellent reason to venture into the desert east of Palm Springs.

11 Gamble House Page **168** • This 1908 Craftsman-style treasure is one of Pasadena's gems, blending elements of rustic native design with touches of Swiss-chalet and Japanese decoration.

12 LA County Museum of Art Page **74** • After a recent massive renovation, this huge storehouse of old and new art easily presents the broadest collection of art in the western US.

13 San Diego Zoo Page **318** • Simply put, the greatest zoo in the country, and one of the best in the world, featuring thousands of animals, including some famous Chinese pandas.

14 Griffith Park Page **83** • A verdant swath of urban greenery on the hills overlooking the city, containing several museums, bucolic glades, great trails and the signature Observatory.

15 Egyptian Theatre Page **89** • The stylishly preserved zenith of movie palaces of the 1920s, with ancient-looking columns, scarabs and friezes, and a solid diet of art-house and independent fare.

16 Enjoying a concert at Disney Hall Page **60** • Frank Gehry's gleaming metallic jewel of a symphonic hall has helped kick-start the creative renaissance of Downtown, and the building's interior is no less eye-opening.

17 Whisky-a-Go-Go Page **258** • Perhaps the most famous rock club on the West Coast, a proving ground for punk and metal groups and a classic venue that's hosted the likes of Buffalo Springfield, Janis Joplin and The Doors.

Basics

Basics

Getting there

Unless you are within a short drive of Southern California, the quickest way to get to the Los Angeles metropolitan area is by flying, the most popular airports being Los Angeles International Airport (LAX) and Orange County's John Wayne International. Amtrak trains provide an alternate approach to LA within the US, while Greyhound buses are a cheaper, if much less enjoyable, option. If you're driving to LA, as many do, it pays to familiarize yourself with the freeway layout beforehand.

Flights from the UK and Ireland

The only **nonstop** flights from Britain to California are from London, most of which land in LA, and take around eleven hours. Flights are often advertised as "direct" because they keep the same flight number but actually land elsewhere first. The first place the plane lands is your point of entry into the US, which means you'll have to collect your bags and go through customs and immigration formalities there, even if you're continuing on to California on the same plane. Many other routings involve a change of aircraft.

Flights from Ireland to LA often require a stopover in London (sometimes Chicago or another US city), and take around fourteen hrs minimum with the stop. Costs from either Ireland or Britain start at $1000 USD (£650) for peak season, or down to $700 (£450) in the low season.

One word of **warning**: it's not a good idea to buy a **one-way** ticket to the States. Not only are they rarely good value compared to a round-trip ticket, but US immigration officials usually take them as a sign that you aren't planning to go home and may refuse you entry.

Flights from the US and Canada

Airfares to LA from within the US and Canada can vary dramatically. Published round-trip prices during the midweek in summer — the high season — on the major airlines start at around $400 from New York and other eastern seaboard cities, $350 from Midwest cities, and $520 from Toronto and Montréal, although airline **promotions** can reduce that price at slack times. More important than your choice of carrier are the conditions governing the ticket – whether it's fully refundable, the time and day, and the **time of year** you travel. The high season is the late spring through late summer. You'll get the best prices during the low season, mid-January to the end of February, and October to the end of November; shoulder seasons cover the rest of the year. Least expensive is a non-summer-season midweek flight, booked and paid for at least three weeks in advance. Keep in mind too that one-way tickets are sometimes more expensive than round-trip tickets.

You can also cut costs by going through a specialist flight agent – either a consolidator, who buys up blocks of tickets from airlines and sells them at a discount, or a discount agent who, in addition to dealing with discounted flights, may also offer student or youth fares.

Flights from Australia, New Zealand and South Africa

If you are coming from Australia or New Zealand, there's very little price difference between airlines and no shortage of flights, via either the South Pacific or Asia. Most flights crossing the Pacific are nonstop, with twelve to fourteen hours' travel time between Auckland/Sydney and LA, though some include stopovers in Honolulu or one of the South Pacific islands. If you go via Asia (a more roundabout route that can work out a little cheaper), you'll usually have to spend a night, or the best part of a day, in the airline's home city.

Travelling from **Australia**, fares to LA from eastern cities cost the same, while from Perth they're about Aus$500 more. Flights from Sydney or Melbourne to LA range between Aus$1200 and Aus$1800, depending on the season, with airline specials and student fares sometimes reducing that by Aus$100–300. Seat availability on most international flights is limited, so it's best to book at least several weeks ahead.

From **New Zealand**, most flights are out of Auckland; add about NZ$200 for Christchurch and Wellington departures. Seasonal prices vary between around NZ$1400 and NZ$1800, again with occasional special deals and student fares reducing those figures significantly.

Travel to California is not particularly cheap from **South Africa**; prices are about the same out of Cape Town or Johannesburg but several hundred rand more from Durban and other smaller cities. Fares start at around R10,000, including all taxes, and rise as high as R15,000 at peak times, which are roughly the same as those from Australia. Direct flights with US or South African carriers invariably involve a refueling stop, often in London or a US city, and the entire trip takes at least a full day. Still, a more roundabout route with one of the national airlines from further north in Africa can be cheaper.

Round-the-world tickets

If you intend to take in California as part of a world trip, a **round-the-world** (RTW) ticket offers the greatest flexibility and can work out far more economically than booking separate flights. The most US-oriented are the 26 airlines making up the "Star Alliance" network; for more details, visit Ⓦwww.staralliance.com.

Six steps to a better kind of travel

At Rough Guides we are passionately committed to travel. We feel strongly that only through travelling do we truly come to understand the world we live in and the people we share it with – plus tourism has brought a great deal of **benefit** to developing economies around the world over the last few decades. But the extraordinary growth in tourism has also damaged some places irreparably, and of course **climate change** is exacerbated by most forms of transport, especially flying. This means that now more than ever it's important to **travel thoughtfully** and **responsibly**, with respect for the cultures you're visiting – not only to derive the most benefit from your trip but also to preserve the best bits of the planet for everyone to enjoy. At Rough Guides we feel there are six main areas in which you can make a difference:

- Consider what you're contributing to the **local economy**, and how much the services you use do the same, whether it's through employing local workers and guides or sourcing locally grown produce and local services.
- Consider the **environment** on holiday as well as at home. Water is scarce in many developing destinations, and the biodiversity of local flora and fauna can be adversely affected by tourism. Try to patronize businesses that take account of this.
- Travel with a purpose, not just to tick off experiences. Consider **spending longer** in a place, and getting to know it and its people.
- Give thought to how often you **fly**. Try to avoid short hops by air and more harmful night flights.
- Consider **alternatives to flying**, travelling instead by bus, train, boat and even by bike or on foot where possible.
- Make your trips "**climate neutral**" via a reputable carbon offset scheme. All Rough Guide flights are offset, and every year we donate money to a variety of charities devoted to combating the effects of climate change.

Rail passes

Amtrak has cut down on the number of **rail passes** in recent years, so now only two cover California. They're mainly useful if you're on an extended tour of the state and have plenty of time to explore your destinations.

The **USA Rail Pass** covers varying time periods, and the longer the period, the more "segments" (individual train rides) you're allowed for travel within the US. For 15 days, eight segments are offered ($389); 30 days gets you twelve segments ($579); and 45 days allows eighteen segments ($749). Alternatively, the **California pass** ($159) covers any 7 days of travel in a 21-day window for routes such as the Pacific Surfliner and San Joaquin, or the in-state portion of national routes such as the Coast Starlight, Southwest Chief, etc. Many trains fill quickly, so it's worth making reservations well ahead.

Trains

If you don't want to fly, **Amtrak** (ⓣ1-800/USA-RAIL, ⓦwww.amtrak.com) is a leisurely but expensive option. Although financially precarious for years, the company has managed to keep running – though rarely ever on time. The trains vary in style, amenities and speed, so it can be worth checking ahead on the type of train that services your route.

To arrive by way of the Midwest and Southwest, ride on the **Southwest Chief**, which begins in Chicago and travels through Kansas City, New Mexico and Arizona before reaching LA (Las Vegas is connected by bus line to this route through Needles, California). The **Sunset Limited** covers more of the South and the Southwest, taking you from Orlando through New Orleans and Texas, and arriving in LA via Palm Springs. Another memorable route is the **Coast Starlight**, which runs between Seattle and San Diego and passes some of the most appealing beachside and mountain scenery anywhere. The shortest route of all, the **Pacific Surfliner**, connects San Diego to San Luis Obispo, with LA roughly on the mid-point of the journey.

One-way cross-country fares can be as low as $150 during the off-season, or as high as $300 during peak periods; always check for **online discounts** of up to 60 percent first, though such fares are offered irregularly. While Amtrak's basic fares are good value, the cost rises quickly if you want to travel more comfortably. **Sleeping compartments**, which include small toilets and showers, start at around $200–300 for one or two people, but can climb as high as $400–1000, depending on the class of compartment, number of nights, season and so on, but all include three meals per day.

Buses

Bus travel is a slow, often agonizing way to get to LA, and in the end you won't really save that much money. **Greyhound** (ⓣ1-800/231-2222, ⓦwww.greyhound.com) is the sole long-distance operator servicing LA, and charges begin at $200–250 round-trip, paid at least seven days in advance, from major cities like New York, Chicago and Miami. The main reason to take Greyhound is if you're planning to visit other places en route.

Foreign visitors and US and Canadian nationals can buy a **Greyhound Discovery Pass**, offering unlimited travel within a set time limit: you can order online at ⓦwww.discoverypass.com. A seven-day pass costs $239, fifteen days for $339, thirty days for $439, and the longest, a sixty-day pass, is $539. The company website has a list of international vendors if you don't want to purchase online. The first time you use your pass, the ticket clerk will date it (which becomes the commencement date of the pass), and you will receive a ticket that allows you to board the bus. Repeat this procedure for every subsequent journey. Greyhound's nationwide toll-free **information service** can give you routes and times, plus phone numbers and addresses of local terminals. You can also make reservations at ⓣ1-800/231-2222.

By car

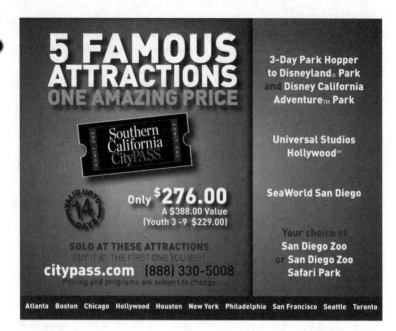

As a city built on, and connected by, large stretches of concrete and asphalt, LA is the perfect place to reach by **car**. There are numerous freeways within the region to hasten your trip (see p.26), and three main routes outside Southern California lead to the metropolis: **Interstate 5**, the north–south corridor that connects LA to Mexico and Canada along the West Coast; **I-10**, a transcontinental east–west route that begins in Jacksonville, Florida, and ends in Santa Monica (or branches off to I-8 south of Phoenix to terminate in San Diego); and **I-15**, running along a mostly deserted stretch of desert before it reaches Las Vegas and drops down into LA's eastern San Gabriel Valley. Another option is **US Highway 101**, the famed coastal route that terminates in Downtown LA, after travelling through the San Fernando Valley and Hollywood, where it is known as the "Hollywood Freeway". If travelling on Hwy-101 beyond LA to the north, you can expect almost double the travel time as on Interstate 5, which goes in the same general direction.

Airlines, agents and operators

Airlines

Aer Lingus ⓦ www.aerlingus.com
Air Canada ⓦ www.aircanada.com
Air New Zealand ⓦ www.airnewzealand.com
Air Pacific ⓦ www.airpacific.com
AirTran ⓦ www.airtranairways.com
Alaska Airlines ⓦ www.alaskaair.com
American Airlines ⓦ www.aa.com
British Airways ⓦ www.ba.com
Cathay Pacific ⓦ www.cathaypacific.com
China Airlines ⓦ www.china-airlines.com
Continental ⓦ www.continental.com
Delta Airlines ⓦ www.delta.com
EgyptAir ⓦ www.egyptair.com
Frontier Airlines ⓦ www.frontierairlines.com
Hawaiian Airlines ⓦ www.hawaiianair.com
JAL (Japan Airlines) ⓦ www.jal.com
JetBlue ⓦ www.jetblue.com
Kenya Airways ⓦ www.kenya-airways.com
KLM ⓦ www.klm.com
Korean Air ⓦ www.koreanair.com
Midwest Airlines ⓦ www.midwestairlines.com
Qantas ⓦ www.qantas.com
Singapore Airlines ⓦ www.singaporeair.com
South African Airways ⓦ www.flysaa.com

Southwest ⓦ www.southwest.com
United Airlines ⓦ www.united.com
US Airways ⓦ www.usair.com
Virgin Atlantic Airways ⓦ www.virgin-atlantic.com
WestJet ⓦ www.westjet.com

Agents and operators

North South Travel UK ⓣ 01245/608 291, ⓦ www.northsouthtravel.co.uk. Friendly, competitive travel agency, offering discounted fares worldwide. Profits are used to support projects in the developing world, especially the promotion of sustainable tourism.
On the Go Tours UK ⓣ 020/7371 1113, ⓦ www.onthegotours.com. Runs group and tailor-made tours to Egypt, India, Sri Lanka, Africa, Jordan, Russia, China and Turkey.
STA Travel UK ⓣ 0871/2300 040, US ⓣ 1-800/781-4040, Australia ⓣ 134 782, New Zealand ⓣ 0800/474 400, South Africa ⓣ 0861/781 781; ⓦ www.statravel.co.uk. Worldwide specialists in independent travel; also student IDs, travel insurance, car rental, rail passes and more. Good discounts for students and under-26s.
Trailfinders UK ⓣ 0845/058 5858, Ireland ⓣ 01/677 7888, Australia ⓣ 1300/780 212; ⓦ www.trailfinders.com. One of the best-informed and most efficient agents for independent travellers.
Travel CUTS Canada ⓣ 1-866/246-9762, US ⓣ 1-800/592-2887; ⓦ www.travelcuts.com. Canadian youth and student travel firm.
USIT Ireland ⓣ 01/602 1906, Northern Ireland ⓣ 028/9032 7111; ⓦ www.usit.ie. Ireland's main student and youth travel specialists.

Online booking

ⓦ **www.expedia.co.uk** (in UK)
ⓦ **www.expedia.com** (in US)
ⓦ **www.expedia.ca** (in Canada)
ⓦ **www.hotwire.com** (in US)
ⓦ **www.lastminute.com** (in UK)
ⓦ **www.opodo.co.uk** (in UK)
ⓦ **www.orbitz.com** (in US)
ⓦ **www.priceline.com** (in US)
ⓦ **www.travelocity.co.uk** (in UK)
ⓦ **www.travelocity.com** (in US)
ⓦ **www.travelocity.ca** (in Canada)
ⓦ **travel.yahoo.com** (in US)
ⓦ **www.zuji.com.au** (in Australia)
ⓦ **www.zuji.co.nz** (in New Zealand)

Arrival

Depending on how you travel, arriving in LA can place you at any number of locations scattered across the city – from the train and bus stations Downtown to the main air terminal by the ocean to the freeways coming in from all directions. However you arrive, you're faced with an unending sprawl that can be a source of bewilderment and frustration. Provided you don't panic, however, this ungainly beast of a city can be managed and even easily navigated, if not necessarily tamed.

By air

All international and most domestic flights use Los Angeles International Airport (**LAX**) sixteen miles southwest of Downtown LA (ⓣ 310/646-5252, ⓦ www.los-angeles-lax.com). **Shuttle** bus A is for intra-airport connections (carrier-to-carrier), while buses B and C serve their respective parking lots around the clock, with parking lot C being the place to board city buses (the citywide MTA and individual city-oriented lines to Santa Monica, Culver City and Torrance) – see p.27 for more details.

To travel between LAX and Downtown's Union Station, the UCLA campus in Westwood (at parking structure 32 on

Kinross Avenue), or the private Van Nuys Airport, the direct-routed **LAX Flyaway** service (Ⓣ1-866/435-9529, Ⓦwww.lawa.aero/flyaway) uses buses in freeway car-pool lanes to provide the most direct airport access on public transit; buses leave every thirty minutes and run around the clock, except at Westwood, where the service runs from 6am to 10pm ($5–7 oneway).

Another way into town is on a minibus; operators include SuperShuttle (Ⓣ1-800/BLUE-VAN, Ⓦwww.supershuttle.com) and Prime Time Shuttle (Ⓣ1-800/RED-VANS, Ⓦwww.primetimeshuttle.com), and run all over town; fares depend on your destination but start around $15 for travel to downtown and the Westside (or up to $40 for more outlying areas), with a journey time of between thirty and sixty minutes. The shuttles run around the clock from outside the baggage reclaim areas, and you should never have to wait more than fifteen or twenty minutes; pay the fare when you board.

Taxis charge at least $35 to West LA or $40 to Hollywood, around $100 to Disneyland, and a flat $46.50 to Downtown from LAX; a $2.50 surcharge applies for all trips starting from LAX (all airport trips are a minimum of $17.50). For more information check out Ⓦwww.taxicabsla.org.

Using the **Metro** system to get to your destination from LAX is difficult. The nearest light-rail train, the **Green Line**, stops miles from the airport, and the overall journey involves two time-consuming transfers (very difficult with luggage) before you even arrive in Downtown Los Angeles. If you'd like to try anyway for $1.50, shuttle service leaves from the lower level of the terminal to access the Metro stop at Aviation Station.

If you're arriving from elsewhere in the US or from Mexico, you can land at one of the **smaller airports** in the LA area. Burbank's Bob Hope Airport (Ⓣ818/840-8840, Ⓦwww.burbankairport.com) is very convenient for the Valley and for Hollywood; Long Beach (Ⓣ562/570-2619, Ⓦwww.longbeach.gov/airport) is best known as the local base for JetBlue and is convenient for the South Bay; Ontario (Ⓣ909/937-2700, Ⓦwww.lawa.org/ont) is farther out yet, in the smoggiest part of the San Gabriel Valley, and only useful for the eastern suburbs; and Costa Mesa's John Wayne Airport (Ⓣ949/252-5200, Ⓦwww.ocair.com) provides the best way to get to Orange County and within reach of Disneyland. All these are well served by car rental firms; if you want to use public transportation, phone the MTA Regional Information Network on arrival (Ⓣ1-800/COMMUTE, Ⓦwww.mta.net), and tell them where you are and where you want to go.

By train

Arriving in LA by **train**, you'll disembark at Union Station (Ⓣ213/624-0171), on the north side of Downtown at 800 N Alameda St. (You can also connect to regional bus lines next door at the Gateway Transit Center.) Union Station is the hub for three main rail lines: **Metrorail**, the subway and light-rail system (see p.27); **Metrolink**, a commuter rail line servicing distant suburbs (see p.28); and Amtrak (Ⓣ1-800/USA-RAIL, Ⓦwww.amtrak.com), whose long-distance trains also stop at outlying stations in the LA area.

Amtrak: departures for Downtown

Anaheim	10 daily	40min
Fullerton (for Disneyland)	10 daily	35min
Las Vegas	1 daily	6hr, with bus connection
Oxnard	5 daily	1hr 35min
Palm Springs	2 daily	2hr 35min
Sacramento	1 daily	14hr
San Clemente	2 daily	1hr 30min
San Diego	12 daily	2hr 50min
San Francisco	5 daily	9–12hr, with bus connection
San Juan Capistrano	12 daily	1hr 20min
Santa Ana	2 daily	50min
Santa Barbara	6 daily	2hr 35min
Ventura	5 daily	1hr 50min

By bus

The main **Greyhound** bus terminal, at 1716 E Seventh St (Ⓣ213/629-8401, Ⓦwww.greyhound.com), is in a seedy section of

Downtown – though access is restricted to ticket holders and it's safe enough inside. There are other Greyhound terminals elsewhere in LA handling fewer services: in Mid-Wilshire at 4910 E Olympic Blvd (☎323/261-5522); Hollywood at 1715 N Cahuenga Blvd (☎323/466-6381); North Hollywood at 11239 Magnolia Blvd (☎818/761-5119); Glendale at 400 W Cerritos Ave (☎818/244-7295); Long Beach at 1498 Long Beach Blvd (☎562/218-3011); and Anaheim at 101 W Winston Rd (☎714/999-1256). Only the Downtown terminal is open around the clock.

Greyhound: departures for Downtown

Anaheim	6 daily	45min
Bakersfield	12 daily	2hr 45min
Las Vegas	12 daily	6–8hr
Oxnard	5 daily	2hr
Palm Springs	4 daily	2hr 40min
Phoenix	10 daily	7–9hr
Sacramento	9 daily	7–10hr
San Diego	18 daily	3hr
San Francisco	14 daily	8–12hr
Santa Barbara	5 daily	2–4hr
Tucson	6 daily	10–12hr

By car

The **main routes** by car into LA are the interstate highways, most of which pass through or by Downtown. From the east, I-10, the **San Bernardino Freeway**, runs south of Downtown then heads to the Westside and the coast, where it's called the **Santa Monica Freeway**. US-60, the **Pomona Freeway**, parallels the faster I-10 through the eastern suburbs. The **Foothill Freeway**, I-210 (formerly Route 66), mainly serves the San Gabriel Valley; while the **Golden State Freeway**, or I-5, is the chief north–south access corridor, with the **San Diego Freeway**, I-405, used commonly as a Westside alternative.

Alternative routes into the city include US-101, the scenic route from San Francisco, which as the **Ventura Freeway** cuts across the San Fernando Valley and Hollywood into Downtown. Hwy-1 follows the entire coast of California and links up with US-101 in Ventura County. Through much of southern California it's known as **Pacific Coast Highway** (PCH), and in LA it uses surface streets through Santa Monica, the South Bay and Orange County.

Getting around

Wherever and however you're going in LA, you should allow plenty of time to get there. This is partly due to the sheer size of the city, but the tangle of freeways and the gridlock common throughout the day can make car trips a grinding haul. Though most buses stop on every corner, some express buses can be a quicker alternative. The Metrorail subway and light-rail system are increasingly attractive options, though at present they serve too few parts of the city to be your only transit option.

Driving and car rental

The best way to get around LA is still to **drive**. All the major car rental firms have branches throughout the city, and most have their main office close to LAX, linked to each terminal by a free shuttle bus. **Parking** is a particular problem Downtown, along Melrose Avenue's trendy Westside shopping streets, and in Beverly Hills and Westwood – the latter with one of the nation's most aggressive meter-enforcement policies. Also watch out for restrictions – some lampposts boast as many as four placards listing dos and don'ts. If you're staying at a hotel in a high-ticket area (especially Downtown, West Hollywood and Beverly Hills), be prepared to plunk down an average of $25–30 per day for hotel parking – street parking is typically banned overnight in many of these areas. Otherwise, at cheap motels and hotels in lower-rent zones, it'll cost you nothing to keep your vehicle overnight.

Car rental agencies

Advantage ⓣ1-800/777-5500, ⓦwww.advantage.com
Alamo ⓣ1-800/462-5266, ⓦwww.alamo.com
Avis ⓣ1-800/230-4898, ⓦwww.avis.com
Budget ⓣ1-800/527-0700, ⓦwww.budget.com
Dollar ⓣ1-800/800-3665, ⓦwww.dollar.com
Enterprise ⓣ1-800/261-7331, ⓦwww.enterprise.com
Fox Rent-a-Car ⓣ1-800/225-4369, ⓦfoxrentacar.com
Hertz ⓣ1-800/654-3131, ⓦwww.hertz.com
National ⓣ1-800/CAR-RENT, ⓦwww.nationalcar.com
Payless ⓣ1-800/PAYLESS, ⓦwww.paylesscar.com
Rent-a-Wreck ⓣ1-800/944-7501, ⓦwww.rentawreck.com
Thrifty ⓣ1-800/847-4389, ⓦwww.thrifty.com

LA's freeways

If you travel at the right time and avoid the gridlock, the **freeways** are the only way to cover long distances quickly; with more than 250 miles of asphalt and twenty major routes, the LA freeway system is the largest in the world.

The system, however, can be confusing, especially since each stretch might have two or three names (often derived from its eventual destination, however far away) as well as a number. Out of an eye-popping, four-level interchange known as "**The Stack**," four major freeways fan out from Downtown: the Hollywood Freeway (a section of US-101) heads northwest through Hollywood into the San Fernando Valley; the Santa Monica Freeway (I-10) runs south of Mid-Wilshire and West LA to Santa Monica; the Harbor Freeway (I-110) goes south to San Pedro – heading northeast it's called the Pasadena Freeway; and the Santa Ana Freeway (I-5) passes Disneyland and continues south through Orange County – north of Downtown it's called the Golden State Freeway. **Other freeways** include the San Diego Freeway (I-405), which roughly follows the coast through West LA and the South Bay; the Ventura Freeway (Hwy-134), which links Burbank, Glendale and Pasadena to US-101 in the San Fernando Valley; the Long Beach Freeway (I-710), a truck-heavy route connecting East LA and Long Beach; and short routes like Hwy-2, which serves the San Gabriel Valley, and Hwy-90, which runs through Marina del Rey. For **shorter journeys** and travelling during rush hour (6–9am and 3–7pm), especially between Hollywood and West LA, the wide avenues and boulevards are a better option (sometimes the only one).

Freeway driving strategies

LA freeway travel presents its own unique challenges. For one, alternate route planning is critical, especially when travelling to Orange County, because **gridlock** can occur at any time of the day. To assist your planning, AM news radio stations (see p.31) provide frequent **traffic updates** identifying where the nasty

Road conditions

The California Department of Transportation (CalTrans) operates a toll-free **24-hour information line** (ⓣ1-800/427-7623) and **web page** (ⓦwww.dot.ca.gov/hq/cgi-bin/roads.cgi) giving up-to-the-minute details of road conditions throughout the state. On a touch-tone phone, simply input the number of the road ("5" for I-5, "299" for Hwy-299, etc) and a recorded voice will tell you about any relevant weather conditions, delays, detours, snow closures and so on. From out of state, or without a touch-tone phone, road information is also available on ⓣ916/445-1534. To check real-time road conditions from a smartphone, use a web page such as ⓦmaps.google.com (with traffic overlay) or ⓦwww.sigalert.com.

MTA offices and information

For **MTA route and transfer information**, phone ⓣ1-800/COMMUTE; be ready to give precise details of where you are and where you want to go. Otherwise, you can check out the MTA website (ⓦwww.metro.net) or go in person to Downtown's Gateway Transit Center, Chavez Avenue at Vignes Street (Mon–Fri 6am–6.30pm), or to Mid-Wilshire at 5301 Wilshire Blvd (Mon–Fri 9am–5pm).

tie-ups are, as does a website such as ⓦwww.sigalert.com.

The **busiest roads** are Highway 101 and the 405 freeway, with particularly hellish confluences at the Downtown "Stack" and the section of the 405 at the 10 freeway. Individual roads present their own difficulties, including the glacially paced 101 south through Universal City, and the antiquated 110 freeway in Highland Park, where exit-ramp speeds suddenly drop to 5 mph. At the LA River, transferring from the south 5 to the south 110 is a hair-raising merge around the base of a cliff, while following the 10 freeway through East LA plunges you briefly, and chaotically, into the confusion of Interstate 5. Finally, tractor-trailer trucks are almost ubiquitous on the Terminal Island Expressway, a short road near the harbour, and on the Long Beach Freeway, or 710, where most of your neighbours on the road will have at least sixteen wheels.

Public transportation

The bulk of LA's **public transportation** is run by the LA County Metropolitan Transit Authority (MTA or "Metro"), whose massive **Gateway Transit Center**, Downtown to the east of Union Station on Vignes Street, serves commuters travelling by Metrorail, light rail, commuter rail, Amtrak, and regional buses. The Center comprises **Patsaouras Transit Plaza**, from where buses depart, the glass-domed **East Portal**, which leads to train connections, and the 26-storey Gateway Tower, which has an MTA **customer service office** on the ground floor (Mon–Fri 6am–6.30pm; ⓣ1-800/COMMUTE, ⓦwww.metro.net).

Metrorail

LA's **Metrorail** subway, express bus and light-rail system has tried for two decades to expand and access areas of the city that its critics claimed it would never reach. For tourists, much depends on location – if you're staying in Hollywood, Pasadena or Long Beach and want to go Downtown without a car (or vice versa), it's pretty useful. Otherwise, the city's other popular areas – notably the Westside – are well out of its reach.

LA's **Metrorail** system encompasses seven colour-coded lines, though extensions are planned in coming years. The **Orange Line express buses** cross the San Fernando Valley and link Canoga Park with North Hollywood, where they connect to the northern terminus for the **Red Line subway**, which heads south under the Hollywood Hills to connect Central Hollywood and Downtown (stopping at the Gateway Transit Center, as do all Downtown routes). The **Purple Line subway** covers the last part of the same ground, from Vermont Avenue to Union Station, but also extends a short distance west to Western Avenue. Of more use to residents than tourists, the **Green Line** light rail runs between industrial El Segundo (where you can pick up an LAX shuttle at Aviation Station; see p.24) and colourless Norwalk in South LA. The **Blue Line** light rail leaves Downtown and heads overland through South Central to Long Beach, while the more appealing **Gold Line**, another light-rail route, connects Downtown with northeast LA, Highland Park and Old Pasadena, before ending at drab Sierra Madre; another section of the Gold Line recently opened for access to East LA. Finally, the Silver Line uses express buses, like those on the Orange Line, to reach the San Gabriel Valley. Note that the Expo Line light rail is due to open by late 2011 and connect downtown LA with Culver City parallelling the I-10 freeway. **All fares** are $1.50 one way, with day passes available for

$6. Trains run daily from 5am to 12.30am, at five- to six-minute intervals during peak hours and every ten to fifteen minutes at other times. No smoking, eating or drinking is allowed while on board.

Other forms of rail transit mainly serve more distant parts of the city. Amtrak, for example, connects to points in Ventura, Riverside, and Orange counties and beyond (see p.192).

Metrolink

As one rail alternative, **Metrolink** commuter trains ply primarily suburban-to-Downtown routes on weekdays, which can be useful if you find yourself in any such far-flung districts, among them places in Orange, Ventura, Riverside and San Bernardino counties. Although casual visitors may find the service useful mainly for reaching the outlying corners of the San Fernando Valley, the system does reach as far as Oceanside in San Diego County, where you can connect to that region's Coaster commuter rail (see p.309) and avoid the freeways altogether. One-way Metrolink fares range from $5 to $14, depending on when you're travelling (most routes run during daily business hours, often to LA in the morning and back to the suburbs in the evening) and how far you're going. For information on specific routes and schedules, call ⓣ1-800/371-LINK or visit ⓦwww.metrolinktrains.com.

Buses

Although initially bewildering, the MTA bus network is really quite simple: the main routes run east–west (eg, between Downtown and the coast) and north–south (eg, between Downtown and the South Bay). Establishing the best transfer point if you need to change buses can be difficult, but with a bit of planning you should have few problems – though always allow plenty of time.

Free brochures are available from MTA offices, as are diagrams and timetables for individual bus routes and regional bus maps showing larger sections of the metropolis. Buses on the major arteries between Downtown and the coast run roughly every fifteen minutes between 5am and 2am; other routes, and the **all-night services** along the major thoroughfares, are less frequent, usually every thirty minutes or hourly. At night, be careful not to get stranded Downtown waiting for connecting buses.

The standard **one-way fare** is $1.50, but **express buses** and any others using a freeway are $2.20–2.90. Put the correct money (coins or bills) into the slot when getting on. Day passes are $6, but if you're staying in LA for a while, you can save some money with a **weekly** or **monthly pass**, which cost $20 and $75, respectively, and also give reductions at selected shops and travel agents. Finally, "EZ Transit" passes give you the option of travelling on MTA and DASH buses, as well as Metrorail trains, for a flat $84 per month.

Two dozen Metro Rapid routes run throughout the region, offering a modified bus service (along special #700 lines) with particular red-coloured identification, waiting kiosks with enhanced displays, and technology to reduce waiting times at red lights. There are also the mini **DASH** buses, which operate through the LA Department of Transportation, or LADOT (ⓣ808-2273 for area codes 213, 310, 323 and 818; ⓦwww.ladottransit.com), with a flat fare of 25¢ for broad coverage throughout Downtown and very limited routes elsewhere in the city. The LADOT also operates quick, limited-stop routes called **commuter express**, though these cost a bit more (90¢–$4) depending on distance.

Other **local bus services** include those for Orange County (OCTD; ⓣ714/636-7433, ⓦwww.octa.net), Long Beach (LBTD; ⓣ562/591-2301, ⓦwww.lbtransit.org), Culver City (ⓣ310/253-6500, ⓦwww.culvercity.org/bus) and Santa Monica (ⓣ310/451-5444, ⓦwww.bigbluebus.com).

Mass transit routes

MTA's transit routes fall into several categories, as outlined below. Whatever you're on, if travelling alone, especially at night, it's best to sit up front near the driver.

#1–99 Local routes to and from Downtown
#100–199 East–west routes between other areas
#100–299 North–south routes between other areas

#300–399 Limited-stop routes (usually rush hour only)
#400–499 Express routes to and from Downtown
#500–599 Express routes for other areas
#600–699 Special service routes/shuttles
#700–799 Metro Rapid service
#800–829 Metrorail subways and light rail lines
#900–929 Metrorail express buses

Major LA bus lines

Metro routes unless otherwise stated.

From LAX bus centre to:
Beverly Hills Santa Monica line #3 or Culver City line #6 to Metro #720
Culver City: Culver City line #6
Downtown #42, #439
Hollywood: Santa Monica line #3 to Metro #4 or #304
Long Beach #232
Santa Monica Santa Monica line #3
Watts Towers #117
West Hollywood Santa Monica line #3 to Metro #4 or #304

To and from Downtown along:
Beverly Blvd #14, #714
Melrose Ave #10
Olympic Blvd #28
Santa Monica Blvd #4, #704
Sunset Blvd #2, #302
Venice Blvd #33
Wilshire Blvd #20, #720

From Downtown to:
Beverly Hills #14, #20, #714, #720
Burbank Studios #96
Exposition Park #81
Forest Lawn Cemetery, Glendale #90, #91
Getty Center #2 or #302 then transfer at UCLA to #761
Hermosa Beach/Redondo Beach #130
Hollywood #2, #302
Huntington Library #79
Long Beach #60
Orange County, Knott's Berry Farm, Disneyland #460
Santa Monica #4, #20, #720
Venice #33, #333

Taxis

You can find **taxis** at most transit terminals and major hotels. Among the more reliable companies are Independent Taxi (☎1-800/521-8294), Checker Cab (☎1-800/300-5007), Yellow Cab (☎1-800/200-1085) and United Independent Taxi (1-800/411-0303). Fares are at least $35 to West LA or $40 to Hollywood, $100 to Disneyland, and a flat $46.50 to Downtown; a $2.50 surcharge applies for all trips starting from LAX (minimum charge from the airport is $15). The driver won't know every street in LA but will know the major ones; ask for the nearest junction and give directions from there. If you encounter problems, call ☎1-800/501-0999, or visit ⓦwww.taxicabsla.org.

Guided tours

One quick and easy way to see LA is on a **guided tour**. The mainstream tours carry large busloads of visitors to the major tourist sights; specialist tours usually carry smaller groups and are often a better, quirkier value; and media studio tours are available on day-trips by most of the mainstream operators, though again you'll save money by turning up on your own. Some of your best bets for touring Downtown and other spots are the **walking tours** offered by the **LA Conservancy** (Sat 10am; 2.5 hr; $10; ☎213/623-CITY, ⓦlaconservancy.org), which typically set off from Pershing Square downtown and concentrate on various aspects of the city's architecture, history and culture. More expensive, Architours (☎323/294-5821, ⓦwww.architours.com) offers walking, driving and custom tours of the art and architecture highlights of the city, with most running 2–3 hrs for $68–75. Also appealing, **Neon Cruises**, 501 W Olympic Blvd, Downtown (June–Nov; $55; ☎213/489-9918, ⓦwww.neonmona.org), are three-hour-long, eye-popping evening tours of LA's best remaining neon art, once a month on Saturdays, sponsored by the Museum of Neon Art. One type of trek to avoid, however, are the uninspired bus tours that focus on the **homes of the stars** (their ivy-covered security gates) and advertise their overpriced services around central Hollywood. For some insight into how an actual film or TV show is made, or just to admire the special effects, there are guided studio tours at Warner Brothers (see p.177), NBC (p.176), Sony (p.119), Paramount (p.95) and Universal (p.177), all near Burbank except for Sony, in Culver City, and Paramount, in Hollywood. On a related note, if you want to be part of the **audience** in a TV show, Hollywood Boulevard, just outside the Chinese Theatre, is the spot to be: TV company reps regularly appear handing out free tickets, and they'll bus you to the studio and back. All you have to do once there is be willing to laugh and clap on cue.

Cycling

Cycling in LA may sound perverse, but in some areas it can be one of the better ways of getting around. There are beachside bike paths between Santa Monica and Redondo Beach, and from Long Beach to Newport Beach, and many equally enjoyable inland routes, notably around Griffith Park and Pasadena. For maps and information, contact the LA Department of Transportation, 100 S Main St, 9th Floor (Ⓣ213/972-4962, Ⓦwww.bicyclela.org); AAA, 2601 S Figueroa St (Mon–Fri 9am–5pm; Ⓣ213/741-3686); or the California Department of Transportation, known as CalTrans, 100 S Main St (Mon–Fri 8am–5pm; Ⓣ213/897-3656, Ⓦwww.dot.ca.gov). The best place to **rent a bike** for the beaches is around the Venice Boardwalk. Prices range from $10 a day for a clunker to $20 a day or more for a mountain bike. Many beachside stores also rent roller skates and rollerblades.

Walking

Although some people are surprised to find sidewalks in LA, let alone pedestrians, walking is in fact the best way to see much of Downtown and districts like central Hollywood, Pasadena, Beverly Hills, Santa Monica and Venice. You can enjoy guided hikes through the wilds of the Santa Monica Mountains and Hollywood Hills free of charge every weekend with a variety of organizations and bureaus, including the Sierra Club (Ⓣ213/387-4287, Ⓦwww.angeles.sierraclub.org), the State Parks Department (Ⓣ818/880-0350, Ⓦwww.parks.ca.gov) and the Santa Monica Mountains National Recreation Area (Ⓣ805/370-2301, Ⓦwww.nps.gov/samo).

The media

Known for its breathless helicopter pursuits of police chases and constant celebrity gossip, LA's local press has a deserved reputation for sensationalism, but you can still find good regional and national media outlets, typically of the print variety. With the growth of cable TV, there are more television viewing choices than ever, though since most channels are owned by the same handful of multinational corporations, the quality has not improved one bit. The same is true for area radio stations; hunt down LA's public radio affiliates for relief from thundering talk-show bombast and rigid pop-music playlists.

Newspapers and magazines

For such a large city, LA supports surprisingly few daily **newspapers**. At the top of the list is the *Los Angeles Times* (Ⓦwww.latimes.com), the most widely read newspaper in Southern California, available at news boxes and dealers throughout town. Upscale hotels often distribute the newspaper to your door for free, sometimes along with a copy of the *New York Times*, *USA Today* or *Wall Street Journal*. However, most other major newspapers, whether domestic or foreign, tend to be found mainly at city and university libraries, and a few magazine stands.

As far as **other dailies** go, the *Los Angeles Daily News* (ⓦwww.dailynews.com) is more conservative than the *LA Times*, with a strong suburban slant; while *La Opinion* (ⓦwww.laopinion.com) is one of the country's major Spanish-language newspapers, and has a large readership in LA. The *Orange County Register* (ⓦwww.ocregister.com), a right-of-centre paper, is mainly found in its namesake macro-suburb and offers little for LA readers.

There are a few good **alternative weeklies**, most notably the free *LA Weekly* (ⓦwww.laweekly.com), found at libraries and retailers everywhere, providing engaging investigative journalism and copious entertainment listings. The *OC Weekly* (ⓦwww.ocweekly.com) is the liberal Orange County counterpart of the *LA Weekly*.

Every community of any size has at least a few free newspapers that cater to the local scene. Many of these are also good sources for listings for bars, restaurants and nightlife within their areas. Both the USC and UCLA campuses have libraries carrying recent overseas newspapers, while day-old **foreign papers** are on sale in Hollywood at the 24-hour World Book and News, 1652 N Cahuenga Blvd.

LA has a few style-conscious **magazines**, foremost among them the monthly *Los Angeles* magazine (ⓦwww.lamag.com), packed with gossipy news and profiles of local movers and shakers, as well as reviews of the city's trendiest restaurants and clubs. There are also dozens of less glossy **zines** focusing on LA's diverse gay and lesbian culture and nightclubs. As for **free** magazines, the touristy *Where LA* (ⓦwww.wherela.com) is a monthly public-relations magazine found in many hotel rooms, and has peppy reviews and listings.

Television

LA **network television** generally offers a steady diet of talk shows, sitcoms, soap operas and the ubiquitous "reality shows", with some Spanish-language and Asian stations on the UHF portion of the dial. An ad-free alternative to the standard fare is KCET, on UHF channel 28 (ⓦwww.kcet.org), LA's public television station and one of the nation's top producers of educational programmes.

Most motel and hotel rooms are hooked up to some form of **cable TV**, though the number of channels available to guests depends on where you stay. (See the daily papers for channels, schedules and times.) Most cable stations are actually no better than the big broadcast networks, though some of the specialized channels are occasionally interesting. Cable News Network (CNN) and Headline News both have round-the-clock news, with Fox News providing a right-wing slant on the day's events. ESPN is your best bet for all kinds of sports, MTV for youth-oriented music videos and programming, and VH-1 for Baby Boomer shows. Home Box Office (HBO) and Showtime present big-budget Hollywood flicks and excellent TV shows, as does American Movie Classics (AMC).

Many major **sporting events** are transmitted on a pay-per-view basis, and watching an event like a heavyweight boxing match will set you back at least $50, billed directly to your motel room. Most hotels and motels also offer a choice of **recent movies** that have just finished their theatrical runs, at around $10 per film.

Major LA broadcast TV stations

KCBS CBS channel 2
KNBC NBC channel 4
KTLA CW channel 5
KABC ABC channel 7
KCAL CBS channel 9
KTTV Fox channel 11
KCOP MyNetwork channel 13
KCVR PBS channel 24 UHF
KCET PBS channel 28 UHF
KMEX Univision channel 34 UHF (Spanish language)
KOCE PBS channel 50 UHF (Orange County)
KVEA Telemundo channel 52 UHF (Spanish language)

Radio

Radio stations are even more abundant than broadcast TV stations, and the majority stick to mainstream commercial formats. **AM stations** offer little beyond news, traffic reports and talk radio, while **FM stations**, particularly the **public** and **college stations**

found between 88 and 92 FM, broadcast diverse programming, from bizarre underground rock to local board meetings. Of these stations, KCRW (89.9) has some of the most diverse programming in LA, from public affairs to dance music, which at night can be anything from trance, dub and trip-hop to ambient. LA also has a range of decent **specialist music** stations – classical, jazz and so on – as well as a sizable number of Spanish-language stations. Finally, check out LA Radiowatch (Ⓦwww.radiowatch.com) for information on up-and-coming **Internet** stations playing tunes over the web – often more unusual and daring than their broadcasted counterparts.

LA radio stations

AM

KFI 640 right-wing talk radio
KFWB 980 news, traffic, talk, sports
KNX 1070 CBS radio: traffic, news, sports
KDIS 1110 Radio Disney
KTLK 1150 left-wing talk

FM

KKJZ 88.1 blues and jazz Ⓦwww.kkjz.org
KXLU 88.9 alternative, progressive and eclectic Ⓦwww.kxlu.com
KPCC 89.3 news, talk, arts and (National Public Radio) NPR Ⓦwww.scpr.org
KCRW 89.9 one of the country's best NPR affiliates, with new music, transatlantic imports and world news Ⓦwww.kcrw.com
KPFK 90.7 leftist opinions, news and music, Pacifica affiliate Ⓦwww.kpfk.org
KUSC 91.5 classical and opera Ⓦwww.kusc.org
KCBS 93.1 eclectic oldies
KLOS 95.5 album rock
KLSX 97.1 Top 40 pop
KRTH 101.1 golden oldies
KIIS 102.7 Top 40 pop
KBIG 104.3 soft rock and pop oldies
KPWR 105.9 rap and R&B
KROQ 106.7 indie rock

Culture and etiquette

If you regularly watch the sort of mainstream movies and TV shows that feature life in California, you'll find you're already familiar with many aspects of the area's culture and etiquette before you arrive. A few points do warrant a mention, though.

Some form of **picture ID** should be carried at all times. A driver's licence will work, though having a passport as well should diffuse any suspicion. If you're stopped when driving you'll be required to produce a driver's licence, the car's registration papers, and verification of insurance (though the latter two will be waived if you are driving a rental).

One point of eternal discussion is **tipping**. Many workers in service industries get paid very little and rely on tips to bolster their income. Unless you've had abominable service (in which case you should tell the management), you really shouldn't leave a bar or restaurant without leaving a tip of at least fifteen to twenty percent, and about the same should be added to taxi fares. A hotel porter deserves roughly $1 for each bag carried to your room; a coat-check clerk should receive the same per coat. When paying by credit card you're expected to add the tip to the bill before filling in the total amount and signing. Smoking is a much frowned-upon activity in California, which has banned it in all indoor public places, including bars and restaurants. In fact, you can spend weeks in the state barely ever smelling cigarette smoke. Nevertheless, cigarettes are sold in virtually any food shop, drugstore or bar, and also from the occasional vending machine.

Possession of under an ounce of **marijuana** is a misdemeanor in California, and the worst you'll get for holding a little of the widely consumed herb is a small fine. Being caught with more than an ounce, however, means facing a criminal charge for dealing, and a possible prison sentence – stiffer if you're caught anywhere near a school. Medical marijuana clinics are an ongoing source of controversy, with locals tending to support them and the authorities regularly cracking down. Other **drugs** are, of course, completely illegal and it's a much more serious offence if you're caught with any.

Shopping

The richest state in the US is something of a shopper's paradise, and here you'll be able to find just about anything your consumer heart may desire. Details of specific shopping locations are given throughout the guide, but here is a general indication of what you are likely to come across.

Malls

Visitors to LA cannot fail to be impressed by the ubiquitousness of the ultimate American shopping venue, the mall. Whether these are of the "strip mall" variety, strung out along major arteries, or showpiece complexes in desirable neighbourhoods, they unabashedly glorify commercialism and consist mostly of well-known multinational chains. The summit of commercial excess is Rodeo Drive (see p.106) in Beverly Hills, where the older Hollywood stars go to shop. For more

Clothing and shoe sizes

Women's clothing									
American	4	6	8	10	12	14	16	18	
British	6	8	10	12	14	16	18	20	
Continental	34	36	38	40	42	44	46	48	
Women's shoes									
American	5	6	7	8	9	10	11		
British	3	4	5	6	7	8	9		
Continental	36	37	38	39	40	41	42		
Men's shirts									
American	14	15	15.5	16	16.5	17	17.5	18	
British	14	15	15.5	16	16.5	17	17.5	18	
Continental	36	38	39	41	42	43	44	45	
Men's shoes									
American	7	7.5	8	8.5	9.5	10	10.5	11	11.5
British	6	7	7.5	8	9	9.5	10	11	12
Continental	39	40	41	42	43	44	44	45	46
Men's suits									
American	34	36	38	40	42	44	46	48	
British	34	36	38	40	42	44	46	48	
Continental	44	46	48	50	52	54	56	58	

creative wanderings, try the alternative strips of Melrose Avenue (see p.95) or La Brea Avenue (p.96).

Arts and crafts

LA is home to many artists, whose paintings, sculptures and other creations can easily be found both in big galleries on the Westside and in smaller shops with a reputation for creativity, such as those around northeast LA. Original artworks will set you back a fair penny, maybe even thousands of bucks, depending on how established the artist is. Quaint gift shops selling attractive items from all over the world also abound and are a good source of souvenirs and presents, even if they are not specifically local.

Farmers' markets, food and drink

One fine tradition that has survived since California's earlier times are "farmers' markets," which pop up regularly around the city. It can come as a pleasant surprise to stumble on a street full of stalls selling fresh country fare in the middle of Hollywood, for example. Most concentrate solely on edible goods, but the larger ones may have a few gift stalls as well. The apotheosis of all such markets is the sprawling Farmers Market (see p.78) in mid-Wilshire.

LA's countless ethnic eateries, bakeries, cake shops, cheese dealers and other delicacy suppliers can also be well worth seeking out, even though it can be time-consuming to reach the many purveyors spread widely across the metropolitan basin. Check out p.297 for a list of selected shops.

Travel essentials

Costs

Despite its high prices in certain neighbourhoods, Los Angeles's decentralized character and economically diverse neighbourhoods make it less expensive than San Francisco or New York, and with a minimum of effort you can find plenty of bargains and reasonably priced goods and services, though of course you won't lack for choice should you want to splurge at one of the city's swankier restaurants or trendy bars.

Accommodation is likely to be your biggest single **expense** in LA: adequate lodging is rarely available for less than $80 per night, although hostels will of course be cheaper (usually $21–25 per night in a dorm bed). An acceptable hotel room will cost $100–150, with fancier hotels charging much more – upwards of $400 in some cases. **Camping** is an alternative only if you're staying in more isolated areas like San Clemente or Santa Catalina Island, or in other spots on the fringes of the metropolis (see "Accommodation", p.205).

Unlike accommodation, prices for **good food** range widely, as do the types of places that serve it, from hot-dog stands to chic restaurants. You could get by on as little as $20 a day per person, but realistically you should aim for around $50 – and remember, too, that LA has plenty of great spots for a splurge. Beyond restaurants, the city has many bars, clubs and live-music venues to suit all tastes and wallets.

In terms of **transportation**, your best bet is probably to rent a car from any of the rental outlets around the airport, for anywhere between $50–80 per day, with good discounts available on the internet for reserving ahead. Regional distances are huge, and if you're headed anywhere beyond central LA or, more specifically, beyond the Westside, you'll undoubtedly find public transit to be a time-consuming hassle. US gas prices are still relatively cheap compared with those in Europe.

Added to the cost of most items you purchase **in LA County** is a total sales **tax of** 9.75 percent. Many LA-area municipalities tack on a hotel tax of 14–16 percent, which can drive up accommodation costs dramatically.

For attractions in the main part of the Guide, **prices** are quoted for adults, with children's rates listed only if they are more than a few dollars less; at some spots, kids get in for half price, or for free if they're under 8. Seniors may sometimes get a break, too, with admissions that usually run a few dollars less than the standard adult rate. Los Angeles also has a few **free** attractions for everyone, but these are mostly historical and cultural monuments like adobes and old railroad stations – with the major exceptions of the Getty Center and Getty Villa (though parking is $15).

Crime and personal safety

With crime going down significantly in the past few years, the lawless reputation of Los Angeles is far in excess of the truth, and you're unlikely to have problems as long as you stick to the main areas of town. At night, though, a few areas – notably Compton, Inglewood, and South Central and East LA – are off limits. By being careful, planning ahead, and taking care of your possessions, you should be able to avoid any problems.

If you're unlucky enough to get **mugged**, just hand over your money; resistance is not a good idea. After the crime occurs, immediately report it to the police so you can later attempt to recover your loss from an insurance provider – unlikely, but worth a try. One prime spot to be mugged is at an **ATM** in a darkened location, where you may be forced to make the maximum withdrawal and hand it over. Needless to say, you should treat ATM use with caution and not worry about looking paranoid.

If your passport is stolen (or if you lose it), call your country's consulate (see list on p.37) and pick up or have sent to you an application form, which you must submit with a notarized photocopy of your ID and a reissuing fee, often at least $30.

Car crime and safety

When driving, keep doors locked and hide valuables out of sight, either in the trunk or the glove compartment, and leave any valuables you don't need for your journey back in your hotel safe. Should a rare "carjacking" occur, in which you're told at gunpoint to hand over your car, you should flee the vehicle as quickly as possible, get away from the scene, and then call the police (☎911). If your car breaks down at night while on a major street, activate the emergency flashers to signal a police officer for assistance. During the day, find the nearest phone book and call for a tow truck. Should you be forced to stop your car on a freeway, pull over to the right shoulder – never the left – and activate your flashers. Wait for assistance either in your vehicle, while strapped in by a seatbelt, or on a safe embankment nearby.

Breaking the law

Whether intentionally or not, foreign visitors may find themselves breaking the law on occasion. Aside from the increasingly steep fines for speeding or parking violations, one of the most common ways visitors bring trouble on themselves is through jaywalking, or crossing the road against red lights or away from intersections. Fines can be stiff, and the police will most assuredly not have sympathy for you if you mumble that you "didn't think it was illegal".

Alcohol laws provide another source of irritation to visitors, particularly as the law prohibits drinking liquor, wine or beer in most public spaces like parks and beaches, and, most frustrating of all to European tourists, alcohol is officially off limits to anyone under 21. Some try to get around this with a phony driver's licence, even though getting caught with a fake ID will put you in jeopardy particularly if you're from out of the country. Driving under the influence, or drunk driving, is aggressively punished throughout the state, with loss of license, fines and potential jail time for those caught breaking the law with a police-enforced "breathalyzer" test. The current limit is a blood-alcohol level of .08, or three drinks within a single hour for a 150-pound person. Other infringements include insulting a police officer (eg, arguing with one) and riding a bicycle at night without proper lights and reflectors.

Electricity

The US operates on 110V 60Hz and uses two-pronged plugs with the flat prongs parallel. Foreign devices will need both a plug adapter and a transformer, though laptops and phone chargers usually automatically detect and cope with the different voltage and frequency.

Entry requirements

Basic requirements for entry to the US are detailed (and should be frequently checked for updates) on the US State Department website Ⓦtravel.state.gov.

Under the Visa Waiver Program (VWP), if you're a citizen of the UK or most other European states, Australia, New Zealand, Japan or other selected countries (36 in all), and visiting the US for less than ninety days, at a minimum you'll need an onward or return ticket, a visa waiver form and a Machine Readable Passport (MRP). The **I-94W Nonimmigrant Visa Waiver Arrival/ Departure Form** can be provided by your travel agency or embassy, or you can get the form online at the US Customs website, Ⓦwww.cbp.gov. The same form covers entry across the US borders with Canada and Mexico (for non-Canadian and non-Mexican citizens). Under no circumstances are visitors who have been admitted under the Visa Waiver Program allowed to extend their stays beyond ninety days. If you're in the Visa Waiver Program and intend to work, study or stay in the country for more than ninety days, you must apply for a **regular visa** through your local US embassy or consulate.

Canadian citizens, who have not always needed a passport to get into the US, should have their passports on them when entering the country. If you're planning to stay for more than ninety days you'll need a **visa**. Without the proper paperwork, Canadians are barred from working in the US.

Citizens of all other countries should contact their local US embassy or consulate for details of current entry requirements, as they are often required to have both a valid passport and a non-immigrant visitor's visa, and additional information may be required, depending on the home country and its current relationship with the US government.

For further information or to get a **visa extension** before your time is up, contact the nearest US Citizenship and Immigration Service office, whose address will be at the front of the phone book under the Federal Government Offices listings. You can also contact the National Customer Service Center at Ⓣ1-800/375-5283 or Ⓦwww.uscis.gov/contact_us.

US Customs

Upon your entry to the US, Customs officers will relieve you of your customs declaration form, which you receive on incoming planes, on ferries and at border crossing points. It asks if you're carrying any fresh foods and if you've visited a farm in the last month.

As well as food and anything agricultural, it's prohibited to carry into the country any articles from such places as North Korea, Iran, Syria or Cuba, as well as obvious no-nos like protected wildlife species and ancient artefacts. Anyone caught sneaking **drugs** into the country will not only face prosecution but also be entered in the records as an undesirable and probably denied entry for all time. For duty-free allowances and other information regarding customs, call Ⓣ202/354-1000 or visit Ⓦwww.customs.gov.

US embassies and consulates abroad

Australia

Canberra (embassy) 21 Moonah Place, Yarralumla ACT 2600 Ⓣ02/6214 5600, Ⓦcanberra.usembassy.gov
Melbourne (consulate) 553 St Kilda Rd, VIC 3004 Ⓣ03/9526 5900
Perth (consulate) 16 St George's Terrace, 13th Floor, WA 6000 Ⓣ08/9202 1224
Sydney (consulate) MLC Centre, Level 10, 19–29 Martin Place, NSW 2000 Ⓣ02/9373 9200

Canada

Calgary (consulate) 615 Macleod Trail SE, Room 1000, AB T2G 4T8 ⓣ403/266-8962
Halifax (consulate) Wharf Tower II, 1969 Upper Water St, Suite 904, NS B3J 3R7 ⓣ902/429-2480
Montréal (consulate) 1155 St Alexandré St, QC H3B 1Z1 ⓣ514/398-9695, ⓦmontreal.usconsulate.gov
Ottawa (embassy) 490 Sussex Drive, ON K1N 1G8 ⓣ613/238-5335, ⓦcanada.usembassy.gov
Québec City (consulate) 2 Place Terrasse Dufferin, QC G1R 4T9 ⓣ418/692-2095, ⓦquebec.usconsulate.gov
Toronto (consulate) 360 University Ave, ON M5G 1S4 ⓣ416/595-1700, ⓦtoronto.usconsulate.gov
Vancouver (consulate) 1095 W Pender St, 21st Floor, BC V6E 2M6 ⓣ604/685-4311, ⓦvancouver.usconsulate.gov
Winnipeg (consulate) 201 Portage Ave, Suite 860, MB R3B 3K6 ⓣ204/940-1800, ⓦwinnipeg.usconsulate.gov

Ireland

Dublin (embassy) 42 Elgin Rd, Ballsbridge 4 ⓣ01/668 8777, ⓦdublin.usembassy.gov

New Zealand

Auckland (consulate) 3rd Floor, Citibank Building, 23 Customs St ⓣ09/303 2724
Wellington (embassy) 29 Fitzherbert Terrace, Thorndon ⓣ04/462 6000, ⓦnewzealand.usembassy.gov

South Africa

Pretoria (embassy) 877 Pretorius St, 0083 ⓣ12/431 4000, ⓕ12/342 2299, ⓦsouthafrica.usembassy.gov

UK

Belfast (consulate) Danesfort House, 223 Stranmillis Road, Belfast BT9 5GR ⓣ028/9038 6100
Edinburgh (consulate) 3 Regent Terrace, EH7 5BW ⓣ0131/556 8315
London (embassy) 24 Grosvenor Square, W1A 1AE ⓣ020/7499 9000, visa hotline ⓣ09042/450 100, ⓦlondon.usembassy.gov

Consulates in California

Australia

Los Angeles 2029 Century Park E, 31st Floor, CA 90067 ⓣ310/229-4800, ⓦwww.dfat.gov.au/missions

Canada

Los Angeles 550 S Hope St, 9th Floor, CA 90071-2627 ⓣ213/346-2700, ⓕ213/620-8827, ⓦwww.dfait-maeci.gc.ca
San Diego 402 W Broadway, 4th Floor, CA 92101 ⓣ619/615-4287, ⓕ619/615-4286

Ireland

Los Angeles 751 Seadrift Drive, Huntington Beach, CA 92648 ⓣ714/658-9832, ⓕ714/374-8972

New Zealand

Los Angeles 2425 Olympic Blvd, Santa Monica, CA 90404 ⓣ310/566-6555, ⓦwww.nzcgla.com

South Africa

Los Angeles 6300 Wilshire Blvd, Suite 600, CA 90048 ⓣ323/651-0902, ⓕ323/651-5969, ⓦwww.link2southafrica.com

UK

Los Angeles 11766 Wilshire Blvd, Suite 1200, CA 90025 ⓣ310/481-0031, ⓕ310/481-2960, ⓦwww.britainusa.com/la

Health

If you have a serious accident while you're in California, emergency services will get to you sooner and charge you later. For **emergencies**, dial toll-free ⓣ911 from any phone. For medical or dental problems that don't require an ambulance, most hospitals have a walk-in emergency room: for your nearest hospital or dental office, check with your hotel or dial information at ⓣ411.

Should you need to see a **doctor**, lists can be found online or in the *Yellow Pages* under "Clinics" or "Physicians and Surgeons". Be aware that even consultations are costly, usually around $95–145 each visit, which is payable in advance. Keep receipts for any part of your medical treatment, including prescriptions, so that you can claim against your insurance once you're home.

For minor ailments, stop by a local **pharmacy**. Foreign visitors should note that many medicines available over the counter at home – codeine-based painkillers, for one – are **prescription-only** in the US. Bring additional supplies if you're particularly brand-loyal.

By far the most common tourist illness in California is **sunburn**: the sun can be fierce, so plenty of protective sunscreen (SPF 30+) is a must. Surfers and swimmers should also watch for strong currents and **undertows** at some beaches: we've noted in the text where the water can be especially treacherous.

Travellers from Europe, Canada and Australia do not require inoculations to enter the US.

Medical resources for travellers

US and Canada

CDC ⓦwwwnc.cdc.gov/travel. Official US government travel health site.
International Society for Travel Medicine ⓦwww.istm.org. Has a full list of travel health clinics.

Australia, New Zealand and South Africa

Travellers' medical and Vaccination Centre ⓣ1300/658 844, ⓦwww.tmvc.com.au. Lists travel clinics in Australia, New Zealand and South Africa.

UK and Ireland

British Airways Travel Clinics ⓣ012776/685-040 or ⓦwww.britishairways.com for nearest clinic.
MASTA (Medical Advisory Service for Travellers Abroad) ⓣ0113/238-7575 or ⓦwww.masta.org for the nearest clinic.

Insurance

The US has no national health-care system and, while major health-care legislation passed in 2010, the implementation dates are far spread out and the law itself is a bit of a patchwork, especially for foreign travellers. You're still well advised to protect yourself from exorbitant medical costs should any injury occur while in the country. Even though EU health-care privileges apply in America, UK residents would do well to take out an **insurance** policy before travelling to cover against theft, loss, and illness or injury. Before paying for a new policy, however, it's worth checking whether you are already covered – some all-risks home insurance policies may cover your possessions when overseas, and many private medical schemes include coverage when abroad.

Internet

The proliferation of wireless hot spots all over the region means anyone travelling with a laptop or PDA should have no trouble getting connected to the **internet**, often at fast speeds at no cost. At some cafés you'll need to use your credit card to sign up for a service, though many other cafés have unsecured access or will give you the password when you buy a coffee or muffin.

If you need to borrow a computer to log on, the best bets are **public libraries**, which almost invariably have **free internet access** – just ask at the front desk. You may have to wait for an opening, or sign up for a later slot. You'll also come across dedicated **cybercafés** with a dozen or more machines usually charged at around $5–10 an hour. Many motels, hotels and hostels also offer Internet access with a machine or two in the lobby, but again, WiFi is taking over.

Laundry

The larger hotels provide laundry service at a price. Cheaper motels and hostels may have self-service laundry facilities, but otherwise you'll be doing your laundry at a laundromat. Found all over the place, they're usually open long hours and have a powder-dispensing machine and another to provide change. A typical wash and dry costs $4–6.

Mail

Post offices are usually open Monday through Friday, from 9am to 5pm, although some are also open on Saturday from 9am to noon or 1pm.

Ordinary **mail** within the US costs 44¢ for letters weighing up to an ounce; addresses must include the zip code, which can be found at Ⓦwww.usps.com. The return address should be written in the upper left corner of the envelope. **Airmail** from California to Europe generally takes about a week. Postcards cost 28¢ or 44¢, depending on size.

Drop mail off at any post office or in the blue mailboxes found on street corners throughout LA. Domestic letters that don't carry a **zip code** are liable to get lost or at least seriously delayed; phone books list zip codes for their service area, and post offices – even abroad – should have zip-code directories for major US cities.

You can have mail sent to you c/o General Delivery (known elsewhere as poste restante), at the main post office in Downtown LA, north of Union Station, at 900 N Alameda St, Los Angeles, CA 90012 (Mon–Fri 8am–5.30pm, Sat 8am–4pm; Ⓣ213/617-4404), which will hold mail for thirty days before returning it to the sender – so make sure the envelope has a return address. Alternatively, any decent hotel will hold mail for you, even in advance of your arrival.

Rules on sending **parcels** are very rigid: packages must be sealed according to the instructions given at the Ⓦusps.com website. To send anything out of the country, you'll need a green **customs declaration form**, available from the post office. Postal rates for airmailing a parcel weighing up to 1 lb to Europe, Australia and New Zealand are $15–18.

Maps

The **maps** in this book should be sufficient in helping you find your way around the main parts of town and their key attractions, with the exception of the Hollywood Hills, whose serpentine passages and switchbacks require highly detailed maps to navigate (and even then, with difficulty). For a folding map, try our rip-proof *Los Angeles Rough Guide Map* ($8.99).

For a more detailed view of the city, Thomas Brothers Publishing has the hefty, spiral-bound, 2009 editions *LA County Thomas Guide* ($19.95) and *Thomas Guide to Los Angeles and Orange Counties* ($34.95), sold at most bookstores. Published yearly for counties across Southern California, the Thomas guides are the best maps available for regional travel, especially for venturing beyond the easily accessed parts of the city into more unfamiliar territory – like the northern deserts, eastern suburbs or Hollywood Hills. If you're staying for several weeks, consider purchasing one if you're travelling anywhere outside central LA. If you're interested in highly detailed views of rural terrain, as well as the urban layout, consider the colourful *Benchmark California Road and Recreation Atlas* ($24.95, published 2009), which best shows national forests, parkland, hiking trails, and minor dirt and gravel roads.

If you happen to be a member, stop by the Automobile Club of Southern California, 2601 S Figueroa St, south of Downtown (Mon–Fri 9am–5pm; Ⓣ213/741-3686, Ⓦwww.aaa-calif.com), for free maps, guides and other information. The national office of the AAA also provides maps and assistance to its members, as well as to British members of the AA and RAC, and Canadian members of the CAA (Ⓣ1-800/222-4357, Ⓦwww.aaa.com).

LA-area travel bookshops can be found under "Shopping", p.301.

Money

With an **ATM card**, you'll be able to withdraw money just about anywhere in LA, though you'll be charged $2–4 for using a different bank's network. Foreign cash-dispensing cards linked to international networks, such as Plus or Cirrus, are also widely accepted. Make sure you have a **personal identification number** (PIN) that's designed to work overseas.

US currency: a note for foreign travellers

One **US dollar** is the rough equivalent of 0.67 pound sterling, 0.75 euro, one Canadian dollar, 1.1 Australian dollars, 1.35 New Zealand dollars and 7.5 South African rand. US currency comes in bills of $1, $5, $10, $20, $50 and $100 **denominations**. All are the same size, though denominations of $5 and higher have in the last few years been changing shades from their familiar drab green – with the $100 bill particularly loaded with high-tech, anti-counterfeiting elements. The dollar comprises one hundred cents, made up of combinations of one-cent pennies, five-cent nickels, ten-cent dimes, and 25-cent quarters. Quarters are most useful for buses, vending machines, parking meters and telephones, so always carry plenty.

Bank hours are generally from 9am to 5pm Monday to Thursday, and until 6pm on Friday; the big local names are Wells Fargo and Bank of America. For banking services – especially currency exchange – outside normal business hours and on weekends, try major hotels or Travelex outlets.

Credit cards are the most widely accepted form of payment for most hotels, restaurants and retailers. Using a credit card can save on exchange-rate commissions. Most major credit cards issued by foreign banks are honoured in the US. Visa, MasterCard, American Express and Discover are the most widely used.

If your credit cards are **stolen**, you'll need to provide information on where and when you made your last transactions, and to access the specific credit card company emergency numbers (on the back of your card).

Opening hours and public holidays

The opening hours of specific attractions – including museums, theme parks, public offices and homes open for tours – are given throughout the Guide, with phone numbers for those sights that are open irregularly, closed until further notice, or accessible only via advance reservation. It's always worth checking ahead, especially if you're planning to visit attractions far from central LA.

As a general rule, most museums are open Tuesday through Saturday (occasionally Sunday, too) from 10am until 5 or 6pm, with somewhat shorter hours on the weekends. Many museums will also stay open late one evening a week – usually Thursday, when ticket prices are sometimes reduced or entry is even free. Government offices, including post offices, are open during regular business hours, typically 8 or 9am until 5pm, Monday through Friday (though some post offices are open Sat morning until noon or 1pm). Most stores are open daily from 10am until 5 or 6pm, while speciality stores can be more erratic, usually opening and closing later in the day, from noon to 2pm until 8 or 9pm, and remaining shuttered for two days of the week. Malls tend to be open from 10am until 7 or 8pm daily, though individual stores may close before the mall does.

While some diners stay open 24 hours, the more typical restaurants open daily around 11am or noon for lunch and close at 9 to 10pm. Places that serve breakfast usually open early, between 6 to 8am, serve lunch later, and close around 2 or 3pm. Dance and live music clubs often won't open until 9 or 10pm, and many will serve liquor until 2am and then either close for the night or stay open until dawn without serving booze. Bars that close at 2am may reopen as early as 6am to grab bleary-eyed regulars in need of a liquid breakfast.

On the national public holidays listed below, banks, government offices and many museums are likely to be closed all day. Small stores, as well as some restaurants and clubs, are usually closed as well, but shopping malls, supermarkets, and department and chain stores increasingly remain open, regardless of the holiday. Most parks, beaches, and cemeteries stay open during holidays, too.

National holidays

New Year's Day Jan 1
Martin Luther King's Birthday observed third Mon in Jan

Presidents' Day third Mon in Feb
Memorial Day last Mon in May
Independence Day July 4
Labor Day first Mon in Sept
Columbus Day second Mon in Oct
Veterans' Day Nov 11
Thanksgiving fourth Thurs in Nov
Christmas Dec 25

Phones

Like most major US cities, LA has an excellent communications infrastructure. Although some areas are better hooked up than others – the Westside, for example – most communication services are more than adequate throughout the region, especially telephone service and email.

If you're making a **telephone** call, note that Los Angeles has thirteen area codes (see below) that, with the rise of ten-digit dialling, you may need to use even if calling from within the same area code. A local call on an increasingly rare public phone usually costs 50¢. Outside the immediate calling zone, you'll have to dial a 1, plus the area code, then the telephone number. Unless you're using a cell phone (and not paying a roaming fee), you'll be charged quite a bit more for out-of-area-code calls than for calls within them.

With excellent **mobile phone** reception in all but the remotest areas, taking your phone to California makes a lot of sense. Ask your provider to confirm that your phone will work on US frequencies (most do these days) and get it set up for international use. **Roaming** calling rates can be pretty high and if you're planning to make a lot of calls it may work out cheaper to **buy a phone** in California, though the lower cost is counterbalanced by the need to tell all your friends your new phone number. Basic, new phones can be picked up for as little as $30.

Calling from your **hotel room** will cost considerably more than if you use a public phone. Fancy hotels often charge a connection fee of at least $1 for most calls (waived if they're toll-free or emergency), and international calls will cost a small fortune. While an increasing number of public phones accept credit cards, these are best avoided, as they can incur astronomical charges for long-distance service, including a high "connection fee" that can bump charges up to as much as $7 a minute.

Any number with ⓣ800, ⓣ866, ⓣ877 or ⓣ888 in place of the area code is **toll-free**. Most major hotels, government agencies and car rental firms have toll-free numbers, though some can be used only within the state of California – dialling is the only way to find out. Numbers with a ⓣ1-900 prefix are toll calls, typically sports information lines, psychic hotlines and phone-sex centres, and will cost you a variable, though consistently high, fee for just a few minutes of use.

Calling home from LA

Australia 00 + 61 + city code
Canada 1 + area code
New Zealand 00 + 64 + city code
Republic of Ireland 00 + 353 + city code
South Africa 00 + 27 + city code
UK and Northern Ireland 00 + 44 + city code

Useful numbers

Emergencies ⓣ911
Directory information ⓣ411
Directory inquiries for toll-free numbers ⓣ1-800/555-1212
Long-distance directory information ⓣ1-(area code)/555-1212
International operator ⓣ00

LA area codes

213 Downtown
310 West Hollywood, Beverly Hills, West LA, Westwood, Santa Monica, Venice, Malibu, South Bay, San Pedro (area code shared with 424)
323 Mid-Wilshire, Hollywood, South Central LA, East LA
424 West Hollywood, Beverly Hills, West LA, Westwood, Santa Monica, Venice, Malibu, South Bay, San Pedro (area code shared with 310)
562 Long Beach, Whittier, Southeast LA
626 Pasadena, Arcadia, San Gabriel Valley
657 Northern Orange County – Anaheim, Garden Grove, Huntington Beach (area code shared with 714)
661 Santa Clarita, far northern LA
714 Northern Orange County – Anaheim, Garden Grove, Huntington Beach (area code shared with 657)
805 Lancaster, northern deserts

818 Burbank, Glendale, San Fernando Valley
909 Pomona, Inland Empire
949 Southern Orange County – Costa Mesa, Newport and Laguna beaches

Photography

With fabulous scenery and great light much of the time, many parts of the LA area can be a **photographer's** paradise. If you have a camera in tow, bring plenty of digital memory or be prepared to periodically visit photo shops and burn your images onto CD. Otherwise, a cell phone camera will do. As ever, try to shoot in the early morning and late afternoon when the lower-angled light casts deeper shadows and gives greater depth to your shots.

It is never a good idea to take photos of military installations and the like, and with the current heightened security, airports and some government buildings may be considered sensitive.

Senior travellers

Seniors are defined broadly in the US as anyone older than 55–65 years of age. Those travelling can regularly find discounts of anywhere from 10 to 50 percent at movie theatres, museums, hotels, restaurants, performing arts venues and the occasional shop. On Amtrak, they can get a fifteen percent discount on most regular fares. On Greyhound the discount is smaller, in the range of five to ten percent. If heading to a national park, don't miss the **Senior Pass**, which, when bought at a park for a mere $10, provides a lifetime of free entry to federally operated recreation sites, as well as half-priced discounts on concessions such as boat launches and camping. In California, low-income seniors (age 62 and above) can apply for a **Golden Bear Pass** ($5; ⓦwww.parks.ca.gov), which allows complimentary parking at all state-operated facilities, though it doesn't cover boating fees, camping and the like.

Time

California runs on **Pacific Standard Time** (PST), which is eight hours behind GMT, and jumps forward an hour for Daylight Savings Time (the second Sunday in March to the first Sunday in November). During most of this eight-month period, when it is noon Monday in California it is 3pm in New York, 8pm in London, 5am Tuesday in Sydney, and 7am Tuesday in Auckland.

Tourist information

California's official tourism website (ⓦwww.visitcalifornia.com) is a reasonable starting point for advance information. Much of the same material is available in its free tourism information packet, which can be ordered online, by calling ⓣ1-877/CALIFORNIA, or by contacting California Tourism, PO Box 1499, Sacramento, CA 95812-1499 (ⓣ916/444-4429 or 1-877/225-4367).

Visitor centres go under a variety of names, but they all provide detailed information about the local area. Typically they're open Monday through Friday 9am–5pm and Saturday 9am–1pm, except in summer, when they may be open seven days a week from 8 or 9am until 6pm or later. These

Visitor centres in and around LA

Anaheim/Disneyland 800 W Katella Ave ⓣ714/991-8963, ⓦwww.anaheimoc.org

Beverly Hills 239 S Beverly Drive ⓣ1-800/345-2210, ⓦwww.beverlyhillscvb.com

Downtown LA 685 S Figueroa St ⓣ213/689-8822, ⓦwww.discoverlosangeles.com

Hollywood at Hollywood & Highland mall, 6801 Hollywood Blvd ⓣ323/467-6412

Long Beach 1 World Trade Center, 3rd Floor ⓣ562/436-3645, ⓦwww.visitlongbeach.com

Pasadena 300 E Green St ⓣ626/795-9311, ⓦwww.pasadenacal.com

Santa Monica 1920 Main St ⓣ310/393-7593, ⓦwww.santamonica.com

West Hollywood in the Pacific Design Center, 8687 Melrose Ave #M38 ⓣ310/289-2525, ⓦwww.visitwesthollywood.com

promotional offices will send you copious material on their respective areas, including glossy promos advertising the swanky hotels and restaurants, plugs for the top sights, and, occasionally, a simple map or two.

You can also pick up free promotional material such as maps, hotel and restaurant pamphlets, and magazine-sized city guides at small kiosks across the city, or at stands in most hotels.

Travellers with disabilities

By the Americans with Disabilities Act, the US is focused on accommodating travellers with mobility problems or other physical disabilities. All public buildings have to be **wheelchair accessible** and provide suitable toilet facilities, almost all street corners have dropped curbs, public telephones are specially equipped for hearing-aid users, and most public transport has accessibility aids such as subways with elevators and buses that "kneel" to let riders board. Even movie theatres have been forced by courts to allow people in wheelchairs to have a reasonable, unimpeded view of the screen. Most hotel and motel chains offer accessible **accommodation**, though the situation may be more problematic at bed-and-breakfasts built a century ago, where a narrow stairway may be the only option.

Transport

Major **car rental** firms can provide vehicles with hand controls for drivers with leg or spinal disabilities, though these are typically available only on the pricier models. Regarding parking regulations, licence plates for the disabled must carry a three-inch-square international access symbol, and a placard bearing this symbol must be hung from the car's rearview mirror.

American **air carriers** must by law accommodate customers with disabilities, and some even allow attendants of those with serious conditions to accompany them for a reduced fare. Almost every Amtrak train includes one or more cars with accommodation for disabled passengers, along with wheelchair assistance at train platforms, adapted on-board seating, free travel for guide dogs, and discounts on fares, all with 24 hours' advance notice. Passengers with hearing impairment can get information by calling ⓣ1-800/523-6590 (TTY) or checking out ⓦwww.amtrak.com.

By contrast, travelling by **Greyhound** and **Amtrak Thruway** bus connections is often trouble. Buses are not equipped with platforms for wheelchairs, though intercity carriers are required by law to provide assistance with boarding, and disabled passengers may be able to get priority seating. Call Greyhound's ADA customer assistance line for more information (ⓣ1-800/752-4841, ⓦwww.greyhound.com).

Information

The California Office of Tourism (ⓦwww.gocalif.ca.gov) has lists of handicapped facilities at places of accommodation and attractions. National **organizations** facilitating travel for people with disabilities include SATH, the Society for the Advancement of Travelers with Handicaps (ⓣ212/447-7284, ⓦwww.sath.org), a non-profit travel-industry grouping made up of travel agents, tour operators, and hotel and airline management; contact them in advance so they can notify the appropriate members. Mobility International USA (ⓣ541/343-1284, ⓦwww.miusa.org) answers transportation queries and operates an exchange programme for people with disabilities. Access-Able (ⓣ303/232-2979, ⓦwww.access-able.com) is an information service that assists travellers with disabilities by putting them in contact with other people with similar conditions.

The City

The City

1

Downtown LA

Visible from a distance as a patch of skyscrapers caged by freeways, **DOWNTOWN LA** has in the last few decades emerged from tourist obscurity to become something of a destination in its own right. Although it lacks the showpiece sights of the much more familiar Westside, it nonetheless contains a number of the region's key historic and artistic attractions. An enjoyable place to visit during the day (though it still shuts down at night), the district features a smattering of grand old movie palaces, modern museums, and a few interesting pieces of architecture – along with some of the city's best hotels and restaurants.

From the city's earliest days, Downtown was the social and cultural hub of the region, where the masses worked, dined, shopped, and came to be entertained. With the advent of the automobile, however, Angelenos moved away from the city centre, paving over orange groves and beanfields in their march outward, and Downtown became a second-rate neighbourhood home to decaying Victorian mansions and downwardly mobile residents.

Until 1960, **City Hall** was, at 28 storeys, the town's tallest structure, and seemed to symbolize the limited public ambitions of the area. However, from the 1960s to the end of the 1980s, Downtown saw a building boom spurred on largely by Canadian and Japanese venture capital. Development replaced the creaky mansions atop Bunker Hill with the glass curtain-walls of international banks. The boom faded during LA's near-depression during the early 1990s, but since then the area has made a slow recovery. To many, the monumental construction of Disney Hall is the singular symbol of Downtown's long-awaited rebirth, while less high-minded souls point to the sports complex of the Staples Center as providing the real lifeblood of the area.

Although the gleaming modernity of Bunker Hill is immediately tempting, a trip Downtown rightfully starts at **the Plaza**, the original nineteenth-century town site and now the remodelled focus of "**El Pueblo de Los Angeles**", a state park that also holds the historic, if over-commercialized, **Olvera Street**. To the south, LA's **Civic Center** is a bland seat of local government, enlivened by the classic form of City Hall and the startling modern brio of the Caltrans building.

Further south stand the antique facades along Spring Street and Broadway. Since their heyday in the 1920s as the respective financial and cultural axes of the city, the two streets have changed considerably. **Broadway** is still a thriving commercial area home to many Hispanic merchants, its once-grand movie palaces now hosting fiery evangelist churches, hectic swap meets, or the occasional revival film. **Spring Street**, on the other hand, became largely deserted through the 1980s and 90s, but since then some of its grand Neoclassical buildings have been renovated into artists' lofts and a few smart shops and restaurants.

Replacing Spring Street as LA's financial axis, **Bunker Hill** has a few museums and modern buildings of note, while north and east of Downtown, **Chinatown** and **Little Tokyo** are interesting for their predictable wealth of ethnic restaurants, though neither is a vital cultural centre – the city's Asian immigrants tend to migrate toward livelier places like Monterey Park and Alhambra. Central American newcomers, by contrast, often end up in **Westlake** or **MacArthur Park**, west of Downtown, while hipsters gravitate to funky, working-class **Echo Park**.

Finally, sealing off Downtown from the spiderweb of freeways to the east, the **LA River** is a bleak concrete channel designed for flood control and, not

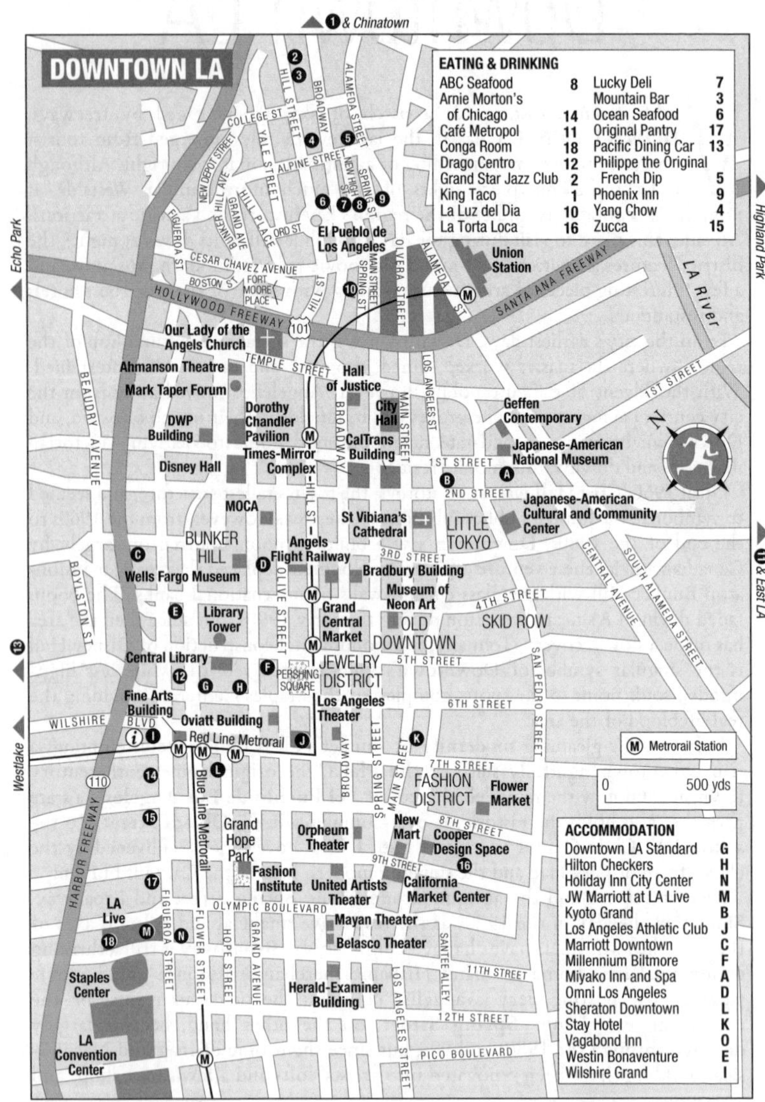

surprisingly, the forbidding setting for dramatic scenes in assorted TV shows and Hollywood action flicks.

Downtown can easily be seen in a day, and if your feet get tired you can hop aboard the **DASH buses** that run frequently to major tourist destinations. The area is also the hub of the MTA networks and easily accessible by public transportation, based around the colossus of Union Station. **Parking** in lots is expensive on weekdays ($10+ per hour), but on weekends is more affordable (a flat $7–10 for up to eight hours); street parking is a good alternative, less so on Bunker Hill, where the meters cost at least $2 per hour.

Some history

For more than two hundred years, the centre of Downtown LA has been slowly shifting. **Spanish colonizers** constructed the first town site, the Plaza, in 1781, but the tract was soon destroyed by fire and rebuilt further southeast in 1818, at the present site of El Pueblo de Los Angeles (see below). While the district was the focus of commercial activity during the Mexican years of rule and the early American period, even then other parts of the LA basin were developing as alternative nodes for housing and commerce.

By the end of the nineteenth century, Downtown's **commercial hub** had relocated to Broadway, thick with department stores and vaudeville theatres, while Spring Street had become the financial nexus. Meanwhile, Broadway and Spring were, along with the 1928 City Hall, the most visible emblems of LA as an emerging American **metropolis** – by then numbering over a million people within its city limits and over two million in surrounding LA County.

Although the Civic Center is still LA's seat of government, its financial and cultural counterparts have since relocated. Cold War-era urban renewal projects led to Bunker Hill's replacing Spring Street in the 1960s as Downtown's financial nucleus, while nothing so far has re-created Broadway's buzzing entertainment zone. Ultimately, it took a handful of huge new showpieces, most prominently Disney Hall, Our Lady of the Angels Catholic Church and the Staples Center, to begin drawing the city's attention back from the Westside, with the hopes of civic boosters riding on the public's appreciation for eye-catching architecture and sports enthusiasm – so far, a moderately successful gamble.

The Plaza and around

Because so much of LA's architectural heritage has been destroyed, it is surprising that **the Plaza** still exists. From the early 1920s on, city planners wanted to demolish it to make way for a larger Civic Center. Luckily, the area was saved by its 1953 designation as **El Pueblo de Los Angeles State Historic Park**, 845 N Alameda St (daily 9am–5pm; free; ⓣ213/625-3800, ⓦwww.ci.la.ca.us/ELP), making it an essential stop on any history trek through LA. In the immediate vicinity of the Plaza, **Union Station** and the adjacent **Gateway Transit Center** together are a sizable hub for train and bus activity throughout the region, while just north sits the latest version of LA's uninspiring **Chinatown**.

Olvera Street

Within El Pueblo de Los Angeles Historic State Park, the square known as **the Plaza** was in 1870 reconstructed into the circular design located just off North Los

Angeles Street. However, the true focus of the early settlement was the **zanja madre**, or "mother ditch", which ran from the then-wild Los Angeles River through what is now **Olvera Street**. The canal was used for domestic and agricultural purposes as early as 1781. In the 1870s, pioneering hydrologist **William Mulholland** had an early job ditch-digging on the watercourse, moving up to all-powerful water superintendent in eight short years.

Open to pedestrian traffic only (daily 10am–7pm; free; Ⓦwww.olvera-street.com), tiny Olvera Street has been closed since 1930 to automobiles; you can trace the original path of the *zanja madre* by a series of marked bricks along its length. The street is at its best when taken over for numerous **festivals** throughout the year, like the Day of the Dead on November 2, and regularly features strolling mariachi bands, Aztec and Mexican-themed processions, and various dancers and artisans.

Olvera Street's re-emergence was the work of one **Christine Sterling**, who, with help from the city government, tore down the slum she found here in 1926 and created much of what remains today. For the next twenty years, she organized fiestas and worked to popularize the city's Mexican heritage while living in the early nineteenth-century **Avila Adobe** at 10 Olvera St (daily 9am–4pm; free). Furnished in the style of the 1840s, it's touted as the oldest structure in Los Angeles (from 1847), though it was almost entirely rebuilt out of reinforced concrete following the 1971 Sylmar earthquake.

Across the street, the **Sepulveda House**, 125 Paseo de la Plaza (daily 9am–4pm; free), is a quaint 1887 Eastlake Victorian and the park's visitor centre, with rooms highlighting different eras in Hispanic cultural history and an informative free film on the history of LA. To get a sense of everything in the historic park, take a free walking tour (Tues–Sat 10am, 11am & noon; Ⓣ213/628-1274, Ⓦwww.lasangelitas.org), which begins at the business office of Las Angelitas del Pueblo next to the Old Plaza Firehouse on the Plaza's south end.

South and west of Olvera Street

Just west of the Plaza, the Catholic Plaza Church, or **La Placita**, 535 N Main St (daily 6.30am–8pm; Ⓣ213/629-3101, Ⓦwww.laplacita.org), is a small adobe structure with a gabled roof that has long been a sanctuary for Central American refugees. From 1861 to 1923 the building was remodelled or reconstructed four times, but it still evokes a sense of the local heritage. Church **masses** occur three or four times daily, with twelve Eucharist services on Sunday.

Just south of Olvera Street, across the Plaza, is a small collection of historic buildings that are in various states of renovation and public use. From the east, the red-brick **Old Plaza Firehouse** (Tues–Sun 10am–3pm; free) was only operational for thirteen years, beginning in 1884, subsequently becoming a saloon, lodging house, and pool hall before reaching museum status in 1960. If you like old firefighting equipment, this is the place for you. Around the corner, LA's original Chinese settlement was centred on the **Garnier Building**, an 1850 brick-and-stone structure that now houses the **Chinese American Museum**, 425 N Los Angeles St (Tues–Sun 10am–3pm; $5; Ⓣ213/485-8567, Ⓦwww.camla.org), featuring exhibits on local Chinese history, society and culture, with items from the nineteenth and twentieth centuries including revealing letters, photos and documents, as well as some contemporary art and the re-creation of a Chinese herb shop c.1900. Another site honouring a historic ethnic group, the Italian Hall, on Cesar Chavez Avenue, is due to open in 2011 as the Italian American Museum (see Ⓦitalianhall.org), and will house artefacts and mementos of a community that flourished here in the early twentieth century.

West across tiny, pedestrianized Sanchez Street, handsome Italianate arches grace the **Pico House**, opened in 1870 as LA's most luxurious hotel; the last Mexican governor of California, Pio Pico, lived here. Pico House is closed to the public, as is the adjacent **Merced Theater**, which dates from the same year and was the city's first indoor theatre.

Lastly, three blocks west, at the top of the hill marking the junction of Sunset Boulevard and Hill Street, the **Fort Moore Pioneer Memorial** is a series of bas-reliefs depicting early political and social figures who provided "for [LA's] citizens water and power for life and energy". This heroic inscription is written on the adjacent wall of what has been described as "the most spectacular man-made waterfall in the United States": an 80-foot-wide, 50-foot-high torrent serving as a colossal monument to the city's aqueous bounty. Not surprisingly, it was shut off thirty years ago.

Union Station and around

The Mission-style **Union Station**, across from the Plaza at 800 N Alameda St, is an impressive architectural landmark that still welcomes rail travellers with the same grandeur it had when it was constructed in the 1930s. Despite train travel's precipitous decline in the US, the terminus remains one of the city's best-preserved monuments to the golden age of railways, replete with grand arches a high clock tower, Spanish-tiled roof, and Art Deco verticality, grand arches and Streamline Moderne lettering. The heart of the region's public transit system, the station serves as the confluence for Amtrak, Metrolink and Metroline commuter trains (see Basics, p.27), as well as the occasional shooting location for all kinds of Hollywood movies. It was used most memorably in *Blade Runner*, as the gloomy, atmospheric police station where Harrison Ford's Deckard is given his mission to kill off four alien "replicants".

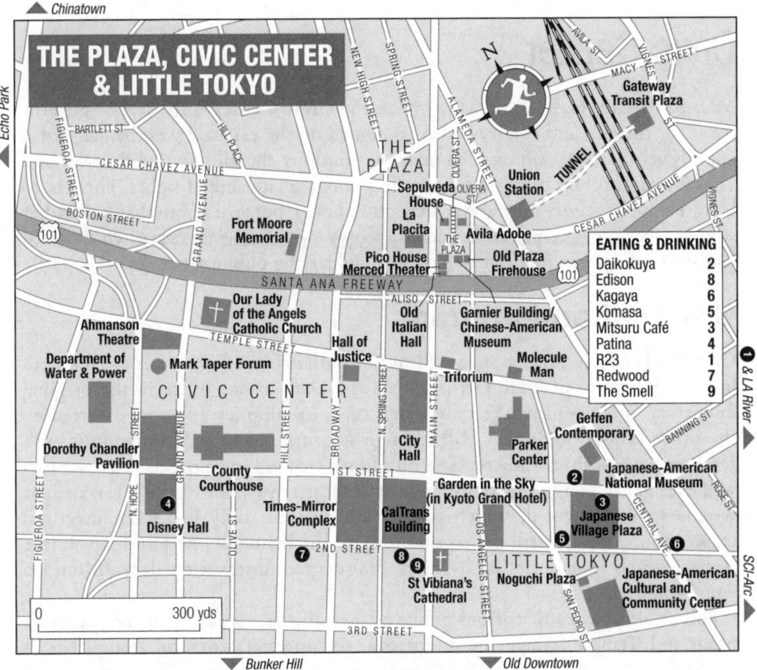

Less interesting is **Gateway Transit Center**, connected to Union Station by tunnel below the train tracks and comprising three distinct parts: the 26-storey **Gateway Tower**, with a customer service centre on its ground floor; **Patsaouras Transit Plaza**, the bus mall itself, decorated with insipid public art; and, under a glass ceiling, the **East Portal**, a light and airy space marred by an Orwellian-looking mural supposedly celebrating LA's ethnic diversity. There's nothing much to see beyond here, just the largest municipal **jail** in the US, Vignes St off N Main St, where celebrities from Paris Hilton to OJ Simpson have cooled their heels in recent decades.

Chinatown

The core of LA's **CHINATOWN** is located between North Broadway and North Hill streets, though it's rather touristy: small and hemmed in by wide boulevards, with a maze of ersatz-Chinese architecture, and narrow pedestrian alleys featuring inauthentic names like Bamboo Lane and Gin Ling Way. The area was established in 1938 following its residents' abrupt transplant from the current site of Union Station, and much of its decor was determined by outsiders more interested in creating a chinoiserie version of exoticism than anything genuine. Still, the surrounding streets away from the core do feature a range of authentic businesses, from excellent restaurants to curiosity shops and herbalists, and on **Chinese New Year**, there's a spirited display of pageantry throughout.

For a more well-rounded sense of contemporary Chinese culture, visit **Alhambra** and **Monterey Park** (see p.145), both lively suburbs located several miles east of Downtown.

Civic Center

Marked by City Hall's great white pillar, the **Civic Center** is the seat of government for the city and county of LA. Bounded on the east and west by San Pedro and Figueroa streets and on the north and south by the Hollywood Freeway and First Street, this hive of bureaucracy offers only a smattering of sights. There is, to be sure, much activity during weekday office hours, but apart from that it's a rather strange scene of desperate homeless people wandering in an often-deserted landscape of spartan modern architecture and jarring public artworks.

City Hall and around

City Hall, 200 N Spring St, is still most familiar from TV reruns as Dragnet's imposing symbol of civic virtue and as the *Daily Planet* office in the original Superman show. Once LA's tallest structure, its silhouette is now dwarfed by the office blocks of Bunker Hill, though it continues to be synonymous with Downtown's political power. The building's crown is as close as most visitors will ever get to seeing the Mausoleum at Halicarnassus, one of the seven ancient wonders of the world, which provided a curious, only-in-LA architectural inspiration. You can still get a good look at the inside of the building on free **tours**, which include its 28th-storey 360-degree observation deck (Mon–Fri 9am–4pm; free).

There's also plenty of curious public art hereabouts, especially at the corner of Main and Temple, where the monstrous, six-storey **Triforium**, from 1975, is decorated with shafts of coloured glass, flashing lights, and loudspeakers strategically placed between its massive concrete legs. After being silent for decades and surviving numerous demolition threats, the sound system in the "polyphonoptic" carillon was finally reactivated at the end of 2006 and the sculpture now offers a sort of retro-1960s light show daily (6–8am & 6–8pm). More compelling is **Molecule Man**, 255 E Temple St, in which sculptor Jonathan Borofsky (better known for his *Ballerina Clown* in Venice; see p.127) used perforated figures to supposedly illustrate the watery composition of the human body. Some see the figures as bullet-riddled bodies – a jab at the adjacent **Parker Center**, former headquarters of the LAPD.

Just to the south, near Spring and First streets, the concrete and glass **Times-Mirror Complex** houses the production facilities for the *Los Angeles Times*. Built in the colossal PWA Moderne style in the mid-1930s, and given a drab expansion in 1973, the building supplanted an earlier version, closer to Broadway, that was bombed, rebuilt, then torn down. Something similar has happened to the newspaper's quality in recent years, which has become enfeebled through endless rounds of budget cuts and corporate tinkering. Still, you can take one of its free, twice-monthly **public tours** (hours vary; by reservation only at Ⓣ213/237-5757, Ⓦwww.latimes.com) if you're interested in seeing how this once-great paper operates.

Much more eye-opening and engaging is the colossal modernist pile of the $165-million **CalTrans Building**, at Main and First streets (Mon–Fri 8am–5pm; free), whose spectacle starts at the ground-level plaza, where the mottled glass-and-aluminum facade towers over the visitor, its exterior panels opening and closing depending on weather and sunlight. Closer to the entrance, in the "outdoor lobby", banded neon tubes spray coloured light in various patterns across four storeys, making it the largest public-art sculpture in the city. On the east side of the building, the large, glassy curtain wall is actually made up of hundreds of photovoltaic cells, contributing five percent of the building's power needs. For this building and others throughout the US, Thom Mayne won architecture's highest honor, the Pritzker Prize, in 2005.

Civic Center West

The municipal buildings in the **Civic Center West** are fairly bland, though not entirely without interest. The **Department of Water and Power Building**, at the corner of Hope and First streets, is a pleasing modern edifice that casts an appealing glow at night with its narrow horizontal bands of light – though its array of once-gleaming fountains have been turned off to save water. Nearby is the 1925 **Hall of Justice**, Broadway and Temple streets, a compelling counterpart to City Hall, with high granite columns typifying the late Beaux Arts style of the time, and famous for hosting the turbulent trial of the Manson Family. Plans are to renovate and reopen it as headquarters of the LA County sheriff's office.

A block west is LA's ecclesiastical colossus, **Our Lady of the Angels** Catholic church, 555 W Temple St (Mon–Fri 6.30am–6pm, Sat 9am–6pm, Sun 7am–6pm; tours Mon–Fri 1pm; free; Ⓣ213/680-5200, Ⓦwww.olacathedral.org). The $200-million concrete seat of the local archdiocese is a truly massive structure, standing eleven storeys tall and capable of holding three thousand people. Dressed in an unattractive shade of ochre, the church's fortress-like exterior suggests a parking garage or prison. However, the interior is a visual delight, with its grand marble altar and giant bronze doors, tapestries of saints, and ultra-thin alabaster screens for diffusing light – not to mention the $30 million worth of art and furnishings laid out in a space longer than a football field.

Little Tokyo and around

Southeast of the Civic Center, **LITTLE TOKYO** is a more vital ethnic core than Chinatown, full of smart shops and restaurants, Buddhist temples, well-heeled visitors, and some worthwhile businesses and cultural institutions. Originally named in 1908, the area, bound by First and Third streets north and south, and Central Avenue and San Pedro Street east and west, was home to thirty thousand Japanese immigrants before they were forced into internment camps in 1942. While the district has returned to prominence, most of LA's Japanese-Americans now live well outside the area.

Little Tokyo

Little Tokyo is best explored on foot, starting at the **Japanese American Cultural and Community Center**, 244 S San Pedro St (Ⓣ213/628-2725, Ⓦwww.jaccc.org), which hosts films, lectures and dance performances, among other things, and is reached via the gentle contours and heavy basalt rocks of **Noguchi Plaza**, designed by modern sculptor Isamu Noguchi, who grew up in nearby Boyle Heights. Inside the centre, the **Doizaki Gallery** (Tues–Fri noon–5pm, Sat & Sun 11am–4pm; free) displays traditional and contemporary Japanese drawing and calligraphy, along with costumes, sculptures and other media. Also on site is the **Japan America Theater** (box office Mon–Sat noon–5pm; Ⓣ213/680-3700), which hosts cultural events such as kabuki theatre, as well as more contemporary plays. Shoehorned between the two and easy to miss is the stunning **James Irvine Garden** (Tues–Fri 9am–5pm; free), with a 170-foot stream running along its sloping hillside. Although it was named after its biggest donor it really owes its existence to the efforts of two hundred volunteers who gave up their Sundays to carve the space out of a flat lot, turning it into the "garden of the clear stream" and making the area seem a world away from LA's expanse of asphalt and concrete. Nearby, the more authentically Japanese **Garden in the Sky**, 120 S Los Angeles St, located on the *Kyoto Grand Hotel*'s third-floor terrace, uses local materials native to Japan. This half-acre strolling garden, or *shuyu*, works the skyline into the setting – a technique known as "borrowed scenery", or *shakkei* – and nicely fits LA City Hall and other modern structures into the landscape of a Zen-like Asian garden.

The most active part of Little Tokyo is **Japanese Village Plaza** (most stores daily 9am–6pm), a touristy outdoor mall near First Street and Central Avenue lined with sushi bars and retailers. Adjacent to the plaza is the area's signature icon: the **Yagura Tower**, a small canopy sitting atop slender wooden beams, built in the style of a traditional Japanese fire tower used to spot forest fires. Across the road at 369 First St, the **Japanese American National Museum** (Tues–Sun 11am–5pm, Thurs closes at 8pm; $9; Ⓣ213/625-0414, Ⓦwww.janm.org), housed in a former Buddhist temple constructed in 1925, has exhibits on everything from origami to traditional furniture and folk craftwork to the internment of Japanese-Americans during World War II.

Geffen Contemporary and Museum of Neon Art

Just north from the Japanese American National Museum is the **Geffen Contemporary**, Central Avenue at First Street (same hours and website as MOCA, to which a ticket entitles same-day admission; see p.61). The Frank Gehry-designed museum, which occupies an old city warehouse and police garage, was initially opened in 1983 as overflow space for the main facility on Bunker Hill. Though there are no permanent installations on view, you're likely to find anything from temporary exhibits on the latest LA architecture to small abstract paintings lining the walls to huge installation pieces occupying similarly huge galleries. Also worth a stop, a few blocks away, is the latest home for the ever-itinerant **Museum of Neon Art**, 136 W 4th St (Thurs–Sat noon–6pm, Sun noon–5pm; $7; Ⓦwww.neonmona.org), where you can check out some enchanting neon signs, kinetic displays and an array of oddball artworks that glow, move, sparkle and otherwise behave in ways foreign to pieces found in most conventional galleries.

St Vibiana's Cathedral and Skid Row

West of Little Tokyo, **St Vibiana's Cathedral**, 114 E Second St, is a modest replica of Barcelona's church of San Miguel del Mar, with a simple white Italianate design. For years the regional seat of the Catholic Church, as well as a sanctuary for recently arrived Latin American immigrants, the 1871 cathedral fell on tough times after it was damaged in the 1994 Northridge earthquake and the archdiocese abandoned it to build Our Lady of the Angels (see p.53) further west, absconding with some of its stained glass and its sarcophagus in the process. Saved from demolition, the cathedral has been redeveloped as a rental complex, making for a wonderfully elegant spot for weddings, art shows and the like (information at Ⓣ213/622-4949, Ⓦwww.vibianala.com).

South of Little Tokyo, off San Pedro Street, is LA's own **Skid Row**, worth avoiding for most outsiders, with a resident population of up to eighteen thousand homeless people – one of the largest concentrations in the US.

SCI-Arc and the Arts District

East of Little Tokyo, not far from the LA River, intriguing art is on display in the **Freight Depot** of the Southern California Institute of Architecture, or **SCI-Arc**, 960 E Third St, adjacent parking on the south end at 345 Merrick St (daily 10am–6pm; free; Ⓣ213/613-2200, Ⓦwww.sciarc.edu), housed in a renovated train depot from 1907 that stretches a full fourth of a mile. Founded in 1972 by Thom Mayne (best known for his CalTrans Building; see p.53), "SCI-Arc" devotes its flowing horizontal spaces to experimental architectural instruction. Not surprisingly, the depot's public gallery hosts all manner of quirky and avant-garde exhibits by its students and faculty, from high-tech computer models to minimalist installations that play off light and shadows. In the neighbourhood just west, an independent cultural scene is developing around classic industrial buildings that have been renovated into lofts and branded as the **Arts District**. If you'd like to check out some of the physical or online galleries in the area, visit Ⓦwww.ladad.com for more information.

Old Downtown

Spring Street Main Street, and Broadway form the axes of **Old Downtown**, a once-thriving district that is trying to recapture its old spark with scattered new investment. To the east, the **Garment District** and **Flower Market** are hives of mercantile energy, representing an urban vitality that the antique banking corridor of Spring and Main streets can only hope to achieve with a smattering of new condos and cafés. Parallelling Spring to the west, Broadway buzzes with street life, though its character has changed, too: whereas movie palaces and fine restaurants once drew white middle-class crowds, its current swap meets and bargain discounters now draw working-class Hispanics.

Spring and Main streets

As the one-time "Wall Street of the West", the imperious banking and commercial buildings of **Spring** and **Main streets** no longer serve their original functions, almost all of them victims of Downtown's financial relocation to Bunker Hill. Still, for those with an interest in LA history, or with a nose for sniffing out the area's emerging arts scene, the streets may offer a few worthwhile attractions (many of which are viewable on LA Conservancy tours of the old strip; see p.29). South from the Civic Center, begin your wanderings at peaceful **Biddy Mason Park**, 333 S Spring St (daily 8am–8pm, weekends open 9am; free), which commemorates a former midwife and slave who won her freedom in an 1855 legal challenge. The small memorial, adorned with camphor and jacaranda trees, provides a timeline of her life, from when she was purchased for $250 (on the property that is now the park), to when she became one of the founders of the local First African Methodist Episcopal Church.

Less than a block away begins the Spring Street **Financial District**, a collection of stately Beaux Arts buildings from one hundred years ago, which is a bit of a misnomer since hardly any of these structures are still used for their intended banking purposes, most of them since converted into condos, shops, eateries and the like. Fourth Street is the main crossing axis of the area, and most of the worthwhile buildings lie along Spring. At no. 408, the 1904 Braly Block is home to the **Continental Building**, which was LA's first "skyscraper", though it only boasts twelve storeys, while the **Farmers and Merchants Bank**, at no. 401, is an eye-catching Neoclassical pile from 1908, rich with grand columns, and the **Security Trust and Savings Bank**, at no. 514, is home to four small theatres presenting intermittent productions and special events. Further south, the one-time **Pacific Coast Stock Exchange**, no. 618, is an example of 1930s Art Deco at its most imposing and heroic, and, at Spring Street's intersection with Seventh Street, the 1911 **I.N. Van Nuys Building** celebrates a San Fernando Valley land baron and wheat farmer in grand Beaux Arts style, with ornamental Ionic columns and white terracotta walls adorning the old office space.

The Fashion District

Without question, the **Fashion District** (most businesses Mon–Sat 10am–5pm; ⓣ213/488-1153, ⓦwww.fashiondistrict.org), is one of the LA's most appealing and frenetic attractions, thick with street vendors hawking everything from hot dogs to bootleg DVDs in a blizzard of mercantile activity, not to mention twenty square blocks of clothing manufacturers and discounters selling fabric for as little as $2 per yard, designer suits, exquisite silk and velvet draperies, and countless other items. On Saturdays, the wholesalers open their doors to the general public, prompting a free-for-all among the fabric obsessed. The biggest retailer here, the **California Market Center**, at Ninth and Los Angeles streets (typically Mon–Fri 9am–5pm; ⓣ213/630-3600, ⓦwww.californiamarketcenter.com), fills three million square feet and seemingly has just as many visitors, especially during the hectic mid-October and mid-March "Fashion Week" (ⓦwww.fashionweekla.com). Just across Los Angeles Street at Santee, the **Cooper Design Space** (ⓣ213/627-3754, ⓦwww.cooperdesignspace.com) offers designer merchandise in a bevy of showrooms, as well as designer studios and offices, while the ultra-chic New Mart, 127 E Ninth St (ⓣ213/627-0671, ⓦwww.newmart.com), is another good stop for shrewd Angelenos trying to avoid the higher-priced Westside boutiques.

To plunge into the fabric-shopping experience at its most colourful and robust, head for the area along Maple Avenue between Sixth and Ninth streets, where businesses (often run by first-generation immigrant families) sell bolts of serviceable fabrics for ultra-cheap prices. Keep in mind, however, that street parking is meagre, parking lots are expensive ($10/hr) and traffic maddening – take a bus, instead. Nearby, at the atmospheric **Flower Market**, 766 Wall St (public hours Mon, Wed & Fri 8am–noon, Tues, Thurs & Sat 6am–noon; entry $2, Sat $1; ⓣ213/627-5527, ⓦwww.laflowerdistrict.com), trade buyers make the rounds as early as 2am, though the public has to wait a few more hours to get its hands on a voluminous selection of blooms; you can buy them for a fraction of the prices charged elsewhere.

Much more tumultuous is **Santee Alley** (between Maple Ave and Santee St, running from Olympic Blvd to 12th St), a visual-information-overloaded agora

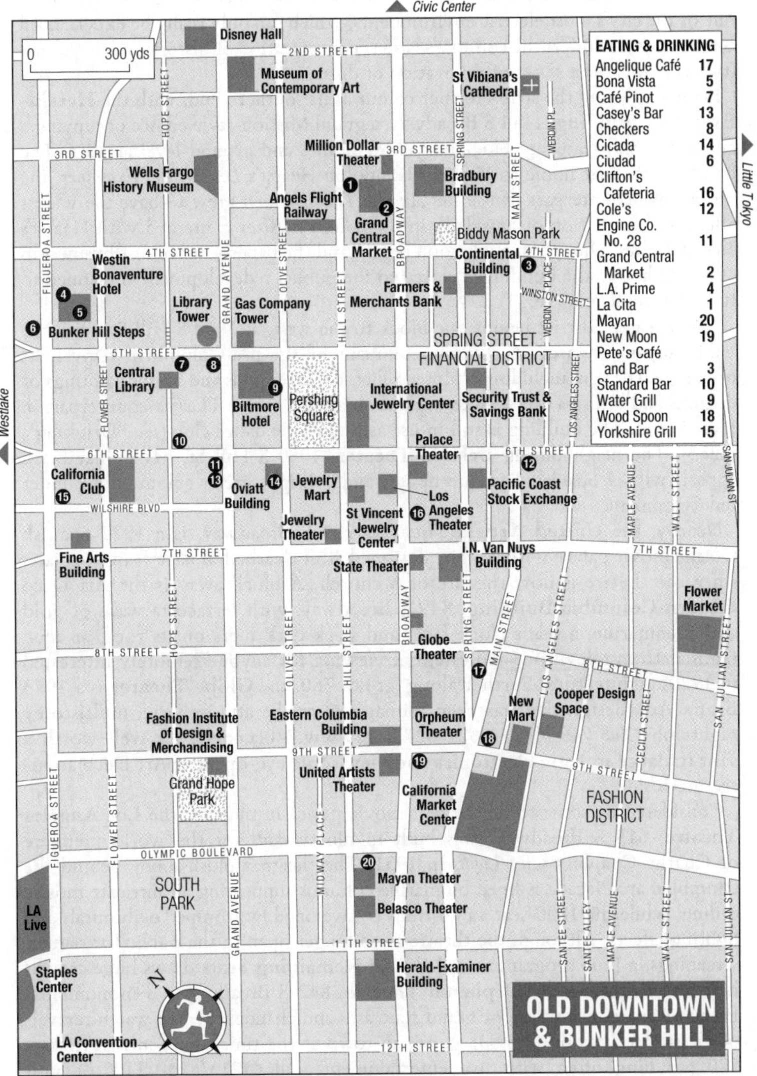

thick with hundreds of vendor shops and little stalls selling everything from the cheapest junky sunglasses to the smartest suits – LA's pint-sized version of New York's Canal Street. Keep in mind, the quality of the goods (and honesty of the dealers) varies widely, so you should haggle without hesitation.

Broadway and the Theater District

Broadway was once the proud axis of LA's most fashionable shopping and entertainment district, brimming with theatres and department stores. Today it's been largely taken over by the clothing and knick-knack stores of a bustling Hispanic community. Combined with blaring salsa music and a hectic street scene, this is one of the city's most electric environments, which can only really be experienced on foot. It's also offers the country's largest concentration of historic movie palaces (twelve), in various states of renovation or disuse.

Begin exploring the strip's former colour at its southern end, with the **Herald-Examiner Building**, 1111 S Broadway, a grand Mission-style edifice occupying a city block and featuring blue-and-yellow domes and ground-level arcades. The building was first home to William Randolph Hearst's *Los Angeles Examiner*, the progressive counterpart of the *Los Angeles Times*, which grew to have the widest afternoon circulation of any daily in the country. After it merged with Hearst's *Herald-Express*, though, trouble soon began, and the paper went out of business in 1989. Although the building is closed to the public, redevelopment is planned to turn it into office space.

The Theater District begins one block to the west, at 1040 S Hill St, with the wild **Mayan Theater**. A stunning remnant of the pre-Columbian revival, its ornamental design, including sculpted reliefs of Aztec gods and bright paintings of dragons and birds, is every bit as outlandish as its Chinese Theatre counterpart in Hollywood. The building is still in use as the *Mayan* dance club (see "Drinking", p.253). The neighbouring **Belasco Theater**, 1050 S Hill St, has similar brash appeal, with a Spanish Baroque design and a bright green colour, now under redevelopment.

Nearby, the **United Artists Theater**, 929 S Broadway, is a 1927 Spanish Gothic movie palace with a lobby designed after a cathedral nave – appropriate, since the theatre is now the site of a church. A block away is the Art Deco **Eastern Columbia Building**, 849 S Broadway, with terracotta walls of gold and aquamarine, a giant clock face, and sleek dark piers on its roof, an icon familiar from television, and essential viewing for anyone remotely interested in 1920s architecture. Further along, at no. 760, the **Globe Theater** is a 1913 Beaux Arts design that has been reimagined as the atmospheric, multistorey nightclub *Club 740* (Ⓣ213/627-6277, Ⓦwww.740la.com); it's well worth a visit to dance to Latin electronica and view some eye-opening Art Deco architecture inside.

Considered by some to be the best movie palace in the city, the **Los Angeles Theatre**, 615 S Broadway, was built in ninety days for the world premiere of Charlie Chaplin's *City Lights* in 1931. The theatre's plush lobby behind the triumphal arch facade is lined by marble columns supporting an intricate mosaic ceiling, while the 1800-seat auditorium is enveloped by trompe l'oeil murals and lighting effects. Although the theatre is no longer open to the public for regular screenings, a June programme called **Last Remaining Seats** draws huge crowds here and to the nearby **Orpheum Theatre**, 842 S Broadway – a monumental French Renaissance palace of grand staircases and chandeliers – to watch revivals of classic Hollywood films. If you're in town at the time, don't miss it (tickets $20 per film, often with live entertainment; call Ⓣ213/623-CITY or visit wlaconservancy.org for details). Near the Los Angeles Theatre, you can take in the Renaissance Revival charm of the **Palace Theatre**, 630 S Broadway, a remodelled nickelodeon from 1911, during one of its occasional public events; check entertainment listings for details.

A few blocks north, the **Million Dollar Theater**, no. 307, is also part of the Last Remaining Seats festival and has appeared in numerous Hollywood movies, renowned for its whimsical terracotta facade, mixing buffalo heads with bald eagles. The former moviehouse was built in 1906 by theatre magnate Sid Grauman, who went on to build the Egyptian and Chinese theatres in Hollywood. Across the street, the 1893 **Bradbury Building**, no. 304 (lobby open Mon–Sat 9am–5pm; free), has perhaps the finest atrium of any structure in the city, each level of its glazed-brick court adorned in wrought-iron railings and open-cage elevators, all atmospherically lit by a skylight. The lobby, which is as far as the public can go, should be recognizable from films such as *Blade Runner*, and LA Conservancy tours often begin here. As you exit on Third Street, the colourful **Grand Central Market**, between Third and Fourth (daily 9am–6pm; ⓣ213/624-2378, ⓦwww.grandcentralsquare.com), provides a good taste of modern Broadway – everything from apples and oranges to carne asada and pickled pig's feet.

Pershing Square and around

The city's oldest park, uninspiring **Pershing Square**, acts as a buffer between Bunker Hill and Old Downtown. Constructed in 1866 and known variously as Public Square, City Park, La Plaza Abaja and St Vincent's Park, it was renamed for the last time in 1918, in honour of World War I general **John Pershing**. However, decades of efforts to revitalize the park have resulted only in a bright purple campanile towering over charmless concrete benches and a dearth of grass and foliage.

The buildings around the square hold more appeal, including the **Millennium Biltmore Hotel** (see p.207), on the west side of the park, its three brick towers rising from a Renaissance Revival arcade along Olive Street. Inside, the grand old lobby has an intricately painted Spanish-beamed ceiling, plus all manner of Baroque flourishes and an elegant bar, exquisite ballrooms and a dark, luminous pool facility.

To the east lies the heart of the **Jewelry District** (most businesses at least Mon–Fri 10am–5pm; ⓣ213/629-3335, ⓦwww.lajd.net), a wholesale and retail zone to which diamond shoppers come to hunt down the cheapest prices for the rock of their choice. One of the more prominent spots, the **International Jewelry Center**, 550 S Hill St, holds more than six hundred jewellers and dealers in precious stones and metals. If this doesn't satisfy your passion for gem shopping, try the **St Vincent Jewelry Center**, 640 S Hill St, a sizable complex with some of the best deals; or the grand **Jewelry Theater**, 411 W Seventh St, which occupies the former Warner Brothers Theater.

Finally, at 617 S Olive St, the Art Deco **Oviatt Building** once housed on its ground floor LA's most elegant haberdashery, catering to dapper types such as Clark Gable and John Barrymore. The elevators, which open onto the street-level exterior lobby, feature hand-carved oak panelling designed and fashioned by elegant Parisian craftsman René Lalique. Equally striking is the intricate 1928 design of the building's exterior, especially its grand sign and **clock** high above, as well as the exquisite **penthouse**, a regular host of weddings and public events (event-related showings by reservation only at ⓣ213/488-9951, ⓦwww.oviatt.com).

Bunker Hill

Developed as a middle-class neighbourhood in the 1870s, **Bunker Hill** was an upscale district for just a few decades; by the 1940s it was little more than a collection of fleabag dives and crumbling Victorian mansions, the very image of the decay of the Downtown district. With its middle class having long since moved to the suburbs, in the 1960s the whole thing was plowed under, and Bunker Hill became the nucleus for Downtown's massive redevelopment as a high-rise corporate enclave, a hive of activity from nine-to-five, and deserted after hours.

The best way to approach Bunker Hill's Financial District is on the Angels Flight Railway, a funicular train originally banished from the hillside along with the residents it once served. In 2010, after a nine-year delay following an accident, the two orange-and-black train cars have once again come out of storage. You can board the train just north of the intersection of Hill and Fourth streets for a quarter, though an escalator at the corner of Olive and Fourth streets will give you the same views of the city for free.

The Music Center and Disney Hall

On the north end, LA has lumped together three leading music and theatre venues – the Dorothy Chandler Pavilion, the Ahmanson Theatre and the Mark Taper Forum – as the blandly modern **Music Center**, north of First Street at 135 Grand Ave (see "Performing arts and film", Chapter 15). However, **Disney Hall**, First Street at Grand Avenue, is a true jewel of modern architecture, a headline-grabbing spectacle based on a 1987 design by architect Frank Gehry, which inspired his later-designed, but earlier-opened, Guggenheim Museum in Bilbao, Spain. The Hall is a 2300-seat acoustic showpiece whose stainless-steel exterior resembles something akin to colossal origami or broken eggshells and is so shiny that the authorities had the metallic facade sanded down in order to reduce its glare. The interior is just as impressive, with a mammoth, intricate pipe organ and rich, warm acoustics; indeed, the Hall is already considered one of the best

Breaching the ramparts of Bunker Hill

Bunker Hill, thick with freeway access ramps, giant boulevards without sidewalks, walled-off skyscraper landscapes, and even signs prohibiting pedestrians, is true to its name – a high-rise corporate enclave, with automatically controlled security doors and private guards to ward off interlopers. When Bunker Hill was being developed in the 1960s and 70s, the financial forces behind the project never considered creating a pedestrian-friendly space Downtown and instead followed the logic of much late-modern design: bigger is better, impersonal is ideal, and cars are always king.

Still, there are a few remedies for dealing with Bunker Hill's layout if you're on foot. The first is to explore the area from the north or south – via Flower and Hope streets and Grand Avenue. By contrast, the east and west sides of the hill are its most "fortified" and difficult to navigate. If you're coming from the east, however, the Angels Flight Railway is your best bet; if you're coming from the west, try Fifth Street, as the east–west streets to the north are among the most inaccessible to pedestrians. Motorists should also realize that while Bunker Hill was made expressly for their driving pleasure, it was not made for convenient, or cheap, parking. Find a lot below the hill and hike up the incline from there, or be prepared to cough up plenty for street parking. Finally, resist the temptation to walk under the hill by way of the Third Street Tunnel; despite its gleaming appearance in films like *Blade Runner*, it remains quite deadly to venturesome pedestrians.

places in the country to hear music, which you can do courtesy of the excellent LA Philharmonic (Ⓦwww.laphil.com; see p.263). Hours and days vary for the free, 60min tours, which run between 10am and 2pm most days of the month (information at Ⓣ213/972-4399, Ⓦmusiccenter.org/visit).

The Museum of Contemporary Art

Just south and across the street from Disney Hall, the **Museum of Contemporary Art**, 250 S Grand Ave (MOCA; Mon & Fri 11am–5pm, Thurs 11am–8pm, Sat & Sun 11am–6pm; $10, students $5, free Thurs 5–8pm; Ⓣ213/626-6222, Ⓦwww.moca.org), is the leading institution for contemporary art in Southern California, designed in 1986 by showman architect **Arata Isozaki** as a "small village in the valley of the skyscrapers", its playful red pyramids offering a welcome splash of colour in a high-rise sea of black, white, and brown.

The **main entrance** to the galleries is below the barrel-vaulted entry pavilion (which opens onto an outdoor sculpture plaza and a gift shop), in a smaller plaza down the stairs from the upper plaza. Much of the museum is used for **temporary exhibitions**, which may include the likes of Donald Judd's prefabricated metal boxes and Ed Kienholz's perverse assemblage art, or explore some of the city's up-and-coming names in photography, sculpture and other media. The bulk of the **permanent collection** draws heavily from the Abstract Expressionist and Pop Art periods and features Franz Kline and Mark Rothko, an important Jackson Pollock work – his imposing, hypnotic *Number Three* – plus ten of Sam Francis's vivid explosions of colour. Also prominent are Claes Oldenburg's papier-mâché representations of hamburgers and fast foods, Andy Warhol's print-ad black telephone, Robert Rauschenberg's *Coca-Cola Plan*, a battered old cabinet containing three soda bottles and angelic wings tacked onto the sides, and Jasper Johns's *Map* – a blotchy diagram of the United States. Other highlights include Alexis Smith's quirky collages, Lari Pittman's painted postmodern hallucinations, Dan Flavin's mesmerizing neon tubes, and Martin Puryear's anthropomorphic wooden sculptures. The museum's strong **photography** collection celebrates the work of Diane Arbus, Larry Clark and Robert Frank, while the impressive selection of **Southern California artists** features the likes of Mike Kelley, Charles Ray and John Baldessari, and ranges from Chris Burden's polemical sculptures to Robert Williams' feverishly violent and satiric comic-book-styled paintings.

The best time to visit MOCA is during an **evening concert** in summer, when jazz and classical music is played outdoors under the silhouette of the red pyramids. At other times, a ticket to MOCA also entitles you to same-day entrance to the Geffen Contemporary, the museum's renovated warehouse for temporary exhibitions on the east side of Downtown (see p.54), and the much cosier branch at the Pacific Design Center in West Hollywood (p.102).

The Financial District

South of MOCA lie the office towers that herald Downtown from a distance. Known as the **Financial District**, the area became LA's money centre in the 1960s and 1970s, making the antique buildings of Spring Street obsolete. There are a handful of interesting sights here if you feel like giving your legs a stretch. A good place to start is the **Wells Fargo History Museum**, just south from MOCA at 333 S Grand Ave (Mon–Fri 9am–5pm; free; Ⓣ213/253-7166, Ⓦwww.wellsfargo history.com). Located at the base of the Wells Fargo Center, the museum displays antique photographs, a two-pound chunk of gold, a re-created assay office from the nineteenth century, and an original Concord stagecoach.

A block away, the shining glass tubes (or giant cocktail shakers) of the **Westin Bonaventure Hotel**, 404 S Figueroa St (see p.207), have become one of LA's most unusual landmarks since the late 1970s. The only LA building by architect John Portman, the structure doubles as a shopping mall and office complex, and is built with a flurry of ramps, concrete columns and catwalks in a soaring six-storey atrium. Step inside for a ride in the glass elevators that climb up the outside walls of the building, giving views over much of Downtown and beyond. From the hotel's 34th-floor rotating bar, *Bona Vista* Lounge (see p.247), you'll get a bird's-eye view of Bunker Hill's skyline, including the **Gas Company Tower**, 555 W Fifth St, a stunning modern high-rise whose crown symbolizes a blue natural-gas flame on its side.

The biggest of the skyscrapers, though, is the cylindrical **Library Tower**, at Grand Avenue and Fifth Street, designed by I.M. Pei's firm and, at 73 storeys, the tallest building west of Chicago. Now owned by US Bank (which has named the tower after itself, to little effect), the off-white tower acquired its familiar moniker from the neighbouring **Richard J. Riordan Central Library**, 630 W Fifth St (Mon–Thurs 10am–8pm, Fri & Sat 10am–6pm, Sun 1–5pm; ⓣ213/228-7000, ⓦwww.lapl.org/central), named for LA's billionaire mayor of the 1990s. The concrete walls and piers of the lower floors form a pedestal for the squat central tower, which is topped by a brilliantly coloured pyramid roof. The library, built in 1926, was the last work of architect Bertram Goodhue, and its striking, angular lines set the tone for many LA buildings, most obviously City Hall. Across Fifth Street, Lawrence Halprin's huge **Bunker Hill Steps**, supposedly modelled after the Spanish Steps in Rome, curve up Bunker Hill between a series of terraces with uneventful outdoor cafés, and ultimately end at the **Source Figure**, one of sculptor Robert Graham's small, creepy nudes at the top.

On the downslope, a reminder of old LA sits at Sixth and Flower streets. **The California Club**, an exclusive social club for the city's elite, was a favourite spot for the **Committee of 25**, an informal group of conservative politicians and businessmen in the 1950s who acted as LA's shadow government behind the club's (still) closed doors. Just over a block south is the more welcoming Romanesque Revival splendor of the 1927 **Fine Arts Building**, 811 W Seventh St (Mon–Fri 8.30am–5pm; free), notable for its grand entry arch featuring gargoyles and griffins, and eye-catching lobby where you'll find medieval-flavoured carvings and the odd modern art exhibit.

South Park

The mostly colourless blocks south of Bunker Hill have been named "**South Park**" by developers apparently lacking irony or access to cable TV. Serene **Grand Hope Park**, a grassy public space between Grand Avenue and Hope Street, just south of Ninth Street, was designed by Lawrence Halprin, and features a whimsical clock tower, wooden canopies and concave fountains with gilt mosaics. Across the park, the **Fashion Institute of Design and Merchandising**, 919 S Grand Ave (Tues–Sat 10am–4pm; free; ⓣ1-800/624-1200, ⓦwww.fashionmuseum.org), trains would-be couturiers and costume designers, throwing the odd fashion exhibition, with items drawn from its collection of twelve thousand pieces of costume and apparel. While the French gowns, Russian jewels and quirky shoes sometimes on display are appealing, the highlight is the annual "**Art of Motion Picture Costume Design**" show that runs from February to April and displays colourful outfits from the history of cinema, from Liz Taylor's Cleopatra garb to the spacey get-ups from *Star Wars*. In August comes a somewhat less interesting show devoted to costumes from television.

Finally, three blocks to the southwest, the LA **Convention Center**, 1201 S Figueroa St (ⓣ213/741-1151 or 800/448-7775, ⓦwww.lacclink.com) and the **Staples Center**, 865 S Figueroa St (ⓣ213/742-7340, ⓦwww.staplescenter.com), are sleek modern structures that have led the way for the redevelopment of the area, but otherwise offer little of interest beyond conventions and Lakers games. Just north of the Staples Center is the retail behemoth **LA Live** (ⓣ213/763-6030, ⓦwww.nokiatheatrela.com/lalive.php), a $2.5-billion shopping and entertainment complex that features theatres, sports facilities and broadcast studios, upper-end hotels, a central plaza, a museum devoted to the Grammy Awards, a bowling alley, and numerous arcades, restaurants and clubs.

Around Downtown

Just west of the Harbor Freeway, the **Temple-Beaudry** and **Pico-Union** barrios are home to thousands of newly arrived immigrants from Central America. Along Wilshire Boulevard, **MacArthur Park** and the **Westlake** neighbourhood, despite the appeal of their faded Victorian architecture, should only be viewed by car when arriving at night – when petty theft and drug dealing are rampant. North of Westlake, **Echo Park** has a pleasantly faded charm and a hipster vibe, and, like **Angelino Heights** to its east, is quite picturesque. Further east is car-friendly **Elysian Park**, a green space that surrounds **Dodger Stadium**. Finally, **Highland Park**, northeast of Downtown, has two decent museums, none very far from the grim concrete channel of the **LA River**.

Westlake and MacArthur Park

If you want to get a real sense of modern LA away from the tourist zones, **Westlake** is a sure bet, the tumultuous centre for countless Latino newcomers to the city, thronged with Panamanians, Hondurans, Salvadorans and many others. The activity centres on the intersection of **Wilshire and Alvarado**, where street vendors hawk their wares in front of busy swap meets, overlooked by the classy sign for the Spanish Colonial Revival **Westlake Theater**, 638 Alvarado St, now promoting a flea market, but there are plans for it to reopen in coming years as a performing-arts venue. A few Angelenos drop by the area for cheap and tasty Mexican food, since the place has something of the atmosphere of Broadway; stick to the well-trafficked areas during the day, and avoid the place after dark.

Across Alvarado, **MacArthur Park** was developed in the 1890s when its surrounding area was a prime LA suburb, and strolling was a favourite pastime. For many decades the park declined because of drug dealing and gang violence, but, while crime is still an issue, the place is much safer than it used to be. With its charming fountain and paddleboats, it might even give you a glimpse of its former appeal. To the south, **Bonnie Brae Street** and **Alvarado Terrace** continue to have a number of quaint Victorian houses. The one functional museum of note in the area is the **Grier-Musser Museum**, 403 S Bonnie Brae St (Wed–Sat noon–4pm; $6; ⓣ213/413-1814), offering a glimpse of the luxurious furnishings and stylish architecture of the nineteenth century, overflowing in six rooms with all manner of Victorian bric-a-brac and precious decor.

Echo Park and Angelino Heights

About a mile north of Westlake along Glendale Boulevard, **Echo Park**, a tranquil arrangement of lotuses and palm trees set around an idyllic lake, was the setting for several scenes in Roman Polanski's film *Chinatown*, and as in that film you can still rent a rowboat (along with paddleboats) from vendors flanking Echo Park Avenue, running along the eastern edge of the lake. The park also appeals for its funky, **bohemian atmosphere**, with countless affordable (for LA) bungalows and apartments surrounding it that house the city's next generation of artists, musicians and filmmakers. To get a flavour of the scene, wander over to the gritty stretch of Sunset Boulevard just north, especially around the Alvarado junction, a hive of cheap clubs and diners and homegrown galleries.

As a different sort of inspiration, in the large, white **Angelus Temple** on the northern side of the lake at 1100 Glendale Blvd, evangelist **Aimee Semple McPherson** used to preach to some five thousand people, with thousands more listening in on the radio. The first in a long line of media evangelists, "Sister Aimee" was tainted by a later romantic scandal and died in 1944, but the building is still used for services by her Four Square Gospel ministry, which dunks converts in its huge water tank during mass baptisms.

Just east of Echo Park on a hill overlooking the city, **Angelino Heights** was LA's first suburb, laid out in the flush of a property boom at the end of the 1880s and connected by streetcar to Downtown. Although the boom soon went bust, a dozen elaborate houses that were built here, especially along **Carroll Avenue**, have survived and been restored – their wraparound verandas, turrets and pediments set oddly against the Downtown skyline and occasionally used in ads for paint, among other things. The best of the lot is the **Sessions House**, no. 1330, a Queen Anne masterpiece with Moorish detail, decorative glass and a circular "moon window". On the first Saturday of the month, you can take a two-and-a-half-hour walking tour of the neighbourhood through the LA Conservancy (first Sat of month 10am; $10; reserve at Ⓣ213/623-CITY, Ⓦlaconservancy.org).

Elysian Park

Two miles north of the Civic Center, quiet **Elysian Park** was laid out in 1886 and has been shrinking ever since. The LA Police Academy first commandeered a chunk of the park for its training facility; later, the Pasadena Freeway sliced off another section. Finally, after city bureaucrats booted a good number of poor Hispanic tenants from the land, **Dodger Stadium** was constructed here in the early 1960s to host the transplanted Brooklyn baseball team. However, even criss-crossed by winding roads, it's still worth a look, especially for its awe-inspiring views of the metropolis – when the smog doesn't intercede.

Beyond the stadium, **Angels Point**, on the upper western rim of the park on Angels Point Drive, is your best vantage point of the city, marked by an abstract industrial sculpture with a palm tree growing out of its centre.

Highland Park

Beside the freeway, a mile from Elysian Park, Highland Park is one of several neighbourhoods north of Downtown that has established a surprising beachhead for the arts in a once-depressed part of the city (see box opposite). It was the very first district annexed to LA, in 1895, and is linked up with the Gold Line Metrorail, with a stop at the **Southwest Museum of the American Indian**, 234 Museum Drive (Ⓣ323/221-2164), which rises castle-like below Mount Washington.

Despite being the oldest museum in Los Angeles, founded in 1907 to house tribal artefacts from all over North America, a seemingly endless seismic renovation has kept the collection off-limits until 2013 at the earliest (see Ⓦtheautry.org for the latest details).

Just down the road, at 200 E Ave 43, the **Lummis House** (Fri–Sun noon–4pm; free; Ⓣ323/222-0546, Ⓦwww.socalhistory.org) is the well-preserved home of Charles F. Lummis, the city librarian who helped develop the Southwest Museum. An early champion of civil rights for Native Americans, and one who worked to save and preserve many of the missions, Lummis built his late-nineteenth-century home as a cultural centre, where the literati of the day would meet to discuss poetry and the art and architecture of the Southwest. The house, named "El Alisal" after the many large sycamore trees that shade the gardens, is an ad hoc mixture of Mission and Medieval Revival styles; its thick walls were made out of rounded granite boulders taken from the nearby riverbed and the beams over the living room are old telephone poles. The solid wooden front doors are similarly built to last, reinforced with iron and weighing tons, while the plaster-and-tile interior features rustic, hand-cut timber ceilings and home-made furniture. It's all a fitting reflection of its rugged owner, one of the few individuals to reach LA by walking – from Cincinnati.

Across the Pasadena Freeway, and two miles north of Downtown, the fenced-off, ten-acre park of **Heritage Square**, 3800 Homer St (Fri–Sun noon–5pm; $10; Ⓣ323/225-2700, Ⓦwww.heritagesquare.org), is an outdoor museum featuring a jumble of eight Victorian structures collected from different places in the city, most transported from Bunker Hill. The strip uncomfortably sites a railway station next to an octagonal house next to a Methodist church, and although the buildings are interesting enough, the adjacent freeway makes this a less than ideal spot to imagine a quaint Victorian world of buggies and gingerbread.

Art in post-industrial LA

Although the Westside grabs most of the attention for attracting artists, in recent years the leading edge of LA's **underground art movement** has been located much further east, in the neighbourhoods of northeast Los Angeles, which have increasingly drawn some of the city's most interesting and enterprising painters, sculptors and architects to the districts of Highland Park, Eagle Rock, Mount Washington and Lincoln Heights.

A good place to start a tour of the burgeoning art scene is **The Brewery**, north of Downtown at 676 S Ave 21 (information at Ⓣ323/222-0222, Ⓦwww.thebrewery.net), a renovated 1920s complex of 22 buildings that's gone from brewing suds to exhibiting designers and architects, with some five hundred artists occupying space in a variety of galleries and art annexes that are open to the public (typically Fri–Sun noon–5pm; free). Most prominent in the complex is Michael Rotundi's striking **Carlson-Reges Residence**, a converted electrical utility building, noteworthy for its jagged architecture and post-industrial decor. (It's not open to the public, but is viewable from outside.)

To learn more about northeast LA's art scene, check out the websites of the **Northeast LA Network** (Ⓦwww.nelanet.org), which can point you in the direction of some two dozen local galleries, and the more comprehensive **Arroyo Arts Collective** (Ⓣ323/850-8566, Ⓦwww.ArroyoArtsCollective.org), which also organizes an annual November Discovery Tour ($10 in advance, $15 on the day), a self-guided driving tour of around one hundred of the best and quirkiest of the area's galleries and private studios.

The LA River

"A beautiful, limpid little stream with willows on its banks" is how water czar William Mulholland once described the **LA River**, the long concrete gutter that serves as Downtown's eastern border, and symbolizes to many the city's asphalt-and-concrete landscape. While the river may have often been tranquil, it was also quite volatile, periodically flooding neighboring communities until, in 1938, a typically drastic solution was imposed: its muddy bottom was transformed into cement and its earthy contours into a hard, flat basin. The river mutated into a flood channel, which it remains, snaking through the city for 58 miles. Although some of the northern sections of the river (mainly through the San Fernando Valley) have been reseeded with trees and foliage, efforts to return the Downtown stretch to its natural state have met with predictable bureaucratic resistance.

Still, the fight continues, with groups like **Friends of the LA River** (Ⓣ1-323/223-0585, Ⓦwww.folar.org) arguing for the restoration of the water-course's old natural contours, and hosting curious monthly, seven-hour "**river tours**" (April–Nov 9am–4pm; $25) exploring the environmental and architectural high- and lowlights of its 51-mile course, by car caravan. To learn more about the character of the waterway and the potential for resurrecting its much-abused ecosystem, you can stop by the idyllic **Los Angeles River Center and Gardens**, 570 W Ave 26 (Mon–Fri 9am–5pm; free; Ⓣ323/221-9939, Ⓦwww.lamountains.com/planning_river.html), for its informative "living river" presentation and exhibit showing the rebirth of the river along eleven upstream miles.

You can also get a good Downtown river view by driving across several eastside bridges, designed in various revival styles – from mild Gothic to quasi-Baroque – or by renting movies. The empty riverbed has been used in numerous films, notably *Grease*, in which the channel hosts a wild drag race, and the *Terminator* series, in which cyborgs run amok in its bleak setting.

2

Mid-Wilshire and the Miracle Mile

The ethnically diverse territory of **MID-WILSHIRE** takes in the general area around **Wilshire Boulevard** between Downtown and Beverly Hills, running parallel to Hollywood to the north. As one of LA's best bets for revisiting the architecture of the early twentieth century, Mid-Wilshire was the site of the fabled *Ambassador Hotel*, where Robert Kennedy Jr was killed, and while that structure has been demolished, there are a number of other proud towers from the early to mid twentieth century that reward a look. Because Wilshire was the principal route of LA's first major suburban expansion in the 1920s, when the middle class began migrating west along the expanding strip, you can literally take a chronological tour of LA history simply by driving west from Downtown along it, from the Art Deco piles of its eastern end, to the auto-centric precinct of the mid-century Miracle Mile, to today's upscale shops and office blocks of the Westside.

Middle-income Asians, old-money whites, working-class African Americans, diverse groups of Hispanics, and a small but growing bohemian contingent live within a few miles of each other along the Wilshire corridor. LA's most industrious ethnic enclave, **Koreatown**, has experienced renewed growth in recent decades with a slew of modernist office towers and three-storey strip malls. To the west, just north of Wilshire Boulevard, many of the old Anglo-Saxon estates in places like **Hancock Park** visually recall their 1920s heyday, and are now populated by members of various ethnic groups, though still only one class – rich.

Further along Wilshire, the **Miracle Mile** is a classic shopping strip that boasts enough remaining Art Deco design to make a visit worthwhile, while the area's western side has been reincarnated as **Museum Row**, a collection of institutions celebrating everything from tar-soaked fossils to automobile culture, but especially noted for the presence of the huge **LA County Museum of Art** – one of the city's essential stops. **Fairfax Avenue**, west of Museum Row, takes you up to the human hive of the **Farmers Market** and through the geographical heart of the city's long-established Jewish population. Further west, the **Third Street** shopping district, along with **La Brea Avenue** to the east, is where the trendy buy designer clothes, eat in smartest cafés, and hobnob with other would-be hipsters. Fittingly perhaps, the west side of Mid-Wilshire is marked by an imposing symbol of mass consumerism, the concrete monstrosity of the **Beverly Center mall**.

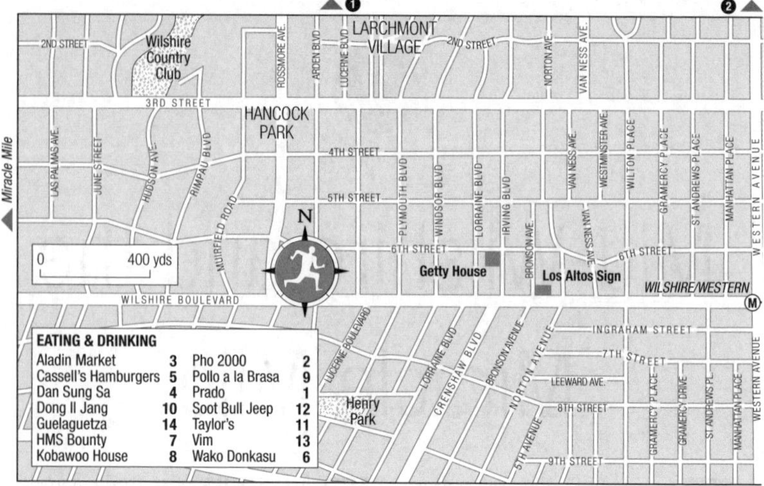

Wilshire Boulevard

Named for oil magnate and socialist Henry Gaylord Wilshire – a unique individual even by LA standards (see box below) – **Wilshire Boulevard** runs from Downtown to Beverly Hills and Santa Monica. The stretch of road from Vermont to Fairfax avenues was for many decades LA's prime shopping strip, until the same middle class that supported this "**linear city**" in the 1920s and 30s disappeared for good in the 1970s and 80s. After a couple of lean decades, many of the strip's once-vacant buildings have re-emerged as the homes of cheap ethnic diners, offices for entertainment companies, and various independent businesses. While

The millionaire socialist

Henry Gaylord Wilshire gained his notoriety from the petroleum industry (also making a fortune selling an electrical device that claimed to restore grey hair to its original colour), and was a scion of a family dynasty, as well as an entrepreneur. By the time he was 30, in the 1880s, he had already come to California and founded the Orange County town of Fullerton. Shortly thereafter, he became heavily involved in progressive causes and before long was in London hanging out with members of the **Fabian Society**, as well as a then-unknown George Bernard Shaw. The turn of the century found Wilshire back in LA, this time buying up chunks of land from Pasadena to Santa Monica, including some of the Westlake neighbourhood west of Downtown (see p.63).

Although Wilshire is often credited with creating his eponymous boulevard, the strip had actually been a wagon trail well before the Spanish had begun to settle in the area. The oil baron developed the street and the property around it, eventually helping the boulevard to connect Downtown with the ocean and creating one of the city's biggest thoroughfares in the process. Wilshire, though, had worse luck than the street he named. After another failed congressional attempt, he lost much of his money in foolhardy investments. Still, he survived long enough to see his beloved route become one of the city's most important streets, a role that it holds to this day.

the Art Deco piles have experienced only scattered renovation (and, occasionally, demolition), they continue to serve as beacons of a lost era, when Zigzag and Streamline Moderne architecture were the rage, and designers built apartment blocks to resemble Egyptian temples and French castles.

East of Vermont Avenue

On its way west, Mid-Wilshire picks up from the area around MacArthur Park and Westlake (see "Around Downtown", p.63) to reach **Lafayette Park**, between Wilshire and Sixth Avenue, where there are a few excellent examples of various historic-revival styles. The 1925 **Park Plaza Hotel**, 607 S Park View St (visits by appointment only at ⓣ213/381-6300, ⓦwww.parkplazala.com), a mixture of Romanesque Revival and Art Deco, is adorned by intricately crafted sculptures of stern angels on the facade, with an exquisite marble lobby regularly used in film shoots. Nearby, the **First Congregational Church**, 540 S Commonwealth Ave, is a 1930 English Gothic-styled cathedral known for its huge and glorious set of pipe organs (half-hour concerts Thurs 12.10pm; free) and, appropriately, the annual Bach Festival (information at ⓣ213/385-1341, ⓦwww.fccla.org). The best example of the period-revival styles may be the historic **Granada Buildings**, 672 S Lafayette Park Place, a shopping and residential complex posing as a charming Spanish Colonial village.

Overall, though, the best and most famous icon in the neighbourhood is the former **Bullocks Wilshire** department store, 3050 Wilshire Blvd, the most complete and unaltered example of Zigzag Moderne Art Deco architecture in the city, with a sturdy terracotta base and dazzling green oxidized-copper tower. Built in 1928, in what was then a suburban beanfield, it was the first department store in LA outside Downtown, and the first to construct its main entrance, a porte-cochere entry for cars, at the back of the structure adjacent to the parking lot – pandering to the automobile in a way that was to become the norm. The era's obsession with modernity and transport extended to the inside, where murals and mosaics featured planes and ocean liners abuzz with activity. The building closed to commerce twenty years ago, and has since reopened as the law library of adjacent **Southwestern University**, which has brought the old beauty back to its original glamour; to inquire about visiting during special events, visit ⓦwww.swlaw.edu/campus/building.

West of Vermont Avenue

The intersection of Wilshire Boulevard and Vermont Avenue is also a fork in the transit system: Red Line subway riders have the option of continuing north toward Hollywood, or heading down Wilshire on the Purple Line to reach a dead end at Western Avenue. The latter line, while meagre at the moment, stands to become one of the country's great transit lines, connecting a broad swath of LA from Downtown to the beach, when it gets built in the coming decade.

In the vicinity, the strikingly modern **St Basil's Roman Catholic Church**, 3611 Wilshire Blvd, was once the seat of the Church in Los Angeles (now Downtown at Our Lady of the Angels; see p.53), and is still LA's foremost example of contemporary ecclesiastical architecture, dating from 1969. The church features twelve severe, looming concrete columns interspersed with stained-glass windows, resplendent teak altars and pews, and a ceiling decorated with over two thousand twisted aluminum tubes; and offers periodic **choral concerts** (information at ⓣ213/381-6191, ⓦwww.stbasilchurch-la.org). Built forty years earlier, the lustrous mosaics, marble and gold of the Byzantine **Wilshire Boulevard Temple**, nearby at no. 3633 (ⓣ213/388-2401, ⓦwww.wilshireboulevardtemple.org), are appropriately stunning.

At the corner of Wilshire and Western stands one of LA's great Art Deco monuments: the **Wiltern Theater**, a former movie palace featuring a bluish Zigzag Moderne facade and a dazzling interior with opulent sunburst motifs and grand columns and friezes. Known as the Warner Bros Western Theater on its completion in 1930, the building was nearly demolished in the 1980s until, unlike other threatened structures in the vicinity, conservationists were able to save it. It's now a concert hall (see p.257), and you'll need to attend a performance for a look inside.

Decades ago, countless **neon signs** used to illuminate the bustling blocks of the Wilshire corridor. Some of them still survive, in various states of renovation and illumination. Neon of note includes the elegant **Gaylord sign**, 3355 Wilshire Blvd, the stylishly Art Deco **Asbury sign**, 2505 W Sixth St, the faux-French **Du Barry sign**, 500 S Catalina Ave, and the gentle script of the **Los Altos Hotel sign**, 4121 Wilshire Blvd. The Museum of Neon Art offers monthly tours of these and many other historic signs (see p.55), or check out ⓦwww.publicartinla.com/neon_signs if you'd like to create your own tour.

Koreatown

To get a good look at LA's cultural diversity, head to the large, amorphous area between Wilshire and Olympic boulevards, especially from Vermont and Western avenues, to find the centre of **KOREATOWN**, the largest concentration of Koreans outside Korea (around two hundred thousand people) and five times bigger than touristy Chinatown and Little Tokyo combined. Unlike the latter two, Koreatown is an active residential and commercial district, noticeably lacking the low-rise buildings and mom-and-pop stores that fit the stereotype of ethnic enclaves elsewhere: the district is loaded with glossy modern buildings and brash signs advertising multistorey minimalls that contain several of the city's better restaurants, especially for Korean barbecue (see p.231). There aren't enough key sites to warrant a lengthy trip, but if you'd like to know more about the place, drop in on the **Korean Cultural Center**, further west at 5505 Wilshire Blvd (Mon–Fri 9am–5pm, Sat 10am–1pm; free; ⓣ323/936-7141, ⓦwww.kccla.org). Along with a museum displaying photographs, antiques and craftwork from Korea and local immigrants, the centre features a gallery with rotating exhibits of fine art, folk work and applied crafts, and puts on periodic theatrical and performing arts productions.

Hancock Park and around

Further west, Wilshire passes through the sloping, tree-lined neighbourhood of **Hancock Park**, named after yet another oil magnate, G. Allan Hancock, who developed this expansive parcel of real estate in the 1920s as an elite suburb. The area has managed to retain both its charm and its well-heeled residents, thanks to its carefully preserved historic revival architecture, especially the restored 1920 **Getty House**, 605 S Irving at Sixth Street, the mayor's official residence. It's open periodically for free tours and public events (check ⓦwww.gettyhouse.org for details), but can be readily appreciated from the street. As for the suggestive name, J. Paul Getty himself didn't reside here – his oil company owned it, along with the surrounding blocks, before donating it to the city in 1975.

There are plenty of other lovely houses in the neighbourhood, which range from mock-Tudor to squat Greek Revival to Medieval Norman fantasy, though none is regularly open to the public. In the small subdistrict of Windsor Square, a few blocks east of Rossmore Avenue, a number of elegant homes are open for annual tours; contact the Windsor Square-Hancock Park Historical Society for more information (ⓣ213/243-8182, ⓦwww.wshphs.org).

Bordering Hancock Park to the west and Wilshire Boulevard to the north, the Mid-Wilshire blocks of **La Brea Avenue** have emerged as one of the city's trendier shopping districts, with weekend visitors coming to sample the edgy galleries, hip boutiques and restaurants, and antique furniture dealers. As a more relaxed, though similarly well-heeled alternative, **Larchmont Village** also has its share of high-end shops and restaurants, located just around Larchmont and Beverly boulevards, on the northern edge of Hancock Park.

The Miracle Mile

Like so many of LA's iconic districts, the **Miracle Mile**, along Wilshire Boulevard between La Brea and Fairfax avenues, was created by a property developer, in this case A.W. Ross, who realized the growing importance of the city's car culture and quickly began developing this stretch of road in 1921. Designed to be best viewed at 25–30mph, the strip's buildings used a horizontal layout, clear and large signage, simplified ornament, and novelties like timed traffic lights to cater to drivers. It worked. And though it never became LA's version of Fifth Avenue as Ross thought it would be, the Miracle Mile was quite a successful enterprise in its time, luring once-big-name department stores like Coulter's, Desmond's, Orbach's and May Company to the then fringes of the city. Inevitably, the westward suburban shift that helped create the Miracle Mile also doomed it, and by the 1970s the area had fallen into decline, its vivid Art Deco designs left to fade and crumble after its department stores had moved away. Recent years have brought nightclubs, galleries, ethnic diners and multimedia offices, though the Mile has a distance to go before it reaches it previous vitality. It's also slow: there are few stretches where you can reach 30mph these days, and the strip has some of LA's worst **congestion**, too.

The route begins with the **Security Pacific Bank Building**, just east of La Brea Avenue at 5209 Wilshire Blvd, an excellent little black-and-gold Zigzag Moderne gem, which gives you a small hint of what LA's greatest Art Deco structure, the **Richfield Building** Downtown, must have looked like before it was summarily destroyed in 1968. Both the original and the tiny version were designed by the firm of Morgan, Walls and Clements, perhaps LA's greatest purveyor of Art Deco and historic revival styles (see box opposite). Just past this is the **Wilson Building**, 5217 Wilshire Blvd, a grand Zigzag tower known for the colossal neon ad on its roof, visible throughout the area; the former **Dark Room**, no. 5370, a Streamline Moderne retail shop with a facade shaped like a camera; and, another Art Deco classic, the former home of **Desmond's**

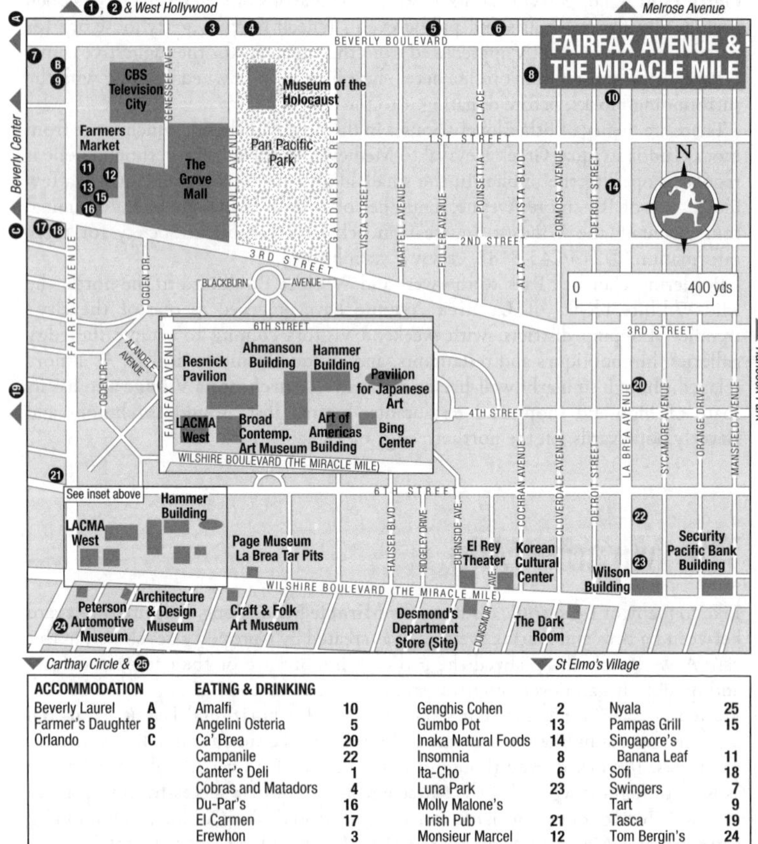

LA's greatest unknown architects

Frank Lloyd Wright's forays into pre-Columbian styles in 1920s Los Angeles are well known, as are Rudolf Schindler's and Richard Neutra's early modernist efforts. However, the firm of **Morgan, Walls and Clements** had equal, if not greater, success in the age of Art Deco, even though its name is now largely forgotten.

The most conspicuous works of Octavius Morgan, J.A. Walls and Stiles O. Clements were the beloved Art Deco movie palaces that have survived the years and re-emerged as shrines to the golden age of Hollywood. The old **Warner Bros Western Theater**, now called the Wiltern (see p.70) and transformed into a performing-arts complex, was a triumph of the Zigzag Moderne style saved from the wrecking ball by community activism in the 1980s. Other of the firm's theatres, such as the **El Capitan** (see p.90), have survived through massive renovation, or by being converted into nightclubs, as in the pre-Columbian fantasy of the **Mayan Theater** (see p.58). Moviehouses aside, the firm's best work included a variety of commercial buildings in a range of styles, most notably the monumental mock-ancient design of the **Samson Tyre and Rubber Company**, now The Citadel shopping complex (see p.145) – a would-be Assyrian temple stranded alongside a busy freeway.

Besides being skilled in period-revival architecture, Morgan, Walls and Clements also produced superb designs in Beaux Arts, as in Downtown's **I.N. Van Nuys Building** (see p.56). Perhaps their most impressive remaining structure, though, is the Spanish Colonial **Chapman Building and Market** (now the Granada Buildings; see p.69), a fanciful creation occupying a full city block and hiding an exotic interior courtyard with assorted clubs and diners.

Although many of the firm's structures were built for commerce, their Andalusian **Adamson House** in Malibu (see p.188), was not, offering the best chance to see what made their romantic escapist designs of the period so appealing to the private, as well as the public, world.

Department Store, no. 5514, with its bold Moderne tower and wraparound corners. The most vibrant classic Deco building may be the **El Rey Theater**, no. 5519, a thriving concert venue (see p.258) with its sleek king's head and flashy neon marquee.

Museum Row

As you continue west, the Art Deco monuments of the Miracle Mile give way to the cultural behemoths of **Museum Row**. The museums begin at **La Brea Tar Pits**, Wilshire at Curson Avenue, where a large pool of smelly tar (*la brea* in Spanish, making the name redundant) surrounds full-sized models of mastodons struggling to free themselves from the grimy muck, a re-creation of prehistoric times when such creatures tried to drink from the thin layer of water covering the tar in the pits, only to become entrapped. Millions of bones belonging to some hundreds of animals (and one set of human bones) have been found here and reconstructed in the adjacent **George C. Page Museum**, 5801 Wilshire Blvd (daily 9.30am–5pm; $7; ⓣ323/934-PAGE, ⓦwww.tarpits.org), a Westside branch of the Natural History Museum in Exposition Park. Throughout the year, researchers are on view outside, cleaning and categorizing the bones of recent finds. Inside, you can examine the mounted remains of many early or extinct creatures, including bison, saber-toothed tigers and giant ground sloths, who met their fate here during the last Ice Age, from forty thousand to one hundred thousand years ago. More recently, oil drillers pumped the liquid black gold from the ground and created an industry as endemic to Southern California as the movie business. In fact, it was a petroleum geologist, **William Orcutt**, who found the modern world's first saber-toothed tiger skull here in 1916. Outside, tar still seeps through the grass, but most of it oozes behind chain-link fences.

Across the street, the **Craft and Folk Art Museum**, 5814 Wilshire Blvd (Tues–Fri 11am–5pm, Sat & Sun noon–6pm; $5; Ⓦwww.cafam.org), has a small selection of handmade objects – rugs, pottery, clothing and so on – with rotating exhibitions featuring the likes of handmade tarot cards, ceramic folk art and highly detailed Asian textiles. Further west, the **Architecture + Design Museum**, 6032 Wilshire Blvd (Tues–Fri 11am–5pm, Sat & Sun noon–6pm; $5; Ⓣ323/932-9393, Ⓦwww.aplusd.org), puts on rotating exhibits of the latest trends in art, photography and architecture. At the intersection of Fairfax Avenue, the **Petersen Automotive Museum**, 6060 Wilshire Blvd (Tues–Sun 10am–6pm; $10; Ⓣ323/930-CARS, Ⓦwww.petersen.org), is spread over three floors, showcasing cars of all makes and models, from the splashiest muscle cars to "million-dollar" vehicles like the 1919 Bentley and 1961 Ferrari. Upper floors are mainly given over to temporary exhibits, where you might find anything from a hot-rod retrospective to a series of "green" low-carbon vehicles. On the ground floor, after you enter, an asphalt path leads you on a winding trek through the city's vehicular history, passing alongside dioramas of LA car worship past and present – from the reconstruction of a Streamline Moderne gas station to a mock-1950s car-hop diner to a 1960s body shop in a suburban garage.

The Los Angeles County Museum of Art

On the west side of the La Brea Tar Pits, the **Los Angeles County Museum of Art**, or LACMA, 5905 Wilshire Blvd (Mon, Tues & Thurs noon–8pm, Fri noon–9pm, Sat & Sun 11am–8pm; $12, pay what you wish after 5pm; Ⓣ323/857-6000, Ⓦwww.lacma.org), is one of the least-known of the most important museums in the US, dwarfed in popular recognition by the Getty Center even though its collection is considerably broader and, in fact, one the largest west of the Mississippi. Since its creation in 1965, the museum's homely beige-and-green blocks have attracted the scorn of architecture critics and have served as plodding, uninspired places to show world art. However, perhaps due to competition from the Getty Center, LACMA has finally undergone and almost finished an extensive renovation and expansion, developing it into the kind of celebrated art venue it should have been all along.

There's no way to see everything in one day. The place is enormous, and concentrated in several huge buildings spread out over a quarter mile along Wilshire Boulevard. Get a map of the complex from the **information desk** in the central courtyard, and note that with the expansion, many of the pieces described below may be shifting around as the museum settles into its final configuration.

The Art of the Americas Building

The **Art of the Americas Building** (formerly the Anderson Building) is home to the museum's collection of **American art**, ranging from the landscapes and portraits of the early-American period up to the homegrown Impressionism and social realism of the turn on the nineteenth century. (More modern American works are often shown elsewhere in the museum.) Although the collection is rotated, typical highlights include the work of John Singleton Copley (the regal *Portrait of a Lady*), Winslow Homer (the dusty realism of the *Cotton Pickers*), Albert Pinkham Ryder (the murky, alluring landscape of *The River*) and Thomas Eakins, whose writhing, nude *Wrestlers* is the sort of expertly crafted, almost erotic work that has made him a favourite among contemporary critics.

Better than most of the pre-modern paintings on display, though, is the impressive assortment of American and Western **furniture**, including bureaus from the Federal period, rough-hewn Craftsman designs, and machine-moulded 1950s modern seats, the best of which are the familiar but fetching laminated-wood chairs of Charles and Ray Eames. Also in the building is a striking selection of Central and South American art, the highlight of which is the **Fearing Collection**, consisting of funeral masks and sculpted guardian figures from the early civilizations of pre-Columbian Mexico.

The Hammer Building

The **Hammer Building** houses the museum's growing collection of **Chinese and Korean art**, of primary interest for its ancient lacquerware trays, hanging scrolls, bronze drinking vessels, glazed stone bowls and jade figurines all spanning nearly seven thousand years of East Asian history. On the floor above, reached by exterior escalator, special exhibitions encompass a broad variety of topics, and there's a small photography gallery with just enough room to focus on one particular artist or era at a time. The corridors on the upper floor continue to the west and connect to the Ahmanson Building.

The Ahmanson Building

The **Ahmanson Building**'s galleries are in many ways still the centrepiece of a trip to LACMA. Continuing on from the Hammer Building, the central attractions of the Ahmanson's third floor are undoubtedly the **European art rooms**. The earliest pieces offer a good overview of Greek and Roman art and continue into the medieval era with religious sculptures, notably a series of stone carvings of the Passion cycle and various shards of ecclesiastical architecture such as Romanesque capitals, Gothic reliefs and so on. The Renaissance and Mannerist eras are represented by compelling works such as Veronese's *Two Allegories of Navigation*, great Mannerist figures filling the frame from an imposing low angle; El Greco's *The Apostle Saint Andrew*, an uncommonly reserved portrait; and Titian's *Portrait of Giacomo Dolfin*, a carefully tinted study by the great Venetian colourist. Northern European painters are well represented by Hans Holbein's small, resplendent *Portrait of a Young Woman with White Coif*, a number of Frans Hals's pictures of cheerful burghers, and Rembrandt's probing *Portrait of Marten Looten*.

In adjacent galleries are Georges de la Tour's *Magdalen with Smoking Flame*, a Caravaggio-influenced chiaroscuro work of a girl ruminating by candlelight while holding an ominous skull; Jean-Jacques Feuchère's wickedly grotesque bronze sculpture, *Satan*; and an excellent set of Rodin's smaller works. Elsewhere are some lesser works by Degas, Gauguin, Renoir and the like, and a few rooms containing ancient **Egyptian and Persian** sculptures and icons, including bronze figures and stone reliefs of Egyptian deities dating back to 3000 BC.

The fourth floor is most interesting for its **South and Southeast Asian** and Islamic art, notably the selection of richly detailed sculptures of Buddha in copper and polychromed wood, watercolour images of Tibetan monks inlaid with gold, and a pantheon of Hindu gods carved in stone, copper and marble. The adjacent **costume and textile gallery** presents a wide assortment of fabrics and clothing from many different eras and cultures – including ancient Persian rugs, embroidered Jacobean gauntlets made of gold and silk, kimonos from feudal Japan, and nineteenth-century New England quilts – but really draws the crowds with occasional shows on **Hollywood costume design**, featuring elegant gowns and outlandish headpieces from the likes of studio legends Edith Head and Adrian.

The people vs Ed Kienholz

Just as Los Angeles was beginning to emerge from the artistic torpor of the 1950s, **Ed Kienholz** made waves with his *Back Seat Dodge '38*, one of his eye-assaulting assemblages of pure modern chaos, a broken-down old Dodge with faded blue paint and dim headlights sitting on an artificial grass mat surrounded by empty beer bottles. An open door reveals two wire-mesh bodies, their grubby clothes ripped and torn, intertwined in an act of sexual frenzy and looking thoroughly decomposed. Ominous, crackly music adds to the sordid effect. Now recognized as a triumph of early social-protest art, and LA art in general, Kienholz's piece was called many other things on its debut in the mid 1960s – indecent, morally depraved, pornographic.

LA County Supervisor **Kenneth Hahn** was one of the loudest voices to vilify both Kienholz and the museum for exhibiting the work, calling for the museum to be shut down unless it was removed. The battle that ensued was resolved with an appropriately ridiculous solution: the piece would be left in the gallery, but its car door would have to be closed most of the time; only when an adult over 18 asked to see the work could the door be opened by a museum guard, and only then if no minors were present in the room.

Both Kienholz and Hahn moved on from the fight relatively unscathed: Hahn became a local legend for funding large-scale social and infrastructure projects; Kienholz went on to establish an international reputation for daring assemblage and installation art, becoming especially influential in Europe, though largely unheralded in his native country.

Appropriately, Kienholz carried his fixation with cars to the grave. When he was buried in 1994, in a strangely modern version of an Egyptian funeral rite, his wife drove him and his possessions down into the grave, burying him along with his favourite car – a Packard.

The Broad Building

Contemporary art is showcased in the **Broad Contemporary Art Museum**, where American and international **modernist** art is the focus. The sizeable Broad Building houses some of the West Coast's largest pieces of art, and features accordingly high ceilings in its rooms and elevator. Among the more prominent pieces are works by abstract expressionists like Mark Rothko and Franz Kline, as well as the splashy, colourful paintings of Sam Francis. Less celebrated, but just as appealing when they're on display, are Mariko Mori's hypnotic video presentation *Miko No Inori*; Bill Viola's *Slowly Turning Narrative*, a huge, rotating projection screen displaying discordant images; and Ed Kienholz's *Back Seat Dodge '38*, looking just as perverse as it did in the 1960s when it caused political outrage (see box above). Other pieces showcase current LA stalwarts such as John Baldessari, Mike Kelley and Chris Burden, but the real eye-openers are by Cindy Sherman, whose self-portrait photographs are stacked four and five high in one huge gallery; Jeff Koons, whose various pop-culture-kitsch pieces are centred around a huge blue-metallic "balloon animal"; and Richard Serra, whose giant, rusted, curving steel walls have the entire ground floor all to themselves. Some of the building is given over to space for rotating exhibitions, which are also on view at the new Resnick Pavilion, a huge, glass-and-marble showpiece designed by Renzo Piano that houses flexible open galleries to accommodate works of any size.

The Pavilion for Japanese Art and other buildings

On the northeast side of LACMA, adjacent to the tar pits, is the **Pavilion for Japanese Art**. This traditional–modern hybrid was designed by maverick architect Bruce Goff, and modelled after traditional *shoji* screens to filter varying levels and qualities of light through to the interior. Rivaling the holdings of the late Emperor Hirohito as the most extensive in the world, the pavilion's collection includes delicately painted screens and scrolls, while elegant ceramics and lacquerware are arranged beside a gradually sloping ramp that starts at the entrance and meanders down through the building, until it reaches a small, ground-floor waterfall that trickles pleasantly in the near silence of the gallery.

Across from the Pavilion, the **Leo S. Bing Theatre** in the **Bing Center** presents a regular series of programmes that focus on classic Hollywood, art house and foreign films, for about the cost of a regular movie (ⓣ323/857-6010). Additionally, the museum houses a research library and the prints and drawings of the **Robert Gore Rifkind Center for German Expressionist Studies**, which includes a library of magazines and tracts from Weimar Germany (by appointment only; call LACMA for details). Finally, on the western end of Museum Row at Fairfax Avenue, inside the 1934 former May Company department store, is **LACMA West**, which, when it isn't showing big-ticket blockbusters, presents children's art – with pieces made to be jumped on, played with and laughed at.

South of Wilshire

A few blocks **south of Wilshire**, around San Vicente Boulevard, the period-revival architecture of **Carthay Circle**, a 1920s property development, is one of LA's best spots to see classic Spanish Colonial homes. A few more blocks to the south, **South Carthay** preserves plenty of 1920s and 30s Historic Revival styles, and has the added benefit of being one of the region's few protected architectural areas (and toured periodically by the LA Conservancy; see p.29). On the western edge of the neighbourhood, the attractive **Center for Motion Picture Study**, 333 S La Cienega Blvd (Mon, Thurs & Fri 10am–6pm, Tues 10am–8pm; ⓣ310/247-3000, ⓦwww.oscars.org/library), houses the esteemed **Margaret Herrick Library**, resembling a Spanish Mission church, whose voluminous and non-circulating collection includes books on actors, filmmaking and festivals, as well as valuable screenplays, film production photographs and etchings. No cell phones are allowed, and you must bring a driver's licence or passport for admittance.

A mile from Wilshire down La Brea Avenue, **St Elmo's Village**, 4836 St Elmo Drive (ⓣ323/931-3409, ⓦwww.stelmovillage.org), is a community arts project now forty years old, worth a look for its colourful murals and sculptures, with many of the local artists present for Sunday-afternoon presentations. It's now also the site of the **Festival of the Art of Survival**, an annual celebration of folk and popular art and music held each Memorial Day, and periodic jazz, African drumming and poetry events.

Fairfax Avenue and around

Just beyond Museum Row, **Fairfax Avenue**, between Santa Monica and Wilshire boulevards, was long the backbone of the city's Jewish culture, full of temples, yeshivas, kosher butcher-shops and delicatessens. The ethnic presence lingers even as encroaching development threatens to turn the area into another homogenized LA retail zone.

At Fairfax's junction with Third Street is the white-clapboard tower of the famed **Farmers Market** (Mon–Fri 9am–9pm, Sat 9am–8pm, Sun 10am–7pm; free; ⓣ323/933-9211, ⓦwww.farmersmarketla.com). Created in 1934 in an act of civic boosterism, it was intended to highlight the region's agrarian heritage, much of which was being paved over to make way for new suburbs. Inside the market is a bustling warren of diners, food stalls and produce stands, popular with locals and out-of-towners to the point where it now sees tens of thousands of visitors daily. This growth has helped fund a monstrous mall next door: **The Grove** (ⓣ323/900-8080, ⓦwww.thegrovela.com), a three-level complex that has taken over much of the market's old parking lot; there's nothing here you haven't seen anywhere else, but it's a pleasant enough place to get your shopping fix, and there's a diverting fountain in the centre with kinetic jets to keep the young ones occupied.

Just north at the corner of Beverly Boulevard, **CBS Television City** is a thoroughly contemporary, sprawling black cube – and something of an architectural eyesore – but also a worthwhile destination if you're in town to sit in an audience for a sitcom, game show or the network's *Late Late Show with Craig Ferguson* (apply online at ⓦwww.cbs.com or call ⓣ818/295-2700 for tickets to this and other programmes). Note, however, that many sitcoms – including those on other networks such as Fox – are taped in the San Fernando Valley at CBS Studio Center (ⓦwww.cbssc.com; to attend a taping, call Audiences Unlimited at ⓣ818/753-3470). To the east, pleasant **Pan Pacific Park**, 7600 Beverly Blvd, once featured the wondrous Pan Pacific Auditorium, a masterpiece of late Art Deco architecture and filming location for the Olivia Newton John kitsch classic *Xanadu*. Although the structure is long gone, a hint of its breezy architectural style is still visible in the lettering and curving pylon of an adjacent sports facility.

Also at the site is the moving Los Angeles **Holocaust Monument** (ⓣ310/204-2050, ⓦwww.laholocaustmonument.com), featuring six black-granite columns (each representing a million Jews killed by the Nazis) inscribed with the events of that horrific period from 1933 to 1945. By 2011 the new Museum of the Holocaust is also due to open in the park (Mon–Thurs 10am–4pm, Fri 10am–2pm, Sun noon–4pm; ⓣ323/651-3704, ⓦwww.lamoth.org), designed to present the terrible history of the Nazi era, using interactive technology and multimedia exhibits to tell the stories of those who were confined to and killed in the concentration camps, personifying their historical legacy with artefacts, photographs, diaries and oral testimony. Other sections of the museum illustrate the various means of resistance – violent or non-violent – employed by victims, and offer a timeline by which German hatred of Jewish people and culture led to the Nuremberg laws, Kristallnacht and eventually the "Final Solution" of state mass murder.

West of the Farmers Market, the **Third Street** shopping district, running from La Jolla Avenue to La Cienega Boulevard, is another of LA's trendy retail zones. Although there are numerous good antique stores, restaurants and coffee shops, most visitors are actually drawn by the huge shopping mall nearby – the imposing **Beverly Center**, Third Street at La Cienega Boulevard (ⓣ310/854-0070, ⓦwww.beverlycenter.com), a brown-plaster fortress that serves as the hub of weekend activity for LA teenagers.

3

Hollywood and West Hollywood

Ever since movies and their stars became international symbols of the good life, **HOLLYWOOD** has epitomized the American dream of glamour, money and overnight success, acting as a magnet to both tourists and hopefuls drawn by the prospect of riches and glory. Even if their real chances of success were infinitesimal, enough people were taken in by the dream to make Hollywood what it is today – a lively mix of wide-eyed visitors, wannabe actors and musicians, and hipsters on the prowl. Nathanael West memorably captured its dark side in his 1938 novel, *The Day of the Locust*, Raymond Chandler made a career out of telling bleak stories of its violence and corruption, and James Ellroy has mined its depravity in lurid detail. Nonetheless, this dark side has only served to enhance Hollywood's romantic appeal, giving it an allure that no amount of myth-busting or bad press can taint.

Hollywood generally follows the contours of Griffith Park, the lower stretch of the eastern Hollywood Hills, Melrose Avenue and part of Sunset Boulevard, excluding West Hollywood. Just beyond the eastern edge, at Griffith Park Boulevard, is a district whose early development was similar to Hollywood's. **Silver Lake**, the initial site of the movie studios, is now a centre for Latin American immigrants and a well-established gay community. To the northwest, **Los Feliz** was home in the 1920s to many of the residences of Hollywood bigwigs, and nowadays is a charming mixed-income community with a few examples of notable architecture on its northern slope. Further north lies **Griffith Park**, the site of LA's famed **observatory**, among other less well-known institutions, and offering some excellent recreational opportunities.

The district's main drag, **Hollywood Boulevard**, is the basis for much LA myth and lore, epitomized by the ever-popular **Walk of Fame**. This strip and its southern neighbour, **Sunset Boulevard**, were the central axes of the golden age of Hollywood, from the 1920s through the early 1950s; even now the stars live above it in exclusive homes in the **Hollywood Hills**, perched on snaking driveways behind locked gates. The **lower Hollywood** stretches of **Santa Monica Boulevard** and **Melrose Avenue** are known for a famous film studio, cemetery and shopping strip, while the economic core of the area lies further west in **WEST HOLLYWOOD**, actually a separate city, attracting a diverse mix of gays and lesbians, pensioners, bohemians and Russian immigrants. Youthful poseurs and music lovers congregate on the legendary **Sunset Strip**, loaded with divey and posy nightclubs and bars, and huge, towering billboards.

Some history

Although you'd never believe it these days, Hollywood started life as a **temperance colony**, created to be a sober, God-fearing alternative to raunchy Downtown LA, eight miles away by rough country road. Laid out and named by real estate wizard H.J. Whitley – justly known as the Father of Hollywood – in 1887, Hollywood was a typical LA property development. The place grew and became an independent city in 1903, still dry enough to keep the teetotalers happy, but linked by streetcar with the rest of the region, giving sinners easy access to the vices of Downtown LA. The district's pious nature was forever changed in 1911, though, when residents were forced, in return for a regular water supply, to be annexed to the now-booming city of Los Angeles. The film industry, meanwhile, gathering momentum on the East Coast, needed a place with guaranteed sunshine, cheap labour, low taxes, diverse scenery and, most importantly, enough distance to dodge Thomas Edison's patent trust, which tried to restrict filmmaking nationwide. Southern California was the perfect spot.

A few offices affiliated to Eastern film companies started appearing Downtown in 1906 and the first true studios opened in nearby Silver Lake, but independent hopefuls soon discovered the cheaper rents in Hollywood (for the full story, see "The Hollywood Studio System", p.351). Producer **Thomas Ince** set up shop here and established a studio that would become a template for later filmmaking companies. While Hollywood soon vaulted to domestic economic success, its international rise was only assured after the World War I; World War II crippled Europe's film industry, ensuring American pop-culture hegemony until the 1950s. At that time, government antitrust actions, television and revitalized European competition damaged the US movie industry, and the American movie business only renewed its financial strength two decades later with the rise of George Lucas, Steven Spielberg and summer blockbusters aimed at teenagers.

In recent years, film production has increasingly been outsourced to far-flung locations from North Carolina to Romania – anywhere that offers a reasonable tax break for filmmaking – while the local industry struggles. Though offices for big-name producers, directors, actors and agents are still based in LA, all of the major studios, except for **Paramount**, have long since moved from Hollywood to digs in Burbank, Culver City and elsewhere.

Almost as long as it's been identified with the movies, the district has been depicted in books and films as being rife with two-bit thugs, hookers and drug abusers – often with a degree of accuracy. Since the late 1990s, though, an influx of urban-renewal money and community involvement has helped to brighten up the place, and city redevelopment schemes are always in the works. The tourists have now come in full force, too, at least on the stretch of Central Hollywood from Vine Street to La Brea Avenue. Beyond this, Hollywood may never be totally sanitized, and most of its true denizens – rock musicians, struggling writers, club-hoppers and petty criminals – prefer it to stay that way.

Silver Lake and Los Feliz

As the original home of the region's film studios, **Silver Lake** and **Los Feliz** are fitting places to begin any in-depth tour of Hollywood. Unfortunately, Silver Lake's movieland heritage survives in only a few dusty pockets; it's more noteworthy now for its striking views of the city and fine modern architecture. Los Feliz has preserved slightly more of its history and maintains a number of landmark buildings, and remains a pleasantly low-key area with less of the pretension found in the Hollywood Hills.

Silver Lake

One of LA's lesser known but still interesting districts, **SILVER LAKE** has a split personality, its lower section having a decidedly funky, grimy feel, and its upper section boasting good views and well-heeled residents. The central body of water, Silver Lake itself, is not a pretty sight – little more than a utilitarian reservoir, built in 1907, just before the area around it briefly became LA's movie capital. With its mainly Hispanic parts near Sunset Boulevard, Silver Lake also has sizable white and Latino gay populations, and the combination gives the place a real vitality, especially evident in the area's varied bars and clubs, where you're apt to come across anything from old-fashioned cocktail lounges to free-wheeling drag shows. The intersection of **Sunset** and **Silver Lake boulevards** is the heart of the neighbourhood, crowded with dingy bars, art studios, offbeat shops, and cheap diners. The best time to come is during the **Sunset Junction Street Fair** in August (see p.286), a bohemian carnival known for its loud music, ethnic food and vintage-clothing stalls, which draws everyone from aging hippies with their families to pierced and tattooed youth looking for a little raucous amusement.

Above Sunset, Silver Lake's hills rise around the reservoir, and from the aptly named **Apex Street** to the east, wealthy residents are afforded great views of the city. The hills to the west are peppered with prime examples of modernist homes by the likes of Gregory Ain, Richard Neutra, R.M. Schindler and Harwell Harris. Occasionally, neighbourhood houses are open to the public for classical-music concerts presented by the Da Camera Society (see "Performing arts and film", p.262).

The east side of Silver Lake is an area once known as **Edendale**. Although most of the district's movie history has been paved over or altered beyond recognition (such as the long-gone Walt Disney studio formerly at 2719 Hyperion Ave), an indication of its fleeting glory remains at 1712 Glendale Blvd, currently a drab storage facility but once the place where movie pioneer Mack Sennett's **Keystone Film Company** employed such legends as Fatty Arbuckle, Charlie Chaplin, Gloria Swanson and the Keystone Kops, using much of the surrounding terrain for shooting locations. If you're a devotee of Laurel and Hardy, wander south to one such location on Vendome Street where, near no. 930, a **long stairway** saw the duo trying to move a grand piano up its incline, in the 1932 film *The Music Box*.

Los Feliz

Named after nineteenth-century soldier and landowner José Feliz, **LOS FELIZ** is a mixed-class neighbourhood that used to hold the glittering mansions of movie stars and studio bosses, a legacy that has left it with no small amount of eye-opening architecture. Just northwest of Silver Lake and occupying a prime perch below Griffith Park, the district numbered among its 1920s denizens Cecil B. DeMille, W.C. Fields and Walt Disney. The legendary animator had his first "studio" here, in still-humble digs at 4649 Kingswell Ave, which was actually little more than rental space in a realty office, where the bathroom had to double as a darkroom.

KCET Studios, 4376 Sunset Blvd, is Hollywood's oldest film studio in continuous use, its original building constructed in 1912 and since expanded into a modern complex housing the local PBS station. Its lot was first home to forgotten studios like Lubin, Essanay, Monogram and Allied Artists, but was later to become the birthplace of great films like the original *Invasion of the Body Snatchers*, and execrable ones like Zsa Zsa Gabor's *Queens of Outer Space*. Tours are, however, only open to subscription members (contributors) of KCET (by reservation at Ⓣ323/953-5289, Ⓦwww.kcet.org). Also remodelled for TV, the old **Vitagraph Studios**, 4151 Prospect Ave, is now the home of Prospect Studios, which mainly uses the facility for taping soap operas (no public admittance). Melodrama and

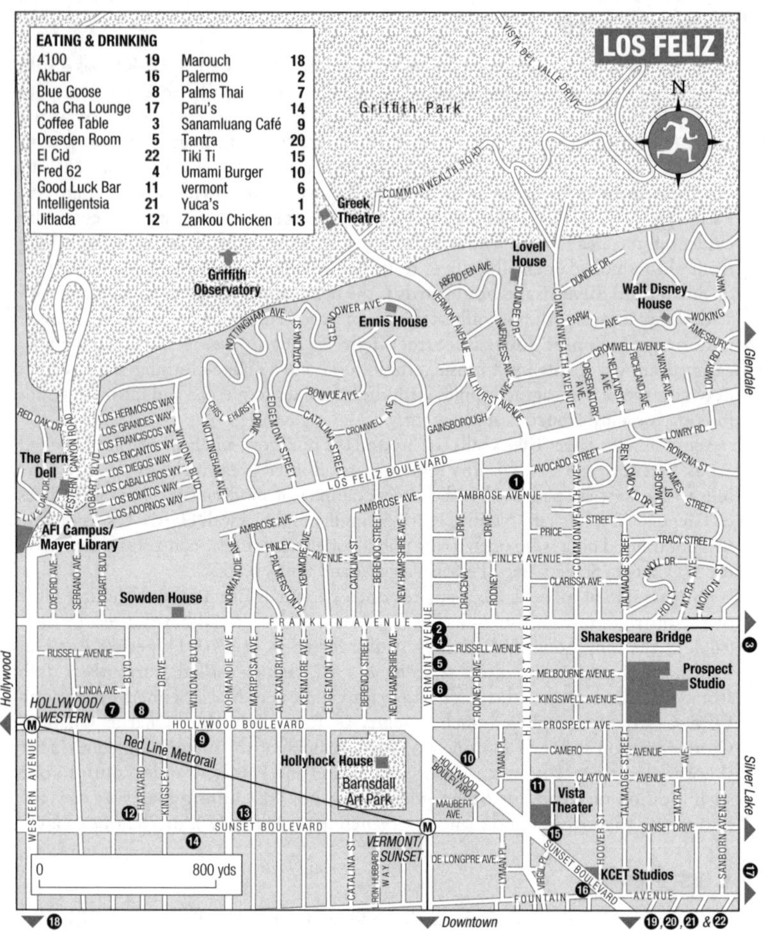

mystery junkies may also want to pass by **4616 Greenwood Place**, the apartment complex used as the exterior of TV's *Melrose Place*, and where Raymond Chandler lived in the 1930s.

More atmospheric is the **Vista Theater**, at the convergence of Sunset and Hollywood boulevards, a lovely, quasi-Egyptian moviehouse (see p.270). The intersection was the legendary spot where **D.W. Griffith** constructed his Babylonian set for the 1916 film **Intolerance**, which cost $2 million and employed fifteen thousand extras. It became one of the biggest bombs in box-office history, and, perhaps symbolically, the colossal film set (featuring elephant statues, hanging gardens and massive pillars) sat for three years, becoming a perverse sort of tourist attraction as it decayed. As an odd epilogue, a stripped-down "re-creation" of the gargantuan film set – complete with elephant pillars and a massive pseudo-Babylonian arch – is now the centrepiece of the giant Hollywood and Highland mall in Central Hollywood (see p.90), and of a Disneyland fake studio lot (see p.194).

Just after the original movie set's destruction, Frank Lloyd Wright began building his first LA house up the road, on a picturesque knoll overlooking the city. Construction of the 1921 **Hollyhock House**, close to the junction of Vermont Avenue at 4800 Hollywood Blvd (Wed–Sun tours at the bottom of the hour 12.30–3.30pm; $7; ⓣ323/662-8139, ⓦwww.hollyhockhouse.net), was largely supervised by Wright's student, **Rudolf Schindler**. Covered with Mayan motifs and stylized, geometric renderings of the hollyhock flower, the house is an intriguingly obsessive dwelling – complete with a fireplace moat and original furniture. The bizarre building was obviously too much for its oil-heiress owner, Aline Barnsdall, who lived here only for a short time, complaining of its leaks, cramped space and inhuman geometry, before donating the house and the surrounding land to the city authorities. She was right: the house works much better as a piece of sculpture than it does as a functional home. It now sits in the **Barnsdall Art Park** (ⓦwww.barnsdallartpark.com), where a number of galleries devoted to the work of regional artists make a pleasant stop while you're waiting for the Hollyhock tour to begin.

Further into the residential heart of Los Feliz are a number of notable sights, including the **Shakespeare Bridge** on Franklin Avenue near St George Street, a 1925 quasi-Gothic charmer with turrets, which leads toward several notable private homes, and the **Walt Disney House**, 4053 Woking Way, an oversized Tudor cottage perched on a high slope, where the cartoon magnate lived in his early career. Further into the hills, Richard Neutra's **Lovell House**, 4616 Dundee Drive, is a stack of blindingly white concrete slabs balanced on delicate stilts that looks quite contemporary for a 1929 building, and in fact was the first steel-frame house in the US. One of LA's landmarks of early modernism, the nickname of the so-called "Health House" reflects the original owner's dedication to wholesome living. More garish is the **Sowden House**, 5121 Franklin Ave, a pink box with concrete Aztec-looking jaws designed by Frank Lloyd Wright's son Lloyd; you can get a pretty good look at this curiosity from the street, but if you can afford a spare $2400, you can stay here for a night (information at ⓣ510/647-9769, ⓦsowdenhouse.com).

Much higher on the slopes above Los Feliz, the **Ennis House**, 2655 Glendower Ave, is the elder Wright's own design, a fascinating experiment built from hundreds of bulky concrete blocks to look like a monumental Mayan temple – one of four similar Wright oddities in LA. The house's imposing, pre-Columbian appearance has added atmosphere to over thirty TV shows and movies, from Vincent Price's *The House on Haunted Hill* to David Lynch's *Twin Peaks* to Ridley Scott's *Blade Runner*. It's no longer open to private tours, but as Glendower curves around it you can see an up-close view of the exterior – still one of the most striking and bizarre private residences on the West Coast.

Finally, Los Feliz is home to the **American Film Institute** campus, Los Feliz Boulevard at Western Avenue, whose **Louis B. Mayer Library** (Mon, Tues & Thurs 9am–5pm, Wed 9am–7pm, Sat 10am–4pm; free; ⓣ323/856-7654, ⓦwww.afi.com) is a non-circulating research facility stuffed with fourteen thousand books, five thousand scripts, and all manner of archives on classic and contemporary movies. AFI's excellent annual **film festival** is a key event in Southern California, attracting silver-screen aspirants from around the country and world.

Griffith Park

Just north of Los Feliz, **Griffith Park** (daily 5am–10.30pm, mountain roads close at dusk; ⓣ323/913-4688) is the nation's largest municipal park, a sprawling combination of gentle greenery and rugged mountain slopes that makes for a good

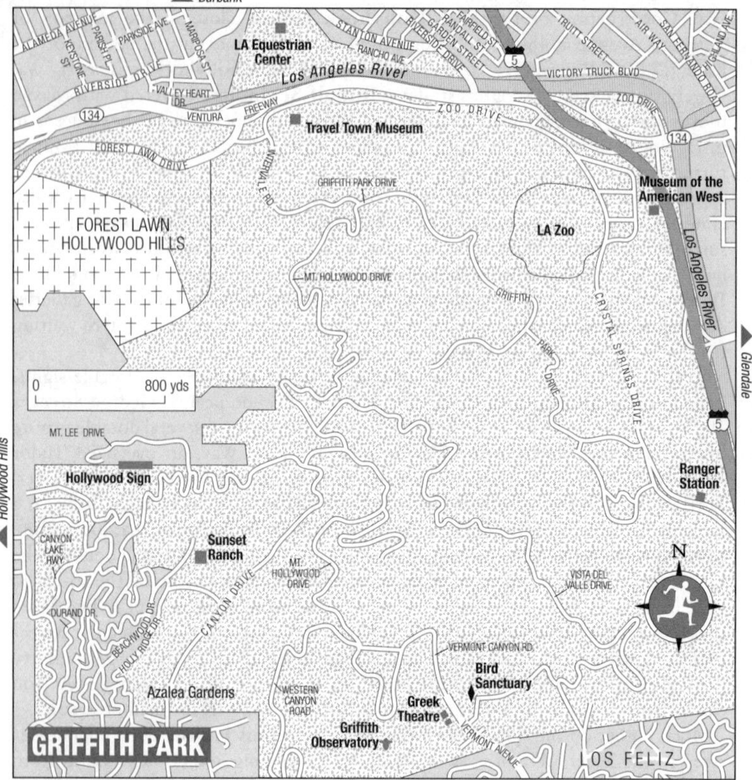

escape from LA's traffic and chaos. With its picture-postcard vistas and striking silhouette, it has become a standard field trip for grade-school kids and a requisite stop for anyone taking a trip through Hollywood. Above the landscaped flat sections, where the crowds gather to picnic or play sports, the hillsides are rough and wild, marked only by foot and bridle paths, leading into steeper terrain that gives great views over the basin and out to the ocean.

The park was acquired by mining millionaire **Griffith J. Griffith** in 1884, but almost immediately, Griffith wanted to be rid of it; he could find no buyers and, in 1896, deeded the space to the city for public recreation. Through the decades it became increasingly important to LA residents' leisure pursuits, even as its slopes have never been fully tamed. Occasional wildfires erupt and in the brush and scorch entire hillsides, sometimes wiping out favourite trails and attractions, either through conflagration or the mudslides that follow.

Near the entrance to the park off Los Feliz Boulevard, Fern Dell Drive leads into the **Fern Dell**, a bucolic glade of ferns that acts as a border between the park to the east and an exclusive neighbourhood to the west. Along Canyon Drive to the northwest, a short hiking trail leads past a rock quarry to the lush **azalea gardens**. Elsewhere, at 2900 N Vermont Ave, a bird sanctuary (daily 10am–5pm; free) offers a limited display of birdwatching, and recently reopened after a 2007 wildfire damaged this and other natural attractions; the **Greek Theatre** (Ⓣ323/665-5857, Ⓦwww.greektheatrela.com), is an open-air amphitheatre that seats nearly five

Park activities

The steeper parts of Griffith Park, which blend into the foothills of the Santa Monica Mountains, offer a variety of **hiking trails,** with some 55 miles in the park overall. You can get maps at the park centres at 4400 and 4730 Crystal Springs Rd (daily during daylight hours; ⓣ323/664-6611). Near the latter ranger station you can rent bikes at Spokes 'n Stuff (summer Mon–Fri 2–6pm, Sat & Sun 10.30am–dusk; $10/hr, cash only; ⓣ323/653-4099), good for touring the upper trails and canyons as well as the easier lower slopes. The highest point in the area – the summit of Mount Hollywood — is a good hike for those in shape, but there are plenty of lesser jaunts if you're not quite up for it. If you'd rather go horseback riding, the **Sunset Ranch**, 3400 N Beachwood Drive, provides one- or two-hour horse rides through the area for $25 and $40 (daily 9am–4pm; ⓣ323/469-5450, ⓦwww.sunsetranchhollywood.com), and the **LA Equestrian Center**, just across the LA River at 480 Riverside Drive, offers horse rentals for $20 per hour or evening rides for $40 (daily 5am–9pm; ⓣ818/840-8401, ⓦwww.la-equestriancenter.com). The park also holds basketball and tennis courts, a swimming pool, a golf course and a baseball field, among other things; contact the park's main number for information on these sites (most are open during general park hours).

thousand beneath its quasi-Greek columns – though if you're not coming for a show (mostly summertime rock, jazz, and country concerts), you'll see just the bland exterior.

More entertaining for some are the caged animals in the **LA Zoo**, 5333 Zoo Drive (daily 10am–5pm, summer closes 6pm; $13; ⓦwww.lazoo.org), home to about a thousand creatures, divided by continent, with pens representing various parts of the world. Despite the zoological inventory, it's crammed and uninspired, especially compared with its San Diego counterpart (see p.318). In the **recreation centre**, Los Feliz Boulevard at Riverside Drive, are various sports facilities, as well as an old-fashioned **carousel** (11am–5pm: summer daily, rest of year Sat & Sun; free) with 68 sprightly horses first carved in 1926 and a rather sizable organ. In the summer the park hosts periodic, free classical-music **concerts** (information at ⓦwww.symphonyintheglen.org).

The Griffith Observatory

The **Griffith Observatory**, at 2800 East Observatory Rd (Tues–Fri noon–10pm, Sat & Sun 10am–10pm; free; ⓣ213/473-0800, ⓦwww.griffithobservatory.org), is unquestionably one of LA's monuments, a domed Art Deco shrine to science, and a favourite shooting location for Hollywood filmmakers. However, it got off to a less than auspicious start. Just after the turn of the twentieth century, Griffith J. Griffith offered $700,000 to the city to build the observatory and theatre on the parkland he had donated. The city declined, principally because "the Colonel" had just been released from California's San Quentin Prison for trying to murder his wife – a 1903 incident in which Griffith, drunk and convinced that his wife was plotting a papal conspiracy, shot Mary Griffith through the eye. Although convicted of attempted murder, Griffith only spent a year in prison, and it wasn't until 1919, after his death, that LA finally took his money and later built the observatory and theatre.

The observatory, finished in 1935, is perhaps most familiar from its use as a backdrop in *Rebel Without a Cause* and numerous sci-fi flicks, ranging from *The Amazing Colossal Man* to *Back to the Future*. It presents an array of high-tech exhibits for young and old alike – highlighted by the twelve-inch Zeiss refracting telescope, a trio of solar telescopes for viewing sunspots and solar storms, and other assorted, smaller telescopes set up on selected evenings for inspecting the firmament at your own pace. A planetarium provides a nice view of the heavens and a theatre gives you the history of the observatory; elsewhere, a full range of modern exhibits covers the history of astronomy and human observation, including a camera obscura, and a 150-foot timeline of the universe provides the lowdown on cosmological history and explains wormholes, black holes and other out-of-this-world notions.

Northern Griffith Park

The **northern end** of the park, over the hills in the San Fernando Valley, is best reached directly by car from the Golden State Freeway (I-5), although you can take the park roads (or explore the labyrinth of hiking trails) that climb the park's hilly core, past some of its wildlife lurking in the brush. The most worthwhile museum in these parts is undoubtedly the **Museum of the American West**, near the junction of the Ventura and Golden State freeways at 4700 Western Heritage Way (Tues–Fri 10am–4pm, Sat & Sun 11am–5pm; $9; Ⓦwww.theautry.org), founded by **Gene Autry**, the "singing cowboy" who from 1929 cut over six hundred discs and was the star of Hollywood Westerns during the 1930s and 1940s as well as his own TV show in the 1950s. Among the many exhibits are buckskin jackets and branding irons, Frederic Remington sculptures of turn-of-the-century Western life, and the truth about the shoot-out at the OK Corral. The comprehensive collection of artefacts is organized into engaging sections on native peoples, European exploration, nineteenth-century pioneers and Romantic painters, the Wild West, Asian immigrants and, of course, Hollywood's versions of all of the above.

More aimed at children is the nostalgic **Travel Town Museum**, 5200 Zoo Drive (Mon–Fri 10am–4pm, Sat & Sun 10am–6pm; free; Ⓦtraveltown.org), a lot full of old trains and fire engines that has more than enough creaky locomotives and antique trucks, plus a miniature train to ride ($2.50), to keep the little ones occupied, perhaps longer than their parents can stand. Bounding Griffith Park's northwest rim, **Forest Lawn Hollywood Hills**, 6300 Forest Lawn Drive (daily 8am–5pm; Ⓣ800/204-3131, Ⓦwww.forestlawn.com), is a cemetery of the stars that, while not quite as awe-inspiringly vulgar as its Glendale counterpart (see p.173), is no less pretentious, with showy gravestones and fancy memorials to such luminaries as Buster Keaton, Stan Laurel, Marvin Gaye and Charles Laughton, as well as the likes of Andy Gibb, Liberace and Jack Webb.

Hollywood Boulevard

From the 101 freeway to the edge of West Hollywood, the central section of Hollywood runs along **Hollywood Boulevard**, whose hub from Vine Street to La Brea Avenue contains the densest concentration of film mythology in the world, with a pervasive sense of nostalgia that draws tourists the world over. The decline that long blighted the area has partly receded in the face of prolonged efforts by local authorities to make the central section more tourist-friendly by attracting new chain stores and malls and luring the annual Oscars ceremony here from its previous Downtown location. Nevertheless the place still has its grungy side after dark away from the main visitor zones, when the assorted scenesters, drunks, drug addicts and prostitutes create a lively, if not entirely savory, mix.

HOLLYWOOD

EATING & DRINKING

Name	No.
25 Degrees	14
Angelli Caffe	34
Arena	38
Astro Burger	39
Avalon	4
Bar Sinister	20
Beauty Bar	19
Blu Jam Cafe	33
Boardners	16
Bourgeois Pig	2
Burgundy Room	18
Cactus Mexican	41
Café des Artistes	25
Cat 'n Fiddle	29
Catalina Bar and Grill	17
Chan Darae	27
Crown of India	36
Dar Maghreb	31
El Floridita	37
The Foundry on Melrose	32
Frolic Room	10
Grub	40
Hotel Café	21
King King	8
Lucky Devils	7
Mario's Peruvian & Seafood	42
Moun of Tunis	23
Music Box	15
Musso and Frank Grill	6
Off Vine	30
Power House	5
The Room	22
Roscoe's Chicken and Waffles	28
The Ruby	12
Shintaro Sushi	1
Stout	24
Tiago Espresso Bar	13
Tomato Pizza Pie Joint	35
Tommy's	11
The Well	9
The Woods	26
Yamashiro	3

ACCOMMODATION

Name	Key
Banana Bungalow	K
Best Western Hollywood Hills	A
Dunes Sunset	O
Holiday Inn Express	E
Hollywood Celebrity	G
Hollywood Hills Magic Hotel	B
Hollywood International Hostel	J
Hollywood Liberty	H
Hollywood Roosevelt	I
Orange Drive Manor	F
Orchid Suites	D
Renaissance Hollywood	C
Saharan	N
Sunset-La Brea Travelodge	M
USA Hostels–Hollywood	L

Mulholland Drive
North Hollywood
Lake Hollywood
Downtown & 11
Los Feliz
0
West Hollywood
31
32, 33, 34, 35 & Santa Monica Blvd
36
37 & 38
Paramount Studios & Hollywood
Forever Cemetery
39, 40, 41 & 42

Hollywood Bowl
Hollywood Bowl Museum
John Anson Ford Theater
Hollywood Heritage Museum
High Tower
Freeman House
Magic Castle
Wattles Mansion
Wattles Garden Park
Runyon Canyon Park
WHITLEY HEIGHTS
HOLLYWOOD HILLS
HOLLYWOOD FREEWAY
Red Line Metrorail
Chinese Theatre
Hollywood & Highland Mall
El Capitan Theater
Egyptian Theater
Hollywood History Museum
Hollywood Gateway Sculpture
Guitar Center
Charlie Chaplin Studios
Crossroads of the World
Hollywood Athletic Club
Janes House
Knickerbocker Hotel
Capitol Records Tower
Frolic Room
Pantages Theater
Amoeba Music
Cinerama Dome
Hollywood Palladium
GOWER GULCH
HOLLYWOOD/HIGHLAND
HOLLYWOOD/VINE
HOLLYWOOD BOULEVARD
SUNSET BOULEVARD
FRANKLIN AVENUE
N. HIGHLAND AVENUE
LA BREA AVENUE
VINE STREET
0 500 yds

Still, the contrasting qualities of faded glamour, modern hype and deep-set seediness also make Hollywood one of LA's best spots for funky bar-hopping and nightclubbing, with a range of cheap options.

Once you cross the freeway and reach Gower Street, you enter the most celebrated stretch of the boulevard. An unofficial dividing line between the east and west sides of this historic district is **Highland Avenue**.

East of Highland Avenue

The junction of **Hollywood and Vine** is perhaps the most famous intersection in Los Angeles, though exactly why is a bit more unclear, since there's little more than the usual dives and knick-knack shops there today. During the early years of film, the rumour spread that any budding star had only to parade around this junction to be "spotted" by big-name film directors, who nursed coffees behind the windows of neighbouring restaurants, as the major studios were in those days all concentrated nearby. In typical Hollywood style, the whole tale was blown wildly out of proportion, and while many real stars like Tom Mix and Rudolph Valentino did pass by, it was only briefly on their way to and from work. The most visible reminder of the legend today is located underground, where the **Red Line** subway stop is decorated with film reels and familiar cinematic imagery. For a look at this and other subway-art highlights, the MTA transit system sponsors free two-hour tours of the most noteworthy installations, beginning at the Hollywood and Highland stop (first Thurs of month 7pm & first Sat 10am; ⓣ213/922-2738, ⓦwww.mta.net/metroart).

Few aspiring stars may loiter at Hollywood and Vine, but many visitors do come to trace the **Walk of Fame**, which officially begins here (see box below), and just north of Hollywood and Vine is a small array of historic pop-culture buildings. The most familiar, the **Capitol Records Tower**, 1750 Vine St, resembles a stack of 45rpm records with its circular floors and top spire; Capitol was the first major

Sidewalk stargazing

As practically any visitor to Hollywood knows, the **Walk of Fame** is a series of metallic stars inlaid into the sidewalk throughout the district, honouring various actual, quasi- and pseudo-celebrities of the past and present, from big-name actors to obscure radio commentators to people only famous for being famous. The laying of the stars began in 1960, instigated by the local **Chamber of Commerce**, which thought that by enshrining the big names in radio, television, movies, music and theatre, it could somehow restore the boulevard's past glamour and boost tourism. However, for every Laurence Olivier or Dustin Hoffman, plenty of dubious choices are also made; the Rolling Stones, for example, took decades to gain a star, long after they were past their prime, while such questionable picks as TV's Judge Judy, Vanna White and the *Rugrats* cartoon characters are enshrined regularly. Selected stars have to part with several thousand dollars for the privilege of being included: among them Marlon Brando (1717 Vine St), Marlene Dietrich (6400 Hollywood Blvd), Michael Jackson (6927 Hollywood Blvd), Elvis Presley (6777 Hollywood Blvd) and Ronald Reagan (6374 Hollywood Blvd). (For the full rundown, visit ⓦwww.hollywoodchamber.net.) Almost every month there's a ceremony for some new luminary, like Michelle Pfeiffer, or curiosity, like Donald Trump, to be "inducted" into the street; check the local newspapers for upcoming ceremonies. Strangely enough, the one major figure to actually die on the Walk of Fame was TV actor William Frawley – better known as Fred Mertz on *I Love Lucy* – who had a heart attack a short distance from his own star at 6322 Hollywood Blvd.

record company based on the West Coast, and used this as its headquarters until the building was sold to a developer in 2006. Nearby, at 6233 Hollywood Blvd, the 1929 **Pantages Theater** (Ⓣ323/468-1770) has one of the city's greatest interiors, a melange of Baroque styling and ornate Art Deco friezes that mainly sees touring stage productions these days, but also served as the glossy site of the Academy Awards throughout the 1950s.

Ivar Avenue and around

Around the corner, a bit of literary history can be found at 1817 Ivar Ave, the site of the rooming house where author and screenwriter **Nathanael West** lived during the 1930s. Gazing over the street's assortment of extras, hustlers and make-believe cowboys, he penned the classic satirical portrait of Hollywood, *The Day of the Locust*, whose apocalyptic finale was inspired by West's witnessing of the Hollywood Hills wildfires in the summer of 1935 (and which, oddly enough, includes a character named Homer Simpson). Down the block, the former **Knickerbocker Hotel**, 1714 Ivar Ave, now a retirement centre, hosted celebrities such as Elvis Presley and was the site for several morbid occurrences over the decades. Here, the widow of legendary magician Harry Houdini conducted a rooftop seance in an attempt to assist her late spouse in his greatest escape of all; later, the hotel had a reputation for rooming some of Hollywood's more unstable characters, and a number of lesser names jumped from its windows; and in 1948 faded silent director D.W. Griffith expired in the hotel's lobby.

Further south on Ivar, between Sunset and Hollywood boulevards, the popular **Hollywood Farmers Market** (Sun 8am–1pm; Ⓣ323/463-3171, Ⓦwww.farmernet.com) offers a hundred vendors selling a variety of produce, from local citrus fruits and avocados to more exotic specimens like cherimoyas. Back up on 6541 Hollywood Blvd, the **Janes House** is a 1903 Queen Anne dwelling that is now the last remaining residential site on central Hollywood Boulevard, though it's been converted into an odd sort of lounge and nightclub (Ⓣ323/308-1911). A block west, you can find the well-worn dining booths of the **Musso and Frank Grill**, no. 6667 (see p.248), a 1919 restaurant that has been a fixture since the days of silent cinema. Here, writers, actors and studio bosses would meet to slap backs, cut deals and drink potent lunches. Not surprisingly, it's better for its drink than its food, and still a major draw for movieland denizens both famous and unknown.

The Egyptian Theatre

Across from the Grill, the **Egyptian Theatre**, 6708 Hollywood Blvd, is a unique, essential Hollywood icon: the very first Hollywood premiere (*Robin Hood*, an epic swashbuckler starring Douglas Fairbanks Sr), took place here in 1922. Financed by impresario Sid Grauman, in its heyday the Egyptian was a glorious fantasy, modestly seeking to recreate the Temple of Thebes, with usherettes dressed as Cleopatra. This great, restored building is managed by the American Cinematheque film foundation, and now plays an assortment of Hollywood classics, avant-garde flicks, and foreign films to small but appreciative crowds (tickets $11). Tourists, however, are encouraged to check out a documentary chronicling the rise of Hollywood as America's movie capital (Sat & Sun 11.40am; $10; Ⓣ323/461-2020 ext 3, Ⓦwww.egyptiantheatre.com). Alternatively, take a 60-minute tour of the facility (Tues–Sun 10.30am–4pm; $7; by reservation only at Ⓣ323/461-2020 ext 121). Much less appealing, the eastern corners of the Hollywood and Highland intersection feature a handful of overpriced tourist traps – wax museum, oddities gallery, world-record hall – that are worthwhile only if you're easily amused and eager to part with your money.

The Hollywood Heritage and Hollywood History museums

A five-minute walk north of the Hollywood and Highland intersection, the **Hollywood Heritage Museum**, 2100 N Highland Ave (Wed–Sun noon–4pm; $7; ⓣ323/874-4005, ⓦwww.hollywoodheritage.org), occupies a historic horse barn that originally stood at the corner of Selma and Vine streets. In 1913, Cecil B. DeMille, Jesse Lasky and Sam Goldfish (later Goldwyn) rented one half of the structure while the barn's owner continued to stable horses in the other. From this base, the three collaborated to make *The Squaw Man*, Hollywood's first true feature film, whose success propelled them to move their operation – including the barn itself – to the current Paramount lot at Marathon Street and Van Ness Avenue. The barn was eventually brought to its present location as a monument to Hollywood history, and now exhibits memorabilia from the early days, including old photos and props and documents signed by the bigwigs of the time (now mostly forgotten).

Just south of the Hollywood and Highland crossing, the **Hollywood History Museum**, 1660 Highland Blvd (Wed–Sun 10am–5pm; $15; ⓦthehollywoodmuseum.com), has four floors of fashion, sets, make-up, and other artefacts taken from movie history, though it has less a feel of a museum than a hodgepodge of castoffs in an overstuffed attic. In the coming years, though, the Academy of Motion Picture Arts and Sciences (see p.105) will be building what promises to be a truly comprehensive film museum near Sunset Boulevard just south of Arclight Cinemas, with acclaimed French architect Christian de Portzamparc designing this showpiece (see ⓦwww.moviemuseum.org for updates).

West of Highland Avenue

Looming on the west side of its eponymous intersection, the **Hollywood and Highland** complex (ⓣ323/467-6412, ⓦwww.hollywoodandhighland.com) is the most prominent sign of the local authorities' attempt to make Hollywood a tourist beacon once more – with a billion dollars of public and private investment, the commitment of a major hotel, boutiques and restaurants, and the relocation of the Oscars to the specially designed **Kodak Theater** (30min tours daily 10.30am–4pm; $15; ⓣ323/308-6300, ⓦwww.kodaktheatre.com). Still, this towering beacon of commerce is not much better than your average suburban shopping mall. That's not to say you shouldn't have a look – the architecture practically begs it. The mall's chosen, perhaps unintentionally ironic, theme is the Babylonian set from the 1916 D.W. Griffith film *Intolerance* from which the mall borrows heavily in its supersized columns, elephant statues poised atop massive pillars, and colossal, pseudo-Babylonian archway.

The mall has nearly surrounded the **Chinese Theatre**, 6925 Hollywood Blvd (ⓣ323/464-8111, ⓦwww.manntheatres.com/chinese), an odd version of a classical Chinese temple, replete with dubious Chinese motifs and upturned dragontail flanks; the lobby's Art Deco splendour and the grand chinoiserie of the auditorium make for interesting viewing. For $12 you can take in a **tour** of the theatre, complete with a look at VIP seating, a lounge, and balconies for the glitterati who attend premieres of big-budget spectaculars. Afterward, linger in the theatre's forecourt to see the handprints and footprints left in cement by Hollywood's big names (see box opposite). You'll probably encounter hundreds of other sightseers as well as celebrity impersonators – Elvis, Marilyn and Star Wars characters among them – low-rent magicians, and assorted oddballs vying for your amusement and money.

Across the street, the similarly impressive **El Capitan Theater**, no. 6834 (see p.270), is a colourful 1926 movie palace, with Baroque and Moorish details and a wild South Seas–themed interior of sculpted angels and garlands, plus grotesque sculptures of strange faces and creatures, and one of LA's great marquees, a multicoloured profusion of flashing bulbs and neon tubes. Admission to the Disney-owned theatre, which mostly shows cartoons and comedies, is worth the price to glimpse the eye-popping old Hollywood architecture. You can also drop in to sample the frat-house antics of ABC's *Jimmy Kimmel Live* talk show (TV tickets at ⓣ866/546-6984, movie tickets at ⓦwww.elcapitantickets.com).

A few doors down, at no. 7000, the **Hollywood Roosevelt** was movieland's first luxury hotel (see p.208). Opened in the same year as the Chinese Theatre, it fast became the meeting place of top actors and screenwriters, its Cinegrill restaurant feeding and watering the likes of W.C. Fields and F. Scott Fitzgerald. In 1929 the first Oscars were presented here, too. Look inside for a view of the fountains and elegantly weighty wrought-iron chandeliers of its marble-floored lobby. Although the glory has faded a bit, the place is still thick with legend: on the staircase from the lobby to the mezzanine, Bill "Bojangles" Robinson taught Shirley Temple to dance; and the ghost of Montgomery Clift (who stayed here while filming *From Here to Eternity*) reputedly haunts the place. Moreover, the hotel is the starting point of in-depth, three-hour **walking tours** led by docents from the Hollywood Heritage organization, who take you around some of the area's historic old piles and point out where various famed and forgotten celebrities did their bidding (every Sat 9am; $10; reserve at ⓣ323/465-6716, ⓦwww.hollywoodheritage.org).

The Hollywood Gateway and around

Hollywood Boulevard's historic stretch largely ends where it hits La Brea Avenue, on the corner of which stands Karl West's **Hollywood Gateway**. This iconic 1993 sculpture features a towering pylon and metallic Art Deco-styled roof supported by caryatids of movie goddesses Dorothy Dandridge, Dolores del Rio, Anna May Wong and Mae West – supposedly a homage to diversity in Tinseltown history, though all four were imprisoned by the stereotypes of the era, making the sculpture strangely resemble a shiny cage. One long block north, at 7001 Franklin Ave, the **Magic Castle** is a Victorian mansion designed as a grand French chateau,

Hollywood impressions at the Chinese Theatre

Opened in 1927 as a lavish setting for premieres of swanky new productions, the **Chinese Theatre** was for many decades *the* spot for movie premieres, and the public crowded behind the rope barriers in the thousands to watch the movie aristocrats arriving for the screenings – a familiar scene memorably satirized in the classic musical *Singin' in the Rain*. The main draw has always been the array of cement **handprints** and **footprints** embedded in the theatre's forecourt. The idea came about when actress Norma Talmadge "accidentally" stepped in wet cement (some say it was a deliberate publicity stunt) while visiting the construction site with owner **Sid Grauman**, a local P.T. Barnum of movie exhibitors who, with the Egyptian Theatre down the block and other such properties, established a reputation for creating movie palaces with gloriously vulgar designs based on exotic themes. The first formally to leave their marks were Mary Pickford and Douglas Fairbanks Sr, who ceremoniously dipped their hands when arriving for the opening of *King of Kings*, and the practice continues today, with celebrity hands, feet, cowboy guns, movie props and assorted other images making impressions in the cement, along with various heartfelt odes to the glories of Sid Grauman. It's certainly fun to work out the actual dimensions of your favourite film stars, and to discover if your hands are smaller than Julie Andrews' or your feet are bigger than Rock Hudson's (or both).

as well as a private club that puts on magic shows and other spectacles; the only non members allowed a look inside are guests at the adjacent *Magic Castle Hotel*.

For a respite from the Hollywood scene, the **Wattles Mansion and Garden Park**, further west at 1824 N Curson Ave (daily dawn–dusk; ⓣ323/969-9106), is a relaxing city park at the edge of the Hollywood Hills. This 1907 estate contains an expansive setting with picturesque grounds, several gardens with Japanese, Italian and native-plant themes, and a palm court. The house is usually off-limits, though no less interesting, with its 1909 Mission Revival design, impressive arcade and craftsman detail.

Lower Hollywood

Although Hollywood Boulevard is the undisputed hub of Tinseltown legend, the actual focus of the early film industry was in **Lower Hollywood** around **Sunset and Santa Monica boulevards**. In the 1910s and 20s, these streets hosted five of the seven major film studios, but a decade later, four had left for more spacious lots in cities like Burbank, which offered huge parcels of land to these studios, with lower taxes than LA. Ultimately, only **Paramount** stayed in its Hollywood location, parked right on **Melrose Avenue**; farther west the street has now become best known for its many independent businesses, mostly boutiques and eateries.

Aside from this area, these streets are grittier and much less touristy than Hollywood Boulevard, and their attractions are more modest and intermittent, aimed at those with a real yen to see the full spectrum of Hollywood. Aside from the west part of Melrose, most of the interesting spots should be explored by car, not on foot, as the strips can get dicey at night.

Sunset Boulevard

Famous as the title of the classic 1950 movie that featured Gloria Swanson as an aging, predatory silent-film star, **Sunset Boulevard** runs all the way from Downtown through Hollywood and into West Hollywood, where it becomes the colourful Sunset Strip (and beyond that runs miles on to the Pacific Ocean). Apart from **RKO** to the south (which went under in 1955) and then-tiny **Universal** (which left in 1915), three filmmaking giants left sizable holes in the landscape when they departed more than seven decades ago. **Warner Bros** (1918–29), **Columbia** (1920–34), and **William Fox Studios** (1924–35) were located within twelve blocks of each other, but all their studio buildings have been destroyed or remodelled beyond recognition.

The big studios weren't the only ones to offer employment to budding actors and crew in the early days. Small upstarts also occupied space along Sunset, and countless performers would try to get the attention of movie producers or casting directors by loitering around the corner of Sunset and Gower Street, the so-called **Gower Gulch**. Although there's not much more than an eponymous minimall at the spot today, in the 1920s film extras in need of a few days' work would show up in the hope of being hired for the latest B-grade Western, as extras or ad hoc stuntmen. The gulch's air of desperation earned it the moniker "**Poverty Row**", which also collectively described the town's smaller studios, such as nearby Columbia, which the legendarily tyrannical Harry Cohn founded (along with Universal), before it grew to become one of the majors – after it left the area.

Down the street from the site of the old Warner Bros studios, the recently refurbished **Hollywood Palladium**, 6215 Sunset Blvd (Ⓣ323/962-7600), was best known for hosting big names in swing, jazz and big-band music, and the place still puts on concerts today, though of the rock, punk and rap variety (see p.257). Across the street, at no. 6360, the white concrete **Cinerama Dome** (Ⓣ323/464-1478, Ⓦwww.arclightcinemas.com) is an unmistakable sight, its eight-hundred-seat hemispheric auditorium now part of a larger retail complex of theatres, shops and eateries. The dome was originally built to screen the three-projector films sweeping Hollywood at the end of the 1950s, but the movie fad faded even before the theatre was completed, in 1963. You can still see blockbusters in the dome on its central large, curved screen. Park in the lot for the adjacent **Amoeba Music** (see p.303), hands down LA's best music "shop", though indie clearinghouse or supermarket would be a better description of this massive vendor of vinyl, CDs and more. Nearby, the delectable Spanish Revival building at no. 6525 was, from the 1920s until the 1950s, known as the **Hollywood Athletic Club**, another of Hollywood's legendary watering holes. The likes of Charlie Chaplin, Clark Gable and Tarzan himself (Johnny Weismuller) lounged beside its Olympic-sized pool, while Johns Barrymore and Wayne held Olympic drinking parties in the apartment levels above, with the Duke himself prone to chucking billiard balls at passing cars below. The place now hosts special parties and private events.

Continuing west, **Crossroads of the World**, 6672 Sunset Blvd, was, when finished in 1936, one of LA's major tourist attractions: its very first mall. The central plaza supposedly resembles a ship, surrounded by shops designed with Tudor, French, Italian and Spanish motifs – the idea being that the shops are the ports into which the shopper would sail. Time has been kind to this place, and it still has a definite, if muted, charm as the headquarters of various local media companies.

Further along, **Charlie Chaplin Studios**, just south of Sunset at 1416 N La Brea Ave, was a 1918 creation, built a year before the Little Tramp teamed with other celebrities to create the United Artists studio. Now owned by the Jim Henson Company, the complex is not open to the public but does exhibit a bit of whimsical, Tudor-flavoured architecture from the street, especially as one of its little entry towers is topped with a statue of Kermit the Frog dressed as Chaplin's most famous character. A few blocks to the west, the **Guitar Center**, 7425 Sunset Blvd (Ⓣ323/874-1060, Ⓦwww.rockwalk.com), is a musical-instrument store catering to every would-be rock god in LA County, and features handprints of your favourite axemen – Eddie Van Halen, Slash and so on – embedded in the style of the movie stars' handprints at the Chinese Theatre.

Santa Monica Boulevard

For a street with such a familiar name, **Santa Monica Boulevard** has few noteworthy attractions, at least in Hollywood proper. Often plied by prostitutes and drug dealers, the boulevard is home to a mix of Russian immigrants, pensioners and gays. For excitement, you're better off heading further west into West Hollywood, where the street becomes a lot more lively – and safer. Still, despite its seediness, this stretch does have the distinction of bordering Hollywood's most famous graveyard.

Hollywood Forever cemetery

The former Hollywood Memorial Park is now known as **Hollywood Forever**, 6000 Santa Monica Blvd (daily dawn–dusk; free; Ⓣ323/469-1181, Ⓦwww.hollywoodforever.com), close to the junction of Santa Monica and Gower and overlooked by the famous water tower of neighboring Paramount Studios. The cemetery displays myriad plots of dead celebrities, most notably in its southeastern corner, a cathedral mausoleum that includes, at no. 1205, the resting place of **Rudolph Valentino**. In 1926, ten thousand people packed the cemetery when the celebrated screen lover died aged just 31, and to this day on each anniversary of his passing (August 23), a certain "**Lady in Black**" will be found mourning – a tradition that started as a publicity stunt in 1931 and has continued ever since. Appropriately enough, the current Lady in Black also serves as a guide to the cemetery, and her regular tours are great opportunities to find out more about the famous and forgotten names buried here (2hr length; $12; by reservation at Ⓔinfo@cemeterytour.com, Ⓦcemeterytour.com). While at Valentino's marker, spare a thought for the more contemporary screen star Peter Finch, who died in 1977 before being awarded a Best Actor Oscar for his role in the film *Network* ("I'm as mad as hell, and I'm not going to take it anymore!"). His crypt is opposite Valentino's and tourists often lean their butts against it while photographing the resting place of the "White Sheik."

Fittingly, outside the mausoleum, the most pompous grave belongs to **Douglas Fairbanks Sr**, who, with his wife Mary Pickford (herself buried at Forest Lawn Glendale), did much to introduce social snobbery to Hollywood. Even in death Fairbanks keeps a snooty distance from the pack, his ostentatious memorial (complete with sculptured pond), only reachable by a shrubbery-lined path from the mausoleum. More visually appealing, on the south side of Fairbanks' memorial lake, stands the appropriately black bust of **Johnny Ramone**, showing the seminal punk pioneer rocking out with dark, mop-top intensity (fellow bandmate Dee Dee Ramone is also interred here, in a more unassuming plot). Further west, one of the cemetery's more animated residents is **Mel Blanc**, "the man of a thousand voices" – among them Bugs Bunny, Porky Pig, Tweety Pie and Sylvester – whose epitaph simply reads "That's All, Folks."

Despite its morbid glamour, the cemetery also has a contemporary function. As you'll see around the Blanc memorial, there are many tightly packed rows of glossy black headstones with Orthodox crosses and Cyrillic lettering. These mark the resting places of **Russian and Armenian immigrants**, who increasingly populate the graveyard just as their living counterparts populate Central and West Hollywood.

Further along Santa Monica

There are only two other interesting sights along this stretch of Santa Monica Boulevard, the first of which is the **Formosa Café**, no. 7156 (see p.248), built around an old, remodelled trolley car, where celebrities from Humphrey Bogart to Marilyn Monroe came to drown their sorrows. Now part of a massive mall complex, it's still open, and its colourful ambience, though faded, makes it an

Laughing on cue

For many visitors, there's no greater highlight of a trip to LA than sitting in a **studio audience** and chuckling or applauding on cue to the comedy stylings of a TV sitcom. While not for everyone, such visits are required viewing for any proper television fanatic or old-movie buff – many production facilities are based in movie studios like Disney and Fox that would otherwise be off-limits to interlopers. Unless stated otherwise in the text, the main agency that handles the business of drumming up eager crowds for (live) laugh tracks is **Audiences Unlimited**. To be a member of an audience and experience the tapings of shows such as *Two and a Half Men* and dozens of others, call Ⓣ818/753-3470 or visit Ⓦwww.tvtickets.com.

excellent spot to savour authentic Hollywood spirits. A block west, at 1041 Formosa Ave, is the independent production facility now known as **The Lot**, which used to be owned by Warner Bros, and before that housed **United Artists Studios** (starting in 1928), the production company of Charlie Chaplin (his second), Douglas Fairbanks Sr, Mary Pickford and D.W. Griffith. With their studio as the symbol of the **star system** in the silent era, these four artists controlled their careers through the company, at least for a while, and helped craft the Hollywood marketing machine that sold movies by celebrity appeal, a system that endures to this day, for better or worse. If you want to venture inside the historic confines, you'll have to reserve space in the audience for whatever TV show might be taping there at the time you arrive; for information, call Audiences Unlimited (see box opposite).

Melrose Avenue

The southerly border of Hollywood, **Melrose Avenue** is home to the district's last major film studio and, further west, offers LA's most famous shopping strip outside Rodeo Drive. It only really gets interesting west of La Brea Avenue, though – anything further east offers the same melange of strip malls, diners and apartment complexes seen everywhere else in central LA.

Paramount Studios

Standing at 5555 Melrose Ave are the grand gates of **Paramount Studios**, for many one of the essential icons of old Hollywood, though the original entrance – which Gloria Swanson rode through in *Sunset Boulevard* – is now inaccessible. The movie company, despite its many changes of ownership over the decades, is still located here and hosts assorted film and TV production facilities, and offers a **tour** as well (2hr; Mon–Fri 10am, 11am, 1pm & 2pm; $35; by reservation at Ⓣ323/956-1777). It isn't quite up to the standard of Universal's theme-park madness or Warner Bros's close-up visit, but if you want to poke around soundstages and a mildly interesting backlot, it may be worth it. However, fans of drawling TV shrink Dr Phil don't need to shell out to watch their hero in action: the lot is readily open to those who've reserved space in the audience (info at Ⓣ323/461-7445, Ⓦwww.drphil.com).

The shopping strip

Synonymous to many with Los Angeles itself – splashy, anarchic, vulgar – the central shopping strip of **Melrose Avenue** came to national prominence in the 1980s for stores with edgy veneers and irreverent attitudes. And although the exteriors of the 1990s soap opera *Melrose Place* were shot at an actual apartment complex in the area – further east in Los Feliz (see p.81) – that programme's blow-dried beautiful people were a world away from the black-clad Gen-Xers and grungy hipsters of the real Melrose. More than anything else, though, what really defined the Melrose experience in its heyday was its widely eclectic selection of shops – junk emporia, perverse novelty stores, tarot-card readers, lingerie merchants, etc – and colourful decor, making a stroll along the strip a truly odd and invigorating experience.

Since then, many of the shops that once defined the avenue have been edged out by steep rents and forced to move to newer digs in zones like Silver Lake, Echo Park and Downtown's northeastern fringe. Melrose is still plenty eccentric, and offers eye-opening boutiques for the likes of leather clubwear and fetish attire, but some things have changed. You might drop a wad for a fancy dress or pick up a sleek pair of chic boots, but you won't see much in the way of antique dealers, toy shops, booksellers or taverns. As for **parking**, you won't find it easily on the avenue itself, but free spots exist on the side streets a block or two north and south of Melrose – as always, though, check the signs for parking restrictions.

The strip begins in earnest at La Brea Avenue. The west end of Melrose beyond Fairfax Avenue is rather dull and mainstream, and turns self-consciously chic and pricey when it reaches West Hollywood, where its colour and vitality dissolve into an uninspiring stretch of elite boutiques, and most of the window-shoppers also vanish.

The Hollywood Hills

Once the exclusive domain of Hollywood's glitterati, the **HOLLYWOOD HILLS** are synonymous with the legendary LA image of celebrities sipping champagne and enjoying the good life, high above the common folk toiling in the urban sprawl. Roughly parallelling Hollywood itself, and forming the eastern end of the Santa Monica Mountains chain, these canyons and slopes offer truly striking views of the basin at night, when LA spreads out like a huge illuminated grid in all directions, seemingly without end. Beyond the stunning views, most of the appealing sights in this area are located just north of Hollywood Boulevard, on narrow, snaking roads that are easy to get lost on. If you want to do serious exploring in these hills, bring a subcompact car, lots of patience, and a detailed map, such as a *Thomas Guide*, or prepare to be befuddled.

The eastern Hollywood Hills

On the eastern side of the area, Beachwood Drive heads into the hills north of Franklin Avenue and was the axis of the **Hollywoodland** residential development, a 1920s product of *Los Angeles Times* news baron **Harry Chandler**, who found ample time for real-estate speculation when he wasn't strong-arming city politicians. The chief reason most people come to the area is for the view of the **Hollywood sign** at the top of Mount Lee above (see box opposite). Unfortunately, there's no public road to the sign (Beachwood comes nearest, but ends at a closed gate) and you'll incur minor cuts and bruises while scrambling to get anywhere near. In any case, infrared cameras and radar-activated zoom lenses have been installed to catch trespassers, and innocent tourists who can't resist a close look are liable for a steep fine. For a much simpler look, check out Ⓦwww.hollywoodsign.org, where the letters are visible day or night, along with a virtual-reality tour of it.

More accessible and, for the most part, more appealing, **Lake Hollywood** is a bucolic refuge from urban life that's great for an hour's walk or jog along its flat perimeter. If you've seen the disaster epic *Earthquake*, you may remember **the lake**'s Mulholland Dam bursting and flooding the LA basin; however, this man-made, 2.5-billion-gallon body of water is anything but fearsome – just a pleasant refuge in the heart of the city. The clear, calm waters of this reservoir, intended for drought relief, are surrounded by clumps of pines in which squirrels, lizards and a few scurrying skunks and coyotes easily outnumber humans. You can't get too near the water, as metal fences protect it from the general public, but the 3-mile-long footpath that encircles it and crosses the dam makes for a relaxed stroll, especially for a glimpse of the stone **bear heads** that decorate the reservoir's curving front wall.

Tales of the Hollywood sign

The **Hollywood sign** began life in 1923 as a billboard for the Hollywoodland development and originally contained its full name; however, in 1949 when a storm knocked down the "H" and damaged the rest of the sign, the "land" part was removed and the rest became the familiar icon of the district. The sign, however, saw plenty of rough times, including during 1960s and 70s when the weatherbeaten letters and one missing "O" of the crumbling sign mirrored the district's own ramshackle condition. Since then there have been regular renovations (the first in 1978, the latest in 2005), and in 2010 the land around the sign was kept out of the hands of property developers when none other than Hugh Hefner plunked down nearly a million dollars to cap a campaign by a land trust to keep the property rugged and pristine.

Despite its preservation, though, the sign's current incarnation has literally lost its radiance: it once featured four thousand light bulbs that beamed the district's name as far away as LA Harbor, but a lack of maintenance and frequent theft put an end to that practice. The public's easy access to the sign is also a distant memory, for it has gained a reputation as a suicide spot, ever since would-be movie star Peg Entwhistle terminated her career and life here in 1932, aged 24. It was no mean feat: from the end of Beachwood Drive she picked a path slowly upward through the thick brush and climbed the 50-foot-high "H", eventually leaping from it to her death. However, stories that this act led a line of failed starlets to make their final exit from Tinseltown's best-known marker are untrue – though many troubled souls have tried and failed to end it all here. Less fatal mischief has been practised by students of nearby Cal Tech, who on one occasion took to renaming the sign for their school, and by other defacers representing USC, UCLA, the US Navy and Fox Television.

There's only one entrance at the time of publication, from the south (the north gate is closed until spring 2011 for construction). To get to the **lake access road** (usually daily 6.30am–7.30pm; information at ⓣ323/463-0830), go north on Cahuenga Boulevard past Franklin Avenue, turn right onto Dix Street and left to Holly Drive and climb up to Deep Dell Place; from there it's a sharp left on Weidlake Drive. Follow the winding street to the gate.

Whitley Heights

West across Cahuenga Boulevard, the charming pocket neighbourhood of **Whitley Heights** is a gem of Spanish Colonial Revival architecture, worth a look for its well-maintained houses and great city views. The district, accessible from Milner Road off Highland Avenue, was laid out in 1918 by business tycoon **Hobart J. Whitley**, an Owens Valley water conspirator who engineered the sale of San Fernando Valley real estate (under his aptly named corporation, "Suburban Homes"). He was also known as the "Father of Hollywood," as his Whitley Heights soon became a movie-star subdivision for such silent-screen greats as Marie Dressler, Gloria Swanson, Rudolph Valentino and the first "Ben Hur", Francis X. Bushman. It gives a hint of the relatively small size of the 1920s movie industry that so many of its stars were able, and willing, to live in such close quarters to each other and to their employers at the base of the hill – unimaginable today. Overall, while the construction of the 101 freeway wiped out a chunk of the neighbourhood in the 1950s, today the elegant, ungated area is well protected from development, and while tours of some homes are occasionally offered by preservation groups such as the LA Conservancy (see p.29), you won't find any tourist brochures available. Just park your car and go for a stroll.

The Hollywood Bowl and around

Near the Hollywood Freeway at 2301 N Highland Avenue, the **Hollywood Bowl** is a natural amphitheatre that's better known for its bandshell, which opened in 1921 and has since become something of an icon. The Beatles played here in the mid-1960s, but the Bowl's principal function is as the occasional summer home of the Los Angeles Philharmonic, which gives evening concerts from July to September (Ⓣ323/850-2000, Ⓦwww.hollywoodbowl.com). These events are less highbrow than you might imagine, many of them featuring fist-pumping crowd-pleasers like *Victory at Sea* and the *1812 Overture*, as well as selections of smooth jazz, film music and other inoffensive fare. More about the Bowl's history can be gleaned from the video inside the **Hollywood Bowl Museum** near the entrance (mid-June to Sept Tues–Sat 10am to showtime, Sun 4pm–showtime; Oct to mid-June Tues–Fri 10am–5pm; free; Ⓣ323/850-2000). It's not an essential stop by any means, but is worth a visit if you have any affection for the grand old structure, which has gone through many different incarnations and composition materials, from concrete and fibreglass to steel and even cardboard (for acoustics). With a collection of musical instruments from around the world, the museum also features recordings of notable symphonic moments in the Bowl's history and architectural drawings by Lloyd Wright, Frank's son (more famous for his Wayfarer's Chapel, p.151, and spooky Sowden House, p.83), who contributed a design for one of the Bowl's many shells. The fifth and newest dates from the summer of 2004.

One of the elder Wright's memorable 1920s residences, the **Freeman House**, is just south of the Bowl at 1962 Glencoe Way (information at Ⓣ323/851-0671), a squat, Mayan-modern hybrid made of concrete "knit-blocks", which doesn't actually seem like much from the outside, but inside offers an outstanding panoramic view of Hollywood, and a close-up look at Wright's geometric decorations and motifs. Unfortunately, like Wright's other major pre-Columbian experiment, the Ennis House (p.83), this one has seen its share of environmental damage (from an earthquake, in this case) and is undergoing a seemingly endless renovation. Another early 1920s design, the **High Tower**, is notable for a different reason. Inaccessible to the public, though viewable at the end of High Tower Drive, the Italian-styled campanile is the literary home of Raymond Chandler's Philip Marlowe – and Elliott Gould, playing Marlowe, lived in a dumpy apartment at the tower's apex in Robert Altman's 1973 film *The Long Goodbye* (see "Films", p.358). The surrounding neighbourhood is pleasant for walking, as many of its streets are pedestrian-only, tree-lined walkways.

The western Hollywood Hills

When he was directing *Chinatown*, Roman Polanski spent many hours in Jack Nicholson's house on **Mulholland Drive**, and later remarked of LA, "There's no more beautiful city in the world … provided it's seen at night and from a distance." With its striking panorama after dark of the illuminated city-grid, stretching nearly to the horizon, Mulholland easily justifies the director's wry comment – and makes the **western Hollywood Hills** a good place to get a glimpse of the LA good life.

Mulholland was once contiguous by car from the Hollywood Hills to the beach, switching names from "Drive" to "Highway" along the way. Nowadays part of Mulholland Drive is no longer accessible a few miles west of the 405 freeway, as this rustic section has been converted to a non-motorized section for hikers and mountain bikers, at least until Topanga Canyon Boulevard. However, the eastern stretch between the 101 and 405 freeways is still the best option, especially at night, when alternating views of brightly lit LA and the San Fernando Valley, to the north, keep drivers dangerously distracted. North of Hollywood, start your journey near the Drive's intersection near 2900 Cahuenga Boulevard West and continue up the hill, first south and then westbound.

Although parking is forbidden at night, daytime views are best experienced at a **roadside pullout** at the crest of Runyon Canyon Park (daily dawn–dusk). Here, telescopes allow you to peek at Hollywood, Downtown, and the many palatial homes. The park itself is a 130-acre delight, which actually improves on the views from Mulholland's crest. If you take the short upper trail, you'll be rewarded with some of the best vistas anywhere in the city. The lower trail is also appealing, descending through switchbacks down the canyon until reaching the striking views of the (often smoggy) city at Inspiration Point. If you have the stamina, take the long hike back up the hill to Mulholland, and keep a look out for B-list celebrities walking their dogs or burning off a few pounds for their next roles; otherwise, leave the park at Fuller Street or Vista Avenue (the only southern exits) and call a cab to take you back up to the top.

From Runyon Canyon's crest, follow Mulholland west past the Woodrow Wilson Drive entrance to the elite subdivision of **Mount Olympus**, a residential exercise in 1970s vulgarity that is to Neoclassical architecture what a toga party is to ancient drama, with faux palazzos, pseudo-Roman statuary, goofy marble urns and snarling stone lions added pell-mell to charmless stucco boxes. Much more appealing is the **Chemosphere**, 776 Torreyson Drive, architect John Lautner's giant, octagonal UFO-like house, balanced on a huge space-age pedestal and

The Case Study Program

Of all the popular architectural images to appear in the decades after World War II, perhaps none has been as recognizable or influential as the one of two women reclining in their evening gowns inside a glass-enclosed home overlooking the illuminated grid of Los Angeles. The photograph was of Case Study House #22, at 1635 Woods Drive in the Hollywood Hills, one of the 36 **Case Study Houses** planned in the LA area in the two decades after the war.

Created by the editor of the influential *Arts and Architecture* magazine, **John Entenza**, the **Case Study Program** was designed to show how industrial materials like glass and steel could be used for elegant, affordably modern homes, using "open-floor" plans to eliminate dining rooms and unnecessary walls – all revolutionary concepts at the time. Surprisingly, for a programme that showcased what were then rather avant-garde structures, it was quite popular locally, selected homes were displayed for the public, and nearly four hundred thousand visitors took a walk through the first six of these open houses. However, despite its popularity and influence, the programme never really came close to its goal of converting the broader American public to the modern mindset, though it did create some pretty impressive works, with many of the biggest names in LA architecture – Richard Neutra, Raphael Soriano, Gregory Ain, among 27 others – eventually taking a stab (check out Elizabeth A.T. Smith's *Case Study Houses*, p.367).

The houses were numbered in the order they were planned, irrespective of when, or if, they were ever built (23 eventually were, all but two in LA). The eighth house in the series was its first masterpiece, Charles and Ray Eames' colourful 1949 steel-and-glass complex, the **Eames House and Studio** (see p.184), a modular construction on the bluffs of Pacific Palisades that's a National Historic Landmark and perhaps the most famous of all the Case Study houses, despite only being assembled in a few days. Unfortunately, with the exception of this structure and Case Study House #22 (see p.100), almost all these houses are now closed to the public, so a drive-by look will have to suffice.

overlooking the San Fernando Valley to the north. Today it's home to Benedikt Taschen, publisher of stylish art and architecture books.

Other architectural treats can be found with sufficient effort as well, notably the stunning **Case Study House #21**, 9038 Wonderland Park Ave, Pierre Koenig's glass-and-steel hillside box, part of the influential Case Study Program (see box, p.99). Koenig's other notable home, **Case Study House #22**, also known as the Stahl House, 1635 Woods Drive, has an even more spectacular layout, famously perched above a cliff with its arch modern design, including a swimming pool. Best of all, the house is even on view for occasional tours ($25–40; information at Ⓣ208/331-1414, Ⓦwww.stahlhouse.com). Unfortunately, most of the area's other houses are hidden away, and there's no real way to explore in depth without your own car, a copy of the latest Thomas Guide map and, if possible, a detailed guide to LA architecture, such as *Los Angeles: An Architectural Guide* (see p.367). If you're more interested in peeking at the homes of the stars, avoid the tourist-trap bus tours and instead check out a master list on the Internet for your own exploring (Ⓦwww.seeing-stars.com is a good place to start).

Mulholland Drive continues past a series of enjoyable parks, including **Fryman Canyon Overlook**, a good place for a hike in the Santa Monica Mountains, and **Coldwater Canyon Park**, a pleasant wayside with a series of short trails.

West Hollywood

Between Hollywood proper and Beverly Hills, **WEST HOLLYWOOD** was for many years the vice capital of LA, with prostitution, gambling and drugs all occupying prominent places on the debauched **Sunset Strip**. The area was incorporated in 1984, a move meant partly to clean up the place and partly to represent the interests of gays, seniors and renters. West Hollywood has since gone on to become one of the most dynamic parts of the region, especially notable for its freewheeling bars and clubs, and housing prices have skyrocketed on many streets. However, West Hollywood is in many ways more akin to Hollywood, in its progressive character and attitudes, than it is to the prosaic wealth of Beverly Hills.

Except for the Sunset Strip – the well-known asphalt artery that features LA's best nightlife and billboards – West Hollywood's principal attractions lie west of **La Cienega Boulevard** around the colossal **Pacific Design Center**. The area east of Crescent Heights Boulevard generally blends with the less inviting parts of lower Hollywood and has little appeal beyond a few clubs and restaurants.

The Sunset Strip

Sunset Boulevard from Crescent Heights Boulevard to Doheny Drive, long known as the **Sunset Strip**, is a roughly two-mile-long assortment of chic restaurants, plush hotels and swinging nightclubs – as great a place to walk along and people watch as it is to drive. During the 1920s, it was a dirt road serving as the main route between the Hollywood movie studios and the early Westside "homes of the stars". F. Scott Fitzgerald and friends spent many leisurely afternoons over drinks around the swimming pool of the long-demolished *Garden of Allah* hotel, and the nearby *Ciro's* nightclub was *the* place to be seen in the 1940s, surviving today as the *Comedy Store* (see p.268). With the demise of the studio system, the Strip declined, only reviving in the 1960s when a happening scene developed around the landmark *Whisky-a-Go-Go* club, which featured seminal rock bands such as Love, The Doors

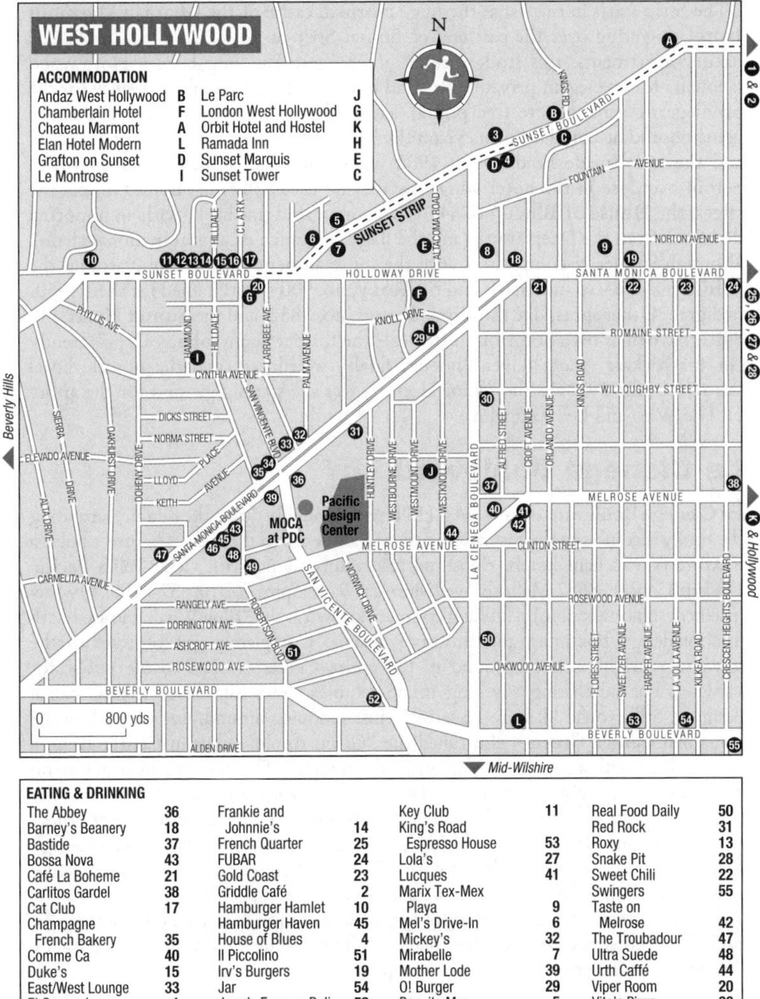

EATING & DRINKING

The Abbey	36
Barney's Beanery	18
Bastide	37
Bossa Nova	43
Café La Boheme	21
Carlitos Gardel	38
Cat Club	17
Champagne French Bakery	35
Comme Ca	40
Duke's	15
East/West Lounge	33
El Compadre	1
The Factory	46
Fat Fish	49
Frankie and Johnnie's	14
French Quarter	25
FUBAR	24
Gold Coast	23
Griddle Café	2
Hamburger Hamlet	10
Hamburger Haven	45
House of Blues	4
Il Piccolino	51
Irv's Burgers	19
Jar	54
Jerry's Famous Deli	52
Jones	26
Katana	3
Key Club	11
King's Road Espresso House	53
Lola's	27
Lucques	41
Marix Tex-Mex Playa	9
Mel's Drive-In	6
Mickey's	32
Mirabelle	7
Mother Lode	39
O! Burger	29
Poquito Mas	5
Rage	34
Rainbow Bar and Grill	12
Real Food Daily	50
Red Rock	31
Roxy	13
Snake Pit	28
Sweet Chili	22
Swingers	55
Taste on Melrose	42
The Troubadour	47
Ultra Suede	48
Urth Caffé	44
Viper Room	20
Vito's Pizza	30
Wa Sushi	8
Whisky-a-Go-Go	16

and Buffalo Springfield. Since the incorporation of West Hollywood, seedier joints such as striptease clubs and head shops have been phased out and this fashionable area now rivals Beverly Hills for movie-industry executives per square foot, though there's still plenty of chic grunge to keep you occupied.

Some tourists come to the Strip just to see the enormous **billboards**, which take advantage of a very permissive, longstanding municipal policy that allows all kinds of gargantuan signs to pop up along the road. The ruddy-faced Marlboro Man is now gone, but there are many more along the Strip to attract your eye: fantastic commercial murals animated with bright colours, movie ads with stars' names in massive letters, and various bored or angry-looking models posing in their underwear.

The Strip starts in earnest at the huge Norman castle of the **Chateau Marmont Hotel**, towering over the east end of Sunset Strip at no. 8221. Built in 1927 as luxury apartments, this stodgy block of concrete has long been a Hollywood favourite for its elegant private suites and bungalows, and you'll pay plenty for the privilege of staying here (see p.209). Howard Hughes used to rent the entire penthouse so he could keep an eye on the bathing beauties around the pool below, and the hotel made headlines in 1982 when comedian John Belushi died of a heroin overdose in the hotel bungalow that he used as his LA home. Across the street, the **House of Blues**, no. 8430, is a corrugated tin shack, with an imported dirt floor from the Deep South (and the flagship branch of an international chain), although it pales in comparison with the more authentic scene found around the **Whisky-a-Go-Go**, no. 8901, and the **Roxy**, no. 9009, both famed for their 1960s pedigree. Other spots, like the **Viper Room**, no. 8852, and the **Sunset Hyatt**, no. 8401, have their own notorious histories – the former being Johnny Depp's trendy lair for rockers where River Phoenix fatally overdosed, and the upscale hotel (known in the 1970s as the "Riot House") was the staging ground for the antics of The Who and Led Zeppelin.

La Cienega Boulevard

La Cienega Boulevard divides West Hollywood roughly down the middle, separating the funky seediness to the east and the snooty affluence to the west. The street holds a mixture of excellent hotels, clubs and restaurants, along with Cesar Pelli's **Pacific Design Center**, 8687 Melrose Ave (Mon–Fri 9am–5pm; ⓣ310/657-0800, ⓦwww.pacificdesigncenter.com), a hulking complex known as the "Blue Whale", loaded with interior-design boutiques and furniture dealers. Completely out of scale to the low-slung neighbourhood around it, the entire Center is open to the public for viewing, but purchasing anything inside requires the assistance of a professional designer. Still, you're likely to be satisfied just snooping around, not so much in the octagonal **Center Green** – also called the "Green Apple" – but in **Center Blue**, a massive barn with a mix of showrooms and boutiques. The most recent structure on the block, the acutely triangular Red Building, is meant for private offices only. The centre also features a Westside branch of the **Museum of Contemporary Art** (Tues–Fri 11am–5pm, Sat & Sun 11am–6pm; free; ⓣ310/289-5223, ⓦwww.moca.org), focusing on architecture and design with a sleek, modern bent, and often participating in shows with the two Downtown branches (see p.54 and p.102).

If you have a taste for contemporary art and design, there's even more to be found on the streets around the area, which are home to any number of fancy designers, art galleries and trendy boutiques.

Schindler House

Back east of La Cienega Boulevard, the **Schindler House**, 835 N Kings Rd (Wed–Sun 11am–6pm; $7), was for years the blueprint of California modernist architecture, with sliding canvas panels designed to be removed in summer, exposed roof rafters, and open-plan rooms facing onto outdoor terraces. Coming from his native Austria via Frank Lloyd Wright's studio to work on the Hollyhock House (see p.82), R.M. Schindler was so pleased with the California climate that he built this house without any bedrooms, romantically planning to sleep outdoors year-round in covered sleeping baskets on the roof. However, like other newcomers unfamiliar with the region's erratic climate, he misjudged the weather and soon moved inside. Now functioning as the **MAK Center for Art and Architecture**, the house plays host to a range of avant-garde music, art, film and design exhibitions (programme information at ⓣ323/651-1510, ⓦwww.makcenter.org).

4

Beverly Hills and West LA

Although Downtown and Hollywood are richer in historic and cultural attractions, **Beverly Hills** and **West LA** are ground zero for tourism in LA (at least outside of Disneyland). Along with neighbouring West Hollywood, they boast the best hotels and restaurants, and relentlessly market themselves as the height of fashion. With its diverse architecture and plentiful gardens, there's more to Beverly Hills than just the elite boutiques of **Rodeo Drive**, but for most visitors, the focus lies within the three sides of the shopping zone known as the **Golden Triangle**. Above Beverly Hills, the canyon roads beyond Sunset Boulevard lead into the well-guarded enclaves of rich celebrities, while to the west, the bland modern towers of **Century City** rise in the distance, with the district's main attraction being its large, eponymous mall.

As with the similar term "Westside", West LA has an amorphous definition, anything from the vaguely defined area between Beverly Hills and Santa Monica to everything west of Hollywood. Whatever the case, it's definitely crossed by the 405 freeway and extends from the mountain foothills to the I-10 freeway. One of West LA's main districts, **Westwood**, is pedestrian-friendly around the so-called "Village" just south of UCLA, and the university itself is full of resplendent buildings and gardens. To the west, along the **Sepulveda Pass**, the wooded wealth of **Bel Air** and **Brentwood** offers little of interest, but the hilltop **Getty Center** is a travertine icon of monumental proportions that's one of LA's crown jewels of art and architecture. West LA's southern neighbour, **Culver City**, is far less conspicuous than other areas, even though it contains several historic movie studios, a renovated downtown area, and a trove of eye-catching, experimental buildings.

Beverly Hills

The world over, **BEVERLY HILLS** is synonymous with suntanned Mercedes-drivers, fur-clad poodle-walkers, and outrageously priced designer clothes, illustrating how successful this city has been in marketing itself to the rest of the world – a glossy soap opera come to life. Inevitably, this self-promotion is more hype than reality, but if you've come here to fawn over celebrities (actual and pseudo) and press your nose against display windows, you won't leave

BEVERLY HILLS

EATING & DRINKING	
A Votre Santé	27
American Tea Room	16
Bar Noir	F
Barney Greengrass	25
Brighton Coffee Shop	21
Chaya Brasserie	6
Crustacean	20
Cut	26
Euro Caffe	17
The Farm of Beverly Hills	13
Fish Grill	5
Il Pastaio	14
Jacopo's	28
Largo	1
Locanda Veneta	7
Matsuhisa	24
Mishima	8
Mr. Chow	22
Nate 'n Al's	15
Nic's Restaurant/ Martini Lounge	12
The Nosh of Beverly Hills	18
Ortolan	10
The Palm	19
Plancha	4
Sofi	11
Spago	23
St. Nick's	9
Sushi Time	3
Talesai	29
Vegan Glory	2

ACCOMMODATION	
Avalon	J
Beverly Hills Hotel	A
Beverly Hilton	E
Beverly Wilshire	D
Crescent	B
Four Seasons Beverly Hills	I
Luxe Rodeo Drive	C
Maison 140	F
Mosaic	H
Peninsula Beverly Hills	G
Tower Beverly Hills	K

West Hollywood
Westwood
Mid-Wilshire
3, 4 & 5
10 & 11
BEVERLY HILLS
GOLDEN TRIANGLE
CENTURY CITY
City Hall
Civic Center & Library
Paley Center for Media
MCA Building
O'Neill House
Spadena House
Gagosian Gallery
Anderton Court
Two Rodeo
Electric Fountain
Creative Artists Agency
Academy of Motion Picture Arts & Sciences
Los Angeles Country Club
Century City Shopping Center
0 500 yds

disappointed. Beverly Hills's sparkling image is also kept up in part by a formidable local police force that keeps the streets free of panhandlers and others it deems undesirable. The heart of Beverly Hills is, of course, **Rodeo Drive**, which slices through Downtown with much pomp and circumstance, though it's not more than a few blocks long and there's little of interest beyond shopping. More picturesque sights are tucked away in the slopes and canyons north of here, where you'll find gated-off mansions to match the area's super-exclusive stores.

Wilshire Boulevard

The "linear city" of **Wilshire Boulevard** picks up west of the Miracle Mile (see p.71) to lead into Beverly Hills in grand style, though at an often glacial pace if you're driving. The first sight of note is the **Academy of Motion Picture Arts and Sciences (AMPAS)**, 8949 Wilshire Blvd, the headquarters of the organization that puts on the Oscars each year (see box below) at the Kodak Theatre (see p.90) and has historically established standards for technical movie craft and style, and is now building its own movie museum in Hollywood (see p.90). The Academy also

"I'd like to thank the Academy..."

The **Academy of Motion Picture Arts and Sciences** was formed in 1927 by titans of the film industry such as Louis B. Mayer, Cecil B. DeMille, Mary Pickford and Douglas Fairbanks Sr. Officially created to advance the cause of filmmaking, it was actually intended to combat trade-union expansion in Hollywood, which it tried to do, unsuccessfully, for ten years. After that, the Academy concentrated instead on standardizing the **technical specifications** of moviemaking – including everything from screenwriting to sound and lighting. To expand its membership and appeal, the Academy began to promote its award show as an event of national significance – if not quite an arts festival on the level of Cannes or Venice, at least an opportunity for starlets to parade past the footlights in the latest haute couture.

This show was, of course, the **Academy Awards**, which began two years after the organization's creation and was designed to give the industry's stamp of approval to its own film product. Called the **Oscar**, an award with many dubious explanations for its name – everything from its being a forgotten acronym to the name of Academy librarian Margaret Herrick's uncle – the Academy's official blessing has generally recognized the most well-crafted work produced by the **studio system**, not necessarily the best films overall. This is why landmark works of cinema such as *Citizen Kane*, *Vertigo*, and *Taxi Driver* have often been ignored and tub-thumping "event" films like *The Greatest Show on Earth*, *Cavalcade*, *Titanic* and *Gladiator* have grabbed the accolades. In recent years, however, perhaps due to the Academy membership's getting younger and more European, actual quality films have won the award – from the Coen Brothers' harrowing *No Country for Old Men* to the Martin Scorsese gangster epic *The Departed* to the bleak and unsentimentalized Iraq war film *The Hurt Locker*. Not surprisingly, ceremonies featuring such artier fare have suffered from lower TV ratings, and Oscar organizers have resorted to including ten Best Picture nominees – a grab-bag sure to pull in the likes of *Avatar* and its millions of viewers.

The awards are not above the occasional debacle. The appearance of a **streaker** during the 1974 show is the most notorious example, and actors Marlon Brando and George C. Scott publicly refused their awards in the early 1970s, with Scott describing the awards as a "meat parade". A good bet, too, are award-winning actors blurting out cringe-inducing hosannas (Sally Field's "You really, really like me!" or Cuba Gooding Jr's histrionics) or, more frequently, reading laundry-list thank-yous to all the people in town who *really* matter: executives, agents, managers, publicists, lawyers, ad infinitum.

offers regular screenings of classics in its excellent Samuel Goldwyn Theater (box office Mon–Fri 9am–5pm; tickets $5), along with exhibits in its **galleries** showcasing items from classic and contemporary American films, from scripts and storyboards to still photographs and animation cels (Tues–Fri 10am–5pm, Sat & Sun noon–6pm; free; ⓣ310/247-3000, ⓦwww.oscars.org/foundation). This stretch of Wilshire features other classic venues, including the Zigzag Moderne **Saban Theatre**, no. 8440 (ⓣ323/655-0111, ⓦwww.sabantheatre.org), built in 1930, and nowadays a home to travelling stage productions; the exuberant neon of the **Fine Arts Theater**, no. 8556 (ⓣ310/360-0455), a theatrical Art Deco-flavoured stage built in 1936, now under renovation; and the once-grand, now subdivided, **Music Hall Theater**, no. 9036 (ⓣ310/478-3836).

The Golden Triangle

Downtown Beverly Hills, successfully labelled the **Golden Triangle** by the city's PR department, is a ritzy wedge between Rexford Drive and Wilshire and Santa Monica boulevards, dotted with some of LA's top retailers, hotels and eateries – all charging the premium you would expect for such prime real estate. Street parking is tough to come by in the area, though there are a few scattered public lots, two of them just off Beverly Drive, north of Brighton Way and Dayton Way, respectively.

Rodeo Drive

Most people's chief reason for visiting Beverly Hills is, of course, **Rodeo Drive**, which cuts right through a three-block area boasting the most exclusive names in international fashion. Some of the bigger names include Barney's, 9570 Wilshire Blvd, and, all on Rodeo itself, Christian Dior, no. 309; Prada, no. 343; Gucci, no. 347; Chanel, no. 400; Hermes, no. 434; and Giorgio Armani, no. 436. (For details on each store, see "Shopping," Chapter 20.) However, Rodeo Drive wouldn't be quite so successful if it didn't appeal to the masses and offer at least something affordable: to wit, a Niketown here, at 9560 Wilshire Blvd, a Cheesecake Factory there, at 364 N Beverly Drive, and so on.

Adjacent to Rodeo Drive and Wilshire Boulevard, **Two Rodeo** (ⓦwww.tworodeo.com) is the area's mock-European tourist corridor, where a cobble-stoned street leads visitors up into a curving path through what is designed to resemble a vaguely French or Italian village, or at least a Disney version of one. However, while a few big-name retailers find residence here, most of the visitors don't do much shopping – snapshots of friends and family are the main draw. True to its LA identity, this Continental fantasy is built on top of a parking garage.

Just to the north of these snooty shops is Frank Lloyd Wright's curious **Anderton Court**, now called "Tallarico", at 328 N Rodeo Drive (ⓣ 310/273-6655), which resembles a boxy, miniature version of New York's Guggenheim museum, with a spiralling ramp crowned by a jagged horn, and is home to a few cramped retailers who must contend with Wright's awkward experiment in space and light. For a complete overview of Beverly Hills shopping and the area's art and architecture, take a trip on the **Beverly Hills Trolley** (40min ride; 11am–4pm: Sat & Sun year-round, also July & Aug & Dec Tues–Sun; $5; ⓣ310/285-2442), departing hourly from the corner of Rodeo and Dayton Way.

The Paley Center for Media and around

A few more interesting sights lie in and around Rodeo's elite commercial zone, most prominently the **Paley Center for Media**, 465 N Beverly Drive (Wed–Sun noon–5pm; $10, kids $5; ⓣ310/786-1000, ⓦwww.paleycenter.org), featuring a collection of more than 140,000 TV and radio programmes, often arranged in informative exhibits on such subjects as political image-making, famous advertising characters, and the best of radio and TV sitcoms, dramas and thrillers. The museum, LA's only real attempt at providing a media museum of scholarly value, has a well-designed theatre for public screenings of old and recent shows, and dozens of booths in which you can personally view your favourite media programmes after filling out a request form. The building itself is immaculate white geometry from the leading practitioner of this style, Richard Meier – more famous for his Getty Center (see p.115) – whose other noteworthy Beverly Hills work is his spartan, garage-like **Gagosian Gallery**, just two blocks west at 456 N Camden Drive (Tues–Sat 10am–5.30pm; free; ⓣ310/271-9400), which shows modern painting, photography and sculpture.

A few blocks northeast at 360 Crescent Drive, and representing a very different sort of architecture, is the former **MCA Building**, now headquarters of a financial firm, a 1939 triumph of the Classical Revival style, whose open forecourt features a lovely Florentine fountain set around classical columns and foliage. It was designed by the city's pioneering black architect, Paul R. Williams, also famed for designing a number of celebrity homes, including those for Frank Sinatra, Lucille Ball and Lon Chaney. Another architectural gem is the adjacent **Beverly Hills City Hall**, a 1932 concoction of Spanish Revival and Art Deco architecture that resembles a squat version of LA's City Hall (see p.52), except for the ornate dome dripping with Baroque details and vivid colours. Within the complex, the **Beverly Hills Municipal Gallery**, 450 N Crescent Drive (Mon–Fri 10am–4pm; free; ⓣ310/550-4796), regularly offers programmes of some interest, focusing on arts and crafts, furniture, antiques and photography. One block east at 444 N Rexford Drive, the **Civic Center and Library** complex is a postmodern Charles Moore confection with Art Deco elements, intended to give a contemporary design nod in City Hall's direction, though it remains much less appealing compared with its neighbour.

Outside the triangle

Just west of the triangle is the **Electric Fountain**, created in 1930 by the Beverly Hills Women's Club, through the efforts of comedian Harold Lloyd's mother. Depicting the history of the West on a circular frieze running along its base, the fountain spews water from the hands of a nameless Tongva native sitting atop its central column, deep in a rain prayer. Across from here, at the intersection of Wilshire and Santa Monica boulevards, sits the former headquarters of **Creative Artists Agency**, where powerbrokers, led by Mike Ovitz, made their company into one of the most feared institutions in town twenty years ago. With its imperious white-marble curtain wall and curved glass, the I.M. Pei design befits the attitude of the company, but agents don't reign quite as supreme these days, and CAA sold the behemoth and moved to Century City in 2007.

Meanwhile, on the north side of Santa Monica Boulevard, a continuous two-mile strip of green is known as **Beverly Gardens**. The most appealing stretch, between Camden and Bedford drives, is home to one of the largest municipal collections of cacti in the world and some fetching rose beds, and is a tranquil setting amid the abundance of prickly plants. The gardens are enlivened with occasional municipal art shows that pepper the grounds with lively, often whimsical sculptures along the roadside.

Further north is the residential side of Beverly Hills, with its winding, palm-lined streets and Mercedes- and Bentley-filled driveways. Although a number of has-been and lesser-known stars live on these streets (grab any guide to the stars to find out who lives where), the real interest is the fanciful architecture. Without a doubt the most peculiar specimen is the **Spadena House**, Carmelita Avenue at Walden Drive, whose sagging roof, gnarled windows and pointed wooden fence have earned it the

The Beverly Hills oil baron

The 1920s were a busy time for millionaire oil magnate **Edward L. Doheny**. Not only did the former mining prospector build the mansion of his dreams, **Greystone**, at the end of the Beverly Hills street that would one day bear his name, but he was also granted the title of Knight of the Equestrian Order of the Holy Sepulchre by the Roman Catholic Church and later had the main library at USC named after him, thanks to a million-dollar donation. Unfortunately, he was also involved in one of the biggest political scandals in US history.

Some three decades before, in 1892, Doheny and partner Charles Canfield struck **black gold** in the Temple-Beaudry district west of Downtown – a spot that quickly became the city's most lucrative terrain, and which is now, ironically, one of its most desperate slums. But around 1909, petro-dollars made Doheny wealthy beyond all imagining, and he put some of his fortune into his elegant mansion in the Exposition Park district (which is still a marvel; see p.141) and invested even more into new wells throughout the city.

By 1921, the one-time miner was a formidable force in both the local and national economy, and he probably didn't need to offer a bribe to the newly installed Interior Secretary, **Albert Fall**, one of President Warren Harding's many corrupt minions, in exchange for preferential drilling leases in the Elk Hills region of Southern California. But he did just that, putting $100,000 in the secretary's wallet. Three years later, after Harding's untimely death, a national scandal was unearthed in Wyoming, where another bribery deal – this one engineered by oil titan Harry Sinclair – had been made over the lucrative **Teapot Dome** lease. Soon enough, the corrupt bargain for the Elk Hills property was uncovered, and Doheny was prosecuted. Over the next six years until 1930, the government tried to put him in prison, but two trials only resulted in acquittals on technicalities. Although the legal result was favourable for Doheny – though not for Fall, who served time – the damage was significant, and the scandal forever blackened his reputation. In a tragic coda to the story, Doheny's son Ned, whom he had originally used to deliver Fall's bribe, died in a mysterious murder-suicide shooting inside the mansion in 1929.

nickname the "Witch's House." Sure enough, before it was relocated here, it was built as the headquarters for a Culver City movie company in 1921. Also outlandish and private, the **O'Neill House**, 507 N Rodeo Drive, looks like a melting birthday cake, with its undulating lines and lopsided, vaguely Art Nouveau shape.

From the lower residential zone, the increasingly curvaceous roads head into the hills and become more upmarket, converging on the pink-plaster **Beverly Hills Hotel**, on Sunset and Crescent Drive (see p.209), constructed in 1912 to attract wealthy settlers to what was then a town of just five hundred people. Much has changed in the intervening years, and the hotel's Mission style has been updated by a slew of renovations, though the core design of the building and its attendant gardens remain intact. Will Rogers, W.C. Fields and John Barrymore were but a few of the celebrities known to frequent the bar here, and the hotel's social cachet still makes its *Polo Lounge* a prime spot for movie execs to power-lunch.

The northern hills and canyons

Above the *Beverly Hills Hotel*, in the **northern hills and canyons**, the gated estates and well-concealed gardens and parks seem a world away from the more touristy confines of the southern portion of town. One idyllic place, the wooded **Virginia Robinson Gardens**, 1008 Elden Way (tours Tues–Fri 10am & 1pm; $10; by appointment only at ⓣ310/276-5367), spreads across six acres of flora, with more than a thousand varieties, including some impressive Australian King Palm trees. To the east, the grounds of the biggest house in Beverly Hills, **Greystone Mansion**, 905 Loma Vista Drive, are now maintained as a public **park** by the city (daily 10am–5pm; free; Ⓦwww.greystonemansion.org), which uses it to disguise a massive underground reservoir. The 50,000-square-foot manor somewhat resembles an imperious English Norman castle and was once the property of oil titan Edward Doheny (see box opposite), built in 1929. Though you can see the mansion's interior in countless films, including *There Will Be Blood*, based on the turbulent life of Doheny, the house itself is rarely open to the public, except for monthly **Music in the Mansion** classical-music concerts (Sun 2pm; $25; Ⓣ310/285-6850). At other times, you can admire the mansion's limestone facade, genteel courtyard (a car turnaround) and intricately designed chimneys, then stroll through the 16-acre park, with its ponds filled with koi and turtles, lovely gardens that are the frequent site of weddings and TV commercials, and expansive views of the LA sprawl below.

Two miles northwest, the oil baron's summer retreat, **Doheny Ranch**, was used for grazing his cattle, but is now good for picnicking and idling, part of 600-acre **Franklin Canyon Park**, an isolated niche of the Santa Monica Mountains National Recreation Area. The canyon is a broad public preserve that also contains two quaint little reservoirs. Although reaching the area may require a detailed map (or a visit to wlamountains.com), you can make the attempt by following Franklin Canyon Drive north into the parkland until you hit a fork in the road. The lake route, to the left, takes you to the upper reservoir, around which you can take a gentle walk amid ducks and old concrete abutments; the ranch route, to the right, leads to short hiking trails and a central lawn, popular with families, school kids and wedding parties. This side of the park also contains several amphitheatres and the **Sooky Goldman Nature Center**, 2600 Franklin Canyon Drive (Ⓣ310/858-7272 ext 131), where you can learn all about the park's ecosystem and geology. More intrepid hikers can head a half-mile north on the Berman Trail to Mulholland Drive, and from there reach parks with terrific views such as Coldwater Canyon Park, just east along the mountain crest.

Further west, in the verdant canyons and foothills above Sunset Boulevard, a number of palatial estates lie hidden away behind security gates. **Benedict Canyon Drive** climbs from the *Beverly Hills Hotel* past many of them, including Harold Lloyd's 1928 **Green**, 1740 Green Acres Place, west off Benedict Canyon, where he lived for forty years. Although the secret passageways and a large private screening room are still intact (and off-limits to the public), the grounds, which once contained a waterfall and a nine-hole golf course, have since been broken up into smaller lots. Apart from the period-revival houses that dominate the area, a smattering of other styles can be found off Benedict Canyon, best among them the **Anthony House**, 910 Bedford Drive, a terrific Craftsman work by Charles and Henry Greene designed for the head of Packard Automobiles, which was originally sited in Hollywood until a later owner moved it here. The house, with its rugged wooden frame and elegant garden, bears more than passing resemblance to the brothers' larger and better-known Gamble House in Pasadena – though this one isn't open to the public.

Century City and around

CENTURY CITY, along with Bunker Hill, is LA's most egregious example of building for the automobile, and one of its least pedestrian-friendly areas, overrun by giant boulevards and dominated by bland, boxy skyscrapers. It is, however, something of a landmark for West LA, its huge, triangular **Century Plaza Towers** visible from far across the Westside, as well as from the air as you approach LAX. Originally part of the 20th Century Fox studio lot, Century City began taking shape in the early 1960s when, because of its desperate financial condition resulting from a string of box-office bombs, the studio sold off much of its acreage, at the height of glass-and-steel corporate modernism. If the buildings seem oddly out of proportion, they are: they were designed to be seen from the windows of cars speeding by on the Beverly Hills Freeway – which mercifully never got built. Nonetheless, the district remains flash-frozen in that era, with the exception of the splashy new building for Creative Artists Agency, 2000 Avenue of the Stars. For most people, though, the only real reason to visit is the **Century City Shopping Center**, 10250 Santa Monica Blvd (see p.293), a single-level, open-air mall loaded with pricey boutiques and department stores.

Perhaps as a result of its overall lack of charm, Century City has appeared in several dystopic Hollywood movies, from *Conquest of the Planet of the Apes* to *Die Hard*. Just south at 10201 Pico Blvd, the current home of **20th Century-Fox** occupies much smaller digs than it used to. And while the company still has offices and movie sets on the premises, the public is kept firmly out.

Around Century City

The area around Century City has a few sights that are worth seeking out if you have the time. East of Century City, below Beverly Hills, is the affecting **Beit HaShoa Museum of Tolerance**, 9786 West Pico Blvd (hours vary, often Mon–Fri 10am–5pm, Sun 11am–5pm; $15; ⓣ310/553-8403, ⓦwww.museumoftolerance.com), an extraordinary interactive resource centre that shows the story of Fascism and the genocide of Jews and other atrocities in contemporary world history. Among other exhibits, it leads the visitor through multimedia re-enactments outlining the rise of Nazism to a harrowing conclusion in a replica gas chamber.

Further west, apart from the **Westside Pavilion**, another of LA's multilevel shopping mall complexes, at Pico and Westwood boulevards, the area's only other sight of note is the colossal **Mormon Temple**, the largest such building outside of Salt Lake City, located on a hilltop some blocks to the north at 10777 Santa Monica Blvd. Visible throughout the mostly flat Westside, the local headquarters of the Latter-day Saints is easily recognized by its 257-foot tower crowned by the 15-foot-tall angel Moroni. Although the main part of the building isn't open to non-Mormons, you can enter the **visitor centre** (daily 9am–9pm; free; ⓣ310/474-1549), and gaze at a 12ft marble sculpture of Jesus. Plus, if for some reason you've come to LA to hunt down long-lost family members, the LDS Church also has an on-site **Family History Center** (Tues–Thurs 10am–9pm, Fri–Sat 9am–5pm; free; ⓣ310/474-9990, ⓦwww.larfhc.org) that holds some 2.4 million microfilm documents for genealogy research, including links to British, Polish, Jewish and African-American databases; the majority of visitors here, perhaps not surprisingly, are not Mormon.

Westwood and UCLA

Just west of Beverly Hills and Century City along Wilshire Boulevard, **WESTWOOD** is divided between the pleasant, low-rise neighbourhood of **Westwood Village** – crowded with students, shoppers and theatre-goers – and the adjacent Wilshire traffic corridor loaded with some of LA's tallest buildings,

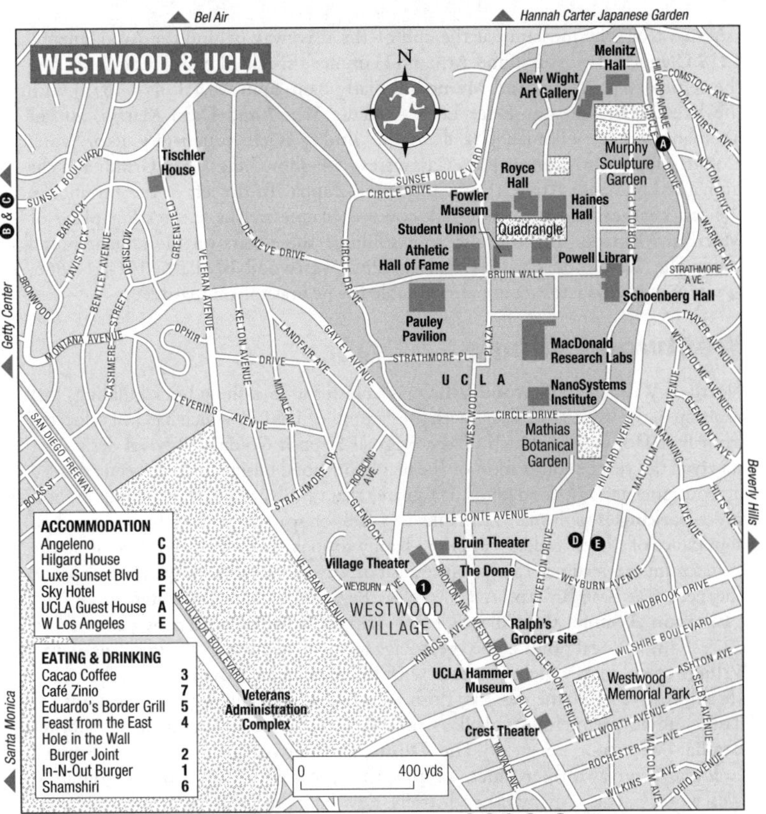

and some of LA's longest and most aggravating waits for a green light. To the south along Westwood Boulevard, there are also pockets of good ethnic diners, with an especially large concentration of Iranian–American (or Persian) businesses.

At the corner of Wilshire and Westwood boulevards, the **UCLA Hammer Museum**, 10899 Wilshire Blvd (Tues–Sat 11am–7pm, Thurs closes 9pm, Sun 11am–5pm; $7, kids free, Thurs free to all; Ⓦhammer.ucla.edu), comprises a sizable art stash amassed over seven decades by the flamboyant oil tycoon **Armand Hammer**. While the Rembrandts and Rubenses may be fairly minor, the nineteenth-century pieces like Van Gogh's intense and radiant *Hospital at Saint Remy* more than make amends. There are some impressive American works as well, such as a Gilbert Stuart regal portrait of George Washington; Thomas Eakins' painting *Sebastiano Cardinal Martinelli*, depicted with blunt, penetrating realism; and John Singer Sargent's *Dr Pozzi at Home*, one of the artist's skilled character studies. However, even more than the works of Old Masters, what you're likely to see at the Hammer these days are its insightful, sometimes risk-taking contemporary and avant-garde exhibits – quite a leap from what the conservative Hammer had in mind when he built the art enclave – everything from bizarre sculptural installations to light and airy minimalist pieces to multimedia works incorporating film, television and even holographic elements.

Across from the museum, at the end of the driveway behind the Avco cinema, 1218 Glendon Ave, you'll find Armand Hammer's speckled marble tomb, sharing the cemetery of **Westwood Memorial** (daily 8am–5pm; ⓣ310/474-1579) with the likes of movie stars Peter Lorre, Natalie Wood and Dean Martin, author Truman Capote, wildman jazz drummer Buddy Rich, tough-guy actor James Coburn, indie film pioneer John Cassavetes, talk-show king Merv Griffin and the unmarked graves of Roy Orbison and Frank Zappa. To the left of the entrance in the far northeast corner, a lipstick-covered plaque marks the resting place of **Marilyn Monroe**. You can also spot some of these stars on the radiant mural inside the Westwood **Crest Theatre**, 1262 Westwood Blvd (ⓣ310/474-7866, ⓦwww.westwoodcrest.com), also notable for its brash neon marquee.

Westwood Village

North of Wilshire, **Westwood Village** is a cluster of low-slung brick buildings that went up in the late 1920s, along with the campus of UCLA, which had just relocated from East Hollywood. Much of the original Spanish Colonial Revival design has survived the years, though most of the neighbourhood businesses have been replaced by boutiques and fast-food joints. It's an area that's easily, and best, explored on foot; street **parking** is nightmarish, thanks to a lack of spaces, steep $5/hr rates, and an abundance of meter readers – only too happy to stick you with a $35 ticket if you're even a minute overtime. Take public transit or, if you're driving, leave your car at the cheaper lot at 1036 Broxton Avenue before beginning your wanderings.

Broxton Avenue, the Village's main strip, is crowded with moviehouses and diners, but its focal point is the great Zigzag spire atop the 1931 **Fox Westwood Village** at no. 961, which, together with the neon-signed **Bruin** across the street, are impressive Moderne designs. Both are used occasionally by movie studios for flashy movie premieres, as well as sneak previews for test audiences. Another familiar Westwood image is **The Dome**, 1099 Westwood Blvd, the Spanish Colonial Revival former offices of the developer who created the surrounding Westwood tract and many other districts, now bedecked with palm trees out front for a nice Mediterranean touch. Also appealing is the one-time **Ralph's Grocery Store**, 1150 Westwood Blvd, a Spanish Romanesque structure whose entryway offers grand pilasters and cylindrical corner tower – a lot of ceremony for today's humble coffeeshop. Among several historic structures west of UCLA, the best is R.M. Schindler's 1949 **Tischler House**, 175 Greenfield Ave, which resembles a highly abstract boat: thick white rectangles jut out from the house's base, while the wooden-gabled living space on top recalls a ship's upper deck.

UCLA

The University of California at Los Angeles, or **UCLA**, is Westwood's dominant feature and one of the country's most prominent academic and athletic institutions, its group of lovely Romanesque Revival buildings spread generously over well-landscaped grounds.

The campus originally occupied the site of the Downtown Library, later moving to Los Feliz, and by the mid-1920s relocated to Westwood, where it became a model of Northern Italian-styled Romanesque design. Intended by architect **George Kelham** to resemble the redbrick structures of Milan and Genoa, the buildings around the central quadrangle, such as the library and science halls, seem to be plucked straight from a Lombard blueprint, giving the campus a classic "collegiate" look. Recent years have seen creative experimentation by the likes of Frank Gehry and Robert Venturi, though the Italian design thumbprint still remains.

Sun, sand and surf

From San Diego to Santa Barbara, Southern California is synonymous with American beach culture and its attendant body worship, sporting prowess and after-hours debauchery. The stereotype has been perpetuated by decades worth of pop music and Hollywood movies that identify the region with the good life by the sea – the fame of celebrity colonies like Malibu doesn't hurt, either. Indeed, the image is a potent one, and has been carefully cultivated since LA started promoting itself as a mecca for sunshine and healthy living in the late nineteenth century.

Santa Monica, late nineteenth century ▲

Scene from *Endless Summer* ▼

Surfer at Malibu ▼

Golden sands

During LA's Victorian-era reign as a land of clean air and citrus groves, salt-water bathing natatoriums, open-air **boardwalks** and carnivals peppered the coast. In 1907 surfing arrived from Hawaii, but the sport had not yet developed a national following, and most Southern Californians were content to enjoy the beach as a backdrop for **pleasure piers** like Venice and Pacific Ocean Park. In later decades, changing demographics and oil-drilling pollution shut down the funfairs, leaving the local beach scene in need of reinvention.

The **1960s** changed everything: the *Gidget* movies popularized the surf scene throughout the world, while more serious adventurers saw the thrills awaiting them in the *Endless Summer* documentaries. The Beach Boys, Jan and Dean and other pop artists sang of the glories of California beach life, while Venice became a home for up-and-coming artists and musicians, like Billy Al Bengston, Robert Williams and Ed "Big Daddy" Roth raising the area's profile by shaking up the staid LA cultural scene and making fortunes in the art world. Soon, **Venice Beach** would be famed for its boardwalk and Muscle Beach, and beach cities named Huntington, Manhattan, Hermosa and Laguna would promote their own indigenous beach scenes.

Surf's up

Although a sport as challenging as **surfing** is not something you can likely pick up on a single trip to California, there are few better places to get started. We've listed sport-rental vendors throughout the guide (see "Sports and Outdoor Activities" for more info; p.276), some of which run their own training sessions or camps.

Each beach in Southern California has its own vibe: some are friendly; others give off a hostile, "locals only" attitude; some are popular with a wide range of surfers, such as Zuma Beach north of Malibu, while more daunting places, like Rincon Point between Santa Barbara and LA, are best suited for pros who know what they're doing. A good source of information on the scene is the *Guide to Southern California Surf Spots* (see p.364); for weather reports, try calling or visiting Watch the Water (Ⓣ310/457-9701, Ⓦwww.watchthewater.org).

Oceanside pursuits

Southern California's beach culture hasn't looked back in the last four decades. Developers have plunked down the predictable condos and made once-funky places like Venice friendly to millionaires, but there are still plenty of prime spots for some memorable **oceanside pursuits**. The beach boardwalk extends from Santa Monica down to Redondo Beach, and is a great place to jog, bike, rollerblade or stroll, divided down the middle just like a miniature LA freeway. Closer to the waves, activities from bronzing to basketball, pumping iron to paragliding, water skiing to windsurfing are available for your amusement, while music fans can duck into a club for a seaside nightcap – you can even camp in some places. But more than anything else, it's the mix of people that defines the beach's appeal. The sand and surf bring together everyone from Hollywood hipsters to working-class immigrant families to Westside jet-setters. And in class- and culture-stratified LA, that's an uncommon and welcome mix.

▲ Venice Beach

▼ Surfers at Santa Barbara

▼ Muscle Beach

Crystal Cove State Park ▲

Zuma Beach ▼

The best LA beaches

These sandy stretches are among the best the Los Angeles region has to offer.

▶▶ **Abalone Cove** Fascinating scenery on the south side of the Palos Verdes Peninsula, where the cove offers tide pools and kelp beds rich with sealife. See p.151.

▶▶ **Carbon Beach** South of Malibu Pier, this is celebrity-watching central on the sands, where actors, agents and lawyers talk shop and negotiate on the famous "Dealmaker's Rock". See p.188.

▶▶ **Crystal Cove State Park** This marvellous beach, in a park spread over two thousand acres along the Pacific Coast Highway, is great for diving, snorkelling and poking around tide pools; you can stay in one of 46 historic bungalows and cottages. See p.200.

▶▶ **Huntington Beach** Beach culture Orange County-style, with regular surfing competitions, and a buzzing, friendly vibe. See p.199.

▶▶ **Leo Carrillo State Beach** At the northern edge of LA county, a favourite spot for surfing as well as camping, with kayaking and fishing also drawing locals in the know. See p.190.

▶▶ **San Clemente** Known to most of the country as the place where "Tricky Dick" Nixon retired, but to surfers as one of the top places in the region to catch a wave. See p.202.

▶▶ **Surfrider Beach** If you've seen *Gidget* or *Beach Blanket Bingo*, you know this longstanding, primetime surf spot. See p.187.

▶▶ **Victoria Beach** Wonderfully secluded alcove of sand that appeals to Laguna Beach residents for its clean water, pristine environs and few tourists. See p.201.

▶▶ **Zuma Beach** A popular beach with a range of fun activities and close proximity to the great arcing hump of Point Dume. See p.190.

The campus and around

A good place to start touring the campus is the **Mathias Botanical Garden**, 405 Hilgard Ave (Mon–Sat 8am–4pm, summer Mon–Fri closes at 5pm; free; ⓣ310/825-1260, ⓦwww.botgard.ucla.edu), a bucolic glade on the east side of the university where you can pick your way along sloping paths through the redwoods and fern groves, past small waterfalls splashing into lily-covered ponds.

Around the corner is the campus hub of the central **quadrangle**, a greenspace bordered by UCLA's most graceful buildings, a terrific place for reading, socializing or frisbee-throwing. The most visually appealing structures here include **Royce Hall**, modelled on Milan's Church of St Ambrosio, with high bell-towers, rib vaulting and grand archways; and the **Powell Library** (hours vary, often Mon–Thurs 7.30am–11pm, Fri 7.30am–6pm, Sat 9am–5pm, Sun 1–10pm; ⓦwww.library.ucla.edu), featuring a spellbinding interior with lovely Romanesque arches, columns, and stairwell. The highlight is the dome above the **reading room**, where Renaissance printers' marks are inscribed, among them icons representing such pioneers as Johann Fust and William Caxton. Other, more current designs are more experimental. Robert Venturi's 1991 **MacDonald Research Labs**, Westwood Boulevard at Young Drive S, is a postmodern take on the greatest hits of classical architecture, featuring off-colour, brick upper storey with irregular windows, a concrete base and quasi-Egyptian colonnade. Even more contemporary, Rafael Vinoly's ultra-modern NanoSystems Institute from 2007 offers a serene steel-and-glass facade that hides its manic array of bridges and catwalks crowding a central courtyard.

UCLA's artistic and cultural attractions are also a strength. The **Fowler Museum of Cultural History**, Bruin Walk at Westwood Plaza (Wed–Sun noon–5pm, Thurs closes 8pm; free; ⓣ310/825-4361, ⓦwww.fowler.ucla.edu), offers an immense range of multicultural art – including ceramics, religious icons, paintings and musical instruments. The museum's highlights include a worldwide selection of native masks, thousands of textile pieces from different cultures, an extensive collection of African and Polynesian art and various folk designs, from simple household implements to elaborate ritual costumes and ceremonial icons. To the northeast, just west of Hilgard Avenue before it meets Sunset Boulevard, the **Franklin Murphy Sculpture Garden** (open 24hr; free; tours at ⓣ310/443-7041) is LA's best outdoor display of modern sculpture, including pieces by such big names as Jean Arp, Henry Moore, Joan Miró, Henri Matisse and Isamu Noguchi. Other notable works include Auguste Rodin's *Walking Man*, a stark nude composed of only a torso and legs, and George Tsutakawa's *OBOS-69*, a fountain resembling a stack of TV sets.

Just north of the Murphy Garden, the **New Wight Art Gallery**, 11000 Kinross Ave (Mon–Fri 9am–4pm; free; ⓣ310/825-0557, ⓦwww.art.ucla.edu/gallery.html), has a less intriguing collection of contemporary art on display. Just east of the Wight Gallery and northeast of the garden, in **Melnitz Hall**, UCLA's **film school** has produced filmmakers like Francis Ford Coppola, Alison Anders and Alex Cox, the more independent-oriented rival to USC's industry-dominated school. The school oversees the massive storehouse of the **UCLA Film and Television Archive**, a treasure-trove of more than 220,000 items, among them classic, foreign and art movies, and a wide range of old TV shows, state journalism footage and even an assortment of Hearst newsreels from the turn of the twentieth century. To check out the collection, make an appointment at 46 Powell Library (where the archive's items are kept), or by calling ⓣ310/206-5388 (Mon–Fri 9am–5pm) or visiting ⓦwww.cinema.ucla.edu. The archive also presents regular screenings of films in the **Billy Wilder Theatre** in the courtyard of the Hammer Museum (see p.111; tickets $9; ⓣ310/206-8013).

UCLA is well known for its athletic prowess, winning more NCAA basketball championships – eleven – than any other team (most of them as a result of the wizardry of legendary coach John Wooden, who died in 2010). Some of this history is on display at the **Athletic Hall of Fame** (Mon–Fri 8am–5pm; free; Ⓦuclabruins.cstv.com/ot/hof.html) near the centre of campus along Bruin Walk east of Young Drive W, where you can check out the school's awards in basketball, football and volleyball, among other sports. UCLA's basketball team plays just west of here, at **Pauley Pavilion** (now undergoing renovation), while the football team's home is the Rose Bowl (see p.169).

For a more contemplative experience, travel just north of campus to UCLA's **Hannah Carter Japanese Garden**, 10619 Bellagio Rd (Tues, Wed & Fri 10am–2pm; free; by appointment only at Ⓣ310/794-0320 or Ⓦwww.japanesegarden.ucla.edu), an idyllic spot featuring magnolias and Japanese maples, and traditional structures and river rocks brought directly from Japan – though four hundred tons of dark-brown rocks were also hauled in from Ventura County to lend the right aesthetic touch. Adding to the calming Zen feel are a pagoda, teahouse, quaint bridges and assorted gold and stone Buddhas.

The Sepulveda Pass and around

The gap through the Santa Monica Mountains known as the **Sepulveda Pass** runs alongside some of LA's most exclusive residential neighbourhoods, dividing Brentwood from Bel Air and some of the areas further north, where you'll find the **Getty Center**, the city's art showpiece. The pass often gives tourists their first views of central LA as they travel south on the 405 freeway into town. The pass contains both the freeway and part of Sepulveda Boulevard – the longest road in LA County, leading from Long Beach into the north San Fernando Valley — which acts as an alternate, more leisurely route, as it meanders through the hills.

Bel Air and Brentwood

BEL AIR, just northwest of UCLA and east of the 405 freeway, is an elite subdivision with opulent black gates fronting Sunset Boulevard and security guards driving about to catch interlopers. For many, this district and Rodeo Drive seem to be the very definition of wealth in the city, though despite its famous name and reputation, very little goes on here, as the only business is the well-known, luxurious **Bel Air Hotel** (see p.211) and the residential architecture is near impossible to see, typically hidden behind thick foliage. For a closer look at the well-heeled, **BRENTWOOD** to the west is a better bet. Known for its most famous former resident, O.J. Simpson (his Tudor mansion has since been razed), Brentwood also has an upscale shopping strip along **San Vicente Boulevard**, with a good range of boutiques and restaurants, and surrounding neighbourhoods with accessible streets and stylish modern architecture. San Vicente's greenway, heading west, is also an enjoyable place to get in a morning jog as the sun rises.

Skirball Cultural Center

Back along Sepulveda Boulevard, near the crest of the Santa Monica Mountains, the compelling **Skirball Cultural Center**, 2701 N Sepulveda Blvd (Tues–Fri noon–5pm, Sat & Sun 10am–5pm; $10; Ⓣ310/440-4500, Ⓦwww.skirball.org), is an institution with several missions. One, its original purpose, is to focus on the history, beliefs and rituals of Judaism, concentrating on the more mystical elements of the faith and offering a broad overview of Judaic treasures, from Hanukkah lamps to a Holy Ark (a cabinet for Torah scrolls) from a German synagogue. The second goal of the Skirball is to be a modern centre for Jewish expression in science, art, philosophy and popular culture, with various rotating exhibits. Finally, the centre looks at the American diaspora in stark photographs of c.1900 immigrants and written mementos of their arduous travel and assimilation (or not); among assorted other historic American artefacts are an early copy of the Declaration of Independence and one of Abe Lincoln's stovepipe hats.

The Getty Center

Off Sepulveda and west of the 405 freeway, Getty Center Drive leads up to the monumental **Getty Center** (Tues–Thurs & Sun 10am–5.30pm, Fri & Sat 10am–9pm; free, parking $15; ⓣ310/440-7300, ⓦwww.getty.edu). A grand 110-acre museum and research complex towering over the city, it was planned and built over fourteen years at a cost of $1 billion to hold the vast art holdings of oil mogul **J. Paul Getty**. To rise up to this gleaming city on a hill by bus, you'll need to take MTA line #761 from UCLA after taking line #2 or #302 from Downtown, or line #720 from Santa Monica; if you come by car, there's a parking lot at the base of the hill; either way, a tram ride can get you up to the complex – a slow, enchanting ride with fine vistas of the metropolis, which you can also get by hoofing it up the slope alongside the track.

Construction of the Center took eight years, from 1989 to 1997. Its architect, **Richard Meier**, designed part of the Center in travertine, a good choice, since it combines the ancient roughness of fossil-bearing sandstone with the austere geometry of high-modernism, ultimately leading some to dub the site the "American Acropolis". However, even the museum curators acknowledge that Getty himself would have been horrified to see such a modernist creation, no matter how brilliant, built in his name, since he was a staunch aesthetic reactionary – preferring the figurative, ornamental and historical to the abstract, severe and contemporary. Except for the photography collection and a handful of twentieth-century works, the building itself is the only thing modern about the place.

Getty started amassing his massive collection in the 1930s, storing much of it in his own house until the first **Getty Museum** opened in 1974 on an ocean bluff near Malibu. That site is now a showcase for the foundation's antiquities (see p.185). The **museum** itself is on the grounds of the Center, which also includes facilities for art research, conservation and acquisition, though none of these are open to the public. Despite the huge investment, the Getty Foundation still has billions in reserve and must, by law, spend hundreds of millions each year from its endowment. Thus, it plays an elephantine role on the international art scene and can freely outbid its competitors for anything it wants. However, it's not immune from outside pressure, as in the ongoing trial in Italy of a Getty director for alleged illegal removal of that country's antiquities. Although the institution didn't explicitly admit fault, it has returned forty ancient works with dubious provenance – from Pompeiian frescos to Greek limestone and marble statues to various bronzes and vases.

The museum itself consists of five two-storey structures that are landscaped around open plazas and shallow fountains, with the collection spread throughout buildings that are linked by bridges and walkways. No matter where you start, you'll find the artworks still heavily influenced by Getty's tastes, long after the oil baron's death.

Breaking for a meal at the Getty

If you spend a full day here – and many do – you'll want to grab a bite in one of the Getty's two central eateries. The **restaurant** (Tues–Sat 11.30am–2.30pm, Sun 11am–3pm; reservations suggested at ⓣ310/440-6810) serves California cuisine and attracts locals who enjoy an elegant setting and upscale pasta, crab cakes and the like. Most visitors, however, head to the lower level for the massive **café** (Tues–Fri 11.30am–5pm, Sat & Sun 11.30am–3pm), which has a broad sampling of international cuisines laid out in the style of a cafeteria, and not much tastier, though much pricier. There are also **seasonal cafés** around the terrace and courtyard, oriented more toward providing snacks and coffee.

Getty gardens

A good place to begin exploring the museum is outside in its **Central Garden**, a concentric array of leafy terraces designed by conceptual artist Robert Irwin. Occupying the middle ground of the complex, the garden is a stunning arrangement, leading crowds along sloping paths through azaleas, bougainvilleas and other plants and flowers, while the austere pavilions loom in the background, making it a multicoloured oasis in a sea of white and beige. More in the style of Richard Meier, perhaps, is the topiary formalism of the **Desert Garden**, on the south end of the complex, where a low-scaled set of hardy plants sits in tight, circular confinement above a cliff of the Santa Monica Mountains, the plants assuming their role as a rigid natural component of Meier's spartan design scheme.

Furniture and decorative arts

One of his greatest enthusiasms was his formidable array of ornate **furniture** and **decorative arts**, with clocks, chandeliers, tapestries and gilt-edged commodes, designed for the French nobility from the reign of Louis XIV, filling several overwhelmingly opulent rooms and dripping with all the gold, silver, silk and velvet you might expect. This part of the collection is primarily geared toward enthusiasts of such antique luxuries, who spend hours poring over the detailed craftsmanship of the fabric and metalwork. As a bonus, the museum offers video and on-site **reproductions** of classic items of furniture, showing in full detail the painstaking steps that went into creating cabinets, bureaus and commodes for the aristocracy.

Painting

The European paintings are principally from the post-Renaissance era, but there are a few notable exceptions, including several from the **Italian Renaissance**. Among these are Andrea Mantegna's stoic but affecting *Adoration of the Magi*, Correggio's *Head of Christ*, a rich portrait that rivals Rembrandt's work for emotional expression, and Titian's *Venus and Adonis*, depicting in muted colours the last moments between the lovers before the latter is gored by a wild boar. Notable **Mannerist** works include Pontormo's *Portrait of a Halberdier*, in which the subject's almost-blank expression has been variously interpreted as arrogant, morose or contemplative, and Veronese's richly detailed *Portrait of a Man*, perhaps of the painter himself – a sword-bearing nobleman gazing proudly down at the viewer.

The finest works from the seventeenth century are **Flemish** and **Dutch**. Among the highlights are Rubens' *Entombment*, a pictorial essay supporting the Catholic doctrine of transubstantiation; Hendrik ter Brugghen's *Bacchante with an Ape*, showing a drunken libertine clutching a handful of grapes, an action mirrored by his pet monkey; and a trio of Rembrandts: *Daniel and Cyrus before the Idol Bel*, in which the Persian king tries foolishly to feed the bronze statue he worships; *An Old Man in Military Costume*, the exhausted, uncertain face of an old soldier; and the great portrait *Saint Bartholomew*, showing the martyred saint as a quiet, thoughtful Dutchman – the knife that will soon kill him visible in the corner of the frame.

While some lesser **French Neoclassical** works are included, notably David's overly slick and unaffecting *Farewell of Telemachus and Eucharis*, one of the best works from the period is Gericault's later *Portrait Study*, a sensitive portrait of an African man. The Getty Center is also known for bidding on **Impressionist** works; these acquisitions read like a laundry list of late nineteenth-century French art: the portrait *Albert Cahen d'Anvers* by Renoir, the inevitable Monet haystacks, and one of Degas' ballet dancers. Van Gogh's *Irises* is also on view, the Getty Trust snatching up the vivid floral icon for an unknown price. Other significant works from the **nineteenth century** include *Bullfight* by Goya, in which the bull stares triumphantly at a group of unsuccessful matadors; J.M.W. Turner's frenzied *Ships at Sea, Getting a Good Wetting*, all hazy colours that look surprisingly modern and abstract; and Caspar David Friedrich's elegant and understated *A Walk at Dusk*, a Romantic painting of a man bowing before a stone cairn during twilight.

Drawings and manuscripts

The museum also boasts a wide collection of **drawings**, among the best of which are Albrecht Dürer's meticulous *Study of the Good Thief*, a portrait of the crucified criminal who was converted on the cross; his *Stag Beetle*, precise enough to look as if the bug were crawling on the page itself; Piranesi's dramatic image of a ruined, but still monumental, *Ancient Port*; and William Blake's bizarre watercolour of *Satan Exalting over Eve*, an expressionless devil hovering over his prone captive.

Also fascinating is the museum's excellent collection of medieval **illuminated manuscripts**, depicting Biblical scenes such as the Passion cycle, as well as notable saints. Exquisitely drawn letters introduce chapters from Scripture, with one of the most interesting volumes being the *Apocalypse with Commentary by Berengaudus*, an English Gothic tome that shows the Book of Revelation in all its fiery detail, including an image of the Four Horsemen of the Apocalypse as stalwart medieval knights.

Sculpture, photography and other arts

The museum's most memorable sculptures are Benvenuto Cellini's *Hercules Pendant*, a small, finely rendered piece of jewellery that shows the ancient hero in shock, mouth agape; Antonio Canova's gracefully Neoclassical rendering of the god *Apollo*; and Gian Lorenzo Bernini's much smaller *Boy with a Dragon* – done when he was only 16 – depicting a plump toddler bending back the jaw of a dragon with surprising ease, either a playful putto or Jesus himself, depending on your view.

Some of the Getty's excellent array of **photographs** include renowned works by Stieglitz, Strand, Weston, Adams Arbus and others, but again, it's the museum's less familiar works that are the most intriguing: an 1849 *Portrait of Edgar Allan Poe*, by an unknown photographer, has the writer staring at the camera with manic intensity; Thomas Eakins's photo study *Students at the Site for "The Swimming Hole"*, showing the artist's pupils jumping naked from a flat rock into a muddy pond; Civil War photographer Timothy O'Sullivan's seemingly doomed wagon train grinding on through the *Desert Sand Hills*; and August Sander's feral *Frau Peter Abelen*, an androgynous woman with slicked-back hair, white culottes, business shirt and tie, holding an unlit cigarette between gritted teeth.

Beyond all this, the museum hosts **temporary exhibitions** of classical and modern work, everything from medieval tapestries and religious icons to old-fashioned lithographs and avant-garde photography. Displays that relate to recently conserved works are also on view in the lobby of the neighbouring **Getty Research Institute**, just west of the main museum entrance (also free; same hours), which allows a brief glimpse into the workings of the rest of this sizable organization – though, unfortunately, no tours are offered.

Culver City

Several miles south of Beverly Hills and Westwood, triangular **CULVER CITY** has a past rich with movie lore and a current face shaped by groundbreaking architectural experiments. An extensive facelift since the 1990s has resulted in more parks and footpaths, streets lined with old-fashioned lampposts and jacaranda trees, and fewer drab streets and buildings. The city centre is sited around the intersection of Washington and Culver boulevards, which hosts a weekly **farmers' market** (Tues 3–7pm; free) on a block-long stretch, a good bet for assorted snacks and seasonal produce. Looming over the intersection is the early-twentieth-century **Culver Hotel** (see "Accommodation", p.211), replete with chequered marble flooring and iron railings. Plenty of Hollywood history took place inside the hotel, which started as Harry Culver's office space, was later purchased by John Wayne, and was often a favourite spot to stay for stars like Greta Garbo and Clark Gable. However, stories of drunken debauchery by the midget cast of the *Wizard of Oz* – who apparently stayed here during the filming – are more Hollywood myth than reality.

Just east, the **Ivy Substation**, at Culver and Venice boulevards, is a 1907 power station for the old Red Car public transit line. Located in a palm-tree-filled park, the Mission Revival building is now used as a 99-seat performing arts venue for

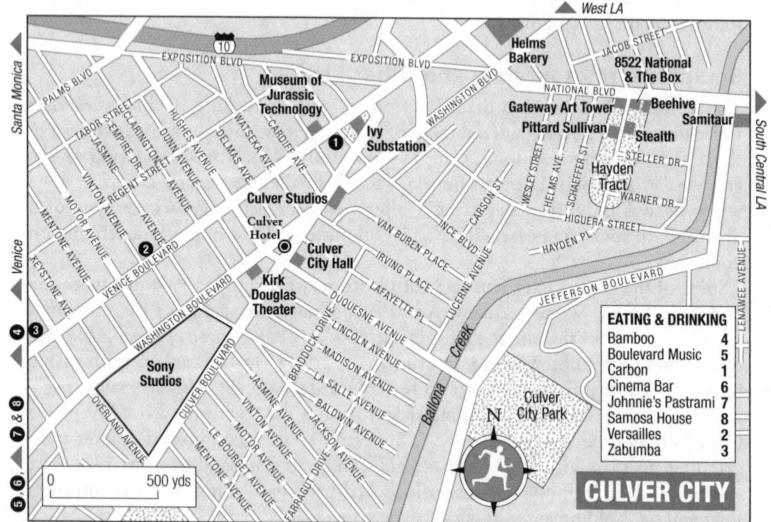

the Actors' Gang Theatre (Ⓣ310/838-4264, Ⓦwww.theactorsgang.com). Other major structures can be found nearby, including the 1931 **Helms Bakery**, 8800 Venice Blvd, a WPA landmark with its original iron lamps, grand sign and fixtures, which is now home to a range of furniture dealers and design showrooms.

West of the *Culver Hotel*, the old Culver Theater, 9820 Washington Blvd at Duquesne Avenue, is a striking 1947 moviehouse with a streamlined marquee and sparkling neon pylon; it has been reborn as the **Kirk Douglas Theater** (Ⓣ213/628-2772, Ⓦwww.taperahmanson.com), named after the star of *Paths of Glory* and *Spartacus*. Not far away, **City Hall**, 9770 Culver Blvd (Mon–Fri 8am–5pm), is notable for its huge, detached facade – a re-creation of the entryway to the previous City Hall, from 1928. Between the facade's freestanding archway and the actual building you'll find a pleasant park with a peek-through movie camera detailing the city's film history.

Culver City movie studios

Without a doubt, Culver City's most significant historic structures are its movie studios, many of which still function, though in different guises. The man responsible for creating the two greatest studio complexes was **Thomas Ince**, a film pioneer and producer who essentially created the mechanized modern industry, with specialized roles for craftspeople and assigned roles for producers, directors, screenwriters and so on, a rigid hierarchy that persists to this day and is still synonymous with the Hollywood "industry" of moviemaking. He was a major film-industry figure until he was mysteriously killed on William Randolph Hearst's yacht. The producer's Ince Studios is still around, though, reborn as **Culver Studios**, at 9336 Washington Blvd – predictably, this Colonial Revival "mansion" is no more than a facade.

Ince's later, bigger creation was **Triangle Pictures**, 10202 Washington Blvd, which he helped build with the financial aid of Harry Culver, a journalist and realtor who founded the city specifically for the movie business. Triangle became **MGM** by the 1920s, helmed by legend Louis B. Mayer, who held on as the studio's tough-as-nails boss for three decades and oversaw the site, creating some of Hollywood's biggest productions during the Golden Age of Movies. The bloom faded in the 1950s and 60s, though, and sections of the lot were sold off to developers and what was left was swallowed up by **Sony** in the 1980s. In today's studio tour (Mon–Fri 9.30am, 10.30am, 1.30pm & 2.30pm; $33; Ⓣ310/244-TOUR, Ⓦwww.sonypicturesstudios.com), you can still stroll past the fine old colonnade, but unfortunately, most of the glorious MGM backlot was torn down, and the lore of that moviemaking giant is given short shrift – the organizers would rather you pay attention to sets from current TV game shows like *Wheel of Fortune* and *Jeopardy*. Sony did undertake a massive renovation of the site to a make it more tourist friendly, but mostly that's consisted of building a new Main Street fronted with faux shop fronts, as with Disneyland or Universal CityWalk. Unlike those places, though, there's not much to buy or eat here, and you're not allowed to wander off on your own.

The Hayden Tract

Most small towns, even in LA, are known for their conservatism in design and architecture. Culver City is a major exception. With architect/artist **Eric Owen Moss**, this city has not only welcomed some bizarre buildings, it has also helped subsidize the business sites for many of his clients and prominently advertised his groundbreaking work. The **Hayden Tract**, one such city-subsidized business strip, has excellent examples of contemporary architecture ranging from austere modernism to cockeyed deconstructivism – and sure enough it sits on a former backlot of a movie studio, once belonging to RKO among others.

In the Tract, you can find a whole series of Moss's designs, including the 1997 **Pittard Sullivan** building, 3535 Hayden Ave, a giant gray box with massive wooden ribs poking out of its sides, somewhat like flying buttresses. Nearby, 8522 National, also known as the **IRS Building**, features a jangled-up facade with a white staircase leading to nowhere. Adjacent to this is **The Box**, with a cubic window riveted to one of its corners and seeming ready to come off its hinges and tumble down onto the street below. One of the best Moss works in the Tract is the **Samitaur**, 3457 S La Cienega Ave, massive, grey warehouse-like offices with skewed lines, sharp points, and a freakish sense of proportion. The overwhelming **Stealth**, 3530 Hayden Ave, is fronted by a massive, dark wall of projecting angles that seems more like the setting for a science-fiction film than a business complex. Even stranger, the **Beehive**, 8520 National Blvd, is a bulbous take on the concept of the (business) hive, with curving bands and a rooftop stairway. Most recently completed is the **Gateway Art Tower**, Hayden Avenue at National Boulevard, a huge column of five steel rings staggered over each other and supporting a dozen digital projectors showing off art and news footage, and allowing you to climb up the structure 72 feet to get a wider view of the odd, but still industrial, neighbourhood around it.

Moss isn't done yet with Culver City, and future years have the architect planning all manner of curious retrofits, additions, and transformations. To learn more about the plans of this pioneering modern architect, head to Ⓦwww.ericowenmoss.com.

The Museum of Jurassic Technology

If movie history and weird architecture aren't enough for you, top off your trip with a visit to the bizarre **Museum of Jurassic Technology**, 9341 Venice Blvd (Thurs 2–8pm, Fri–Sun noon–6pm; $5; Ⓦwww.mjt.org), on the northern edge of Culver City. As much an art museum as a science centre, this institution has little to do with distant history or roving dinosaurs. Rather, it tries to find the intersection between the scientifically possible, the culturally mythical, and the artistically absurd. In practice, this means it features a great range of oddities from the pseudo-factual to the paranormal to the just plain creepy. Examples include exhibitions of folk superstitions, most memorably the image of dead mice on toast used as a cure for bedwetting; written and oral narratives of crank scientists and researchers, many of whom have reputedly disappeared under strange circumstances or gone mad; a portrait gallery honouring the dogs of the Cold War-era Soviet space programme; and a collection of unearthly insects, such as an Amazonian bug that kills its prey through the use of a giant head-spike. For such curious efforts, museum creator David Wilson was the winner of a MacArthur Fellowship in 2001.

5

Santa Monica and Venice

Located on the western edge of LA, **SANTA MONICA** and **VENICE** offer two different sides of LA, both well heeled: Santa Monica, the trendy liberal enclave with smart restaurants, shops and coffeehouses; and Venice, the offbeat focus of experimental architecture, vibrant beach culture and fringe galleries. Still, driving north on Main Street it can be hard to discern exactly where Venice stops and Santa Monica starts. Both places also share moderate temperatures – they're cooler than the rest of the basin, with average midsummer temperatures sitting comfortably around 19°C (66°F). Perhaps for this reason, these areas have become home to at least one-quarter of LA's population of British and Irish expatriates, many of whom can be spotted in the local Euro-friendly pubs, clubs and diners.

As the epitome of Southern California's laid-back sun-and-surf culture, the two cities have little of the pretension of Beverly Hills and West LA, and much in the way of easygoing attitudes and pleasantly low-scale development. Santa Monica's population is relatively stagnant because of the steep price of new housing and, like other parts of the Westside, is still fairly WASPy. Multiculturalism, however, has been long established in Venice, which was one of the few coastal cities not to use restrictive covenants to keep blacks from living there. It was also an alternative melting pot of sorts in the 1960s, when the place was shambling, attracting a number of up-and-coming artists and musicians inspired by the mix. Since then, the district has prospered, but continues to be home to a much wider range of classes and races than Santa Monica.

Further south, the colourless real-estate tract of **Marina del Rey** offers few spots of interest, but the adjacent **Ballona Wetlands** have much natural appeal. **Playa del Rey**, meanwhile, maintains a certain faded charm, which takes an eerie turn near the airport, around the site of LA's only urban ghost town.

Santa Monica

A low-slung, oceanside burg with a relaxed air and easy access to the rest of LA, **Santa Monica** is a great spot to visit, a compact and friendly bastion of breezy charm. The city is well served by public transit and near enough to the airport, and serves as the terminus for a number of bus (and, by 2015, light rail) lines that fan out to serve the rest of the basin to the east.

SANTA MONICA

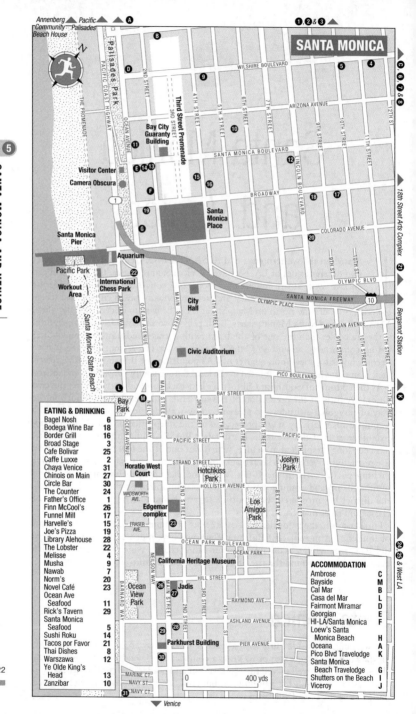

Annenberg Community Beach House ▲ Pacific Palisades ▲ ▲ A

1, 2 & 3 ▲

C, 6, 7 & 8 ▶

18th Street Arts Complex ▶

21 ▶

Bergamot Station ▶

K ▶

24, 25 & West LA ▶

▼ Venice

Wilshire Boulevard · Arizona Avenue · Santa Monica Boulevard · Broadway · Colorado Avenue · Olympic Blvd · Santa Monica Freeway · Olympic Place · Michigan Avenue · Pico Boulevard · Bay Street · Bicknell St · Pacific Street · Strand Street · Hollister Avenue · Wadsworth Ave. · Fraser Ave. · Ocean Park Boulevard · Ocean Park · Hill Street · Raymond Ave. · Ashland Avenue · Pier Avenue · Marine Ct. · Navy St · Navy Ct.

The Promenade · Pacific Coast Highway · Ocean Avenue · 2nd Street · 3rd Street · 4th Street · 5th Street · 6th Street · 7th Street · 9th Street · 10th Street · 11th Street · 12th St · Lincoln Boulevard · Main Street · Appian Way · Neilson Way · Barnard Way · Beverly Ave · 7th Street

Palisades Park · Bay City Guaranty Building · Third Street Promenade · Visitor Center · Camera Obscura · Santa Monica Place · Santa Monica Pier · Aquarium · Pacific Park · International Chess Park · Workout Area · City Hall · Santa Monica State Beach · Civic Auditorium · Bay Park · Horatio West Court · Hotchkiss Park · Joslyn Park · Los Amigos Park · Edgemar complex · California Heritage Museum · Ocean View Park · Jadis · Parkhurst Building

0 — 400 yds

EATING & DRINKING

Bagel Nosh	6
Bodega Wine Bar	18
Border Grill	16
Broad Stage	3
Cafe Bolivar	25
Caffe Luxxe	2
Chaya Venice	31
Chinois on Main	27
Circle Bar	30
The Counter	24
Father's Office	1
Finn McCool's	26
Funnel Mill	17
Harvelle's	15
Joe's Pizza	19
Library Alehouse	28
The Lobster	22
Melisse	4
Musha	9
Nawab	7
Norm's	20
Novel Café	23
Ocean Ave Seafood	11
Rick's Tavern	29
Santa Monica Seafood	5
Sushi Roku	14
Tacos por Favor	21
Thai Dishes	8
Warszawa	12
Ye Olde King's Head	13
Zanzibar	10

ACCOMMODATION

Ambrose	C
Bayside	M
Cal Mar	B
Casa del Mar	L
Fairmont Miramar	D
Georgian	E
HI-LA/Santa Monica	F
Loew's Santa Monica Beach	H
Oceana	A
Pico Blvd Travelodge	K
Santa Monica Beach Travelodge	G
Shutters on the Beach	I
Viceroy	J

As little as a century ago, most of the land between Santa Monica and what was then Los Angeles was covered by ranch lands and citrus groves, interrupted by the outposts of Hollywood and Beverly Hills. Like so much of the state, the land was owned by the **Southern Pacific Railroad**, whose chief Collis Huntington tried to make Santa Monica into the port of Los Angeles, losing out to Phineas Banning and other established interests in San Pedro and Wilmington – a blessing in disguise. The linking of the beachfront with the rest of Los Angeles by the suburban streetcar system, known as the **Red Cars**, meant the town grew into one of LA's premier getaways – a giant funfair city that was the inspiration for Raymond Chandler's anything-goes "Bay City", memorably described in *Farewell My Lovely*. While working- and middle-class residents flocked to the Santa Monica Pier for its thrill rides and freewheeling atmosphere, the town's elite sailed out to the gambling boats anchored offshore to indulge in a bit of illicit excitement beyond the reach of the local authorities, and the business bigwigs entertained mistresses and underworld cronies in private beachside cabanas and well-guarded enclaves. These days the offshore gambling ships and most of the bathing clubs are long gone, and there's no longer any place where a celebrity is really free from public scrutiny. The result is that Santa Monica is now among LA's more elegant seaside towns, with a relative absence of seamy drama or high-rolling hijinks.

The city lies across Bundy Drive from West LA, and splits into three general areas: **oceanside** Santa Monica, holding a fair bit of its history and tourist attractions, sits on the coastal bluffs and includes the pier, Third Street Promenade, and beach; **Main Street**, running south from the pier into Venice, is home to designer eateries and quirky shops; and **inland** Santa Monica is split between exclusive neighbourhoods and art galleries, to the north, and acres of apartment blocks and quiet bungalows, to the south.

Santa Monica Pier and around

A busy tourist attraction jutting out into the bay at the foot of Colorado Avenue, the **Santa Monica Pier** (Ⓣ310/458-8900, Ⓦwww.santamonicapier.org) was

Healing the Bay

Although Los Angeles has a well-deserved reputation for its noxious air, its **water pollution** has also been a significant problem. Cities and districts from Santa Monica to Palos Verdes have the bad luck of being trapped next to nearly all of LA's outlets for wastewater and sewage, with streetside **storm drains** emptying the runoff from a 5000-mile network of LA urban sprawl and a single treatment centre – **Hyperion**, near LAX – handling the task of cleaning up the collective filth. You can see the pollution problem in full colour just by walking past one of the Santa Monica Bay's storm drains after a major rainstorm, and seeing the rainbow slick of detritus floating along. Still, there have been improvements to the bay in the last two decades since **Heal the Bay** and other environmental groups were formed: Hyperion no longer freely dumps sewage as it once did, and chemical companies have stopped flushing DDT offshore.

If you really feel the need to catch the California waves, make sure to do so well away from city piers – often the most polluted zones – and don't wade within one hundred yards of a beachside drain or venture into the water within three days after a storm, when runoff, sewage, bacteria and algae combine to form a vile aquatic stew. To check out the sands beforehand, visit the Heal the Bay website at Ⓦwww.healthebay.org, which also provides updates on the latest progress in the fight against water pollution, and click on the colour-coded beach map detailing which areas are fine for swimming or fishing.

constructed in 1874, and was once one of LA's prime diversions, offering nerve-jangling rides and a heady carnival atmosphere, while remaining fairly tame compared with the raucous Pacific Ocean Park that took shape a few decades later to the south (see box, p.126). Rebuilt and reconstructed several times, it was often threatened with demolition, narrowly averting this fate on several occasions in the 1970s (thanks largely to citizen advocacy groups). However, it later developed a reputation as a hangout for gangs and petty thugs from outside the area, and many visitors stayed away, especially at night when skirmishes between hoodlums and cops often took place, and business suffered accordingly. Since then, the local police have made their presence felt and nearly all of the violent crime is long gone, and nightly tourist traffic is once again visible, attracting everyone from business workers to teens and families. But unless you really want to try the watered-down rides or are eating or drinking here, it's hard to find reason to linger on the pier for more than an hour.

Although dominated by an assortment of fast-food stands, video-game parlours, and watering holes, the pier's most obvious appeal is its restored 1922 wooden **carousel** (late March to Sept Mon–Thurs 11am–5pm, Fri–Sun 11am–7pm; Oct to early March Thurs & Mon 11am–5pm, Fri–Sun 11am–7pm; $2, 50¢ kids per ride), in its own squat building and offering more than forty colourful hand-carved horses. The roller coaster and other thrill rides of **Pacific Park** (hours vary, often summer daily 11am–11pm, Sat & Sun closes 12.30am; unlimited rides $21; ⓦwww.pacpark.com) may catch your eye, but the place is an overpriced attempt to lure suburban families, and you're better off saving your money for a real theme park. Instead, consider visiting the **Santa Monica Pier Aquarium**, below the pier at 1600 Ocean Front Walk (Tues–Fri 2–6pm, Sat & Sun 12.30–6pm; $5, kids 12 and under free; ⓦwww.healthebay.org/smpa), which is run by the Heal the Bay environmental group; here you can find out about marine biology and get your fingers wet touching sea anemones and sea stars.

To the south, kids can clamber about on the chunky stone sculptures of a **children's park**, and near the end of the pier, anglers cast their lines into the murky depths of Santa Monica Bay. Below the pier, **Santa Monica State Beach** is a popular strip of sand, tightly packed with visitors on weekends – one of the iconic images of LA fun in the summer sun. Swimming (or fishing) here is a gamble, though, because of contaminants from nearby storm drains (see box, "Healing the Bay", p.123), but the less than sparkling water doesn't keep some locals from venturing out into it.

Just south of the pier, Santa Monica features LA's original "Muscle Beach," which predates Venice's own, more famous version, though it's a bit on the small side. Still, there are enough rings, bars and other athletic equipment here to make it suitable for would-be bodybuilders and fitness fans, without the same pressure you'll get from the muscle mavens in Venice. If you'd rather match wits than flex biceps, visit the adjacent **International Chess Park**, a fancy name for a serviceable collection of chessboards that attracts a range of players from rank amateurs to slumming pros. There's also a human-size chessboard on the premises, though it's doubtful you'll find enough living pawns willing to stand in the sun for several hours while you plot your next move. Finally, a **bike path** begins at the pier and heads twenty miles south to Palos Verdes, a stretch that ranks as one of the area's top choices for bicycling. It's busy enough that, if you're walking or running, you should keep well to the side and let the speedy cyclists have the centre. To join in, you can rent bicycles, surfboards or rollerblades at equipment-rental shacks by the pier, or just stroll along taking in the local colour.

Palisades Park

North of the pier along Ocean Avenue, **Palisades Park** is a palm- and cypress-tree-lined strip that affords stunning views stretching from Malibu to Palos Verdes – all the while sitting precariously atop high bluffs that are constantly being eroded. At least half of the **cliffside sidewalk** around the edge is usually fenced off, as it has a tendency to tumble down the bluffs, especially after heavy rains. Inside the park, you may want to stop by the **visitors information office** (daily 10am–4pm, summer 9am–5pm; ⓣ310/393-0410, ⓦwww.santamonica.com), in a kiosk just south of Santa Monica Boulevard, at 1400 Ocean Ave. The centre's handy map shows the layout of the town and the routes of the Santa Monica Big Blue Bus transit system, a useful Westside complement to the MTA network (ⓣ310/451-5444, ⓦwww.bigbluebus.com).

Nearby, the **Camera Obscura**, 1450 Ocean Ave (Mon–Fri 9am–2pm, Sat & Sun 11am–4pm; free; ⓣ310/458-8644), entertains by way of an old-fashioned device that prefigures modern photography. Inside a darkened room, you can view images of the outside world projected onto a circular screen by a rotating mirror on the roof – the sort of tool artists like Jan Vermeer once used as a visual aid for painting. On clear days, the clarity of the images can be startling. The camera is located within a social centre for the elderly ("Camera Obscura" is written with verve on the facade), so make sure to ask someone inside for access to this upstairs room.

Finally, at the end of Wilshire Boulevard on Ocean Avenue stands the austere statue of the city's namesake, **Santa Monica**, the mother of St Augustine, a serene white pillar at the edge of the Pacific Ocean.

Below the Palisades

At the turn of the twentieth century, optimistic realtors attempted to call Santa Monica the "**Zenith City by the Sunset Sea**", testimony to the place's growing reputation as a swanky resort town. More catchy, though, was the moniker "The Gold Coast", which described the strip of sand north of the Santa Monica Pier and below the Palisades. This was the site of some of LA's swankiest hotels – including the Queen Anne colossus of the **Arcadia**, finished in 1887 – and great beach houses occupied by a wealth of Hollywood personalities. The largest still standing, the **North Guest House**, at 415 Palisades Beach Rd, was built as the servants' quarters of a massive 120-room house, now demolished, which William Randolph Hearst built for his mistress, actress Marion Davies. MGM boss Louis B. Mayer owned an adjacent Mediterranean-style villa, which was later rumored to be the place where the Kennedy brothers had their secret liaisons with Marilyn Monroe. As the lone survivor of the era, the Guest House has undergone a massive renovation as part of the site of the Annenberg Community Beach House, which allows tours of the Guest House's fetching Colonial Revival quarters (open Mon 11am–3pm, free tours 11am & 1pm; ⓦwww.annenbergbeachhouse.com). More appealing for families, perhaps, is the public pool (daily 8.30am–8pm; access $10) graced by handmade tiles and an adjacent modern pool house. (There's also an event house on site for special exhibits.) It's all well worth your leisure time, and part of a huge project funded by the Annenberg Foundation to open the site to the public after a half-century of governmental dithering, lawsuits and lack of funding.

The Third Street Promenade

Two blocks east of Ocean Avenue, between Wilshire and Broadway, the **Third Street Promenade** is a pedestrian stretch that's one of LA's most densely touristed, especially on summer weekends. It's fun to hang out in the cafés, bars and night-clubs, or play a game of pool, and the promenade can be really busy at night, when huge numbers of tourists and locals jostle for space with sidewalk poets, swinging jazz bands and street lunatics, under the watchful eyes of water-spewing **dinosaur sculptures** draped in ivy. The mall is anchored at its southern end by **Santa**

Monica Place (Ⓦwww.santamonicaplace.com), originally built by architect Frank Gehry, and one of his less inspired works, but has been newly remodelled and reopened as a lively outdoor retail complex with contiguous access to the Promenade. Towering over the shopping strip and topped by a colourful clock, the **Bay City Guaranty Building**, Third Street at Santa Monica Boulevard, is a Zigzag Moderne marvel that was for years Santa Monica's tallest building.

Main Street

The key attraction on the south side of town is **Main Street**, ten minutes' walk from the pier, whose collection of classy boutiques, bars and restaurants makes it one of the most popular shopping districts on the Westside. The big chain stores are here and there, but there are still enough quirky local operations to make a visit here worthwhile. The best of these is **Jadis**, 2701 Main St (Ⓣ310/396-3477), a prop-rental operation with LA's finest display window: a collection of mannequins posed in various demented dioramas from 1930s horror films, such as a mad scientist's lab, and surrounded by all sorts of antiquated technical junk and contraptions. It's open (very) irregular hours, sometimes during Sunday afternoons, with a small but worthwhile donation to visit.

To make for a more comprehensive tour of the stretch, you can travel between Main Street and the Third Street Promenade on the **Tide Ride** (every 15min; Sat noon–8pm, Sun noon–10pm; Ⓣ310/451-5444), ponying up a mere 50 cents to hit all the shopping highlights. One of the few actual sights, the **California Heritage Museum**, no. 2612 (Wed–Sun 11am–4pm; $5; Ⓣ310/392-8537, Ⓦwww.californiaheritagemuseum.org), is the city's effort to preserve some of its architectural past. Two houses were moved here to escape demolition. One house – the museum itself – hosts temporary displays on California cultural topics, from old fruit-box labels to modern skateboards, and has permanent exhibits on regional pottery, furniture, quilts and decorative arts. The other house is known as The Victorian (Ⓣ310/392-4956, Ⓦwww.thevictorian.com), and is now a special-event venue. There are also several noteworthy buildings on and around Main Street, including the angular grey volumes and strange geometry of Frank Gehry's **Edgemar** shopping development, no. 2415, and the more traditional **Parkhurst Building**, south on Main Street at Pier Avenue, a 1927 Spanish Colonial Revival gem. Among the most important structures, the cool white arches and simple boxlike shapes of Irving Gill's 1919 **Horatio West Court**, north of Edgemar at 140 Hollister Ave, prefigured the rise of local modernism by about twenty years, with a generous helping of austere Mission Revival.

Bisecting the central part of Main Street, **Ocean Park Boulevard** once offered some of the city's most evocative sights. The entire beachfront between here and Venice used to be the site of a resort community developed by Abbot Kinney, the man behind the design of Venice itself. Along with vacation bungalows, a wharf, and a colourful boardwalk, the neighbourhood also featured the largest and wildest of the old amusement piers: the fantastic **Pacific Ocean Park**, with a huge rollercoaster, a giant funhouse and a boisterous midway arcade. Against the sanitized fun zones like Disneyland, though, the old piers began to look faded and depressing by the 1950s, and went steadily downhill, languishing for a time as a makeshift obstacle course for daredevil surfers (best seen in the film *Dogtown and Z-Boys*; see p.360) before being demolished in the mid-1970s.

Inland Santa Monica

Although **inland Santa Monica** provides less interest than the coastal strip, there are a handful of interesting attractions that make a visit here worthwhile. **Wilshire**

Boulevard is the main commercial axis of this area, but a mile north, **San Vicente Boulevard** is a more appealing diversion, a grassy tree-lined strip and a joggers' freeway that leads east to the wealthier confines of Brentwood. LA's true health mania is visible just two blocks north of San Vicente, along Adelaide Drive between First and Seventh streets. Here an entire stair-climbing culture has evolved along the giant **Santa Monica Stairs** that connect Santa Monica with the Pacific Palisades stretch of Entrada Drive. On any given morning, crowds of locals trot up and down the street, just waiting for a chance to descend down the bluffs and charge back up again, red-faced and gasping for air. You, too, may wish to descend the steps, to get a glimpse of the tonier confines of Pacific Palisades, Santa Monica's even more well-heeled neighbour to the north (see p.183).

Two blocks south of San Vicente, the pricey restaurants and boutiques of **Montana Avenue** mark the upward mobility of the area, but offer little you haven't seen elsewhere in West LA. The area does have one curiosity in the wild **Gehry House**, 22nd St at Washington Ave. Now partially hidden by foliage and remodelled for the worse, Frank Gehry's domicile shattered conventional notions of architecture on its completion in 1978: not a unified design at all, but what appears to be random ideas thrown together helter-skelter and bundled up with concrete walls and metal fencing.

Bergamot Station and around

Inland Santa Monica has many fine **galleries** with works by emerging local and international artists. **Bergamot Station**, the city's aesthetic hub, is a collection of former tramcar sheds at 2525 Michigan Ave, near the intersection of 26th and Cloverfield, which houses a multitude of small art galleries (most open Tues–Fri 10am–6pm; free). Many of LA's latest generation of artists have shown here, and the highlight is the **Santa Monica Museum of Art** (Tues–Sat 11am–6pm; $5; ⓣ310/586-6488, ⓦwww.smmoa.org), a good space to see some of the most engaging and curious work on the local scene, in temporary exhibitions ranging from simple painting shows to complex, space-demanding installations. Among the regular displays, don't miss the **Gallery of Functional Art** (free; ⓣ310/829-6990, ⓦgalleryoffunctionalart.net), offering an array of mechanical gizmos and eccentric furniture like cubist lamps and neon-lit chairs. If you want to check out more art, visit the **18th Street Arts Complex**, further inland at 1639 18th Street (Mon–Fri 11am–5.30pm; ⓣ310/453-3711, ⓦwww.18thstreet.org), a hip and modern centre for various types of art, much of it experimental.

Venice

South of Santa Monica, **Venice** was laid out in the marshes of Ballona Creek in 1905 by developer Abbot Kinney as a fantasy replica of the northern Italian city. While most of the architecture and canals have long since disappeared, the lingering pseudo-European atmosphere has since proved just right for pulling in the artsy crowd he was aiming at. Even the mainstream commercial enterprises get into the spirit. Main Street, for instance, is the former home of the offices of advertising firm **Chiat/Day**, just south of Rose Street, marked by Claes Oldenburg's huge pair of binoculars that overshadow the entrance. A block north is the grotesque **Ballerina Clown**, an enormous sculpture by Jonathan Borofsky perched above the intersection of Rose Avenue and Main Street, its lithe body and stubbly clown mask making for a disturbing combination. Elsewhere, a strong alternative arts scene thrives around the **Beyond Baroque** literary centre in the old City Hall, 681 Venice Blvd (Ⓣ310/822-3006, Ⓦwww.beyondbaroque.org), a good place to get a flavour of the work of local artists, catch one of the regular book readings, or sign up for a workshop in poetry, prose or drama.

Venice Beach and Boardwalk

The quintessential California sand strip of **Venice Beach** really draws the crowds, and nowhere else does LA parade itself quite so openly, colourfully and aggressively as it does along the **Venice Boardwalk**, a wide pathway tracking alongside the

sands that's packed on weekends and all summer long with jugglers, fire-eaters, Hare Krishnas and roller-skating guitar players. You'll have no difficulty picking up your choice of cheap sunglasses, T-shirts, sandals and whatever else you need for a day at the beach. In the sands beyond are several squat concrete walls and towers that make up an officially sanctioned **graffiti park**, where the designs might include anything from the Virgin of Guadelupe to abstract tagger self-portraits to cryptic letters spelling out mysterious, indecipherable phrases. South of Windward Avenue along the Boardwalk is **Muscle Beach**, a legendary outdoor weightlifting centre where stern-looking, would-be Schwarzeneggers pump serious iron, high-flying gymnasts swing on the adjacent rings and bars, and serious games of basketball take place on the concrete courts – don't show your face if you can't hit the rim. Contact the Venice Beach Recreation Center, 1800 Ocean Front Walk (Ⓣ310/399-2775, Ⓦwww.laparks.org/venice), for information on the activities and contests that occur here. Rollerbladers, skateboarders, volleyball players and bicyclists are ubiquitous throughout the area, and there are **rental shacks** along the beach for picking up skates, surfboards or bikes.

Beyond the beach, the rather basic **Venice Pier** stretches into the ocean off Washington Boulevard, but don't expect much in the way of carnival fun or thrill rides – the pier doesn't offer a great deal of entertainment value these days, since it's used mostly for fishing in the often-polluted bay. Incidentally, be warned that Venice Beach at night can be a **dangerous** place. It's illegal to walk after dark on the beach, when various miscreants have been known to appear, but you should have no problem supping at a beachside café or browsing at a nearby record store.

Windward Avenue and around

Windward Avenue is Venice's main artery, running from the beach into what was the Grand Circle of the canal system, now paved over and ringed by a number of galleries. In the vicinity, colourful giant **murals** – depicting everything from a shirtless Jim Morrison (1811 Ocean Front Walk) to Botticelli's Venus on rollerskates (Windward at Speedway Avenue) – cover the walls of the original structures, while a Renaissance-style **arcade**, around Windward's intersection with Pacific Avenue, is alive with health-food shops, knick-knack stores and rollerblade-rental stands. Left over from the district's high-art phase a hundred years ago, a handful of **classical columns** are painted in Day-Glo colours that Kinney would no doubt have gasped at, while others retain their original black-and-white colouring. Look closely at some of the columns and you'll see an odd touch: on their Ionic capitals are engraved the faces of local businessmen – a pointed reminder of Venice's entrepreneurial roots, and its early hubris.

This area has also become home to some of LA's most inventive artists and designers, whose offices are scattered around Windward Avenue and the Windward Circle. You'll see the fruits of their labours in the small boutiques and far-out houses throughout the district, but especially to the south, along Ocean Front Walk (see p.130). Lovers of **experimental architecture** may also want to visit the section of town between California Avenue and Venice Boulevard (around Superba and Amorosa courts and Linden Avenue and Lincoln Boulevard), where Thom Mayne's **Morphosis** architecture firm has created numerous colourful, bizarre structures, among them Venice III, a deconstructed steel box covered with tent-like structures, and the 2-4-6-8 House, looking like an oversized playpen perched above the ground.

Just a few blocks south from Windward, the five remaining **canals** are still crossed by their original 1904 bridges – quaint wooden structures that are among LA's few touches of Americana – and you can also sit and watch ducks paddle around in the still waters. It's a great place to walk around, though if you're in a car, there's only one way to see the area – heading north on Dell Avenue between Washington and Venice boulevards. Whether you walk or drive, you'll get an eyeful of eclectic residential styles, modernist cubes and Tudor piles mixed in with Colonial bungalows and postmodern sheds, all of them now worth millions. There's no organized way to take a boat trip through the canals; if you happen to get friendly with a resident, you may be able to talk your way into a **rowboat ride** around the canals – many homes have the skiffs docked right next to their back yards.

To the north, running diagonally between Venice Boulevard and Main Street, the shopping strip of **Abbot Kinney Boulevard** features a range of fine restaurants, funky clothing stores and arty boutiques, and makes a handy shortcut to get through the district. Even here, you can find the home of the odd celebrity – Dennis Hopper's **Hopper Studio**, 326 Indiana Ave, the ultimate in maximum-security architecture: a slanted, corrugated-steel box with no windows, incongruously surrounded by a quaint, white picket fence.

Ocean Front Walk

Between Marina del Rey and the ocean lies narrow Pacific Avenue, home to some of LA's better contemporary architecture. Park either at the channel-side lot on the south side, near Via Marina street, or along the curb on the north side, and follow **Ocean Front Walk** (actually the same route as the Venice Boardwalk further north) for a pleasant stroll by the sands and the colourful modern houses. From Venice Pier, the intersecting streets are named alphabetically and nautically – from Anchorage Street to Yawl Court. Among the more eye-catching sights are Antoine Predock's groundbreaking **Douroux House**, 2315 Ocean Front Walk, whose heavy concrete frame hosts rooftop bleachers and a big red window that pivots toward the sea, allowing the ocean breezes to easily sweep through the cubic structure; and Frank Gehry's **Norton House**, 2509 Ocean Front Walk, which features a curious boxy room projecting above the rest of the structure – a visual ode to the beach's lifeguard stations.

South of Venice

At its nadir in the 1950s and 60s, Venice was confronted with a new and unwelcome neighbour to the south: **Marina del Rey**, a massive real-estate tract that blotted out the old city's coastal views with highrises. The whole area is ringed by chain restaurants, giant hotels, office complexes and apartment superstructures, and the upscale marina exudes a distinct sense of exclusivity. However, you can get out on the water, by boat tour or by renting a kayak, through several local outfitters; Marina del Rey Boat Rentals, 13719 Fiji Way (Ⓣ310/574-2822, Ⓦboats4rent.com), is one of the more convenient of these, offering single kayaks for $15/hr and sailboats for about three times as much. Check out Ⓦwww.visitmarinadelrey.com for a list of other options.

Along the south end of the area, at the end of Fiji Way, **Fishermen's Village** is Marina del Rey's top visitor attraction, an array of low-end seafood joints and endless trinket and T-shirt shops. There's not much to see here, but you can rent bikes and roller blades from the rental stands, and then head to the channel-side walking and biking **path** that stretches from the end of Fiji Way out to the end of the spit. Not only is this the place where the Christmas **regatta** takes place, but it's also a good spot to watch yachts and speedboats make a leisurely sail into the marina. On the south side of the channel, Fiji Way dead-ends near a path that can take you to the end of the jetty, from where it's a short jog south over a channel **bridge** crossing Ballona Creek, really a storm drain, into the marginally more interesting district of **Playa del Rey**.

Ballona Wetlands

Further south down Lincoln Boulevard, Marina del Rey gives way to the wide expanse of the six-hundred-acre **Ballona** (pronounced *BY-oh-na*) **Wetlands**, encompassing bodies of fresh and salt water that are home to two hundred major bird species and a host of other creatures. Although off limits to humans, this natural preserve can be toured at a distance, starting by heading west on Jefferson Boulevard (off Lincoln) and taking a left onto Culver Boulevard. While conspicuous wildlife might be hard to spot, you will get a sense of the uniqueness of this landscape in the heavily urbanized LA basin.

Before Abbot Kinney created what is now Venice, the wetlands of this mid-coastal area stretched all the way to the border of the community of Ocean Park. Because of the area's proximity to the LA airport (then called "Mines Field"), **Howard Hughes** in the 1940s located his airplane-manufacturing facility on its the eastern side, and at its peak the plant had countless huge hangars and engineering facilities, as well as the nation's longest private runway; it was also the place where the notorious **Spruce Goose** was built. Hughes Aviation lasted a half-century here, until several decades after its founder's death, but in 1994 relocated elsewhere. That's when the preservation battles for the wetlands began in earnest.

For well over fifteen years developers and environmentalists battled for permanent control of this prime real estate, with the old aviation site (and parcels around it) eventually turning into an 1100-acre tract of new condos and commercial structures called **Playa Vista**. Several hundred acres have been preserved as a concession (most west of Lincoln Boulevard); for more information on the wetlands, check out Ⓦwww.ballona.org.

Playa del Rey

To the west from the wetlands, Culver Boulevard leads to the former resort community of **Playa del Rey**, once an essential link in the Red Car transit line and the site of grand hotels, restaurants and a funicular railway, but since reduced to a faded collection of commercial shacks and condos. The **lagoon**, nestled near the beach along Pacific Street, is a popular spot for dog-walking, but you're better off heading up Vista del Mar to a high bluff above the main part of Playa del Rey, to the neighbourhood of **Palisades del Rey**, which makes for a pleasant, hilly hike past some fine views of the ocean. There used to be more to this neighbourhood (including historic houses by the likes of R.M. Schindler), and to Playa del Rey overall, but the need for a sound barrier between LAX and the ocean did much to ruin its idyllic setting. In the 1960s, when the county condemned the property here, more than eight hundred homes were destroyed and an entire neighbourhood all but disappeared. The result is one of LA's strangest attractions: a modern-day **ghost town** stretching for several miles from Waterview Street to Imperial Highway along Vista del Mar. Chain-link fences guard the empty streets, now lined by crumbling housing foundations and defunct street lights. The only residents these days are some fifty thousand **El Segundo blue butterflies** that have moved in since the south end of the area was turned into an ecological preserve. Head to Sandpiper Street to survey the surreal scene close up, or at least until the next blaring takeoff of a jumbo jet makes you jump back in your car.

6

South Central and East LA

The districts of **South Central** and **East LA** are far removed from the tourist circuit, and avoided by most visitors to the city, many of whom believe any venture south of the I-10 freeway to be an open invitation to murder, mugging or some other unpleasantry. In truth, while these places can be dicey and should be avoided at night, the ghetto stereotypes are blown out of proportion. Crime has gone down dramatically in the last decade, and in selected districts a number of interesting museums and historic-revival homes can be found, especially on the northern side of South Central around Exposition Park and West Adams.

Contained mostly within the boundaries of the 405, 605 and 10 freeways, South Central and East LA make up a large portion of the LA basin, encompassing diverse cultures, with neighbouring communities often separated by major differences in language, ethnicity and religion. Hispanic population growth is a constant throughout these areas, as it is throughout the rest of LA: as late as the 1980s, the racial makeup was 75 percent black; twenty years later, it's 60 percent Latino, and increasing yearly.

South Central LA

Without doubt, **SOUTH CENTRAL LA** does not rank on the city's list of prime attractions, and the city's authorities have even tried to rebrand it as "South LA", which would make the area even more amorphous than it already is (since most residents associate that name with the harbour area). According to most definitions, South Central is a big oval chunk bordered by Alameda Street and the 10 and 405 freeways (the latter forming the western and curving southern border of the area). Typically made up of detached bungalows enjoying their own patch of palm-shaded lawn, South Central nevertheless has serious poverty in places, especially the closer you go toward districts like Watts and Compton. Taking advantage of the desperate conditions, the district's gangs infamously riddled the area with bullets in the 1980s and 90s, although as a result of various gang truces and better police interdiction, some of the mayhem has decreased.

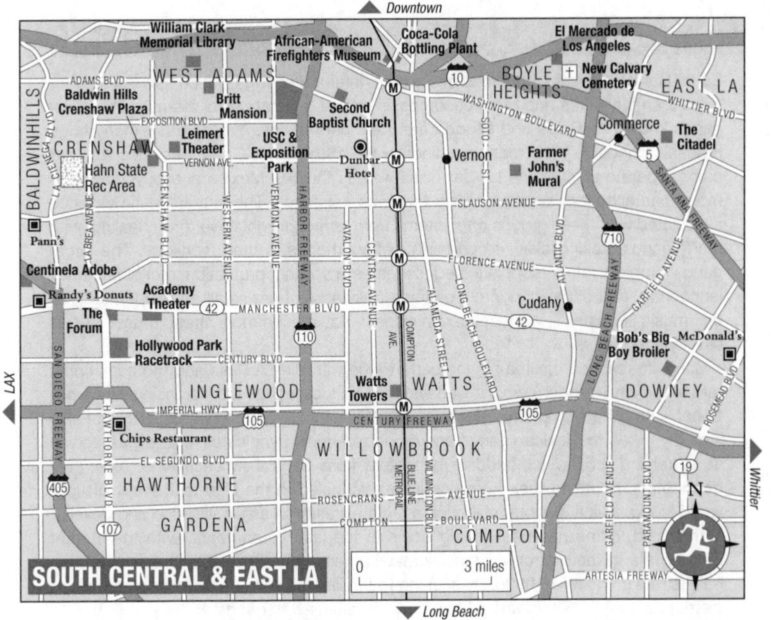

Most out-of-area commuters obliviously zip through the area on the Harbor Freeway (I-110), which is largely confined to its own walled-off channel. Nonetheless, if you have the time, there are several compelling sights to be found, including the historic homes of **West Adams**, several museums in **Exposition Park**, and the folk-art masterpiece of the **Watts Towers** – which should all be seen in daylight.

Some history

Like other parts of the city, much of South Central LA was settled in the nineteenth century by **Mexican immigrants** when the area was still governed by Mexico, and its large land tracts divided up as ranchos. Later, after the US took control of the land and California became the 31st state in 1850, **white Protestants** began migrating from the Midwest, drawn by the sunny weather, low cost of living, and favourable job market, continuing into the early twentieth century. By the time of World War II, West Adams was still among the chicest neighbourhoods of LA, universities like USC and Pepperdine had taken root in the area, and a young George H.W. Bush (the elder) moved his family to work in the burgeoning oil town of Compton.

Although LA had the largest African-American settlement on the West Coast at the time, it was the war that brought blacks in great numbers from the South and the East Coast to work in defence-related industries, especially aerospace. Born or raised in South Central LA were such notables as jazz musicians Dexter Gordon, Charles Mingus and Eric Dolphy, United Nations undersecretary Ralph Bunche, dance choreographer Alvin Ailey, and Hollywood actress Dorothy Dandridge. Most of the new residents were unpleasantly surprised to experience a taste of the Old South in new LA – or, more specifically, the racism of the white Midwest transplants. The rampant, blatant discrimination of the time ensured the widespread presence of **colour bars** and **restrictive covenants** – social codes and

The gangs of LA

South Central LA is the heartland of the city's infamous **gangs**, which have existed for more than fifty years and often encompass several generations of a family. The black gangs known as **Crips** and **Bloods** are the most famous, but there are many huge Hispanic gangs as well, most prominently the **18th Street Gang** who, despite their name, operate all over the LA basin, as well as the US, Mexico and beyond – with more than sixty thousand members by some estimates. The characteristic violence associated with these groups often stems from territorial fights over drug dealing, with many gangs staking claim to certain neighbourhoods in their monikers. The larger gangs employ rather sophisticated schemes involving protection rackets, money laundering, and expansion into legitimate businesses from small retail operations to the music industry – all tactics reminiscent not of common street thugs, but of old-style mobsters.

Gang life reached a climax in the early 1990s with the LA Riots and the peak crime rate of the city's modern era. Nowadays, though, local gangs are increasingly **international**, with chapters not only reaching other cities throughout the western US, but also strongly linked to Mexican gangs and organized-crime syndicates. Indeed, LA serves as a training ground for budding gangsters from Central America who, after their deportation, return to their home countries schooled in the high-tech ways of first-world killing, inflicting more misery on a region already awash in violence and poverty.

That said, crime has been going down in the last fifteen years, with the current murder rate in the metropolis (and somewhat less so in South Central) is less than half its rate in the mid-1990s. By sticking to familiar areas in the day and well-policed districts at night, visitors should have few problems with gangs.

housing bylaws that kept blacks out of white neighbourhoods. African-Americans were hemmed in by avenues like Western and Slauson for their home-buying, and faced extreme hostility from whites whenever they ventured out of their neighbourhoods to buy groceries, meet friends or watch movies. Because of this, areas like Central Avenue and West Adams became segregated, though culturally rich, enclaves for blacks, with a thriving entertainment scene in the former and excellent architecture in the latter.

The **Civil Rights Era** and changing demographics put an official end to the old ways of segregation in the 1950s and 60s, and LA's southern neighbourhoods have become a diverse blend of blacks, Hispanics and Asians, with many districts changing character in just a few decades. However, many problems persist, and what was formerly political and social apartheid has instead become de facto **economic segregation**, for both blacks and Latinos. While poorer residents are still confined to the desperate ghettos of Watts and Compton, the more middle-class areas toward the north – namely, West Adams – have improved materially, to the point where white gentrification is now the key issue. Whatever the struggle, South Central continues to be as socially turbulent as it is culturally diverse.

Inglewood

Bordered by the San Diego Freeway (I-405) on the western edge of South Central, **INGLEWOOD** is, as the city bordering LAX, the first area most air travellers experience in LA – mainly to fight through the traffic congestion when heading north to a Westside hotel. It's also well known for the **Hollywood Park Racetrack** (Ⓣ310/419-1549, Ⓦwww.hollywoodpark.com), a landscaped track that has been around for more than seventy years, with lagoons and state-of-the-art widescreen TV for closing viewing of the ponies. Next door are the white pillars that ring **The Forum**, 3000 W Manchester Blvd, the seventeen-thousand-seat arena that was the former headquarters of LA's Lakers (basketball) and Kings (hockey). These days it's been converted into one of the country's biggest mega-churches, owned by Faithful Central Bible Church, though pop and rock concerts are still regularly held here during the week (Ⓣ310/330-7300, Ⓦwww.thelaforum.com).

Unless you're here to play the horses or hear a concert, Inglewood's best attraction is its **pop architecture**. The grand **Academy Theater**, 3141 W Manchester Blvd, now a church, was built in 1939 to house the Oscars ceremony (it never did), and features a giant Moderne spire and spiky neon globe that beckon to worshippers, while further west, the **Loyola Theater**, at Sepulveda and Manchester boulevards, is a late Streamline Moderne design with a sweeping, red goose-neck curve on its facade, which now serves as medical office space. Not far away at 805 Manchester Blvd, **Randy's Donuts** (Ⓣ310/645-4707, Ⓦrandys-donuts.com) is one of LA's more surreal icons, a 1954 fast-food shack topped by a giant brown donut, easily visible on your way to and from LAX, with pretty good junk food to boot; while **Pann's** (Ⓣ323/776-3770, Ⓦwww.panns.com), a mile north at La Tijera Boulevard and Centinela Avenue, still serves comfort food in what is perhaps the greatest 1950s "Googie"-style diner of all, with a big neon sign, pitched and gabled roof, exotic plants, gravel roof and a wealth of primary colours. Other classic diners are in fairly shopworn condition, except for the striking **Chips Restaurant**, a few miles south at 11908 Hawthorne Blvd (Ⓣ310/679-2947), showcasing one of LA's great signs, three aquamarine columns supporting a sparkling set of letters (plus cheap comfort food, too), and the zesty **Wich Stand**, 4508 Slauson Ave, graced with a towering, neon-lit pylon, though it no longer serves "De Luxe" hamburgers and deviled-egg sandwiches – it's now a health-food store, *Simply Wholesome* (Ⓣ323/294-2144).

Centinela Adobe

Just south of *Pann's*, the historic **Centinela Adobe**, 7643 Midfield Ave (Sun 2–4pm; free; weekday tours by appointment at Ⓣ310/671-2075), was once home to Ignacio Machado, an heir to one of the Mexican founders of Los Angeles. It's the oldest building in the area, dating from 1834 and furnished with antiques and replicas, including a good array of Victorian clothing and furniture, and offering details on Machado's life and his surrounding Aguaje de Centinela rancho, a 2200-acre land parcel granted him by the Mexican government. Also on site is the **Daniel Freeman Land Office**, built in 1887, a centre for historic preservation, and a storehouse of curios and memorabilia recalling Inglewood city history and culture, from the town's origins as the site of LA's first chicken and chinchilla farms to its rise as a centre for brick production and, later, as a home to the aerospace and defense industries.

Crenshaw, Leimert Park and Baldwin Hills

Just to the north, **CRENSHAW** and adjacent **Leimert Park** form the contemporary hub of middle-class African-American social activity in LA. This is most vibrant along **Crenshaw Boulevard**, a busy stretch of restaurants and book and record stores, as well as the **Baldwin Hills Crenshaw Plaza shopping mall**, 3650 W Martin Luther King Jr Blvd (Ⓣ323/290/6636, Ⓦwww.crenshawplaza.com). The stunning **Leimert Theater**, 3314 43rd Place, an Art Deco gem by architects Morgan, Walls and Clements (see box, p.73), features a towering oil-derrick sign with neon accents. It's now being (slowly) redeveloped as a performing-arts centre; see Ⓦvisiontheatre.org for the latest news. The theatre stands in the heart of

Leimert Park Village, several blocks of lively shops and decent restaurants. There are also a few solid jazz, R&B and blues **clubs** here, notably the *World Stage*, 4344 Degnan Blvd (concerts Thurs–Sat; ⓣ323/293-2451, ⓦwww.theworldstage.org), which doubles as an arts centre with creative workshops for up-and-coming writers, musicians and poets. Also here is the legendary institution *Babe & Ricky's Inn*, 4339 Leimert Blvd (ⓣ323/295-9112, ⓦwww.bluesbar.com), which serves up solid helpings of soul food as well as blues five nights a week.

West and above Crenshaw and Leimert Park, the black upper-middle class resides in pleasant **Baldwin Hills**, named after Wall Street gambler and Santa Anita racetrack-builder E.J. "Lucky" Baldwin. Just before he died in 1909, Baldwin acquired the old Rancho La Cienega, which encompassed the hills and was named after the misspelled Spanish word for "marsh". (He also built an estate east of Pasadena that's now home to the LA County Arboretum; see p.173.) Later, the area would host the Olympic Village for LA's 1932 summer games and become the site of a catastrophic 1963 dam-burst and flood. This was due in no small part to environmental damage from area oil drilling, which continues to this day, though in fewer spots than before. To relax or burn off some calories around here, **Kenneth Hahn State Recreation Area**, 4100 S La Cienega Blvd (daily 6am–dusk; ⓣ323/298-3660), offers 319 acres of attractive turf (the occasional oil patch notwithstanding) overlooking central LA, with seven miles of trails, a lake for fishing, two baseball diamonds, picnic tables and a sandy volleyball court. There's also a scenic overlook at 6300 Hetzler Rd, off Jefferson Boulevard (daily 8am–dusk; $6), which provides expansive panoramas of the metropolis, with the best view accessed via a steep trail or even steeper stairway.

West Adams

The main reason to visit the **West Adams** neighbourhood, along Adams Boulevard from Crenshaw Boulevard to the vicinity of the 110 freeway, is for its architecture – featuring classic houses in styles from Victorian to Craftsman to all manner of historic revivals. In the last decade, the district has even experienced a small revival, with new homeowners arriving to renovate the grand old properties, as the area begins to harken back to its one-time glory days. As one of LA's few racially mixed neighbourhoods in the early part of the twentieth century, it was one of the spots where movie stars tended to live, known in the 1920s and 30s as "**Sugar Hill**" and full of notable celebrities such as movie-musical director Busby Berkeley, and (literal) silent-film heavyweights Fatty Arbuckle and Theda Bara. After World War II and the demise of racist restrictive property covenants, many wealthy blacks began moving in as well, including Ray Charles, Little Richard and Joe Louis. Unfortunately, the politics of the 1950s and 60s took their toll on the neighbourhood, partly because of the construction of the **Santa Monica Freeway** (I-10), which slashed the area in half and enforced a de facto segregation on its residents. However, this official policy of malign neglect also led developers to ignore the neighbourhood, instead of plowing it under in the name of urban renewal.

The historic mansions

These days, West Adams holds three different historic-preservation zones, though many of the grand houses and mansions have become religious institutions. The bulk of the most notable structures can be found near Adams' intersection with Arlington Avenue. In this vicinity, Berkeley's estate, the 1910 **Guasti Villa**, 3500 W Adams Blvd, is a graceful Renaissance Revival creation thick with columns, pools and fountains, plus a stone labyrinth, which all might fit nicely in Italy but is now home to a New Age spiritual centre. If you feel like meditating in, or taking a tour of, these historic grounds, contact ⓣ323/737-4055 or ⓦwww.peacelabyrinth.org. Nearby, the **Lindsay House**, no. 3424, a terracotta curiosity with a heavy stone facade and unique tilework (the first owner was a tile manufacturer), has become Our Lady of Bright Mount, a Polish Catholic church (ⓣ323/734-5249); and just north, the **Marquis House**, 2302 W 25th St, is a jumble of eclectic Victorian touches from 1904 whose main claim to fame is its role as the Fisher funeral home in the TV series *Six Feet Under*; and the **South Seas House**, 2301 W 24th St (Mon–Fri 8am–10pm, Sat 10am–4pm; ⓣ323/373-9483), is a community centre that you can visit to sample the place's odd 1902 blend of Victorian and Polynesian architecture. Further east, the **Britt Mansion**, 2115 W Adams, is a 1910 Neoclassical gem with grand white columns and adjoining gardens. It's now home to the sports organization LA84, whose library boasts a large selection of books and publications on athletics (Mon–Fri 10am–5pm; free; ⓦwww.LA84Foundation.org).

William Clark Memorial Library

The finest library in West Adams, however, is the striking French Renaissance **William Clark Memorial Library**, 2520 Cimarron St (Mon–Fri 9am–4.45pm; free; ⓣ323/731-8529, ⓦwww.humnet.ucla.edu/humnet/clarklib), with its elegant symmetry, yellow-brick walls, formal gardens and grand entrance hall – a splash of Continental elegance in an unexpected LA setting. As millionaire heir to a copper fortune, founder of the LA Philharmonic, and a US Senator from Montana, Clark amassed this great collection before donating it to UCLA, which continues to oversee it. Besides rare volumes by Pope, Fielding, Dryden, Swift and Milton, plus a huge set of letters and manuscripts by Oscar Wilde, the library includes four Shakespeare folios, a group of works by Chaucer, and copies of key documents in American history pertaining to the Louisiana Purchase and the like. Four annual **exhibitions** are given of selected works from the collection.

USC

The **USC** (University of Southern California) campus, a few miles south of Downtown, and easily accessed along Jefferson or Exposition boulevards, is a wealthy enclave in one of the city's poorer neighbourhoods. For many years a breeding ground for political and economic fat cats, the university was well known for hatching LA's shadow rulers for the secretive "**Committee of 25**", supplying Richard Nixon with gung-ho advisers like H.R. Haldeman, and generally acting as the reactionary force in the local academic scene.

Today, USC or, to wags, the "University of Spoiled Children", is among the most expensive universities in the country, its undergraduates thought of as more likely to have rich parents than fertile brains. Mostly, though, it's been known for its sporting prowess: within fifteen years of the school's 1874 founding, it already had a **football** team, becoming the first university in Southern California to play the game. They remain a dominant force today, and famous alumni include O.J. Simpson, who, before his courthouse escapades, collected college football's highest honour, the Heisman Trophy, when he played here.

Though largely white and conservative, there have even been a few small steps to integrate the **campus** more closely with the local, mainly black and Hispanic, community. Based on an Italian Romanesque style similar to that of UCLA, USC's 1920s buildings are much more forbidding, though they exhibit nice detail and ornament. The lack of greenspace at times gives the campus the appearance of a concrete desert, and the austere character of its modern buildings can, in places, look like something out of a desolate de Chirico painting. Unlike UCLA, where you can visit to idle away the time, you go to USC strictly to get something done.

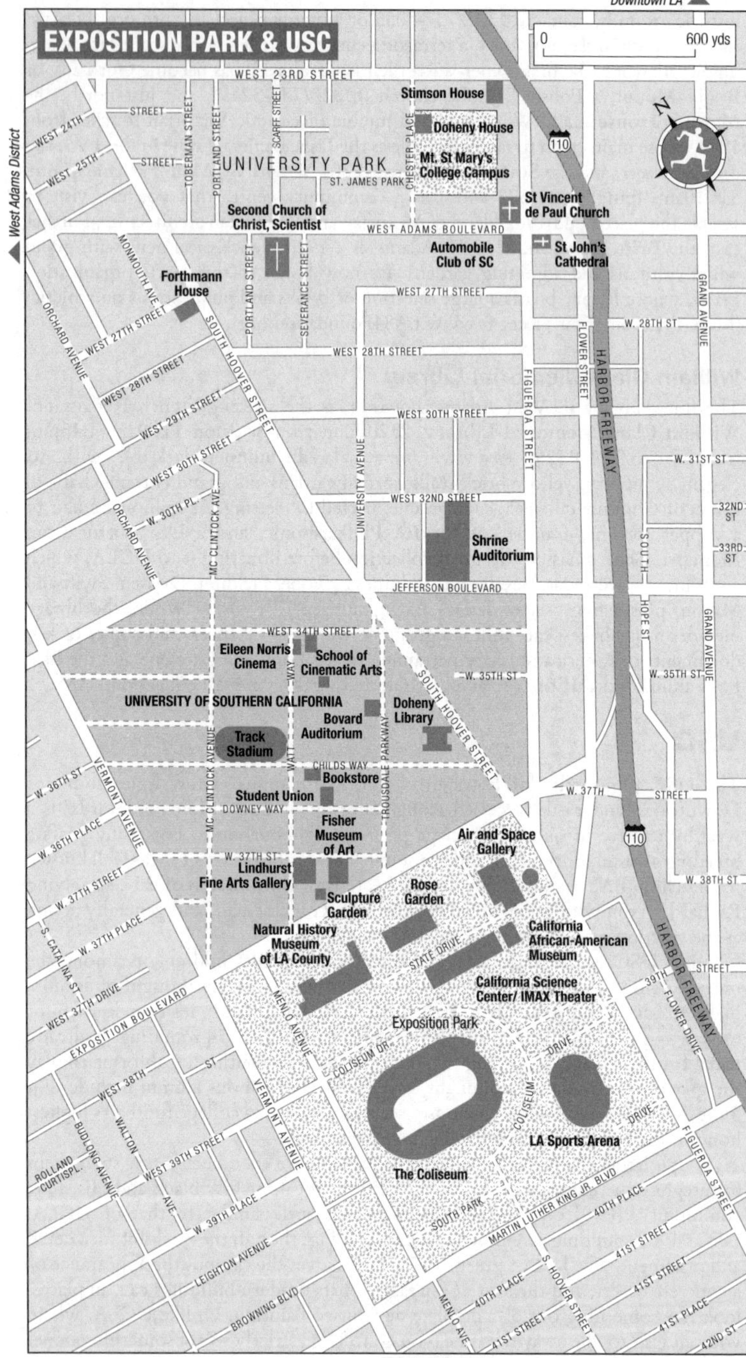
EXPOSITION PARK & USC
Downtown LA
0
600 yds
West Adams District
South Central LA
WEST 23RD STREET
STREET
WEST 24TH
WEST 25TH
TOBERMAN STREET
PORTLAND STREET
SCARFF STREET
CHESTER PLACE
UNIVERSITY PARK
ST. JAMES PARK
Stimson House
Doheny House
Mt. St Mary's
College Campus
St Vincent
de Paul Church
Second Church of
Christ, Scientist
WEST ADAMS BOULEVARD
Automobile
Club of SC
St John's
Cathedral
110
N
Forthmann
House
MONMOUTH AVE.
ORCHARD AVENUE
WEST 27TH STREET
WEST 28TH STREET
WEST 29TH STREET
WEST 30TH STREET
W. 30TH PL.
SOUTH HOOVER STREET
PORTLAND STREET
SEVERANCE STREET
W. 28TH ST
GRAND AVENUE
FLOWER STREET
HARBOR FREEWAY
FIGUEROA STREET
WEST 30TH STREET
W. 31ST ST
UNIVERSITY AVENUE
WEST 32ND STREET
32ND
ST
33RD
ST
SOUTH
HOPE ST
Shrine
Auditorium
MC CLINTOCK AVE.
ORCHARD AVENUE
JEFFERSON BOULEVARD
WEST 34TH STREET
Eileen Norris
Cinema
School of
Cinematic Arts
WAY
W. 35TH ST
W. 35TH ST
UNIVERSITY OF SOUTHERN CALIFORNIA
Doheny
Library
Bovard
Auditorium
Track
Stadium
WATT
TROUSDALE PARKWAY
CHILDS WAY
Bookstore
Student Union
DOWNEY WAY
MC CLINTOCK AVENUE
VERMONT AVENUE
W. 36TH ST
W. 36TH PLACE
W. 37TH
STREET
Fisher
Museum
of Art
Air and Space
Gallery
W. 37TH ST
Lindhurst
Fine Arts Gallery
Sculpture
Garden
Rose
Garden
W. 38TH ST
W. 37TH STREET
W. 37TH PLACE
S. CATALINA ST
Natural History
Museum
of LA County
STATE DRIVE
California
African-American
Museum
California Science
Center/ IMAX Theater
39TH
STREET
FLOWER DRIVE
HARBOR FREEWAY
WEST 37TH DRIVE
EXPOSITION BOULEVARD
MENLO AVENUE
Exposition Park
COLISEUM DR.
DRIVE
COLISEUM
DRIVE
WEST 38TH
ST
WALTON
BUDLONG AVENUE
ROLLAND
CURTIS PL.
VERMONT AVENUE
WEST 39TH STREET
AVE.
The Coliseum
LA Sports Arena
FIGUEROA STREET
W. 39TH PLACE
SOUTH PARK
MARTIN LUTHER KING JR. BLVD
40TH PLACE
41ST STREET
LEIGHTON AVENUE
BROWNING BLVD
MENLO AVE.
40TH PLACE
S. HOOVER STREET
41ST STREET
41ST STREET
41ST PLACE
42ND ST

The campus

While sizable, USC's campus is reasonably easy to get around. You might find it easiest, however, to take the free fifty-minute **walking tour** (four tours daily; by reservation at ⓣ213/740-6605, ⓦwww.usc.edu), which departs from the Admission Center, reachable off McCarthy Way west of Figueroa Street. Without a guide, a good place to start is the **Doheny Library**, between Childs Way and Trousdale Parkway (hours vary, often Mon–Thurs 9am–8pm, Fri & Sat 9am–5pm, Sun noon–5pm; ⓣ213/740-2924), an inviting Romanesque pile named after the famous LA oil baron, where you can pick up a campus map and investigate a large stock of overseas newspapers and magazines.

USC's art collection is housed in the **Fisher Museum of Art**, 823 Exposition Blvd (Tues–Sat noon–5pm; free; ⓣ213/740-4561, ⓦfisher.usc.edu), showing a wide range of art, from international and multicultural to avant-garde and contemporary. It stages several major international exhibitions each year and has a broad permanent collection, best for its nineteenth-century American works, including works from Thomas Cole and Albert Bierstadt. For more local efforts, the **Helen Lindhurst Fine Arts Gallery**, room 103 in Watt Hall, 850 W 37th St (Mon–Thurs 9am–7pm, Fri 9am–4.30pm; free; ⓣ213/740-2787), focuses on contemporary and experimental works from student and regional artists. If music is more to your interest, note that the **Bovard Auditorium**, 3551 Trousdale Pkwy (concert line ⓣ213/740-4211), is one of five concert venues on campus that hosts regular performances by students, faculty and guest performers.

There's plenty of bad public art on campus; one of the few compelling pieces is Jenny Holzer's **First Amendment**, in the **sculpture garden** around Harris Hall, Bloom Walk east of Watt Way – a work commemorating the Hollywood Ten, those writers and directors blacklisted for refusing to rat out their colleagues as Communists in the McCarthy era. Steps of stone slabs lead to ten circular benches, all of which are inscribed with the names and writings of the persecuted filmmakers.

Finally, the campus is also home to the **School of Cinematic Arts**, a mainstream rival to the UCLA film school in Westwood. Ironically, **Steven Spielberg** couldn't get in to USC when he applied, but nowadays his name is hallowed here, and writ large on the wall of the sizeable and expensive sound-mixing centre he later funded. You can sometimes catch a good classic or foreign flick at the nearby **Eileen Norris Cinema**, just east of Watt Way at 3507 Trousdale Parkway.

Just across the street from USC lies the most exotic piece of architecture in the area, the **Shrine Auditorium**, 665 W Jefferson Blvd (tickets and info at ⓣ213/748-5116, ⓦwww.shrineauditorium.com), best known as the former venue of the Oscars ceremony, which looks like a vestige of an *Arabian Nights* set in Hollywood. This 1926 Islamic-inspired fantasy, with its onion domes and streetside colonnade, is still in use as a venue for travelling religious revival shows, pop concerts, circuses, pageants and award ceremonies.

Exposition Park

Once known as Agricultural Park because of its produce vendors and farming exhibits, **Exposition Park**, just south of USC with its main entrance near 3800 S Figueroa St (parking $8; ⓣ213/763-0114), is one of the better parks in LA, incorporating lush gardens and several modest museums. Along with being a favourite lunchtime picnic spot for school kids, the park's big draw is the **California Science Center**, one of a cluster of **museums** off Figueroa Street at 700 State Drive (daily 10am–5pm; free; ⓣ213/744-7400, ⓦwww.californiasciencecenter.org), whose highlights include scores of working models and quirky, fun displays aimed at making the world of science more lively to youngsters. Exhibits include a walk-in periscope, imitation earthquake and a demonstration wind tunnel. Three of the museum's attractions – a "high-wire" bicycle, motion simulator and rock-climbing wall – cost $7 jointly. In the same complex, an **IMAX Theater** (tickets $8.25, kids $5) plays a range of eye-popping documentaries on a gigantic, seven-story curved screen. Nearby, the **Air and Space Gallery** (free; same hours and info as the Science Center), marked by a jet stuck to its white cubic facade, offers a series of satellites and telescopes and a slew of airplanes and rockets. The building itself was designed by Frank Gehry, and prefigures some of his later, better work. Close by, the **California African-American Museum**, 600 State Drive (Tues–Sat 10am–5pm, Sun 11am–5pm; free; ⓣ213/744-7432, ⓦwww.caamuseum.org), has diverse temporary exhibitions on the history and culture of black people in the Americas, including musical instruments from Africa and the Caribbean, shows devoted to the life and legacy of performers like Ella Fitzgerald, and painting and sculpture by local artists.

On a sunny day, take a stroll through Exposition Park's **Rose Garden**, 701 State Drive (mid-March to Dec daily 9am–dusk; free; ⓣ213/765-5397), planted on the site of a former racetrack in the park's early days. The flowers are at their most fragrant in April and May, which is when the bulk of the visitors come by to admire the sixteen thousand rose bushes and the charm of their setting. Finally, near the centre of the park, the grand **Coliseum**, 3939 S Figueroa St, was the site of the 1932 and 1984 Olympic Games. Since then, though, it's seen its glory days fade, with the Raiders pro-football team long gone. However, stiff demand for home games for the USC football team, one of the top squads in the country, allows them to charge a minimum of $75+ per game for nosebleed seats, and much more for anything better (ⓣ213/740-GOSC, ⓦwww.usctrojans.com). Otherwise, the imposing grand arch on the facade and muscular, headless commemorative statues create enough interest to make the place worth a quick look.

Natural History Museum of Los Angeles County

In the northwest corner of Exposition Park, the **Natural History Museum of Los Angeles County**, 900 Exposition Blvd (daily 9.30am–5pm; $9; ⓣ213/763-3466, ⓦwww.nhm.org), is an explosion of Spanish Revival architecture with echoing domes, travertine columns and a marble floor. Nearly one hundred years old, it's the park's most striking building and its best museum, with the biggest collection. Foremost among the exhibits is a tremendous stock of dinosaur bones and fossils, and some imposing skeletons (usually casts), including the crested "duck-billed" dinosaur, the skull of a Tyrannosaurus rex, and the astonishing frame of a Diatryma, a huge, flightless prehistoric bird. More contemporary (relatively speaking) bones of Ice Age-era ground sloths, mammoths, lions and the like are sometimes on view – many of them dug out of the muck of the La Brea Tar Pits, where the Page Museum is a satellite of this one (see p.73). Other exhibits cover rare sharks, the combustible native plant chaparral, and a spellbinding insect zoo – centred around a sizable ant farm – add to the appeal, but there's a lot here beyond strict natural history, so you should allow several hours at least for a comprehensive look around. In the fascinating Pre-Columbian Hall, you'll find Mayan pyramid murals and the complete, reconstructed contents of a Mexican tomb, while the Californian history sections document the early (white) settlement of the region during the Gold Rush era and after, with some evocative photos of LA in the 1920s. Topping everything off is the breathtaking gem collection: several roomfuls of crystals, and a tempting display of three hundred pounds of gold, safely off-limits to prying fingers.

University Park

Just to the north of USC and Exposition Park, around West Adams Boulevard and Figueroa Street, is **University Park**, a pocket of some of LA's most important early twentieth-century architecture, and an eastern extension of the historic West Adams district (see p.136). The intersection of Adams and Figueroa features three of LA's best period-revival designs from the 1920s: **St John's Cathedral**, 514 W Adams Blvd (Ⓣ213/747-6285, Ⓦwww.stjohnsla.org), a lovely Italian Romanesque Revival showpiece that features plenty of Venetian glass and Italian marble and gold mosaics, as well as the modern image of Martin Luther King Jr in stained glass; the church-like **Automobile Club of Southern California**, 2601 S Figueroa St (Ⓣ213/741-3686), a Spanish Baroque-style structure with a high octagonal tower and Mexican terrazzo tile; and the grand **St Vincent de Paul Church**, catercorner to St John's at 621 W Adams Blvd (Ⓣ213/749-8950), oil baron Edward Doheny's monumental donation to the faith, an ornamental Spanish Baroque-inspired creation with a sparkling, tiled dome and richly detailed steeple. Just to the north, the **Stimson House**, 2421 S Figueroa St, is a Romanesque castle-home, surely one of LA's most distinctive and photo-ready marvels. Made in 1891 of ruddy red sandstone, it appears ripe and ready for a Crusader battle and now serves, fittingly enough, as a Christian religious institution.

One long block to the west, **Chester Place** and **St James Park** are pedestrian-friendly zones loaded with the stunning residences of some of LA's most prominent citizens of the early twentieth century. The area's centrepiece is the palatial **Doheny House**, 8 Chester Place (Mon–Fri 8am–5pm; Ⓣ213/477-2767), a triumph of Victorian opulence, built in 1899 for the petroleum magnate himself, and the precursor of what would be LA's first gated community. Designed as a hybrid of various European revival styles, the place is overflowing with luxury – everything from Siena marble flooring to a Great Hall thick with Corinthian pillars to a golden glass dome cast by Louis Comfort Tiffany, plus a fetching palm conservatory and immense dining hall built to seat one hundred guests. After the 1958 death of Edward Doheny's wife Estelle, this and the surrounding property were given to **Mount St Mary's College**, and the house is now just one of several elegant buildings on campus. Periodically, the Da Camera Society offers chamber concerts (see p.262) played under the mansion's beautiful, reverberant dome. Once every three months, there's also a tour of the mansion and grounds that's well worth checking out if you're in town ($25; by reservation only at Ⓣ213/477-2962, Ⓦwww.dohenymansion.org).

Right by here are more intriguing period-revival creations, including the Forthmann House, 2801 S Hoover Blvd, a soap maker's nearly ideal 1887 Victorian house (now owned by USC), with a few French touches as well, including a mansard tower; and the **Second Church of Christ, Scientist**, 948 W Adams Blvd, a Neoclassical jewel with 40-foot-high Corinthian columns and a copper dome that shelters a thousand souls; it's now the centre for a New Age spiritual institute.

Central Avenue

The focus of African-American commerce and culture during the interwar years, **Central Avenue** had a vigour that has never been recaptured. With pre-1960s segregation and restrictive housing covenants prohibiting blacks from living in most of LA, this avenue from Eighth Street to Vernon Avenue became the hub for numerous restaurants, nightclubs and jazz halls.

With the end of official segregation, Central Avenue inevitably declined, but there are still several appealing sights amid the abandoned lots and strip malls. A superb example of Streamline Moderne architecture lies at the north end of the street: the **Coca-Cola Bottling Plant**, 1334 S Central Ave, looking like a huge, landlocked ocean liner, complete with rounded corners (with oversized Coke-bottle sculptures), porthole windows and ships' doors. Besides being in excellent condition, the plant is still churning out product for the soft-drink giant. Nearby at 1401 S Central Ave, the **African-American Firefighter Museum** (Tues & Thurs 10am–2pm, Sun 1–4pm; free; Ⓣ213/744-1730, Ⓦwww.aaffmuseum.org) is housed in Engine Company #30, LA's first all-black fire station, which protected the area from 1913 to 1980, and now displays a modest collection of historic equipment and memorabilia.

Eleven blocks south, pioneering black architect Paul R. Williams' first major building, the **Second Baptist Church**, 2412 Griffith Ave (Ⓣ213/748-0318, Ⓦwww.sbcla.org), is a striking Romanesque Revival church built in 1924 for a congregation dating from 1885, making it LA's oldest black religious institution. Further south, the **Dunbar Hotel**, 4225 S Central Ave, was the first US hotel built specifically for blacks and patronized by many prominent African-Americans – W.E.B. DuBois and Duke Ellington among them – during the 1930s through the 1950s. The hotel is only visible in its lobby and facade, as it is now a home for the elderly. It does, however, host the **Central Avenue Jazz Festival** in late July (details at Ⓣ213/473-7009, Ⓦwww.centralavejazz.org), which gives a hint of the area's swing and vigour in the old days.

Watts

Now more Hispanic than black, **WATTS** provides only one (very) compelling reason to visit, and only during the day: the Gaudí-esque **Watts Towers**, sometimes

"To Serve and Protect"

The **Los Angeles Police Department** – despite its slogan of "To Serve and Protect" – has had a longstanding reputation as one of the most brutal police forces in the nation. This notoriety began early on but was regularized in the 1950s when the LAPD's paramilitary tactics were developed under super-cop **William Parker**. In reaction to decades of police mistreatment of local blacks, the district of Watts first achieved notoriety as the scene of the six-day **Watts Riots** of August 1965. The arrest of a 21-year-old African American man, **Marquette Frye**, on suspicion of drunken driving, gave rise to bricks, bottles and slabs of concrete being hurled at police and passing motorists during the night of the 11th. The situation had calmed by the next morning, but by the following evening both young and old were on the streets, venting an anger generated by years of abuse by the police force and other white-dominated institutions. Weapons were looted from stores and many buildings set afire (though few residential buildings, black-owned businesses or community services, such as libraries and schools, were torched); street barricades were erected, and the events then took a more serious turn. By the fifth day the insurgents were approaching Downtown, which led to the callout of the **National Guard**: 13,000 troops arrived, set up machine-gun placements and road blocks, and imposed a curfew, causing the rebellion to subside. In the aftermath of the uprising, which left 36 dead, one German reporter said of Watts, "It looks like Germany during the last months of World War II." Watts hit the headlines for a second time in 1975, when members of the **Symbionese Liberation Army** (SLA), who had kidnapped publishing heiress Patty Hearst, fought a lengthy – and televised – gun battle with police until the house they were trapped in burned to the ground.

Despite all the violence, nothing had changed by the 1980s when chief **Daryl Gates** hit the headlines for his new and disturbing LAPD tactics: the department's own tank bashed down the walls of alleged drug suspects, its helicopter gunships were thick in the skies over South Central LA, and the chief himself proudly argued, in front of called the Rodia Towers, at 1765 E 107th St (30-minute tours every half-hour Thurs & Fri 11am–3pm, Sat 10.30am–3pm, Sun 12.30–3pm; $7; ⓣ213/847-4646), a half-mile north off the 105 freeway on Wilmington Avenue. Constructed from iron, stainless steel, old bedframes and cement, and adorned with bottle fragments and some seventy thousand crushed seashells, these striking pieces of folk art are shrouded in mystery. Their maker, Italian immigrant **Simon Rodia**, had no artistic background or training, but laboured over the towers' construction from 1921 to 1954, refusing offers of help and unwilling to explain their meaning or why he was building them. Once finished, Rodia left the area, refused to talk about them, and faded into obscurity. The towers, the tallest standing at almost 100 feet, managed to stave off bureaucratic hostility and structural condemnation for many decades, and at least one close encounter with the wrecking ball, before finally being declared a cultural landmark. One especially good time to come is during the late-September weekend that hosts the Saturday Day of the Drums Festival and Sunday Watts Towers Jazz Festival, both signature events in the city.

Compton

Between Watts and the LA Harbor, the few districts are of passing interest. Despite its fame as the home of many of LA's rappers, as well as tennis champs Serena and Venus Williams, **COMPTON** is not a place where strangers should attempt to sniff out the local music scene. Oddly enough, the town's most famous resident was none other than former president George Bush (Sr), who lived here when the city was

Congress, that casual drug users should be taken out and shot. Gates was, however, finally forced out by the **riots of 1992**, in which three white Los Angeles police officers were unexpectedly acquitted of using excessive force after they were videotaped kicking and beating African-American motorist **Rodney King**. What few predicted was the scale and intensity of the response to the verdict, which was partly fuelled, ironically enough, by the almost total lack of a police presence during the first evening's bloodshed. Beginning in South Central LA, where motorists were pulled from their cars and attacked, the situation quickly escalated into a tumult of arson, shooting and looting that spread from Long Beach to Hollywood. It took the imposition of a four-day dusk-to-dawn curfew, and the presence on LA's streets of several thousand well-armed National Guard troops, to restore calm – whereupon the full extent of the rioting became known. The **worst urban violence** seen in the US since the bloody, Civil War-era New York draft riots had left 58 dead, nearly 2000 injured, and caused an estimated $1 billion worth of damage.

Prompted by the Rodney King case, the **Christopher Commission** was set up to investigate racial prejudice within the LAPD, but its recommendations were blatantly ignored. The **Rampart police scandal** in 2000 revealed evidence of possible hit-squad tactics and other vigilante actions by members of the LAPD, confirming people's worst fears that the cops were beyond civilian, or even anyone's, control. While politicians and Westsiders expressed shock at such charges, no one in South Central was very surprised. After that, however, New York's trailblazing former police chief **William Bratton** was brought in and things have slowly improved. In the last decade, as with other cities in America, crime rates in Los Angeles have declined markedly and many once-fearsome neighbourhoods have seen levels of street violence subside. Still, **gang violence** remains a regular occurrence, and it acts as a reminder that, while large stretches of the city may be safer than ever, the familiar ghettos and barrios of South Central and East LA continue to smoulder, just waiting for the next spark.

still known for its oil wells, and when whites were still in power. With the white flight of the 1950s and 60s, though, investment capital dried up and Compton hasn't recovered – though decreasing in the last decade, the city's murder rate is still among the highest in the country. At the south edge of town, though, history buffs secure in their cars can stop at the **Dominguez Ranch Adobe**, just off the 91 freeway at 18127 S Alameda St (Sun & Wed 1, 2 & 3pm; ⓣ310/603-0088, ⓦdominguezrancho.org), which chronicles the social ascent of the adobe's founder, Juan Jose Domínguez. One of the soldiers who left Mexico with Padre Junípero Serra's expedition to found the California missions, he was rewarded for his long military service in 1782 by the granting of 75,000 acres of surrounding land. The six main rooms of the handsome 1826 Mission-style adobe are on display and worth a look for anyone intrigued by pre-American California.

East LA

You can't visit LA without being aware of the Hispanic influence on the city's demography and culture, whether through the thousands of Mexican restaurants, the innumerable street names in Español or, most obviously, the preponderance of Spanish spoken on the streets in dialects from Tijuana to Oaxaca, from Guatemala to Peru. Of the many Hispanic neighbourhoods all over the city, the most enduring is **EAST LA**, which begins two miles east of Downtown, across the LA River.

There was a Mexican population here long before the white settlers came, and from the late nineteenth century onward millions more arrived, chiefly to work as agricultural labourers in orchards and citrus groves. As the white inhabitants gradually moved west towards the coast, the Mexicans stayed, creating a vast Spanish-speaking community that's one of the most historic in the country, as well as one of the most insular and unfamiliar to outsiders.

Activity in East LA tends to be outdoors, in cluttered markets and busy shopping pavilions. Non-Hispanic visitors are thin on the ground; you are unlikely to meet any hostility on the streets during the day – but avoid the whole area after dark. **Guadalupe**, the Mexican depiction of the Virgin Mary, appears in mural art all over East LA, nowhere more strikingly than at the junction of Mednik and Cesar Chavez avenues. Lined with blue tile, the mural serves as an unofficial shrine where worshippers place fresh flowers and candles.

Other than the street life and murals, there are few specific "sights" in East LA other than the mausoleum of **New Calvary Cemetery**, 4201 E Whittier Ave (daily 8am–5pm, spring & summer closes 6pm; ⓣ323/261-3106). Rivalling City Hall for sheer audacity, the monumental 1902 tomb piles on the styles, with Corinthian columns and pilasters, an Egyptian-pyramid roof and a few Byzantine domes, plus some sculpted angels thrown in for good measure. Beyond its exterior panache, the cemetery is also the resting place of rich, old-time Angelenos like Edward Doheny, jazz great Jelly Roll Morton, and movie stars like Lionel and Ethel Barrymore, and Lou Costello.

For a more animated scene, stroll along **Cesar Chavez Avenue**, preferably on a Saturday afternoon – the liveliest part of the week – going eastward from Indiana Street, and check out the wild-pet shops for their free-roaming parrots and cases of boa constrictors, or the **botánicas** that offer remedies from a wide selection of magical herbs, ointments and candles. Just as lively is **El Mercado de Los Angeles**, 3425 E First St (daily 10am–8pm; ⓣ323/268-3451, ⓦwww.elmercadodelosangeles.com), an indoor market somewhat similar to Olvera Street (see p.49), but much more authentic. Outdoor murals depict a Maya god and warrior, as well as actor Edward James Olmos, and various shops sell clothing, Latin American food, and arts and crafts; the top floor, where the restaurants are located, is the most musical, with mariachi bands playing daily well after midnight.

Monterey Park

Of the nearby districts, the only one of conceivable interest is **MONTEREY PARK**, northeast of East LA, a reasonably safe area that has the highest percentage of Asian residents of any city in the nation (62 percent) and is a major gateway for Taiwanese and mainland Chinese immigrants arriving in the US. It's also home to a number of excellent authentic Chinese restaurants, as well as many nightclubs, ethnic grocers and theatres, on its main drag, **Atlantic Boulevard**.

Whittier and around

Well to the southeast of East LA, and almost to the border of Orange County, the small town of **WHITTIER**, originally founded by Quakers and named after Quaker poet John Greenleaf Whittier, offers a few interesting sights. It was here

The dirty heart of Southeast LA

Near interstates 5 and 710 south of East LA and east of South Central, **Southeast LA** is generally made up of low-grade industrial sites and their dingy bedroom communities. As one of the main US centres for (often illicit) new arrivals, population density in some places has become overwhelming – the tiny town of **Cudahy** packs nearly 25,000 people on one square mile of land, and not surprisingly has one of the country's highest poverty rates – while in other industrial towns, residential zones are practically forbidden, sweatshops evade labour laws, and drug and contraband smuggling are major industries.

If, for some reason, you should wind up here, there are a few sights surprisingly worth checking out, starting in **Vernon**, an inhospitable burg whose only highlight is the **Farmer John's Mural**, 3049 E Vernon Ave, a bucolic idyll on a meat-packing plant, painted by a Hollywood set designer in the 1960s. It depicts a team of little pigs scampering about a farm, cavorting with a family, and managing to scale the building walls – an amusing scene that almost makes you forget the ugly business inside. Further east, in Commerce, is **The Citadel**, right off I-5 at 5675 Telegraph Rd (daily 10am–8pm; ⓣ323/888-1724, ⓦwww.citadeloutlets.com), modelled on the ancient Assyrian architecture of Khorsabad in the Middle East; note the massive battlements and carvings of priests and warriors on the huge facade. Built by the architecture firm of Morgan, Walls, and Clements (see box, p.73), this structure started life as the Samson Tyre and Rubber Company, was a backdrop for the 1950s spectacular *Ben Hur*, then abandoned, and finally restored and turned into a fashion outlet.

To the south, the community of **Downey** is unremarkable in itself, but does feature a pair of pop-architecture icons. The most famous is the country's original **McDonald's**, 10207 Lakewood Blvd (ⓣ562/622-9248), opened in 1953, a year before the chain officially started. Boasting a much more exuberant, colourful design than the mansard-roofed clones of today, this *McDonald's* also features big yellow-neon arches that stretch over and into the building itself, plus a winking chef named "Speedee" atop its 60-foot-high sign. Still in Downey, and even more fun, is Bob's Big Boy Broiler, 7447 Firestone Blvd (ⓣ562/928-2627, ⓦwww.bobsbigboybroiler.com), a neon monument to the zesty "Googie" architecture style of 1950s diners, recently restored with its glorious sign and old-fashioned car hops, and more than meriting a stop for a burger and fries.

that **Richard Nixon** – a Quaker himself – was raised, went to law school, and started his first law office. (His birthplace and library is in the Orange County town of Yorba Linda; see p.198.) You can find out more at the engaging **Whittier Museum**, 6755 Newlin Ave (Sat & Sun 1–4pm; free; ⓣ562/945-3871, ⓦwww.whittiermuseum.org), where docents lead a tour past a treasure-trove of historic city artefacts and assorted gizmos ranging from a working model of an oil derrick to replicas of a Pacific Electric Red Car. Other highlights include an old-fashioned barn and Victorian cottage, a rebuilt version of a Quaker meeting hall, and the desk Tricky Dick used in his first law office.

For a look at another politician who had an even harder time of it, there's the engaging **Pio Pico State Historic Park**, 6003 Pioneer Blvd (Sat & Sun 9am–4pm; free; ⓣ562/695-1217 ext 102, ⓦwww.piopico.org), a 9000-acre tract that used to be the ranch of **Pio Pico**, the last Mexican governor of California, and centred around an **adobe** full of Victorian furnishings and artefacts tracing his life. Constructed in 1853, the house saw Pico lose his governorship, re-emerge on the LA City Council, make a fortune in real estate and finally go bankrupt, eventually dying penniless.

Several miles south, at 10211 Pioneer Blvd, the **Clarke Estate** (tours Tues & Fri 11am–2pm; free; ⓣ562/868-3876) is a mix of Mission Revival and early-modern styles, and a popular wedding spot, with elegantly landscaped grounds. Spartan white arches give way to Mediterranean balconies, and Tuscan columns are used to offset a number of pre-Columbian reliefs and icons – giving a hint of what LA would have looked like if it had been colonized by Italians and Mayans, instead of Spaniards. Neighbouring **Heritage Park**, 12100 Mora Drive (daily 7am–9pm; free), is also worth a look for its collection of re-created, local historic buildings, including a windmill, conservatory and carriage barn from the 1870s and 80s, accompanied by a pretty English garden and an 80-ton locomotive that sits on railroad lines dating back to the 1870s as well.

Workman and Temple Family Homestead Museum

If you've already ventured this far for historic attractions, you might as well head north to the **Workman and Temple Family Homestead Museum**, 15415 E Don Julian Rd (tours on the hour Wed–Sun 1–4pm; free; ⓣ626/968-8492, ⓦwww.homesteadmuseum.org), a historic estate that's the lone point of interest in the drab **CITY OF INDUSTRY**. Here, docents will lead you around the place where an early emigrant party first staked a regional land claim and constructed this historic Spanish Colonial house around an 1840 adobe, complete with expansive grounds. There's a smokehouse and water tower, as well as a cemetery that contains the graves of many figures from regional history, including that of Pio Pico. The house itself is striking, full of carved wooden details, wrought-iron railings and tiled stairways, and the glimmering centrepiece – stained-glass windows depicting steadfast family members on their westward trek to Southern California.

7

The South Bay and LA Harbor

Stretching south of LAX and South Central, all the way to the edge of Orange County, the oceanside cities of the **South Bay** and the **LA Harbor** share little in common except their proximity to the sea and insularity from the rest of the metropolis. Overall, though, the area's balmy climate and windswept scenery make this one of the city's most appealing regions, at least by the shoreline.

The South Bay begins south of the airport, with three **south beach cities** that are smaller and more suburban than LA's other seaside towns, and worth a brief idyll. Further south, and visible all along this stretch of the coast, the **Palos Verdes Peninsula** occupies a wild, craggy stretch of coastline, with some rustic parks and pricey real estate, while rough-hewn **San Pedro** is a gritty working town that forms part of the site for the LA Harbor. Its counterpart, **Long Beach**, is best known as the home of the *Queen Mary*, even though it is also the region's second-largest city, with nearly half a million people. Both San Pedro and Long Beach form the **LA harbor** – a massive complex consisting of so many ship passages, trucking routes and artificial islands that the huge Vincent Thomas Bridge had to be built to carry travellers over the entire works.

The most enticing place in the area is **Santa Catalina Island**, located twenty miles offshore and easily reached by ferry. Little visited, the interior of the island remains largely a wilderness, with many unique forms of plant and animal life, and there's just one significant centre of population, **Avalon**, a charming town in which the main form of motorized transport is the golf cart.

South beach towns

Several miles south of LAX along the coast, you'll find few interesting sights, just a steam plant, oil refineries and a sewage-treatment centre. Soon after, though, the main access route, **Vista del Mar**, rises up a bluff as it hugs the coastline, and an eight-mile strip of beach towns begins – Manhattan, Hermosa and Redondo beaches. Sitting on small, gently sloped hills, these **south beach towns** are linked by **The Strand**, a beach boardwalk used heavily by local joggers and roller skaters. Each town has at least one municipal pier and a beckoning strip of white sand,

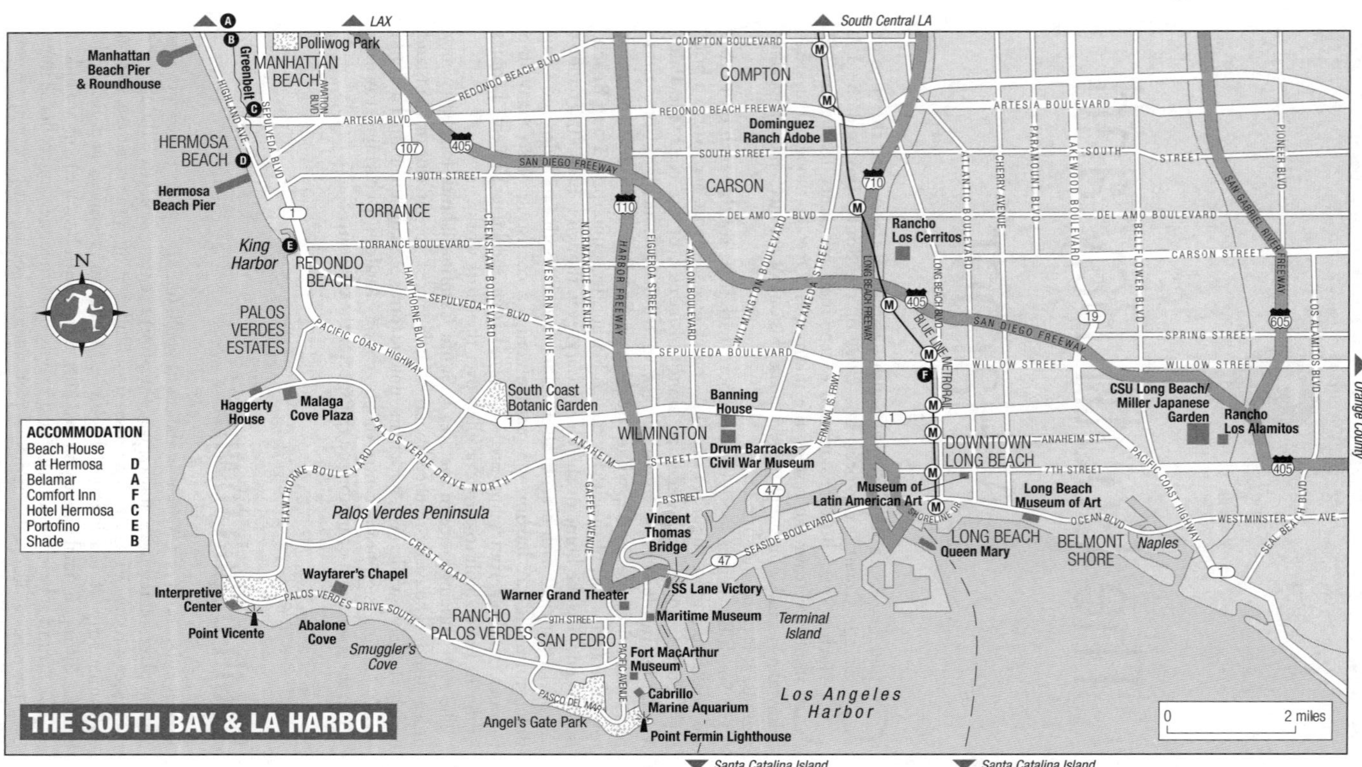
THE SOUTH BAY & LA HARBOR
ACCOMMODATION
Beach House at Hermosa D
Belamar A
Comfort Inn F
Hotel Hermosa C
Portofino E
Shade B
N
0
2 miles
LAX
South Central LA
Orange County
Santa Catalina Island
Santa Catalina Island
Manhattan Beach Pier & Roundhouse
Polliwog Park
MANHATTAN BEACH
Greenbelt
HERMOSA BEACH
Hermosa Beach Pier
TORRANCE
King Harbor
REDONDO BEACH
PALOS VERDES ESTATES
Haggerty House
Malaga Cove Plaza
South Coast Botanic Garden
Palos Verdes Peninsula
Wayfarer's Chapel
Interpretive Center
Point Vicente
Abalone Cove
Smuggler's Cove
RANCHO PALOS VERDES
SAN PEDRO
Warner Grand Theater
Angel's Gate Park
Point Fermin Lighthouse
Cabrillo Marine Aquarium
Fort MacArthur Museum
Maritime Museum
SS Lane Victory
Vincent Thomas Bridge
Terminal Island
Los Angeles Harbor
WILMINGTON
Banning House
Drum Barracks Civil War Museum
COMPTON
Dominguez Ranch Adobe
CARSON
Rancho Los Cerritos
Museum of Latin American Art
DOWNTOWN LONG BEACH
Long Beach Museum of Art
LONG BEACH
Queen Mary
BELMONT SHORE
Naples
CSU Long Beach/ Miller Japanese Garden
Rancho Los Alamitos
COMPTON BOULEVARD
REDONDO BEACH BLVD
REDONDO BEACH FREEWAY
ARTESIA BLVD
ARTESIA BOULEVARD
AVIATION BLVD
SEPULVEDA BLVD
HIGHLAND AVE.
SAN DIEGO FREEWAY
SOUTH STREET
190TH STREET
DEL AMO BLVD
DEL AMO BOULEVARD
TORRANCE BOULEVARD
CARSON STREET
SEPULVEDA BOULEVARD
PACIFIC COAST HIGHWAY
HAWTHORNE BLVD
CRENSHAW BOULEVARD
WESTERN AVENUE
NORMANDIE AVENUE
HARBOR FREEWAY
FIGUEROA STREET
AVALON BOULEVARD
WILMINGTON BOULEVARD
ALAMEDA STREET
LONG BEACH FREEWAY
LONG BEACH BLVD
BLUE LINE METRORAIL
ATLANTIC BOULEVARD
CHERRY AVENUE
PARAMOUNT BLVD
LAKEWOOD BOULEVARD
BELLFLOWER BLVD
SAN GABRIEL RIVER FREEWAY
PIONEER BLVD
LOS ALAMITOS BLVD
SPRING STREET
WILLOW STREET
TERMINAL IS. FRWY
ANAHEIM STREET
ANAHEIM ST
7TH STREET
B STREET
GAFFEY AVENUE
PALOS VERDE DRIVE NORTH
HAWTHORNE BOULEVARD
CREST ROAD
PALOS VERDES DRIVE SOUTH
9TH STREET
PACIFIC AVENUE
PASCO DEL MAR
SEASIDE BOULEVARD
SHORELINE DR
OCEAN BLVD
WESTMINSTER AVE.
SEAL BEACH BLVD
405
110
710
605
107
19
1
47

with most spots fronting the ocean equipped for surfing and beach volleyball. A major international surf festival across all three towns takes place at the end of July (Ⓦwww.surffestival.org), a good time to see the California leisure life at its finest.

Because of the towns' relative isolation from the rest of the LA basin, there are few public transit choices, other than Metro bus route #232, which connects LAX Bus Center with Long Beach and provides access to all three towns along the way. Alternately, you can connect to the Green Line light rail (via the Blue Line from Downtown) and get off at the Marine/Redondo station and transfer to the #126 line, which runs to Manhattan Beach.

Manhattan Beach

Accessible along the bike path from Venice, or by car via Pacific Coast Highway or Vista del Mar, **MANHATTAN BEACH** is the most northern of the three towns, a likeable place with a well-to-do air, home mainly to white-collar workers whose stucco houses sit near the beach, along the main drag of **Highland Avenue**. The **beach** is the main reason to visit: **surfing** is a major local pastime, along with beach volleyball. To play, just rent a ball at one of the rental shacks found along the beach. However, there's not much to do on Manhattan Beach's **pier**, save for visiting the aptly named **Roundhouse**. At the **aquarium** (Mon–Fri 3pm–dusk, Sat & Sun 10am–dusk; $2; Ⓣ310/379-8117, Ⓦwww.roundhouseaquarium.org) inside you can peer at sharks and lobsters, and fiddle around with the helpless creatures in a tide-pool "touch tank".

Inland, the main attraction is **Polliwog Park**, Manhattan Beach Blvd at N Peck Ave (daily 8am–dusk; Ⓣ310/802-5410), which features swimming pools, rose and botanical gardens, picnic tables, gazebos and a Frisbee golf course. In the summer the park is one of fifteen, mostly beachside locations that hosts "**Shakespeare by the Sea**" (June–Aug Thurs–Sun usually between 7–8pm; free; Ⓦwww.shakespearebythesea.org), a series of local performances of the Bard's works, usually a few selected comedies that rotate between the sites. It's better than you might expect since, this being LA, there's always a large pool of actors to draw from.

Hermosa Beach and Redondo Beach

To the south, **HERMOSA BEACH**, across Longfellow Avenue, has a bit of a bohemian feel – or as much of one as is possible in a town with scads of million-dollar homes. It also has a thriving beachside strip, which is most energetic near the foot of the **pier** on Twelfth Street, with a selection of lively restaurants and clubs. The area has long been a major hangout for revellers of all stripes, and a good time to come is during the **Fiesta Hermosa** (Ⓦwww.fiestahermosa.com), a three-day event held twice a year, over Memorial Day and Labor Day, when you'll find music (including surf rock), tasty food, and displays of regional arts and crafts. Apart from ocean-based activities, the town boasts the lush **Hermosa Valley Greenbelt** – a former railroad easement that's now been turned into a long, grassy strip running between Valley Drive and Ardmore Avenue, which connects to Manhattan Beach and makes a good place to relax or to work out on any of several bike and jogging paths.

Further south, despite its familiar name and fine views of Palos Verdes' stunning greenery, **REDONDO BEACH**, across Herondo Street, is less inviting than its relaxed neighbour, with hardly any noteworthy sights beyond the beachside boardwalk. Condos and hotels front the beach, and the yacht-lined King Harbor is off limits to curious visitors. However, the town does hold a good number of prime seafood eateries, the best of which are noted on p.242.

The Palos Verdes Peninsula

South of the beach towns, the **PALOS VERDES PENINSULA**, a great green mound marking LA's southwest corner, is known for its rugged beaches and secluded coves, sweeping views of the coastline, and some of the most expensive real estate in Southern California, or the nation for that matter. Originally intended as a "millionaires' colony" by 1920s developers, Palos Verdes has more or less worked out according to plan, with several gated communities like **Rolling Hills**, numerous multimillion-dollar estates, and an armada of private security guards making sure the place stays as exclusive as it looks. Despite this, the Palos Verdes Peninsula is one of the best spots for experiencing nature in the South Bay (especially along Palos Verdes Drive), with sea cliffs and tide pools, and its oceanside scenery is nothing less than awe-inspiring. Keep in mind, though, that it's assumed none of the residents need public transportation, so almost none is available (though the local transit authority offers irregular summer bus service on a few routes, for $2.50 a ticket; see ⓦwww.palosverdes.com/pvtransit for details).

North Palos Verdes

The northwest section of the peninsula is largely ungated and accessible, with most attractions located near the coast of **PALOS VERDES ESTATES**, the first city founded on the peninsula, in 1939, and the one with the most significant architecture and public greenspace. Nearly one-third of its space is preserved as parkland, on which you may come across a roaming herd of up to 150 officially protected peacocks. The town itself has a pseudo-European air, with a complete absence of stop lights along circuitous streets that overlook the ocean, and tightly controlled commercial development. Indeed, the town's early overseers were so committed to the period-revival aesthetic that all new designs, housing or otherwise, had to be reviewed and approved by an officially sanctioned "**art jury**" – surely the only time this has ever happened in LA.

The best place to soak in this "Old World" atmosphere is at **Malaga Cove Plaza**, Palos Verdes Drive at Via Corta, a Spanish Revival-flavoured commercial and civic centre. Here, the main draw is the **Neptune Fountain**, a smaller replica of a 1563 structure in Bologna, Italy, of the same name, featuring a bronze sculpture and mock-late-Renaissance design. Elsewhere, much of the city's seaside architecture has a strong Mediterranean flair. One of the few examples open to the public is the **Haggerty House**, 415 Paseo del Mar, a 1927 Italian-villa-style mansion that has been reincarnated as the Neighbourhood Church (ⓣ310/378-9353, ⓦwww.neighbourhoodchurchpve.org). For a different sort of experience, you might try locating the **Malaga Dunes**, a small ten-acre pocket of what was once an extensive ancient sand-dune ecosystem that led all the way up to the Ballona wetlands (see p.131). Now, this sandy terrain is all that remains,

Hiking tours of Palos Verdes

Once a month, the Palos Verdes Peninsula Land Conservancy offers **hiking tours** of some of the most invigorating spots on Palos Verdes, from Malaga Dunes to Portuguese Bend, including marshes, canyons, cliffs and other dramatic vistas. The treks typically take place the second Saturday of the month, are free, and last two to three hours, sometimes in rather rugged environs, and focus on the ecological, historical or cultural value of a given area – information you're not likely to discover very easily otherwise (information at ⓣ310/541-7613, ⓦwww.pvplc.com).

though it's worth exploring for its rich variety of birdlife, eucalyptus grove and unusual habitat. To get there, go just east of the intersection of Palos Verdes Drive North and Palos Verdes Drive West, where the dunes lie on the hillside across the ravine. For more information or to take one of its occasional tours, contact the Palos Verdes Peninsula Land Conservancy (see box opposite).

South Coast Botanic Garden

Inland on the north peninsula, there are few compelling sights save the **South Coast Botanic Garden**, 26300 Crenshaw Blvd (daily 9am–5pm; $8; ⓣ310/544-1948, ⓦwww.southcoastbotanicgarden.org), a relaxing spot that was first home to a diatomite pit for 37 years, mined for single-celled algae fossils used for industrial purposes, and then to a giant landfill. In the 1950s and 60s, LA dumped 3.5 million tons of its trash here, creating one of the bigger eyesores in the region, but since 1961, the landfill has been covered by layers of soil and successfully reclaimed as a garden, filled with exotic bromeliads, a cactus garden, palm trees, ferns, fuchsias, dahlias, herbs and flowering plants, and even a small French-style garden. The only sign of its former life is the terrain itself, which, thanks to the subsiding of the garbage below, has a weirdly undulating landscape, peppered here and there with "exhaust" pipes that allow for the release of carbon dioxide and methane from the chemical stew beneath.

South Palos Verdes

South of Palos Verdes Estates along Palos Verdes Drive, the beaches are more easily visited, and worthwhile for their significant natural attractions, one of which is the promontory of **Point Vicente**, sitting on high cliff walls above the Pacific Ocean. An **interpretive centre**, 31501 Palos Verdes Drive W (daily 10am–5pm; donation; ⓣ310/377-5370), here provides displays on the history of the region, the area's biology and geology, and especially the presence of **whales** – which you might see from the point during their seasonal migrations (Dec & Jan and March & April), when they swim close enough to photograph. Nearby, a **lighthouse**, 31550 Palos Verdes Drive W (second Sat of month 10am–3pm; free; ⓣ310/541-0334, ⓦwww.palosverdes.com/pvlight), dates from 1926 and towers nearly two hundred feet above sea level in a dramatic cliffside setting.

Further south, **Abalone Cove**, reached from a parking lot at 5970 Palos Verdes Drive South via a quarter-mile walk, boasts a cobblestoned beach, rock and tide pools, and, offshore, kelp beds alive with sea urchins, rock scallops and the rare abalone. Don't be tempted to make off with any, though, since the place is an **ecological reserve** (Mon–Fri noon–4pm, Sat & Sun 9am–4pm; parking $5; ⓣ310/377-1222), and the authorities take a dim view of anyone stealing the cove's namesake.

The Wayfarer's Chapel and Portuguese Bend

While you're in the area, don't miss the **Wayfarer's Chapel**, 5755 Palos Verdes Drive, a masterpiece of pitched glass and wood that was designed by Frank Lloyd Wright's son, Lloyd. A tribute to the eighteenth-century Swedish scientist and mystic Emanuel Swedenborg, and funded by the Swedenborgian Church, the ultimate aim is for the redwood grove around the chapel to grow and entangle itself in the glass-framed structure – a symbolic fusing of human handiwork with the forces of nature. Unsurprisingly, the place is one of LA's top choices for weddings. The **visitor centre** (daily 10am–5pm; ⓣ310/377-7919, ⓦwww.wayfarerschapel.org) lays out the history and architecture of the chapel, and can send you on your way with a self-guided walk through the dramatic site.

A half-mile south, the coast at **Portuguese Bend** provides another striking ocean vista, and was once the place where Portuguese whalers hunted grey whales for their blubber, which was harvested for its oil. The Bend occupies a 1400-acre preserve that, while ill-suited for home building and road construction (given the geological "slippage" in the form of landslides), is great for hiking and biking. See Ⓦwww.pvplc.org/land/portuguesebend for information on trails and scenic vistas at this and other protected lands in the area.

San Pedro

Forming part of the site of the LA Harbor, scruffy **SAN PEDRO**, at the south-eastern edge of the Palos Verdes Peninsula and due south of downtown LA by 20 miles, is a diverse blue-collar town settled by immigrants from Portugal, Greece, Mexico and the Balkans. As one of several places along the West Coast where labour strife erupted during the Depression, the city has a long tradition of populism and a nagging antipathy toward the city of Los Angeles, which annexed it in 1909, despite local opposition. And indeed, everything about San Pedro, from its low-rise, old-time buildings to its maritime atmosphere, gives it a unique flavour that bears little in common with any place else in the metropolis. Many locals use the American pronunciation (PEE-dro) for the town name, rather than the Spanish one.

Downtown San Pedro

San Pedro's harbour abuts the district's **downtown** and forms part of the massive Port of Los Angeles – with Long Beach, the biggest in the United States. The focus of all shipping activity is the man-made **Terminal Island**, across the harbour's main channel. While you'll have to keep your distance from the docks and machinery, there are some points along the channel worth investigating. Still don't bother with downtown's heavily promoted **Ports o' Call Village** – a dismal batch of wooden and corrugated-iron huts supposedly capturing the flavour of seaports around the world by way of its T-shirt and junk-food vendors.

A good place to start is the **SS Lane Victory**, in Berth 94, off Swinford Street, across from the shipyard (daily 9am–3pm; $3; Ⓣ310/519-9545, Ⓦwww.lanevictory.org). The huge, ten-thousand-ton cargo ship was built in the shipyard in 1945 for World War II, also operated in Korea and Vietnam, and today is maintained by the Merchant Marine. Tours lead through its many cramped spaces, including the engine and radio rooms, crew quarters, galley and bridge. The ship offers all-day summertime **cruises** to Santa Catalina Island (one weekend per month July–Sept; $130, kids $80; Ⓣ310/519-9545), involving onboard meals, historical re-enactments with captured stowaway spies, and dogfights with old-fashioned biplanes and Japanese and American air squadrons. Overhead is the towering **Vincent Thomas Bridge**, California's third-longest suspension bridge, completed in 1963 to take over the work of transporting sailors and fishermen to and from Terminal Island.

There's more nautical history at the **Maritime Museum**, further south at Sampson Way at Sixth Street (Tues–Thurs 10am–5pm, Fri noon–5pm, Sat 10am–5pm; $3; Ⓣ310/548-7618, Ⓦwww.lamaritimemuseum.org). Occupying the old ferry tower, the museum is a storehouse for artefacts from the glory days of San Pedro's fishing industries, focusing on everything from old-fashioned clipper-ship voyages to contemporary diving expeditions. Besides plenty of model ships, the museum has interesting exhibits on Native American seacraft, navigation devices and artful scrimshaw from the whaling era. Four blocks west of the Maritime Museum, old downtown San Pedro has been refurbished in recent years, thanks in part to the restoration of the opulent **Warner Grand Theater**, 478 W Sixth St (Ⓣ310/548-7672, Ⓦwww.warnergrand.org), a terrific 1931 Zigzag Moderne moviehouse and performing-arts centre with dark geometric details, grand columns and sunburst motifs, a style that almost looks pre-Columbian. Also part of the clean-up effort is the **San Pedro Trolley** (Fri–Sun noon–9.30pm; $1), a collection of three classic 1908 Pacific Electric Red Cars (two replica trolleys, one restored) linking most of the city's major attractions, running alongside Harbor Boulevard and connecting the SS *Lane Victory* with the Cabrillo Marina at 22nd Street.

Fort MacArthur Museum

To the south, the **Fort MacArthur Museum**, 3601 S Gaffey St (Tues, Thurs, Sat & Sun noon–5pm; free; Ⓣ310/548-2631, Ⓦwww.ftmac.org), is sited on the former Battery Osgood. This gun emplacement was at the original **Fort MacArthur**, a military post built in the late nineteenth century and named after General Arthur MacArthur – Douglas's dad. During the Cold War, the fort became a launch site for the early Nike-Ajax and later nuclear-warhead-equipped Hercules missiles, one of sixteen such sites in LA (the only other one now open to the public can be found in the Santa Monica Mountains; see "San Vicente Mountain Park", p.190). Reflecting its history, the fort's museum displays a clutch of military uniforms and old photographs, scads of antique radio equipment, as well as assorted disarmed bombs, mines and missiles.

Point Fermin

At the tip of San Pedro, about a mile south of the trolley terminus, is **Point Fermin**, a cape that, at the end of the eighteenth century, explorer George Vancouver named for an early Franciscan missionary, Padre Fermín Lasuén. On the cape's far end, across Paseo del Mar, **Point Fermin Park** is a verdant, palm-laden strip of land sitting atop ocean bluffs that mark LA's southernmost point, as well as a Monarch butterfly wintering location. Hidden on the seaward edge of the bluffs, (poorly) blocked off by chain-link fences, sits what's left of an early twentieth-century resort now known as **Sunken City**, where the crumbling streets and housing foundations, much of them covered in graffiti, are officially off limits to the public. Despite the perilous footing in places and countless warning signs, risk-takers will enjoy exploring one of the strangest and most evocative landscapes in LA. Fans of *The Big Lebowski* will recognize this as the spot where Walter and the Dude try to dispose of Donny's ashes, to little avail.

Inland, **Point Fermin Lighthouse**, 807 Paseo del Mar (Tues–Sun 1–4pm, tours usually on the hour; donation suggested; Ⓣ310/241-0684, Ⓦwww.pointfermin lighthouse.org), once contained a 6600-candlepower light and beamed it 22 miles out to sea. Ending its service during World War II, the lighthouse fell into disrepair until, in 2004, it was spruced up and opened to the public. Now you can get a sense of its quaint old Victorian style and take a peek from the chamber where the light used to beam; there's also an outdoor whale-watching station where you can read up on the winter migrations. Bottle-nosed dolphins can often be seen during their fall departure and spring return as well.

Just north, on a windswept hill overlooking the Pacific, is **Angel's Gate Park**, 3601 Gaffey St (daily 10am–5pm), which has sports facilities, a swimming pool and cultural centre with occasionally interesting art exhibits (same as park hours; free). At the top of the hill, a central pagoda contains the **Korean Bell of Friendship**, a 17-ton copper-and-tin gift from South Korea. Inscribed with Korean characters and twelve lines representing the signs of the zodiac, the bell has no clapper; instead, a hefty log strikes the instrument only Korean and American independence days, and New Year's Eve. It's a fine spot for photos and, not surprisingly, a regular backdrop for weddings.

Cabrillo Marine Aquarium and beyond

Below the bluffs is the excellent **Cabrillo Marine Aquarium**, 3720 Stephen White Drive (Tues–Fri noon–5pm, Sat & Sun 10am–5pm; $5, kids $1, parking $1/hr; ⓣ310/548-7562, ⓦwww.cabrilloaq.org), where a diverse collection of marine life has been assembled into tanks and assorted exhibits: everything from predator snails and sea urchins to larger displays on otters, seals and whales. Fully visible from the aquarium, a short jetty extends to a 1913 **breakwater** that is over 9200ft long, constructed from three million tons of rock hauled over from Santa Catalina Island, and marks the harbour entrance. At the end of it sits the **Angel's Gate Lighthouse**, a 75-foot-tall Romanesque-styled monolith that blasts its automated foghorn twice per minute, using a rotating green light to direct ships into the protected harbour and helping them avoid the rock seawall.

Wilmington

North of San Pedro, **WILMINGTON** is the centre of LA's petroleum industry, and holds the third-largest oil field in the entire US, extending from the Palos Verdes Peninsula to the bay outside Long Beach. The city's stark industrial landscape, dotted with derricks and refineries and massive towers spurting jets of flame, has been on display in Hollywood films such as *Terminator 2*. However, it's also the home of several key structures from LA history. The first, the grand **Banning House**, 401 East M St (guided tours at the bottom of the hour Tues–Thurs 12.30–2.30pm, Sat & Sun 12.30–3.30pm; $5; ⓣ310/548-7777, ⓦwww.banningmuseum.org), is an 1864 Greek Revival estate that was the residence of mid-nineteenth-century entrepreneur **Phineas Banning**, who made his fortune when the value of his land increased astronomically as the harbour was developed. Through his promotion of the rail link between Wilmington and Downtown LA, he also became known as "the father of Los Angeles transportation", and helped push for the creation of a breakwater and lighthouse as well. His 23-room house remains an engaging spot to visit, full of opulent Victorian touches (chandeliers, elegant place settings and the like) and several restored carriages and stagecoaches kept in an outside barn.

Also in town is the **Drum Barracks Civil War Museum**, 1052 Banning Blvd (tours Tues–Thurs 10am & 11.30am, Sat & Sun 11.30am & 1pm; $5; ⓣ310/548-7509, ⓦwww.drumbarracks.org), originally part of a military base called Camp Drum and named for its commander, Richard Drum. Today, the only building remaining is the rickety barracks, housing a hodgepodge of nineteenth-century military antiques and artefacts, notably a 34-star US flag and an early version of a machine gun, as well as a complement of guns and muskets. In the 1860s, this base was the Southwest headquarters for the US Army, which processed volunteers here before sending them to fight in the battles in the East, and a staging point for attacks on Confederate troops in neighbouring Arizona and New Mexico. In later decades it became a base for federal soldiers fighting the native tribes of the Southwest.

Long Beach

Along with San Pedro, **LONG BEACH** is the home of the Port of Los Angeles and a sizable Southern California city in itself, with many acres of tract homes and flat, sprawling development. Not surprisingly, almost all of its interesting sights are grouped near the water, away from the port to the west, as are the tourist-oriented attractions around **Shoreline Drive** and the historic architecture of **downtown**. Long Beach Transit connects downtown with the major shoreline sights by AquaBus shuttle ($1) or AquaLink water taxi ($5); information at Ⓣ562/591-2301, Ⓦwww.lbtransit.org.

Long Beach near the shore has some of the best *c*.1900 buildings on the coast. Inland from downtown, however, it's a different story – bleak housing projects that run continuously north into impoverished South Central LA. The only real point of interest is **Rancho Los Cerritos**, 4600 Virginia Rd, northeast of the junction of the 405 and 710 freeways (Wed–Sun 1–5pm, tours Sat & Sun on the hour; free; Ⓣ562/570-1755, Ⓦwww.rancholoscerritos.org), the centre of what was once a 27,000-acre tract that was part of a 1784 Spanish land grant of 300,000 acres. This U-shaped adobe dates from 1844 and sits on five leafy acres with a number of cypress and black locust trees, a delightful garden of roses, herbs and exotic plants, and an

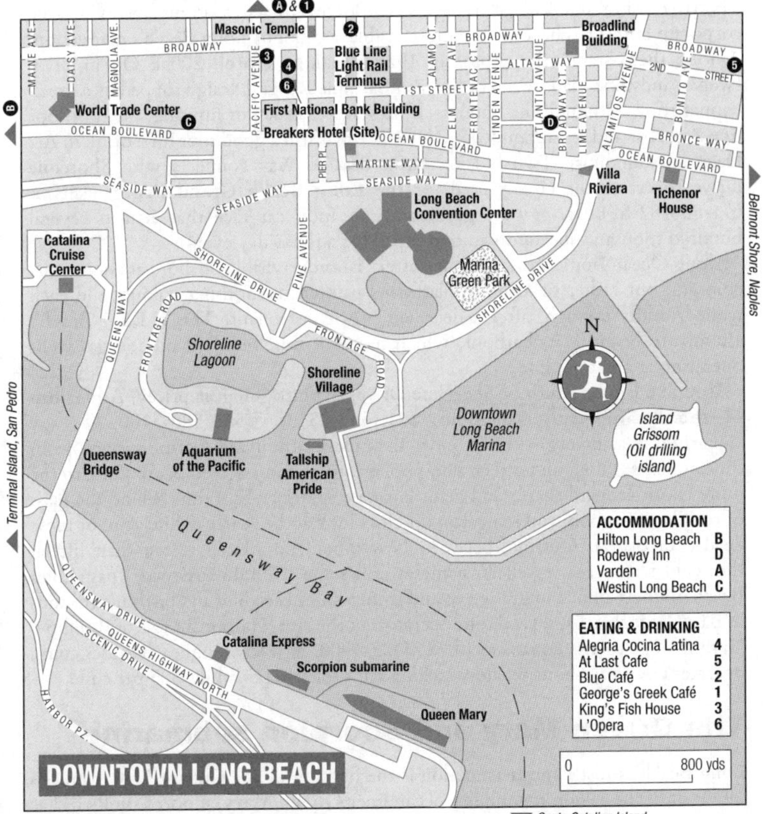

antiquated water tower. The orchard features the kind of citrus fruits, avocados, nuts and cherimoyas that once flourished here. Fortunately, the site is easily accessible, via the 710, to Long Beach's more prominent attractions near the harbour.

Shoreline Drive and around

Since the early 1900s, Long Beach has sold itself as a splashy resort and, while it's difficult to imagine a romantic getaway nestled behind an industrial port basin, the city keeps trying. Its major seaside amusements now sit close to the curving strip of **Shoreline Drive**, an area that was much more of an entertainment centre a century ago than it is today.

Around 1910, Long Beach developed its municipal pier, known as "**The Pike**", which teemed with street vendors and throngs of tourists queuing up for such thrilling rides as the Jack Rabbit Racer and Salt Water Plunge. These days, the focus of attention is **Shoreline Village**, just south of Shoreline Drive (Ⓦwww.shorelinevillage.com), a ragtag collection of middling shops and restaurants. Aside from the bikes, boats and rollerblades for rent here, the only real draw is the **Tallship American Pride**, a 130ft cutter which is a simulation of an 1848 vessel, offering tourists three-hour whale-watching outings with lunch provided (Sat & Sun 10am–1pm & 1.30–4.30pm; $35–45; by reservation only at Ⓣ714/970-8801, Ⓦwww.americanpride.org).

North of Shoreline Village, along Ocean Boulevard, a row dominated by upscale corporate hotels has become the most visible symbol of Long Beach's renovation. Among them stands the appealing 1926 **Breakers Hotel**, 200 E Ocean Blvd, twelve sandstone-clad stories of Spanish Baroque Revival design topped by a green copper roof. Although the hotel itself now serves as senior housing, the top-floor *Sky Room* bar and restaurant (Ⓣ562/983-2703) is still a good spot for a drink in Art Deco surroundings. Two blocks south, Seaside Way connects with Shoreline Drive to create the circuit used for the **Long Beach Grand Prix** (tickets at Ⓣ1-888/82-SPEED, Ⓦwww.gplb.com), an Indy car race that attracts several hundred thousand spectators in mid-April for a three-day event.

Along Ocean Boulevard, the four pastel "**islands**" visible offshore are not resort colonies, but rather oil-drilling platforms painted in soothing colours and each named, oddly enough, after a deceased NASA astronaut. This is Long Beach's attempt to beautify its harbour, which has over four hundred oil and gas wells operating at any one time.

Around a lagoon south of Shoreline Drive, the intriguing, if pricey, **Aquarium of the Pacific** (daily 9am–6pm; $21, kids $13; Ⓣ562/590-3100, Ⓦwww.aquariumofpacific.org) exhibits more than eleven thousand marine species, from the familiar sea lions and otters, tide-pool creatures and assorted ocean flora, to the more exotic leopard sharks and giant Japanese spider crabs. From behind the glass of the Shark Lagoon, you can get an up-close look at the pearly-white grins of these deadly predators. Outside, between November and March, more than fifteen thousand fellow sea travellers' nemeses cruise the "**Whale Freeway**" past Long Beach on their annual migration to and from winter breeding and birthing grounds in Baja California. Of several tour operators in the area, Harbor Breeze, at Rainbow Harbor next to the aquarium (Ⓣ562/432-4900, Ⓦwww.longbeachcruises.com), operates good two-hour whale-watching trips for $40 per adult, $25 per child.

The Queen Mary and Scorpion submarine

Long Beach's most famous attraction is the flagship of the Cunard Line from the 1930s until the 1960s, the mighty ocean liner **Queen Mary**, moored on Pier H at the end of Queens Highway South (daily 10am–6pm; $25 self-guided tours, kids $13; combo tickets with Aquarium of the Pacific $35, kids $19; ⓣ562/435-3511, ⓦwww.queenmary.com). It was acquired by the city in 1964 with the sole aim of boosting tourism, which it has succeeded in doing, well beyond expectations. The ship lies across the bay, opposite Shoreline Village, and is accessible either by a lengthy walk or Long Beach Transit (see p.155). Now a luxury hotel, with somewhat overpriced rooms for what you get ($130), the ship offers exhibits that include extravagantly furnished lounges and luxurious first-class cabins, and a wealth of gorgeous Art Deco details in its glasswork, geometric decor and chic streamlining; there are also stores and restaurants, and even a wedding chapel. The site hosts numerous festivals throughout the year, from a celebration of all things Scottish to a reggae fest. In addition, various lounges, clubs and cabarets compete for your attention, and there are assorted "ghost" walks and Halloween events that try to make you believe the old boat is haunted. Also on site, the **Scorpion submarine** (same hours as Queen Mary; $11, or combo ticket $33; ⓦwww.russiansublongbeach.com) was used in the service of the Soviet, and then Russian, navy until 1994, carrying a payload of 22 nuclear weapons and powered by creaky diesel engines. Its antiquated technology and cramped crew quarters are, however, really only worth a look for those with a flair for Cold War nautical technology or anyone determined to prove they're not claustrophobic.

Downtown Long Beach

Running from Magnolia Avenue to Alamitos Boulevard and Ocean Boulevard to Tenth Street, **downtown Long Beach** offers a wide array of boutiques, antique dealers and diners, many of them around a three-block strip known as **The Promenade**, which can get quite busy on weekend nights. The downtown core is easily reached from Downtown LA via the Blue Line light rail, which terminates two blocks west of the Promenade at **Pine Avenue**. Beyond its nightlife, the area is excellent for having some of LA's best-preserved architecture – historic-revival buildings that have since been reborn as hotels, artists' lofts, galleries and nightclubs. Highlights include the **First National Bank Building**, 115 Pine Ave, a 1900 Beaux Arts structure with a resplendent clock tower; the 1903 **Masonic Temple**, 835 Locust Ave, whose stately columns and imperious facade now front condos; and the **Broadlind Hotel**, 149 Linden Ave, a graceful if faded neo-Italian Renaissance gem that's been closed for years.

Further east is the striking **Villa Riviera**, 800 E Ocean Blvd (ⓦwww.villariviera.net), a fourteen-storey Gothic Revival apartment block, recognizable by the high dormers on its pitched copper roof, pointed octagonal turret and narrow ground-level archways. The Villa was the second-tallest building in all of LA when built in 1929, and is still one of its most impressive. Just down the block, the 1904 **Tichenor House**, 852 E Ocean Blvd, a private, U-shaped Craftsman residence with Japanese touches, was designed by the famed firm of Greene & Greene (see Pasadena's Gamble House, p.168). Several blocks north, the **Museum of Latin American Art**, 628 Alamitos Ave (Wed, Fri–Sun 11am–5pm, Thurs 11am–9pm; $9; ⓣ562/437-1689, ⓦwww.molaa.com), is devoted to the broad subject of Hispanic art. Showcasing artists from Mexico to South America, the absorbing collection includes big names like Diego Rivera and José Orozco, as well as lesser-known newcomers working in styles that range from high modernism to magical realism. Four blocks west, **St Anthony Roman Catholic Church**, 600 Olive Ave (ⓣ562/590-9229), is one of LA's most colourful and eye-opening churches, an appealing mishmash of historic styles constructed in 1933 and remodelled two decades later. Note the eye-catching neo-Gothic stained glass and hexagonal turrets, along with the facade's sizable Byzantine golden mosaic, depicting the Virgin Mary amid flocks of angels.

East Long Beach

A mile east from the Villa Riviera, the **Long Beach Museum of Art**, 2300 E Ocean Blvd (Tues–Sun 11am–5pm; $7; ⓣ562/439-2119, ⓦwww.lbma.org), is partly housed in a stately 1912 Craftsman home, along with a newer pavilion, featuring a decent collection of early modernism, folk art, video art and Southern Californian art. A mile further, the affluent **Belmont Shore** district is full of designer shops and yuppified cafés, though there's not much to see.

From here, Second Street crosses man-made Alamitos Bay to reach the island community of **Naples**, supposedly designed after the Italian city – if that city was loaded with rows of T-shirt and trinket vendors. While the thin, circular **canal** may give you a romantic thrill during hour-long boat rides (daily 11am–11pm; $75 for two people; call Gondola Getaway for details ⓣ562/433-9595, ⓦwww.gondolagetawayinc.com), the place is still little more than a tacky aquatic suburb thronged with tourists.

Two miles north, **Rancho Los Alamitos**, 6400 Bixby Hill Rd (Wed–Sun 1–5pm, tours every half-hour; free; ⓣ562/431-3541, ⓦwww.rancholosalamitos.com), is a grand version of the typical nineteenth-century adobe, with six historic buildings and plenty of antiques and relics from the Spanish and Mexican eras. Built in 1806, the renovated ranch house is noteworthy for its four acres of gardens, where you can wander amid herbs, roses, cacti, jacaranda and oleander planted along the terraces and landscaped walks. Nearby, the campus of California State University at Long Beach is best known for its towering, dark-blue aluminum **Pyramid**, an athletic complex, but is mainly worth visiting for the **Earl Burns Miller Japanese Garden**, 1250 Bellflower Blvd (Tues–Fri 8am–3.30pm, Sun noon–4pm; free; ⓣ562/985-8885, ⓦwww.csulb.edu/~jgarden), a peaceful spot amid weeping willows, bamboo and Japanese maples.

Santa Catalina Island

Overlooked by many visitors, **SANTA CATALINA ISLAND** is an inviting mix of uncluttered beaches and wild hills twenty miles off the coast. Claimed by the Portuguese in 1542 as San Salvador, and renamed by the Spanish in 1602, the island's most longstanding inhabitants were the Tongva Indians, who in 1811 were forced to resettle on the mainland. Since then, the island has been in private ownership, and has over the years grown to be something of a resort – a process hastened by businessman **William Wrigley Jr** (part of the chewing-gum dynasty), who financed the Art Deco-styled **Avalon Casino**, the island's major landmark, in the 1920s, and used the island as a spring-training site for his baseball team, the Chicago Cubs, until the early 1950s.

Since 1975 the island has been almost entirely owned by the **Catalina Island Conservancy**, which maintains a sizable nature preserve here, and in more recent years Catalina has become a popular destination for boaters and nature lovers, and its small marina swells with luxury yachts and cruise ships in summer. Even so, the elegant hotels are unobtrusive among the whimsical architecture, and cars are rare – there's a ten-year waiting list to ferry one over. Consequently, most of the three thousand islanders walk, ride bikes or drive electrically powered golf carts.

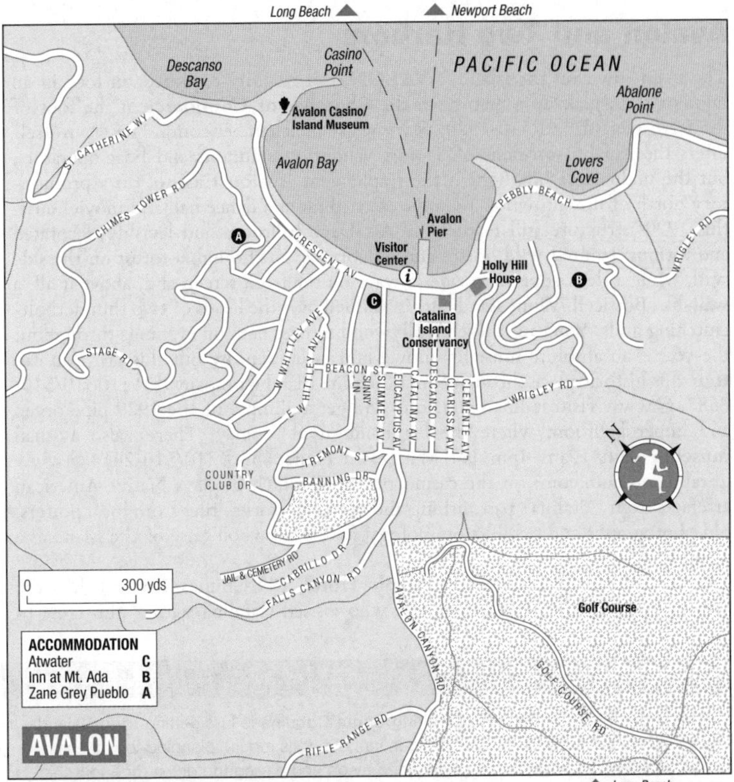

Long Beach
Newport Beach
PACIFIC OCEAN
Descanso Bay
Casino Point
Avalon Casino/ Island Museum
Abalone Point
Avalon Bay
Lovers Cove
PEBBLY BEACH
ST CATHERINE WY
CHIMES TOWER RD
CRESCENT AV
Avalon Pier
Visitor Center
Holly Hill House
WRIGLEY RD
Catalina Island Conservancy
STAGE RD
W WHITTLEY AVE
E W HITTLEY AVE
BEACON ST
SUNNY LN
SUMMER AV
EUCALYPTUS AV
CATALINA AV
DESCANSO AV
CLARISSA AV
CLEMENTE AV
WRIGLEY RD
TREMONT ST
COUNTRY CLUB DR
BANNING DR
JAIL & CEMETERY RD
CABRILLO DR
FALLS CANYON RD
AVALON CANYON RD
Golf Course
GOLF COURSE RD
RIFLE RANGE RD
0 300 yds
ACCOMMODATION
Atwater C
Inn at Mt. Ada B
Zane Grey Pueblo A
AVALON

Long Beach
SANTA CATALINA
Parsons Landing
Silver Peak
Isthmus Cove
Two Harbors
Catalina Cabins
Two Harbors
Newport Beach
Catalina Harbor
Airport-in-the-Sky
Little Harbor
Blackjack
PACIFIC OCEAN
Ben Weston Beach
Mt. Orizaba
Frog Rock
Avalon
Pebbly Beach
Hermit Gulch
See Avalon map
China Beach
Salta Verde Beach
Silver Beach
Wrigley Memorial & Botanical Garden
Seal Rock
0 5 miles

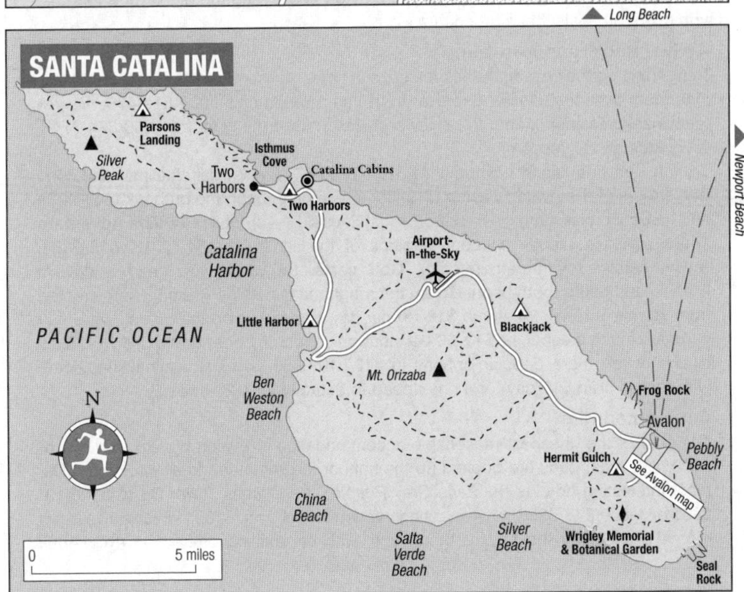

Avalon and Two Harbors

The main town on the island, **AVALON**, can be fully explored on foot in an hour or two; pick up a map from the **Chamber of Commerce** at the foot of the ferry pier (Ⓣ310/510-1520, Ⓦwww.catalinachamber.com). The town itself offers the usual assortment of T-shirt vendors, restaurants and boat operators, but the undeniable highlight is the resplendent **Avalon Casino**, on a promontory north of downtown at 1 Casino Way. Built as a dance hall and moviehouse, this 1920s structure still features an Art Deco ballroom and lavishly decorated auditorium: painted wild horses and unicorns roam through a forest on the side wall, while a sleek superhero rides a wave on the front screen and, above it all, a waif-like Botticelli Venus stands atop a seashell over the heads of two thunderbolt-clutching gods. You can still see Hollywood movies here on evenings throughout the year – an absolute must for movie buffs who venture out this far. You can **tour** this historic place through Santa Catalina Island Company ($19; Ⓣ310/510-8687, Ⓦwww.visitcatalinaisland.com) and get a glimpse of the 1929 pipe organ and upper ballroom where the big bands used to play. There's also a small **museum** (daily 10am–4pm, Jan–Mar closed Thurs; $5; Ⓣ310/510-2414 Ⓦwww.catalinamuseum.com) on the casino premises, which displays Native American artefacts from Catalina's past, fishing and ranching stories, tiles from local potters, old photographs and exhibits on biology, and Hollywood's use of the island as a scenic backdrop.

To the south, the **Zane Grey Pueblo Hotel**, 199 Chimes Tower Rd, is the former home of the Western author, who visited Catalina with a film crew to

Visiting the island

One of the major challenges of **visiting Santa Catalina** is just getting to the island itself. It's not difficult to get accommodation, but does require planning to make sure you don't end up staying in an overpriced resort and paying top dollar for a tour that you might otherwise take for cheap.

Arrival and transportation

Depending on the season, ferries run several times daily and cost $65–70 round trip. Operators include Catalina Express, from Long Beach (Ⓣ1-800/481-3470, Ⓦwww.catalinaexpress.com), and, from Newport Beach, Catalina Flyer (Ⓣ1-800/834-7744, Ⓦwww.catalina-flyer.com).

Santa Catalina Island Company (Ⓣ310/510-8687, Ⓦwww.visitcatalinaisland.com) offers tours of the Avalon Casino ($19–30), bus trips through the outback ($43–120), and harbour cruises and glass-bottom-boat rides ($18–42), while **Catalina Adventure Tours** provides slightly cheaper versions of the same ($17–64; Ⓣ310/510-2888, Ⓦwww.catalinaadventuretours.com). **Golf carts**, for which you need a driver's licence, and **bikes** (both banned from the rough roads outside Avalon) can be rented from stands in town. Bikes run $12–40 per day, depending on the model, while golf carts are much steeper, at $40–60 per hour only. Near the boat dock, Brown's Bikes is one of the more popular options (Ⓣ310/510-0986, Ⓦwww.catalinabiking.com), with rentals from $12/day for a one-speed to $40/day for a 21-speed.

Accommodation

The cost of the cheapest reasonable accommodation in Avalon hovers upwards of $100, and most beds are booked up throughout the summer and at weekends. The most interesting hotel is the *Zane Grey Pueblo*, 199 Chimes Tower Rd (Ⓣ310/510-0966 or 1-800/378-3256, Ⓦwww.zanegreypueblohotel.com; $150), which has sixteen rooms overlooking the bay or mountains, with an enticing off-season (Nov–April) shoot *The Vanishing American* and liked the place so much that he stayed, building for himself this "Hopi pueblo" house, complete with beamed ceiling, stark white walls, and thick wooden front door. The hotel rooms (see box below) are themed after his books, and the pool is shaped like an arrowhead. Similarly, the **Inn on Mt. Ada**, at 398 Wrigley Terrace Rd on the south hillside of Avalon, was the 1921 Colonial Revival home of William Wrigley and is now an elegant hotel (see box below), with sweeping ocean views and a fine garden. Also striking is the **Holly Hill House**, 718 Crescent Ave, an 1890 Queen Anne cottage on a high bluff overlooking the bay, with an elegant, striped conical tower, and wraparound verandas. This and other local landmarks are viewable on the History Walk (Tues & Sat 2pm; $10; by reservation at ⓣ310/510-2414 ext 1) presented by Catalina Island Museum.

Several miles southwest of Avalon, the **Wrigley Memorial and Botanical Garden**, 1400 Avalon Canyon Rd (daily 8am–5pm; $5; ⓣ310/510-2897), administered by the Catalina Island Conservancy, displays all manner of natural delights on 38 acres, but is especially strong on native, endangered plants, such as indigenous varieties of manzanita, ironwood mahogany and the wild tomato – a poisonous member of the nightshade family. Also fascinating is the Wrigley memorial, where a striking **cenotaph**, made from Georgia marble, blue flagstone and red roof-tiles, honours the chewing-gum baron. A grand tiled staircase leads to an imposing Art Deco mausoleum where Wrigley was to have been interred – though he's buried elsewhere. While in the vicinity, you can check out the **Nature Center at Avalon Canyon**, 1202 Avalon Canyon Rd (daily 10am–4pm, winter closed Thurs; free; ⓣ310/510-0954), which has

weekday rate of $75. The cheapest overall is usually the *Atwater*, 125 Sumner Ave (May–Oct only; ⓣ310/510-2500 or 1-800/626-1496; $100), though there are units here that reach $390. If you really have a bundle to spend, the *Inn on Mt. Ada*, 398 Wrigley Rd (ⓣ1-800/608-7669, ⓦwww.innonmtada.com; $415), is the final word in Catalina luxury. One interesting choice is the *Banning House Lodge*, near Two Harbors (ⓣ310/510-4228; $213), a rambling Craftsman home that has twelve bed-and-breakfast rooms with a courtyard, continental breakfast and private baths. The only ultra-budget option is the basic Catalina Cabins (Nov–April only; ⓣ310/510-2800; $35–45), at Two Harbors, which have a shared kitchen and barbeques, but mostly bare-bones facilities. For more primitive camping facilities, Hermit Gulch is the closest site to Avalon and the busiest. Four other sites in Catalina's interior – Blackjack, Little Harbor, Parsons Landing and Two Harbors (all $14 per person, kids $7) – are much more distant, but also roomier. Book at ⓣ310/510-8368 or ⓦwww.scico.com/camping.

Outdoor activities

The waters around Catalina are rich in yellowtail, calico bass, barracuda, and sharks. On the pier in Avalon, Joe's Rent-a-Boat (ⓣ310/510-0455, ⓦwww.joesrentaboat.com) can get you started **fishing** with basic runabouts starting at $55/hour or $275/day, as well as kayaks ($15/hr) and pedal boats ($15/hr) for pleasure cruising using your own horsepower. On Descanso Beach beyond the Casino, Descanso Beach Ocean Sports (ⓣ310/510-1226, ⓦwww.kayakcatalinaisland.com) has similar kayak-rental rates, as well as **snorkelling** packages ($68/four hrs) and guided kayak tours ($40–80). **Snorkel** and **scuba** gear is available for rent at Catalina Divers Supply, on the pier and at the Casino (ⓣ310/510-0330 or 1-800/353-0330, ⓦwww.catalinadiverssupply.com), for $30 per day for a complete snorkel set, and $60 for the full scuba package.

displays on the endemic flora and fauna and the island, its unique ecosystem, and the importance of conservation to the area.

Northwest of Avalon, the small, isolated resort town of **TWO HARBORS** holds only about three hundred souls and sits on a little strip of land that connects Cherry Cove and Catalina Harbor. With a large marina and campground, the town is suitable enough for outdoor activities like kayaking, snorkeling, and scuba diving, but otherwise there's little to see.

The island interior

If you have the opportunity and a few spare days to explore it, venture into the rugged **island interior**, comprising 42,000 acres of wilderness, untouched by anything but the occasional wildfire (the latest was in 2007), and home to many indigenous creatures and plants, and more than one hundred types of native birds. You can take a **bus tour** if time is short (see box, p.160); if it isn't, get a map and a free **wilderness permit**, which allows you to hike and camp, from the Chamber of Commerce or from the **Catalina Island Conservancy**, 125 Claressa Ave (daily 8.30am–4.30pm; ⓣ310/510-2595, ⓦwww.catalinaconservancy.org), which owns and manages 88 percent of the island's land; mountain biking (the only type allowed in the outback) requires a $35 permit.

There are some unique **animals** roaming about the wildlands, among them the rare Catalina Shrew and the Catalina Mouse, bigger and healthier than its mainland counterpart thanks to abundant food and lack of natural enemies. There are also foxes, ground squirrels, pigs, bald eagles and quail, along with **buffalo**, descended from a group of fourteen left behind by a Hollywood crew filming Zane Grey's *The Vanishing American* in 1924; there is now a sizable herd of 150 or more wandering about the island.

8

The San Gabriel and San Fernando valleys

Running north of central LA, below the crests of their respective mountain ranges, lie the expansive **SAN GABRIEL** and **SAN FERNANDO VALLEYS**, which start close to one another a few miles north of Downtown and span outwards in opposite directions – east to the deserts around Palm Springs for the sloped foothills of the San Gabriel, west to Ventura on the California coast for the relatively flat San Fernando.

In the San Gabriel Valley, on the east side of the Verdugo Mountains, **Pasadena** is a small, patrician town full of great architecture and diligent historic preservation, for years the province of old money but more recently enlivened by tourist shopping dollars. The neighbouring cities of **South Pasadena** and **San Marino** also have their charms, particularly the latter's Huntington Library and Gardens, though the rest of the San Gabriel Valley holds much more dispersed pleasures – worth a look only if you're staying in the LA region for at least a week.

North of the Hollywood Hills, the San Fernando Valley offers an even more sprawling landscape, stitched together by seemingly endless ribbons of asphalt under a boiling summer sun. The upper-middle-class suburb of **Glendale** is mainly home to the famous cemetery Forest Lawn; while **Burbank**, further west, is studio central, accommodating the likes of Warner Bros, NBC, and, in its own municipal enclave, Universal – only Disney Studios can't be visited on a tour. Further west are the bulk of LA's suburbs, known collectively as **"the Valley"**, with historic attractions here and there, but mostly known for their copious mini malls. At the apex of the triangular San Fernando Valley, places like **San Fernando** have a rich heritage, while further north, exciting **Magic Mountain** easily outdoes Disneyland for death-defying rides.

The San Gabriel Valley

Set at the foothills of the San Gabriel Mountains, the **San Gabriel Valley** escapes the derision that Angelenos pile upon the San Fernando Valley. However, though it has genuine cultural cachet in many places, its eastern side has some of the basin's worst smog, blown this way from central LA.

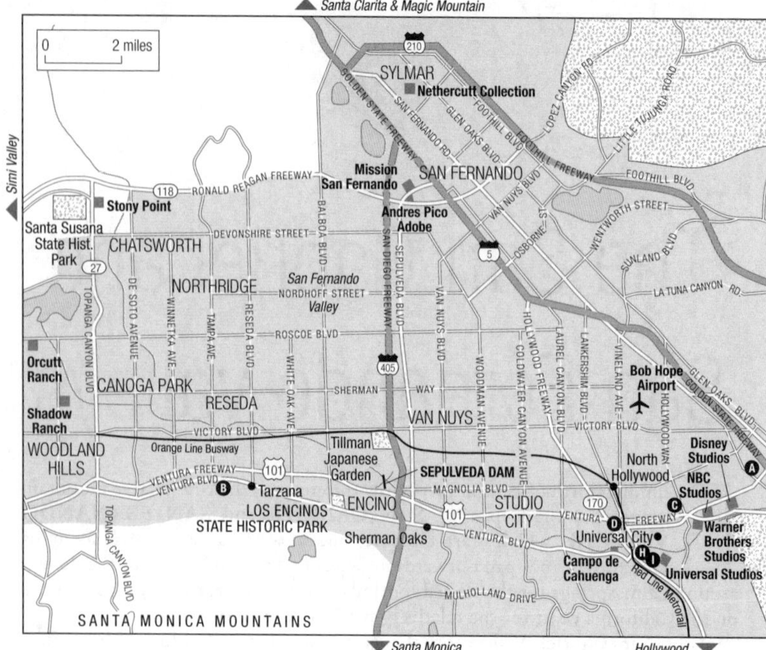

After its early settlement by native Tongva tribes and the later arrival of Spanish soldiers and missionaries, the San Gabriel Valley had become by the beginning of the twentieth century a choice region for American agriculture, growing predominantly grapes and citrus crops. Railroads brought new migrants, and by the 1950s, the foothills of the San Gabriel Mountains developed into another populous arm of LA, with suburban ranch houses and swimming pools taking the place of ranches and orange groves. One thing that has not changed, however, is the torrential flooding. Thanks to its specific climate and geography, the Valley has always been a prime spot for **winter deluges**: great cascades of water sweep down the hillsides, turning into mudslides by the time they reach the foothills, and then charging through the canyons and destroying all in their wake – including encroaching homes. This problem has been an occasional impediment to hillside growth, but with the creation of huge "**catch basins**" to contain the mudslides, real-estate developers have been able to push growth further up into the mountains.

Pasadena

At the western edge of the San Gabriel Valley, **PASADENA** is a mix of old-fashioned charm and contemporary appeal. Located ten miles northeast of Downtown LA, and connected to it by the rickety Pasadena Freeway (110 north), Pasadena was, like much of LA, settled by Midwesterners (in this case from Indiana) and even today retains a measure of its patrician style and genteel habits. The **Rose Parade**, an annual New Year's Day event dating back to 1890, is one reflection of this heritage – LA's most famous festival – as are the grand estates of the **Arroyo Seco** neighbourhood and the stylish Spanish Revival architecture of downtown Pasadena.

In the 1970s and 80s, Pasadena was in a slump, its greying population dying and leaving behind a number of decaying estates and an unkempt downtown.

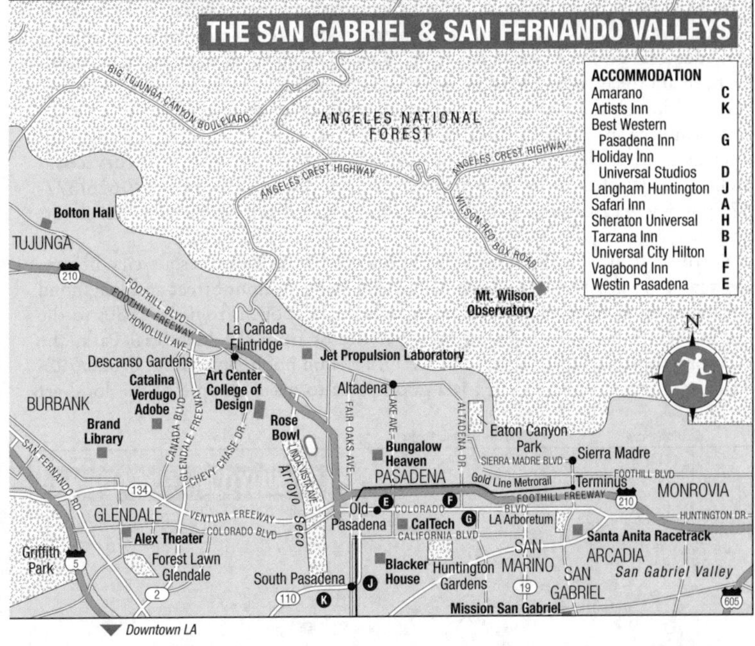

However, once urban-renewal dollars began flowing in the 1990s, tourists rediscovered the town, especially its **Old Pasadena** commercial strip and architectural treasures like the **Gamble House**. Not surprisingly, most of the city's appeal can be found either in the blocks surrounding Old Pasadena or in Arroyo Seco; while the burg stretches miles eastward, there's little reason to venture in that direction unless you're searching for cheap accommodation.

If you're in need of information, go to the **Pasadena Visitors Bureau**, 300 E Green St (Mon–Fri 9am–5pm, Sat 10am–4pm; Ⓣ626/795-9311, Ⓦwww.pasadenacal.com), which provides **maps** and booklets detailing self-guided tours of city architecture and museums. The local preservation society, **Pasadena Heritage**, offers regular tours of area landmarks – including an excellent 90min overview of Old Pasadena on the first Saturday of the month (9am; $10; reserve at Ⓣ626/441-6333, Ⓦwww.pasadenaheritage.org).

Downtown Pasadena

Bordered by Lake Avenue, California Boulevard, and the 210 and 710 freeways, **downtown Pasadena** is one of LA's few traditional downtowns, with fine municipal architecture and worthwhile restaurants and shops. It's easily navigable on foot as well: most places of interest are located near **Colorado Boulevard**, the city's commercial axis. On and around this boulevard, between Fair Oaks and Euclid avenues, is **Old Pasadena** (Ⓦwww.oldpasadena.org), a mix of antique sellers, book stores, cafés, boutiques and theatres, which gets quite crowded on weekends. It's also worth a visit in early October, when the PasadenART Weekend occurs (Ⓦwww.pasadenaartweekend.com), a three-day mix of museum exhibits, an art walk around the local galleries and other art-themed events that can be quite engaging. The handy **Gold Line** light rail (see p.27) links to Downtown LA, with the stop at Memorial Park being the most convenient for Old Pasadena.

Just south of Colorado Boulevard is the fascinating **Castle Green**, also known as "Hotel Green", 99 S Raymond St, formerly a 1903 resort that centred around a now-demolished hotel across the street. Later additions included the apartments that remain today, plus a **bridge** that crossed Raymond Avenue to link the structures. Although the walkway, which was billed as the "Bridge of Sighs" after the Venetian version, has been sliced in half and now stops in mid-air, its design still fascinates, with everything from Spanish-tiled domes and turrets to curvaceous arches. The Castle itself offers occasional tours of the site ($20; info at ⓣ626/577-6765, ⓦwww.castlegreen.com), which is understandably popular for film shoots and weddings.

North of Colorado Boulevard, the **ruins** of the old Romanesque city library, located in what is now **Pasadena Memorial Park**, Walnut Street and Raymond Avenue, hint at the building's grandeur when it was open from the 1880s to the 1930s, before being demolished in 1954. Across from the Memorial Park, the **Armory Center**, 145 N Raymond Ave (Tues–Sun noon–5pm; free; ⓣ626/792-5101, ⓦwww.armoryarts.org), is a good place to get a glimpse of the local art

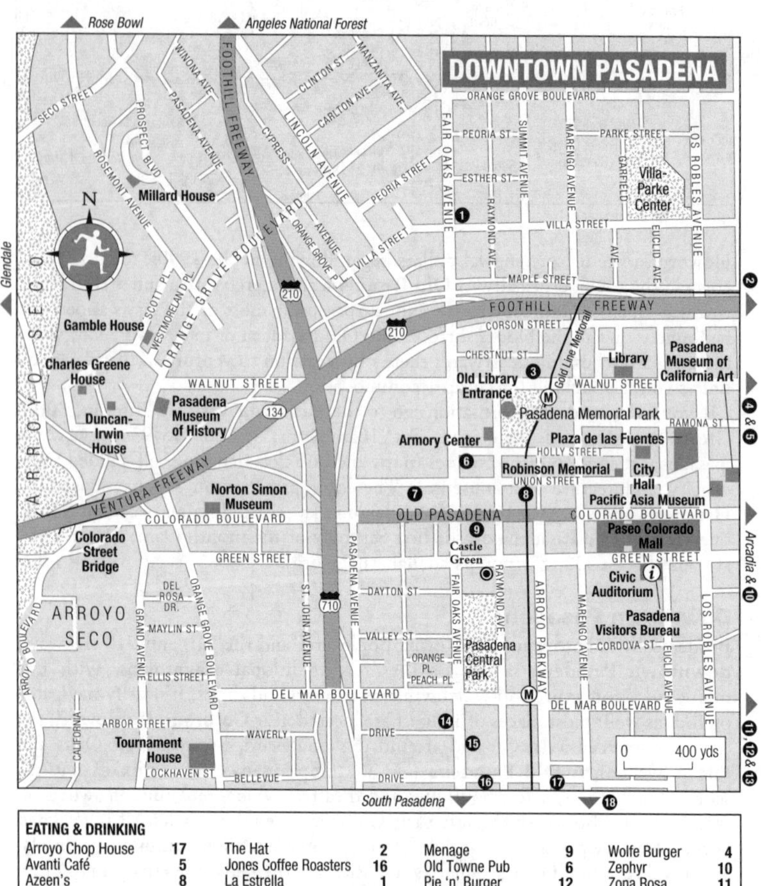

EATING & DRINKING

Arroyo Chop House	17	The Hat	2	Menage	9	Wolfe Burger	4
Avanti Café	5	Jones Coffee Roasters	16	Old Towne Pub	6	Zephyr	10
Azeen's	8	La Estrella	1	Pie 'n' Burger	12	Zona Rosa	11
Café Santorini	7	Magnolia	13	Rose Tree Cottage	18		
Gale's	15	Marston's	3	Saladang	14		

scene, showing a mix of community folk art and professional avant-garde and modernist creations. Further east, on Garfield Avenue at Union Street, you'll find two nine-foot bronze sculptures – strange, disembodied heads gazing out at an intersection – of the great baseball pioneer **Jackie Robinson** and his brother, **Frank**, winner of a silver medal at the 1936 summer Olympics in Berlin. The Robinsons were raised in town and Jackie went to junior college here before transferring to UCLA. In the brothers' eyeline is the city's grand centrepiece, **Pasadena City Hall**, 100 N Garfield Ave (Mon–Fri 9am–5pm; ⓣ626/744-7073), one of several city buildings in Mediterranean styles – in this case 1920s Spanish Baroque Revival. Set on a wide city plaza, the structure has a large, tiled dome and imposing facade with grand arches and columns, and an elegant garden with a patio and fountain, all of which make it more impressive than LA's City Hall.

Plaza de las Fuentes and around

Across Euclid Avenue from City Hall, **Plaza de las Fuentes** is landscape architect Lawrence Halprin's postmodern public square, with colourful tile work, bubbling little fountains and quirky sculptures, which makes a good spot to enjoy the sun or read a book.

The engaging **Pacific Asia Museum**, diagonally southeast at 46 N Los Robles Ave (Wed–Sun 10am–6pm; $9; ⓣ626/449-2742, ⓦwww.pacificasiamuseum.org), is modelled after a Chinese imperial palace, with a sloping tiled roof topped with ceramic-dog decorations, inset balconies and dragon-emblazoned front gates. For 25 years, until 1948, this was the home of collector Grace Nicholson, who started the expansive collection, which now includes thousands of historical treasures and everyday objects from Korea, China and Japan, including decorative jade and porcelain, various swords and spears, and a large cache of paintings and drawings. In the museum's peaceful **courtyard garden**, koi fish rest in pools beneath marble statues and a variety of trees native to the Far East. Just around the corner, the **Pasadena Museum of California Art**, 490 E Union St (Wed–Sun noon–5pm; $7; ⓣ626/568-3665, ⓦwww.pmcaonline.org), offers an eye-opening focus on the many aspects of the state's art since it became part of the Union in 1850, with a strong tilt to the contemporary, in all kinds of media from painting and photography to installation and digital art. Kenny Scharf's colourful graffiti murals, which jump off the walls with lurid primary hues and comic-book-like characters, are unfortunately confined to the walls of the museum's parking garage.

Bungalow Heaven and CalTech

Two miles northeast of Old Pasadena, the **Bungalow Heaven** historic district, bordered by Washington and Orange Grove boulevards and Hill and Catalina avenues, features some eight hundred quaint Craftsman bungalows that offer a glimpse of what much of the city looked like in the early 1900s. For Arts and Crafts enthusiasts, the neighbourhood association puts on a yearly **tour** on the last Sunday in April ($18–20; information at ⓣ626/585-2172, ⓦwww.bungalowheaven.org), peeking into six to eight of the classic structures. Further south, the commercial strip of **South Lake Avenue** (ⓦwww.southlakeavenue.com) has seven hundred or so mostly chain retailers, worth a stroll if you're in the mood to shop.

A few blocks east of Lake Avenue on California Boulevard, the **California Institute of Technology**, or **CalTech**, campus is best known for its "cool nerd" students and media-friendly seismologists who inevitably pop up on the local news every time a major temblor rumbles through LA. However, CalTech is worth visiting for its splendid assortment of pre-World War II architecture, notably the Spanish Baroque-inspired buildings of LA Central Library designer **Bertram Goodhue** and the Islamic-styled work of Edward Stone. Two-hour

architecture tours depart from the Spanish Colonial-style Atheneum, 551 S Hill Ave (Sept & Oct & Jan–June fourth Thurs of month, Nov third Thurs; 10.30am; free; reserve at ⓣ626/395-6328, ⓦwww.caltech.edu), while for your own, self-guided campus tour, get a brochure from the visitor centre at 315 S Hill Ave (Mon–Fri 9am–5pm).

The Norton Simon Museum

Just across the 710 freeway from downtown Pasadena, the collections of the **Norton Simon Museum**, 411 W Colorado Blvd (Wed–Mon noon–6pm, Fri closes 9pm; $8, students free; ⓣ626/449-6840, ⓦwww.nortonsimon.org), merit at least an afternoon of wandering through its dramatic, intimate galleries, which feature some of the best examples of Old World art on the West Coast.

The museum's focus is **Western European painting** from the Renaissance to early modernism. It's a massive collection, much of it rotated, but most of the major pieces are usually on view. Highlights include Dutch paintings of the seventeenth century – notably Rembrandt's vivacious *Titus, Portrait of a Boy* and Frans Hals's austerely aggressive *Portrait of a Man* – and Italian Renaissance work including Botticelli's tender *Madonna and Child with Adoring Angel*, Giorgione's leering *Bust Portrait of a Courtesan*, and Raphael's lovely modelling of the serene figures of the *Madonna and Child with Book*. There's a good sprinkling of French Impressionists and post-Impressionists: Monet's light-dappled *Mouth of the Seine at Honfleur*; Manet's plaintive *Ragpicker*; and Degas' *The Ironers*, capturing the extended yawn of a washerwoman. Other highlights include Jan Steen's *Wine is a Mocker*, an image of rural peasants assisting a drunken bourgeoise as she lies pitifully in the dirt; and Tiepolo's *The Triumph of Virtue and Nobility over Ignorance*, in which the winged, angelic victors gloat over their symbolic conquest of the wretched, troll-like figure of Ignorance.

Unlike the Getty Center (see p.115), the Norton Simon also boasts a solid collection of **modernist greats**, from Georges Braque and Pablo Picasso to Roy Lichtenstein and Andy Warhol, with figures such as Robert Irwin, Richard Diebenkorn, Ed Kienholz and Ed Ruscha adding a California bent to the collection. As a counterpoint to the Western art, the museum has a fine collection of **Asian art**, including highly polished Buddhist and Hindu figures, some inlaid with precious stones, and many drawings and prints – the highlight being Hiroshige's masterful series of coloured woodblock prints, showing nature in quiet, dusky hues.

The Arroyo Seco

The isolated pocket northwest of the junction of the 134 and 210 freeways, known as **Arroyo Seco**, or "dry riverbed" in Spanish, is home to some of LA's best residential architecture – a reminder of Pasadena's genteel upper-end traditions. Orange Grove Avenue leads into the neighbourhood from central Pasadena and takes you to the **Pasadena Museum of History**, 470 W Walnut St at Orange Grove (Wed–Sun noon–5pm; $5, kids free; ⓣ626/577-1660, ⓦwww.pasadenahistory.org), which has fine displays on Pasadena's artistic and cultural legacy and is surrounded by tasteful gardens. The museum is most interesting for the on-site **Feynes Mansion** (tours by appointment at ⓣ626/577-1660; $4), which, decorated with its original furnishings and paintings, is an elegant 1905 Beaux Arts mansion that was once the home of the Finnish Consulate. Much of the folk art on display comes from Pasadena's "twin town" of Jarvenpää in Finland.

It's the **Gamble House**, 4 Westmoreland Place (hour-long tours every 20–30min Thurs–Sun noon–3pm; $10; ⓣ626/793-3334, ⓦwww.gamblehouse.org), though, that's Pasadena's architectural centrepiece, the crown jewel in the rich architectural legacy of the brothers **Charles and Henry Greene**. Built in 1908 for David Gamble, of the consumer-products giant Proctor & Gamble, this masterpiece of Southern Californian Craftsman architecture helped give rise to a style that's replicated all over the state, freely combining elements from Swiss chalets and Japanese temples in a romantically sprawling, shingled mansion. The interior too was crafted with exacting attention to detail, and all the carpets, cabinetry and lighting fixtures were designed for the house. The area around the Gamble House has at least eleven other private homes by the two brothers, including **Charles Greene's house**, 368 Arroyo Terrace, and the picturesque **Duncan-Irwin House**, around the corner at 240 N Grand Ave, a perfect two-story Craftsman with stone lanterns and a rustic stone wall out front, with shrubs and foliage wending their way into the design. Also worth a look is San Marino's Blacker House (see p.170), considered their best home after this one.

A quarter of a mile north of here is Frank Lloyd Wright's "La Miniatura", also known as the private **Millard House**, which you can glimpse through the gate around 585 Rosemont Ave, a small, concrete-block house supposedly designed to look like a jungle ruin, with thick foliage growing over Mayan-style architecture. The preservation organization Pasadena Heritage hosts tours that discuss this and other notable homes, in the Arroyo Seco and elsewhere (see p.165). Several miles north at 1700 Lida St, Craig Ellwood's **Art Center College of Design**, a monumental steel-and-glass span crossing a natural ravine, is home to one of the area's best schools for groundbreaking modern design. It also hosts eye-catching, often experimental modern sculptures and installations in the **Williamson Gallery** (Tues–Sun noon–5pm, Fri closes 9pm; free; Ⓣ626/396-2446, Ⓦwww.artcenter.edu/williamson).

The Rose Bowl and Tournament House

North of the arroyo, the historic 104,000-seat **Rose Bowl** was built in 1922, just off Arroyo Boulevard at Rose Bowl Drive and out of use most of the year. As a national historic landmark, it's where one of college football's five Bowl Championship Series games is played in early January, meaning every fifth year the Rose Bowl officially gets to decide the champion. It's also home to a popular monthly

Arroyo culture

The neighbourhood around the **Arroyo Seco** has shifted somewhat through the years. Orange Grove Boulevard, several blocks east of the Arroyo proper, was around the turn of the twentieth century lined with a series of grand estates, tagged "**Millionaires' Row**", with the local gentry using the Arroyo itself as a source of wood and a place to picnic. (The palaces went into decline by the mid-twentieth century, to be replaced eventually by the apartment blocks visible today.) At the time the Row was at its grandest, just after 1900, the Arroyo Seco was being built up by numerous **Arts and Crafts**-movement intellectuals, many from the East Coast. They were inspired by the English example of William Morris, and preached a return-to-nature philosophy that reacted against precious Victorian ornamentation along with industrialized culture in general. Built in the Arroyo's wooded lots amid craggy rocks and rugged cliffsides, the resulting Craftsman monuments were manifestations of a new **Arroyo culture**, its artisan practitioners prized for working with wood, clay and stone. Not surprisingly, one of their heroes was Charles Lummis, famed for his eponymous boulder house in Highland Park (see p.65), and an equally prominent intellectual of the time. Architects Charles and Henry Greene and Frank Lloyd Wright were all attracted by the Arroyo too, if not full believers in its attendant ideology. The culture faded, however, as much of the area was bought up by wealthy Angelenos in 1910–30. Fortunately, the architecture has been largely preserved – even as prices on the homes have predictably skyrocketed.

flea market (second Sun of month; $8, reserve tickets at ⓣ323/560-7469, ⓦwww.rgcshows.com) and, in the autumn, the place where the UCLA football team plays its home games (tickets at ⓣ310/825-2101, ⓦwww.uclabruins.com).

To the south on Arroyo Boulevard, pass under the monumental spans of the **Colorado Street Bridge**, a 1486-foot monolith of curving concrete, built in 1913, to reach the **Tournament House**, 391 S Orange Grove Blvd (tours Feb–Aug 2pm & 3pm; free; ⓣ626/449-4100, ⓦwww.tournamentofroses.com), the administrative headquarters of the annual **Rose Parade**, which began in 1890 to publicize the mild Southern California winters, and now attracts over a million visitors every year to watch its marching bands and elaborate flower-emblazoned floats. The mansion itself is a pink 1914 Renaissance Revival gem, once owned by gum king William Wrigley, and well worth a look for its grand manor and surrounding gardens – containing up to 1500 types of roses.

South Pasadena

For all its historic architecture and small-town appeal, **SOUTH PASADENA** only exists as it is today because of a successful series of lawsuits over the past thirty years fighting the completion of the **710 freeway**, which would have divided the town in half and wiped out a thousand homes and seventy-odd historic sites. The city's main strip, **Fair Oaks Avenue**, used to be part of the famous **Route 66**, and it's here where you can find such eye-catching sights as the landmark, now-closed **Rialto Theater**, no. 1023, a faded 1925 movie palace that's also been a theatrical stage and vaudeville venue. **Meridian Avenue**, which parallels Fair Oaks Avenue several blocks west, takes you through the quaint Victorian-era homes south of the 110 freeway and into the larger residences north of it. On the southern end, the **Meridian Iron Works**, 913 Meridian Ave (Thurs 3–8pm, Sat 1–4pm; free; ⓣ626/799-9089, ⓦwww.sppreservation.org), is a sturdy old pile from 1887 that houses a cosy museum covering the history of the ironworks (and its former lives as a hotel, blacksmith and bicycle dealer), as well as the city itself, including assorted curios from a local ostrich farm.

To the north, Meridian Avenue runs into posh **Buena Vista Street**, notable for two grand dwellings by Charles and Henry Greene: the **Garfield House**, no. 1001, a 1904 Swiss-style chalet with numerous Craftsman elements that was once the home of murdered US President James Garfield's widow; and the adjacent **Longley House**, no. 1005, the brothers' first commission, an eclectic 1897 mix of revival styles from Romanesque to Moorish to Georgian. A few blocks east, at the end of Oaklawn Avenue, the Greene's 1906 **Oaklawn Bridge**, a restored concrete relic with vine-draped river-rock portals, spans the railway gully of the former Southern Pacific and Santa Fe line, which has been reincarnated for use by the Metrorail **Gold Line**, connecting Pasadena with Downtown LA.

San Marino

East of South Pasadena, uneventful **SAN MARINO** is known for some of LA's most privileged residents and widest neighbourhood streets. One of the most notable structures is the **Blacker House**, 1177 Hillcrest Ave, Charles and Henry Greene's 1907 Craftsman marvel, with dark wooden beams, horizontal layout, rustic appearance and Asian-influenced details. Unlike the larger Gamble House, you can't get into this one for regular tours, but it is worth a stop just to admire the design from the street.

Beyond architecture, there's little of interest in town beyond the legacy of railway and real-estate magnate **Henry Huntington**, preserved in his museum and gardens. Before hitting the museum, check out **El Molino Viejo**, 1120 Old Mill Rd (Tues–Sun 1–4pm; free; ⓣ626/449-5458, ⓦwww.old-mill.org), a weathered structure of brick, adobe stone and wooden beams, and built as a flourmill in 1816 by Spanish missionaries from Mission San Gabriel. Nowadays the old mill, with walls up to five feet thick in places, presents a few historical exhibits and photographs, plus an art gallery, gardens and diagrams of how water generated the power to make flour. Just to the west, the towering **Huntington Hotel**, atop a hill at 1401 S Oak Knoll Ave (see "Accommodation", p.214), began life as the *Wentworth Hotel* in 1906, later to be taken over by Huntington (and now part of the Langham chain). The hotel's Mediterranean-style main building boasts attractive gardens out back, and, further away, small bungalow-style residences for its swankiest guests.

The Huntington Library and Gardens

Without question, though, San Marino's highlight is its marvellous **Huntington Library, Art Collections and Botanical Gardens**, just off Huntington Drive at 1151 Oxford Rd (Mon & Wed–Fri noon–4.30pm, Sat & Sun 10.30am–4.30pm; $15 weekdays, $20 weekends; ⓣ626/405-2100, ⓦwww.huntington.org). This broad cache of art is based on the collections of Henry Huntington, the nephew of childless multimillionaire Collis P. Huntington, who owned and operated the Southern Pacific Railroad – which in the late-nineteenth century had a virtual monopoly on transportation in California. Henry, groomed to take over the railroad from his uncle, was dethroned by the board of directors and took his sizable inheritance to LA. Once there, he bought up the existing streetcar routes and combined them as the Pacific Electric Railway Company, which in turn controlled the Red Car line that soon became the largest transit network in the world, and helped make Huntington the largest landowner in the state. He retired in 1910, moving to the manor house he had built in San Marino, devoting himself full time to buying rare books and manuscripts, and marrying his uncle's widow Arabella and acquiring her collection of English portraits.

You can pick up a self-guided **tour** from the bookstore and information desk in the entry pavilion. The **library**, right off the main entrance, is a good first stop, its two-storey exhibition hall containing many manuscripts and rare books, among them a Gutenberg Bible, a folio of Shakespeare's plays, Thoreau's manuscript for *Walden*, Thomas Jefferson's architectural plans, John Audubon's *Birds of America*, and the **Ellesmere Chaucer**, a c.1410 illuminated version of *The Canterbury Tales*. Displays trace the history of printing and of the English language from medieval manuscripts to a King James Bible, from Milton's *Paradise Lost* and Blake's *Songs of Innocence and Experience* to first editions of Swift, Coleridge, Dickens, Woolf and Joyce.

The **Huntington Gallery**, a grand neoclassical mansion with an interior done out in Louis XIV carpets and later French tapestries, has works by Van Dyck and Constable and the stars of the whole collection – Gainsborough's *Blue Boy* and Reynolds' *Mrs Siddons as the Tragic Muse*. More striking are Turner's *Grand Canal, Venice*, a vibrant, hazily sunlit image of gondolas on the water, and Blake's mystical *Satan Comes to the Gates of Hell*, showing the ghostly, bearded figure of Death facing off with spears against a very human Satan and a serpentine Eve. Elsewhere, the **Scott and Erburu Galleries** display paintings by John Singleton Copley, Frederic Church, Benjamin West, Edward Hopper and Mary Cassatt, Wild West drawings and sculpture, and work by the architects Greene & Greene.

For all the art and literature, though, it's the grounds that make the Huntington truly worthwhile. The acres of beautiful themed **gardens** surrounding the buildings include a Desert Garden with the world's largest collection of desert plants, including twelve acres of cacti; lush rose, palm and subtropical gardens; a sculpture garden full of Baroque statues; and a Japanese garden dotted with koi ponds, cherry trees, and "moon bridges". While strolling through these botanical splendours, you might also visit the Huntingtons themselves, buried in a neo-Palladian **mausoleum** designed by John Russell Pope at the northwest corner of the estate, beyond the rows of an orange grove, built as a marble Greek temple and claimed to be the inspiration for the later 1930s Jefferson Memorial in Washington, DC.

North of Pasadena

The cities and districts **north of Pasadena**, such as **Altadena** and **La Cañada Flintridge**, sit on hillsides that lead into the **Angeles National Forest**, a 650,000-acre wilderness in the San Gabriel Mountains that is a favourite weekend spot for locals. There are numerous activities in the forest, from fishing and hunting to water skiing, biking and hiking. You can also **camp** (most free–$12) at any one of some fifty locations; most have five to twenty campsites, but the larger ones, Chilao and Los Alamos, hold around one hundred each. Keep in mind that some, but not all, parts of the forest require a $5 Northwest Forest Adventure Pass, which you can acquire from one of the three visitor centres or online. For locations, maps and the full range of activities on offer, contact the Forest Center (Ⓣ626/796-5541, Ⓦwww.fs.fed.us/r5/angeles).

The Jet Propulsion Laboratory and Descanso Gardens

In the foothills of La Cañada Flintridge is one of the cornerstones of America's military-industrial complex: the **Jet Propulsion Laboratory** (JPL), 4800 Oak Grove Drive (2hr tours alternate by week, Mon or Wed 1pm; free; by reservation only at Ⓣ818/354-9314, Ⓦwww.jpl.nasa.gov), devoted to the development of satellites, missiles and rockets, and secretive government projects. The tours are very popular, and you'll have to reserve well in advance and bring some form of ID – a visa or passport if you're a foreigner. Despite the JPL's obvious military mission, the lab chooses to focus on more PR-friendly displays, including replicas of the solar-system-exploring *Voyager* craft and the *Magellan* and *Galileo* vehicles that mapped Venus and Mars; photos from the Saturn-bound *Cassini* craft; and exhibits on the Hubble telescope, killer asteroids and Hollywood's version of outer space.

West off Foothill Boulevard, **Descanso Gardens**, 1418 Descanso Drive, La Cañada Flintridge (Fri–Mon 9am–5pm, summer also Tues–Thurs 9am–8pm; $8, kids $3; Ⓣ818/949-4200, Ⓦwww.descansogardens.org), squeezes all the plants you might see in the region's mountains into 155 acres of landscaped park, especially brilliant in spring when the wildflowers are in bloom. The centrepiece is a live-oak forest loaded with camellias, and there's also a Japanese teahouse and garden, with a narrow red footbridge, and a tranquil bird sanctuary for migrating waterfowl.

Angeles National Forest and around

North from the 210 freeway, the **Angeles Crest Highway** (Hwy-2) heads into the mountains above Pasadena, through an area once dotted with resorts and wilderness camps; to park in many areas, you'll need a Northwest Forest Adventure Pass (see opposite). One of the most scenic trails here, a rugged eleven-mile round trip, follows the route of the **Mount Lowe Scenic Railway**, once one of LA's biggest tourist attractions, a funicular that hauled tourists 1500 feet up to Echo Mountain, to the remains of "**White City**" – formerly a mountaintop resort of two hotels, a zoo and an observatory. Today, you'll see little more than crumbling walls, but the trail's expansive views of the basin can be striking when smog isn't a problem. To follow the old route of the railway (which ended service in 1937), drive north on Lake Avenue in Altadena until it ends at the intersection of Loma Alta Drive. Find a parking spot and head east along the trailhead. The site's historical committee (Ⓣ562/868-8919, Ⓦwww.mtlowe.net) offers information on the background and topography of this special place, along with a number of current and antique trail maps. More fine hiking in Altadena can be found further east in **Eaton Canyon Park**, 1750 N Altadena Drive, a natural refuge on 190 acres, and good for its hiking and horse riding trails. The on-site **nature centre** (Tues–Sun 9am–5pm; free; Ⓣ626/398-5420, Ⓦwww.ecnca.org) provides more information on the region's geology, flora and fauna.

Further north, the Angeles Crest Highway heads up to Mount Wilson, high enough to be a major site for TV broadcast antennae. At the peak, the **Mount Wilson Observatory** has a small **museum** (April–Nov 10am–4pm; $1; free tours Sat & Sun 1pm; Ⓣ626/440-9016, Ⓦwww.mtwilson.edu) where you can browse astronomical displays detailing the work of Edwin Hubble, who, aside from having a famous telescope named after him, developed the theory of cosmological expansion. The observatory was built by the Carnegie Institution in 1904, and although the last century of growth has added much light pollution, Carnegie researchers still find it useful, even if most of their groundbreaking discoveries are made in the Andes mountains. To peer through the 60-inch **observatory telescope** itself you'll need to go through the Mount Wilson Observatory Association (Ⓦwww.mwoa.org), which reserves blocks of time for its members ($20 fee) for viewing, and arranges regular group tours of the facility.

East of Pasadena

East of Pasadena, the San Gabriel Valley becomes a patchwork of small cities with a few appealing sights scattered across large distances. The one feature these places share is Foothill Boulevard, which before it was displaced by the Foothill Freeway (Hwy-210) was famously known as **Route 66**. The strip has declined in recent decades, though sections of the road have been smartened up with fresh neon and retro-flavoured building renovations. The Gold Line light rail runs from Downtown LA to Old Pasadena up to Sierra Madre, but isn't really convenient for accessing these far-flung sights.

Arcadia, Sierra Madre and San Gabriel

If you follow Foothill Boulevard out of Pasadena, you'll come to **ARCADIA**, a colourless suburb whose **LA County Arboretum**, 310 N Baldwin Ave (daily 9am–4.30pm; $5; Ⓣ626/821-3222, Ⓦwww.arboretum.org), contains many impressive gardens and waterfalls, and, of course, a great assortment of trees, arranged by their native continents. The gardens are grouped around various themes, from carnivorous plants and tropical blooms to rose and palm gardens, and native wildflowers and vegetables. This was the 127-acre home of Elias "Lucky" Baldwin, who made his millions in the silver mines of Nevada's Comstock Lode in the 1870s, settled here in 1875, and built a fanciful white mansion along a palm-tree-lined lagoon (later used in the TV show *Fantasy Island*) on the site of the 1839 Rancho Santa Anita. Nearby, Baldwin also bred horses and raced them on a track that has since grown into the **Santa Anita Park**, 285 W Huntington Dr (racing Oct to early Nov & late Dec to late April Wed–Sun; $5 admission; Ⓣ626/574-RACE, Ⓦwww.santaanita.com), still the most famous racetrack in California, with a Depression-era steel Art Deco frieze along the grandstand.

The foothill district of **SIERRA MADRE**, on the northern edge of Arcadia, lies directly beneath Mount Wilson and is worth a visit if you're a hiker. A fifteen-mile eight-hour round-trip trail up to the summit makes for an excellent, if tiring, trek; to find the route, take Baldwin Avenue north from the 210

Aqua in Los Angeles

On the north end of the San Fernando Valley, I-5 runs past two of LA's main reservoirs, the water carried by the **California Aqueduct**, travelling from the Sacramento Delta, and the **LA Aqueduct**, coming from the Owens Valley and Mono Lake on the eastern slopes of the Sierra Nevada Mountains.

How LA acquired the latter water source, however, is a shady matter indeed. Acting on behalf of water czar **William Mulholland**, agents of the city, masquerading as rich cattle barons interested in establishing ranches in the Owens Valley, bought up most of the land along the Owens River in the first years of the twentieth century before selling it, at great personal profit, to the city of Los Angeles. Tellingly, when the first rush of water was brought to the city with great fanfare, Mulholland publicly pronounced his triumph with the memorable command, "There it is! Take it!" The Owens Valley farmers didn't take this subterfuge lying down, however, and resorted to **dynamiting** sections of the aqueduct in later years. The violent tactics proved of little use, though, for as soon as the water began flowing, LA's San Fernando Valley began to blossom with suburbs, along with huge profits for its new Downtown property owners. These were the region's major bigwigs, bankers and real estate magnates who, with the *Los Angeles Times* as their propaganda organ, trumpeted the development as the height of civic duty, even as they were employing Mulholland's agents to trick the valley farmers into selling their land for a fraction of its potential value.

There is little doubt that the LA Aqueduct has served the interests of the city well, bringing water to two million people, but the morality and legality of such a distant supply of water is still disputed. After much controversy, various court decisions in the last sixteen years have required that the endangered Mono Lake area – the salty home of fascinating tufa (gnarled limestone) columns – be removed from the clutches of LA's water empire. This result (along with California's losing its grip on a generous portion of the Colorado River's water) has forced the city finally to get down to serious **water-management** policies, controlling the amount of the precious fluid used to water people's lawns and fill their swimming pools.

freeway until it becomes Mount Wilson Trail and ends at the trailhead. Part of the trail follows the **Mount Wilson Toll Road**, a narrow, antique route that was open to horses and cars for 45 years (until 1936) and, amazingly, hosted the occasional auto race as well; the Toll Road itself is an 18-mile round trip that terminates near the Mount Wilson Observatory (see p.173). South of Sierra Madre stands the valley's original settlement, the church and grounds of **Mission San Gabriel Arcangel**, 428 S Mission Drive (daily 9am–4.30pm; $5; ⓣ626/457-3035, ⓦsangabrielmission.org), in the heart of the small town of **SAN GABRIEL**. The mission was established here in 1771 by Junípero Serra and the current building finished in 1812. Despite decades of damage by earthquakes and the elements, the church and grounds have been repaired and reopened, their old winery, cistern, kitchens, gardens and antique-filled rooms giving some sense of mission-era life.

The San Fernando Valley

Home to eight-lane boulevards, countless minimalls, and nonstop tract housing, the **San Fernando Valley** is often derided by LA Westsiders as the epitome of dull, faceless suburbia. And indeed, other than theme parks and movie-studio tours, the valley has pretty sparse attractions; the more historically interesting sites are perched at the periphery of the Valley, while the concrete-and-asphalt suburbs sit closer to central LA.

The Valley's 1769 Spanish discovery predated the settlement of Los Angeles. After the US took possession of California and the Southern Pacific Railroad cut through it, the Valley rapidly transformed, going from a nineteenth-century tract of wheat fields and ranchos to an early twentieth-century expanse of citrus groves to a post-World War II dynamo of industry, media and, above all, suburban housing. The spark that made all this development possible was the 1913 construction of the LA Aqueduct (see box opposite). Today, the agricultural ghosts are apparent only in streets with idyllic names like Orange Grove, Walnut and Magnolia, and "bucolic" is the last word anyone would use to describe this sun-blasted desert of concrete and asphalt.

Glendale

West of Pasadena, beyond the Verdugo Mountains, **GLENDALE** is an upper-middle-class suburb that extends from Griffith Park all the way past the northern reaches of foothill cities like La Cañada Flintridge. At least its downtown is compact, south of the 134 freeway along Brand Boulevard. Apart from a handful of serviceable boutiques and restaurants (among them the terrific *Porto's Bakery*; see p.227), you'll find the **Alex Theater**, 268 N Brand Blvd, a striking piece of green-and-yellow Art Deco with a towering pylon, which now serves as a performing-arts venue (information at ⓣ818/243-ALEX, ⓦwww.alextheatre.org).

North of the 134, the city has a smattering of noteworthy sites, such as the modest **Catalina Verdugo Adobe**, 2211 Bonita Drive (grounds daily 7am–dusk; free), the oldest home in Glendale, dating from 1828 and retaining something of its original look, though a north wing was added later. Though the adobe itself is not open to the public, the gardens contain the knotty remains of the **Oak of Peace**, which, when it was alive, was said to be more than five hundred years old. It stood where in 1847 Mexican leaders agreed to surrender to US troops in the Mexican-American War, though the treaty signing occurred elsewhere two days later. To the northwest in Brand Park, the **Brand Library and Art Center**, or "El Miradero", 1601 W Mountain St (Tues & Thurs noon–8pm, Wed 10am–6pm, Fri & Sat 10am–5pm; free; ⓣ818/548-2051, ⓦwww.brandlibrary.org), looks like nothing else in LA. This white oddity from 1902 is said to be modelled on the East India Pavilion at Chicago's 1893 Columbian Exposition, and features a striking quasi-Islamic Spanish design of domes and minarets, now containing art and music books and periodicals. Plus, there are art exhibitions, musical recitals, lectures and numerous special events held here throughout the year. Also located in Brand Park is the so-called **Doctors House** (tours Sun 2–4pm; $2; ⓦwww.glendalehistorical.org/doctors.html), a charming Eastlake residence from 1888, which was named for three physicians who lived there successively. You can take a look at period decor, a projecting roofline and dormers, latticed white porches, and gardens with a gazebo.

Forest Lawn Glendale

For most visitors, the main reason to come to Glendale is to visit the city's famous branch of **Forest Lawn Cemetery**, 1712 S Glendale Ave (daily 8am–5pm; free; ⓣ1-800/204-3131, ⓦwww.forestlawn.com), at the vanguard of the American way of death for nearly a century. Founded in 1917 by one Dr Hubert Eaton, this soon after became *the* place to be buried, its pompous landscaping and pious artworks attracting celebrities by the dozen to fill out the plots. The graveyard's success has allowed it to expand throughout the LA region, notably with a branch near Griffith Park, in the Hollywood Hills (see p.86).

It's best to climb the hill and see the cemetery in reverse from the **Forest Lawn Museum** (open during park hours; free), whose hodgepodge of worldly artefacts includes coins from ancient Rome, Viking relics, medieval armour and a mysterious, sculpted Easter Island figure, discovered being used as ballast in a fishing boat in the days when the statues could still be swiped from the island. How it ended up here is another mystery, but it is the only one on view in the US. The museum also hosts regular shows that may feature assorted art, stained glass and funerary sculptures, among other things.

Next door to the museum, the **Hall of the Crucifixion-Resurrection** houses the colossal *Crucifixion* by Jan Styka – an oil painting nearly 195ft tall and 45ft wide, which you're only allowed to see during the ceremonial unveiling every hour on the hour. Besides this, Eaton owned a "re-creation" of Leonardo da Vinci's *Last Supper*, created in stained glass instead of fresco; it's housed in the Memorial Court of Honor, which is stuffed with replicas of Michelangelo's sculptures. Realizing that he only needed one piece to complete his trio of "the three greatest moments in the life of Christ", he commissioned *The Resurrection* – which is unveiled every half-hour. If you can't stick around for the ceremonial showings (with both, in any case, the size is the only aspect that's impressive), you can check out the scaled-down replicas just inside the entrance.

Oddly, Forest Lawn chooses to coyly downplay the presence of so many Hollywood glitterati lying in its grounds. Therefore, bring a cemetery tour booklet (found easily online or from a local bookseller) and, from the museum, walk down through the terrace gardens – loaded with sculptures modelled on the greats of classical European art, along with an ungainly thirteen-foot rendering of George Washington – to the **Freedom Mausoleum**, where you'll find a handful of the cemetery's better-known graves. Just outside the mausoleum's doors, Errol Flynn lies in an unspectacular plot (unmarked until 1979), rumoured to have been buried with six bottles of whisky at his side, while a few strides away is the grave of Walt Disney, who is not in the deep freeze as urban legend would have it. Inside the mausoleum you'll find Clara Bow, Nat King Cole, Jeanette MacDonald and Alan Ladd placed close to each other on the first floor. Downstairs are Chico Marx and his brother Gummo, the Marx Brothers' agent and business manager.

Back down the hill, the **Great Mausoleum** is chiefly noted for the tombs of Clark Gable (next to Carole Lombard, who died in a plane crash just three years after marrying him) and Jean Harlow, in a marble-lined room that cost over $25,000, paid for by fiancé William Powell. Amid all this morbid glamour, the cemetery has actually been the site of thousands of **weddings**, not least being Ronald Reagan's star-crossed wedlock with Jane Wyman in 1940.

Burbank

Although Hollywood's name is synonymous with the movies, in reality many of the big studios moved out of Tinseltown long ago, and much of the business of making films (and TV shows) is located west of Glendale in otherwise boring **BURBANK**. Hot, smoggy and ugly, Burbank nonetheless has an official "Media District" bustling with activity. **Disney** is the most visible of the studios, with Robert A.M. Stern's starry wizard-hat building, Riverside Drive at Keystone Street, visible from the 101 freeway just east of the Buena Vista St exit, housing hundreds of animators. Less appealing is Disney's other public face, its **Studio Office Building**, 500 S Buena Vista St, a clumsy effort from Michael Graves that has five of the Seven Dwarfs propping up the building's roof. As for touring the studio, forget it – the secretive company would rather have you plunk down your cash in Disneyland.

Nearby, **NBC**, 3000 W Alameda St (box office open Mon–Fri 9am–4pm; $8; reserve at ⓣ818/840-3537), offers an engaging 75min tour of its production

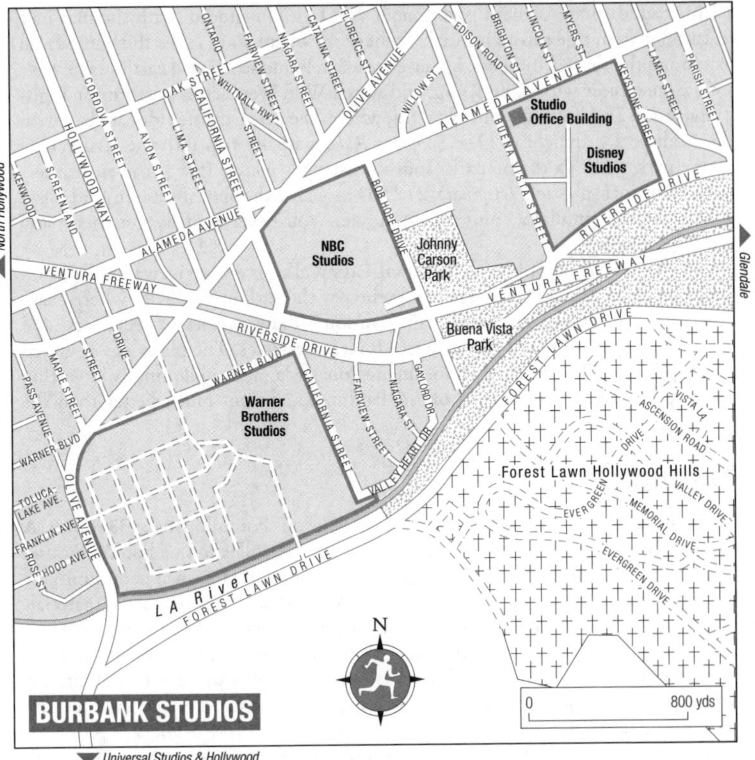

facility, even though only a handful of shows currently tape there. The studio also gives you the chance to be in the audience for the taping of a TV programme (phone ahead for free tickets), such as *The Tonight Show*. **Warner Brothers**, 4000 Warner Blvd at Hollywood Way, offers a tour (Mon–Fri 8.30am–4pm; $48; ⓣ818/972-TOUR, ⓦwww2.warnerbros.com/vipstudiotour) that takes you past the sound stages, around the production offices, and to the outdoor sets for movies and TV shows. Ultimately, you won't get to see any actual filming, but if you want to see a working environment of a studio, it's worth the money.

Beyond the studios, Burbank's greatest attraction is the oldest **Bob's Big Boy** in existence, 4211 W Riverside Drive (ⓣ818/843-9334, ⓦwww.bobs.net), a well-preserved "Googie"-style coffee shop from 1949, and home of the "Double Deck" hamburger. It's been used for a host of Hollywood flicks, and for good reason: the 70-foot-tall pink-and-white neon sign is a knockout. Occasionally on Friday nights, the restaurant hosts stylish hot-rod shows in the parking lot (5–10pm), and every Saturday and Sunday night, you can chow down on your burgers and fries with old-fashioned car-hop service (5–10pm).

Universal Studios and CityWalk

Just to the south along the 101 freeway, the largest of the backlots belongs to **Universal Studios** (hours vary, often summer daily 8am–10pm; rest of year daily 10am–6pm; two-day minimum ticket $69, kids $59; ⓣ818/508-9600, ⓦwww.universalstudioshollywood.com), where the four-hour-long "tours" are more like a trip around an amusement park than a visit to a film studio, with the first half featuring a tram ride through a make-believe set where you can see the house from *Psycho* and the shark from *Jaws*, experience a San Francisco-styled earthquake, have a close encounter with King Kong, and watch Wild West actors performing high-flying stunts and holding gunfights. Elsewhere, the other theme rides are based on the studio's TV franchises (*The Simpsons Ride*, a wacky trip into the Krustyland theme park within a theme park) and films such as *Jurassic Park* (close encounters with prehistoric plastic), *Terminator 2* (a 3-D movie with robot stuntmen) and *Shrek 4-D* (a motion simulator, plus a 3-D movie). You never actually get to see any filming, though.

Also part of the complex is **Universal CityWalk** (Ⓦwww.citywalkhollywood.com), an outdoor mall that's free to all who pay the parking fee ($14), where chain diners draw masses of families, chain boutiques draw gaggles of teenagers, and giant TV screens run ads for the latest Universal releases. The place was designed by shopping-mall architect extraordinaire Jon Jerde, and while mildly diverting for its pint-sized reproductions of LA landmarks, it's not much better than the usual massive mall.

Tujunga

Seven miles north of Glendale and Burbank on Foothill Blvd, **TUJUNGA** (tah-HUNG-ah) is mainly notable for its remarkable collection of boulder houses and bungalows built in the 1910s and 20s, the inspiration of a small community of Socialists who, like the dwellers in Pasadena's Arroyo Seco, believed earthy materials like wood and stone made for the best, and most moral, forms of construction. Their restored 1913 clubhouse, **Bolton Hall**, 10106 Commerce Ave (Tues & Sun 1–4pm; free; Ⓣ818/352-3420), hints at their aims, with a rocky central tower and interior with exposed wooden beams. This striking creation was LA's second historic monument (after the Avila Adobe; see p.50), and displays a good selection of antiques from its rich history – it has also doubled as the town's city hall, and its jail. Curiously enough, the structure's name actually honours an author named "Bolton Hall", a friend of the developer who gave rise to the surrounding town.

The western San Fernando Valley

Beyond Burbank, the **western San Fernando Valley** suburbs of Los Angeles – some of the more well known of which are **North Hollywood**, **Sherman Oaks**, **Van Nuys** and **Reseda** – are often collectively called "the Valley", immediately bringing to mind strip malls, fast-food joints and endless asphalt. The Valley is also the capital of America's **porn industry**, with internet demand making the low-rent video studios and distributors here an integral part of the local economy – all of it kept discreetly behind the closed doors of unmarked warehouses and office suites.

The first of the Valley's official points of interest is **Campo de Cahuenga**, across from Universal Studios – and a Red Line subway stop – at 3919 Lankershim Blvd, in North Hollywood (Sat & Sun 10am–2pm; donation; Ⓣ818/762-3998 ext 2, Ⓦwww.campodecahuenga.com). This is where generals John Frémont and Andres Pico signed the 1847 Treaty of Cahuenga between the US and Mexico – which led to the more famous Treaty of Guadalupe Hidalgo – thus ending the Mexican-American War, and later allowing the US to officially acquire California and the rest of the Southwest. The adobe on the grounds has recently been renovated to a condition more closely approximating its mid-nineteenth-century look, but it's still only a replica of an original 1840s structure. Every January you can watch a historical re-enactment of the events that made the site famous.

Several miles north, the **North Hollywood Arts District** (Ⓦwww.nohoartsdistrict.com), located around Magnolia and Lankershim boulevards between Burbank and the western San Fernando Valley (and accessible by the Metrorail Red Line), was named "NoHo" by county bureaucrats as a play on New York's SoHo. Otherwise it has little in common with that fabled place, its many performing-arts centres, theatres, and restaurants too spread out to make for any sort of easy strolling. Among the highlights are the 1926 El Portal Theatre, 5269 Lankershim Blvd (Ⓣ818/508-4200, Ⓦwww.elportaltheatre.com), which began as a vaudeville venue but now attracts mid-range theatrical productions, and the NoHo Arts Center, 11136 Magnolia Blvd (Ⓣ818/508-7101), which presents a regular rotation of mostly contemporary plays.

About six miles west off Burbank Boulevard in Van Nuys, the 6.5-acre **Tillman Japanese Garden**, 6100 Woodley Ave, near the 405 freeway (grounds Mon–Thurs noon–4pm, Sun 10am–4pm; hour-long tours by reservation only Mon–Thurs; $3; Ⓣ818/751-8166, Ⓦwww.thejapanesegarden.com), is a pleasant spot adorned with stone lanterns, bonsai trees, low bridges, a teahouse, and artful streams, islands and pools; the site uses reclaimed water from a nearby treatment plant and sits in the giant flood plain behind the **Sepulveda Dam**, visible along Burbank Blvd west of the 405 freeway. Thanks to Hollywood, the dam is perhaps the most famous sight in this part of the Valley, a monolithic, futuristic wall of concrete towers and abutments that's appeared in everything from *Grease* and *Escape from New York* to *Iron Man 2*.

Due southwest off Ventura Boulevard, the district of **Encino** sits near **Los Encinos State Historic Park**, 16756 Moorpark St (Wed–Sun 10am–5pm; free; Ⓣ818/784-4849, Ⓦlos-encinos.org), which includes all that remains of an original Native American settlement and later Mexican hacienda, along with an extensive cattle and sheep farm. In addition to a blacksmith's shop and lake fed by a natural spring, the main attraction is an 1849 adobe house, featuring high-ceilinged rooms that open out onto porches, shaded by oak trees (in Spanish, *encinos*), and kept cool by the two-foot-thick walls.

The Shadow and Orcutt ranches

At the western end of the Valley on Vanowen St, in **West Hills**, are a few minor historic points of interest, including the **Shadow Ranch**, 22633 Vanowen St (grounds Mon–Fri 9am–9pm, Sat & Sun 9am–5pm; free; Ⓣ818/883-3637), the centre of a 23,000-acre ranch that was controlled by land moguls I.N. Van Nuys and Isaac Lankershim, with some seventy barns and a thousand head of cattle. These days, the once-huge tract has been subdivided and sold off, and the thirteen-acre property is mainly notable for its great stand of eucalyptus trees imported from Australia over 120 years ago, along with a main ranch house that hosts occasional arts-and-crafts shows. To the northwest is the **Orcutt Ranch**, 23600 Roscoe Blvd (daily dawn–dusk; free; Ⓣ818/346-7449), where there's an impressive plot of ancient oaks, some five hundred rose bushes, and citrus trees and bamboo too, alongside a 1926 Spanish Colonial Revival ranch house with a romantic grotto and a large sundial. The ranch originally belonged to William Orcutt, the oil geologist who first found fossils in the La Brea Tar Pits, and initially spread out over two hundred acres – about ten times its current size.

The northern San Fernando Valley

A few miles east of Orcutt Ranch, Topanga Canyon Boulevard heads into the far northwest reaches of the Valley to **Stony Point**, just off Hwy-118, a bizarre sandstone outcrop that has been used for countless Westerns, usually for a climactic gun battle, and in recent decades as a venue for LA's contingent of rock climbers (for information, check out Ⓦwww.sowr.com). The area has a desolate spookiness about it, part of Santa Susana Pass State Historic Park (daily 8am–dusk; free; Ⓣ310/455-2465, see Ⓦwww.parks.ca.gov for directions), which includes the Old Santa Susana Stage Road that was part of the stagecoach route for travel between LA and San Francisco in the nineteenth century. Later, it was used as a hideout by the legendary late-nineteenth-century bandit Joaquin Murrieta, and during the late 1960s as a hangout for the Manson family, who lived for a time at the **Spahn Ranch**. The ranch had been part of a silent-film-era movie ranch where countless Westerns were filmed, and later, episodes of *Bonanza* and *The Lone Ranger*, but the entire works burned in 1970 and the place now appeals mainly for its scenic, rugged hiking trails.

San Fernando and Sylmar

At the northern tip of the Valley, the San Diego, Golden State, and Foothill freeways join together at I-5, the quickest route north to San Francisco. Standing near the junction, at 15151 San Fernando Mission Blvd in the small town of **SAN FERNANDO**, the church and many of the historic buildings of **Mission San Fernando Rey de España** (daily 9am–4.30pm; donation suggested; Ⓣ818/361-0186) had to be completely rebuilt following the 1971 Sylmar earthquake. With its nicely landscaped courtyards and gardens, it's an evocative spot that also offers a good collection of pottery, furniture and saddles, along with an old-time blacksmith's shop. Unexpectedly, in 2005 comedian Bob Hope was interred at the site, in his own memorial garden underneath a red hemispheric shell.

Also in the vicinity, another key nineteenth-century site can be found at 10940 Sepulveda Blvd, the **Andres Pico Adobe** (Mon 10am–3pm & third Sun of month 1–4pm; free; Ⓣ818/365-7810, Ⓦwww.sfvhs.com), the estate and grounds of the eponymous Mexican general who fought off American troops, at least for a while, in the 1840s. This lovely, two-storey brick adobe was built in 1834, with an upper

Earthquakes in Los Angeles

The devastating 6.7 magnitude **earthquake** that shook LA on the morning of January 17, 1994, was one of the most destructive natural disasters in US history. Fifty-five people were killed, two hundred more suffered critical injuries, and the economic cost was estimated at $8 billion. The tremor toppled chimneys and shattered windows all over Southern California, with the worst damage concentrated at the epicentre in the San Fernando Valley community of **Northridge**, where a dozen people were killed when an apartment building collapsed. At the northern edge of the Valley, the I-5/Hwy-14 interchange was destroyed, killing one motorist and snarling traffic for at least a year; while in West LA, the Santa Monica Freeway overpass collapsed onto La Cienega Boulevard at one of LA's busiest intersections. The Northridge event followed a quake in the eastern desert around **Landers** a few years earlier, and just eclipsed LA's previous worst earthquake in modern times, the 6.6 magnitude temblor of February 9, 1971, which had its epicentre in **Sylmar** – also in the Valley.

Small earthquakes happen all the time in LA, but in the unlikely event a sizable one strikes when you're in LA, protect yourself under something sturdy, such as a heavy table or a door frame, and well away from windows or anything made of glass. In theory, all the city's new buildings are "quake-safe"; the extent of the crisis in January 1994, however, forced the city to re-examine and reinforce buildings – though as the quake recedes in memory, the job seems to diminish in perceived importance. So when the inevitable "**Big One**", a quake in the 8+ range, arrives, no one knows exactly what will be left standing.

storey added in 1873 – which is the year to which the adobe has been restored. It's crammed with period furnishings and historical bric-a-brac, and makes a good spot for a stroll in an idyllic setting.

Up the road in nearby **SYLMAR**, the wondrous **Nethercutt Collection**, 15200 Bledsoe St (tours only Thurs–Sat 10am & 1.30pm; free; by reservation at ⓣ818/364-6464, ⓦwww.nethercuttcollection.org), is a storehouse for all kinds of Wurlitzer organs, old-time player-pianos, cosmetic paraphernalia, Tiffany stained glass and classic French furniture, collected by J.H. Nethercutt, the chairman of Merle Norman Cosmetics, and his wife Dorothy. There's also two dozen antique cars on view from the 1920s and 30s. Even more worthwhile, however, is the adjoining **Nethercutt Museum** (self-guided tours Tues–Sat 9am–4.30pm; free; reservations not needed), a stunning showroom filled with 130 collectors' vintage automobiles such as Packards, Mercedes and Bugatti. The eye-popping highlights are the Duesenbergs, splendid machines driven by movie stars in the Jazz Age, including a silver 1933 Arlington Torpedo with curvaceous lines, sinuous bumpers and an array of exposed chrome pipes.

North of the valleys

The expanding exurbs **north of the valleys** offer several compelling historical and cultural sights along or near the I-14 freeway, which leaves the San Fernando Valley to make a harsh trek into the periphery of the Mojave Desert – still part of huge Los Angeles County. To the far north of San Fernando, the remains of the former company town of **Mentryville**, three miles west of I-5 at 27201 W Pico Canyon Rd (grounds daily 9am–dusk; free; ⓦwww.mentryville.org), are where California's very first oil well was dug, in 1876. The boom only lasted a few decades and the site was a ghost town for many years. These days the red-and-white barn, one-room 1880s schoolhouse, and thirteen-room Victorian mansion of town founder Charles Alexander Mentry evoke some of the city's old character, and are slowly being restored. For the more adventurous, trails lead away from the townsite into the hills of surrounding **Pico Canyon**, which is a popular site for hiking, mountain biking and horseriding.

To the east, in the town of **SANTA CLARITA**, the **William S. Hart Ranch and Museum**, 24151 San Fernando Rd (Wed–Fri 10am–1pm, Sat & Sun 11am–4pm; June–Aug Wed–Sun 11am–4pm; free; ⓣ661/254-4584, ⓦwww.hartmuseum.org), was named after a silent-movie star who made 65 westerns and is still considered one of the all-time cowboy greats. It holds a fine assemblage of native artworks, Remington sculptures, displays of spurs, guns and lariats, Hollywood costumes and authentic cowhand duds, housed in a Spanish Colonial Revival mansion on a sizable 265-acre ranch.

Nearby **Six Flags Magic Mountain**, Magic Mountain Parkway at I-5 (hours vary, often summer daily 10am–10pm; rest of year Sat & Sun 10am–8pm; $60, kids $35, $15 parking; ⓦwww.sixflags.com/parks/magicmountain), has some of the wildest roller coasters and rides in the world – highlights include the Viper, a huge orange monster with seven loops; the appropriately named Goliath, full of harrowing 85mph dips; Déjà Vu, a high-speed gut-wrencher that twists and jerks you in several different directions at once; and Tatsu, which sends you through the requisite loops while strapped in face-down at a 90-degree angle. The adjacent water park, **Hurricane Harbor** (same hours; $30, kids $20; ⓦwww.sixflags.com/parks/hurricaneharborla), provides aquatic fun if you don't mind getting splashed by throngs of giddy pre-adolescents.

The I-14 freeway, also called the Antelope Valley Freeway, branches off from I-5 into an extension of the Mojave Desert and takes you to 932-acre **Vasquez Rocks Park**, off Agua Dulce Canyon Road at 10700 W Escondido Canyon Rd (Ⓣ661/268-0840), whose startlingly jagged, diagonally uplifted rocks and an undulating terrain make for one of Hollywood's favourite film locations: everything from *The Flintstones* to *Dracula* to *Star Trek* has been shot here. Further up I-14, near the remote desert burg of **LANCASTER**, the awe-inspiring **Antelope Valley Poppy Reserve**, on Lancaster Drive, spreads over nearly 1800 acres. The reserve comes alive in late April as the site of the annual **California Poppy Festival** (during event, 10am–6pm; tickets $8; Ⓣ661/723-6075, Ⓦwww.poppyfestival.com), when the eye-blinding, fiery blooms appear in a sea of fluorescent orange.

9

Malibu and the Santa Monica Mountains

Home to some of LA's most expensive real estate, and largely free from smog and crime, **MALIBU** and the **SANTA MONICA MOUNTAINS** represent the good life in Southern California. Any Angeleno lucky enough to make it almost immediately tries to move here. The area features some of LA's most picturesque scenery, its rambling canyons, striking valleys and dense forests making up a large, pristine wilderness on the western edge of the metropolis.

With their attendant beauty, the mountain residences are also under constant threat from natural dangers, built on eroding cliffs forever sliding into the ocean and blackened by summer hillside fires, which leave a slick residue of burnt chaparral – a perfect surface for the floods and mudslides that come just a few months later. The periodic arrival of El Niño-driven wet weather only makes the situation more dire, with watery calamities a constant, inescapable threat, sometimes with whole neighbourhoods being washed away.

From **Pacific Palisades**, a chic district just northwest of Santa Monica, to rustic **Topanga Canyon**, a wooded neighbourhood with an arty flair, to beautiful **Point Dume**, a whale-watching promontory, these areas are best navigated by car on the popular beachside motorway, the Pacific Coast Highway (also known as "PCH" or Highway 1). North of PCH, **Mulholland Highway** provides an alternative trip through the area, winding through the Santa Monica Mountains and skipping Malibu entirely, instead reaching the ocean less than a mile from LA County's distant northwest boundary – at one of its prime spots for surfing.

Pacific Palisades

Driving north on PCH beyond the bluffs of Santa Monica, you reach the sandy crescent of **Will Rogers State Beach** and, on the other side of the road, **PACIFIC PALISADES**, once an upper-crust community of artists and writers, but now the home of media-industry millionaires. No amount of wealth, however, has been able to keep the district's hillsides from slowly falling into the ocean. With each winter's storms, more of the place gets washed away by erosion or mudslides, blocking traffic on PCH and shrinking the backyards of the clifftop homes.

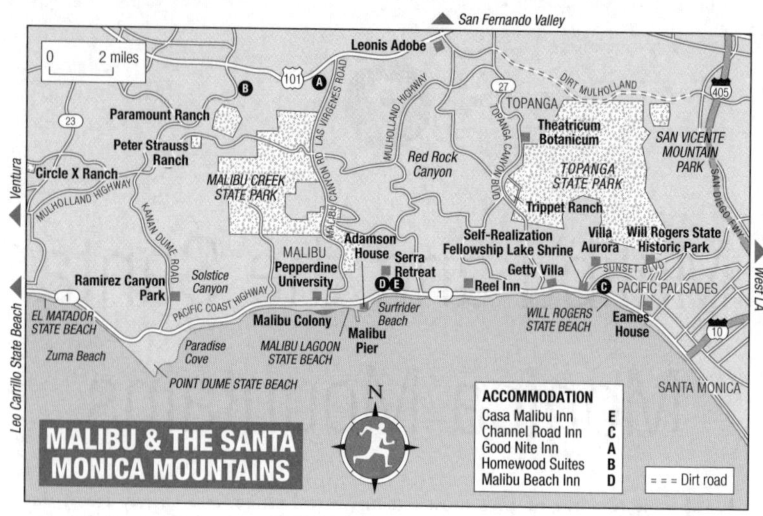

The Eames House and around

You can't visit most of the homes of the elite, with the exception of the **Eames House**, also known as Case Study House #8, just off PCH at 203 Chautauqua Blvd, perhaps the most influential house of post-war LA. Fashioned out of prefabricated industrial parts in 1947 as part of the renowned Case Study Program (see box, p.99), the compound boasts a main residential unit and an adjacent studio building, both resembling large, coloured metal-and-glass boxes, and surrounded by a grove of eucalyptus trees. The house's builders, Charles and Ray Eames (his wife), were one of the city's most creative couples in the 1950s, contributing thoughtful designs for art and architecture, furniture and cinema. For modern architecture fans, this is probably the most beloved spot in LA; the Eames family still owns and uses the structure, and the site has been declared a National Historic Landmark. However, only the grounds and exterior are viewable (Mon–Fri 10am–4pm, Sat 10am–3pm; free; by appointment at ⓣ310/459-9663, ⓦwww.eamesfoundation.org).

The nearby **Entenza House**, at no. 205, which was #9 in the Case Study Program, isn't quite up to the standard of the landmark next door, but this steel-framed structure was nonetheless built by the same architect, Charles Eames, with help from Eero Saarinen. Also in this glorious pocket of modern architecture is Richard Neutra's **Bailey House**, no. 219, which was #20 in the Program and features a steel-and-glass design with wood accents – more homey looking than the usual modernist house. Best of the more contemporary buildings in Pacific Palisades is the **Schwartz House**, just north, off W Channel Road at 444 Sycamore St, designed in 1994 by Pierre Koenig, more famous for his late-1950s Case Study House #22 (see box, p.100). His unique design includes a black-steel frame and foundation pivoted at a 30-degree angle from the rest of the boxy gray house, which has the function of keeping the living room and bedrooms out of the full glare of the rising sun.

Will Rogers State Historic Park

Continue north on Chautauqua Boulevard, then east on Sunset Boulevard to **Will Rogers State Historic Park** (summer daily 8am–dusk; rest of year daily

8am–6pm; free, parking $12; ⓣ310/454-8212), a steep climb from the MTA bus (#2, #302) stop. This was the home and ranch of Depression-era cowboy philosopher and journalist **Will Rogers**, one of America's most popular figures of the time, and renowned for saying that he "never met a man he didn't like" – though it's less well known that he was a socialist who was also, ironically, mayor of Beverly Hills. His isolated Pacific Palisades estate did much to attract Hollywood celebrities, many of whom were his friends, away from central LA, which at the time was quite a trip. The overgrown ranch-style house serves as an informal **museum**, filled with cowboy gear and Native American art (free tours Thurs & Fri 11am, 1pm & 2pm, Sat & Sun on the hour 10am–4pm). The surrounding 200-acre park has miles of foot and bridle paths, the most appealing being the three-mile trek up to Inspiration Point, where you can enjoy magnificent vistas of the Pacific and the sweeping curve of Santa Monica Bay. Closer to the ranch, visitors can drop by the **polo grounds** where matches take place during the spring and summer (April–Oct Sat 2–5pm, Sun 10am–1pm).

Castellammare

On the western side of Pacific Palisades, the mock Italian villas and Spanish Colonial estates of **Castellammare** sit precariously on steep hillsides and cliffs. Just before it reaches PCH, Sunset Boulevard takes a large, curving descent around the **Self-Realization Fellowship Lake Shrine**, 17190 Sunset Blvd (Tues–Sat 9am–5pm, Sun 1–5pm; free; ⓣ323/225-2471, ⓦwww.yogananda-srf.org), a religious monument created in 1950 by Paramahansa Yogananda, whose life and works are recounted in a **museum** detailing the spiritual leader's progressive thoughts on ecumenism, global peace and the like. The ten-acre lake shrine is an ode to world faiths, featuring symbols and credos of the major religions. Visitors are invited to circle the lake on a literal path of spiritual enlightenment, pausing to view such sights as the **windmill chapel**, a church built as a replica of a sixteenth-century Dutch windmill, along with a massive archway topped with copper lotus flowers, a houseboat that the shrine's Indian founder once used, a bird refuge, and gardens with religious symbols. The giant, gold-domed **temple** looming above on the hilltop at 17080 Sunset Blvd is usually off limits, except for occasional meditation and physical-spiritual exercise sessions (information at ⓦwww.lakeshrine.org).

Up the bluffs from Sunset, the **Villa Aurora**, 520 Paseo Miramar, is an idyllic 1927 Spanish Colonial-style structure that was conceived as a public-relations project by the *LA Times*, which devoted a series of articles to the construction of the house and all its modern amenities – dishwasher, electric fridge, gas range, three-car garage – and stunning Mediterranean style, carried through in the Spanish tile, wrought-iron balconies, and alluring gardens. Later, as the home of writer Lion Feuchtwanger, it became the focus of German emigres, hosting salons attended by Bertolt Brecht, Thomas Mann, Kurt Weill, Arnold Schoenberg and Fritz Lang, as well as Charlie Chaplin, and has since been reborn as a nonprofit organization that presents lectures, poetry readings, film screenings and music recitals of contemporary artists from Europe (usually free; ⓣ310/454-4231, ⓦwww.villa-aurora.org).

The Getty Villa

Just west of Sunset Boulevard's intersection with PCH, the **Getty Villa**, 17985 PCH (Wed–Mon 10am–5pm; free, parking $15 or take Metro Bus #534; by reservation only at ⓣ310/440-7300, ⓦwww.getty.edu), was originally the site of the full Getty Museum, until that site was reconstructed on a West LA hilltop (see p.115) and this one underwent significant renovation. It now serves as the Getty

Foundation's spectacular showcase for its wide array of Greek and Roman antiquities. If classical art is your forte, this should be your one essential stop in Southern California. Modelled after a Roman country house buried by Mount Vesuvius in 79 AD, the villa is built around fetching gardens, one an expansive courtyard complex surrounding a long, shallow pool and peppered with black, faintly menacing replicas of stern-looking Roman heads, the other a pleasant herb garden that shows the kinds of plants used for cooking two millennia ago.

Inside, the museum is based around a two-storey peristyle and courtyard, where a quaint pool is surrounded by more austere black statues. The rooms are grouped in themes ranging from religious and mythic to theatrical to martial. Highlights include the *Getty Kouros*, a rigidly posed figure of a boy that conservators openly state could be a later forgery, as well as Athenian vases, many of them the red-ground variety, and ancient kylikes, or drinking vessels, and ceremonial amphorae, or vases given as prizes in athletic contests. Not to be missed is a wondrous Roman skyphos, a fragile-looking blue vase decorated with white cameos of Bacchus and his friends, properly preparing for a bacchanalia. Keep in mind that because of the dubious provenance of some of the collection's holdings (dating from the days when high-ticket art was routinely shipped out of the Mediterranean region with little oversight), the Italian government recently forced the Getty to send up to forty priceless items back to the Old World. Despite this, there's more than enough statues, vases, vessels, sculptures and oddments to keep you occupied, and the site well merits a full afternoon of exploration.

Topanga Canyon

Around Topanga Canyon Boulevard north of PCH, **Topanga Canyon** is a stunning natural preserve. With hillsides covered in golden poppies and wildflowers, 150 thousand acres of these mountains and adjacent seashore have been protected as the **Santa Monica Mountains National Recreation Area** (Ⓦwww.lamountains.org) – striking evidence that LA offers a lot more than just asphalt, smog and movie stars. Boasting fine views and fresh air, the area is wilderness in many places, and you can still spot a variety of deer, coyote and even the odd mountain lion. However, the mountains are not without an element of danger, especially in winter and early spring, when mudslides cause damage that can prevent you from traversing certain trails. Otherwise, rangers offer free guided hikes throughout the mountains most weekends (information at Ⓣ818/597-9192). Also, there are self-guided trails through the canyon's huge, 11,000-acre **Topanga State Park**, off Old Topanga Canyon Boulevard at the crest of the mountains, with spectacular views over the Pacific. In fact, there are so many trails and options for scenic wandering that it's easy to get lost if you don't prepare beforehand with a decent map and plenty of water. A good starting point for visitors is **Trippet Ranch**, east of Old Topanga Canyon Boulevard on Entrada Road, which offers the Musch Trail, an easygoing trek through prime wildflower country, with terrain less challenging than that of other parts of the park. The local Audubon Society leads monthly birdwatching hikes through this and other LA-area nature zones, with the Topanga jaunt taking place the first Sunday of the month (8am–noon; free; reserve at Ⓣ310/455-1401, Ⓦlosangelesaudubon.org). If you'd like to find out more about the area, go to the Santa Monica Mountains **visitor centre** in neighbouring Thousand Oaks, 401 W Hillcrest Drive (daily 9am–5pm; Ⓣ805/370-2301, Ⓦwww.nps.gov/samo), which has maps and information.

The nearby community of **TOPANGA**, further up Topanga Canyon Boulevard, was a proving ground for West Coast rock music in the 1960s and 70s, when Neil Young, the Byrds, Canned Heat, Emmylou Harris, Joni Mitchell, Jim (and Van) Morrison and many other artists moved here and held all-night jam sessions in the fabled Topanga Corral nightclub (burned in 1986) or in sycamore groves along Topanga Creek. A less salubrious arrival was Charles Manson, whose followers managed to kill a resident in 1969. One of the few conventional attractions is the **Will Geer Theatricum Botanicum**, 1419 Topanga Canyon Blvd, a wooded outdoor amphitheatre that usually runs a pair of good summer performances of Shakespeare, and another pair of more modern works (June–Oct Fri–Sun; $10–50; information and tickets at ⓣ310/455-3723, ⓦwww.theatricum.com). Named after and founded by Will Geer, TV's Grandpa Walton, who moved here to get away from the Hollywood blacklist in the 1950s, the theatre also presents a range of other musical and dramatic performances throughout the year, for similar prices. If you're around for Memorial Day weekend, drop by the area for **Topanga Days** (at the **Topanga Community House**, 1440 Topanga Canyon Blvd; $20; ⓣ310/455-1980, ⓦwww.topangadays.com), a country-flavoured fair with art-and-craft booths, music and vegetarian-oriented cuisine.

Before leaving the area, don't miss **Red Rock Canyon**, off Old Topanga Canyon Road at 23601 Red Rock Rd, a stunning red-banded sandstone gorge that was formerly a Boy Scout retreat and is now a state park. The colourful rock formations, surrounding gardens, and riparian wildlife give you a good reason to leave your car behind and go explore the area on the canyon's eponymous trail.

Malibu

Further up PCH, past a long stretch of gated beachfront homes, lies **MALIBU**, the very name of which conjures up images of beautiful people lazing on palm-fringed beaches and consuming cocktails. However, getting to the beach itself is a notorious problem for the public here (see box). As you enter the small town, the succession of tourist-oriented surf shops and unassuming restaurants around **Malibu Pier** (primarily for fishing, at 23000 PCH) don't exactly reek of big money, but the secluded estates just inland are as valuable as any in the entire US.

Surfrider Beach and around

Adjacent to the pier, **Surfrider Beach** (daily 8am–dusk; ⓣ818/880-0350), also known as Malibu Lagoon State Beach, is a major surfing nexus, first gaining notice when the sport was brought over from Hawaii and mastered by Southern California pioneers. The waves are best in late summer, when storms off Mexico cause them to reach upwards of eight feet – not huge for serious pros, but big enough for you. This was the surfing capital of the world in the early 1960s, with the movies *Gidget* and *Beach Blanket Bingo* helping draw the masses. Adjoining the beach is a nature reserve and lagoon good for birdwatching, along with seasonal guided tours that showcase, among other things, the sea life in the marshes and tide pools (information at ⓣ310/456-8432). A small **museum**, 23200 PCH (Wed–Sat 11am–3pm; donation), gives you the historical rundown, from the Chumash era up to the arrival of Hollywood movie stars. Special emphasis is given to **May K. Rindge** (widow of entrepreneur Frederick Rindge), who, up until the 1920s, owned all of Malibu. Employing armed guards and dynamiting roads to keep travellers from passing through, Rindge operated her own roads and private railroad and fought for

Reaching the beach in Malibu

Visitors to Malibu commonly believe that all **beaches** in the area, aside from the officially marked state or county variety, are off limits to interlopers – not surprising considering the sands are located in the very backyards of the gated communities that hug the Malibu shoreline. In reality, the sand along Santa Monica Bay is **open to visitors** below the "mean high-tide line", which means that as long as you stay off the private beachside territory above that line (you should stick to where the sand is wet and/or matted, instead of dry and hilly), you can go anywhere you please, looking at the guarded domains of the rich and famous – of which there are many, as any guide to stars' homes will tell you. The challenge, however, is in finding the **pedestrian rights-of-way** that give access to the beach. The urban explorers group LA Urban Rangers has published a free, online map (available at Ⓦlaurbanrangers.org) showing some eighteen access points, with perhaps the most notable one being the Zonker Harris Access Way, at 22706 PCH, named after the perpetually stoned burnout in the syndicated comic strip.

Keep in mind also that many of these public-access points have been the subject of a number of **lawsuits** in recent years, with the wealthy sometimes putting up barriers — or misleading "Private Property" signs — to the less well heeled, and aggrieved beach lovers seeking their revenge in court. If possible, don't let these things deter you, for the above access points are all legally protected and well established. Make sure to report any illegal obstructions to public access to the state coastal commission (Ⓣ805/585-1800), which tries to rigorously enforce the rules and can provide additional information on any public easement in the area.

As an another interesting expedition, find the easement around 22126 PCH to access Carbon Beach, aka "Billionaire's Beach", which lines many of the back doors of the elite, and even features a prominent, legendary "**Dealmaker's Rock**", where the rich and famous (or at least their producers, lawyers and agents) cut deals in bathing suits and jogging sweats. Even better, what decent works of architecture there are in Malibu can be spotted in full glory along this beach. There are few better than Richard Meier's stunning **Ackerberg House**, 22466 PCH, which looks like a nondescript wall of cement and white tile from the street, but from the beach looks exactly as its architect intended: a 1986 practice run for the Getty Center, rendered small, with the same rigidly geometric form clad in white-steel panelling and wraparound windows.

years to prevent the Southern Pacific Railroad from laying down track through her property, as well as the state of California from building the Pacific Coast Highway across her land. She ultimately lost her legal battle in the state supreme court, and her money in the Depression; the road was built in 1928.

Before her mother went broke, Rindge's daughter and her husband hired architect Stiles O. Clements, of the legendary firm of Morgan, Walls and Clements (see box, p.73), to design the magnificent **Adamson House** (grounds 8am–sunset, house tours Wed–Fri 10.30am–3.30pm, Sat 10.30am–3pm; $5; Ⓦwww.adamsonhouse.org), on the grounds of the Malibu Lagoon museum. One of LA's finest pieces of Spanish Colonial architecture, the opulent house features Mission and Moorish Revival elements, such as individually carved teak doors, glazed ceramic tiles, detailed ironwork, and Spanish and Middle Eastern furnishings, as well as expansive gardens and a pool and fountain.

The Malibu Colony and Serra Retreat

After May Rindge's mischief finally ceased, her son took over the ranch and quickly sold much of the land, establishing the **Malibu Colony**, along Malibu

Colony Drive off Malibu Road, as a haven for movie stars. Unless you take a long oceanside trek (see box opposite) to see the estates of the glitterati from the sands, there's very little to see here because the public is barred admittance. If you're after a glimpse of the stars, visit the **Malibu Country Mart**, 3835 Cross Creek Rd, where celebrities are regularly seen munching on veggies or sipping espressos, or shopping at any of a few dozen high-end boutiques.

To the northeast, spiritual relaxation can be found at the **Serra Retreat**, 3401 Serra Rd (Ⓣ310/456-6631, Ⓦwww.serraretreat.com), a nondenominational religious haven named for Franciscan friar and missionary Junípero Serra, one of several such retreats operated by the friars throughout the West. You can enjoy a weekend getaway here in one of the hundred rooms ($180–240 total cost), wander the flower gardens or get a fantastic hilltop view of the Pacific. The retreat was originally meant to be the **Rindge Mansion**, but construction was mothballed during the Depression and the half-built property given over to the Franciscans, who after a 1970 fire rebuilt it after the missions of old.

Pepperdine to Solstice Canyon

Pepperdine University, 24255 PCH, moved north of downtown Malibu after abandoning its Art Deco digs in South Central LA in 1971, and is mainly notable for its sloping green lawns and gigantic white cross. The campus's **Frederick R. Weisman Museum of Art** (Tues–Sun 11am–5pm; free; Ⓦarts.pepperdine.edu/museum) sometimes puts on good shows of modern abstraction and California art.

Across from Pepperdine, the six-acre, hilltop **Malibu Bluffs State Park**, at the intersection of Malibu Canyon Rd at 24250 PCH, is a prime spot for whale watching in the winter months (Nov–March), when you may spot orcas or baleen whales, depending on the time and weather. Further up, the less-crowded shoreline of **Dan Blocker County Beach**, 26000 PCH – dedicated to the actor who played Hoss in TV's *Bonanza* – is the most appealing sight before you get to Corral Canyon Road, which leads you into **Solstice Canyon Park**, one of LA's hidden treasures. A mile down placid Solstice Canyon Creek on the Solstice Canyon Trail is a rustic **cabin** from 1865 sitting in a state of arrested dilapidation – supposedly the oldest stone structure in Malibu. Past the cabin are the atmospheric remains of a modern estate known as **Tropical Terrace**, built in 1952, which was once surrounded by a ranch stocked with buffalo, camels, giraffes and African deer. Burned in 1982, the basic structure of the house is still standing, as are its surrounding brick steps, garden terraces – with inlaid horseshoes and bits of coloured glass – and a partially visible bomb shelter, with trees sprouting through the concrete and vines covering the brickwork. As you continue on, take the Sostomo Trail and Deer Valley Loop for a rugged, four-mile round trip up to the crest of the mountains and an awe-inspiring view of the Pacific and Santa Monica Bay all the way down to Palos Verdes. Several other trails here are worth the jaunt, ranging from one to two miles and taking you past assorted small seasonal waterfalls, oak groves and the odd bit of wildlife such as deer and bobcat.

Point Dume and beyond

Several miles northwards up the coast from downtown Malibu, **Point Dume**, named after the Franciscan padre Francisco Dumetz in 1793, is the tip of a great seaward promontory of lava from an ancient volcano, offering fine vistas of Santa Monica Bay. Along with being a popular whale-watching spot from November to

March, it also features some excellent strips of sand. **Zuma Beach** (most beaches in the area daily 7am–10pm; parking $7–10), north at 30000 PCH, the largest of the LA County beaches, is popular for its surfing, scuba diving and fishing; it's also where the surprise ending of the original *Planet of the Apes* was filmed. On the east side of the point, at 28128 PCH, **Paradise Cove** is a private beach that makes for a fine walk, with superb views of fancy houses perched by the shore. Parking, unfortunately, is $20, so you're best off hoofing it for a mile heading east from Point Dume County Beach, at the tip of the promontory.

North of Point Dume and PCH, **Ramirez Canyon Park**, at 5750 Ramirez Canyon Rd, in Ramirez Canyon Park (Wed tours 1–4pm; $35; by reservation only at ⓣ310/589-2850, ⓦwww.lamountains.com), is a 22-acre complex of houses and gardens that Barbra Streisand donated to the Santa Monica Mountains Conservancy in 1993. Amid extensive flower, herb and fruit gardens, you can get a glimpse into her former properties, constructed in styles ranging from Art Nouveau to Craftsman to Art Deco.

Several miles up the coast from Point Dume, at 32215 PCH, the rocky and wonderfully picturesque **El Matador State Beach** was where the opening shots of the movie musical *Grease* were filmed, and still has the flair of a secluded private beach, and is well worth a stop if you've made it this far. Another five miles north, where Mulholland Drive reaches the ocean, **Leo Carrillo** ("ca-REE-oh") **State Beach Park**, 35000 PCH, marks the northwestern border of LA County – about 30 miles north of Santa Monica. The mile-long sandy beach is divided by Sequit Point, a bluff with underwater caves, tide pools and a tunnel you can pass through at low tide, and is also one of LA's best campgrounds (see p.217). The beach has starred in quite a few Hollywood flicks, much like its namesake: Carrillo was an actor who appeared in nearly one hundred films and was best known as Pancho in the 1950s TV show *The Cisco Kid*. Today, his surname is synonymous with some of LA's best surf.

Mulholland Drive and Highway

Best known as the road running along the crest of the Hollywood Hills, Mulholland Drive continues a mile west of the 405 freeway before turning into "Dirt Mulholland", as it's known, a bumpy, rocky, winding dirt road that's closed to cars but is good for its hiking and mountain biking access to the heart of the Santa Monica Mountains, with some awe-inspiring vistas and abundant greenery along the way. While in the area, don't miss the towering hilltop of the unusual ten-acre **San Vicente Mountain Park**, 17500 Mulholland Hwy, on the eastern side of Dirt Mulholland about a mile from the paved section of the road. A decommissioned military site, it was used between 1956 and 1968 as a radar centre and launching pad for Nike anti-aircraft missiles, to be fired in the event of a Soviet bomber run over LA. A zigzagging stairway leads to a hexagonal viewing platform on top of the command tower, where you can ponder the Cold War while staring down at striking vistas of the San Fernando Valley. Around Topanga Canyon Boulevard, Mulholland Drive becomes paved again and heads north to the 101 freeway. Just west of the Mulholland freeway entrance, the **Leonis Adobe**, 23537 Calabasas Rd (Wed–Sun 1–4pm, Sat opens 10am; $4; ⓣ818/222-6511, ⓦwww.leonisadobemuseum.org), is an 1844 ranch and adobe (remodelled in 1880) that's worth a look. The grounds of this lovely Spanish estate include a blacksmith, windmill, barn and restored carriage, as well as the engaging **Plummer House**, a

Victorian-era home relocated from Hollywood and now the rancho's visitor centre, where you can see exhibits on the estate's history.

About two miles south of Mulholland Drive's intersection with the 101, another road, Mulholland Highway, branches off and heads back into the mountains, where it continues past some interesting sites before terminating at the beach at the far end of LA County.

Malibu Creek State Park and Paramount Ranch

Mulholland Highway offers quite the scenic drive, at times via dizzying switchbacks and narrow cliffside passages. There are many excellent state and regional parks here and plenty of movie history, too. Perhaps the most notable site is **Malibu Creek State Park**, just south of Mulholland Highway on Las Virgenes Road (daily dawn–dusk; ⓣ818/880-0367), a 4000-acre park that was once home to early Chumash tribes. It much later belonged to 20th Century-Fox studios, which filmed many Tarzan pictures here, as well as the original *Planet of the Apes*, and used the chaparral-covered hillsides to simulate South Korea for the film and TV show *M*A*S*H*. The park features countless gorgeous vistas, lagoons, buttes and canyons, as well as sheer cliffs and the lovely watercourse of Malibu Creek itself; there's also the odd sight of Rindge Dam, a 1926 creation of one-time Malibu land baron May K. Rindge, which was been filled in with sediment and now acts as a 100-foot-tall waterfall. The park is known for its fishing, rockclimbing, and birdwatching – and wildlife viewing in general, since it's rich with eagles, mule deer, bobcats and cougars. Pick up a map at the visitor centre or at a kiosk to avoid getting lost on its nearly fifteen miles of hiking trails. If you're planning to pitch your tent and camp, make a reservation beforehand (see p.217).

Further west on Mulholland, **Paramount Ranch**, 2813 Cornell Rd (daily 8am–5pm; 818/222-6511), is another old studio lot dating from 1927, with a few short trails and an intact Western movie set used in films starring Gary Cooper, W.C. Fields and Hopalong Cassidy, and TV programmes like *The Rifleman*, *The Cisco Kid* and *Dr. Quinn Medicine Woman*. Film and TV crews still occasionally shoot here on weekdays, though generally without public notice.

West to the ocean

A few miles west of Cornell Road, at 30000 Mulholland Hwy, the charming **Peter Strauss Ranch** (ⓣ805/370-2301) was once the site of the **Lake Enchanto Resort**, a top LA amusement spot from the 1930s through the 1950s, until a nearby dam burst and washed it away. Resurrected variously as a resort and a nudist colony, the property passed into the hands of actor and producer Peter Strauss, who, after yet another dam burst, turned it over to the Santa Monica Mountains Conservancy. Although a few hints of the old days remain – such as a disused swimming pool and terrazzo patio – the park is a pretty low-key attraction, with a short walking trail, aviary and cactus garden.

Mulholland continues westward until it reaches the Pacific Ocean near Leo Carrillo State Beach Park (see opposite), passing a number of excellent parks and striking vistas along the way, most of them controlled and protected by the Santa Monica Mountains Conservancy (information at ⓦwww.nps.gov/samo). The most worthwhile of these is the stunning scenery of Circle X Ranch, north of Mulholland at 12896 Yerba Buena Rd, whose various trails take you past rocky crags, sandstone peaks and chaparral-covered hillsides, as well as a fern-bedecked grotto.

10

Orange County

Now that the abundant citrus groves that inspired its name are long gone, **ORANGE COUNTY** has more of a reputation for insular, suburban conservatism than it does for fruit. The long-standing stereotype painted the place as a West Coast version of Levittown – where tract homes and asphalt stretched to the horizon and anyone not conforming to bourgeois propriety wasn't allowed admittance. These days, the county has become more multicultural, with rising numbers of Latino immigrants transforming cities like Santa Ana, and other newcomers from Southeast Asia, India and Eastern Europe developing their own communities as well. Indeed, Orange County's fractured social landscape of libertarian beach cities, reactionary old-line suburbs, burgeoning immigrant districts, and hordes of itinerant tourists is mainly stitched together by the ubiquitous freeway system.

The original heart of the 1940s and 50s suburbs, **inland Orange County** is famous as the domain of Mickey Mouse and Knott's Berry Farm, with the other handful of diversions too spread out to be handily seen by public transit. More appealing, the **Orange County coast** is a collection of relaxed seaside towns with both easygoing "surfer-dude" attitudes and upscale, beach-condo snootiness. It's hard to identify the southern limit of the coastal cities: they just blend into even more housing colonies as you head further south – a seemingly endless exurban stretch between LA and San Diego.

Inland Orange County

Located in the heart of **INLAND ORANGE COUNTY**, the first modern theme park, **Disneyland**, was opened in 1955 by Walt Disney, who correctly divined that the area around **Anaheim** would become the next great population centre in Southern California. It did, but not as he intended: for miles around the park stretch nothing but strip malls, motels and knick-knack shops. Nonetheless, this suburb and those around it continue to grow rapidly, drawing immigrants by the thousands. **Westminster**, for example, is now the site of Little Saigon, a centre for Vietnamese expatriates, and is the most fervent bastion of anti-Communism in Southern California, long after the end of the Cold War.

One thing hasn't changed: Disneyland still dominates the area. Elsewhere, the thrill rides at **Knott's Berry Farm** are superior to those of the Magic Kingdom, the **Crystal Cathedral** is an imposing reminder of the potency of the evangelical movement, and the **Richard Nixon Presidential Library and Museum** is a good spot to find out about the illustrious life and career of Tricky Dick. Other isolated spots of interest can even be found in places like **Santa Ana** and **Fullerton** – places usually well off the tourist trail.

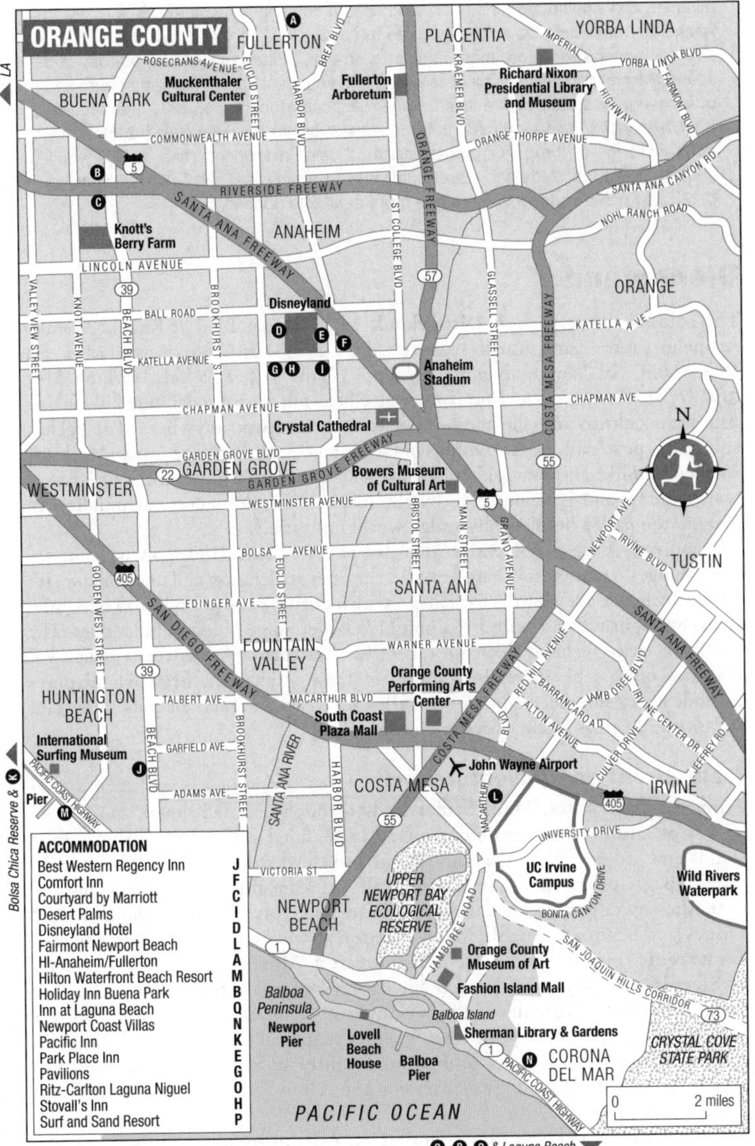

Planning a trip to Disneyland

Depending on traffic, Disneyland is about 45 minutes by **car** from Downtown LA on the Santa Ana Freeway (I-5). By **train** from Downtown (there are a dozen daily), it's a thirty-minute journey to Fullerton, from where OCTD buses will drop you at Disneyland or Knott's Berry Farm. By **bus**, MTA #460 from Downtown takes about ninety minutes, and Greyhound runs six to ten buses a day and takes 45 minutes to get to Anaheim, from where it's an easy walk to the park.

As for **accommodation**, most people try to visit Disneyland just for the day and spend the night somewhere else, or at home. If you must stay in this rather drab and often overpriced area, we've listed some reasonable options on p.214; alternately, the *HI-Anaheim/Fullerton* hostel is the cheapest bet in the area (see p.216). If you don't want to eat the park's greasy fast food or its overpriced "fine dining", you'll need to leave the place and travel a fair way in Anaheim. The "Eating" listings on p.227 and p.245 suggest some of the more palatable options.

Disneyland

The colossal theme park of **Disneyland**, 1313 Harbor Blvd at Katella Avenue, Anaheim (hours vary, usually summer daily 8am–1am; rest of year Mon–Fri 10am–6pm, Sat 9am–midnight, Sun 9am–10pm; $72, $62 kids, parking $14; ⓣ714/781-4565, ⓦdisneyland.com), is, for better or worse, a defining bulwark of American culture and the most influential theme park anywhere. For such a culturally powerful place, Disneyland occupies less than one square mile of Anaheim (unlike Disneyworld in Florida, which sits on 46 square miles of Disney-owned turf), and is hemmed in by the low-end developments surrounding it, making the park a hermetically sealed world unto itself.

If you only have an expensive, one-day pass to Disneyland, you will not see everything, no matter how hard you try: the lines are lengthy and unavoidable. It's wisest to choose a few of the top rides – which during peak periods may have lines with two-hour waiting periods – alongside a larger range of less popular ones. The admission price includes them all, except for **California Adventure**, which will cost you quite a bit more. In addition to these attractions, **firework displays** explode every summer night, and **parades** and special events celebrate important occasions – such as Mickey Mouse's birthday.

Main Street and Adventureland

From the front gates, **Main Street** leads through a scaled-down, camped-up replica of Disney's Missouri hometown c.1900, filled with souvenir shops, food stands and arcades. Note that the second and third storeys of the false-fronted buildings get progressively smaller in scale, tricking the eye into believing the structures are taller than they really are. From here you can hop on the pint-sized Disneyland Railroad (usually two or three run at one time) that encircles the park **for a scenic tour**, or hail a horse-drawn streetcar. Most people just plow directly to **Sleeping Beauty's Castle**, a pseudo-Rhineland palace that employs the same progressive-scale technique as the windows on Main Street. Familiar from the Disney company logo, the castle was recently reopened to fascinating effect, with narrow corridors and stairs leading to brightly coloured, three-dimensional scenes from the classic Disney cartoon and a few modern special effects to enhance the mood.

Radiating out clockwise from Main Street, **Adventureland** was built near the height of the Tiki craze in the 1950s, most evident in the famed Jungle Cruise. The creaky old ride still has its fans, who revel in the "tour guides" making crude puns about the fake animatronic beasts creaking amid the trees, and a few fake piranhas thrown in recently to provide more (tame) thrills. Nearby, Tarzan's Treehouse offers catwalks in the branches of a huge artificial tree and rustic rooms with assorted playthings target an audience of 8 year olds. Ultimately, if you're going to spend any time at all in this section, get in line for the **Indiana Jones Adventure**. Two hours of waiting in line are built into the ride, with an interactive archeological dig and 1930s-style newsreel show leading up to the main feature – a speedy journey along 2500ft of skull-encrusted corridors, loosely based on the movie trilogy *Indiana Jones*, in which you face fireballs, burning rubble, venomous snakes and a rolling-boulder finale.

The nearby **New Orleans Square**, clockwise to the northwest of Adventureland, is the site of **Club 33**, Walt's ultra-exclusive dinner club for his chums in the corporate and political elite, which even today offers membership by invitation at a (last-reported) entry cost of $10,000. Still, there's a decade-plus waiting list to get into the club, where microphones were once hidden in the chandeliers to record the comments of unsuspecting dinner guests. It's also the only place in the park where alcohol is served. Although you definitely can't get in, you can spot the club's door, marked with a "33". The door is located next to the facade of the *Blue* restaurant *Bayou*, which, despite its jaw-dropping prices for steak and seafood, has some of the best dining ambience in Orange County: a darkly romantic waterfront scene with dim lighting, old-fashioned Southern decor, and imitation crickets chirping in the distance. (Reserve early at ⓣ714/956-6755, the reservation line for all Disneyland restaurants, or ⓣ714/781-3463 for priority seating.)

From your table, you'll be able to see crowds lining up for the square's signature ride, the **Pirates of the Caribbean**, a renowned boat-trip through underground caverns, with drunken pirates singing, laughing skeletons, and all manner of ruddy-cheeked yokels hooting and bellowing for your amusement. The ride is perhaps best known these days as the inspiration for the Johnny Depp film franchise. Nearby, another of Disneyland's best rides, the **Haunted Mansion**, features a riotous "doom buggy" tour in the company of the house ghouls, with a nightmarish elevator ride to start the trip off in skin-crawling fashion and plenty of creepy portraits to stare at along the way, culminating with a ghost hitching a ride in your buggy.

Frontierland and Fantasyland

Among the smallest of the various themelands, **Frontierland** should be a lot more fun than it is. Supposedly the area takes its cues from the Wild West and the tales of Mark Twain, but the main reason you'll want to come here is for the rollercoaster and a movie tie-in. The coaster is Thunder Mountain Railroad, a rather slow-moving trip through a rocky landscape resembling a cartoon version of a Hollywood Western, but more interesting is Pirate's Lair, which has taken over most of the old Tom Sawyer Island. Themed around Disney's movie franchise *Pirates of the Caribbean*, it's a nice continuation of the older Pirates of the Caribbean ride (see above), and lets you poke around the spooky Dead Man's Grotto for hidden treasure, explore the skeletons littered through a shipwreck at Smuggler's Cove, and watch (live) singing and stunt-performing pirates at various spots around the island. Nearby, the focus of **Critter Country** is Splash Mountain, a fun log-flume ride in which you can expect to get drenched. Young children and those with a flair for the surreal will find amusement in adjacent The Many Adventures of Winnie the Pooh, in which you follow Pooh Bear as he has bizarre dreams and encounters strange creatures in the Hundred Acre Wood.

Across the drawbridge from Main Street, **Fantasyland** is either wondrous or dull, depending on your age. The highlight, Mr Toad's Wild Ride, is a jerky funhouse voyage through Victorian England featuring a trip into hell. The other rides are much tamer, such as those involving Peter Pan flying over London, Snow White being tormented by the wicked witch, and Alice in Wonderland descending down the rabbit hole. It's a Small World gets the most extreme reactions, with children delighting in this boat tour of the world's continents – in which four hundred animated dolls sing the same cloying song over and over again – and adults finding it a slow, gurgling torture test. The one Fantasyland roller coaster, the Matterhorn, is somewhat entertaining for its phony cement mountain and goofy abominable snowman appearing when you round a corner, though the dips and curves are rather gentle compared with most coasters these days.

Tomorrowland and Toontown

On the park's northern end, **Toontown**, a cartoon village with goofy sound effects and Day-Glo colours, is aimed only for the under-10 set, with the exception of Roger Rabbit's Car Toon Spin, which jerks you around in a cartoon taxi through a loony landscape based on scenes from the 1988 movie.

On the eastern side of the park, **Tomorrowland** is Disney's vision of the future. Here, the Space Mountain roller coaster – the best in the park – zips through the pitch-blackness of "outer space"; the late Michael Jackson is celebrated once more in the Captain EO Tribute, a 17-minute 3-D film juiced up with various special effects; and the Finding Nemo Submarine Voyage picks up where its predecessor, 20,000 Leagues Under the Sea, left off, giving you a quick underwater tour of notable aquatic scenes from a hit movie. This idea of the future occasionally looks like a hangover from the past – note rides such as Autopia, where you drive a miniature car at a glacial pace. However, this fun zone has been updated somewhat in recent years, with new rides like the Jules Verne-inspired Astro Orbiter offering carnival-style thrills as you get spun around in a "rocket" contraption, and Buzz Lightyear Astro Blasters combining a ride into the world of the film franchise *Toy Story* with a video-game-like laser-blasting competition.

California Adventure

The newest part of Disneyland is **California Adventure**, technically a separate park but connected to the main one in architecture, style and spirit. Aside from its slightly better food, California Adventure is really just another "land" to visit, albeit a much more expensive one. For a single-day admission ticket to both parks, you'll have to shell out $97, or $87 for kids; the one-park price for California Adventure is $72 and $62, as it is for Disneyland. Such high prices and the comparative lack of thrills have really punctured the hype that Disneyland built up for this park, so unless you're hopelessly obsessed by all things Disney, you're better off avoiding the place.

There are a handful of highlights if you do visit: Grizzly River Run is a fun giant-inner-tube ride, splashing through plunges and "caverns"; Soarin' Over California is an exciting trip on a mock-experimental aircraft that buzzes through hairpin turns and steep dives; and the **Pacific Pier** zone has a slew of old-fashioned carnival rides – from California Screamin', a sizable roller coaster, to the Ferris-like Mickey's Fun Wheel – that only faintly recall the wilder, harder-edged midways of California's past. There's also a rather tame zone devoted to Tinseltown, the **Hollywoodland**, which, aside from a few theatres, special-effects displays, and the Tower of Terror (a shock-drop ride in a haunted hotel), is mainly notable for its design, which loosely borrows from the movie set of D.W. Griffith's 1916 failure *Intolerance* – exotic columns, squatting elephants and so on (a design also used in the Hollywood and Highland mall; see p.90).

Knott's Berry Farm

Though making up a distinct minority, partisans of **Knott's Berry Farm**, four miles northwest of Disneyland, off the Santa Ana Freeway at 8039 Beach Blvd (hours vary, usually summer Sun–Thurs 9am–11pm, Fri & Sat 9am–midnight; rest of year Mon–Fri 10am–6pm, Sat 10am–10pm, Sun 10am–7pm; $55, kids $24; ⓣ714/220-5200, ⓦwww.knotts.com), claims it's every bit as good, if not better, than Disneyland – at least for thrill rides. And unlike Disneyland, this park can easily be seen in one day, as long as you concentrate on the roller coasters. Although there are ostensibly six themed lands here, several of them consist only of familiar carnival rides, fast-food stands, and dodgy versions of history. **Camp Snoopy** is the Knott's version of Disney's Toontown, enlivened by the presence of the Sierra Sidewinder roller coaster, while the **Wild Water Wilderness** isn't really a theme area at all, but simply the site of the moderately exciting Bigfoot Rapids giant-inner-tube ride. In the **Ghost Town** part of the park, the GhostRider roller coaster delivers excellent thrills with its old-fashioned wooden design and "haunted mine train" theme. The gut-wrenching, inverted Silver Bullet is also a chiller, sending you around multiple loops and rolls that can easily, and happily, induce nausea.

Beyond this, **Fiesta Village** is home to Montezooma's Revenge, the original one-loop coaster, and Jaguar, a high-flying coaster that spins you around the park concourse. The **Boardwalk** is all about heart-thumping thrill rides: the Boomerang, a forward-and-back coaster that spends a lot of time upside down; Supreme Scream, a delightfully terrifying freefall drop; Xcelerator, a coaster with a stomach-churning catapult mechanism; and the Perilous Plunge, a hellish drop at a 75-degree angle that's far more exciting than any old log-flume ride. This Boardwalk, Knott's version of a carnival midway, with its death-defying rides and vomit-inducing thrills, easily puts Disney's Pacific Pier to shame. The adjacent Knott's water park, **Soak City U.S.A.** (June–Sept only, hours vary but generally daily 10am–5pm or 6pm; $26, kids $20; ⓦwww.knotts.com), offers fourteen rides of various heights and speeds, almost all of them involving the familiar water slides – either with or without an inner tube – which can really bring out the sweltering masses on a hot summer day.

Around Disneyland

South of Disneyland just off the Santa Ana Freeway, in otherwise uneventful **GARDEN GROVE**, the giant **Crystal Cathedral**, 12141 Lewis St (tours Mon–Sat 9am–3.30pm; free; ⓣ714/971-4013, ⓦwww.crystalcathedral.org), is a hugely garish Philip Johnson design of tubular space-frames and plate-glass walls that forms part of the vision of televangelist Robert Schuller. The sermon-spectacles inside reach their climax with the special **Christmas production** (late Nov to early Jan; $35–45; reserve at ⓣ714/544-5679), using live animals in biblical roles and people disguised as angels suspended on ropes.

A more worthwhile attraction lies in the nearby burg of **SANTA ANA**, where the splendid **Bowers Museum of Cultural Art**, 2002 N Main St (Tues–Sun 10am–4pm; $18 weekdays, $20 weekends; ⓣ714/567-3600, ⓦwww.bowers.org), features anthropological treasures from early Asian, African, Native-American and pre-Columbian civilizations, and includes artefacts as diverse as ceramic Mayan icons, hand-crafted baskets from native Californians, and highly detailed Chinese funerary sculpture.

Fullerton

North of Disneyland, drab **FULLERTON** surprisingly has a few interesting sights, among them the 26-acre **Fullerton Arboretum**, in the northeast corner of the California State campus at 1900 Associated Rd (daily 8am–4.30pm; donation; ⓣ714/278-3579, ⓦfullertonarboretum.org). Its series of themed gardens, ranges from desert succulents to Mediterranean plantings to forested groves, and includes cycads, palms, cacti, rare fruits and even the kind of citrus groves that used to grow in abundance in Orange County. In the middle of the arboretum stands the **Heritage House** (tours Sat & Sun 2–4pm; $2), an 1894 Eastlake Victorian that, with its historic displays and vintage decor, harkens back to a more bucolic time.

Much more unusual is the presence in Fullerton of an esteemed institution such as the **Muckenthaler Cultural Center**, 1201 W Malvern Ave (Wed–Sun noon–4pm; free; ⓣ714/738-6595, ⓦthemuck.org), located in an attractive 1924 Renaissance Revival mansion and hosting a range of cultural events and rotating exhibits. The specialities here are ceramics and international art, with Native-American art and textiles, African craftwork and jewellery, and contemporary Korean ceramics only a few of the highlights. There are also classical and world music performances and examples of decorative arts, drawings and textiles from around the globe.

The Richard Nixon Presidential Library and Museum

Mickey Mouse may be its most famous resident, but Orange County's most infamous was 37th US president Richard Milhous Nixon, born in 1913 in what is now freeway-caged **YORBA LINDA**, eight miles northeast of Disneyland. Here, off Imperial Hwy, the **Richard Nixon Presidential Library and Museum**, 18001 Yorba Linda Blvd (Mon–Sat 10am–5pm, Sun 11am–5pm; $10; ⓣ714/993-5075, ⓦwww.nixonlibrary.gov), exhibits items like the presidential limousine, campaign relics, and the little house where the future president was born. In July 2007 control over the site was handed over to the federal government, making it one of the nation's officially approved presidential libraries, and access to the Watergate tapes and other crucial documents from Nixon's era has become more open. Still on view is the **World Leaders Gallery** of Nixon's heyday, with Mao, Brezhnev and de Gaulle among them, cast in bronze and arranged in rigid poses, and the very **helicopter** he used as president, and when he was whisked away from the White House after resigning in disgrace.

There's also a re-creation of the **East Room** of the executive mansion, replicated in architecture and decor. It's an odd tribute, given that Nixon was always uncomfortable in Washington and did all he could to escape it. Even in death, he avoided lying in state and made provision for his memorial service to take place here, where he's buried.

On your way out, stop by the **gift shop** to see its most popular item, a picture of Nixon greeting a zonked-out Elvis in the Oval Office, on the occasion of the president's granting the King – ironically, as it turned out – honorary status as a federal agent in the war on drugs.

The Orange County coast

A string of upscale towns stretching from the edge of the LA Harbor to San Diego County 35 miles south, the **ORANGE COUNTY COAST** is suburbia with a shoreline: swanky beachside houses line the sands, and the general ambience is easygoing, affluent, and conservative or libertarian, depending on the area. As the names of the main towns suggest – **Huntington Beach**, **Newport Beach** and **Laguna Beach** – the best reasons to come here involve sea and sand, though a handful of museums and festivals can also make for interesting excursions as well. To the far south, **San Juan Capistrano** merits a stop as the site of the best kept of all the Californian missions, and **San Clemente** is a surfing hotspot.

The fastest way to **travel** from LA to San Diego skips the coast by passing through Orange County on the inland San Diego Freeway, the 405. The coastal cities, though, are linked by the more appealing **Pacific Coast Highway (PCH)**, part of Hwy-1, which you can pick up from Long Beach. OCTD bus #1 rumbles along PCH every 30–40min during the day, though Greyhound connections mostly run inland. **Amtrak** connects Downtown LA (or Disneyland) to San Juan Capistrano, though you can travel all the way along the coast from LA to San Diego using local buses for about $6–8 – but allow a full day for the trip. A pricier, but more worthwhile, transit option is the Metrolink commuter train line (see p.28), which not only connects Downtown LA with Orange County down to San Clemente ($12.50), but continues on to Oceanside in San Diego County ($14.50), from where you can pick up that region's Coaster and connect to downtown San Diego.

Huntington Beach

Starting on the north coast, **HUNTINGTON BEACH**, or "**Surf City USA**," is the most free-spirited of the beach communities and one that you don't need a fortune to enjoy. It's a compact place composed of cafés and shops grouped around the foot of a long **pier**, off PCH at Main Street. Here, you can find the **Surfers Walk of Fame**, appropriately honouring the greats of the sport – this is where California **surfing** began in 1907, imported from Hawaii to encourage curious day-trippers to visit on the Pacific Electric Railway (whose chief, Henry Huntington, the town was named after). Top surfers still flock here to take a crack at notable stretches like Bolsa Chica, Dog and Huntington State beaches, and there are also regular lifeguarding, kite-flying, and, especially, surfing competitions. A good time to come is during one of the **Surf City Nights**, Main St between Walnut and Orange aves (Tues 5–9pm; free), when spirited local musicians perform and a farmers' market takes place. Another highlight is the **International Surfing Museum**, 411 Olive Ave (Mon–Fri noon–5pm, Sat & Sun 11am–6pm; free; ⓣ714/960-3483, ⓦwww.surfingmuseum.org), which features exhibits on such legends as Corky Carroll and Duke Kahanamoku, historic posters and information on world surfing contests, and traditional and contemporary boards, including one shaped like a Swiss Army Knife.

Several miles north, nature lovers won't want to miss the **Bolsa Chica State Ecological Reserve**, PCH at Warner Avenue, a sizable wetland preserve that's been kept out of the hands of local developers by state regulation. Taking a one-and-a-half-mile loop walk will get you acquainted with some of the current avian residents of this salt marsh, including a fair number of herons, egrets and grebes, and even a few peregrine falcons and endangered snowy plovers. Self-tours are free, and guided tours are available on the first Saturday of the month (9–10.30am; $1; groups by reservation at ⓣ714/840-1575, ⓦwww.amigosdebolsachica.org).

Newport Beach and Corona del Mar

Ten miles south from Huntington Beach, **NEWPORT BEACH**, with its myriad yachts and yacht clubs, is upmarket even by Orange County standards. The town is spread around a natural bay that cuts several miles inland, and although there are hardly any conventional "sights" in town, the obvious place to hang out is on the thin **Balboa Peninsula**, an artificial formation created from infill, accessed along Balboa Boulevard, which runs parallel to the three-mile-long beach. The most socially active section, with a number of bars and restaurants, is about halfway along, around **Newport Pier** at the end of 20th Street. To the north, beachfront homes restrict access; to the south, around **Balboa Pier** (the second of the city's piers), there's a marina from which you can hop on the *Catalina Flyer*, which leaves for Santa Catalina Island (1hr 15min trip, leaves daily 9am, returns 4.30pm; $68 total; ⓣ800/830-7744, ⓦwww.catalinainfo.com).

On the peninsula itself, the one highlight is Rudolph Schindler's modernist **Lovell Beach House**, 1242 Ocean Ave, finished in 1926. Raised on five concrete legs, its living quarters cantilevered over the sidewalk, the blocky white concrete-and-glass house made the architect's international reputation and could easily pass for a product of four decades after.

Across the main harbour channel from the peninsula, the Newport Beach district of **CORONA DEL MAR** is mainly worth a stop for its **Sherman Library and Gardens**, 2647 E Pacific Coast Highway (daily 10.30am–4pm; $3; ⓣ949/675-5458, ⓦwww.slgardens.org), devoted to the horticulture of the American Southwest. Among the many vivid blooms raised in its botanical gardens are cacti, orchids, roses and an array of different herbs. Due north from the gardens, is the **Orange County Museum of Art**, 850 San Clemente Drive (Wed–Sun 11am–5pm, Thurs closes 8pm; $12; ⓣ949/759-1122, ⓦwww.ocma.net), one of the county's few modern art institutions on par with its LA rivals. Its collection focuses on contemporary work from California artists like Lari Pittman, Edward Ruscha and Ed Kienholz, and there are periodical retrospectives of great twentieth century figures as well as Southern Californian up-and-comers.

A short distance west, San Joaquin Hills Road leads you to Backbay Drive, which makes a marvellous trip around the edge of one of Orange County's natural wonders, the **Upper Newport Bay Ecological Reserve**, 2301 University Drive (daily 7am–dusk; $3 weekdays, $5 weekends; ⓣ949/923-2290, ⓦwww.ocparks.com/uppernewportbay), a thousand-acre preserve where you can see a great range of birds, including falcons, pelicans, terns and rails, some of them endangered. The preserve – and its hills, wetlands and inlets – also presents excellent opportunities for hiking, kayaking, horse riding and cycling. The **interpretive centre** (Tues–Sun 10am–4pm; free) provides an overview of the area's ecology and geology.

Crystal Cove State Park

Back along PCH, the area between Newport and Laguna beaches offers an inviting, unspoiled three-mile chunk of coastline, **Crystal Cove State Park** (daily 6am–dusk; free; parking $15; ⓦwww.crystalcovestatepark.com). Its two thousand acres of rugged inland terrain are good for hiking, horseriding, and biking, on trails that cross hilly peaks and ravines. Bluffs tower over the beach, and a fascinating twelve-acre Historic District contains 46 beachside bungalows and cottages (dorm room $31 per person, private cottages $125–191; see "Accommodation", p.217) that provide a hint of the rustic character of the shoreline when they were constructed in the 1920s and 30s. Crystal Cove also has some excellent stretches for surfing, diving, and snorkelling, exploring the aquaculture of the offshore "underwater park", or just poking around on the beach among the coves and tide pools.

Laguna Beach

Six miles south of Crystal Cove, nestled among the crags around a small sandy beach, charming and laid-back **LAGUNA BEACH** is just as well heeled as every

The festivals of Laguna Beach

Laguna Beach hosts a number of large summer **art festivals** over six weeks in July and August. The best known is the **Pageant of the Masters**, in which the participants pose in front of a painted backdrop to portray a famous work of art. It might sound ridiculous, but it's actually quite impressive and takes a great deal of preparation – something reflected in the prices: $15–150 for shows that sell out months in advance. You may, however, be able to pick up cancellations on the night (shows begin at 8.30pm; ⓣ949/497-6582 or 1-800/487-3378, ⓦwww.foapom.com). The idea for the pageant was hatched during the Depression as a way to raise money for local artists, and the action takes place at the Irving Bowl, close to where Broadway meets Laguna Canyon Road, a walkable distance from the bus station. The pageant is combined with the **Festival of the Arts** (daily 10am–11.30pm; $7; information as above) held at the same venue, featuring the work of 150 local artists.

The excitement of both festivals waned in the 1960s, when a group of hippies created the alternative **Sawdust Festival**, 935 Laguna Canyon Rd (July & Aug 10am–10pm; $7.75, season pass $15; ⓣ949/494-3030, ⓦwww.sawdustartfestival.org). These days, it's just as established as the other two, but easier to get into, featuring artists setting up makeshift studios to demonstrate their skills.

other spot along this part of the coast, though it has the benefit of a flourishing arts scene in its many street-side galleries.

PCH passes through the centre of Laguna, a few steps from the small main **beach**. From the beach's north side, a walkway twists around the coastline above a protected **ecological area**, enabling you to peer down on the ocean and, when the tide's out, scamper over the rocks to observe the tide-pool activity. In the vicinity is the **Laguna Art Museum**, 307 Cliff Drive (daily 11am–5pm; $15; ⓣ949/494-8971, ⓦwww.lagunaartmuseum.org), which has changing exhibitions from its stock of Southern California art from the 1900s to the present. A few miles south is relaxed **South Laguna**, where the secluded **Victoria** and **Aliso beaches** are among several below the bluffs.

About two and a half miles inland from downtown Laguna Beach is one sight not to be missed by lovers of sea life, the **Friends of the Sea Lion Marine Mammal Center**, 20612 Laguna Canyon Rd (daily 10am–4pm; free; ⓣ949/494-3050, ⓦwww.pacificmmc.org), a rehabilitation centre that lets you watch as underweight, injured or otherwise threatened seals and sea lions are nursed back to health.

San Juan Capistrano

Four miles south of South Laguna and three miles inland, along the I-5 freeway, most of the small suburb of **SAN JUAN CAPISTRANO** is built in a Spanish Colonial style derived from the **Mission San Juan Capistrano**, right in the centre of town at Ortega Highway and Camino Capistrano (daily 8.30am–5pm; $9; ⓣ949/234-1300, ⓦwww.missionsjc.com), a short walk from the Amtrak stop. The seventh of California's missions, founded by Junípero Serra in 1776, the mission was so well populated within three years that it outgrew the original chapel. Soon after, the **Great Stone Church** was erected, the ruins of which are the first thing you see as you walk in. A full-sized replica – now a church – is just northwest of the mission.

The mission's main **chapel** is small and narrow, decorated with Indian drawings and Spanish artefacts from the mission's earliest days, and set off by a sixteenth-century altar from Barcelona. In a side room is the chapel of **St Pereguin**, a tiny room kept warm by the heat from the dozens of candles lit by hopeful pilgrims who arrive here from all over the US and Mexico. Other restored buildings include the kitchen, smelter and workshops for dyeing, weaving and candle-making. The complex is also noted for its **swallows**, popularly thought to return here from their winter migration every March 19. They sometimes do arrive on schedule, but the birds are more likely to show up as soon as the weather is warm enough, and when there are enough insects on the ground to provide a decent homecoming banquet.

San Clemente

Five miles south of San Juan Capistrano down I-5, the sleepy town of **SAN CLEMENTE** is a pretty little place, its streets contoured around the hills, creating an almost Mediterranean air. It's also home to some of Orange County's better surfing beaches, especially toward the south end of town, and a reasonable campground, too (see "Accommodation", p.217). Around the city's southern tip, San Clemente had a brief glimmer of fame when President Richard Nixon convened his **Western White House** here from 1969 to 1974, regularly meeting cronies and political allies. The 25-acre estate is located off Avenida del Presidente and visible from the beach, but off limits to interlopers.

Listings

Listings

Accommodation

There are plenty of options for **accommodation** in Los Angeles, whether you seek budget motels or world-class resorts. Finding somewhere that's good value *and* well located can be trickier, but it's far from impossible, especially if you don't mind a short drive or light-rail trip between your hotel room and your destination. If money is the issue and you must stay in an ultra-budget motel farther from the action, you'll need to be choosy about the district you pick, as getting across town can be a time-consuming business. Either that or stay in a better-located hostel, if you don't mind a loud atmosphere.

You can often find worthwhile deals by booking online through a site such as Hotwire or Priceline. An adequate **motel** or low-end **hotel** will start at $70 for a double, and if you're comfortable in the familiar two-storey, neon-lit 1960s motel built around a shallow swimming pool, with minimal amenities, you'll find many options. For pricier accommodations, LA has a seemingly limitless collection of high-end **hotels** and **resorts** that rival the best in the world for views, comfort and amenities – and you can expect to pay a small fortune for some of them ($500–1000 a night in some cases). **Bed-and-breakfasts** are slowly becoming more common in LA (typically based on a Victorian-architecture or country-cottage theme), but the few that do exist tend to be expensive.

For those on a tight budget, a dozen **hostels** are dotted all over the city, many in good locations with desirable amenities – though at some, stays are limited to a few nights, and at others, the nonstop party atmosphere can be grating. **Camping** is also an option – from the beach north of Malibu, throughout Orange County, on Santa Catalina Island, and in the San Gabriel Mountains – but you'll need a car (or a boat) to get to these campgrounds.

Where to stay

LA is so big that if you want to avoid constantly having to cross huge, congested expanses, it makes sense to divide your stay between several districts. Prices and options vary widely by area, and except for the most desirable spots – Beverly Hills, West Hollywood, Malibu, beachside Santa Monica – you can find standard chain hotels that are reasonably affordable. **Downtown** has both swank hotels and drab, basic dives, though the tendency these days is more toward the upper end. **Hollywood** provides a good range of choices, a few of them historic hotels and some classic roadside motels, along Hollywood and Sunset boulevards, while **West Hollywood** has some of the most chic and trendy accommodation in town, with predictably high prices. **West LA** and **Beverly Hills** are predominantly upper-range territory, with very expensive establishments in Century City and the relatively few bargains around the Westwood campus of UCLA, and better deals

Accommodation prices

The **accommodation prices** quoted are for the least-expensive double room in each establishment throughout most of the year. As with most major cities, however, rates can fluctuate wildly, rising steeply during the busiest periods – holidays, summer weekends, popular conventions, etc – or dropping similarly when chance discounts are offered. The steepest fluctuations are noted in the review. Bear in mind also that in Los Angeles all room rates are subject to a fourteen percent **room tax** in addition to the rates listed below.

in more out of the way locations such as Culver City. Staying in **Santa Monica** can be costly near the ocean and inexpensive further inland, while just south, **Venice** offers a cheaper alternative, though higher-ticket properties are making headway in recent years. If all else fails, **Marina del Rey** to the south has a number of clean chain hotels grouped near the marina.

Among options further out from central LA, the **South Bay** has a fair selection of low- to mid-range hotels strung along the Pacific Coast Highway, with higher-end hotels in **Long Beach**. The upscale choices in the **San Gabriel** and **San Fernando valleys** are around Pasadena and Universal City, respectively, and many chain alternatives can be found everywhere else, including North Hollywood, Burbank and further out. The limited selections in **Malibu** are almost all upper-end resorts or inns (worth the trip if you have the money), except for several dingy roadside motels along PCH – located well out of town. Finally, the least inspired accommodations in **Orange County** tend to be right around Disneyland, though Anaheim has a handful of good choices here and there, while the Orange County coast has many more appealing choices, from luxury hotels to quirky motels to inexpensive youth hostels.

Note that accommodation listings appear in the relevant chapter maps throughout the guide.

Hotels and motels

Hotels and **motels** are listed by neighbourhood, with specific accommodation options for gay and lesbian travellers listed in Chapter 16, "Gay and lesbian LA"– though most LA hotels are gay friendly. We've also listed a few affordable places to stay near the airport should you be arriving late or leaving early (see p.210).

On the whole, you can comfortably stay throughout LA by **spending** around $125 a night, but there are plenty of bare-bones spots charging far less. Paying $250 will get you an elegant, entry-level room in a swanky hotel, and beyond that anything is possible, with suites often going for $400 and up. Lower on the food chain, many affordable chain hoteliers offer basic suites for around $180.

Listed **amenities** include features that are not always standard to hotel rooms in the area, such as hot tubs, CD and DVD players, iPod docks, flatscreen TVs, fireplaces, internet access, kitchenettes, refrigerators, on-site gyms, sun decks and saunas. More common in-room amenities – the likes of ironing boards, hairdryers, cable TV, coffee makers, free newspapers, free morning bagels and juice, etc – are not listed, except in truly low-end accommodation where their presence comes as a surprise. Finally, note that parking in Los Angeles is uniformly expensive; a few places in out of the way locales will have free parking, but if you want to stay anywhere reasonably popular, per-night rates start at $10–15 and can go as high as $30–35 at the most elegant hotels downtown, in West Hollywood, or in Beverly Hills.

Downtown and around

Comfort Inn 2717 W Sunset Blvd ⓣ213/413-8222, ⓦwww.comfortinn.com. Central to Silver Lake and Echo Park, a solid chain bet for clean and modern furnishings, with gated parking, microwaves and free breakfast. Not too far from Dodger Stadium, either. $115

Downtown LA Standard 550 S Flower St ⓣ213/892-8080, ⓦwww.standardhotel.com. The downtown branch of LA's self-consciously trendy chain has sleek, modern furnishings but rather minimal amenities. It's best for its rooftop bar. Although billed as a "business hotel", the party scene is pretty much constant. Avoid the posy, depressing West Hollywood branch. $159

Hilton Checkers 535 S Grand ⓣ213/624-0000 or 1-800/HILTONS, ⓦwww.hiltoncheckers.com. One of the great LA hotels, with sleek modern appointments in historic 1920s architecture, and nicely furnished rooms, gym, rooftop deck with pool and spa, and swanky *Checkers* restaurant (see p.228). Terrific Downtown views, too. $169

JW Marriott at LA Live 900 W Olympic Blvd ⓣ213/765-8600, ⓦwww.lalivemarriott.com. The main reason to stay at this Marriott, instead of the other Downtown, is for the close access to the LA LIVE entertainment complex and the Staples Center. But unless you've come to town for that, the overpriced rooms here aren't worth the extra money. $179

Kyoto Grand Hotel 120 S Los Angeles St ⓣ213/629-1200, ⓦwww.kyotograndhotel.com. Sleek, Japanese-styled business hotel with gym, beauty salon and straightforward rooms, as well as three decent restaurants. An authentic Japanese garden is also a draw for its fetching scenery. $139

Los Angeles Athletic Club 431 W Seventh St ⓣ213/625-2211, ⓦwww.laac.com. Beaux Arts brick-and-terracotta charmer that's home to an exclusive club, but the top three floors make up a hotel with 72 serviceable rooms and nine expensive suites, all with free WiFi and flat-screen TVs; a real plus is free use of the club's gym equipment, and handball and basketball courts, plus a whirlpool and sauna. $139

Marriott Downtown 333 S Figueroa St ⓣ213/617-1133, ⓦwww.marriott.com. Palm-tree-laden pool area, spacious rooms, and health club add some charm to this chain business hotel with clean and modern rooms, centrally located near the 110 and 101 freeways, and Bunker Hill sights such as Disney Hall and MOCA. $159

Millennium Biltmore 506 S Grand Ave at Fifth St ⓣ213/624-1011 or 1-800/222-8888, ⓦwww.thebiltmore.com. Renaissance Revival architecture from 1923, combined with modern luxury: a health club modelled on a Roman bathhouse, cherub and angel decor, and a view overlooking Pershing Square. The well-appointed rooms match the stateliness of the design. All things considered, Downtown LA's best deal for luxury. $179

Miyako Inn and Spa 328 E First St ⓣ213/617-2000, ⓦwww.miyakoinn.com. Despite the grim, concrete-box exterior, this mid-priced hotel offers comfortable rooms with fridges, plus on-site gym, spa, massage room and free internet access. $149

Omni Los Angeles 251 S Olive St at Fourth St ⓣ213/617-3300 or 1-800/327-0200, ⓦwww.omnilosangeles.com. Fancy Bunker Hill hotel with plush, elegant rooms, swimming pool and weight room. Excellent location adjacent to MOCA and the Music Center. One of the best deals in LA. $135

Sheraton Downtown 711 S Hope St ⓣ213/488-3500, ⓦwww.sheraton.com. A block from the Metrorail line, this business hotel offers smart but standard corporate rooms just south of Bunker Hill, with a spa and health club on site, and internet access. $149

Stay Hotel 636 S Main St **ⓣ**213/213-7829, **ⓦ**www.stayhotels.com. Rock-bottom-priced lodging near a dicey section of the Old Bank District, offering internet access and some rooms with DVD players, but mostly small, no-frills accommodation. Rooms with shared bathroom $50, add $20 for private bathroom. Also some dorm rooms for $25 per person.

Vagabond Inn 3101 S Figueroa St ⓣ213/746-1531 or 1-800/522-1555, ⓦwww.vagabondinn.com. The cheapest place to stay near USC and the Shrine Auditorium, a few miles south of Downtown. Ultra-basic chain-motel rooms, with an on-site pool. $89

Westin Bonaventure 404 S Figueroa St, between Fourth and Fifth Sts ⓣ213/624-1000 or 1-800/228-3000, ⓦwww.westin.com. Modernist luxury hotel with five glass towers that resemble cocktail shakers, a six-storey atrium with a "lake", and elegant, conic-shaped rooms. A breathtaking exterior elevator ride ascends to the rotating cocktail lounge, Bona Vista (see p.247). $149

Wilshire Grand **930 Wilshire Blvd ⓣ213/688-7777 or 1-888/773-2888, ⓦwww.wilshiregrand.com.** Large, somewhat faded Bunker Hill hotel with health club and pool. Mainly geared toward business travellers heading to the nearby convention centre. The rooms are rather bland, but special discounts can knock up to $20–30 off the price. $135

Mid-Wilshire

Beverly Laurel **8018 Beverly Blvd at Laurel Ave ⓣ323/651-2441.** While the coffee shop here, *Swingers* (see p.223), attracts most of the attention, the motel has nice retro-1960s touches, albeit plain rooms. Good location, not far from the Fairfax District and Beverly Hills. $129

Farmer's Daughter **115 S Fairfax Ave ⓣ323/937-3930 or 1-800/334-1658, ⓦwww.farmersdaughterhotel.com.** Conveniently located across from (naturally) the farmers' market, a boutique property with internet access, DVD players, flat-screen TVs and elements of the Midwestern kitsch. Recently renovated. $179

Orlando **8384 W Third St ⓣ323/658-6600, ⓦwww.theorlando.com.** Elegant, well-appointed rooms make this one of the area's better boutique hotels, with plasma TVs, DSL access, swimming pool, hot tub and fitness centre. Good location for accessing the Beverly Center mall. $169

Oxford Palace **745 S Oxford Ave ⓣ213/389-8000, ⓦwww.oxfordhotel.com.** Adequate choice for business travellers with free WiFi, straightforward rooms and a few suites. Located near the heart of Koreatown, just around the corner from the Wiltern Theater. $125

Hollywood

Best Western Hollywood Hills **6141 Franklin Ave between Gower and Vine ⓣ323/464-5181, ⓦwww.bestwesterncalifornia.com.** Reliable chain hotel, with nice amenities such as free WiFi, iPod docks, microwaves, fridges and heated pool, at the foot of the Hollywood Hills. $199

Dunes Sunset **5625 Sunset Blvd ⓣ323/467-5171.** On the dingy eastern side of Hollywood, but far enough away from the weirdness of Hollywood Blvd to feel safe. Adequate motel rooms with free WiFi and free parking and convenient to major sights. $99

Holiday Inn Express **2005 N Highland Ave ⓣ323/850-8151 or 1-877/859-5095, ⓦwww.hiexpress.com.** Massive and well placed, near the heart of Hollywood Boulevard and the Chinese Theatre. Clean and modern rooms with flat-screen HDTVs and internet access. Other amenities include pool, spa, gym and business centre. $169

Hollywood Hills Magic Hotel **7025 Franklin Ave ⓣ323/851-0800, ⓦwww.magiccastlehotel.com.** One of the unheralded deals in these parts, a boutique hotel with studios and suites with kitchens, CD and DVD players, free WiFi, plus continental breakfast. An added plus is that guests can buy tickets to the adjacent Magic Castle (see p.91) – otherwise off-limits to the general public. $195

Hollywood Celebrity **1775 Orchid Ave ⓣ323/850-6464 or 1-800/222-7017, ⓦwww.hotelcelebrity.com.** Good choice on the affordable boutique scene, with great location in central Hollywood and rooms with charming furnishings and free breakfast and free high-speed internet. $139

Hollywood Liberty **1770 Orchid Ave ⓣ323/962-1788, ⓦwww.hollywoodlibertyhotel.com.** Creaky but clean old spot near the centre of the tourist district, featuring WiFi access and free breakfast. Good value for the area, but don't expect much in the way of amenities. $99

Hollywood Roosevelt **7000 Hollywood Blvd ⓣ323/466-7000, ⓦwww.hollywoodroosevelt.com.** The first hotel built for the movie greats in 1927. The place reeks of atmosphere, with cabanas and suites, plus a Jacuzzi, fitness room and swimming pool. However, many of the old-fashioned rooms can be a bit cramped for modern travellers. $219

Orchid Suites **1753 Orchid Ave ⓣ323/874-9678 or 1-800/537-3052, ⓦwww.orchidsuites.com.** Roomy, if spartan, suites with cable TV, free WiFi, kitchenettes, laundry room and heated pool. Very close to the most popular parts of Hollywood and adjacent to the massive Hollywood & Highland mall; good value. $129

Renaissance Hollywood **1755 N Highland Blvd ⓣ323/856-1200, ⓦwww.renaissancehollywood.com.** The centrepiece of the Hollywood & Highland mall, with arty, boutique-style rooms and suites and a prime location in the heart of Tinseltown. $239

Saharan **7212 Sunset Blvd at Poinsettia Place ⓣ323/874-6700, ⓦwww.saharanhotel.com.** A classic 1950s-style motel: double-decker layout with standard rooms built around a pool, plus cheesy neon sign and brash colour scheme. The cheapest decent digs you'll find in Hollywood. $99

Sunset–La Brea Travelodge 1401 N Vermont St ⓣ323/665-5735, ⓦwww.travelodge.com. A cheap bet east of Hollywood's major sights, with adequate rooms, free parking, sundeck and pool. Not the prettiest area, but just two blocks south of Barnsdall Park and a Metrorail stop. $89

West Hollywood

Andaz West Hollywood 8401 Sunset Blvd ⓣ323/656-1234, ⓦwww.westhollywood.andaz.hyatt.com. What used to be the legendary *Hyatt West Hollywood* has been smartly remodelled into this ultra-modern, very chic property with designer furnishings, free WiFi, widescreen TVs and rooftop deck and pool. $250

Chamberlain 1000 Westmount Drive ⓣ310/657-7400, ⓦwww.chamberlainwesthollywood.com. Sumptuous hotel just off the Strip, within easy walking distance of major attractions. The impressive suites include sunken living rooms, internet access, DVD players, fireplaces, balconies and refrigerators. $250

Chateau Marmont 8221 Sunset Blvd at Crescent Heights Blvd ⓣ323/626-1010, ⓦwww.chateaumarmont.com. Iconic Norman Revival hotel, which resembles a dark castle or Hollywood fortress and has hosted all manner of celebrities. Come for the history, but don't expect any kind of deal. Largely suites and bungalows, up to $3000. Cheapest rooms are around $370

Elan Hotel Modern 8435 Beverly Blvd ⓣ323/658-6663, ⓦwww.elanhotel.com. Very good-value boutique hotel, located in a busy shopping zone just north of the Beverly Center mall. Rooms are appointed in smart style, with free WiFi, breakfast and wine and cheese in the later afternoon. Also has fitness centre and spa. $179

Grafton on Sunset 8462 Sunset Blvd ⓣ323/654-4600, ⓦwww.graftononsunset.com. Mid-level boutique hotel with bright and trendy furnishings, CD and DVD players, iPod docks, and flat-screen TVs, plus a pool and fitness centre. $169

Le Montrose 900 Hammond St ⓣ310/855-1115, ⓦwww.lemontrose.com. Excellent spot with splashy modern stylings, featuring upscale restaurant and rooftop tennis courts, pool and hot tub. Most rooms are suites with amenities such as kitchenettes, balconies and fireplaces. $279

Le Parc 733 N West Knoll Drive ⓣ310/855-8888 or 1-800/578-4837, ⓦwww.leparcsuites.com. Graceful apartment hotel in a residential area not far from major sights, with simple studios, more spacious one- and two-bedroom suites, stereos, refrigerators, balconies, kitchenettes, plasma TVs, and rooftop pool and hot tub with views of the hills. $259

London West Hollywood 1020 N San Vicente Blvd ⓣ1-866/282-4560, ⓦwww.thelondonwesthollywood.com. Arty, Euro-flavoured hotel whose lovely rooms have upscale contemporary decor, balconies and kitchens. Public areas include an exquisite lobby, pool, Jacuzzi and gym. One of the most tasteful and elegant of the upper-end hotels in West Hollywood. $319

Sunset Marquis 1200 N Alta Loma Rd ⓣ310/657-1333 or 1-800/858-9758, ⓦwww.sunsetmarquishotel.com. A lush hangout for musicians, with private cabanas around two pools, plus a hot tub, sauna and weight room. There are very pricey villas set in gardens; most rooms are smart suites with kitchens, balconies and patios. $299

Sunset Tower 8358 Sunset Blvd ⓣ323/654-7100, ⓦwww.sunsettowerhotel.com. An Art Deco landmark now converted into an upper-end luxury hotel, featuring automotive radiator-grill decor and 1930s Zigzag Moderne style, but also modern boutique amenities, 24hr gym, spa and pool, along with prime views of the Sunset Strip. $295

Beverly Hills and Century City

Avalon 9400 W Olympic Blvd ⓣ310/277-5221, ⓦwww.avalonbeverlyhills.com. Located in south Beverly Hills, this hipster hotel boasts mid-modern furnishings with in-room CD players, internet access and balconies. The chic poolside bar is where Entourage types pose and cut actual Hollywood deals. $168

Beverly Hills Hotel 9641 Sunset Blvd ⓣ310/276-2251 or 1-800/283-8885, ⓦwww.beverlyhillshotel.com. The pinnacle of hotels in LA and the classic Hollywood resort, with a Mission-style design surrounded by its own exotic gardens. Rooms have marbled bathrooms, VCRs, Jacuzzis and other such luxuries, and the famed Polo Lounge restaurant is here for proper celebrity-watching. $475

Beverly Hilton 9876 Wilshire Blvd ⓣ310/274-7777 or 1-800/922-5432, ⓦwww.hilton.com.

Prominent white, geometric hotel at the corner of Wilshire and Santa Monica boulevards. Business centre, pool and gym, and in-room plasma TVs, boutique decor, and balconies. $205

Beverly Wilshire 9500 Wilshire Blvd ☎310/275-5200, www.fourseasons.com. Located near the heart of Rodeo Drive, amid countless boutiques and chic department stores, this refurbished 1928 hotel has stylish modern rooms with HDTVs, three restaurants, palatial architecture, and views overlooking Beverly Hills. $595

Century Plaza 2025 Avenue of the Stars ☎310/277-2000, www.centuryplaza.hyatt.com. In the middle of Century City, a huge, crescent-shaped hotel offering stylish rooms with outstanding views from Beverly Hills to the ocean. Amenities include pools, spa, health club, business centre and car rental outlets. $259

Crescent 403 N Crescent Drive ☎310/247-0505 or 1-800/451-1566, www.crescentbh.com. Near Beverly Hills City Hall and Rodeo Drive, a formerly low-end property that's been smartened up a bit, though it still has its creaky side. Offers free breakfast and Internet access. Considering the price, it's mainly worth it if you're after a central location over all else. $179

Four Seasons Beverly Hills 300 S Doheny Drive ☎310/273-2222 or 1-800/332-3442, www.fourseasons.com/losangeles. One of the most famous luxury hotels in town, featuring designer-furnished rooms with balconies, elegant traditional decor, and decent artworks, along with pool and health-club facilities. Ultra-high prices attract A-list celebs in droves. $495

Intercontinental Century City 2151 Avenue of the Stars ☎310/284-6500 or 1-800/496-7621, www.intercontinental.com. Century City stalwart with access to sights in West LA and Beverly Hills. Business-oriented rooms with balconies and on-site pool, sauna, gym and spa. $219

Luxe Hotel Rodeo Drive 360 N Rodeo Drive, Beverly Hills ☎310/273-0300, www.luxehotels.com. The self-appointed bastion of luxury on central Rodeo, where the rooms have boutique furnishings and all the amenities you'd expect. You might even spot a celebrity, or at least a lot of rich tourists. $229

Maison 140 140 S Lasky Drive ☎310/281-4000, www.maison140.com. High-profile entry for swank hipsters; the cosy rooms have CD and DVD players and internet access, and there's a saloon bar, fitness room and complimentary breakfast. $165

Mosaic 125 S Spalding Drive ☎310/278-0303, mosaichotel.com. Boutique hotel featuring elegantly furnished rooms with CD players, plasma TVs, free internet access and fridges, and pool, sauna and fitness room. Located near the Golden Triangle shopping zone, but far enough away to sit in its own quiet, leafy setting. $249.

Peninsula Beverly Hills 9882 Little Santa Monica Blvd ☎310/551-2888 or 1-800/462-7899, beverlyhills.peninsula.com. Luxury celebrity digs featuring ultra-chic rooms, suites and villas thick with graceful furnishings and decor, along with pool, sundeck, cabanas, rooftop gardens, whirlpool and weight room. $495; more than double for suites

Tower Beverly Hills 1224 Beverwil Drive ☎310/277-2800, thetowerbeverlyhills.com. Decent accommodation if the bigger-name places are booked. This one has business-standard guestrooms, a health club, pool, gym and some rooms with views and balconies. $159

LAX area

Embassy Suites LAX North 9801 Airport Blvd, just east of LAX ☎310/215-1000 or 1-800/695-8284, www.embassysuites.com. Affordable luxury from this hotel giant, offering in-room wet bars, refrigerators, internet access and microwaves in spacious, two-room suites. Other features include spa, weight room, sauna, pool and airport shuttle. $115

Holiday Inn Express West LA 10330 W Olympic Blvd ☎310/553-1000, www.hiexpress.com. Located between Century City and the Westside Pavilion mall, offering adequate rooms with VCRs and fridges, and suites with lofts and spiral stairways. $159

La Quinta Inn and Suites 5249 W Century Blvd, just east of LAX ☎310/645-2200, www.lq.com. Safe chain choice featuring comfortable and well-equipped rooms with free net access, plus pool, gym, laundry room, two restaurants, a bar and free 24hr LAX shuttles. $95

Renaissance 9620 Airport Blvd ☎310/337-2800 or 1-800/228-9898, www.renaissancehotels.com. One of the best of the LAX-area hotels: swanky wood-and-marble decor, ample rooms, and pool, spa and health club. Elegant suites also available with tasteful appointments and good views. $105

Travelodge LAX 5547 W Century Blvd ⓣ310/649-4000, ⓦwww.travelodge.com. Reliable, basic chain motel with free continental breakfast and WiFi, gym, pool and airport shuttle. $75

West LA

Bel Air 701 Stone Canyon Rd ⓣ310/472-1211 or 1-800/648-1097, ⓦwww.hotelbelair.com. Perhaps LA's poshest hotel, located in a thickly overgrown canyon, with lush gardens and waterfall. Go for a beautiful brunch by the Swan Pond if you can't afford the rooms, which will cost you at least $500–600 for their exquisite decor, spaciousness and luxury amenities. Currently being remodelled; reopening summer 2011.

Best Western Royal Palace 2528 S Sepulveda Blvd ⓣ310/477-9066, ⓦwww.bestwesternroyalpalace.com. The name overstates it more than a little, but if you want a cheap room and don't mind staying near the junction of the 405 and 10 freeways, this is the place: with microwaves and a pool, hot tub and fitness centre. $109

Brentwood Inn 12200 Sunset Blvd ⓣ310/476-9981, ⓦwww.thebrentwood.com. Unassuming little spot that's been around since 1947, but spruced up with boutique furnishings, including flatscreen TVs and high-speed internet access. $149

Carlyle Inn 1119 S Robertson Blvd ⓣ310/275-4445, ⓦwww.carlyle-inn.com. Just north of Pico Boulevard, a hotel close enough to Beverly Hills to make an affordable visit worthwhile. Basic rooms include fridges, and there's also high-speed WiFi, and a smallish gym. $179

Culver Hotel 9400 Culver Blvd ⓣ310/838-7963 or 1-800/888-3-CULVER, ⓦwww.culverhotel.com. Stately old pile in the middle of Culver city with antique decor, chequered marble floors, and old-time iron railings in the lobby. Cosy rooms have good views of the city, but the age of the hotel is often apparent. $159

Hotel Angeleno 170 N Church Lane at Sunset Blvd and 405 freeway ⓣ310/476-6411, ⓦwww.jdvhotels.com/angeleno. Cylindrical concrete eyesore below the Getty Center, but offers boutique furnishings, pool, spa, weight room and rooftop restaurant. All rooms have balconies, some with terrific views across the Westside. Somewhat noisy, right by the 405 freeway. $165

Luxe Sunset Boulevard 11461 Sunset Blvd ⓣ310/476-6571 or 1-800/HOTEL-411, ⓦwww.luxehotels.com. Upper-end spot with impeccable, smartly designed rooms with marble bathtubs, free WiFi, and refrigerators. There are two pools, spa, tennis courts and a health club, plus a free shuttle to nearby Getty Center. $229

Westwood and UCLA

Hilgard House 927 Hilgard Ave ⓣ310/208-3945 or 1-800/826-3934, ⓦwww.hilgardhouse.com. A pleasant, friendly spot with clean, tasteful rooms and excellent location for UCLA. Offers in-room fridges and free WiFi, and some higher-end units come with Jacuzzis and kitchens. $179

Sky Hotel 2352 Westwood Blvd ⓣ310/475-4551, ⓦwww.skyhotella.com. Good-value choice with simple boutique furnishings, rooms with high-speed internet, iPod stations and plasma TVs, gym and business centre. Continental breakfast included. $165

UCLA Guest House 330 Young Drive E ⓣ310/825-2923, ⓦwww.hotels.ucla.edu. Excellent choice for official visitors to the UCLA campus, with rooms offering basic amenities (including complimentary breakfast), use of nearby university recreation centre and kitchenettes available for small extra fee. $143

W Los Angeles 930 Hilgard Ave ⓣ310/208-8765 or 1-800/421-2317, ⓦwww.whotels.com. Chain luxury in Westwood, featuring well-decorated – though not huge – suites with CD players, iPod docks, and Internet access, plus pool, spa, health club and ample parking. $279

Santa Monica and Venice

Ambrose 1255 20th St, Santa Monica ⓣ310/315-1555, ⓦwww.ambrosehotel.com. Excellent choice for inland Santa Monica with Craftsman-styled decor and boutique rooms that have internet access. Continental breakfast included. $229

Bayside 2001 Ocean Ave at Bay St, Santa Monica ⓣ310/396-6000, ⓦwww.baysidehotel.com. Just a block from Santa Monica beach and Main Street, making the price steeper than you'd expect. Adequate rooms on the lower end; higher-priced units offer ocean views, fridges, internet access and kitchenettes. $189

Cal Mar 220 California St, Santa Monica ⓣ310/395-5555, ⓦwww.calmarhotel.com. Good for its central location, plus garden suites have CD/DVD players and dining rooms, kitchens and balconies, and there's a heated pool, fitness room and airport shuttle. $179

Casa del Mar 1910 Ocean Way, Santa Monica ⓣ310/581-5503, ⓦwww.hotelcasadelmar.com. Restored from an old landmark building, this luxury choice is on a beachside strip crowded with upscale hotels, not far from the pier and Promenade. Tasteful rooms feature California-modern decor and internet access, and there's a pool, spa, and garden. For all this, rates start at $350

Fairmont Miramar 101 Wilshire Blvd, Santa Monica ⓣ310/576-7777, ⓦwww.fairmont.com. Swanky hotel that's a fixture near the north end of the Promenade, with designer-furnished suites and tropical-flavoured bungalows ($500+) near the pool, salon, spa, fitness centre and fine views over the Pacific. One of the best luxury choices in town. $349

Georgian 1415 Ocean Ave, Santa Monica ⓣ310/395-9945 or 1-800/538-8147, ⓦwww.georgianhotel.com. A stunning blue-and-gold Art Deco gem, renovated with an airy Californian interior design. Rooms are elegant, if small, though pricier suites offer more space and better views, from Malibu to Palos Verdes. $249

Inn at Venice Beach 327 Washington Blvd, Venice ⓣ310/821-2557 or 1-800/828-0688, ⓦwww.innatvenicebeach.com. A good choice for visiting the beach and the Venice canals, with simple, tasteful rooms with balconies and refrigerators. Other choices in the area are mostly chain-oriented. $209

Loew's Santa Monica Beach 1700 Ocean Ave at Pico Blvd, Santa Monica ⓣ310/458-6700, ⓦwww.loewshotels.com. As with similar hotels on this stretch by the beach, the value of this prominent hotel is somewhat lacking, since the rooms can be a bit too cosy and overpriced. They do, however, come with boutique furnishings and high-speed net access, and the location is hard to beat. $379

Oceana 849 Ocean Ave, Santa Monica ⓣ310/393-0486 or 1-800/777-0758, ⓦwww.hoteloceanasantamonica.com. Almost all-suite hotel with courtyard, good oceanside views, pool, spa, fitness room, in-room kitchens and CD players. Located at the base of trendy Montana Avenue, giving some explanation for the steep prices. $405

Ramada Limited 3130 Washington Blvd, Venice ⓣ310/821-5086, ⓦwww.ramada.com. Located between Venice and Marina del Rey, a good budget choice offering clean rooms with free WiFi and a pool, spa, weight room and complimentary breakfast. A far better option than the grubby, low-end motels littering nearby Lincoln Boulevard. $109

Ritz-Carlton Marina del Rey 4375 Admiralty Way ⓣ310/823-1700, ⓦwww.ritzcarlton.com. A beautiful luxury hotel with all the high-end accoutrements, including rooms with balconies, swimming pool, spa, weight room and garden terrace overlooking the marina. $259

Shutters on the Beach 1 Pico Blvd at Appian Way, Santa Monica ⓣ310/458-0030 or 1-800/334-9000, ⓦwww.shuttersonthebeach.com. The seafront home to the stars, a white-shuttered luxury resort south of the pier. Amenities include hot tubs, pool, spa, sundeck, ground-floor shopping and ocean views. $485

Su Casa Venice Beach 431 Ocean Front Walk ⓣ310/452-9700, ⓦwww.sucasavenicebeach.com. Centrally located beach digs that can be booked by the day, week or month, with a dozen studio rooms and suites, flatscreen TVs, Net access, and laundry (which you'll need, with the limited maid service). $195

Travelodge Santa Monica – Pico Blvd 3102 Pico Blvd ⓣ310/450-5766, ⓦwww.travelodge.com. Clean and basic chain lodging on the eastern edge of town, in a grim, colourless building – but with free WiFi and breakfast. Good fallback if you don't want to pay top dollar for a beachfront spot. $129

Venice Beach House 15 30th Ave, Venice ⓣ310/823-1966, ⓦwww.venicebeachhouse.com. A quaint B&B in a 1911 Craftsman house, with nine comfortable rooms and suites finished with lush period appointments and themed around famous guests, such as Charlie Chaplin and Abbot Kinney. True to the name, it's right next to the beach. $150

Venice on the Beach 2819 Ocean Front Walk ⓣ310/437-4103, ⓦwww.veniceonthebeachhotel.com. Groovy beachside spot whose simply furnished rooms boast microwaves, fridges and net access; some with patios by the sands. Two-night minimum stay on weekends. Excellent, hard-to-find value for the area. $140

Viceroy 1819 Ocean Ave, Santa Monica ⓣ310/451-8711, ⓦwww.viceroysantamonica.com. Luxury option with great bay views and trendy designer decor, and rooms with CD players, on-site pool and lounge. Worth a try, though there are better values in the area. $395

The South Bay and LA Harbor

Beach House at Hermosa 1300 Strand, Hermosa Beach ⓣ310/374-3001, ⓦwww.Beach-House.com. The height of luxury in the South Bay, offering two-room suites with fireplaces, wet bars, balconies, hot tubs, stereos and refrigerators, with many rooms overlooking the ocean. On the beachside concourse of the Strand. $349

Belamar 3501 Sepulveda Blvd, Manhattan Beach ⓣ310/750-0300, ⓦwww.larkspurhotels.com. Good choice for the South Bay, offering boutique-flavoured rooms with DVD players, iPod docks and free WiFi, and some units with balconies. Also has pool and Jacuzzi, gym, business centre and gardens. A good deal, considering the area. $179.

Comfort Inn 200 E Willow St, Long Beach ⓣ562/426-7611, ⓦwww.comfortinn.com. Very good motel accommodation and one of the best deals in the area, a property with clean rooms with free WiFi and free breakfast, business centre, gym and pool. Not too far from the *Queen Mary*. $109

Hilton Long Beach 710 W Ocean Blvd ⓣ562/983-3400, ⓦwww.hilton.com. Chic corporate property whose rooms have the usual style and amenities, with the added plus of prime location near many Downtown sights. The hotel also has a gym, pool and business centre. $139

Hotel Hermosa 2515 PCH, Hermosa Beach ⓣ310/318-6000, ⓦwww.hotelhermosa.com. In a bustling part of town, off a busy stretch of PCH between Hermosa and Manhattan beaches, one of the cheaper hotel options, with free WiFi. Bland rooms variously have balconies, sea views and Jacuzzis, and there are some suites with lofts. A short walk to the beach. $119

Portofino Hotel and Yacht Club 260 Portofino Way, Redondo Beach ⓣ310/379-8481, ⓦwww.hotelportofino.com. Serviceable suite-hotel by the ocean. The best choices are the well-furnished, comfortable two-room suites with hot tubs and vistas over the elite playground of King Harbor. $249

Rodeway Inn 50 Atlantic Ave at Ocean Blvd, Long Beach ⓣ562/435-8369, ⓦwww.rodewayinn.com. Inoffensive chain-motel a block from the beach and a good base for exploring Long Beach and its downtown and harbour area. Has internet access. $95

Shade 1221 N Valley Drive, Manhattan Beach ⓣ310/546-4995, ⓦwww.shadehotel.com. The bleeding edge of trendiness in the South Bay, this boutique property's designer lobby and smart rooms – many with hot tubs – resemble an upscale salon. It offers a chic lounge, pool and spa, though there are better deals around for this price. $395

Varden 335 Pacific Ave ⓣ562/432-8950, ⓦwww.thevardenhotel.com. A 1920s building modernized with sleek white contemporary decor and cosy rooms with free WiFi, flat-screen TVs and a few boutique touches. Plus, its location a block from Pine Avenue makes this a great choice. $109

Westin Long Beach 333 E Ocean Blvd, Long Beach ⓣ562/436-3000, ⓦwww.westin.com. A solid bet for bayside luxury at surprisingly affordable prices, right by the convention centre, with spa, fitness centre, pool and business-oriented rooms. $189

The San Gabriel and San Fernando valleys

Amarano 322 N Pass Ave ⓣ818/842-8887, ⓦwww.thegraciela.com. Smart boutique choice whose stylish rooms have plasma TVs, DVD and CD players, iPod docks and free WiFi. Also with onsite pool, gym, sauna and rooftop sundeck with Jacuzzi. $169

Artists Inn 1038 Magnolia St, South Pasadena ⓣ626/799-5668 or 1-888/799-5668, ⓦwww.artistsinns.com. Themed B&B with ten rooms and suites (some with spas and fireplaces) honouring famous painters and styles. Best of all is the Italian Suite, with an antique tub and sun porch. Located just two blocks from a Gold Line Metro stop. $140

Best Western Pasadena Inn 3600 E Colorado Blvd ⓣ626/793-0950, ⓦwww.bestwesterncalifornia.com. Comfortable chain lodging with clean rooms, internet access, fridges and pool. Much closer to Arcadia's LA County Arboretum than to Old Pasadena. $75.

Holiday Inn Universal Studios 4222 Vineland Ave, North Hollywood ⓣ818/980-8000 or 1-800/238-3759, ⓦwww.beverlygarland.com. Two-tower complex with standard chain-style rooms (some with balconies), but also with pool, tennis courts, gym and sauna, and close to Universal Studios CityWalk. $159

Langham Huntington 1401 S Oak Knoll Ave, Pasadena ⓣ626/568-3900, ⓦpasadena.langhamhotels.com. Landmark 1906 hotel, located in residential Pasadena on an imposing hilltop. Spacious grounds and courtyards, gym, spa, tennis court and terrific San Gabriel Valley views. The elegant rooms are a bit on the small side, though they offer (paid) WiFi, CD players and flat-screen TVs. $175

Safari Inn 1911 W Olive St, Burbank ⓣ818/845-8586, ⓦwww.safariburbank.com. A classic mid-century motel, renovated but still loaded with Pop-architecture touches. Features a pool fitness room, Burbank airport shuttle and in-room fridges, plus free breakfast. $99

Sheraton Universal 333 Universal Terrace, Universal City ⓣ818/980-1212 or 1-800/325-3535, ⓦwww.starwoodhotels.com/sheraton. A large high-rise hotel on the south end of the Universal Studios lot, with health club, spa, pool and good restaurant, and spacious rooms with superior valley views. Easily accessible off the 101 freeway. $179

Tarzana Inn 19170 Ventura Blvd, San Fernando Valley ⓣ818/345-9410, ⓦwww.tarzanainn.com. A half-mile south of the 101 freeway, this is a handy motel for exploring the Santa Monica Mountains that lie further south. Rooms feature free WiFi and complimentary breakfast. Also pool. $89

Universal City Hilton 555 Universal Terrace, Universal City ⓣ818/506-2500, ⓦwww.hilton.com. A sleek high-rise neighbour to the *Sheraton Universal*, with similar appointments and amenities – pool, spa and health club – though a much better-looking, sparkling steel-and-glass edifice. Located within an easy stroll of CityWalk. $149

Vagabond Inn 1203 E Colorado Blvd at Michigan Ave, Pasadena ⓣ626/449-3170, ⓦwww.vagabondinn.com. Friendly budget chain motel, recently renovated and usefully placed for exploring Pasadena, with flat-screen TVs, free net access, pool and continental breakfast. $89

Westin Pasadena 191 N Los Robles Ave, Pasadena ⓣ626/792-2727, ⓦwww.westin.com. Located in the Plaza de las Fuentes, this imposing pastel creation has Spanish Revival touches such as Mission-style arches and bright, fancy tiling. Rooms have paid internet access and stylish decor, but location is the best feature, near Old Pasadena and City Hall. $159

Malibu and the Santa Monica Mountains

Casa Malibu Inn 22752 PCH ⓣ310/456-2219. Located opposite Carbon Beach and featuring superb, well-appointed rooms – facing a courtyard garden or right on the beach – with great modern design and some in-room fireplaces, Jacuzzis and balconies. $169

Channel Road Inn 219 W Channel Rd at PCH ⓣ310/459-1920, ⓦwww.channelroadinn.com. Romantic getaway nestled in lower Santa Monica Canyon, with ocean views, hot tub and free bike rental. Enjoy complimentary grapes and champagne in the sumptuous rooms, each priced according to its view. $235

Good Nite Inn 26557 Agoura Rd, Calabasas ⓣ818/880-6000, ⓦwww.goodnite.com/calabasas. A good deal if you don't mind driving, this double-decker chain motel boasts a pool and spa, and offers simple rooms at affordable rates in a rustic suburb on the north side of the Santa Monica Mountains. A fifteen-minute drive to the ocean. $59

Homewood Suites 28901 Canwood St Agoura Hills ⓣ818/865-1000, ⓦwww.hwsagourahills.com. Drab suburban location off the 101 freeway, but well placed for easy travel down Kanan Road to Point Dume, Malibu Creek State Park, and other great sights in the Santa Monica Mountains. The suites are smart and clean with kitchens, and there's a pool, gym, laundry and complimentary breakfast. $99

Malibu Beach Inn 22878 PCH ⓣ310/456-6445 or 1-800/4-MALIBU, ⓦwww.malibubeachinn.com. Sunny Spanish Colonial resort by the Malibu Pier on chic, celebrity-thick Carbon Beach, with fireplaces, tiled bathtubs, seaward balconies, DVD players, continental breakfast and oceanside hotel deck. $495

Anaheim

Comfort Inn 300 E Katella Way ⓣ714/772-8713, ⓦwww.comfortinn.com. Reliable chain spot offering rooms with continental breakfast, free internet access and parking, fridges and microwaves, on-site pool and spa, and shuttle to Disneyland, a mile away. $75

Courtyard by Marriott **7621 Beach Blvd, Buena Park ⓣ714/670-6600, ⓦwww.courtyard.com/snabp.** The best bet for visiting Knott's Berry Farm, with in-room fridges and internet access, plus free parking, pool, spa, bar and restaurant. $99

Desert Palms **631 W Katella Ave ⓣ1-888/788-0466, ⓦwww.desertpalmshotel.com.** Rooms and suites with fridges, microwaves, high-speed net access, and buffet breakfast – and suites also with kitchenettes. The hotel usually offers agreeable rates, even during conventions. $115

Disneyland Hotel **1150 W Cerritos Ave at West St ⓣ714/956-6400, ⓦdisneyland.disney.go.com.** A thousand cookie-cutter rooms in a huge, monolithic pile – but an irresistible stop for many. Also with pools, faux beach and interior shopping. The Disneyland monorail stops outside – though park admission is separate. The most fun of three similarly overpriced Disney hotels. $319

Holiday Inn Buena Park **7000 Beach Blvd ⓣ714/522-7000, ⓦwww.holidayinn.com.** Good lodging not far from the Magic Kingdom and Knott's Berry Farm, offering standard rooms with limited amenities, plus gym, pool and spa, and much cheaper rates than the Disney equivalent. $80

Park Place Inn **1544 S Harbor Blvd ⓣ714/776-4800, ⓦwww.parkplaceinnandminisuites.com.** Best Western chain hotel right across from Disneyland, with the customary clean rooms and some mini-suites with fridges and microwaves, plus pool, sauna, Jacuzzi and continental breakfast. $119

Pavilions **1176 W Katella Ave ⓣ714/776-0140, ⓦwww.pavilionshotel.com.** Convenient chain hotel offering basic rooms with fridges, free WiFi and microwaves, as well as a pool, spa, sauna and shuttle to Disneyland. $68

Stovall's Inn **1110 W Katella Ave ⓣ714/778-1880, ⓦwww.stovallsinn.com.** Tasteful, clean chain accommodation near Disneyland, with fitness centre, two pools, two spas and in-room fridges and microwaves. $79

The Orange County coast

Best Western Regency Inn **19360 Beach Blvd, Huntington Beach ⓣ714/962-4244, ⓦwww.bestwesterncalifornia.com.** A few miles from the beach, but still worth it for clean and reliable rooms, pool, Jacuzzi and continental breakfast. $99

Fairmont Newport Beach **4500 MacArthur Blvd ⓣ949/476-2001, ⓦwww.fairmont.com.** Hard to top this brand of luxury on the coast – plasma TVs, CD/DVD players and marble baths are some of the chic amenities offered, with pool, gym and spa. $129

Hilton Waterfront Beach Resort **21100 PCH, Huntington Beach ⓣ714/845-8000, ⓦwww.waterfrontbeachresort.hilton.com.** A towering high-rise whose luxurious rooms have private balconies, and there's a serpentine pool, spa and rentals of everything from surfboards to rollerblades. Rooms have LCD TVs, fridges, microwaves and views of gardens or the ocean. $309

Inn at Laguna Beach **211 N Coast Hwy ⓣ949/497-9722, ⓦwww.innatlagunabeach.com.** Great spot right on the beach, featuring many luxury rooms with ocean views, plus CD players, boutique decor and free continental breakfast; there's also a pool and spa and easy access to the main downtown sights. Two-night minimum weekend stay. $229

Newport Coast Villas **23000 Newport Coast Drive ⓣ949/464-6000, ⓦwww.marriott.com.** Among the swankiest of Marriott's Orange County properties, boasting luxury villas and suites chock full of amenities on well-landscaped grounds. $399.

Pacific Inn **600 Marina Drive, Seal Beach ⓣ1-866/466-0300, ⓦwww.sealbeachinn.com.** Sited between Long Beach and the major Orange County coastal cities, this unassuming spot has pleasant rooms and suites which have, at a minimum, WiFi and complimentary breakfast. Some units have Jacuzzis, fridges and wet bars, and there's an on-site pool and gym. $149

Ritz-Carlton Laguna Niguel **PCH at One Ritz-Carlton Drive ⓣ949/240-2000, ⓦwww.ritzcarlton.com/resorts/laguna_niguel.** Stunning property best for its oceanside beauty (on the cliffs overlooking the sea around Dana Point) and swanky rooms and suites rich with luxurious appointments. The high-end amenities – such as pool, spa and racquet club – are everything you'd expect when paying $425 a night.

Surf and Sand Resort **1555 S Coast Hwy, Laguna Beach ⓣ1-888/869-7969, ⓦwww.surfandsandresort.com.** Among the best of the coast's hotels, with terrific oceanside views, easy beach access, and luxurious rooms and suites with many features, including balconies. Rates begin at $500.

Hostels

As you might expect, **hostels** occupy the bottom of the price scale, offering dorm rooms and beds for somewhere around $18–28, depending on whether you're a member of their organization. Many hostels also offer cut-rate single and double rooms for $45–90. You can expect little more from your stay than a clean, safe bed, somewhere to lock your valuables, and a typically colourful crowd of visitors – sometimes making for quite the party atmosphere. Some hostels also offer tours of local sights, while others organize volleyball, pizza parties and the like. There may be a three to five night maximum stay, though this is generally enforced only when demand outstrips supply.

Banana Bungalow 5920 Hollywood Blvd ⓣ323/469-2500 or 1-877/977-5077, ⓦwww.bananabungalow.com. Popular hostel just east of the main Hollywood action, with airport shuttles, internet, tours to Venice Beach and theme parks, and in-room kitchens and many other amenities. Dorms $25–27, private doubles $69–99. Also a similarly priced branch in West Hollywood at **603 N Fairfax Ave ⓣ323/655-2002.**

Big Bear Hostel 527 Knickerbocker Rd, Big Bear Lake ⓣ909/866-8900, ⓦwww.adventurehostel.com. One of the region's best bets if you've got a car, a mountainside spot with plenty of activities, from skiing and snowboarding in winter to jet-skiing, hiking and parasailing in summer. Two-hour drive from LA. Dorm beds $24–29, private rooms $39–49.

HI-Anaheim/Fullerton 1700 N Harbor Blvd at Brea, Fullerton ⓣ714/738-3721, ⓦwww.hihostels.com. Convenient and comfortable, five miles north of Disneyland on the site of a former dairy farm. The hostel's excellent facilities include a grass volleyball court, golf driving range and picnic area. There are only twenty dorm beds, so reservations are a must. $25

HI-LA/Santa Monica 1436 Second St, Santa Monica ⓣ310/393-9913, ⓦwww.hilosangeles.org. A few blocks from the beach and pier, the building was LA's Town Hall from 1887 to 1889, and retains its historic charm, with a pleasant inner courtyard, internet café, movie room and 260 beds. Reservations essential in summer. $39

HI-LA/South Bay 3601 S Gaffey St, Bldg #613, San Pedro ⓣ310/831-8109, ⓦwww.hihostels.com. Sixty beds in old US Army barracks, with a panoramic view of the Pacific Ocean. Ideal for seeing San Pedro, Palos Verdes and the Harbor Area. Dorms $25; private rooms $47. During Oct–May only open to groups of 20 or more.

Hollywood International 6820 Hollywood Blvd ⓣ323/463-2770 or 1-800/557-7038, ⓦwww.hollywoodhostels.com. Centrally located, with game room, gymnasium, patio garden, kitchen and laundry. Offers tours of Hollywood, theme parks, Las Vegas and Tijuana. Dorms $17, private rooms $40.

Orange Drive Manor 1764 N Orange Drive, Hollywood ⓣ323/850-0350, ⓦorangedrivehostel.com. Centrally located hostel (right behind the Chinese Theatre), offering tours to film studios, theme parks and homes of the stars. Dorm beds $25–35, private rooms $59–79.

Orbit Hotel and Hostel 7950 Melrose Ave ⓣ323/655-1510 or 1-877/ORBIT-US, ⓦwww.orbithotel.com. Retro-1960s hotel and hostel with sleek furnishings and modern decor, offering complimentary breakfast, movie screening room, patio, café, private baths in all rooms, and shuttle tours. Dorms $22–28, private rooms $55–89.

Surf City Hostel 26 Pier Ave, Hermosa Beach ⓣ310/798-2323 or 1-800/305-2901, ⓦsurfcityhostel. Good location near popular beachside strip, the Strand, and numerous restaurants, clubs and bars. Also has kitchen and laundry, and offers shuttles to Disneyland and other major theme parks and shopping zones. Shared rooms $25–30 or private doubles $60–70.

USA Hostels – Hollywood 1624 Schrader Blvd ⓣ323/462-3777 or 1-800/LA-HOSTEL, ⓦwww.usahostels.com. A block south of the centre of Hollywood Boulevard, near major attractions, and with a game room, private baths, main bar, internet access and garden patio, as well as airport and train shuttles. Shared rooms $36–39 and private rooms $82–92.

Campgrounds

Reserve America (☎1-800/444-7275, www.reserveamerica.com) processes reservations at many of the **campgrounds** listed below and can help you find an alternative if your chosen site is full. It charges a $8 fee per reservation per night up to a maximum of eight people per site, including one vehicle.

Mainland

Bolsa Chica ☎714/846-3460 or 1-800/444-7275. Facing the ocean in Huntington Beach, near a thousand-acre wildlife sanctuary and birdwatchers' paradise, with fishing opportunities as well. $50–65 for campers with a self-contained vehicle. No tent camping.

Chilao Recreation Area on Hwy-2, 26 miles north of I-10 ☎818/899-1900, www.fs.fed.us/r5/angeles. The only campground in the San Gabriel Mountains reachable by car, though there are others accessible on foot. Bears are active in the area. For details, contact the Angeles National Forest Ranger Station at 701 N Santa Anita Ave, Arcadia (☎626/574-5200). $12, with $5 vehicle pass; open April to mid-Nov.

Crystal Cove State Park 8471 Pacific Coast Hwy, north of Laguna Beach ☎949/494-3539 or 1-800/444-7275. Two thousand acres of woods and nearly four miles of coastline (rich with tide pools) make this tent-camping park a good, and affordable, choice for all manner of hiking, horseriding, snorkelling, scuba diving and surfing. $25. Also with restored vintage beach cottages (dorm-style $33–98, private $125–191; www.crystalcovebeachcottages.com), which are often reserved many months in advance.

Doheny State Beach 25300 Dana Point Harbor Drive ☎949/496-6171 or 1-800/444-7275. Often packed with families, especially on weekends. Located at southern end of Orange County, not far from Dana Point Harbor. $35, add $10 for beachfront sites.

Leo Carrillo State Beach Park northern Malibu ☎818/706-1310 or 1-800/444-7275. Pronounced "Ca-REE-oh", it's near one of LA's best surfing beaches, with campsites in sight of the ocean. About 25 miles northwest of Santa Monica on Pacific Coast Hwy, not far from the end of Mulholland Highway. $35

Malibu Creek State Park 1925 Las Virgenes Rd, in the Santa Monica Mountains ☎818/706-8809 or 1-800/444-7275. A rustic campground in a park that can become crowded at times. Sixty sites in the shade of huge oak trees, almost all with fire pits, solar-heated showers and flush toilets. One-time filming location for TV show *M*A*S*H*. $35

Point Mugu State Park 9000 W Pacific Coast Hwy ☎818/880-0363 or 1-800/444-7275. On the northwestern edge of the Santa Monica Mountains, this oceanside park has five miles of shoreline, with sand dunes and canyons, and the waters are good for surfing and fishing. $25–35

San Clemente State Beach 3030 Avenida del Presidente, two miles south of San Clemente ☎714/492-7146 or 1-800/444-7275. A prime spot for hiking, diving and surfing, around an area that was once home to Richard Nixon's "Western White House". $35–60

Santa Catalina Island

Campgrounds on **Santa Catalina Island** are all processed through the Catalina Island Company (☎310/510-8368, www.scico.com/camping), which charges $12–16 for adult use, $6–8 for kids, and usually requires reservations. Island transportation by boat or bus is not included; see box on p.160 for more details on getting around the area.

Blackjack Not for the timid – an isolated site high up near the island's centre, poised at 1600 feet. It's a rugged nine-mile trek from the nearest town, Avalon (which has its own, much tamer Hermit Gulch, below), with limited facilities except for barbecues, fire pits, toilets and showers.

Boat-in Sites If you have access to watercraft, use it to reach these fine, secluded spots northeast of Avalon, where you have to bring your own cooking implements (fires not allowed) and all facilities are primitive, without running water. Nine locations with seventeen specific sites.

Hermit Gulch Only a mile and a half from the boat launch at Avalon, this campground is popular and easy to access, with barbecues, picnic tables and a few tepees. Provides a good jumping-off point for exploring the island.

Little Harbor Sited on the island's south side, it's accessible by hiking or by bus. Fire rings are available, but the main draw is the pair of sandy beaches, good for swimming in a relaxed, isolated setting. Kayak and snorkel gear available for rent.

Parsons Landing Remote site on the island's northern tip; eight camp sites with no showers or fresh water, but offering fire rings, picnic tables and, for a fee from a lockbox, firewood and bottled water. Boating is the obvious choice for arrival, though the site is accessible on foot with a two and half mile hike from Emerald Bay, or seven miles from Two Harbors.

Two Harbors Located on a lovely isthmus near the island's centre, a tourist-oriented campground a short distance from the hamlet of Two Harbors, offering standard tent sites, with firewood, fresh water, BBQs and fire rings also available.

Eating

Since the arrival of California cuisine in the 1980s, LA has been one of the major locations on the country's fine dining map, its **restaurants** and **cafés** attracting high-profile chefs and generating a national culinary buzz. Even almost thirty years later, the city's gastronomic trendsetters are still going strong, from old favourites such as *Wolfgang Puck*, who helped get the ball rolling, to newcomers specializing in a variety of Cal-cuisine hybrids, incorporating everything from Northern Italian to pan-Asian. The range of cuisines in LA stretches far beyond the influence of California-style dishes like salmon glazed with saffron and shiitake mushrooms, to encompass everything from exclusive supper clubs to the dingiest burger shacks. Besides the fast-food drive-ins that were invented here, LA is the birthplace of such enduring favourites as the cheeseburger, hot fudge sundae, French dip sandwich and Caesar salad.

For many of the restaurants listed, you won't need to **reserve** ahead, though you should make the effort on weekends, during the peak season or major holidays, and at the most expensive or trendy places, provided they allow it. For **dinner**, expect to pay \$7–10 per person for simple fast food, \$10–25 for most ethnic diners and old-fashioned, steak-and-potatoes American restaurants, and \$35–70 for the latest hot spots of any sort (and this doesn't include tax, tip or alcohol). To sample great food without paying a bundle, go for **lunch** at those upscale eateries that offer it, where you can typically eat for about half of what you might shell out at dinner. The price breaks do not, however, continue downward at those establishments that offer **breakfast**, and unless you're going for a rock-bottom meal at *Denny's* or at *Norm's* diners, you'll end up paying \$10–15 for any sort of edible morning repast.

No matter where you choose to eat, though, don't reach for a cigarette – in 1993, health-conscious LA helped lead the nation in banning **smoking** in restaurants, and the state of California then followed with a blanket tobacco prohibition in restaurants and bars.

Cuisines

Budget food is both iconic and plentiful in LA, ranging from good sit-down meals in street-corner coffee shops to the greasy grub at burger shacks – so much so that we've included a special section that leads off the reviews. Almost as common, and just as cheap, is **Mexican food**, nearly an indigenous LA cuisine. Mexican burrito stands and lunch-trucks are often the city's best deals, serving tasty and filling food for as little as \$5–7 per person; they're at their most authentic in East LA, although there's a broad selection of examples all over the city. The cuisines of the rest of **Latin America** have made plenty of inroads, too, from the piquant flavours of Honduras and Nicaragua and the blending of Peruvian cuisine with local seafood (aka "Peruvian seafood"), to hot, garlicky platters of Argentine beef.

The city lacks a wide selection of **African** restaurants, other than those based on the cuisines of North Africa. Those that do exist are mainly found in small strips around Hollywood and Mid-Wilshire. **Moroccan** food is typically flavourful, often with a little belly dancing thrown into the mix, though not concentrated in any one neighbourhood. The best **Ethiopian** restaurants are in a small pocket around Olympic Boulevard in Mid-Wilshire, and are fairly inexpensive. Aside from such singular cuisines, pan-African hybrids have made some headway on the menus of adventurous restaurants, mixing the grains, spices and vegetables of Africa with the foods of the Caribbean, Europe and the American South.

Old-fashioned **American** cuisine, with its massive steaks, baked potatoes and mountainous salads, doesn't ride the wave of LA food trendiness, but does have its adherents – even among chefs. Some nouveau diners market upscale "comfort food" such as designer meatloaf and inventive grilled-cheese sandwiches, with prices to match the creativity. Generally, American fare is available across LA, costing as little as $10 for a gut-busting blowout in a roadside "greasy spoon", to well over $100 for a full meal with a choice porterhouse served amid chandeliers in a luxury steakhouse.

Much more conspicuous is the juggernaut of **California cuisine**, which not only adds bold new twists to American cooking, but often combines with other cuisines (such as Japanese and Indian) to produce some unusual variations. In its original form, "Cal-cuisine" uses fresh, locally available ingredients, more likely grilled or poached than fried, and is stylishly presented with a nod to French *nouvelle cuisine*. In its more recent and decadent incarnation, it's an excuse to mix and match discordant flavors on the same plate, with dubious results – there's only so much apple-cinnamon-glazed beef heart one can stand.

As a sidelight of American cuisine, spicy **Cajun** food is affordable as well as enjoyable, and there are a number of serviceable establishments sprinkled throughout the region, which tend toward the spicier, seafood-oriented elements of the cuisine.

Restaurants specializing in food from the **Caribbean** – namely Jamaican – are more visible in West LA and Santa Monica than in Hollywood. With few exceptions, local Caribbean restaurants leave subtlety behind in exchange for sweat-inducing flavours and spices, added to staples like plantains, yucca root and jerked chicken. However, **Cuban** restaurants (and bakeries, where you can find them) offer more complex flavours, and number among the city's finest restaurants.

LA's most fashionable districts offer many delicious **Chinese** and dim sum restaurants, which can easily set you back $30. More authentic and less pricey outlets tend to be located Downtown, notably in Chinatown, where you can get a good-sized meal for around $10–20. **Vietnamese** food is quite reliable here, both in its authentic variety – namely in the Orange County suburbs of Santa Ana or Westminster – and in its Cal-cuisine incarnation, often employed as a hybrid with *nouvelle* French fare.

French restaurants proper are among LA's fanciest; look to those on the Westside for the most expensive prices, and bistros in the San Gabriel Valley and Downtown for cheaper fare. On the other hand, LA's **Greek** restaurants provide fairly traditional dishes for inexpensive prices, but are fairly thin on the ground, sometimes better known for their frenetic nightly singing and dancing than for their menus.

Indian restaurants are growing in popularity, with restaurant menus embracing California dishes to create hybrids like curry polenta and duck tandoori, though more traditional meals are almost always offered as well. Most of the Indian restaurants in Hollywood or West LA charge $15–20 for a full meal, less for a vegetarian dish. **Pakistani** variants on Indian cuisine can be equally delicious, though of course without pork (or alcohol), and are located in roughly the same areas as Indian eateries.

In the 1980s LA became home to some of the country's best regional **Italian** restaurants, with those specializing in Northern Italian food usually being the most expensive. An equally appealing phenomenon is the **designer pizza**, invented at West Hollywood's (now Beverly Hills') *Spago* restaurant by celebrity chef Wolfgang Puck, and topped with elk, shiitake mushrooms, or whatever comes to mind. None of this comes cheap, however: the least elaborate designer pizza will set you back $15–20. On the other hand, LA's **traditional pizza** joints are generally tasty and affordable, with their chequered table cloths and thatch-wrapped chianti bottles.

Japanese cuisine is available throughout LA and, not surprisingly, Little Tokyo is among the top choices. *Udon* and *soba* spots are more noticeable as you head further west. Along with French cooking, Japanese cuisine is one of the favourites used by Cal-cuisine chefs for their culinary experiments, making many "Japanese" restaurants more pan-Asian or international in style, and fair representatives of the city's latest cultural trends, especially on the Westside. By contrast, outside the giant mini-malls and diners of Koreatown, **Korean** cuisine tends to be limited to isolated pockets in the Westside and the northern suburbs. Spicy barbecued ribs and *kim chee* (pickled cabbage) are among the more traditional dishes; expect to pay $20 per person for a good-sized meal.

LA's various **Middle Eastern** restaurants can be affordably palate-pleasing. Aside from citywide falafel and pita chains, excellent examples of this cuisine are found in strip-mall eateries. In health-food or vegetarian restaurants, the old-style Levantine cooking becomes all but unrecognizable, containing ingredients such as avocado, bean sprouts, tofu and kasha.

Russian and **Eastern European** restaurants are uncommon in LA outside of isolated ethnic enclaves – particularly present in Mid-Wilshire, the eastern side of West Hollywood, and in the San Fernando Valley around Ventura Boulevard.

Spanish cooking, along with **tapas bars**, has made a growing dent in LA's culinary culture. While classic Spanish restaurants are choice spots for a pitcher of sangría and savoury seafood and pork dishes, the latest tapas bars offer "little plates" of anything that comes to mind – meatballs, sushi, garlic fries – hardly Spanish, often quite salty, and definitely expensive, once you finish counting all the plates you need to make a filling meal.

Authentic **Thai** food might be one of the city's best offerings, both for its spicy flavours and reasonable prices. Thai food is at its best and least pretentious in the less trendy sections of town, such as mini-malls in Hollywood and storefronts in Mid-Wilshire. Though lacking wholly in atmosphere, such locales just about guarantee a delicious meal.

There are a number of worthwhile seafood-only restaurants, predominantly along the coast, with a strong concentration near Malibu, Santa Monica and Newport Beach. However, some oceanside restaurants are better for their views than their food, and by venturing just a mile or so inland, you can find a better meal than you might at a restaurant located within sight of whales and seagulls.

Mind- and body-fixated LA has a wide variety of **vegetarian** and **wholefood** restaurants, the bulk of them on the Westside and many along the coast as well, some of which can be very good value ($8–10 or so). If you'd rather have a picnic than visit a restaurant, try the area's frequent **farmers' markets**, loaded with organic produce and frequently advertised in the press.

Finally, LA is littered with **celebrity-owned** outfits, but the food is usually so unremarkable and the prices so steep at these vanity eateries we haven't listed them. For chowing down, celebrity-watching or just enjoying a nice view, you're better off practically anywhere else.

All restaurants and cafes are listed in the relevant chapter maps throughout the guide.

Coffee shops, delis and diners

At its best, budget food in LA is doled out in the many small **coffee shops, delis** and **diners** that offer soups, omelettes, sandwiches, and a slew of comfort food. If you're not considered about things like salt, fat and cholesterol, it's easy to eat this way and never have to spend much more than $10 for a full meal. There are, of course, the usual fast-food franchises on every street; better are the local chains of **hamburger stands**, most open until midnight or 1am. Some, such as *Fatburger* and *In-N-Out Burger*, are increasingly well known across the US; others, like the ever-popular *Tommy's*, are favourites only in LA and sworn by their proponents to be the greatest anywhere.

Sadly, the best of the 1950s "Googie"-style **drive-ins** have either been torn down or remodelled beyond recognition. However, some spots, including *Pann's* near Inglewood, continue to cater to fans of old-fashioned formica-countered diners, with their neon signs, boomerang roofs, and belly-stuffing steak-and-eggs breakfasts.

Downtown

Clifton's Cafeteria 648 S Broadway ⓣ213/627-1673. The main reason to come to this classic 1930s cafeteria institution is for its cornucopia of bizarre decor: redwood trees, a waterfall, even a mini-chapel. The food is secondary – adequate meatloaf, mac and cheese, turkey – but it is cheap. Daily 6.30am–7.30pm.

Cole's 118 E Sixth St ⓣ213/622-4090. In the same seedy spot for 102 years, this is LA's oldest restaurant – and recently restored. The food hasn't changed much over the decades, and the rich, hearty "French dipped" sandwiches – a dish invented at this very spot – are still loaded with steak, pastrami or brisket. Sun–Wed 11.30am–10pm, Thurs 11.30am–11pm, Fri & Sat 11.30am–1am.

Grand Central Market 317 S Broadway ⓣ213/624-9496. Selling plenty of tacos, deli sandwiches and Chinese food, plus seafood, cookies and other sweets, and a few more exotic items, like pigs' ears and lamb sweetbreads. A fun, cheap place to eat. Daily 9am–6pm.

Langer's Deli 704 S Alvarado St ⓣ213/483-8050. "When in doubt, eat hot pastrami", says the sign. Helpful, but you still have to choose from over twenty ways of eating what is easily LA's best pastrami sandwich. Located in a dicey spot, but curbside pick-up is available. Mon–Sat 8am–4pm.

Mitsuru Café 117 Japanese Village Plaza ⓣ213/613-1028. Features old-time favourites like squid balls, teriyaki rice and ramen, but the highlight is the imagawayaki – sweet azuki red-bean paste baked in batter resembling a fat pancake. Mon–Sat 11am–9pm, Sun 11am–7pm.

Original Pantry Café 877 S Figueroa St ⓣ213/972-9279. There's always a queue for the hearty portions of meaty American cooking – chops and steaks, mostly – in this old-time diner (in business 86 years) owned by former mayor Dick Riordan. Breakfast is by far the best option. Mon–Fri 24hr.

Philippe the Original French Dip 1001 N Alameda St, Chinatown ⓣ213/628-3781. Renowned cafeteria near Union Station where you can tuck into juicy, artery-clogging French dips – loaded with turkey, pork, beef, ham or lamb – at one of the long communal tables. The staff are uniformly sour, but it's a filling treat for less than $6. Daily 6am–10pm.

The Yorkshire Grill 610 W Sixth St ⓣ213/623-3362. New York-style deli and neighbourhood fave since 1947, with big sandwiches, pastrami, patty melts, pancakes and friendly service for under $10. Mon–Fri 6am–4pm, Sat 6am–2pm.

Mid-Wilshire

C&J's Cafe 5501 W Pico Blvd ☎323/936-3216. Completely off the tourist circuit, but has a savoury selection of cheap breakfasts like omelettes and huevos rancheros and lunches with burgers, chops, eggs, fried chicken and French toast. Mon–Sat 6.30am–6pm, Sun 7am–5pm.

Canter's Deli 419 N Fairfax Ave ☎323/651-2030. Iconic LA deli with huge sandwiches and excellent kosher soups served by famously aggressive waitresses in pink uniforms and running shoes. Live music nightly in Canter's adjoining "Kibitz Room" 'til 1.40am. Deli open 24 hours.

Cassell's Hamburgers 3266 W Sixth St ☎213/480-8668. No-frills takeout hamburger stand that some swear by, serving up nearly two-thirds of a pound of beef per bun. Mon–Sat 10.30am–4pm.

Chef Marilyn's Soul Food Express 5068 W Pico Blvd ☎323/931-3879. The name says it all. A great place to fill up on super-cheap pan-fried chicken, hush puppies and sides like ham hocks, candied yams and black-eyed peas, plus peach cobbler. Take-out only. Also in the West Adams district at **2638 Crenshaw Blvd ☎323/737-8101.** Both daily 10.30am–9pm.

Du-Par's 6333 W Third St ☎323/933-8446. A longstanding LA institution, located in the Farmers Market, which draws a whole host of old-timers for its gut-busting comfort food, from chicken pot pie to cheeseburgers to fruit pies. Daily 24hr.

Oki Dog 5056 W Pico Blvd ☎323/938-4369. An essential LA stop for all lovers of "red hots", in this case wieners wrapped in tortillas and crammed with all manner of gooey, super-caloric ingredients – from pastrami to cheese to chili. Mon–Thurs 9am–10pm, Fri & Sat 9am–midnight, Sun 9am–11pm. Also a branch closer to Hollywood at **860 N Fairfax Ave (☎323/655-4166)**; Mon–Thurs 7.30am–2am, Fri & Sat 7.30am–3am.

Swingers in the Beverly Laurel Motor Lodge, 8018 Beverly Blvd at Laurel Ave ☎323/653-5858. Affordable all-American comfort food – omelettes, sandwiches, meatloaf, chili – served in a strangely trendy motel environment, luring a large crowd of hipsters and poseurs, as well as a few movie-star wannabes. Also at **802 Broadway, Santa Monica (☎310/393-9793).** Both daily 6.30am–4am.

Hollywood

25 Degrees 7000 Hollywood Blvd, inside Hollywood Roosevelt Hotel ☎323/785-7244. Bring your creativity to this fancy spot, the top of the gourmet burger pile in town, where you can pack your homemade burger with fried eggs, avocado, prosciutto, pesto, even artisan cheeses, along with more traditional toppings. Daily 24hr.

Astro Burger 5601 Melrose Ave ☎323/469-1924. Not just burgers, but garden burgers and garden dogs, as well as grilled-vegetable sandwiches and other veggie meals, are the appeal of this diner – along with the late hours: Mon–Thurs 7am–midnight, Fri & Sat 7am–1am, Sun 9am–midnight.

Fred 62 1854 N Vermont Ave, Los Feliz ☎323/667-0062. Designed like something out of the 1950s – with a soda fountain, streamlined booths and 24-hr operation – this restaurant offers stylish, affordable Cal-cuisine twists on familiar staples like salads, burgers and fries, and a tempting array of pancakes and omelettes, too.

KFC 340 N Western Ave ☎323/467-7421. The chain-food chicken meals are as generic as ever, but the postmodern architecture is striking: a giant, 40-foot-high "bucket" and a little white cube, featuring the Colonel's face, balancing precariously on top. The towering interior ceiling and spiral staircases inside reward a look. Daily 10am–11pm.

Lucky Devils 6613 Hollywood Blvd ☎323/465-8259. Pretty touristy and hit or miss for many of its offerings, this joint is worth it for its handful of savoury burgers, with Cal-cuisine toppings like arugula, gruyere cheese and tomato chutney, and prices $10–15 each. Sun–Thurs 11.30am–10pm, Fri & Sat 11.30am–midnight.

Pink's Hot Dogs 709 N La Brea Ave ☎323/931-4223. The quintessence of chili dogs. Depending on your taste, these monster hot dogs – topped with anything from bacon and chili cheese to pastrami and swiss – are lifesavers or gut bombs. Sun–Thurs 9.30am–2am, Fri & Sat 9.30am–3am.

Roscoe's Chicken and Waffles 1514 N Gower St ☎323/466-7453. An unlikely spot for Hollywood's elite, this diner attracts all sorts for its fried chicken, greens, goopy gravy and thick waffles. One of five area locations. Daily 8am–midnight, weekends closes at 4am.

Tommy's 2575 Beverly Blvd ☎213/389-9060. One of the prime LA spots for big, greasy, tasty burgers and scrumptious fries – and, many would say, the best. Located right off the 101 freeway in a somewhat grim section of East Hollywood. Still, even though there are thirty other metro locations, this is the one you should visit. 24hr.

Umami Burger 4655 Hollywood Blvd ☎323/669-3922. Cutting-edge burger joint with many inventive offerings (most $9–12) flavoured with various types of chilis, port and stilton, truffles and aioli, and other clever choices. Daily noon–11pm, weekends until midnight. Also in Hollywood at **1520 N Cahuenga Blvd (☎323/469-3100)** and two other citywide locations. Call for hours.

West Hollywood

Barney's Beanery 8447 Santa Monica Blvd ☎323/654-2287. Two hundred bottled beers, plus hot dogs, hamburgers and bowls of chili served in a hip, grungy environment, which used to be a rock-star haunt. Angelenos can be divided up by those who love or hate the place – but everybody knows it. The flagship of a growing chain. Mon–Fri 10am–2am, Sat & Sun 9am–2am.

Duke's 8909 Sunset Blvd ☎310/652-3100. A favourite of visiting rock musicians (the clubs *Roxy* and *Whisky-a-Go-Go* are nearby), this coffee shop serves staples like steak and eggs and omelettes also attracts a motley crew of night owls and bleary-eyed locals who've managed to hang on 'til daybreak. Daily 8am–midnight.

Griddle Café 7916 Sunset Blvd ☎323/874-0377. The postmodern Hollywoodized version of a diner, where the pancakes come with various outlandish toppings (Oreos, breakfast cereal and the like), the cheesecake French toast will make you cheer, and half the crowd is there hoping to be seen by slumming producers and casting directors. Mon–Fri 7am–4pm, Sat & Sun 8am–4pm.

Hamburger Hamlet 9201 Sunset Blvd ☎310/278-4924. It's been around sixty years and maintains a clubby atmosphere, but the grub's still the same greasy fare: French dips, chili, cheeseburgers, onion rings and even prime rib, with a few sops to modernity like ginger salmon. Higher prices than other burger spots, though. Mon–Thurs 11am–10pm, Fri & Sat 11am–11pm, Sun 10am–10pm.

Hamburger Haven 8954 Santa Monica Blvd at Robertson Blvd ☎310/659-8796. A funky burger shack serving hot patties inside and at outdoor tables. Especially busy on weekend nights, when refugees from nightclubs in the area drop by in various states of inebriation. Sun 11am–7pm, Mon–Thurs 10.30am–9pm, Fri–Sat 10.30am–10pm.

Irv's Burgers 8289 Santa Monica Blvd ☎323/650-2456. A divey, old-time burger joint where you can sup on rib-stuffers like cheese-, bacon- and fishburgers, patty and tuna melts, and the ever-popular chorizo and egg breakfast. Most items less than $8. Mon–Fri 7.30am–7pm, Sat 8am–7pm.

Mel's Drive-In 8585 Sunset Blvd ☎310/854-7201. Calorie-packing milkshakes, fries and, of course, burgers make this fun 24-hour diner a must if you've got the late-night munchies. Grab a spot outdoors to watch the Sunset Strip parade of clubgoers strut by in all their glory.

O! Burger 8593 Santa Monica Blvd ☎310/854-0234. Tasty vittles like mushroom and garden burgers, burgers made from grass-fed beef and various veggie bowls make this organic eatery a winner. Daily 11.30am–9.30pm.

Beverly Hills and West LA

The Apple Pan 10801 W Pico Blvd, West LA ☎310/475-3585. Grab a spot at the counter and enjoy freshly baked apple pie and delicious "hickoryburgers" across from the imposing Westside Pavilion mall. An old-time joint that opened just after World War II. Tues–Sun 11am–midnight, weekends closes 1am.

Benito's Taco Shop 11614 Santa Monica Blvd, West LA ☎310/442-9924. Beef, pork or fish rolled up in a flour tortilla, for just a few bucks. Most combos are also under $5, making this a good spot to gulp and run. One of three 24hr *Benito's* in the area.

Brighton Coffee Shop 9600 Brighton Way, Beverly Hills ☎310/276-7732. This simple eatery provides welcome relief from the Golden Triangle shopping zone by offering solid diner food, with especially fine omelettes, salads and sandwiches. Mon–Sat 7am–5pm, Sun 9am–3pm.

Hole in the Wall Burger Joint 11058 Santa Monica Blvd ☎310/312-7013. Trendy handcrafted burgers that you can create from a bevy of nouveau ingredients – cranberry mayo, pretzel buns, zucchini pickles and fried eggs – with prices starting at $10. Cash only. Mon–Sat 11am–9pm.

In-N-Out Burger 922 Gayley Ave, Westwood ☎1-800/786-1000. The best-looking fast-food place in town, selling famously greasy hamburgers in an award-winning pop art building – a red-and-white box with zingy yellow boomerang signs. Daily 10.30am–1am.

Islands 10948 W Pico Blvd, West LA ☎310/474-1144. The prototypical "dude" burger joint, one in a chain of Tiki-themed diners in the region, where you can knock back brewskis, chow on decent burgers, and stuff your maw with nachos, fries and all kinds of other appealingly greasy grub. Daily 11.30am–10pm, weekends open until 11pm.

John o' Groats 10516 W Pico Blvd, West LA ☎310/204-0692. Excellent breakfasts and lunches (mostly staples like bacon and eggs, sandwiches, scrambles, oatmeal and waffles), but come at an off hour; the morning crowd can cause a headache. Daily 7am–3pm.

Johnnie's Pastrami 4017 S Sepulveda Blvd, Culver City ☎310/397-6654. A wonderfully dumpy 1950s diner where fans line up for the massive pastrami sandwiches, which cost around $8 and are prepared before your eyes in all their dripping, steaming glory. Sun–Thurs 10am–2.30am, Fri & Sat 10am–3.30am.

Nate 'n' Al's 414 N Beverly Drive ☎310/274-0101. The best-known deli in Beverly Hills, popular with movie people and one of the few reasonably priced places in the vicinity. Get there early to grab a booth. Daily 7am–9pm.

The Nosh of Beverly Hills 9689 Little Santa Monica Blvd, Beverly Hills ☎310/271-3730. Filling breakfasts and homemade bagels, pies and deli fare are the favourites at this unassuming diner, a hangout of movie-industry lawyers and producers, none of whom you'll recognize. Daily 7am–4pm, Sun closes at 3pm.

Santa Monica and Venice

Bagel Nosh 1629 Wilshire Blvd, Santa Monica ☎310/451-8771. Drab ambience may be left over from the 1970s, but this neighbourhood favourite appeals for its sizable breakfasts of omelettes and bagel sandwiches, picked up from an old-fashioned short-order counter. Mon–Fri 6.30am–2.30pm, Sat & Sun 7.30am–3pm.

Café 50's 838 Lincoln Blvd, Venice ☎310/399-1955. Grubby little diner that's nonetheless kept going for years because of its savoury eats – pancakes, French toast, milkshakes – cheap prices and rock 'n' roll jukebox. Daily 7am–11pm.

Café Montana 1534 Montana Ave, Santa Monica ☎310/829-3990. The eclectic menu is highlighted by solid breakfasts, salads, sandwiches and pasta, in an upmarket section of Santa Monica. Avoid the overpriced, underwhelming dinners. Mon–Thurs 8am–9.30pm, Fri & Sat 8am–10pm, Sun 8am–9pm.

The Counter 2901 Ocean Park Blvd, Santa Monica ☎310/399-8383. Another snazzy variation on LA's "custom-built" burger trend, where you can choose from the likes of smoked bacon, guacamole, horseradish mayo, garlic aioli, goat cheese and dozens of other unfamiliar (and familiar) toppings to create your own delightful, if pricey, burger. One in a regional chain. Mon–Sat 11am–10pm, Sun 11.30am–9pm.

Father's Office 1018 Montana Ave, Santa Monica ☎310/736-2224. If you're as interested in watching celebrities as in chowing down, this chic burger joint is a good spot for its upmarket offerings with top-notch prices. Mon–Wed 5–10pm, Thurs 5–11pm, Fri 4–11pm, Sat noon–11pm, Sun noon–10pm.

Mo's Place 203 Culver Blvd ☎310/822-6422. The kind of good-time dive where you can get slapped on the back by an old-timer while sinking your teeth into a burger, listening to the jukebox and watching sports on TV. Just about the only gig in Playa del Rey. Daily 10am–1am.

Norm's 1601 Lincoln Blvd, Santa Monica ☎310/450-6889. One of the last remaining diners with "Googie"-style architecture, this local chain has fifteen other LA branches and serves breakfasts and lunches for around $7. Open 24hr.

Rae's Diner 2901 Pico Blvd, Santa Monica ☎310/828-7937. Solid 1950s diner with heavy comfort food (such as chicken-fried steak, eggs, waffles). Its turquoise-blue facade and interior has appeared in many films, notably *True Romance*. Daily 5.30am–10pm.

South Central and East LA

Bob's Big Boy Broiler 7447 Firestone Blvd, Downey ☎562/928-2627. Way down in southeast LA, this 1950s neon fast-food monument has recently been saved and restored, with its glorious sign and old-fashioned car hops (present daily 4–10pm), making a good pairing with the other classic *Bob's* in Burbank (see below). Sun–Thurs 7am–midnight, Fri & Sat 7am–2am.

Chips 11908 Hawthorne Blvd, south of Inglewood ☎310/679-2947. A solid array of comfort food from sandwiches to burgers, served in a classic 1955 "Googie" diner with a fabulous neon sign. Daily 7am–5pm.

The Donut Hole 15300 Amar Rd, La Puente ☎626/968-2912. Twenty miles east of Downtown LA, this pop-culture icon, like *Randy's Donuts* (see below), is shaped like a giant donut – except you can actually drive through it, picking up a hot sack of fried, sugared dough from deep inside a tunnel of comfort food. Cash only. 24hr.

Pann's 6710 La Tijera Blvd, Inglewood ☎310/337-2860. One of the all-time great "Googie"-style diners, where you can't go wrong with the burgers or biscuits and gravy – and you can always jog off the calories amid the oil wells of Baldwin Hills, just to the north. Sun–Wed 7am–9pm, Thurs–Sat 7am–11pm.

Randy's Donuts 805 W Manchester Ave, Inglewood ☎310/645-4707. This pop-art fixture is hard to miss, thanks to the colossal donut sitting on the roof. Excellent for its piping-hot treats, which you can pick up at the drive-through on your way to or from LAX. 24hr.

The South Bay and LA Harbor

East Coast Bagels 5753 E PCH, Long Beach ☎562/985-0933. Located in a mini-mall, but with a wide selection of bagels ranging from New York staples to California hybrids like a jalapeno-cheddar bagel. Be aware, they run out of the top choices early. Daily 7am–5.30pm.

Hof's Hut 6257 E 2nd St, Long Beach ☎562/598-4070. Part of a local chain that serves up reliable, affordable burgers, salads, sandwiches and pies, plus steak and pork chops. Daily 6am–10pm, weekends until 11pm.

Johnny Reb's 4663 N Long Beach Blvd ☎562/423-7327. The waft of BBQ ribs, catfish, fried green tomatoes, okra and hush puppies alone may draw you to this prime Southern spot, where the portions are large and the price is cheap. Daily 7am–9pm, weekends closes at 10pm.

The Local Yolk 3414 Highland Ave, Manhattan Beach ☎310/546-4407. As the name suggests, everything here is made with eggs, and there are good muffins, French toast and pancakes, too. Breakfast and lunch only. Daily 6.30am–2.30pm.

Ocean View Café 229 13th St, Manhattan Beach ☎310/545-6770. Enjoyably light breakfasts with omelettes and breakfast burritos, and soup and baguettes for under $10, in a pleasant hillside setting on a quiet pedestrian path overlooking the Pacific. Daily 9.30am–4pm.

Pier Bakery 100-M Fisherman's Wharf, Redondo Beach ☎310/318-5348. A small but satisfying menu, featuring the likes of jalapeno-cheese bread, churros and cinnamon rolls. Probably the best food around in this touristy area. Daily 8am–7pm.

The San Gabriel and San Fernando valleys

Art's Deli 12224 Ventura Blvd, Studio City ☎818/762-1221. Long-time film-industry favourite (mainly for old-timers, not for the nubile), with a range of hefty, scrumptious sandwiches, salami, lox and soups like the traditional chicken-noodle. Daily 7am–9pm.

Bob's Big Boy 4211 W Riverside Drive, Burbank ☎818/843-9334. The inimitable chain diner, fronted by the plump burger lad, was saved from demolition through the efforts of "Googie"-style architecture preservationists, and still appeals for its burgers and fries. See also p.225. 24hr.

Carney's 12601 Ventura Blvd, Studio City ☎818/761-8300. The place to come if you really want to chow down on burgers and chili dogs in an old railway car. Sun–Thurs 11am–10pm, Fri & Sat 11am–midnight. A neighbourhood institution, as is the branch on the Sunset Strip at **8351 Sunset Blvd ☎323/654-8300**. Sun–Wed 11am–midnight, Thurs–Sat 11am–3am.

Dr Hogly-Wogly's Tyler Texas Bar-B-Q 8136 Sepulveda Blvd, Van Nuys ☎818/780-6701. Long lines snake out the door here for some of the best brisket, chicken, sausages, ribs and beans in LA, despite the depressing surroundings in the middle of nowhere. Daily 11.30am–10pm.

Fair Oaks Pharmacy and Soda Fountain 1526 Mission St, South Pasadena ☎626/799-1414. A historic 1915 highlight along the former Route 66, this fabulously restored soda fountain serves many old-fashioned drinks, from lime rickeys to egg creams. Daily 9am–9pm, Sun 10am–7pm.

The Hat 491 N Lake Ave, Pasadena ☎626/449-1844. Give your arteries a workout at this very popular spot selling agreeable burgers, "world-famous pastrami", onion rings, chilli cheese fries and French dip sandwiches. Several Valley locations. Mon–Sat 9am–10pm, Sun 10am–10pm.

Jim's Famous Quarterpound Burger 915 W Duarte Rd, Monrovia ☎626/447-5993. If you find yourself way out in the San Gabriel Valley, stop at this fine spot for giant burgers, fries and ice cream, along with avocado cheeseburgers, chilli, beef dips, pastrami burgers and tuna melts. Daily 7am–10pm.

Pie 'n' Burger 913 E California Blvd, Pasadena ☎626/795-1123. Classic coffee shop, with primo omelettes and cheeseburgers and excellent pies, from Dutch apple and lemon to custard and meringue to mince meat. Mon–Fri 6am–10pm, Sat 7am–10pm, Sun 7am–9pm.

Porto's Bakery 315 N Brand Blvd, Glendale ☎818/956-5996. Popular and delicious café serving flaky Cuban pastries, scrumptious sandwiches, cheesecakes soaked in rum, croissants, tarts and tortes, and cappuccino. Also at **3614 W Magnolia Blvd, Burbank ☎818/846-9100.** Both Mon–Sat 7am–7pm, Sun 7am–4pm.

Rose Tree Cottage 801 S Pasadena Ave, Pasadena ☎626/793-3337. Scones, shortbread, and high tea in an English-styled setting. Reservations are essential for afternoon tea Tues–Sun 1pm, 2.30pm & 4pm. Also offers a shop with various goods from the UK for sale, daily 10am–6pm.

Wolfe Burgers 46 N Lake St, Pasadena ☎626/792-7292. Knockout gyros, chili, tamales, fries and burgers – a longstanding Valley favourite. Daily 7am–10pm, Sun opens at 8am.

Orange County

Angelo's 511 S State College Blvd, Anaheim ☎714/533-1401. Straight out of TV's *Happy Days*, a drive-in complete with roller-skating car-hops, neon signs, vintage cars and good burgers. Daily 10am–11pm, until 1am on weekends.

Duke's 317 PCH, Huntington Beach ☎714/374-6446. Best to stick to staples like steak and salad at this frenetic beachside favourite, known more for its prime location near the pier. Mon–Sat 11.30am–2.30pm & 5–9.30pm, Sun 10am–2.30pm & 4.30–9.30pm.

Harbor House Café 34157 PCH, Dana Point ☎949/496-9270. Excellent breakfasts, particularly its overstuffed omelettes – around 25 of them, with a veritable laundry list of options. Also at Sunset Beach, north of Huntington Beach, at **16341 PCH ☎562/592-5404**. Both 24hr.

Heroes 125 W Sante Fe Ave, Fullerton ☎714/738-4356. The place to come if you're starving after hitting the theme parks. Knock back one of the one hundred beers available or chow down on comfort food like hamburgers, chili, ribs or meatloaf. Daily 11am–11pm, weekends closes at 1am.

Mimi's Cafe 1400 S Harbor Blvd, Anaheim ☎714/956-2223. Huge servings, low prices, and solid breakfasts and lunches, with a large menu of sandwiches, pasta and burgers. Part of a sizeable chain in Los Angeles and Orange counties, and popular in both. Daily 7am–11pm.

Ruby's 1 Balboa Pier, Newport Beach ☎949/675-RUBY. The first and finest of the retro-streamline 1940s diners in this chain – in a great location at the end of Newport's popular pier. Mostly offers the standard burgers, fries and soda fare. Daily 7am–9pm, weekends until 10pm.

Zinc Café 344 Ocean Ave, Laguna Beach ☎949/494-2791. A popular breakfast spot also offering simple soup and salad meals and other vegetarian fare, with some tasty desserts. One of three Orange County coast locations. Daily 7am–4.30pm.

Restaurants

The listings below generally follow the chapter divisions of our guide, grouping **restaurants** first by neighbourhood, then by cuisine. A number of speciality categories appear in boxes.

All restaurants and cafes are listed in the relevant chapter maps throughout the guide.

Downtown

American, Californian and Cajun

Arnie Morton's of Chicago 735 S Figueroa ⓣ213/553-4566. The place to come for a predictably succulent steak experience, this swank chain restaurant serves sizable slabs of beef, salads and desserts, with predictably steep prices. Mon–Fri 11.30am–11pm, Sat 5–11pm, Sun 5–10pm.

Café Metropol 923 E Third St ⓣ213/613-1537. One of several restaurants attempting to bring eateries (and people) back to a formerly grim part of town. The area may still be industrial, but this artsy, midpriced spot is worth a visit for its hearty panini, salads, burgers, pizza and pasta. Hours vary by season, often Mon–Fri 8.30am–10pm, Sat 10am–midnight, Sun 10am–4pm.

Checkers in the Hilton Checkers hotel, 535 S Grand Ave ⓣ213/624-0000. One of the most elegant Downtown restaurants, serving top-rated and top-priced California cuisine, with flat-iron steak salad, garlic ravioli and short-rib pot pie among the better offerings. Daily 5.30–9.30pm, also Mon–Fri 6.30am–2.30pm, Sat & Sun 7am–2pm.

Engine Co. No. 28 644 S Figueroa St ⓣ213/624-6996. Longtime favourite for all-American fare, featuring expensive grilled steaks and seafood, plus lamb shank and chicken pot pie, served with great fries in a renovated 1912 fire station. Mon–Fri 11.30am–9pm, Sat 5–9pm.

L.A. Prime inside the Westin Bonaventure hotel, 404 S Figueroa St ⓣ213/612-4743. Plump slabs of tender Midwestern beef are the draw at this pricey New York-style steakhouse, while the side orders and desserts hold their own. Killer views from the hotel's 35th floor. Sun–Thurs 5.30–10pm, Fri & Sat 5.30–11pm.

New Moon 102 W Ninth St ⓣ213/624-0186. Worthwhile for its location near the Garment District and its reasonably priced mix of solid Chinese-American cooking – chow mein, wonton soup, sweet and spicy chicken, and the like. Mon–Fri 11am–5pm, Sat 11am–3pm.

Pacific Dining Car 1310 W Sixth St ⓣ213/483-6000. Here since 1921, a would-be English supper club where the Downtown elite used to cut secret deals. Located inside an old railroad carriage, it's open 24hrs for very expensive and delicious steaks. Breakfast is the best value.

Patina 141 S Grand Ave ⓣ213/972-3331. Fancy, ultra-swank Disney Hall branch of one of LA's top eateries, where you can devour Maine lobster, Jidori chicken and foie-gras ravioli, among other supreme items on the menu, if you're prepared to drop a wad of cash. Tues–Sat 5–9.30pm.

Water Grill 544 S Grand Ave ⓣ213/891-0900. One of the upper-end spots for munching on California cuisine in LA, with the focus on seafood prepared in all manner of colourful and ever-changing ways – mint bass ceviche, big-eye tuna with pomegranate cous cous and so on. Mon & Tues 11.30am–9pm, Wed–Fri 11.30am–10pm, Sat 5–10pm, Sun 4.30–9pm.

Chinese and Vietnamese

ABC Seafood 708 New High St ⓣ213/680-2887. Pork buns, egg tarts and dim sum are the reasons to schlep to this Chinatown joint, which looks like it's been around for eons. Doles out decent dumplings and rolls no matter how creaky the surroundings. Daily 8am–10pm.

Lucky Deli 706 N Broadway ⓣ213/625-7847. Hard to beat for an authentic experience, this Chinese eatery serves up BBQ pork buns, dumplings, hum bao and egg custard like a champ. Not much atmosphere, but plenty cheap. Mon–Fri 9am–9pm, Sat & Sun 9am–10pm.

Ocean Seafood 750 N Hill St ⓣ213/687-3088. Busy Cantonese restaurant serving inexpensive and excellent food – dim sum, crab, shrimp and duck are among many standout choices. Daily 9am–10pm, weekends opens 8am.

Pho 79 29 S Garfield Ave, Alhambra ⓣ626/289-0239. Consider venturing out to this ethnic suburb northeast of Downtown to sample some excellent Vietnamese food, including, of course, their signature pho soups. Daily 9am–9pm, weekends 'til 10pm.

Phoenix Inn 301 Ord St, Chinatown ⓣ213/629-2812. Newly renovated and ready to tempt your taste buds to nice effect, with an array of noodle soups, hot pots, fried noodles and tofu items. The seafood, duck and sliced prime rib are also worth a go. Daily 5pm–1am.

Yang Chow 819 N Broadway ☎213/625-0811. Solid, affordable Chinese restaurant, where you can't go wrong with the Szechuan beef, duck or any shrimp dish. Sun–Thurs 11.30am–9.45pm, weekends closes at 10.45pm.

French

Angelique Café 840 S Spring St ☎213/623-8698. A marvellous and affordable Continental eatery in the middle of the Garment District, where you can sit on the quaint patio and dine on well-crafted pastries for breakfast or savoury sandwiches, rich casseroles and fine salads for lunch. Mon–Fri 11.30am–10pm, Sat 8am–10pm.

Café Pinot 700 W Fifth St ☎213/239-6500. Located next to the LA Public Library, this elegant restaurant adds a touch of French to its nouvelle California cuisine, and is good for its risotto, tuna nicoise, lamb loin and steak. Mon–Fri 11.30am–2.30pm & 5–9pm, Sat 5–10pm, Sun 4.30–9pm.

Italian and pizza

Cicada 617 S Olive St ☎213/488-9488. Lodged in the stunning Art Deco Oviatt Building (see p.59), this Northern Italian restaurant offers fine pasta for half the price of its fish, duck and steak entrees – but is still very expensive. Daily 5.30–9.30pm.

Drago Centro 525 S Flower St ☎213/228-8998. Hard to go wrong with this delicious upscale Italian fare, from affordable panini and small plates under $10 to a fabulous four-course meal for $48. Molto bene. Mon–Fri 11.30am–2.30pm & 5–10.30pm, Sat 5–10.30pm, Sun 5–9pm.

Zucca 801 S Figueroa St ☎213/614-7800. Italian bistro setting near the Convention Center that serves up Cal-cuisine-styled Italian fare, making good midpriced pizza, pasta, salads and desserts, and much pricier seafood and beef offerings. Mon–Thurs 11.30am–2.30pm & 5–9pm, Fri 11.30am–2.30pm & 5–10pm, Sat 4.30–10pm.

Japanese

Daikokuya 327 E 1st St ☎213/626-1680. One of a number of affordable Little Tokyo restaurants congregated in the same general area, this one's nice menu of noodle soups, rolls, gyoza and various combos merit a taste. Mon–Thurs 11am–midnight, Fri & Sat 11am–1am, Sun noon–8pm.

Kagaya 418 E 2nd St ☎213/617-1016. A solid staple of the Little Tokyo area, which provides a range of choices of beef wraps, various noodles and more oddball dishes with fried eel and egg custard – almost all good and almost all very expensive. Tues–Sat 6–10.30pm, Sun 6–10pm.

Komasa 351 E 2nd St ☎213/680-1792. Appealing sushi that, while not exactly cheap, is more affordable than comparable spots in Little Tokyo, and good for its sashimi, hand rolls and various tempura offerings. Tues–Sun 5.30–11pm.

R23 923 E 2nd St ☎213/687-7178. Poised on LA's industrial east side near the river, but worth a try for its middle- to upper-end eel tempura, crab au gratin, oysters with sea urchin and other creative choices. Mon–Fri 11.30am–2.30pm & 5.30–10pm, Sat 5.30–11pm, Sun 5.30–10pm.

Mexican and Latin American

El Taurino 2306 W 11th St ☎213/738-0961. Tacos, burritos and especially tostadas are the draw at this popular and authentic eatery south of Westlake – where the green and red salsas burn all the way down. Daily 11am–11pm.

King Taco 2904 N Broadway ☎323/222-8500. The most centrally located diner in a chain of many ultra-cheap shops around Downtown (this one north of Chinatown), with many varieties of savory tacos, tamales, quesadillas and burritos. Daily 8.30am–11pm, weekends 'til 2am.

La Luz del Día 107 Paseo de la Plaza ☎213/628-7495. Authentic Mexican eatery on Olvera Street with fiery burritos, enchiládas and tacos carnitas, served in sizeable enough portions to make you sweat with a smile. Mon–Thurs 11am–9pm, Fri & Sat 11am–10pm.

La Torta Loca 855 Santee St ☎213/627-2424. With tasty $2 tacos, scrumptious Cuban burritos, various quesadillas, and dozens of cheap and filling tortas, this Cuban joint deserves a lengthy stop if you're anywhere near the Garment District. Daily 6am–4pm.

Wood Spoon 107 W 9th St ☎213/629-1765. Solid Brazilian choice that kicks up its heels with a range of interesting items like shrimp dumplings, croquettes, pork burgers and yam fries. Tues–Fri 11am–3pm & 5–10pm, Sat noon–3pm & 6–11pm.

Rough Guide favourites

Fine dining

At the following restaurants – good for business dinners or impressing your date – you'll need to book ahead and, likely, dress up too. Meals can easily run about $100 or more per head, including drinks.

Checkers p.228
Chinois on Main p.239
Cicada p.229
Claes Seafood p.245
Cut p.236
Engine Co. No. 28 p.228
Geoffrey's p.240
Giorgio Baldi p.240
LA Farm p.239
L.A. Prime p.228
Lucques p.235
Matsuhisa p.238
Melisse p.239
Mr Chow p.237
Ortolan p.237
Pacific Dining Car p.228
The Palm p.236
Saddle Peak Lodge p.243
Spago p.236
Valentino p.240
Water Grill p.228

Spanish

Ciudad 445 S Figueroa St ⓣ213/486-5171. Ceviche, empanadas and rabbit paella are some of the highlights at this colourful, if pricey, Mexican-influenced spot, where the live Latin music competes with the delicious food for your attention. Mon–Thurs 11.30am–9pm, Fri 11.30am–11pm, Sat 5–11pm, Sun 5–9pm.

Mid-Wilshire

African

Awash 5990 W Pico Blvd ⓣ323/939-3233. Rib-stuffing Ethiopian fare just south of the main mid-Wilshire action, where you can get savoury favourites like kifto and chicken tibbs, and some good veggie combos, for quite affordable prices. Daily noon–9.30pm.

Nyala 1076 S Fairfax Ave ⓣ323/936-5918. One of several reasonably priced Ethiopian favourites along Fairfax, serving staples like *doro wat* (marinated chicken) and *kitfo* (chopped beef with butter and cheese) with spongy *injera* bread. Daily 11.30am–10.30pm.

American, Californian and Cajun

The Gumbo Pot 6333 W Third St, in the Farmers Market ⓣ323/933-0358. Ever-popular, delicious and affordable Cajun fare. Try the full-flavoured gumbo yaya of chicken, shrimp and sausage, along with the fruit-and-potato salad. Daily 9am–9pm, weekends until 10pm, Sun until 8pm.

Hatfield's 6703 Melrose Ave ⓣ323/935-2977. A fixture on the local foodie scene that's whipped up a big (deserved) reputation — for rotating items like rack of lamb, duck breast, smoked pork belly and outstanding desserts. Expensive, but the seven-course menu ($59) is great, or the simple three-course menu ($19) for lunch. Daily 6–10pm, also Mon–Fri 11.45am–2.15pm.

Luna Park 672 S La Brea Ave ⓣ323/934-2110. Reliable Cal-cuisine spot that serves up soup and sandwiches for lunch, and anything from short ribs to flat-iron steak to jalapeno grits for dinner. Mon–Thurs 11.30am–10.30pm, Fri 11.30am–11.30pm, Sat 5.30–11.30pm, Sun 10am–10pm.

Tart 115 S Fairfax Ave, in the Farmer's Daughter hotel ⓣ323/556-2608. Some imaginative offerings – fried chicken with honey, sweet-potato hash, crispy alligator – make this mid-priced California cuisine spot worthwhile for adventurous eaters. Mon–Fri 7.30am–10pm, Sat 8am–11pm, Sun 8am–3pm.

Taylor's 3361 W Eighth St ⓣ213/382-8449. Old-fashioned American meat in a darkly lit, old-school steakhouse ambience, priced a bit more reasonably – though still expensively – than at similar Westside spots. Mon–Fri 11.30am–9.30pm, Sat 4–10.30pm, Sun 4.30–9.30pm.

Caribbean

Prado 244 N Larchmont Blvd ⓣ323/467-3871. A stylish, affordable spot in the Larchmont Village shopping zone, better than the standard Caribbean offerings in LA, with a broad range of tasty items, from black-pepper shrimp and jerk chicken to Jamaican tamales. Mon–Fri 11.30am–3pm

& 5.30–10pm, Sat 4.30–10.30pm, Sun 4.30–9.30pm.

Chinese and Vietnamese

Genghis Cohen 740 N Fairfax Ave ⓣ323/653-0640. Familiar Chinese dishes with a Yiddish touch: the menu features fine Szechuan beef, dumplings, pan-fried noodles and kung pao chicken. Sun–Thurs noon–10.30pm, weekends noon–11.30pm.

Pho 2000 215 N Western Ave ⓣ323/461-5845. One of four Koreatown restaurants specializing in hot, spicy bowls of the Vietnamese soup pho. Cheap and authentic, it draws a loyal crowd of regulars. Cash only. Mon–Thurs 11am–9pm, Fri & Sat 11am–2am.

French

Monsieur Marcel 6333 W Third St ⓣ323/939-7792. Within the Farmer's Market is this fabulous French bistro, where you can sup on such delights as duck foie gras, goat-cheese salad and peach duck breast for moderate to high prices, and more affordable sandwiches for lunch. Also offers its own gourmet market. Mon–Fri 11am–9pm, Sat 9am–9pm, Sun 9am–7pm.

Greek

Papa Cristos 2771 W Pico Blvd ⓣ323/737-2970. Consider venturing to this grim neighbourhood near the 10 freeway to sample the authentic delights at this Greek joint, including delicious gyros, Greek sausage, caviar, and hefty portions of lamb chops or roast chicken for under $10. The real thing. Tues–Sat 9am–10pm, Sun 9am–4pm.

Sofi 8030 W Third St ⓣ323/651-0346. A pleasant, comfortable place near the farmers' market, serving well-prepared Greek items like stuffed grape leaves, grilled octopus and moussaka to a loyal crowd — soon to include you. Daily 11.30am–2.30pm & 5.30–11pm, Sun opens at 5.30pm.

Indian

Aladin Market 139 S Vermont Ave ⓣ213/382-9592. Highly authentic South Asian fare in a drab setting, incorporating flavours of India, Bangladesh and Burma in various rice, curry and seafood dishes, with many entrees under $6. Daily 9am–11pm.

Italian and pizza

Amalfi 143 N La Brea Ave ⓣ323/938-2504. Sample appetizers like tuna tartare, many fine pizzas and pastas, and pricier items like rack of lamb and Cajun tuna. The eclectic menu even includes risotto and a sirloin burger. Mon–Thurs 11.30am–3pm & 6pm–midnight. Fri & Sat 6pm–1am.

Angelini Osteria 7313 Beverly Blvd ⓣ323/297-0070. Excellent Old World-flavoured spot that offers a fine selection of pasta and antipasti, as well as veal and lamb chops, Dover sole, and rotating items like oxtail, veal shank and porchetta. Generally pricey, but with many affordable options. Tues–Fri noon–2.30pm & 5.30–10.30pm, Sat & Sun 5.30–10.30pm.

Ca' Brea 346 S La Brea Ave ⓣ323/938-2863. One of LA's best-known, and best, choices for Italian cuisine, with especially solid pasta, osso buco and risotto. Getting in is difficult, so reserve ahead and expect to pay a bundle. Mon–Sat 5.30–10.30pm, also Mon-Fri 11.30–2.30pm.

Campanile 624 S La Brea Ave ⓣ323/938-1447. Incredible but very expensive Northern Italian food. If you can't afford a full dinner, just try the dessert or pick up some of the city's best bread at *La Brea Bakery* next door (see p.300). Mon–Fri 11.30am–2.30pm & 6–10pm, Sat 9.30am–1.30pm & 5.30–11pm, Sun 9.30am–1.30pm.

Japanese

Ita-Cho 7311 Beverly Blvd ⓣ323/938-9009. Not the most authentic fare around, but still appealing for the tasty and affordable sashimi, sushi, grilled squid and eggplant dishes, served in a chic Westside atmosphere that attracts its share of celebs. Mon–Fri 11.30am–2.30pm & 5.30–11pm, Sat 6–11pm.

Wako Donkasu 3377 Wilshire Blvd #112 ⓣ213/381-9256. Somewhat hard-to-find Koreatown joint in a mini-mall. Highlighted by pork and fish cutlets, crispy chicken, and bowls of soba and udon noodles — all cheap and very tasty. Mon–Sat 11am–9.30pm, Sun noon–8pm.

Korean

Dong Il Jang 3455 W Eighth St, Koreatown ⓣ213/383-5757. Cosy, affordable restaurant where the meat is cooked at your table and the food is quite good, especially the grilled chicken, kimchi fried rice and roasted gui prime rib. The sushi bar is an added draw. Daily 11am–10pm.

Kobawoo House 698 S Vermont Ave #109, Koreatown ⓣ213/389-7300. Korean fishhouse where the seafood comes in spicy soups or made into pancakes. There are also a good kimchee, pork belly, barbequed beef and other authentic choices. Daily 11am–11pm.

Soot Bull Jeep 3136 W Eighth St, Koreatown ☎213/387-3865. A genuine Korean BBQ joint, where you'll appreciate just how delicious slow-cooked, heavily spiced slabs of chicken, pork and steak really are – and at moderate prices, too. Daily 11am–10.30pm.

Mexican and Latin American

El Cholo 1121 S Western Ave ☎323/734-2773. One of LA's best Mexican restaurants, despite the wait to get in during peak hours. Offers a solid array of staples like enchiladas and tamales, with some vegetarian options. Mon–Thurs 11am–10pm, Fri & Sat 11am–11pm, Sun 11am–9pm.

Guelaguetza 3014 Olympic Blvd, Koreatown ☎213/427-0608. Primo eatery that appeals for its authentic Mexican fare from Oaxaca – delicious *molés*, savoury stews and soups – though for prices that are a bit higher than at comparable eateries. Mon–Fri 9am–10pm, Sat 8am–11pm, Sun 8am–10pm. Also at **3337 W Eighth St (☎213/427-0601)**, daily 8am–10pm.

Pampas Grill 6333 W Third St, in the Farmers Market ☎323/931-1928. Delivers on the promise of spicy, delicious Brazilian fare with its selection of hearty churrasco, including linguica, leg of lamb and various barbeque temptations. Daily 11am–9pm.

Pollo a la Brasa 764 S Western Ave ☎213/382-4090. Worth a stop in this anonymous neighbourhood to sample the terrific Brazilian barbequed chicken, which comes with spicy sauces and low prices to keep you coming back. Wed–Sun 11am–8pm.

Middle Eastern

Haifa 8717 W Pico Blvd ☎310/888-7700. Located south of Wilshire, this moderately priced Mediterranean spot rewards a visit if you love falafel, kabobs and shawarma, all of it prepared kosher. Sun–Fri 11.30am–9pm.

Spanish

Cobras and Matadors 7615 Beverly Blvd ☎323/932-6178. Expensive tapas restaurant just down the street from Pan Pacific Park. You can sample all your favourite Castilian delights in a hushed, intimate setting. Daily 6–11pm, weekends until midnight.

Tasca 8108 W Third St ☎323/951-9890. A great choice for upper-end tapas, with faves like arancini, braised short ribs and baby octopus, along with a nice selection of salads and wines. Sun–Thurs 5.30–10pm, Fri & Sat 5.30–11pm.

Thai and Southeast Asian

Singapore's Banana Leaf 6333 W Third St, in the Farmers Market ☎323/933-4627. A fine hole in the wall where you can sample Malaysian cuisine at its spiciest and most savoury: delectable curry soups, satay and tandoori dishes. Mon–Fri 9am–9pm, Sat 9am–8pm, Sun 10am–7pm.

Vim 831 S Vermont Ave ☎213/386-2338. Authentic Thai and Chinese food at low prices. The seafood soup, pan-fried noodles and pad Thai are especially pleasing. Daily 11am–10pm, until midnight on weekends.

Vegetarian and wholefood

Inaka Natural Foods 131 S La Brea Ave ☎323/936-9353. Located in the trendy La Brea district and featuring healthy fare including veggie plates, stir fries, hot pots and other Japanese-influenced items. Tues–Fri noon–2.30pm & 6–9.30pm, Sat 5.30–9.30pm, Sun 5.30–9pm.

Hollywood

African

Dar Maghreb 7651 Sunset Blvd ☎323/876-7651. Set in a faux-African palace, done up in ogee arches and antique decor, this eatery's rich, pricey Moroccan dishes, including *b'stilla* (a pastry stuffed with chicken, chickpeas and spices), almost take a backseat to the frenetic belly-dancing. Mon–Sat 6–11pm, Sun 5.30–10.30pm.

Moun of Tunis 7445 Sunset Blvd ☎323/874-3333. Mouthwatering Tunisian fare, including lemon chicken and kebabs, presented in huge, multi-course meals, heavy on the spices and rich on the exotic flavours – plus belly-dancing regularly. Daily 5.30–11pm.

American, Californian and Cajun

Blu Jam Café 7371 Melrose Ave ☎323/951-9191. Scrumptious and popular breakfast place that appeals for its great hashes, scrambles, omelettes and eggs benedict, and burgers, wraps and panini for lunch. Daily 8am–4pm, weekends until 5pm.

The Foundry on Melrose **7463 Melrose Ave ☎323/651-0915.** Fine Cal-cuisine choice serving such succulent dishes as rabbit with gnocchi, mustard-glazed short ribs, and miso pork belly; also with compelling desserts such as peanut-butter bread pudding. Various fixed-priced menus available, $29–49. Daily 6–11pm.

Grub **911 Seward St ☎323/461-3663.** Set in a little house south of Central Hollywood, this is a fine spot for affordable comfort food, especially for breakfast: cinnamon-vanilla French toast, chorizo burritos and inventive omelettes. Flavourful soups, chili and salads are on the lunch menu. Mon–Thurs 11am–9pm, Fri 11am–10pm, Sat & Sun 9am–3pm & 5–9pm.

Off Vine **6263 Leland Way ☎323/962-1900.** Dine on eclectic Cal cuisine – Cornish game hen with cornbread, turkey breast with jalapeno relish – in a renovated but still funky Craftsman bungalow. Daily 11.30am–2.30pm & 5.30–10.30pm.

Providence **5955 Melrose Ave ☎323/460-4170.** Near the top of the LA pricey-food heap, and for good reason: the place is swarming with foodies, who come for the black sea bass, foie gras ravioli, lump blue crab and plenty of other tremendous choices. In a word — go. Mon–Fri 6–10pm, also Fri noon–2.30pm, Sat 5.30–10pm, Sun 5.30–9pm.

Vermont **1714 N Vermont Ave ☎323/661-6163.** One of the better Cal-cuisine eateries in the area. The entrees are predictable enough – roasted chicken, crab cakes, ravioli – but the culinary presentation is effective and, on occasion, inspired. Daily 5.30pm–1am, also Tues–Fri 11.30am–3pm.

Caribbean

El Floridita **1253 N Vine St ☎323/871-8612.** Lively Cuban restaurant where the dance floor swings on the weekends and there's live music regularly throughout the week. The menu features solid standards like plantains, croquetas and yucca, all affordably priced. Daily 4–10pm, also Mon–Fri 11am–4pm.

Chinese and Vietnamese

Hunan Cafe **7986 W Sunset Blvd ☎323/822-1208.** Tasty eats in Central Hollywood. You can sup on spicy chicken and beef and noodle dishes and wonton soup for not more than a couple of bucks. Mon–Sat noon–10pm, Sun 4–9.30pm.

Pho Café **2841 Sunset Blvd ☎213/413-0888.** Traditional Vietnamese restaurant transformed by Silver Lake trendiness into a hipster hangout, with the usual pho soup and egg rolls, plus a decent selection of rice noodle dishes. It's cheap, but cash only. Daily 11am–midnight.

French

Café des Artistes **1534 N McCadden Place ☎323/469-7300.** With a French chef at the helm and French customers at the tables, this cosy, pricey spot is at its best with such treats as osso buco, braised ribs, steak tartare and an array of seafood dishes. Daily 5.30pm–midnight, closes at 2am Thurs–Sat.

Indian

Crown of India **6755 Santa Monica Blvd ☎323/465-3321.** Despite the drab neighbourhood around it, the tikka masala, vindaloo, korma and naans at this authentic spot are consistently first rate and moderately priced. Daily 11am–10pm, weekends until 11pm.

Paru's **5140 Sunset Blvd ☎323/661-7600.** Indian vegetarian cuisine with a kick, highlighted by some very good curries, samosas and pilaf dishes. The stuffed dosa is a particular treat. Mon–Fri 4–11pm, Sat & Sun 1–10pm.

Tantra **3705 Sunset Blvd ☎323/663-8268.** Popular and reasonably priced Silver Lake eatery where you can dig into favourites like lamb curry and vindaloo, chicken tikka and much more. There's a mild hipster vibe, so try to grab a seat before it fills up. Daily 5–11pm.

Italian and pizza

Angeli Caffe **7274 Melrose Ave ☎323/936-9086.** Refreshingly basic pizza styles – baked in a wood-burning oven – make this a worthwhile, mid-priced stop, as do the tasty panini and croquettes. Tues–Thurs 11.30am–2.30pm & 5–10pm, Fri 11.30am–2.30pm & 5–11pm, Sat & Sun 5–10pm.

Palermo **1858 N Vermont Ave ☎323/663-1178.** As old as Hollywood, and with as many devoted fans, who flock here for the rich Southern Italian pizzas, cheesy decor, and gallons of cheapish red wine. Sun, Wed & Thurs 11am–midnight, Mon 11am–10.30pm, Fri & Sat 11am–1am.

Tomato Pie Pizza Joint **7751 Melrose Ave ☎323/635-9993.** A great place to grab a slice, with the usual staples, plus pies with pesto, eggplant parmigiana, hot wings and breakfast-style eggs and cheese on top. Also serves decent pastas, subs and salads. Daily 11am–9pm.

Vivoli Cafe 7994 Sunset Blvd ⓣ323/656-5050. A fine spot for dining on fairly authentic, affordable Italian fare including caprese, calamari, pastas, pizza and palate-pleasing chicken, beef and veal entrees. Daily 11am–10pm, weekends 'til 11pm.

Japanese

Shintaro Sushi 1900 N Highland Ave ⓣ323/882-6524. Just north of the centre of Hollywood, some of the town's best sushi, and not too pricey, with a selection of rolls, sushi and sashimi, and other favourites, including enjoyable cooked presentations of salmon, scallops and albacore tuna. Mon–Sat 5.30–11pm, also Mon–Fri 11.30am–2.30pm.

Yamashiro 1999 N Sycamore Ave ⓣ323/466-5125. Although the food is an overpriced letdown, this place is still a must-see for its outstanding gardens, koi ponds, palatial design and terrific view from the Hollywood Hills – just order a salad to get the best value. Daily 5.30–10pm, weekends until 11pm.

Mexican and Latin American

Cactus Mexican 950 Vine St ⓣ323/464-5865. A good spot to keep the evening going while you're club-hopping in Hollywood, with rib-stuffing tacos, quesadillas and burritos that'll make you hiccup with a smile. Daily 11am–2am, Sun closes 11pm.

El Compadre 7408 W Sunset Blvd ⓣ323/874-7924. With potent margaritas, live mariachi bands, and cheap Mexican standards, this is a music-loving gourmand's delight. One of several locations, most of them in more distant parts of the metropolis. Daily 11am–2am.

Mario's Peruvian & Seafood 5786 Melrose Ave ⓣ323/466-4181. Delicious and authentic Peruvian fare: supremely tender squid, rich and flavourful mussels, among many other compelling choices. Inexpensive, too. Sun–Thurs 11.30am–8pm, Fri & Sat 11.30am–9.30pm.

Yuca's 2056 N Hillhurst Ave ⓣ323/662-1214. A small, hidden jewel serving considerable burritos, Yucatan pork and beef tacos al fresco, and which despite its small size has garnered a national following. Mon–Sat 11am–6pm.

Middle Eastern

Marouch 4905 Santa Monica Blvd ⓣ323/662-9325. Although located in a nondescript part of town, this fine Lebanese restaurant provides rich sustenance with its flavourful *kabobs*, *baba ganoush*, stuffed grape leaves and *shawarma*, at very manageable prices. Tues–Sun 11am–11pm.

Zankou Chicken 5065 Sunset Blvd ⓣ323/665-7845. The top Middle Eastern value in town (and part of a citywide chain), with delicious garlicky chicken cooked on a rotisserie and made into a sandwich, plus all the traditional salads – tabouli, hummus and the like. Daily 10am–midnight.

Thai and Southeast Asian

Chan Darae 1511 N Cahuenga Blvd ⓣ323/464-8585. Terrific Thai food, and the locals know it, flocking here for a mid-priced range of scrumptious staples such as tom yum soup and pad Thai. Daily 11am–11pm.

Jitlada 5233 Sunset Blvd ⓣ323/667-9809. In a dreary mini-mall, but the spicy chicken, squid, oxtail curry, papaya salad and fishball and other seafood curries more than make up for the setting. Affordable prices, too. Mon–Sat 11am–10.30pm, Mon opens 5pm.

Palms Thai 5273 Hollywood Blvd ⓣ323/461-7053. A popular only-in-LA locale, swamped nightly not due to the dishes served – though the fairly priced Thai standards are well done – but for the kitschy entertainment, namely "Thai Elvis", a surprisingly convincing King. Daily 11am–2am.

Sanamluang Café 5176 Hollywood Blvd ⓣ323/660-8006. You can't beat the cheap, excellent and plentiful noodles, or the squid salad and spicy shrimp soup, at this nearly-all-night Thai eatery. Daily 11am–3.30am, Sun closes midnight.

West Hollywood

American, Californian and Cajun

Café La Boheme 8400 Santa Monica Blvd ⓣ323/848-2360. The dark-red, brothel-like decor is matched by the indulgent melange of Cal-cuisine flavours enlivening the pasta, risotto and steak entrees. Daily 5–10pm, weekends until 11pm.

Jar 8225 Beverly Blvd ⓣ323/655-6566. An upper-end steakhouse featuring all the usual red-meat fare – prime rib, T-bone and even a pot roast – with an inspired Cal-cuisine flair, also with savoury items like fried clams and duck-fried rice. Mon–Sat 5.30–10pm, Sun 10am–2pm & 5.30–9.30pm.

Lucques 8474 Melrose Ave ⓣ323/655-6277. Expensive but tasty eatery that doles out comfort food for the culinary elite – spiced lamb ribs, wild mushroom lasagna and grilled cornbread are but a few of the items you might find on the rotating menu. Mon–Sat 6–10pm, Sun 5–10pm, also Tues–Sat noon–2.30pm.

Mirabelle 8768 Sunset Blvd ⓣ310/659-6022. In the centre of the Sunset Strip action is this fine eclectic eatery with a little bit of everything – from rack of lamb and short ribs to gnocchi and calamari – with prices to match the smart clientele. Sun 4pm–midnight, Mon–Fri 11am–midnight, Sat 10am–1am.

Taste on Melrose 8454 Melrose Ave ⓣ323/852-6888. Fancy nouveau diner fare with plenty of panache, with the seafood, tuna tartare, artichoke risotto and tequila-lime hanger steak among the favourites. Hours vary, often daily 11.30am–10pm.

Chinese and Vietnamese

Kung Pao China 7853 Santa Monica Blvd ⓣ323/848-9888. Back-to-basics spot for tasty and affordable Chinese fare. The pork ribs, wontons and pan-fried chicken keep regulars coming back. Daily 11am–10pm, opens at noon Sat & Sun.

French

Bastide 8475 Melrose Place ⓣ323/651-5950. Elegant, upper-end French dining with a dash of panache, from the leek risotto to the steak with bone-marrow broth to the port salmon, plus delicious desserts. Mon–Thurs 6–10pm, Fri & Sat 5.30–10.30pm.

Comme Ca 8479 Melrose Ave ⓣ323/782-1104. Set along a formidable stretch for French dining, this Gallic winner focuses on affordable burgers and sandwiches for brunch before hauling out the big guns – duck confit, rack of lamb, steak – for the pricey supper. Still, a bit less expensive than you might think. Mon–Fri 11.30am–3pm & 5.30–11pm, Sat & Sun 10am–3pm & 5.30–11pm.

Italian and pizza

Frankie & Johnnie's 8947 Sunset Blvd ⓣ310/275-7770. Amid all the big rock clubs, an old favourite for its sizable pizzas loaded with greasy and healthy ingredients alike. Check out the ink-scrawled messages on the walls, which include praise from famous regulars, from Don Knotts to Fred Durst. Mon–Sat 11am–2am, Sun noon–midnight.

Il Piccolino 350 N Robertson Blvd ⓣ310/659-2220. Superb Italian dining with favourites such as grilled lobster, octopus carpaccio and langoustine shrimp giving a hearty element of seafood to the inspired selection of dishes. Mon–Sat 11.30am–10pm.

Vito's Pizza 846 N La Cienega Blvd ⓣ310/652-6859. A neighbourhood staple that, while not large, draws the crowds for its delicious pies, which include a mean Margherita and slices that recall East Coast pizza in all its thin-crusted and succulent glory. Sun–Wed 11am–10pm, Thurs–Sat 11am–midnight.

Japanese

Katana 8439 Sunset Blvd ⓣ323/650-8585. A prototypical Westside sushi house: stunning ambience with high production values, fine and tasty sashimi and hand rolls and a killer price tag. Bring the attitude. Sun–Wed 6–11pm, Thurs–Sat 6pm–12.30am.

Wa Sushi 1106 N La Cienega Blvd ⓣ310/854-7285. Located on the upper story of a minimall, this delightful eatery serves an affordable array of sashimi, seafood carpaccio, hand rolls, and other Japanese favourites presented with an inventive verve and delicious effect – a potent and rare combination. Tues–Sun 5.30–11pm.

Mexican and Latin American

Bossa Nova 685 N Robertson Blvd ⓣ310/657-5070. Fascinating Brazilian eatery with a menu that includes South American staples (shrimp croquettes, fried yucca) and more unexpected items such as chicken skewers, filet mignon and pasta. Even with the surprises, much of it is quite good and affordable. Sun–Wed 11am–midnight, Thurs 11am–1am, Fri & Sat 11am–4am.

Carlitos Gardel 7963 Melrose Ave ⓣ323/655-0891. Rich and delectable upper-end Argentine cuisine that is heavy on the beef and spices, with sausages and garlic adding to the potent kick. Mon–Fri 11.30am–2.30pm & 6–11pm, Sat 6–11pm, Sun 5–10pm.

Poquito Mas 8555 Sunset Blvd ⓣ310/652-7008. Grab a chicken enchilada or shrimp burrito, the top choices at this popular low-priced LA chain. Daily 10am–10pm.

Thai and Southeast Asian

Galanga Thai Fusion 7440 Santa Monica Blvd ☎323/851-4355. Very fine, affordable Thai spot that serves some seriously tasty fish and noodle dishes, green papaya salad, curries, soups and plenty more for a mostly local crowd. Mon–Sat 11am–9.45pm.

Sweet Chili 8276 Santa Monica Blvd ☎323/654-2892. Authentic Southeast Asian beef and noodle salads, spicy curries and assorted barbeque items make this little diner a valuable spot for cheap ethnic eats. Daily 11am–10.30pm, weekends opens at 4.30pm.

Vegetarian and wholefood

Real Food Daily 414 N La Cienega Blvd ☎310/289-9910. Tempeh burgers, hemp bread and various soups and salads draw a crowd at this vegan restaurant. Also a branch at **514 Santa Monica Blvd, Santa Monica (☎310/451-7544)**. Both daily 11.30am–10pm.

Beverly Hills and West LA

African

Koutoubia 2116 Westwood Blvd, West LA ☎310/475-0729. Authentic Moroccan lamb, couscous and seafood, in a comfortable environment enlivened by belly-dancing and a touch of North African style. Can be expensive, though (entrees $20–25). Tues–Sun 6–11pm.

American, Californian and Cajun

Barney Greengrass 9570 Wilshire Blvd, Beverly Hills ☎310/777-5877. Though dining in a department store while stargazing might not be everyone's idea of fun, this Barney's eatery has consistently pleasing Cal-cuisine, including delicious sandwiches, bagels and drinks. You will pay handsomely to eat here, of course. Mon–Sat 8.30am–6pm, weekends 'til 7pm, Sun 9am–6pm.

Cut 9500 Wilshire Blvd, Beverly Hills ☎310/276-8500. This Wolfgang Puck steakhouse designed by Richard Meier looks like the Getty Center cafeteria. Nonetheless, if you like (and can afford) steaks that cost up to $100, Kobe short ribs and Maine lobster, this is the place. Mon–Sat 5.30–10pm, weekends until 10.30pm.

The Farm of Beverly Hills 439 N Beverly Drive ☎310/273-5578. Go for a tasty lunch, and avoid the overpriced dinners, at this Beverly Hills Cal-cuisine power diner, where the rotating menu may feature items such as steak, braised duck and ham, at mid to high prices. Also in the Grove mall, **Third St at Fairfax Ave (☎323/525-1699)**. Daily 7.30am–10pm.

The Palm 9001 Santa Monica Blvd, Beverly Hills ☎310/550-8811. It you can get past the pretentious atmosphere and high prices, you'll enjoy some excellent steaks and seafood and perhaps be amused by the celebrity cartoons on the walls, or the odd celebrity behaving cartoonishly. Mon–Thurs noon–10pm, Fri noon–11pm, Sat 5–11pm, Sun 5–9.30pm, also Mon–Fri noon–3pm.

Spago 176 N Cañon Drive, Beverly Hills ☎310/385-0880. Flagship restaurant that helped nationalize Cal-cuisine (in a different, now-closed location), and still good for supping on Wolfgang Puck's latest concoctions, among them designer pizzas. Mon–Sat noon–2.15pm, also Sun–Fri 6–10pm, Sat 5.30–11pm.

Caribbean

Bamboo 10835 Venice Blvd, Culver City ☎310/287-0668. In a section of West LA full of enticing ethnic restaurants, this one stands out for its chicken curry dishes, paella with swordfish and spicy Caribbean-flavoured pizza, as well as its reasonable prices. Daily 11am–10pm, weekends 'til 11pm.

Versailles 10319 Venice Blvd, Culver City ☎310/558-3168. Bustling, authentic Cuban restaurant with hearty dishes, including excellent and affordable fried plantains, shrimp, garlic lemon chicken and black beans and rice. Also nearby at **1415 S La Cienega Blvd ☎310/289-0392 and three other area locations**. Daily 11am–10pm, weekends 'til 11pm.

Chinese and Vietnamese

Chung King 11538 W Pico Blvd, West LA ☎310/477-4917. Chinese restaurant serving spicy, mid-priced Szechuan food, including hot-and-sour soup, ginger duck, fried wontons and bum-bum chicken and other house specialities. Daily 11am–10pm, weekends until 11pm.

Feast from the East 1949 Westwood Blvd ☎310/475-0400. The pad Thai, Chinese chicken salad, spicy tofu, stir fries and other favourites always please at this appealing neighbourhood eatery, and the prices are under control, too. Mon–Sat 11am–9pm.

Mr Chow 344 N Camden Drive, Beverly Hills ☎310/278-9911. An ultra-pricey hangout where Chinese food comes in a wide variety of flavours and spices – though you can find better in town for much cheaper. The main appeal is the stargazing. Mon–Fri noon–2.30pm & 6–11.30pm, weekends opens at 6pm.

French

Ortolan 8338 W Third St ☎323/653-3300. Fixture on LA's French cuisine map, mixing up the old style with inventive quirks, which may include rotating items such as foie gras terrine, eggs and caviar, cherry duck and roasted sweetbreads. None of this comes cheap – $85–145 for the fixed-priced menu. Tues–Sat 6–10pm.

Greek

Chicken Dijon 2224 Sawtelle Blvd, West LA ☎310/477-0800. Despite its un-Greek name, this joint serves up mid-priced and flavourful Greek fare from mezze samplers and pita sandwiches to garlic rotisserie chicken, with most items under $10. Daily 11.30am–9pm.

Indian

Nizam 10871 W Pico Blvd, West LA ☎310/470-1441. Small Indian haunt, where hefty portions of curried lamb and tandoori chicken go for fairly cheap prices, with a buffet for less than $8. Daily 11.30am–2.30pm & 5.30–10pm, weekends 'til 11pm.

Samosa House 11510 W Washington Blvd, Culver City ☎310/398-6766. Indian vegetarian fare that appeals for its inexpensive prices as well as its range of flavourful choices, but especially for the $8 fixed-price meal. Connected to its own ethnic market. Daily 10am–9pm.

Italian and pizza

Anna's Italian 10929 W Pico Blvd ☎310/474-0102. Comfy haven of old-school cooking, where the sauces are rich, red and drippy (or white and gooey), the pastas are piled on, and you might even spot a pinkie ring or two. Mon–Fri 11.30am–11pm, Sat 4pm–midnight, Sun 4–11pm.

Il Pastaio 400 N Canon Drive ☎310/205-5444. Ever-popular Beverly Hills fave serving fine, affordable food – tasty Northern Italian offerings such as risotto (prepared in a range of ways), many traditional pastas, and veal, pork and seafood entrees. Mon–Wed 11.30am–1pm, Thurs–Sat 11.30am–midnight, Sun 11.30am–10pm.

Jacopo's 326 S Beverly Drive, Beverly Hills ☎310/858-6446. Favourite local spot that has some of LA's best pizza, served piping hot and thin and crispy, in the New York style, and fairly cheap. Daily 11.30am–11pm.

Locanda Veneta 8638 W Third St, Beverly Hills ☎310/274-1893. Whether it's the

Best restaurants for celebrity-watching

If you're less interested in eating fine cuisine than in catching a glimpse of your favourite film and TV stars, there are a number of places where you can watch **celebrities** go through their paces of alternately hiding from, and then mugging for, the public. Practically any upper-end eatery is a likely spot to find the stars, but some places just have that special cachet. Note that one of the most famous spots for celebrity watching, **The Ivy**, 113 N Robertson Blvd in Beverly Hills (☎310/274-8303), with its excessively high prices, is not listed because it's become something of a tourist trap – recommended only to those obsessed with spotting the glitterati at whatever cost.

Barney Greengrass p.236
Chinois on Main p.239
Crustacean p.238
Cut p.236
Drago p.240
The Farm of Beverly Hills p.236
Father's Office p.225
Frankie & Johnnie's p.235
Geoffrey's p.240
Ita-Cho p.231
LA Farm p.239
Locanda Veneta see above
Lucques p.235
Matsuhisa p.238
Mr Chow p.237
Nate 'n' Al's p.225
The Palm p.236
Patina p.228
Spago p.236
Valentino p.240

scrumptious ravioli, risotto, veal or carpaccio, you can't go wrong at one of LA's culinary joys. Expensive, but not unreasonably so. Mon–Fri 11.30am–2.30pm & 5.30–10pm, Sat 5.30–11pm, Sun 5–10pm.

Japanese

Matsuhisa 129 N La Cienega Blvd, Beverly Hills ⓣ310/659-9639. The biggest name in town for sushi, charging the highest prices. Essential if you're a raw-fish aficionado with a wad of cash; combo lunches at $20–25, or fixed-prices meals offered at $75–120. Daily 5.45–10.15pm, also Mon–Fri 11.45am–2.15pm.

Mishima 8474 W Third St ⓣ323/782-0181. Great miso soup, softshell crab salad, and udon and soba noodles, at very affordable prices, at this popular Westside eatery. Tues–Sun 11.30am–10pm.

Mori Sushi 11500 W Pico Blvd ⓣ323/479-3939. A subtly stylish spot that resists trendiness, but still offers up some of the city's finest sushi, almost always delicious and always fresh and not farmed. Mon–Fri noon–2pm & 6–10pm, Sat 6–10.30pm.

Sushi Time 8103 Beverly Blvd ⓣ323/658-6700. Excellent value at this unassuming, low-key spot which offers many affordable hand rolls – including toro tuna – and crab, urchin and other seafood delights. Mon–Sat 11.45am–2.30pm & 5.30–9pm.

Mexican and Latin American

Eduardo's Border Grill 1830 Westwood Blvd, Westwood ⓣ310/475-2410. Quietly appealing neighbourhood Mexican restaurant that serves up a tasty range of meaty tacos and burritos and other staples to a following of local customers. Mon–Sat 11.30am–10pm, Sun 11.30am–9pm.

Monte Alban 11927 Santa Monica Blvd, West LA ⓣ310/444-7736. Forget the tacky mini-mall setting and focus on the fine, affordable selection of mole sauces and Mexican staples that make any trip here a reward. Daily 8am–1pm, weekends until midnight.

Plancha 8250 W Third St ⓣ323/951-9911. Though this minimal eatery has the usual burritos and fajitas, it's best for its spicy fish tacos, tiger tacos with garlic shrimp, and taquitos. Meals are filling and prices are super-cheap, around $5 for three tacos. Sun–Thurs 9am–midnight, Fri & Sat 11am–1am.

Tacomiendo 11462 Gateway Blvd ⓣ310/481-0804. In an anonymous area near the 405 and 10 freeway junction, but offers some of LA's best and cheapest Mexican fare, with scrumptious and huge burritos and solid tamales and tacos as well, including a few veggie options. Daily 9am–10pm.

Middle Eastern

Shamshiri 1712 Westwood Blvd, West LA ⓣ310/474-1410. Top Iranian restaurant in the area, offering delicious kebabs, pilafs and exotic sauces for moderate cost. Daily 11.30am–10.30pm, weekends 'til 11pm.

Seafood

Crustacean 9646 Little Santa Monica Blvd, Beverly Hills ⓣ310/205-8990. Dressy eatery that draws the swells and a few tourists for its array of roasted crab, prawn ravioli, Maine lobster and other inspired seafood entrees. Jacket required. Mon–Fri 11.30am–2.30pm & 5.30–10.30pm, Sat 5.30–11.30pm, Sun 5–9pm.

Fish Grill 7226 Beverly Blvd ⓣ323/937-7162. Just south of Beverly Hills, this unassuming diner serves up tasty meals like fish sandwiches and tacos, chowders, fish and chips, and salmon and tuna wraps, mostly under $10. Sun–Thurs 11am–9pm, Fri 11am–2.30pm.

La Cevicheria 3809 W Pico Blvd, West LA ⓣ323/732-1253. Among the city's best values for Mexican-styled seafood, including prime ceviche, shrimp combos, crab and octopus tostadas and spicy soups, mostly for under $11. Sun & Tues–Thurs 11am–8pm, Sat & Sun 11am–9pm.

Thai and Southeast Asian

Chaya Brasserie 8741 Alden Drive, Beverly Hills ⓣ310/859-8833. Pan-Asian bistro with moderate to expensive prices and a chic clientele that munches on delicious soy-glazed black cod, sushi rolls and big-eye tuna tartare, along with steak and pasta. Merits a splurge. Daily 11.30am-2.30pm & 5–11.30pm, weekends until midnight.

Talesai 9198 Olympic Blvd, Beverly Hills ⓣ310/271-9345. Excellent curried seafood, satays and Cal-cuisine-leaning noodle dishes served to knowing gourmets in a drab strip mall. Daily 5.30–9.30pm, also Mon–Sat 11.30am–2.30pm.

Vegetarian and wholefood

À Votre Santé 13016 San Vicente Blvd, Brentwood ⓣ310/451-1813. Scrambled tofu and fried vegetables are on the menu – along

Rough Guide favourites

Round-the-clock dining

25 Degrees p.223
Benito's Taco Shop p.224
Bob's Big Boy p.225
Canter's Deli p.223
The Donut Hole p.226
Du-Par's p.223
Fred 62 p.223
Harbor House Café p.227
Mel's Drive-In p.224
Norm's p.225
Original Pantry p.222
Pacific Dining Car p.228
Randy's Donuts p.226
Tommy's p.224

with veggie and turkey burgers – at this mid-priced Westside chain. Mon–Fri 8.30am–10pm, Sat 9am–10pm, Sun 9am–9pm.

Vegan Glory 8393 Beverly Blvd ☎323/653-4900. Although the name overstates its case a little, this is still appealing, affordable vegan fare with a pan-Asian influence, everything from pad Thai and pan-fried soy "chicken" to papaya salad and various spicy curries. Daily 11am–10pm.

Santa Monica, Venice and Malibu

American, Californian and Cajun

17th Street Café & Bakery 1610 Montana Ave, Santa Monica ☎310/453-2771. Seafood, pasta, sandwiches, eggs and burgers at moderate prices in a casual, unpretentious atmosphere in a chic part of town. Best for breakfast or lunch, or its selection of baked goods. Daily 8am–9.30pm.

Aunt Kizzy's Back Porch 523 Washington Blvd, Marina del Rey ☎310/578-1005. Serving up hushpuppies, chicken, braised oxtail and sweet potato pie, this is one of the few places to get decent soul food in this part of LA. Mon–Fri 11.30am–9pm, Sat 11.30am–10pm, Sun 4–9pm.

Hal's 1349 Abbot Kinney Blvd, Venice ☎310/396-3105. Popular restaurant in a hip shopping zone in Venice, with a range of well-done, somewhat expensive American standards, including marinated steaks, turkey burgers and salmon dishes. Daily 11.30am–2am, weekends opens 10am.

LA Farm 3000 W Olympic Blvd, Santa Monica ☎310/453-2204. Delicious, though very expensive, California cuisine, with an accent on steak and seafood. The main draw is the celebrity-watching: here the stars dine in peace, unless you have other ideas. Mon–Fri 11am–4pm & 5pm–midnight, Sat 5.30pm–1am, Sun 5.30–10pm.

Melisse 1104 Wilshire Blvd, Santa Monica ☎310/395-0881. Top of the line in some people's minds for LA dining, this French eatery offers a fixed-price $105 menu that may include duck breast with cherries, Sonoma sausage and a wide range of seafood. Well chosen and delicious. Tues–Thurs 6–9.30pm, Fri & Sat 6–10pm.

Sauce on Hampton 259 Hampton Drive ☎310/399-5400. It's all about organic eats at this Venice diner that crosses a lot of culinary boundaries. Ahi tuna wraps, prosciutto sandwiches and meatloaf are among the creative, inexpensive offerings you might enjoy. Daily 9am–10pm.

Uncle Darrow's 2560 Lincoln Blvd, Venice ☎310/306-4862. A bit east of the main beach action, but worth a stop if you like savoury, midpriced catfish, gumbos and other down-home Cajun and Creole cooking. Mon–Thurs 11am–9pm, Fri 11am–10pm, Sat 7am–10pm, Sun 7am–9pm.

Caribbean

Babalu 1002 Montana Ave, Santa Monica ☎310/395-2500. The pancakes at this pan-ethnic, Caribbean-influenced restaurant are delightful, as are the sweet potato tamales, fried plantains, mango shrimp and crab enchiladas. Mon–Fri 11am–10pm, Sat 8am–11pm, Sun 8am–10pm.

Chinese and Vietnamese

Chinois on Main 2709 Main St, Santa Monica ☎310/392-9025. Expensive Wolfgang Puck restaurant, skilfully mixing nouvelle French and pan-Asian cuisine – catfish in ginger and ponzu sauce, duck pancakes, curried oysters – for a ravenous yuppie crowd. Mon–Sat 6–10pm, also Wed–Fri 11.30am–2pm, Sun 5.30–10pm.

Dragon Palace 2832 Santa Monica Blvd ☎310/829-1462. Hot shredded beef, pan-fried noodles, spicy shrimp and scallops, and General Tso's Chicken are among the featured treats at this engaging Chinese diner. Most items $6–10. Mon–Thurs 10am–9.30pm, Fri & Sat 10am–10pm.

Indian

Nawab 1621 Wilshire Blvd, Santa Monica ⓣ310/829-1106. Though there are few surprises on the menu, pleasing renditions of Indian standards like chicken vindaloo and tikka masala do the trick. Mon–Fri 11.30am–2.30pm & 5.30–10pm, Sat & Sun noon–3pm & 5.30–10pm.

Italian and pizza

Abbot's Pizza Company 1407 Abbot Kinney Blvd, Venice ⓣ310/396-7334. Named after the old-time founder of the district, this home of the bagel-crust pizza gives you your choice of alfredo, tomato or two kinds of pesto sauce. Daily 11am–11pm. Also at **1811 Pico Blvd, Santa Monica ⓣ310/314-2777.** Daily 10am–10pm.

Drago 2628 Wilshire Blvd, Santa Monica ⓣ310/828-1585. Among LA's superchic Italian eateries, this one serves various Cal-cuisine-oriented dishes and pastas in an appropriately stuffy setting. Daily 11.30am–3pm & 5.30–11pm, weekends opens 5.30pm.

Giorgio Baldi 114 W Channel Rd, Pacific Palisades ⓣ310/573-1660. Very fine Italian food just north of Santa Monica.Great for its pastas and seafood entrees, and especially ravioli, with a correspondingly high price tag – around $25 a plate. Tues–Sun 6–10pm.

Joe's Pizza 111 Broadway, Santa Monica ⓣ310/395-9222. New Yorkers can quit complaining about LA pizza at this mini-chain based out of, naturally, New York. Features the requisite crispy, thin pizza prepared with aplomb. Also in West Hollywood at **8539 Sunset Blvd ⓣ310/358-0900.** Both Mon–Thurs 10am–midnight, Fri & Sat 10am–3am, Sun 11am–midnight.

Valentino 3115 W Pico Blvd, Santa Monica ⓣ310/829-4313. Some call this the best Italian cuisine in the US, and the specialities, particularly veal osso buco and lobster fettucine, are sure to please, though your pocketbook won't be quite so lucky (entrees $25–30). Reservations and formal wear mandatory – expect to be ignored otherwise. Tues–Thurs 5–10pm, Fri & Sat 5–10.30pm.

Japanese

Chaya Venice 110 Navy St, Venice ⓣ310/396-1179. Elegant mix of Japanese and Mediterranean foods in an arty sushi bar, with items such as miso-marinated sea bass and squid-ink paella ($25–30), excellent service and a suitably snazzy clientele. Mon–Fri 11.30am–2.30pm & 5pm–midnight, Sat 5pm–midnight, Sun 5–10pm.

Musha 424 Wilshire Blvd, Santa Monica ⓣ310/576-6330. Among the top choices on the LA sushi scene, this spot prepares fish with striking invention and culinary precision. Try the sashimi, the lobster roll, the ponzu duck – the results are almost uniformly great. Mon–Sat 6–11.30pm.

Sushi Roku 1401 Ocean Ave, Santa Monica ⓣ310/458-4771. While a bit on the stuffy side, this upscale eatery has fine sushi – including mackerel, monkfish, octopus and crab rolls, among other treats. Mon–Fri 11.30am–2.30pm & 5.30–11.30pm, Sat noon–11.30pm, Sun 4.30–10.30pm.

Mexican and Latin American

Border Grill 1445 Fourth St, Santa Monica ⓣ310/451-1655. Nice place to sup on delicious shrimp, pork, plaintains and other nuevo Latin American-flavoured fixings, with excellent desserts, too. Prices are on the expensive side, but the ambience is swinging. Daily 11.30am–10pm, weekends 'til 11pm.

Marix Tex-Mex Playa 118 Entrada Drive, Pacific Palisades ⓣ310/459-8596. Flavourful fajitas and big margaritas are the best picks at this rowdy beachfront cantina. Also at **1108 N Flores St, West Hollywood ⓣ323/656-8800.** Daily 11.30am–11pm, weekends opens 11am.

Tacos Por Favor 1406 Olympic Blvd ⓣ310/392-5768. Uninspired looking from the outside, but this humble eatery has some of the city's best chow, including great tacos and tortas, and hefty burritos that can easily break your belt – but not your wallet. Daily 9am–8pm, Sun closes 5pm.

Russian and Eastern European

Warszawa 1414 Lincoln Blvd, Santa Monica ⓣ310/393-8831. Pleasant, if a bit pricey, establishment with fine Polish cuisine. Don't miss the hearty potato pancakes, pierogi and borscht. Tues–Sat 6–11pm, Sun 5–10pm.

Seafood

Geoffrey's 27400 PCH, Malibu ⓣ310/457-1519. One of Malibu's most upscale spots for steak, seafood and sunset-watching. The pricey Cal-cuisine-inspired menu is almost secondary to the fun of watching the Tinseltown luminaries drop in. Mon–Fri 11.30am–10pm, Sat 10am–11pm, Sun 10am–10pm.

The Lobster 1602 Ocean Ave, Santa Monica ☎310/458-9294. There are few great seafood eateries in town with a fine view, too – but *The Lobster*, along with excellent upscale cuisine. The crab cakes, oysters, and titular (grilled) crustacean are among the top choices. Mon–Sat 11.30am–3pm & 5–10pm, weekends 'til 11pm.

Ocean Avenue Seafood 1401 Ocean Ave, Santa Monica ☎310/394-5669. One of the more reliable of the upscale fishhouse choices in town, with a nice selection of fresh, raw oysters, lobster, steak and crab cakes. Sun–Thurs 11.30am–10pm, Fri & Sat 11.30am–11pm.

Santa Monica Seafood 1000 Wilshire Blvd ☎310/393-5244. Primo seafood café and oyster bar that features very good chowders and cioppino, as well as Scottish loch salmon and good old fish and chips. Also has a good adjoining fish market. Mon–Sat 11am–9pm, Sun 11am–8pm.

Thai and Southeast Asian

Thai Dishes 1910 Wilshire Blvd, Santa Monica ☎310/828-5634. Affordable, straightforward Thai meals geared toward diners not interested in anything too spicy or rough on the palate. Part of a citywide chain. Daily 11am–10.30pm, weekends opens at noon.

Vegetarian and wholefood

Figtree's Café 429 Ocean Front Walk, Venice ☎310/392-4937. Tasty veggie food and grilled fresh fish on a sunny patio just off the Boardwalk. Health-conscious yuppies come in droves for inexpensive breakfasts. Glacial service, however. Daily 8am–6pm, weekends until 7pm.

Inn of the Seventh Ray 128 Old Topanga Rd, Topanga Canyon ☎310/455-1311. The ultimate New Age restaurant in a supremely New Age area, serving vegetarian and other wholefood meals in a relatively secluded setting. Excellent desserts, too. Daily 11.30am–3pm & 5.30–10pm, Sun opens at 9.30am.

South Central and East LA

American, Californian and Cajun

Harold and Belle's 2920 Jefferson Blvd, South Central ☎323/735-9023. One of the most authentic and affordable of the Cajun-cuisine restaurants in town, offering fine gumbo, po' boy sandwiches, and crayfish, catfish and shrimp, along with sides like corn on the cob. Daily 11.30am–9pm, weekends until 10pm.

Phillips Barbeque 4307 Leimert Blvd, Leimert Park ☎323/292-7613. An excellent, and cheap, Southern joint that appeals for its authentic smoky sauces and spicy marinades, full set of sides like potato salads, and fine desserts. Also at **2619 Crenshaw Blvd ☎323/731-4772.** Both Tues–Thurs 11am–10pm, Fri & Sat 11am–11pm, Sun 11am–6pm.

Woody's 3446 W Slauson Ave ☎323/294-9443. What some claim as LA's best barbeque is, unfortunately, located in one of its grimmer corners. Come during the day and get your fill of some rich beef ribs and gut-stuffing pork sausages. Pretty inexpensive, too. Also at **475 S Market St in Inglewood (☎310/672-4200)**. Daily 11am–11pm.

Mexican and Latin American

Ciro's 705 N Evergreen Ave, East LA ☎323/267-8637. A split-level cave of a dining room, serving enormous platters of shrimp and mole specials. The garlic shrimp, avocado salsa and flautas are the main draw, and they also offer takeout. Tues–Sun 7am–8pm.

El Tepayac 812 N Evergreen Ave, Boyle Heights ☎323/268-1960. Not located in the best area, between Downtown and East LA, but merits a stop to sup on some sizable rellenos, burritos and enchiladas, for not more than a few bucks. Daily 6am–10pm, weekends until 11pm.

Paco's Tacos 6212 W Manchester Ave, Westchester ☎310/645-8692. Potent margaritas and filling burritos are the highlights at this eatery near LAX, part of an affordable local chain. Also at **4141 S Centinela Ave (☎310/391-1616)**. Daily 10am–10pm.

The South Bay and LA Harbor

American, Californian and Cajun

At Last Café 204 Orange Ave ☎562/437-4837. Enthralling mix of Cal cuisine and comfort food – Thai beef salad, mac and cheese, flat-iron steak – with most entrees surprisingly less than $15. Easily the best value in the South Bay, or LA itself. Tues–Sat 11am–8pm.

Lasher's 3441 E Broadway, Long Beach ☎562/433-0153. Set in a little house east of

Downtown, a fine choice for steak, seafood and pasta, with notable bacon scallops and fried green tomatoes, at the upper end of what you'll pay in this port town. Daily 5–9pm, also Sun 10am–3pm.

New Orleans 140 Pier Ave, Hermosa Beach ☎310/372-8970. Deep-South Cajun cuisine featuring lip-smacking jambalaya, gumbo, po' boy sandwiches and fried oysters, for higher prices than you might expect. Mon, Thurs & Fri 11.30am–2pm & 5–9pm, Sat noon–10pm, Sun noon–9pm.

Rock 'n' Fish 120 Manhattan Beach Blvd, Manhattan Beach ☎310/379-9900. Whether you're in the mood for halibut, sea bass, shrimp or just a good old prime rib, this cosy surf 'n' turf eatery is a decent, affordable spot to indulge. Just make sure to reserve ahead. Daily 11.30am–10pm, weekends until 11pm.

Greek

George's Greek Cafe 135 Pine Ave, Long Beach ☎562/437-1184. Centrally located and affordable restaurant where you can indulge in some tasty gyros, dolmas and souvlaki, as well as several fine combo plates. Sun–Thurs 10am–11pm, Fri & Sat 10am–midnight. Two other area locations.

Italian and pizza

L'Opera 101 Pine Ave, Long Beach ☎562/491-0066. Swank Italian dining – mixed with a fair bit of Cal-cuisine style – in a historic old building near the centre of Long Beach's downtown activity. Mon–Fri 11.30am–10pm, Fri & Sat 5–10.30pm, Sun 5–9pm.

La Sosta Enoteca 2700 Manhattan Ave, Hermosa Beach ☎310/318-1556. Among the best options for Italian fare in the South Bay, with a broad swath of excellent pasta, risotto and seafood choices, as well as supreme wine and desserts. Tues–Thurs 6–11.30pm, Fri–Sun 6pm–midnight.

Mangiamo 128 Manhattan Beach Blvd, Manhattan Beach ☎310/318-3434. Like the name says, "Let's eat!" Fairly pricey but interesting for the speciality Northern Italian seafood – and near the beach, too. Daily 5–10.30pm.

Mexican and Latin American

By Brazil 1615 Cabrillo Ave, Torrance ☎310/787-7520. Hearty and affordable Brazilian fare, mostly grilled and barbequed chicken and beef dishes; go to inland Torrance for a taste. Daily 11am–9.30pm, weekends opens at noon.

El Pollo Inka 1100 PCH, Hermosa Beach ☎310/372-1433. Cheap Peruvian-style chicken, catfish and hot and spicy soups to make your mouth water. Daily 11am–11pm. Three other South Bay locations. Sun–Fri 11am–9pm, Sat 11am–9.30pm.

Pancho's 3615 Highland Ave, Manhattan Beach ☎310/545-6670. Big portions of old favourites like tacos and burritos, and fairly cheap for the area. Adequate and convenient, and very good – for the South Bay. Daily 11am–10pm, weekends until 11pm.

Seafood

Bluewater Grill 665 N Harbor Drive, Redondo Beach ☎310/318-3474. The South Bay outpost of an Orange County favourite (see p.245), featuring a slew of mid-priced fresh fish – salmon and catfish to crabs and oysters – though it brings in a few more tourists than the other branch. Daily 11.30am–10pm, weekends 'til 11pm.

Kincaid's Bay House 500 Fishermans Wharf, Redondo Beach ☎310/318-6080. A dramatically placed fishhouse serving old-fashioned meals of crab, lobster and prawns, as well as more adventurous offerings such as spicy ahi tacos and calamari fried in buttermilk. Mon–Sat 11am–10pm, Sun 11am–9pm.

King's Fish House 100 W Broadway #500, Long Beach ☎562/432-7463. Esteemed seafood restaurant with a full selection of salmon, tuna, oysters and sea bass. One in a local chain of upmarket eateries. Sun & Mon 11.30am–9pm, Tues–Thurs 11.30am–10pm, Fri & Sat 11.30am–11pm.

Quality Seafood 130 Intl Boardwalk, Redondo Beach ☎310/372-6408. Seafood eateries are just about the only reason to hang out in this seaside town, and here you can indulge in a fine oyster bar and pick from a great selection of crabs, clams, shrimp and other shellfish, prepared while you watch. Daily 10.30am–6.30pm, weekends 'til 7.30pm.

Spanish

Alegria Cocina Latina 115 Pine Ave, Long Beach ☎562/436-3388. Tapas, gazpacho and a variety of *platos principales* served with sangría on the patio, to the beat of live flamenco on weekends. Central location near the harbour in Downtown Long Beach. Mon–Thurs 11.30am–10pm, Fri 11.30am–midnight, Sat 5pm–midnight, Sun 5–10pm.

Vegetarian and wholefood

Good Stuff 1286 The Strand, Hermosa Beach ☎310/374-2334. Many veggie choices, as well as healthy seafood, wraps and sandwiches, at this link in a chain of reliable South Bay restaurants. Daily 7am–4pm.

The Spot 110 Second St, Hermosa Beach ☎310/376-2355. A wide selection of inexpensive vegetarian dishes, based on Mexican and other international cuisines and free of refined sugar and any animal products. Daily 10am–10pm.

The San Gabriel and San Fernando valleys

African

Marrakesh 13003 Ventura Blvd, Studio City ☎818/788-6354. Zesty Moroccan restaurant in the Valley, where filling couscous and lamb dishes are served amid lush furnishings and belly-dancing. Set price dinners $24–35 per person. Daily 5–9.30pm, weekends until 10pm.

American, Californian and Cajun

Arroyo Chop House 536 S Arroyo Pkwy, Pasadena ☎626/577-7463. Elegant steakhouse with a mouth-watering selection of filet mignon, prime rib, savoury soups, and desserts. Bring several credit cards, though. Sun–Thurs 5–9.30pm, Fri–Sat 5–9.45pm

Granville Cafe 121 San Fernando Blvd, Burbank ☎818/848-4726. California cuisine with a casual spin, featuring artichoke pizza, gourmet mac and cheese, ahi sandwiches and bacon-avocado melts, mostly in the $10–15 range and mostly quite good. Also in Glendale at **807 Americana Way ☎818/550-0472.** Both Mon–Thurs 11am–10pm, Fri 11am–11pm, Sat 9am–11pm, Sun 9am–10pm.

Marston's 151 E Walnut St, Pasadena ☎626/796-2459. This little house makes fine digs for breakfast and lunch, with the omelettes, French toast, pancakes, among the highlights. Mon–Tues 7am–2.30pm & 5.30–9.30pm, Wed–Sat 5.30–9.30pm, also Sat–Sun 8am–2.30pm.

Saddle Peak Lodge 419 Cold Canyon Rd, Calabasas ☎818/222-3888. At this elite eatery on the San Fernando Valley side of the Santa Monica Mountains you can devour anything from albacore sashimi to Alaska halibut to elk tenderloin. Wed–Fri 6–9pm, Sat 5–10pm, Sun 10.30am–2pm & 5–9pm.

Chinese and Vietnamese

Lee's Garden 1428 S Atlantic Blvd, Alhambra ☎626/284-0320. As with many of the Chinese restaurants in the San Gabriel Valley, a fine neighbourhood eatery that has a range of authentic staples – pork dumplings, oyster pancakes, etc – at affordable prices. Mon–Sat 11.30am–10pm.

NBC Seafood 404 S Atlantic Blvd, Monterey Park ☎626/282-2323. Worth a trip out to this ethnic-food enclave east of downtown for some of the city's best dim sum, served authentically in the Cantonese style, for manageable prices. Daily 9am–9.30pm.

Ocean Star 145 N Atlantic Blvd, Monterey Park ☎626/308-2128. A rather huge venue specializing in dim sum, with the fried shrimp, dumplings and salty chicken among the highlights. Popular and affordable. Mon–Sat 10am–10pm.

French

Café Bizou 14016 Ventura Blvd, San Fernando Valley ☎818/788-3536. Bringing affordable French cuisine to the northern valleys, this mid-priced restaurant serves succulent lobster tail, rack of lamb, risotto and salads. Two other LA locations. Daily 5–10pm, also Mon–Fri 11.30am–2.30pm, Sat & Sun 11am–2.30pm.

Julienne 2649 Mission St, San Marino ☎626/441-2299. While the pâté and croque monsieur are decent, the ham and brie on a pretzel roll, sirloin burger and rich desserts like bread pudding French toast are even better at this excellent, mid-priced French restaurant. Breakfast and lunch only. Mon–Fri 7am–10.45am & 11.30am–3.30pm, Sat 7.30am–11.15am & 12.30–3.30pm.

Greek

Café Santorini 64 W Union St, Pasadena ☎626/564-4200. A fine mix of mid-range Greek and Italian food – capellini, souvlaki, risotto, baba ganoush, hummus and the like. Located in a relaxed plaza and offering some patio dining. Daily 11am–10pm, weekends until midnight.

Great Greek 13362 Ventura Blvd, Sherman Oaks ☎818/905-5250. Old World enterprise serving delicious, midpriced dolmas, kebabs, meatballs and moussaka to ethnic music beats and fervent dancing. Daily 11.30am–10pm, weekends until 11pm.

Italian and pizza

Avanti Cafe 111 N Lake Ave, Pasadena ⓣ626/577-4688. A lip-smacking place to get your (affordable) gourmet pizza fix, in styles ranging from seafood, glazed apple, prosciutto or duck sausage to good old pepperoni, sausage and anchovies. Mon–Thurs 11am–10pm, Fri & Sat 11am–11pm, Sun 11.30am–10pm.

Gale's 452 S Fair Oaks Ave, Pasadena ⓣ626/432-6705. Northern Italian cuisine presented with flair, and featuring fine, mid-priced dishes such as beef carpaccio, rosemary lamb chops and a full range of savoury pastas. Tues–Thurs 11.30am–9pm, Fri & Sat 11.30am–10pm, Sun 5–9pm.

Panzanella 14928 Ventura Blvd, Sherman Oaks ⓣ818/784-4400. Some of the best Italian cuisine in LA adds a dash of California creativity, but stays true to the simple, delicious character of traditional pasta, rice and beef dishes. Mon–Sat 5.30–11pm, Sun 5.30–10pm.

Japanese

Kyoto Sushi 4454 Van Nuys Blvd, Sherman Oaks ⓣ818/986-7060. Small but popular eatery with several types of sushi, sashimi and seasonal macrobiotic dishes. Good food for moderate cost, especially the combo platters under $15. Mon–Fri 11am–2.30pm & 5.30–10pm, Sat 5–10pm.

Shiro 1505 Mission St, South Pasadena ⓣ626/799-4774. One of the few top-notch restaurants in South Pasadena, perhaps the only one. The expensive seafood – particularly the grilled catfish and salmon carpaccio – is the highlight of the extensive menu. Tues–Sun 6–9pm, weekends until 9.30pm.

Sushi Don 4816 Laurel Canyon Blvd, North Hollywood ⓣ818/762-8720. Hands down LA's best value for sushi: a broad range of scrumptious hand rolls, sushi and sashimi, mostly for $5–10 each, and good salads and rice bowls to boot. Daily 11.30am–8.30pm.

Sushi Nozawa 11288 Ventura Blvd, Studio City ⓣ818/508-7017. Excellent, if expensive, sushi served to trendy regulars who don't mind being berated by the imperious chef: if you sit at the bar, he will decide what you'll eat. Period. Mon–Fri noon–2pm & 5.30–10pm.

Mexican and Latin American

Don Cuco 3911 W Riverside Drive ⓣ818/842-1123. Top-notch quesadillas, spicy soups, burritos and potent margaritas are the prime draws at this small Burbank eatery, which is priced a bit higher than at comparable Mexican restaurants in the area. One of several in a Valley chain, the other closest at **214 N Brand Blvd, Glendale (ⓣ818/553-1123).** Daily 11am–10pm, weekends 'til 11pm.

Izalco 10729 Burbank Blvd, North Hollywood ⓣ818/760-0396. Salvadoran cuisine presented with style, from plantains and pork ribs to corn cakes and pupusas, for affordable prices. Daily 10am–10pm, weekends opens 9am.

La Estrella 502 N Fair Oaks Ave, Pasadena ⓣ626/792-8559. Delicious old favourite for Mexican cuisine, where you can get great tacos, burritos, ceviche and tostadas for inexpensive prices. Two other Valley locations. Daily 10am–11pm.

Señor Fish 618 Mission St, South Pasadena ⓣ626/403-0145. Somewhat drab-looking joint with great, cheap fish tacos, seafood burritos and charbroiled halibut. Daily 11.30am–9pm.

Middle Eastern

Azeen's 110 E Union St, Pasadena ⓣ626/683-3310. Esteemed, stylish haunt for rich and flavourful Afghani cuisine such as kebabs, meat pastries and dumplings, an appealing mix of Persian and Indian foodways. Daily 5.30–9.30pm, also Mon–Fri 11.30am–2pm.

Carousel 304 N Brand Ave, Glendale ⓣ818/246-7775. A Lebanese charmer in downtown Glendale, chock full of Levantine cultural artefacts and authentic food, from roasted chicken and quail to several different kinds of kebab. Tues–Thurs 11.30am–9.30pm, Fri & Sat 11.30am–midnight.

Thai and Southeast Asian

Saladang 363 S Fair Oaks Ave, Pasadena ⓣ626/793-8123. Don't miss out on the pad Thai, curry, spicy soups and noodles and salmon at this chic and delicious spot. The restaurant's annex, Saladang Song, offers even spicier Thai concoctions. Daily 8am–10pm.

Sanamluang Café 12980 Sherman Way, North Hollywood ⓣ818/764-1180. The noodles, skewers, soups and salads at this late-night Thai eatery are hot, cheap and unbeatable. Daily 11am–2am.

Orange County

American, Californian and Cajun

Bayside 900 Bayside Drive ☎949/721-1222. Upscale Newport Beach California cuisine focusing on tapas (most dishes under $10) such as Scottish salmon, crab cakes and lobster salad, plus good steaks and sandwiches. Mon–Fri 11.30am–10pm, Sat 5–11pm, Sun 11am–3pm & 5–11pm.

Five Crowns 3801 E Coast Hwy, Corona del Mar ☎949/760-0331. A steak and rib joint that doles out ample meaty fare amid mildly kitschy Olde English decor. Mon–Thurs 5–9pm, Fri & Sat 5–10pm, Sun 10am–2.30pm & 4–8.30pm.

Memphis Cafe 2920 Bristol St, Costa Mesa ☎714/432-7685. Fine Southern dining set in a trendy club environment, with a range of shrimp, fried chicken, cornbread and more at higher prices than you might expect (entrées $15–25). Mon–Sat 11am–3pm & 5–10pm, weekends 'til 10.30pm, Sun 5–9.30pm.

Sage 2531 Eastbluff Drive, Newport Beach ☎949/718-9650. Fancy establishment catering to Cal-cuisine lovers, featuring savoury delights like blue crab cakes, cioppino, salmon penne and balsamic salmon. Mon–Sat 11.30am–9.30pm, weekends 'til 10pm, Sun 10.30am–9pm.

Chinese and Vietnamese

Anh Hong 10195 Westminster Ave, Garden Grove ☎714/537-5230. Terrific Vietnamese restaurant known for its traditional, affordable favourites (including broiled pork with vermicelli noodles) and "seven courses of beef", a panoply of red meat in all its glory. Daily 3–10pm, weekends opens 11am.

Favori 3502 W First St, Santa Ana ☎714/531-6838. What may be Orange County's best Vietnamese food: delicious garlic shrimp, barbecued pork, salty squid and baked catfish, all for decent prices. Daily 11am–10pm.

Italian

Onotria 2831 Bristol St ☎714/641-5952. Costa Mesa favourite that emphasizes its considerable wine list. The compelling menu features creative entrees such as peppercorn salmon filet, habanero seafood stew, poached octopus and pumpkin gnocchi, for mid- to high prices. Mon–Sat 5.30–10pm, also Mon–Fri 11.30am–2.30pm.

Villa Nova 3131 W Coast Hwy, Newport Beach ☎949/642-7880. Old-time Italian seafood in a classy setting for locals and out-of-towners alike. The pastas (including a fine gnocchi) and veal scallopine draw crowds, so reserve ahead. Daily 5pm–midnight, Sun from 4pm.

Mexican and Latin American

Fiesta Grill 418 Seventh St, Huntington Beach ☎714/969-7689. Only a few blocks from the beach, this is a choice spot for picking up fish tacos and shrimp burritos for low prices before you enjoy a day on the sands. Daily 11.30am–9.30pm.

Los Primos Cantina 488 E 17th St, Costa Mesa ☎949/650-1486. If you find yourself roving around here looking for cheap, authentic Mexican fare, stop at this joint for very filling burritos, tostadas and other reasonable choices. Daily 11am–10pm.

Taco Mesa 647 W 19th St, Costa Mesa ☎949/642-0629. Low-priced, tasty burritos, quesadillas, chilaquiles and tacos, as well as more unexpected choices like stuffed jalapenos and calamari tacos, at this reliable Orange County chain. Daily 8am–10pm.

Middle Eastern

Zena's 2094 N Tustin St, city of Orange ☎714/279-9511. A friendly Lebanese spot offering a selection of gyros, kebabs, baba ganoush, stuffed grape leaves, shawarma and other traditional, inexpensive favourites. Daily 11am–10pm, Sun closes at 8pm.

Seafood

Bluewater Grill 630 Lido Park Drive, Newport Beach ☎949/675-3474. Delectable, relatively affordable seafood standards – ahi tuna, salmon, oysters, lobster and the like – accompanied by appealing ocean views from the patio. Daily 11am–10pm, weekends 'til 11pm, Sun opens 10am.

Claes Seafood in the Hotel Laguna, 425 S Coast Hwy, Laguna Beach ☎949/376-9283. One of Orange County's best seafood spots, where you can sample pricey ahi tuna and halibut with a Cal-cuisine spin, indoors with a fine view of the Pacific. Daily 5–9.30pm, also Sun 9am–2pm.

Crab Cooker 2200 Newport Blvd, Newport Beach ☎949/673-0100. The hefty plates of crab legs and shrimp and steaming bowls of chowder at this small inexpensive diner make the long lines a bit more bearable. Daily 11am–9pm, weekends until 10pm.

13

Bars and clubs

Nightlife in Los Angeles is some of the best and most frenetic in the country, and the image of swingin' singles or bleary-eyed drunks ensconced in their favourite watering holes is just as iconic to the city as anything produced by Hollywood. Weekend nights are the busiest at the various bars and clubs, but during the week things are cheaper and often just as enjoyable. For uninterrupted drinking, there are **bars** and lounges on seemingly every other corner, especially in Hollywood, where lower-end dives welcome a mixed crowd of grizzled old-timers and slumming hipsters, and shameless velvet-rope scenes cater to wannabe celebrities who feel the need to pay $200 for a bottle of fancy vodka. However, don't get too carried away with the libertine spirit: **smoking is banned** under California law.

Bar styles tend to go in and out of fashion quickly, changing from month to month, often according to music and showbiz trends. What follows are descriptions of some of the more established bars in LA, generally those that have been around for at least a year or two; the trendiest joints sometimes only last a few months, disappearing once they lose their buzz and their exorbitant overhead finally catches up with them.

If you want something of the bar atmosphere without the alcohol, visit one of LA's many **coffeehouses**, which can be relaxed and fun, but sometimes carry a bit of attitude. Given the West Coast's taste for expensive coffee concoctions, coffeehouses can offer a refreshing break from the bar scene, especially if you want some culture – in the form of alternative music and performing arts.

LA's many **clubs** often double as live music venues (for which, see Chapter 14), but in this section we've tried to focus on entertainment that's readily available from night to night, and especially on weekends. When big-name touring DJs pull up, door charges can be as much as going to a live rock concert; more often, however, such big names are the exception and the usual scene will be based around local DJs – who in LA may even be national calibre. There will often be a bar attached to the club (allowing for overlap with that category), but unless the lounge itself is the reason people come, we've tried to focus on the beats.

Bars

As you'd expect, LA's **bars** reflect their locality: a clash of artists, musicians and yuppies Downtown; serious hedonists and leather-clad rockers in Hollywood; actual or (more often) self-styled movie stars and producers in West Hollywood and West LA; a mix of tourists and locals in Santa Monica; a more oddball selection in Venice; and the random assortment of interesting characters in the valleys. A few hard-bitten bars are open the legal maximum hours (from 6am until 2am daily), though the busiest hours are between 9pm and midnight. During

happy hour, usually 5–7pm or 4–6pm, drinks are cheap and there'll often be a selection of "pub grub" to nosh on.

Downtown

Bona Vista at the Westin Bonaventure hotel, 404 S Figueroa St ⓣ213/624-1000. Thirty-five floors up, this constantly rotating cocktail lounge spins faster after a few of the expensive drinks, and offers an unparallelled view of the sun setting over the city.

Casey's Bar 613 S Grand Ave ⓣ213/629-2353. This old-time Irish pub with dark wood-paneled walls has a friendly, rousing ambience that has made it something of a local institution.

Edison 108 W Second St ⓣ213/613-0000. One of LA's best uber-chic bars, a place with stunning antique industrial decor, retro-flavoured lounge music, upmarket food (such as blue-crab fritters and truffle mac and cheese), a nice (though pricey) range of inventive cocktails, and a smart dress code. Wed–Sat only.

Little Cave 5922 N Figueroa St, Highland Park ⓣ323/255-6871. This cramped but fun little joint is worth a visit for its killer drinks, much cheaper than in swankier parts of town, and self-consciously divey atmosphere.

Mountain Bar 475 Gin Ling Way ⓣ213/625-7500. Hidden in a nook in Chinatown, this bar is a good spot if you want to knock back your well drinks and cocktails in a colourful environment loaded with Asian decor. Plus, a happening club scene downstairs and live music above.

Pete's Café and Bar 400 S Main St ⓣ213/617-1000. A retro-flavoured bar in the handsome digs of an old bank building, which despite the dicey environs draws a nightly crowd of business types and a few artsy loft-occupiers. Good food, too, like shrimp skewers and Thai turkey burgers.

Redwood 316 W Second St ⓣ213/617-2867. Solid Downtown choice for serious drinking and cheap all-American grub since 1943, now remade into a "pirate bar" featuring skull-and-crossbones decor and patrons kitted out like Blackbeard. Also offers live music and affordable drinks.

Standard Hotel Bar 550 S Flower St ⓣ213/892-8080. LA's poseur pinnacle: a rooftop playpen where the silk-shirted-black-leather-pants crowd goes to hang out in red metallic "pods" and sprawl out on an Astroturf lawn, against a backdrop of corporate towers. You'll have to navigate the velvet-rope scene and pay a $20 cover charge – drinks are almost as much.

Mid-Wilshire

Dan Sung Sa 3317 W Sixth St ⓣ213/487-9100. If you're looking for an authentic taste of Koreatown, this welcoming bar is a good place to start, with affordable drinks and hearty food like barbequed meats, spicy soups and skewers (and more curious items like gizzards and intestines).

El Carmen 8138 W Third St ⓣ323/852-1552. Groovy faux dive-bar with a south-of-the-border theme pushed to the extreme, with black-velvet pictures of Mexican wrestlers, steer horns, stuffed snakes, signature margaritas and a good range of different tequilas.

H.M.S. Bounty 3357 Wilshire Blvd ⓣ213/385-7275. An authentic dive experience. Advertising "Food and Grog", the scruffy bar is a hot spot for hipsters and grizzled old-timers who come for the dark ambience, cheap and potent drinks, and kitschy nautical motifs dating from 1937.

Molly Malone's Irish Pub 575 S Fairfax Ave ⓣ323/935-1577. Self-consciously authentic Irish bar, from the food (corned-beef sandwiches, burgers and other gut-stuffers) to the music (mostly grinding rock and Celtic folk) to the shamrocks swirled into the creamy head of your Guinness.

St. Nick's 8450 W Third St ⓣ323/655-6917. A few blocks from the colossal Beverly Center mall sits this oddly popular dive bar, good for getting sloshed for cheap, and without the pretentious attitudes on view at lounges just a few blocks north.

Tom Bergin's 840 S Fairfax Ave ⓣ323/936-7151. Old-time drinking joint from 1936, a great place for Irish coffee (supposedly invented here), Irish beer and of course, Irish whiskey. The savoury pub grub – fish and chips, shepherd's pie – hits the spot, and stays there.

Hollywood

4100 4100 Sunset Blvd, Silver Lake ⓣ323/666-4460. Although it continues the annoying LA trend of naming itself after its street address, this murky bar does boast inventive pan-Asian decor, moody lighting and a mix of gays, straights and imbibing tourists.

Beauty Bar 1638 N Cahuenga Blvd ☎323/464-7676. A drinking spot devoted to hair, nails and cosmetics, featuring 1950s-style retro-decor and a cocktail list to match; there's also dancing. One of ten in a national chain.

Blue Goose 5201 Sunset Blvd ☎323/667-1400. Comfortable lounge where you can plunge into a soft couch (or a potent cocktail) or try your luck at karaoke. A good, functional drinker's hangout with minimal pretension.

Boardner's 1652 N Cherokee Ave ☎323/462-9621. Former historic dive bar now remodelled into sleek, yuppie-friendly confines for tasteful drinking (and a decent happy hour) with an impressively dark and luminous set design. Also offers regular electronica, indie rock and burlesque shows.

Burgundy Room 1621 Cahuenga Blvd ☎323/465-7530. A classic place to get down and dirty with the old Hollywood dive-bar vibe, with a lively rock and punk jukebox, minimal decor, stiff drinks, and a growling crowd of regulars.

Cat and Fiddle 6530 Sunset Blvd ☎323/468-3800. Boisterous but comfortable and convivial British-styled pub with darts, decent pub grub, English beers on tap and live jazz on Sun nights. See also "Live music", p.260.

Cha Cha Lounge 2375 Glendale Blvd ☎323/660-7595. The overwhelming kitsch of the art design is what appeals at this East Hollywood dive bar, where the drinks are cheap, the DJ tunes good enough, and the food service nonexistent. Still, for a colourful atmosphere the place is hard to top.

The Dresden Room 1760 N Vermont Ave ☎323/665-4298. One of the neighbourhood's classic bars, best known perhaps for its evening show (Tues–Sun 9pm), in which the husband-and-wife lounge act of Marty and Elayne takes requests from the crowd of old-timers and hipsters.

Formosa Café 7156 Santa Monica Blvd ☎323/850-9050. Started in 1925 as a watering hole for Charlie Chaplin's adjacent United Artists studios, this creaky old spot is still alive with the ghosts of Bogie and Marilyn. Imbibe the potent spirits but steer clear of the insipid food.

Frolic Room 6245 Hollywood Blvd ☎323/462-5890. Classic LA bar that feels airlifted from a half-century ago, decorated with Hirschfeld celebrity cartoons and steeped in a dark Hollywood ambience. Right by the Pantages Theater.

Good Luck Bar 1514 Hillhurst Ave ☎323/666-3524. A hip Los Feliz retro-dive, this cramped little hangout is popular for its cheesy pseudo-Chinese decor and tropical drinks straight from the heyday of *Trader Vic's*. Located near the intersection of Sunset and Hollywood blvds.

Musso and Frank Grill 6667 Hollywood Blvd ☎323/467-7788. Simply put, if you haven't had a drink in this landmark 1919 bar, you haven't been to Hollywood. It also serves overpriced diner food. Soak in the dark, clubby atmosphere like you're a player.

Power House 1714 N Highland Ave ☎323/463-9438. Enjoyable, long-standing hard-rockers' watering hole just off the most touristy part of Hollywood Blvd. Other than the handful of curious tourists, few people get here much before midnight.

The Room 1626 N Cahuenga Blvd ☎323/462-7196. Small, dark bar with acceptably stiff drinks and decent music, attracting a crowd of relaxed scenesters and more jittery poseurs. Good if you like to boogie to the thumping sounds of dance pop and hip hop.

Smog Cutter 864 N Virgil Ave ☎323/660-4626. Dive bar that attracts a mix of boozers and hipsters. Don't miss the karaoke scene, which, like the liquor, can be pleasantly mind-numbing.

Stout 1544 N Cahuenga Blvd ☎323/469-3801. A truly "stout" brick cube of a place that's known for its inventive burgers and microbrewed beer – both quite good, and its thirty brews on tap and 4am closing time provides its true watering-hole bona fides.

Tiki Ti 4427 W Sunset Blvd ☎323/669-9381. Tiny grass-skirted cocktail bar straight out of *Hawaii-Five-O*, packed with kitschy pseudo-Polynesian decor and (hopefully) no more than a handful of patrons – it's pretty cosy inside.

The Well 6255 W Sunset Blvd ☎323/467-9355. Good-time lounge with a fine central bar, murky mood lighting, and not too much pretension. Decent pub grub, too.

The Woods 1533 N La Brea Ave ☎323/876-6612. With its chunky wooden decor and dramatic mood lighting, this well-placed bar sticks to its eponymous bucolic theme with a dash of kitsch. A decent jukebox and strong drinks keep its patrons satisfied.

West Hollywood

Bar Lubitsch 7702 Santa Monica Blvd ☎323/654-1234. Despite the German-film-director name, this fun, moody lounge has a Russian theme and the drinks lean heavily on all things vodka, either served in cocktails or straight-up as cold as a Moscow winter.

Barney's Beanery 8447 Santa Monica Blvd ☎310/654-2287. Well-worn pool room/bar, stocking over one hundred beers, with a solid, rock'n'roll-hedonist history highlighted by the antics of Jim Morrison, among others. It also serves all-American, rib-stuffing food; see p.224.

Jones 7250 Santa Monica Blvd ☎323/850-1726. Pizza-and-pasta Italian joint with serviceable food, but more of a drinking (and posing) scene for semi-employed actors and writers. Buzzing LA atmosphere makes it more fun for spectating out-of-towners than for locals.

Lola's 945 N Fairfax Ave ☎213/736-5652. It has beer and wine, but martinis are the theme at this swanky joint, with more than fifty interesting, inventive choices on offer, from the Big Banana to the Caramel Apple to the Garlic Mashed Potato.

Rainbow Bar & Grill 9015 Sunset Blvd ☎310/278-4232. Leave your Dockers and penny loafers at home for this scruffy lounge that for decades has been catering to the hard-rawkin' crowd on the Strip – it's a lot more authentic (and generous with its pours) than the posier lounges to the east.

Red Rock 8782 Sunset Blvd ☎310/854-0710. Energetic watering hole with a wide array of drafts on tap and a broad assortment of customers. The main patrons, though, are the high-fiving dudes who cheer on their favourite sports teams on the plentiful TV screens.

Snake Pit 7529 Melrose Ave ☎323/653-2011. One of the decent bars along the Melrose shopping strip, small and not too showy, with a mix of locals and tourists who come to slurp down tropical concoctions and other drinks.

Beverly Hills and West LA

The Arsenal 12012 W Pico Blvd ☎310/575-5511. Lively and engaging West LA scene that offers fine pub food (notably the salt-and-pepper calamari), a dancefloor with pop and hip hop sounds, and tasty cocktails mostly under $10.

Bar Noir in the Maison 140 hotel, 140 S Lasky Drive, Beverly Hills ☎310/271-2145. A swank lounge in a small hotel, with much effort spent on the quasi-Asian decor and dark and atmospheric set design. Worth a look to see how the beautiful people imbibe.

Liquid Kitty 11780 Pico Blvd, West LA ☎310/473-3707. As its quirky name might suggest, this bar is aimed solidly at the hipster contingent, with a fine selection of cocktails, kitschy antique burlesque and erotica on TV, and nightly lounge and dance music to set the mood.

Nic's Restaurant and Martini Lounge 453 N Canon Dr ☎310/550-5707. Although it has the pricey drinks, rubberneckers eager to spot celebs, and self-consciously hip decor common to most Beverly Hills bars, this one appeals for its ice-cold vodka tastings (in a separate room) and primo Cal-cuisine. By default the best bar in this town.

Q's Billiards 11835 Wilshire Blvd, Brentwood ☎310/477-7550. Not exactly free of the pretension or meatmarket vibe that plagues West LA bars, but close enough. It's a good spot to knock back a brew in a packed college atmosphere, watch a sports game, play a game of pool and listen to DJs.

Santa Monica and Venice

Beechwood 822 Washington Blvd ☎310/448-8884. Smart neo-modern design with a few Asian touches in this Venice bar that offers savoury Cal cuisine to go along with its mid-priced beer and cocktail menu. Many young, smashing people all around.

Encounter 209 World Way, at LAX ☎310/215-5151. A Space Age-themed bar inside architect Eero Saarinen's futuristic Theme Building, overlooking the LAX parking lot. Well worth a visit to sample the potent Day-Glo drinks (if not the food) while watching the jets land.

Finn McCool's 2700 Main St, Santa Monica ☎310/452-1734. Despite the dubious name, a worthwhile Irish pub with neo-Celtic artwork, a tasty selection of Emerald Isle brews and hefty platters of traditional fare that call for a pint of Guinness.

Hinano Café 15 Washington Blvd, Venice ☎310/822-3902. Low-attitude chill bar – one of the older ones in Venice – right by the beach, with pool tables and shambling decor. A good place to drink without many tourists around, though the Boardwalk is just a few feet away.

Library Alehouse 2911 Main St, Santa Monica ⓣ310/314-4855. Presenting the choicest brews from West Coast microbreweries and beyond, this spot offers a nice range of well-known and obscure labels and a decent selection of food.

O'Brien's 2226 Wilshire Blvd, Santa Monica ⓣ310/829-5303. A fun, tub-thumping scene serving Irish food and brews to an animated crowd of locals and Irish expats.

The Otheroom 1201 Abbot Kinney Blvd, Venice ⓣ310/396-6230. Relaxed hipster vibe with murky lighting, comfy sofas, and low-energy buzz that are well suited for making friends (or more) with the locals.

Rick's Tavern 2907 Main St, Santa Monica ⓣ310/392-2772. Dark and humming neighbourhood joint off the Main Street shopping strip, with sports on TV and boisterous regulars on the bar stools.

Ye Olde King's Head 116 Santa Monica Blvd, Santa Monica ⓣ310/451-1402. Very British joint with jukebox, dartboards, (real) football and rugby on screen, and signed photos of all your favourite rock dinosaurs. Don't miss the steak-and-kidney pie, afternoon tea, or the fish and chips.

The San Gabriel and San Fernando valleys

Clearman's North Woods 7247 N Rosemead Blvd, San Gabriel ⓣ626/286-3579. A kitsch-lover's delight with fake snow on the outside and moose heads on the walls inside. A great place for devouring steaks and drinking like a fiend while throwing peanut shells on the floor.

The Colorado 2640 E Colorado Blvd, Pasadena ⓣ626/449-3485. A bright and lively spot along a rather bleak Pasadena stretch, offering salty bartenders, cheap drinks and a couple of pool tables amid hunting-based decor.

Cozy's Bar & Grill 14048 Ventura Blvd, Sherman Oaks ⓣ818/986-6000. Listen to an excellent range of blues musicians, or come by any time to throw darts, shoot pool or knock back a few. A friendly, laid-back San Fernando Valley spot with a devoted clientele.

Ireland's 32 13721 Burbank Blvd, Van Nuys ⓣ818/785-4031. One of the San Fernando Valley's better spots for quaffing Irish drafts, powering down traditional stews and chops, watching European football and soaking up the traditional atmosphere, shamrocks and all.

Laurel Tavern 11938 Ventura Blvd, Studio City ⓣ818/506-0777. About as enticing as Valley watering holes get if you don't like your bars too divey – in this case the scrumptious Cal cuisine, good range of microbrews and cocktails and (reasonably) laid-back clientele make for a warm and toasty vibe.

Magnolia 492 S Lake Ave, Pasadena ⓣ626/584-1126. Stylish lounge that's plenty chic and modern, but offers enough of the retro-speakeasy atmosphere – dramatic lights, striking decor, well-groomed patrons – to give you a solid buzz, to go along with your tingle from the pricey cocktails.

No Bar 10622 Magnolia Blvd, North Hollywood ⓣ818/753-0545. Dark and moody decor, a quietly hip clientele and a solid jukebox make this trendy-divey joint an appealing, low-attitude spot for inspired drinking.

Old Towne Pub 66 N Fair Oaks Ave, Pasadena ⓣ626/577-6583. Somewhat hard-to-find location that, for its cheap drinks, lack of pretension, and easygoing vibe, ranks first among the dive bars in town, much better than the posier lounges littering Old Pasadena.

Coffeehouses

You can find **coffeehouses** throughout LA, from hole-in-the-wall dives to sanitized yuppie magnets. Although straightforward java joints are alive and well throughout the metropolis, familiar tourist routes such as Melrose Avenue and Santa Monica's Main Street boast more inventive spots to grab a jolt. The listings below go beyond java, focusing on unique establishments that, while serving coffee (and perhaps tea, food and alcohol), also offer diversions like art, music, poetry or eye-popping decor. You can find the best of these coffee joints in Hollywood, West LA, Santa Monica and the valleys. If you feel safer in a chain coffeehouse, try LA's own *Coffee Bean & Tea Leaf*, which has outlets everywhere (see ⓦcoffeebean.com), before resorting to the ubiquitous java mermaid.

Hollywood and West Hollywood

Bourgeois Pig 5931 Franklin Ave, Los Feliz ☎323/464-6008. Ultra-hip environment and overpriced cappuccinos – you really pay for the atmosphere, but the rotating selection of curious artworks, agreeable java and colourful people-watching make it worthwhile.

Coffee Table 2930 Rowena Ave, Los Feliz ☎323/644-8111. Casual, unpretentious space with affordable coffees and relaxed surroundings. Also good for its breakfasts of omelettes, French toast and the usual staples.

Downbeat Cafe 1202 N Alvarado St, Echo Park ☎213/483-3955. East of Silver Lake, this café appeals for its flavourful sandwiches, bagels and desserts, and serves a fine batch of java to a crowd of loyal locals. Plus, true to the name, it offers regular live jazz performances.

Intelligentsia 3902 W Sunset Blvd, Silver Lake ☎323/663-6173. More stylish than your average coffeehouse, and linked to a fine seller of beans, this café has delicious and pricey brews and a youngish crowd that provides a good sense of the East Hollywood hipster scene.

King's Road Espresso House 8361 Beverly Blvd, West Hollywood ☎323/655-9044. Sidewalk café in the center of a busy shopping strip, with good breakfasts and lunches. Popular with the in-crowd as well as a few interloping tourists.

Stir Crazy 6903 Melrose Ave ☎323/934-4656. Cosy haunt that provides a glimpse of what this stretch of Melrose used to be like before the chain retailers moved in. Mellow attitudes, decent java and free WiFi make this place a great option.

Tiago Espresso Bar 7080 Hollywood Blvd ☎323/466-5600. Located near the corner of La Brea Avenue, this spot offers a good range of coffee, tea and maté, and four hours of WiFi with food or drink purchase.

Beverly Hills and West LA

American Tea Room 401 N Canon Dr, Beverly Hills ☎310/271-7922. If you don't mind dropping a wad for some of the city's best tea — in countless varieties and flavours — come to this upscale vendor of the leaf, where you can also drink its many fine offerings.

Cacao Coffee 11609 Santa Monica Blvd, West LA ☎310/473-7283. Fun and friendly joint with all kinds of kitsch and quirky decor, free WiFi, and good snacks and excellent coffee served to an amenable crowd of regulars. Open until 3am.

Café Zinio 1731 Westwood Blvd, West LA ☎310/575-9999. Potent espresso is the main draw at this Westwood-area joint, which also features free WiFi, late-night hours (until 1am), a good array of pastries and panini and the opportunity to puff on a hookah.

Euro Caffe 9559 S Santa Monica Blvd ☎310/274-9070. As the name would suggest, the focus of this little cafe is providing the Continental experience with well-prepared (and properly sized) espressos and cappuccinos, a tasty set of pastries and panini and rather upper-end prices.

Insomnia 7286 Beverly Blvd, north of Mid-Wilshire ☎323/931-4943. A chic spot for chugging cappuccinos while admiring the vivid art on the walls — or tapping out a screenplay on a laptop like the other regulars. Cash only; paid WiFi.

Urth Caffè 8565 Melrose Ave ☎310/659-0628. Customers at this high-priced tea-and-java vendor tend toward navel-gazing and celebrity-watching, but the food and coffees are certainly tasty enough, and the atmosphere is pleasant and fairly well scrubbed. Also at **267 S Beverly Drive, Beverly Hills (☎310/205-9311), and 2327 Main St, Santa Monica (☎310/314-7040).**

Santa Monica and Venice

Abbot's Habit 1401 Abbot Kinney Blvd, Venice ☎310/399-1171. Prototypical Venice coffeehouse, with rich, tasty coffee, snacks and desserts, artwork on the walls, occasional music and spoken-word events and a smooth neighbourhood vibe. Also in West Hollywood at **7554 W Sunset Blvd ☎323/512-5278.**

Café Bolivar 1741 Ocean Park Blvd, Santa Monica ☎310/581-2344. Just as much as the coffee, the small and delightful sandwiches and salads, thoughtful artworks, free WiFi and welcoming air are the draw at this South American-themed cafe.

Caffe Luxxe 925 Montana Ave, Santa Monica ☎310/394-2222. Some of the best espressos, macchiatos and cappuccinos in town (as in, LA) draw loyal customers to this smallish place, which stands out on a busy strip thick with chain coffee-grinders. Also in Brentwood at **11975 San Vicente Blvd ☎310/394-2222.**

Funnel Mill 930 Broadway, Santa Monica ⓣ310/393-1617. Somewhat spare digs create the right atmosphere for the purity of the drink – coffee or tea – at this smart café where the technique of the barista is refined to an art. Be serious about your sipping if you come here.

Novel Café 2507 Main St, Santa Monica ⓣ310/396-7700. Used books and high-backed wooden chairs set the tone. Good coffees, teas and pastries hit the spot, along with free WiFi, making for a nice place to linger. One in a citywide chain of seven.

Rose Café 220 Rose Ave, Venice ⓣ310/392-4191. A somewhat pricey, though not pretentious, place for coffee, meals, pastries and occasional music. A neighbourhood favourite, located near the Santa Monica border.

Tanner's Coffee 200 Culver Blvd, Playa del Rey ⓣ310/574-2739. Free WiFi and good coffee and desserts make this cafe appealing – that and the fact it's just about the only place to get a decent cup o' joe in the neighbourhood. Also in West LA at **11901 Santa Monica Blvd ⓣ310/479-4533.**

UnUrban Coffee House 3301 Pico Blvd, Santa Monica ⓣ310/315-0056. A combination alternative coffeehouse and performance space, worth a look for its open-mike, music and comedy nights, as well as free WiFi.

The South Bay and LA Harbor

Coffee Cartel 1820 S Catalina Ave, Redondo Beach ⓣ310/316-6554. Comfy-cosy coffeehouse with a relaxed setting that presents some interesting acoustic music and poetry readings.

Java Man 157 Pier Ave, Hermosa Beach ⓣ310/379-7209. Welcoming atmosphere at this converted house that offers free WiFi, rotating displays of local artwork, location not far from the beach, and serviceable coffee, sandwiches and desserts.

North End Café 3421 Highland Ave ⓣ310/546-4782. A fancy spot for swillin' mud in Manhattan Beach, with the added allure of hearty sandwiches and a solid breakfast menu for those headed to the beach, which happens to be only a few blocks away.

Portfolio 2400 E Fourth St, Long Beach ⓣ562/434-2486. The kind of place where you're encouraged to browse the artworks for sale as you sip your latte. Also open-mike nights and music shows.

Sacred Grounds 468 W Sixth St, San Pedro ⓣ310/514-0800. Combo coffeehouse and club that offers musical and open-mike performances and has a steady bohemian pulse.

San Gabriel and San Fernando valleys

Aroma Coffee and Tea 4360 Tujunga Ave, Studio City ⓣ818/508-0677. In a remodelled house, this is a mellow spot where you can enjoy beverages with cakes and scones, either on the garden patio or in the living room, or check out the selection of books at the back.

Coffee Gallery 2029 N Lake Ave, Altadena ⓣ626/398-7917. An appealing spot to lounge on sofas, munch on pastries, and browse artworks and various art and culture books while you sip your espresso. Also offers a small performance space at the back.

Jennifer's Coffee Connection 4397 Tujunga Ave #B, Studio City ⓣ818/769-3622. Warm and approachable joint in a strip mall, regularly presenting occasional comedy and music and offering free WiFi.

Jones Coffee Roasters 537 S Raymond Ave, Pasadena ⓣ626/564-9291. Small place with limited seating that nonetheless features some of the Valley's best-brewed coffee, with beans for sale and the usual beverages on offer, presented with dash and skill.

Lulu's Beehive 13203 Ventura Blvd, Studio City ⓣ818/986-2233. Good not only for a jolt of java, but also for a dose of artwork, along with occasional musical performances.

Zephyr 2419 E Colorado Blvd, Pasadena ⓣ626/793-7330. Converted Craftsman house with a nice and homey vibe, and a patio where you can smoke a hookah or just linger with a coffee while enjoying the free WiFi. Also with occasional music performances.

Zona Rosa 15 El Molino Ave, Pasadena ⓣ626/793-2334. One of the city's high points for excellent, inventive coffee drinks (often brewed from South American beans), an arty atmosphere, and periodic live music of the Latin jazz, mariachi and salsa variety.

Clubs

The **club** scene in LA is one of the most energetic in the country, ranging from posey industry hangouts to industrial noise cellars, with everybody claiming to be a rock musician or movie industry bigshot. Some of the hottest clubs – especially those catering to the hip hop or electronica scenes – are the most transient, disappearing within a few months of emerging as a "classic stop" for club-hopping. (As a result, you should always check the *LA Weekly* before setting out.) The ones we've listed below are the more established, meaning they've been around for at least two or three years.

Weekend nights are the busiest, but during the week things are often cheaper and just as fun. Always, the best time to turn up is between 11pm and midnight. **Cover charges** range widely (anywhere from $5 to $25; call ahead), depending on the venue, night and whether a notable DJ is performing. The **minimum age** is 21, and it's normal for ID to be checked, so bring your passport or other photo ID. (Some establishments that don't serve alcohol or that separate the bar from the rest of the club admit patrons under 21.) Prohibitive dress codes are common only at the "velvet rope" clubs that supposedly cater to movie brats and starlets, but more often to drunken suburban kids playing dress-up (and paying $15 for watered-down drinks).

Most of the top clubs are either in Hollywood or along a ten-block stretch of the Sunset Strip in West Hollywood. Beverly Hills and West LA are a lifeless desert, Downtown is home to a handful of itinerant clubs, Santa Monica has a smattering of compelling spots, and the San Fernando Valley's more rough-and-ready scene is usually confined to the weekends. (For gay and lesbian clubs and discos, see p.272.)

Downtown and Mid-Wilshire

Bordello **901 E First St ⓣ213/687-3766.** True to its name, this is an extravagantly decorated, plush set for serious drinking and partying, where the nightly entertainment may be anything from an up-and-coming indie band to a jazz or blues concert to a cabaret freakshow.

El Rey Theater **5515 Wilshire Blvd ⓣ323/936-6400.** Favourite old neighbourhood movie palace turned into a club and performing-arts space; check listings for periodic dance-club nights and other special events.

Jewel's Catch One **4067 W Pico Blvd ⓣ323/734-8849.** Sweaty barn catering to a mixed crowd of gays and straights on two wild dancefloors. A longtime favourite for club-hoppers of all sorts. Especially busy Fri–Mon, though located in the middle of nowhere.

La Cita **336 S Hill St ⓣ213/687-7111.** A sweaty, hip-shaking scene in the heart of Downtown, this dance club draws a crowd with its great bar, cheap drinks, thumping electronica – both Euro and Latin – and the opportunity to dance your drunk off.

Mayan **1038 S Hill St ⓣ213/746-4287.** Formerly a pre-Columbian-styled movie palace, now catering to a mixed crowd and hosting Latin rhythms and nonstop disco, salsa and house tunes on three dancefloors.

Velvet Room **3470 Wilshire Blvd ⓣ213/381-6006.** A curious Koreatown experience, where the DJs spin like mad, the atmosphere is intense, the crowd young and buzzing, and it costs several hundred dollars to "rent" a table to sit down. Bring your best credit card.

Hollywood

Arena **6655 Santa Monica Blvd ⓣ323/462-0714.** Work up a sweat to funk, hip hop, Latin and house sounds on a massive dancefloor inside a former ice factory. Gay-friendly scene, playing host to different, ever-changing club nights.

Avalon **1735 N Vine St ⓣ323/462-3000.** Major dance club spinning old-school faves along with the usual techno and house, with the occasional big-name DJ dropping in. Prices are among the most expensive in town.

Bar Sinister **1652 N Cherokee ⓣ323/462-1934.** A collection of sprightly dance beats most nights of the week, then memorably spooky goth music and anemic-looking vampire types on Saturdays. Connected to *Boardner's* bar (see p.248).

Dragonfly **6510 Santa Monica Blvd ⓣ323/466-6111.** Unusual decor, two large dance rooms, and house and disco club nights and live music. Also presents burlesque shows and various retro-themed evenings.

El Floridita **1253 N Vine St, Hollywood ⓣ323/871-8612.** Quality Mexican and Cuban food plus a fine mix of Cuban and salsa music, played to mostly local, lively crowd.

King King 6555 Hollywood Blvd ⓣ323/960-5765. A crowd of lively regulars hits this primo Hollywood spot for live dance music, with house, funk, rap and retro-pop all on the DJ docket.

Little Temple 4519 Santa Monica Blvd ⓣ323/660-4540. East Hollywood scene themed around moody Asian decor, with tasty beverages like coconut martini. The clientele is expressive and schmoozy and tunes range from hip hop to reggae, soul and funk.

The Ruby 7070 Hollywood Blvd ⓣ323/467-7070. Wide-ranging, feverish dance nights take turns Thurs–Sun, covering everything from modern electronica and grinding industrial to perky house and retro-1980s cheeze.

Three Clubs 1123 N Vine St ⓣ323/462-6441. Dark, perennially trendy bar and club which has live bands playing retro, rock, and funk music, with frenetic weekend club nights, and burlesque and comedy shows, too. Colourless exterior and lack of good signage makes the joint even hipper.

West Hollywood

The Abbey 692 N Robertson Blvd ⓣ310/289-8410. West Hollywood party central 2010: a crazy, busy club scene in the heart of gay WeHo that nonetheless caters to a mixed crowd with its great people watching, go-go dancers and atmosphere so buzzing it could make you deaf.

The Factory 652 N La Peer Drive ⓣ310/659-4551. Mixed straight and gay crowd grooving to DJs spinning house and retro most nights of the week. One of West Hollywood's more popular clubs.

Key Club 9039 Sunset Blvd ⓣ310/274-5800. A hot spot on the lively west side of the Strip, attracting a young, happening group for hip hop and electronica. Music scene is quite varied, often including live-music acts (see p.258) and special events.

Hyde Lounge 8029 W Sunset Blvd ⓣ323/655-8000. Completely overpriced poser scene only worth a visit to get past the velvet rope (with any luck) and watch celebrities boozing, dancing or otherwise embarrassing themselves.

Ultra Suede 661 N Robertson Blvd ⓣ310/659-4551. Heavy on modern technopop, played to a mixed gay and straight crowd. Neighbour to *The Factory*, and draws much of the same crowd.

The Viper Room 8852 Sunset Blvd ⓣ310/358-1880. Excellent live acts, with occasional DJs spinning a mix of hip hop, dance and other styles. See also "Live music", p.258.

West LA

Carbon 9300 Venice Blvd, Culver City ⓣ310/558-9302. Though hardly central, a good spot for eclectic nightly DJs, whose turntables glow with Latin, retro, jungle, drum & bass, hip hop, soul and rock beats, depending on the night.

Santa Monica and Venice

Bodega Wine Bar 814 Broadway, Santa Monica ⓣ310/394-3504. Overpriced though agreeably chic spot that, as per the name, has a broad selection of vino (and beer) on offer, as well as DJs spinning pop, hip hop and electronica. A number of stylish rooms to host private parties, too.

Circle Bar 2926 Main St, Santa Monica ⓣ310/450-0508. Old-fashioned dive that mainly draws a crowd of high-fiving party dudes who get plastered on the pricey but potent drinks and struggle to keep the beat on the dancefloor. Venice is well within staggering distance.

The Gaslite 2030 Wilshire Blvd ⓣ310/829-2382. Though it features a small dancefloor, the real appeal of this hip, kitschily decorated club is its karaoke. Santa Monicans rush to this place on weekends for a chance to sing – so get there early, or you won't.

Zanzibar 1301 Fifth St, Santa Monica ⓣ310/451-2221. DJs spinning sounds with a house, hip hop, and soul bent, but also with an international flair – reggae, cumbia, bossa nova – thrown in for good measure.

San Gabriel and San Fernando valleys

Bigfoot Lodge 3172 Los Feliz Blvd ⓣ323/662-9227. On the far side of East Hollywood in dreary Atwater, this is nevertheless a prime draw for its nightly DJs, who set feet to stomping with retro-pop and rock tunes, with glam, goth and rockabilly thrown in as well.

Coda 5248 Van Nuys Blvd, Sherman Oaks ⓣ818/783-7518. Its sleek, darkly lit atmosphere is fairly hip for the Valley, but not as posey as you might think, drawing locals for its bouncy blend of rap, pop and retro.

Menage 54 Colorado Blvd ☎626/793-0608. Pasadena is hardly prime turf for dance clubs, but this will do in a pinch — a two-storey pop club where the price and pretension can sometimes get out of hand, although it's mostly a scene for locals and interloping tourists.

Verdugo 3408 Verdugo Rd ☎323/257-3408. Cramped and crowded venue that offers a great taste of the south Glendale scene, not far from Forest Lawn in fact, with regular DJ nights, good brews and a lively crowd.

14

Live music

Los Angeles has an overwhelming choice of **live music**. Besides local acts, there are always plenty of big national and international names on tour, from major artists to independents. Most venues open at 8pm or 9pm; headline bands are usually on stage between 10pm and 1am. Cover charges range widely from $3 to $100 (or more), and you should phone ahead to check set times and whether the gig is sold out. For admission, you will often need to be 21 and will likely be asked for ID. As ever, the *LA Weekly* is the best source of **listings**.

The music scene

Just about any musical form can be heard in LA, whether on the biggest concert stages or in the dingiest bars. Ever since the nihilistic punk bands of thirty years ago drew the city away from its spaced-out, pop-country slacker image, LA's **rock** scene has been second to none, peaking in popularity in the 1980s with the Sunset Strip's own brand of "hair metal" and more recently having an alternative or indie tinge. The old **punk** scene has been revitalized with up-and-coming bands, and heavy metal can still be found here and there. The influence and popularity of **hip hop** is also considerable, whether mixed in dance music by Westside DJs or in its more authentic form in inner city clubs (best avoided by out-of-towners).

Surprisingly, **country music** is fairly common, at least away from trendy Hollywood, and the valleys are hotbeds of **bluegrass** and **swing**. There's also **jazz**, played in a few genuinely authentic downbeat clubs, though more commonly found in diluted form in upscale restaurants. Latin **salsa** music is immensely popular in some circles, and can be found in a few Westside clubs; and there's a small live **reggae** scene, occasionally featuring big names but more often sticking to local bands.

Concert halls and performance spaces

LA's **concert halls** and **performance spaces** are scattered throughout the region, with a concentration Downtown and in Hollywood.

Major concert venues

Carpenter Performing Arts Center 6200 Atherton St, on the campus of Cal State Long Beach ⓣ562/985-7000, ⓦwww.carpenterarts.org. A major arts space in the South Bay, attracting mostly mid-level entertainers in pop, folk, jazz, country, world music, and dance.

Cerritos Center for the Performing Arts 12700 Center Court Drive, Long Beach ⓣ1-800/300-4345 or 562/916-8500, ⓦwww.cerritoscenter.com. North of downtown Long Beach, a top draw for mainstream country, gospel, classical, pop and jazz acts – usually nothing too quirky or adventurous.

Ford Amphitheatre **2850 Cahuenga Blvd, Hollywood ⓣ323/461-3673, ⓦwww.fordamphitheater.org.** An open-air venue presenting eclectic productions that include a range of pop and rock concerts. Also features a more cosy 87-seat venue for alternative theatrical performances strangely called "[Inside] the Ford".

The Forum **3900 W Manchester Blvd, Inglewood ⓣ310/330-7300, ⓦwww.thelaforum.com.** Despite being converted into a mega-church for Sunday services, this huge venue with giant columns still hosts the occasional mainstream performance.

Gibson Amphitheatre **100 Universal City Plaza ⓣ818/622-4440, ⓦwww.hob.com/venues/concerts/universal.** A huge but acoustically excellent auditorium putting on regular rock shows by radio-friendly headliners. Located on the Universal Studios lot.

Greek Theatre **2700 N Vermont Ave, Griffith Park ⓣ323-665-5857 or 323/665-1927 ⓦwww.greektheatrela.com.** Outdoor, summer-only (May–Oct) venue hosting mainstream rock and pop acts, and occasional indie rockers, with seating for five thousand. Parking can be a mess, so come early.

Grove of Anaheim **2200 E Katella Ave, Anaheim ⓣ714/712-2700, ⓦwww.thegroveofanaheim.com.** Orange County concert space showcasing old-time performers and mid-level entertainers in soul, country, pop, rock, jazz and comedy.

Hollywood Palladium **6215 Sunset Blvd, Hollywood ⓣ323/962-7600, ⓦwww.livenation.com/venue/hollywood-palladium-tickets.** Once a big-band dance hall, with an authentic 1940s interior and star-studded history, and now a venue for all manner of hard rock, punk, alternative, dance and rap outfits.

Honda Center **2695 E Katella Blvd, Anaheim ⓣ714/704-2400, ⓦwww.hondacenter.com.** A nineteen-thousand-seat sports arena that draws the usual big-ticket events in music and entertainment, with a smaller "Theatre" configuration for less mainstream rock groups.

Kodak Theatre **6801 Hollywood Blvd, Hollywood ⓣ323/308-6300, ⓦwww.kodaktheatre.com.** Part of the colossal Hollywood & Highland mall, a media-ready theatre partly designed to host the Oscars, as well as major and minor pop and rock acts and special events.

Nokia Theatre **777 Chick Hearn Court ⓣ714/763-6030, ⓦwww.nokiatheatrelalive.com.** Grand auditorium that's part of the colossal LA Live complex. To pay off the overhead, the theatre only books the safest pop, children's, country and rock acts.

Orpheum Theatre **842 S Broadway, Downtown ⓣ1-877/677-4386, ⓦwww.laorpheum.com.** Terrific old movie palace (see p.58) that's now been spruced up as a major-league concert venue, hosting a broad range of acts including alternative bands and singer-songwriters.

Staples Center **865 S Figueroa St, Downtown ⓣ213/742-7340, ⓦwww.staplescenter.com.** Big, glassy sports arena (home to the LA Lakers) with millions of municipal and corporate dollars behind it. A good showcase for Top 40 rock and pop acts.

Wiltern Theater **3790 Wilshire Blvd, Mid-Wilshire ⓣ323/388-1400, ⓦwww.wiltern.com.** A striking blue Zigzag Art Deco movie palace, converted into a top performing space for standard pop and rock acts as well as hip hop and alternative groups.

Small venues

You can hear live music in small venues, such as bars and clubs, all over LA, though most major rock and alternative spots are in Hollywood or West Hollywood, with many right on the Sunset Strip.

Rock and pop

Downtown and Mid-Wilshire

Canter's Kibitz Room **419 N Fairfax Ave, Mid-Wilshire ⓣ323/651-2030, ⓦwww.cantersdeli.com.** Located next to *Canter's Deli*, and featuring an assortment of pop, rock and jazz artists – as well as audience members on open-mike nights – performing in a retro-1950s lounge space. Free.

The Echo **1822 Sunset Blvd ⓣ213/413-8200.** Like the name says, an Echo Park club with scrappy indie-rock bands playing in a dark, intense little hole for a crowd of serious rockers. For similar music in a much bigger space, check out the Echoplex, below the Echo in the same building, with an entrance at 1154 Glendale Blvd (☎213/413-8200).

El Rey Theater 5515 Wilshire Blvd, Mid-Wilshire ☎323/936-4790. Although not as famous as its Sunset Strip counterparts, this rock and alternative venue is possibly the best spot to see explosive new bands and enduring oldsters.

Mr T's Bowl 5621 N Figueroa Ave, Highland Park ☎323/960-5693. Former bowling alley remodelled into a quirky bar with a regular crowd of hipsters and freaky local characters. On weekends, there's live music, with a strong punk-rock bent. Otherwise, DJs spin dance favourites.

The Smell 247 S Main St, Downtown ☎213/625-4325. A funky space with cool art grunge and frenetic rock and punk music for cheap prices. A good place to check out the latest groups bubbling under the LA music scene.

Hollywood and West Hollywood

Cat Club 8911 Sunset Blvd ☎310/657-0888. Hard, meaty jams can be heard here, mainly rock, punk and rockabilly – which should come as no surprise, since the owner's a former Stray Cat.

Hotel Café 1623 N Cahuenga Blvd, Hollywood ☎323/461-2040. The small stage comfortable surroundings and brick-lined walls give this well regarded spot for acoustic acts and singer-songsmiths, as well as indie bands, a charming intimacy. Usually has the best line-up for this sort of thing in town.

Key Club 9039 Sunset Blvd ☎310/274-5800. A hot spot in the liveliest section of the strip, attracting young hipsters for its regular concerts in the rock, punk and metal vein, with occasional lighter fare as well. Also has DJ and club nights.

The Music Box 6126 Hollywood Blvd ☎323/464-0808, ⓦwww.henryfondatheater.com. A charming, renovated old theatre that began life in 1926 and now hosts alternative rock, rap and dance musicians, as well as DJs and club nights.

Pehrspace 325 Glendale Blvd ☎213/483-7347. Curious combination art gallery/music venue that has a small but loyal following for its performances of little-known indie and avant-garde artists in an intimate setting. If you want to get a sense of the deepest roots of the LA music scene, this is the place – in an East Hollywood strip mall.

The Roxy 9009 Sunset Blvd ☎310/276-2222. An intimate club showcasing the music industry's new signings and boasting a great sound system, too. Punk and hip hop dominate. On the western – but still hectic – end of the strip.

Spaceland 1717 Silver Lake Blvd ☎213/661-4380. Doesn't have the national rep of places like the Roxy and Whisky, but you're unlikely to find a better spot in LA to catch up-and-coming rockers and other acts, including punk and alternative musicians.

The Troubadour 9081 Santa Monica Blvd ☎310/276-6168. Fabled 1960s mainstay that's been through a lot of incarnations in its forty-plus years. Used to be known for folk and country rock, then metal, now for various flavours of indie rock.

The Viper Room 8852 Sunset Blvd ☎310/358-1881. Great live acts, plus a famous owner (Johnny Depp) and a headline-grabbing past have helped boost this club's hipness quotient. Expect almost any musician to show up on stage.

Whisky-a-Go-Go 8901 Sunset Blvd ☎310/652-4202. For many years LA's most famous Rock 'n' Roll club, legendary for the antics of Jim Morrison among others, and nowadays featuring lesser-known hard rock, metal and alternative acts.

West LA

Cinema Bar 3967 Sepulveda Blvd, Culver City ☎310/390-1328. If you want a break from the Hollywood posers, but want to get down 'n' dirty with an underground band (of any stripe), this small, out-of-the-way spot is a great bet — pretty much the only thing going on in this part of town.

The Joint 8771 Pico Blvd, West LA ☎310/275-2619. A dark, small neighbourhood venue with assorted punk screamers and occasionally decent rock and alternative groups. Poseurs need not apply.

Largo at the Coronet Theatre, 366 N La Cienega Blvd, West LA ☎23/855-0350. Offers some compelling live acts, often of the acoustic singer-songwriter variety, with the odd rock or comedy show as well.

Room 5 143 N La Brea Blvd, West LA ☎323/938-2504. Intimate venue that's a good spot in this part of town to catch a live set by a singer-songwriter, small acoustic band, or other low-decibel performer. Also with comedy nights.

Santa Monica and Venice

14 Below 1348 14th St ☎310/451-5040. At this tiny bar, pool tables and a fireplace compete for your attention with rangy rock, folk and blues acts that perform nightly.

Broad Stage 1310 11th St, Santa Monica ☎310/434-3200. Sleekly modern venue on the campus of Santa Monica City College, which presents a variety of eclectic performances from alternative rock, theatre, dance and opera, to political debates and all manner of other unexpected amusements.

Talking Stick 1411 Lincoln Blvd ☎310/450-6052. Agreeable coffee shop in a minimall that hosts some of Venice's more interesting home-grown acts, including acoustic musicians, various rockers and world beat performers. A mixed but interesting bag.

South Bay and Long Beach

The Lighthouse 30 Pier Ave, Hermosa Beach ☎310/376-9833. Near the beach, this old favourite has a broad booking policy that spans rock, jazz and reggae as well as karaoke and occasional comedy.

San Gabriel and San Fernando Valleys

CIA 11334 Burbank Blvd, North Hollywood ☎818/506-6353. A truly odd venue where art and music collide, with curious visual installations (often with circus clown and freak show themes) and sounds from punk to avant-garde.

LaBrie's Lounge 806 E Colorado St, Glendale ☎818/243-1522. Longtime club that's recently been given a long overdue remodelling and spiffed up into a solid venue for LA's upcoming rockers and singer-songwriters.

Sagebrush Cantina 23527 Calabasas Rd, Calabasas ☎818/222-6062. About as close as the western San Fernando Valley gets to having a live-music scene, this Mexican restaurant offers 1970s-leaning rock cover bands several nights of the week to an appreciative crowd.

Country and folk

Hollywood and West LA

Boulevard Music 4136 Sepulveda Blvd, Culver City ☎310/398-2583. This unglamorous music store manages to host some fairly interesting folk acts on weekends, from roots country to delta blues, with international groups adding more to the mix.

Molly Malone's Irish Pub 575 S Fairfax Ave, west of Mid-Wilshire ☎323/935-1577. Local favourite for its colourful clientele and mix of traditional Irish music, American folk, indie rock, bluegrass and country. See also p.247.

Santa Monica

Finn McCool's 2702 Main St ☎310/452-1734. A serviceable spot for quaffing draughts, this Irish bar also offers twice-weekly performances of folk tunes from the Emerald Isle; see "Bars", p.249.

McCabe's 3103 W Pico Blvd ☎310/828-4497. LA's premier acoustic guitar shop; long the scene of some excellent and unusual folk and country shows, with the occasional alternative act thrown in as well.

Rusty's Surf Ranch 256 Santa Monica Pier ☎310/393-7437. Not that great for food, but does offer surf music – and displays of old-time longboards – and rock, pop, folk and even karaoke. A popular spot for tourists, near the end of the pier.

South Bay and Long Beach

Cowboy Country 3321 E South St, Long Beach ☎562/630-3007. Pull out your best line-dancing moves and your fanciest boots for this two-storey country scene with three dance floors. Very popular with self-styled cowpokes for its country DJ sets and live performances.

San Gabriel and San Fernando Valleys

California Traditional Music Society 16953 Ventura Blvd, Encino ☎818/817-7756, Ⓦwww.ctmsfolkmusic.org. Organization that puts on periodic performances of ancient and modern folk music, also offering education and training and Sunday jam sessions.

Celtic Arts Center 5062 Lankershim Blvd, North Hollywood ☎818/760-8322. A celebration of all things Celtic and Gaelic (and not just Irish, either), offering monthly concerts, dance lessons and, best of all, free Monday night Céili dances followed by traditional-music jam sessions.

Cowboy Palace Saloon 21635 Devonshire St, Chatsworth ☎818/341-0166. Worth a trip to this distant corner of the San Fernando Valley for plenty of tub-thumping country-and-western concerts, courtly line dancing and down-home helpings of Sunday BBQ.

Kulak's Woodshed **5230 Laurel Canyon Blvd, North Hollywood ⓣ818/766-9913, ⓦwww.kulakswoodshed.com.** Puts on nightly shows in a cramped but colourful space, ranging from country, folk and spoken-word to performance art and poetry. Must be a member to enter ($5 fee); join via the website.

Viva Fresh Cantina **900 Riverside Drive, Burbank ⓣ818/845-2425.** A Mexican restaurant on the far side of Griffith Park, where you can hear some of LA's most engaging country, bluegrass and honky-tonk artists performing regularly.

Jazz, blues and reggae

Downtown

Grand Star Jazz Club **943 Sun Mun Way ⓣ213/626-2285.** Solid Chinatown haunt for live jazz and blues, plus some hip hop and funk thrown in as well. Also features DJ spinning breakbeats and other dance tunes.

Hollywood and West Hollywood

Cat 'n' Fiddle Pub **6530 Sunset Blvd, Hollywood ⓣ323/468-3800.** An English-style pub with worthwhile jazz performers on Sun from 7pm until 11pm; no cover. See also "Drinking", p.248.

Catalina Bar and Grill **6725 W Sunset Blvd ⓣ323/466-2210.** This central Hollywood jazz institution offers a wide range of sounds from many kinds of performers, as well as good acoustics, filling meals and potent drinks. It can get pricey, though, with tickets usually $25–50.

House of Blues **8430 Sunset Blvd, West Hollywood ⓣ323/848-5100.** Over-commercialized mock sugar shack, with good but pricey live acts. Very popular with tourists, as it's the flagship of a national chain for mainly blues and rock. Cover can reach $40 or more.

West LA

Industry Café and Jazz **6039 Washington Blvd, Culver City ⓣ310/202-6633.** Ethiopian eatery that also serves soul food, as well as frenetic jazz sounds from cooking local musicians – nicely, for no cover.

The Mint **6010 W Pico Blvd, south of Mid-Wilshire ⓣ323/954-9400.** A small, intense spot that's off the beaten path but worth the ramble to hear the latest in the city's avant-jazz sounds, as well as singer-songwriters, with decent food and drink, too.

Vibrato Grill and Jazz **2930 Beverly Glen Circle, West LA ⓣ310/474-9400.** You're not going to find anything too challenging at this Bel Air club, but for traditional and smooth jazz sounds, it may fit the bill.

Santa Monica

Harvelle's **1432 Fourth St ⓣ310/395-1676.** Near the Third Street Promenade, this stellar blues joint has for more than seven decades offered different performers nightly, with a little funk, R&B and burlesque thrown in as well.

South Central LA

Babe and Ricky's Inn **4339 Leimert Blvd ⓣ323/295-9112.** Long a top spot for blues on Central Avenue, this premier music hall continues to attract quality, nationally known acts at its more recent Leimert Park location. Also fun weekly jam sessions.

Fais Do-Do **5247 W Adams Blvd ⓣ323/954-8080.** West Adams club in a dicey section of town that appeals for its broad sweep – live bands playing New Orleans-flavoured jazz and ragtime, DJs spinning old-school funk and soul and oddball chamber music and other odd entertainment.

South Bay and Long Beach

Blue Café **217 Pine Ave, Long Beach ⓣ562/436-3600.** An eclectic array of music in downtown Long Beach, with an accent on blues and rock shows.

Café Boogaloo **1238 Hermosa Ave, Hermosa Beach ⓣ310/318-2324.** One of the better spots in the South Bay for blues, along with occasional New Orleans jazz and swing, and DJ dance sets.

San Gabriel and San Fernando Valleys

The Baked Potato **3787 Cahuenga Blvd W, North Hollywood ⓣ818/980-1615.** A small but legendary contemporary jazz spot, where many reputations have been forged. Don't come looking for bland lounge jazz/muzak – expect to be surprised.

Café Cordiale **14015 Ventura Blvd ⓣ818/789-1985.** Jazz and blues are at the top of the agenda at this friendly eatery in Sherman Oaks, which also puts on regular performances from soul, funk and R&B stalwarts. Decent California cuisine, as well.

Jax 339 N Brand Blvd, Glendale ☎818/500-1604. A combination restaurant and performing stage where you can take in a good assortment of jazz, from traditional to contemporary. No cover.

Vitello's 4349 Tujunga Ave, Studio City ☎818/769-0905. Broadway toe-tappers, old-time jazz and lively samba are the norm in this cosy lounge with passable Italian food. The highlight, though, is open-mike night, when some of the Valley's more curious characters arrive to belt out a few operatic arias and show tunes.

Latin and salsa

Conga Room at LA Live 800 W Olympic Blvd, Downtown ☎213/745-8771. The mainstream version of Latin music, taking place in a fancy setting, for which you will help foot the bill through the steep cover. The music on hand varies, but mostly ranges from salsa to merengue.

El Cid 4212 W Sunset Blvd, Silver Lake ☎323/668-0318. A good place to enjoy tapas and Mexican food as well as move to the sounds of salsa, flamenco and other Latin rhythms.

El Floridita 1253 N Vine St, Hollywood ☎323/871-8612. Decent Mexican and Cuban food complements a fine line-up of Cuban and salsa artists, who play on weekends and jam on other nights. Also presents salsa lessons.

Luminarias 3500 Ramona Blvd, Monterey Park ☎323/268-4177. Hilltop restaurant with live weekend salsa reckoned to be as good as its Mexican food. No cover.

Mama Juana's 3707 Cahuenga Blvd W, Studio City ☎818/505-8636. Spanish–Mexican restaurant that also features old-style south-of-the-border music on the order of mambo and bossa nova, as well as salsa, merengue and Latin jazz. Menu choices rotate monthly to different Latin cuisines.

Zabumba 10717 Venice Blvd, West LA ☎310/841-6525. In a colourful building amid drab surroundings, this Brazilian venue, with good ethnic eats, is more bossa nova than straight salsa, but it's still great, and very lively.

15

Performing arts and film

Los Angeles offers a wealth of **performing arts** options all over the metropolis. The city's range of highbrow cultural offerings was at one time quite limited, confined to art-house cinemas and a handful of mainstream playhouses, but in the last few decades LA has firmly established itself in the performing-arts field thanks to a solid push from old money and corporate interests, and considerable grassroots interest in alternative theatre and other performances. The city boasts a world-class classical-music **orchestra** with the renowned conductor Gustavo Dudamel, along with smaller regional symphonies and chamber-music groups. The fields of **opera** and **dance** are represented by several noteworthy companies, with the chief alternative entity (Long Beach Opera) consistently surpassing the mainstream one (LA Opera). **Theatre** is always a growth industry here, with more than a thousand shows produced annually (and more than one hundred running at any one time), plenty of actors to draw from, and a burgeoning audience for both mainstream and fringe productions. **Cabaret** caters to a smaller crowd of lounge-act, torch-song and kitsch fans, but **comedy** is a much bigger draw – especially for first-time visitors to town. Not surprisingly, though, it's **film** that is still the chief cultural staple of the region, and there is no shortage of excellent theatres in which to catch a flick.

Classical music

LA's **classical-music** scene is second to none in the US. Under the guidance of wunderkind conductor Gustavo Dudamel, and housed in the stunning Disney Hall, the **LA Philharmonic** should be one of the first tickets you buy if you're interested in the performing arts. Less well known, though still intriguing, are the city's smaller performing groups, which tend to float from art centres to universities to church venues, drawing a loyal, though limited, audience. Your best bet for following the cultural trends is to watch the press, especially the *LA Times*, for details. In any case, you can expect to pay from $15 to $120 for most concerts, and more for really big names.

Classical music companies

Da Camera Society Rotating venues ⓣ213/477-2929, ⓦwww.dacamera.org. This organization's "Chamber Music in Historic Sites" series provides a great opportunity to hear classical, Romantic and modern chamber works in stunning

settings, from grand churches to private estates, including such inspired sites as Doheny Mansion near USC. Ticket prices vary widely, depending on the venue, and can run anywhere from $35 to $105.

Long Beach Symphony Office at 110 W Ocean Blvd, Suite 22, Long Beach ⓣ562/436-3203, ⓦwww.lbso.org. A light alternative to LA's heavier repertoire, playing mainstream favourites like Tchaikovsky and Beethoven, interspersed with pops selections. Principal venue is the **Long Beach Performing Arts Center.** $20–65.

Los Angeles Chamber Orchestra rotating venues ⓣ213/622-7001 ext 215, ⓦwww.laco.org. Appearing at UCLA's Royce Hall, Glendale's Alex Theatre, Downtown's Zipper Concert Hall and Santa Monica's Broad Stage, the orchestra presents a range of chamber works – not all canonical – from different eras. Concerts vary widely by price and seating choices. Most tickets $10–50.

Los Angeles Master Chorale Disney Hall, First St at Grand Ave, Downtown; also at rotating venues ⓣ213/972-2782, ⓦwww.lamc.org. Classic works, along with lighter madrigals and pops favourites, are showcased by this choral institution, now performing in Disney Hall. $25–120.

Los Angeles Philharmonic Disney Hall, Downtown, and Hollywood Bowl ⓣ323/850-2000, ⓦwww.laphil.org. The biggest name in the city's music scene performs regularly during the year, and conductor Gustavo Dudamel always provides a rousing programme, from powerful Romantic works to craggy modern pieces, with a special accent on Latin American works. The LA Phil is the cornerstone of high culture in the city – even the Creative Chair is pioneering modernist John Adams. $20–150.

Pacific Serenades Office at 1201 W 5th St, Downtown ⓣ213/534-3434, ⓦpacser.org. Chamber-music concerts from Jan to June in the LA area, usually highlighting new composers and taking place at sites like Pasadena's Neighbourhood Church and the UCLA Faculty Center (both $32) and various private homes ($55).

Pacific Symphony Orchestra Orange County Performing Arts Center, 615 Town Center Drive, Costa Mesa ⓣ714/755-5788, ⓦwww.pacificsymphony.org. Suburban orchestra that draws big crowds for its stylish performances of canonical works, performed in the sparkling Segerstrom Concert Hall or, in summer, at the outdoor Verizon Wireless Amphitheater. $25–105.

Pasadena Symphony At Ambassador Auditorium, 131 St John Ave ⓣ626/793-7172, ⓦwww.pasadenasymphony.org. This esteemed symphony veers between the standard warhorse repertoire and a few more contemporary pieces ($30–80), while the pops symphony plays on the Rose Bowl lawn, west of downtown, with a huge range of prices ($10–900).

Southwest Chamber Music ⓣ1-800/726-7147, ⓦwww.swmusic.org. A nationally recognized performing and recording troupe that offers a wide range of music, from medieval to modern. Venues include the wintertime (Oct–April) series at the Norton Simon Museum and Downtown's Colburn School of Performing Arts, summer concerts at the Huntington Library, and regular open rehearsals at Pasadena's Armory Center. $38; students $10.

Classical music venues

Bing Theater 5905 Wilshire Blvd, Mid-Wilshire ⓣ323/857-6010, ⓦwww.lacma.org. When it isn't hosting movie revivals, this auditorium at the LA County Museum of Art provides a fine space for classical concerts, which occur periodically during the year ($25). Plus, free Friday-night jazz in the courtyard April–Nov.

Disney Hall First St at Grand Ave, Downtown ⓣ323/850-2000, ⓦwww.laphil.com. LA's most renowned cultural attraction (along with the Getty Center) and home of the LA Philharmonic. A striking Frank Gehry design that hosts a range of music and arts groups.

Dorothy Chandler Pavilion At the Music Center, 135 N Grand Ave, Downtown ⓣ213/972-7211 or 972-7460, ⓦwww.musiccenter.org. Longstanding warhorse of the arts community, used by LA Opera and other top names, but no longer by the LA Philharmonic.

The Hollywood Bowl 2301 N Highland Ave, Hollywood ⓣ323/850-2000, ⓦwww.hollywoodbowl.org. Hosts LA Philharmonic concerts, usually of the pops variety, and various jazz and world-beat groups, for open-air concerts during the summer.

John Anson Ford Amphitheatre 2850 Cahuenga Blvd, Hollywood ⓣ323/461-3673, ⓦwww.fordamphitheater.org. An open-air venue that has eclectic productions by local classical and operatic groups, world music shows, as well as sporadic pop and rock concerts.

Redcat 631 W 2nd St, Downtown ⓣ213/237-2800. ⓦwww.redcat.org. Multidisciplinary arts space in Disney Hall and overseen by the estimable California Institute of the Arts (CalArts). A terrific venue for seeing a range of visual art, hearing risk-taking and experimental music, and enjoying multimedia productions that may incorporate dance, theatre, poetry and cinema.

Segerstrom Concert Hall 615 Town Center Drive, Costa Mesa ⓣ714/556-2787. A polished glass and steel marvel that showcases performances of the Pacific Symphony, and is part of the Orange County Performing Arts Center complex (ⓦwww.ocpac.org), which also presents dance, theatre and other high-culture offerings in sleekly modern style.

Shrine Auditorium 665 W Jefferson Blvd, South Central ⓣ213/749-5123; box office at 655 S Hill St. Huge 1926 Moorish-domed curiosity that hosts touring pop acts, choral gospel groups and countless award shows – though not the Oscars any more.

Thornton School of Music On the USC campus, South Central ⓣ213/740-6935, ⓦwww.usc.edu/schools/music. A fine array of venues, from 90–1200 seats, for sonatas, concertos and other works (usually Sept–May), with most tickets $18. During the season, weekly concerts sometimes feature name guest conductors.

UCLA Center for the Performing Arts ⓣ310/825-4401, wwww.uclalive.org. Coordinates a wide range of touring companies in music, theatre and dance (Sept–June), and runs a fine dance series, often with an experimental bent.

Zipper Concert Hall 200 S Grand Ave, Downtown ⓣ213/621-2200. Part of the esteemed performing-arts Colburn School across from Disney Hall, this warm and modern facility hosts a broad range of troupes, from dance to classical, as well as Southwest Chamber Music and the Los Angeles Chamber Orchestra.

Opera and dance

The few major **opera** companies in LA and Orange counties are either old-line institutions that focus on the warhorses of the repertoire, or newcomers that make more of an effort to cross artistic boundaries and programme contemporary works. **Dance** performances tend to be grouped around major events, so check cultural listings or call the venues listed below for seasonal information.

Opera companies and venues

Casa Italiana Opera Company At St Peter's parish church, 1051 N Broadway, Downtown ⓣ1-800/595-4849, ⓦwww.casaitaliana.org. About four times during the year, and at Christmas, this company stages workshops in which singers in training perform popular Romantic Italian operas, from Puccini to Verdi and Mascagni, for an affordable price. $50.

LA Opera At the Music Center, 135 N Grand Ave, Downtown ⓣ213/972-8001, ⓦwww.losangelesopera.com. With Plácido Domingo at the helm, this institution stages mainstream productions between Sept and June, from heavy *opera seria* to lighter operettas. For better or worse, the undisputed opera heavyweight in town. $20–240.

Long Beach Opera Rotating venues ⓣ562/432-5934, ⓦwww.longbeachopera.org. Although eight years older than LA Opera, this company presents the freshest and edgiest work in town, from lesser-known pieces by old masters to craggy new works by local composers to bizarre hybrids of hitherto unrelated pieces (eg Strauss Meets Frankenstein!). One of the most groundbreaking companies in the nation — cheap, too. $45–100.

Dance companies and venues

Carpenter Center 6200 Atherton St, on the campus of Cal State Long Beach ⓣ562/985-7000, ⓦwww.carpenterarts.org. The South Bay's major arts space, hosting periodic dance and comedy shows, lectures and spoken-word artists and touring arts groups.

Cerritos Center for the Performing Arts 12700 Center Court Drive, Southeast LA ⓣ1-800/300-4345, ⓦwww.cerritoscenter.com. Located in distant Cerritos on the Orange County border, this is one of LA's better-known and funded venues, home to mainstream classical, opera and dance performances, as well as big-name pop and jazz performers.

Japan America Theater 244 S San Pedro St, Little Tokyo ⓣ213/680-3700, ⓦwww.jaccc.org. Intriguing theatrical, dance and performance works drawn from Japan and the Far East, mixing traditional and contemporary styles.

Los Angeles Ballet office at 11755 Exposition Boulevard, West LA ⓣ310/998-7782, ⓦwww.losangelesballet.org. Features a Nov–May programme with standards like the Nutcracker and a good number of new and modern works. Shows at Glendale's Alex Theatre, UCLA sites and other rotating venues.

Pasadena Dance Theater 1985 Locust Ave, Pasadena ⓣ626/683-3459, ⓦwww.pasadenadance.org. One of the San Gabriel Valley's more prominent dance venues, hosting diverse groups throughout the year.

Theatre

LA **theatre** is an active and energetic scene. You can expect to find most any kind of stage production on any given night in one of the city's venues, including huge Broadway juggernauts, obscure hole-in-the-wall shows, avant-garde carnivals, edgy agit-prop, and even revivals of classic works by the likes of Shaw and Ibsen. Aside from the nationally touring mega-hits, some of the productions to attract the most attention are multi-character one-person shows and irreverent stagings of canonical works, with Shakespeare most often in the crosshairs.

Since the region is home to a wealth of **film actors**, there is always a good pool of thespians for local productions. Depending on the play, you may even find semi-popular TV actors or big celebrity names on stage, their presence occasionally impromptu and unannounced. While the bigger venues host a predictable array of shopworn musicals and hidebound classics, there are over a hundred "Equity waiver" theatres with fewer than a hundred seats – typically 99 – enabling non-Equity cardholders (who don't belong to Actors' Equity, the theatrical labour union) to perform. This means a lot of fringe performances take place, for which prices can be very low, and the quality can vary greatly. But you may catch an electrifying surprise now and again – check the *LA Weekly* for a sense of what's out there.

Tickets are less expensive than you might expect: a big show will set you back at least $40–50, or up to $100–125 for some blockbusters (matinees are cheaper), with smaller shows around $10 to $20. A quick way through the maze of LA's theatres is to phone the **LA Stage Alliance** (ⓣ213/614-0556, ⓦwww.lastagealliance.com) and ask for the availability of discount tickets for a given show, under its LA StageTIX program.

Major theatres

Actors' Gang Theater 9070 Venice Blvd, Culver City ⓣ310/838-GANG, ⓦwww.theactorsgang.com. A cross between a major and an alternative theatre; having fewer than a hundred seats keeps it cosy, though it does host the odd spectacular or socially conscious production that features semi-famous names from film or TV.

Ahmanson Theatre at the Music Center, 135 N Grand Ave, Downtown ⓣ213/628-2772, ⓦwww.taperahmanson.com. A two-thousand-seat theatre hosting colossal travelling shows from Broadway. If you've seen a major production advertised on TV and on the sides of buses, it's probably playing here.

Alex Theatre 216 N Brand Blvd, Glendale ⓣ818/243-3622, ⓦwww.alextheatre.org. A gloriously restored movie palace – with a great neon spike and quasi-Egyptian forecourt – hosting a fine range of musical theatre, dance, comedy and film.

Freud Playhouse in MacGowan Hall on the UCLA campus, Westwood ⓣ310/825-2101, ⓦwww.uclalive.org. A nearly six-hundred-seat venue that features a mix of mainstream and contemporary pieces – plus risk-taking experimental works. Along with Royce Hall (see p.113), occasionally hosts performances by visiting major troupes.

Geffen Playhouse 10886 Le Conte Ave, Westwood ⓣ310/208-5454, ⓦwww.geffenplayhouse.com. A five-hundred-seat, Spanish Revival building that often hosts one-person shows. There's a decided Hollywood connection, evident in the crowd-pleasing nature of many of the productions and the frequent presence of semi-familiar names from television and the movies.

International City Theatre 300 E Ocean Ave, Long Beach ⓣ562/436-4610, ⓦwww.ictlongbeach.org. Part of the Long Beach Performing Arts Center, this is an enjoyable, affordable spot for mainstream comedy and drama.

Mark Taper Forum At the Music Center, 135 N Grand Ave, Downtown ⓣ213/628-2772, ⓦwww.taperahmanson.com. Theatre in the three-quarter round, with familiar classics and, less frequently, assorted new plays. Don't expect fringe-theatre radicalism, though.

Pantages Theater 6233 Hollywood Blvd, Hollywood ⓣ323/468-1700, ⓦwww.nederlander.com/wc. Quite the stunner: an exquisite, atmospheric Art Deco theatre, in the heart of historic Hollywood, hosting inoffensive off-Broadway productions like *Shrek the Musical*.

Pasadena Playhouse 39 S El Molino Ave, Pasadena ⓣ626/356-PLAY, ⓦwww.pasadenaplayhouse.org. A grand old space refurbished to provide enjoyable mainstream entertainment. Actors are often a mix of youthful professionals and aging TV and movie stars.

Ricardo Montalbán Theatre 1615 N Vine St, Hollywood ⓣ323/871-2420, ⓦwww.themontalban.com. Named for the actor best known as Mr Roarke from *Fantasy Island*, this venue presents a range of productions dealing with Latino ethnic identity, as well as children's theatre, in a classic building in the heart of Hollywood.

South Coast Repertory 655 Town Center Drive, Costa Mesa ⓣ714/708-5555, ⓦwww.scr.org. Orange County's major theatre entry, where you can watch well-executed performances of the classics on the main Segerstrom Stage, and edgier works by new writers on the smaller, 150-seat Argyros Stage.

Small and alternative theatres

A Noise Within 234 S Brand Blvd, Glendale ⓣ818/240-0910, ⓦwww.anoisewithin.org. A very mainstream performance space in downtown Glendale, focusing heavily on the classics, with a strong emphasis on Shakespeare, Molière and the like.

Actors Forum Theatre 10655 Magnolia Blvd, North Hollywood ⓣ818/506-0600, ⓦwww.actorsforumtheatre.org. Unpredictable venue that hosts a range of topical dramas, one-person shows, and the odd production from nontraditional playwrights.

The Complex 6476 Santa Monica Blvd, Hollywood ⓣ323/465-0383, ⓦwww.complexhollywood.com. An association of five small theatres and five studios putting on innovative works with lesser-known actors you may not see anywhere else.

Highways 1651 18th St, Santa Monica ⓣ310/315-1459, ⓦwww.highwaysperformance.org. Located in the 18th Street Arts Complex, an adventurous performance space that offers a range of topical drama and politically charged productions, with a strong bent toward the subversive.

Hudson Theaters 6539 Santa Monica Blvd, Hollywood ⓣ323/856-4252, ⓦwww.hudsontheatre.com. Socially conscious "message" plays alternate with more satiric, comedic works at this venue for upcoming actors. The complex consists of three stages, each with less than a hundred seats, plus a coffeehouse and art gallery.

Kirk Douglas Theatre 9820 Washington Blvd ⓣ213/628-2772, ⓦwww.centertheatregroup.org. A nice sprucing up of the long-closed Culver Theatre into a three-hundred-seater that hosts modern, alternative and offbeat productions. Part of the Center Theatre Group, which also runs the stodgier Ahmanson Theatre and Mark Taper Forum.

Knightsbridge Theatre 1944 Riverside Drive, Glendale ⓣ323/667-0955, ⓦwww.knightsbridgetheatre.com. On the edge of Griffith Park, a prime spot for classical theatre, from Shakespeare to Molière. The occasional modern show, too.

Lee Strasberg Theatre 7936 Santa Monica Blvd, West Hollywood ⓣ323/650-7777, ⓦwww.strasberg.com. Although Method acting as once taught by the master Strasberg is plentiful here, all types of plays are performed, with a strong bent toward character-driven pieces. You can sometimes spot stars in the crowd, or on stage.

Lonnie Chapman Group Repertory 10900 Burbank Blvd, North Hollywood ⓣ818/700-4878, ⓦwww.thegrouprep.com. A troupe that tends toward plays involving serious social themes – though some musicals and comedies are staged, too.

Los Angeles Theatre Center 514 S Spring St, Downtown ⓣ213/489-0994, ⓦthelatc.org. A new bid to bring modern theatre into the heart of a gentrifying part of town, in the classic 1907 Security Trust and Savings Bank building. Productions are infrequent, but sometimes interesting.

Manual Archives 3320 W Sunset Blvd, Silver Lake ⓣ323/667-0156. A very curious version of puppet theatre, aimed more at adults than kids, which puts on shows involving not just puppets, but mannequins, dioramas, automata and conceptual artworks, to great subversive effect. Check ahead for programme info, since the Archives only puts on a few shows a year.

Matrix Theater 7657 Melrose Ave ⓣ323/852-1445, ⓦwww.matrixtheatre.com. Lower Hollywood theatre offering uncompromising productions that often feature some of LA's better young actors and playwrights.

Odyssey Theater Ensemble 2055 S Sepulveda Blvd, West LA ⓣ310/477-2055, ⓦwww.odysseytheatre.com. Well-respected Westside theatre company with a modernist bent, offering a range of quality productions on three stages for decent prices.

Open Fist Theatre 1625 N La Brea Ave, Hollywood ⓣ323/882-6912, ⓦwww.openfist.org. As you might expect from the name, biting and edgy works are often the focus at this small theatre company, employing a limited cast of spirited unknowns.

Pacific Resident Theatre 703 Venice Blvd, Venice ⓣ310/822-8392, ⓦwww.pacificresidenttheatre.com. Solid mix of productions at this compelling small venue. Away from the centre of the theatre action, but worth a visit if you like good, old-fashioned drama.

Powerhouse Theatre 3116 Second St, Santa Monica ⓣ213/674-6682, ⓦwww.powerhousetheatre.com. On the border of Venice, this alternative theatre presents risk-taking experimental shows; perhaps the best of its kind in town. Located in a former electrical station for the old Red Car transit line.

Stages Theatre Center 1540 N McCadden Place, Hollywood ⓣ323/465-1010, ⓦwww.stagestheatrecenter.com. With three stages offering twenty to one hundred seats, this is an excellent place to catch a wide range of comedies and dramas.

Steve Allen Theater 4773 Hollywood Blvd ⓣ323/666-4268. An intriguing East Hollywood grab bag of entertainment, ranging from vaudeville-style productions, underground theatre and one-person comedy shows, to vintage and oddball films, experimental music, variety shows and cartoons. Needless to say, it's well worth a shot for the daring.

Theatre West 3333 Cahuenga Blvd W, Hollywood ⓣ323/851-7977, ⓦwww.theatrewest.org. A classic venue with a lengthy track record that's always a good spot to see inventive, sometimes odd, productions by a troupe of excellent young up-and-comers.

Theatricum Botanicum 1419 N Topanga Canyon Blvd, Topanga Canyon ⓣ310/455-3723, ⓦwww.theatricum.com. Terrific spot showing a range of classic (often Shakespeare) and modern plays amid an idyllic outdoor setting. Founded by Will Geer – TV's Grandpa Walton.

Comedy

LA has a broad range of **comedy** clubs. While rising stars and beginners can be spotted on the "underground" open-mike scene, most of the famous comics, both stand-up and improv, appear at the more established clubs in Hollywood, West LA, or the valleys. These venues usually have a bar and put on two shows per evening, generally starting at 8pm and 10.30pm – the later one being more popular. The better-known places are open nightly, but are often solidly booked on weekends. Cover charges can vary dramatically depending on the night and the performer (often $5–25), and may include a two-drink minimum; call ahead for info.

Acme Comedy Theater 135 N La Brea Ave, Mid-Wilshire ⓣ323/525-0202, ⓦwww.acmecomedy.com. A solid venue for sketch and improv comedy, as well as variety and theme-comedy shows.

Bang Improv Theater 457 N Fairfax Ave, Mid-Wilshire ⓣ323/653-6886, ⓦwww.bangstudio.com. One-person shows and long-form improv are the specialities at this small theatre/comedy club, with the more popular shows running on weekends. Classes also offered.

Comedy & Magic Club 1018 Hermosa Ave, Hermosa Beach ⓣ310/372-1193, ⓦwww.comedyandmagicclub.info. Notable South Bay comedy space where Jay Leno sometimes tests material. Tickets can run up to $30, depending on the performer.

Comedy Store 8433 W Sunset Blvd, West Hollywood ⓣ323/656-6228, ⓦwww.thecomedystore.com. LA's premier comedy showcase, and popular enough to comprise three rooms – which means there's usually space, even at weekends.

Groundlings Theater 7307 Melrose Ave ⓣ323/934-4747, ⓦwww.groundlings.com. Only the gifted survive at this pioneering improv venue, where Pee Wee Herman and many past and future Saturday Night Live cast members have got their start.

Ha Ha Café 5010 Lankershim Blvd, North Hollywood ⓣ818/508-4995, ⓦwww.hahacafe.com. Amateur and a few professional comedians face off for your amusement nightly, at this combination comedy club and café space around the NoHo Arts District. Also offers open-mike nights.

The Ice House 24 N Mentor Ave, Pasadena ⓣ626/577-1894, ⓦwww.icehousecomedy.com. The comedy mainstay of the Valley, very established and often amusing, with plenty of old names and the occasional big name.

The Improv 8162 Melrose Ave, Mid-Wilshire ⓣ323/651-2583, ⓦwww.improv.com. Long-standing brick-walled joint known for hosting some of the best acts working in the area, in both stand-up and improv. One of LA's top comedy spots, and the forerunner of a national chain of such clubs – so book ahead.

iO West 6366 Santa Monica Blvd, Hollywood ⓣ323/962-7560, ⓦwest.ioimprov.com. In the heart of old Hollywood, a spot for those who like their improv drawn out and elaborate, with comedy routines more like short theatre pieces than a set of wacky one-liners.

LA Connection 13442 Ventura Blvd, Sherman Oaks ⓣ818/710-1320, ⓦwww.laconnectioncomedy.com. Cosy space for sketch comedy, group antics and individual jokesters. Something of a training ground for new comics, including children.

The Laugh Factory 8001 Sunset Blvd, West Hollywood ⓣ323/656-1336, ⓦwww.laughfactory.com. Nightly stand-ups of varying standards and reputation, with the odd big name. Prominent location of the east end of the Sunset Strip.

Second City Studio Theatre 6560 Hollywood Blvd, Hollywood ⓣ323/464-8542, ⓦwww.secondcity.com. Groundbreaking comedy troupe with numerous branches, this one hosting nightly improv and sketch comedy sometimes built around lengthy routines.

Film

Many feature **films** are released in LA months (or years) before they play anywhere else in the world, sometimes only showing here and nowhere else. A huge number of cinemas focus on new releases, though there are also plenty of venues for silver-screen classics, independent or art-house films and foreign flicks. Tickets tend to be around $11–13, with cheaper prices for matinees and screenings of films that aren't current releases (around $6–8). For **cheap** or **free films**, the USC campus often has interesting free screenings aimed at film students (announced on campus notice boards), and the Hammer Museum's **Billy Wilder Theatre** shows films drawn from UCLA's extensive archive (ⓣ310/206-8013 or ⓦwww.cinema.ucla.edu).

Of the countless venues for **mainstream cinema**, the most notable are in Westwood and Hollywood. For **art houses** and **revival theatres**, there are a few worthwhile choices, mostly scattered across the Westside. Finally, the grand **movie palaces**, described in greater depth elsewhere in this guide, are here listed only as actual movie theatres; many others have been converted into performing-arts venues, concert spaces, churches or, depressingly, swap meets and flea markets. The still-functional movie palaces Downtown are open, once a year in June, for the "Last Remaining Seats" festival (see p.58), run by the LA Conservancy – catch it if you have the chance.

Mainstream cinema

AMC Century 15 In the Century City mall, 10250 Santa Monica Blvd, Century City ⓣ310/289-4AMC. One of the best places to see new films in LA. The theatres are somewhat boxy, but if you're after crisp projection, booming sound and comfy seating, there are few better choices.

AMC CityWalk Stadium 19 End of Universal City Drive, Burbank ⓣ818/508-0588. At Universal CityWalk, one of LA's best giant multiplexes. Despite all the screens, though, only five or six films are typically shown, with multiple theatres reserved for each.

ArcLight 6360 Sunset Blvd, Hollywood ⓣ323/464-4226, ⓦwww.arclight cinemas.com. Probably the most carefully shown films in LA (for a commercial venue), with all-reserved seats in fourteen theatres, top-of-the-line projection, good sightlines, wide seats and — best of all — the iconic Cinerama Dome, a white hemisphere that has the biggest screen in California. Three other citywide locations.

Bruin 948 Broxton Ave, Westwood ⓣ310/208-8998. Aggressive remodelling has made it smaller than it used to be, but this 1930s moviehouse remains a city landmark for its wraparound marquee and sleek Moderne styling. Shows contemporary films.

Laemmle Playhouse 7 42 Miller Alley, Pasadena ⓣ626/844-6500. Comfortable Old Pasadena venue showing a mix of mainstream and independent productions; convenient for shopping and dining, too.

Majestic Crest 1262 Westwood Blvd, Westwood ⓣ310/474-7866. A riot of neon and flashing lights outside, with glowing murals of Old Hollywood inside. Typically shows Disney flicks, in one of the last single-screen cinemas in town.

Pacific 14 at the Grove W Third St at Fairfax Ave, Mid-Wilshire ⓣ323/692-0829. This part of town used to be a hotbed of movie-watching; now the few theatres left are in a mall multiplex. Offers the usual amenities – stadium seats, pre-movie ads, overpriced food – of most chains.

Regal 14 at LA Live 800 W Olympic Blvd, Downtown ⓣ1-877/835-5734. Between parking and a movie ticket, it'll cost you $20 just to see a Hollywood flick at this multiplex, but if you want huge screens, deeply sloped stadium seats, booming Dolby sound and all the 3D/special effects wizardry you can stand, there are few better spots in the city.

Village 961 Broxton Ave, Westwood ⓣ310/248-6266. One of the most enjoyable places to watch a movie in LA, with giant screen, fine seats, good balcony views and modern sound system. A frequent spot for Hollywood premieres, it has a marvellous 1931 exterior, particularly the white spire on top.

Art houses and revival theatres

Aero 1328 Montana Ave, Santa Monica ⓣ310/466-FILM, ⓦwww.aerotheatre.com. The American Cinematheque film organization, presents classic and art-house movies in this fine old venue from 1940. The fare is eclectic and intelligently programmed.

Bing at the LA County Art Museum, 5905 Wilshire Blvd, Mid-Wilshire ⓣ323/857-6010. Offers engaging retrospectives highlighting famed actors and directors, as well as full-priced evening programmes of classic, independent, foreign, art-house and revival cinema.

Cinefamily 611 N Fairfax Ave, south of West Hollywood ⓣ323/655-2510, ⓦwww.cinefamily.org. Boasting some of the most inspired movie-buff showings in town, this vintage theatre presents silent films (with live accompaniment) and cult, foreign, avant-garde and long-forgotten flicks, along with more familiar classics and indie films. It's also got a great concession stand and comfortable seating. Top-notch, all around.

The Landmark 10850 W Pico Blvd, West LA ⓣ310/470-0492, ⓦwww .landmarktheatres.com. From the roadside you'd never guess this huge, twelve-screen multiplex – with comfortable furnishings including couches, excellent sound and projection – would show independent films, but it does. These qualities make it one of the best venues for un-Hollywood fare in town.

Los Feliz 3 1822 N Vermont Ave, Hollywood ⓣ323/664-2169. Having successfully avoided a descent into the porn-movie market in the 1960s, this theatre now shows international and indie fare, plus the occasional blockbuster, on its three small screens.

Monica 4-Plex 1332 Second St, Santa Monica ⓣ310/394-9741. An antidote to the big houses showing mainstream schlock on the

Third Street Promenade, this is the closest nearby theatre (a block away) where you can see a mix of indie and art-house fare.

New Beverly Cinema 7165 Beverly Blvd, south of Hollywood ⓣ323/938-4038. Worthwhile for its excellent art films and revival screenings. All screenings are double features, carefully chosen, and cheap too ($7).

Nuart 11272 Santa Monica Blvd, West LA ⓣ310/281-8223. Classics, indies, documentaries and foreign-language films, and the main option for independent filmmakers testing their work. Sometimes offers brief December previews of Oscar contenders.

Old Town Music Hall 140 Richmond St, El Segundo ⓣ310/322-2592, ⓦwww.otmh.org. An old-fashioned spot to see historic movies, with accompanying organ or piano music on some nights. Unfortunately it resides in a grim industrial location south of LAX.

Royal 11523 Santa Monica Blvd, West LA ⓣ310/478-3836. Though it doesn't quite live up to its regal name, this vintage spot is a prime location for independent fare in a spacious, classically ornamented theatre.

Sunset 5 8000 Sunset Blvd, West Hollywood ⓣ323/848-3500. This art-house complex sits on the second floor of the Sunset Plaza shopping centre, and shows an array of edgy, independent flicks.

Movie palaces

Listed here are historic theatres where you can see regularly scheduled films amid the splendour of the golden age of theatrical architecture. For information on movie palaces that are generally closed, such as the Los Angeles (see p.58), Orpheum (see p.58) and Palace (see p.59), refer to individual descriptions in the guide.

Avalon 1 Casino Way, Santa Catalina Island ⓣ310/510-0179. Located in the stunning Casino building, this great old moviehouse is a riot of mermaid murals, gold-leaf motifs, and an overall design sometimes called "Aquarium Deco". Presents mostly mainstream movies.

Chinese 6925 Hollywood Blvd, Hollywood ⓣ323/464-8111. Landmark cinema showing mainstream fare with a large main screen, six-track stereo sound and wild chinoiserie interior (see p.90), plus the famed forecourt where celebrities have laid down countless handprints.

Egyptian 6712 Hollywood Blvd, Hollywood ⓣ323/466-FILM, ⓦwww.americancinematheque.com. Thanks to the American Cinematheque film group, this historic 1922 moviehouse has nightly showings of revival, experimental and art films, and has been lovingly restored as a kitschy masterpiece of Egyptian Revival – all grand columns, winged scarabs and mythological gods (see p.89).

El Capitan 6834 Hollywood Blvd, Hollywood ⓣ323/467-7674. Whether or not you enjoy the typically kiddie-oriented fare offered in this Disney-owned venue, the twice-restored splendour of this classic Hollywood movie palace is bound to impress.

Vista 4473 Sunset Drive, Hollywood ⓣ323/660-6639. A lovely 1923 moviehouse with very eclectic offerings – from mindless action flicks to micro-budgeted indie productions – and wonderfully weird pseudo-Egyptian decor, located near the intersection of Sunset and Hollywood boulevards.

Warner Grand 478 W Sixth St, San Pedro ⓣ310/548-7672, ⓦwww.warnergrand.org. Definitely worth a trip down to LA Harbor to see this restored 1931 Zigzag Moderne masterpiece, with dark geometric details, majestic columns and sunburst motifs – a style that almost looks pre-Columbian. Having been restored twice, the theatre is now a repertory cinema and performing arts hall.

16

Gay and lesbian LA

Although nowhere near as nationally prominent as San Francisco's, LA's **gay and lesbian scene** is similarly well established, and the city as a whole is generally quite welcoming in its urban core and inner suburbs (less so the farther out you go). The best known gay-friendly area is the city of **West Hollywood**, which has become synonymous with the (affluent, white-male) gay lifestyle, not just in LA but all over California. Santa Monica Boulevard, east of Doheny Drive and west of Fairfax Avenue, in particular has a wide range of restaurants, shops and bars aimed at gay men, though less flashy lesbian-oriented businesses can also be found here and there. West Hollywood is also the site of LA's exuberant **Gay Pride Parade**, held annually in June. Another well-established community with a strong gay and lesbian presence is **Silver Lake**, traditionally more working class, especially along Hyperion Boulevard and part of Sunset Boulevard. Even Orange County has its pockets of gay and lesbian culture on the coast, and especially in the upscale confines of **Laguna Beach's** trendy restaurants and bars.

Gay couples will find themselves readily accepted at most LA **hotels**, but the most well-known gay-oriented establishment is the *Ramada Plaza West Hollywood*, at 8585 Santa Monica Blvd (ⓣ310/652-6400, ⓦwww.ramadaweho.com; $135), which has clean and comfortable rooms with high-speed net access, a pool and a gym, and is very much a popular scene and hub of social activity.

Listed here are **restaurants**, **bars** and **clubs** that cater mainly to gay men and lesbians. The most read local gay publication, though it's also distributed nationally,

Local contacts and resources

AIDS Project Los Angeles 611 S Kingsley Drive, Hollywood ⓣ213/201-1600, ⓦwww.apla.org. Has office-based programmes and services and also sponsors fundraisers throughout the year, including a well-attended annual six-mile walkathon in October.

LA Gay and Lesbian Center 1625 N Schrader Blvd, Hollywood ⓣ323/993-7400, ⓦwww.laglc.org. Provides information on gay and lesbian LA and publishes two informative monthly newsletters. Various organizations and groups meet here, and there are numerous special events throughout the year. Also counselling and health-testing.

One Institute and Archives 909 W Adams Blvd, South Central LA ⓣ213/741-0094, ⓦwww.onearchives.org. The world's biggest library of rare gay and lesbian books and magazines, artworks and information on gay and lesbian culture, social issues and politics. Open Tues & Fri 1.30–5.30pm, Wed & Thurs 3.30–9pm, Sat 11am–5pm. Also displays selected works in its Gallery and Museum in West Hollywood, at 626 N Robertson Ave (same phone), Fri 4.30–8.30pm, Sat & Sun 1–5pm.

is *The Advocate* (Ⓦwww.advocate.com); other gay-oriented publications feature weekly club and event listings, community information and topical articles, and can be found at eateries and retailers around LA – often for free.

Restaurants and cafés

The Abbey 692 N Robertson Blvd ⓣ310/289-8410. A popular spot for excellent, all-American food and drink that increasingly caters to a mixed crowd, with a positive, upbeat vibe and sizable lounge with convivial atmosphere. Often packed, though.

Champagne French Bakery 8917 Santa Monica Blvd, West Hollywood ⓣ310/657-4051. Convenient bakery and coffee shop with serviceable pastries and baked treats in a central location – good for an inexpensive breakfast or lunch on the main drag. One of several LA locations.

Coffee Table 2930 Rowena Ave, Silver Lake ⓣ323/644-8111. A neighbourhood coffee-house with low-fat sandwiches and health food, along with a smattering of tasty desserts.

Fat Fish 616 N Robertson Blvd, West Hollywood ⓣ310/659-3882. Enjoyable and upscale pan-Asian and Cal-cuisine restaurant with inventive cocktails and good sushi. Half-priced hand rolls during happy hour are the main reason to come here.

French Quarter 7985 Santa Monica Blvd, West Hollywood ⓣ310/654-0898. Located inside the French Market Place is this New Orleans–themed restaurant that's more of a draw for its convivial atmosphere than its inauthentic cuisine (eg, Mongolian flat-iron steak).

Golden Bull 170 W Channel Rd, Pacific Palisades ⓣ310/230-0402. Long a staple of the gay community, this old-style steak-and-seafood restaurant and bar has potent cocktails and a relaxed atmosphere near the ocean, not far from Santa Monica.

Marix Tex-Mex Playa 118 Entrada Drive, Pacific Palisades ⓣ310/459-8596. Flavorful fajitas and big margaritas in this rowdy beachfront cantina, which attracts mixed gay and straight crowds. An even livelier, much gayer branch at 1108 N Flores St, West Hollywood ⓣ323/656-8800.

Mark's 861 N La Cienega Blvd, West Hollywood ⓣ310/652-5252. Familiar standby for Cal-cuisine, dishing up the likes of crab cakes, truffle fries, steaks and lamb chops.

Bars and clubs

Mid-Wilshire

Faultline 4216 Melrose Ave ⓣ323/660-0889. Busy scene with plenty of frenetic action inside – driving house beats and testo-sterone-fuelled mayhem – catering to a mix of bears and other visitors. Near Koreatown, in a dicey area.

Jewel's Catch One 4067 W Pico Blvd ⓣ323/734-8849. Longtime favourite on the local club scene, a sweaty barn catering to a mixed crowd and covering two wild dance floors.

The Plaza 739 N La Brea Ave ⓣ323/939-0703. Nondescript joint hosts wild, mind-blowing drag shows before a gay Latino crowd, but one that's increasingly mixed. Power up for the night by munching on monster hot dogs from neighbouring *Pink's* (see p.223).

Silver Lake

Akbar 4356 Sunset Blvd ⓣ323/665-6810. A gay-oriented, but somewhat mixed, crowd frequents this cosy, unpretentious Silver Lake scene, which also has (male) go-go dancers and various dance nights and themed events.

Eagle LA 4219 Santa Monica Blvd ⓣ323/669-9472. Longtime leatherman bar that's a very popular hairy/daddy scene with grungy but friendly vibe and various fetish nights.

Le Bar 2375 Glendale Blvd ⓣ323/660-7595. Quiet and welcoming bar in a bland section of Silver Lake, with good drinks and DJs. Not as much attitude as in some West Hollywood spots.

MJ's 2810 Hyperion Ave ⓣ323/660-1503. Thumping neighbourhood hangout with

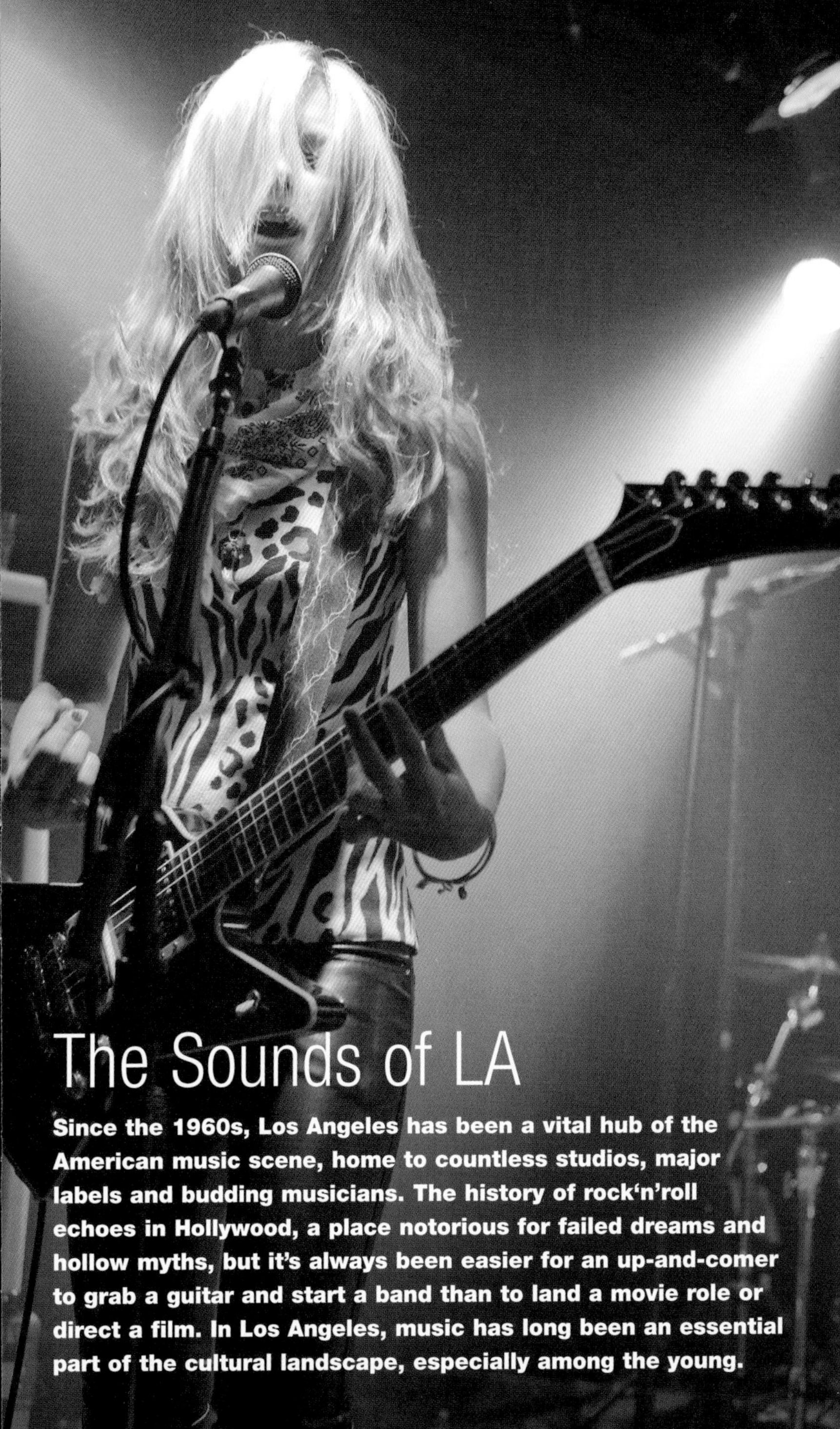

The Sounds of LA

Since the 1960s, Los Angeles has been a vital hub of the American music scene, home to countless studios, major labels and budding musicians. The history of rock'n'roll echoes in Hollywood, a place notorious for failed dreams and hollow myths, but it's always been easier for an up-and-comer to grab a guitar and start a band than to land a movie role or direct a film. In Los Angeles, music has long been an essential part of the cultural landscape, especially among the young.

Monterey Pop Festival ▲

The Doors ▼

The Beach Boys ▼

Early years

In the 1950s, LA witnessed the **birth of rock'n'roll**, with the emergence of such homegrown talent as Ritchie Valens and The Platters, and the efforts of local producers such as Phil Spector and Jack Nitzsche. In marked contrast, the major New York labels, backed by Wall Street financial resources, dominated the industry and propped up greying big-band crooners and insipid teen idols.

Stylistically, the LA sound was defined in the early 1960s by **surf rock**, exemplified by the pleasant harmonies of the **Beach Boys** and Jan and Dean, and by pop vocalists like Frankie Avalon, who sang anodyne tales of apple-cheeked youth and puppy love.

The gold rush, and after

It wasn't until the mid-1960s that the major-label recording industry really took root in town, as The Doors, Buffalo Springfield, Frank Zappa and Love rose to the top of the club scene. The 1967 **Monterey Pop Festival** brought LA and San Francisco bands to prominence, and a flood of record deals went to once-obscure acid-rockers. "After the Gold Rush" (as Neil Young would put it), the Sunset Strip was awash in drugs and criminals, of which Charles Manson was the most infamous. At the same time, super-agents like David Geffen and Elliot Roberts began building their empires, taking the music-money muscle away from New York.

By the early 1970s, stupefied by a blizzard of cocaine, LA's musicians spawned the **country-rock** sound, defined by the Eagles, Jackson Browne, Gram Parsons and Linda Ronstadt, who sang about the city as a spaced-out pleasure zone, to great commercial success.

Rock reactions

The music haze cleared around 1978, with the emergence of an energetic **punk** scene first headed by groups such as the Germs and X, later dominated by Orange County hardcore bands like Black Flag, Circle Jerks, Fear and The Adolescents. Huntington Beach was a notable birthplace of violent trends like slam dancing.

The major labels reacted to the threat of punk with **heavy metal**, which had been around since Led Zeppelin's first American tour at the dawn of the 1970s. At the end of the decade, LA's own Van Halen rose to the top of the charts. The style really hit its commercial stride in the 1980s, with Mötley Crüe and Guns N' Roses; many lesser imitators like Ratt and Poison found chart success as well.

▲ Dr Dre

Rap and beyond

Near the end of the "hair metal" era, by the late 1980s, the city's **hip-hop** artists created their own unique sound. Leading the way were rappers such as NWA, Snoop Dogg, Ice Cube, Ice T and, especially, Dr Dre, who almost single-handedly elevated the **West Coast sound** to prominence: Laid-back beats, an undertone of funk and soul, and a lyrical emphasis on violence and hedonism.

▼ Jane's Addiction

Since then, alternative or **indie rock** has claimed the creative mantle, its roots extending back to bands like Jane's Addiction, Hole and Red Hot Chili Peppers. These days, with the exception of major-name artists like Beck and Silversun Pickups, many LA bands are content with more limited success in exchange for creative freedom via self-distribution, online promotions and web-based fan clubs.

▼ Silversun Pickups

Whiskey-a-Go-Go ▲

Sunset Strip Music Festival ▼

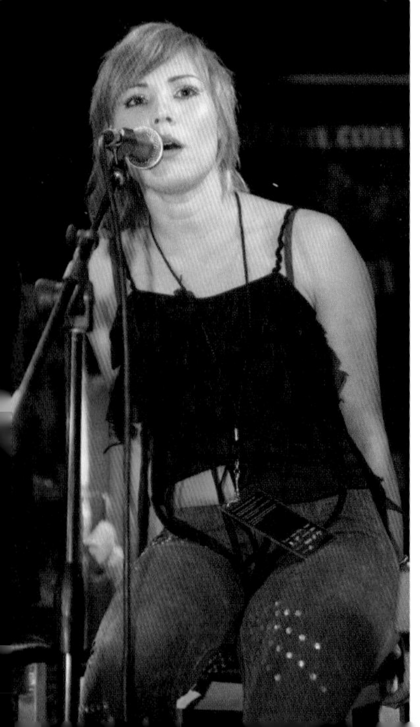

Famous LA music sites

▸▸ **Barney's Beanery** (see p.224). An LA staple since 1920, this bar really became (in)famous for the drunken antics of Jim Morrison and Janis Joplin in the 1960s, and the Olympian drinking of Charles Bukowski.

▸▸ "**Beatle Manor**", 356 St Pierre Rd, Bel Air. One of three hideouts where the Fab Four decamped during their mid-60s tours, when playing at the Hollywood Bowl.

▸▸ **Chateau Marmont** (see p.209). A grand Norman castle that hosted a slew of spectacles, among them Jim Morrison's painful attempt to play Tarzan on a drain pipe and John Belushi's overdose on a coke-and-heroin speedball.

▸▸ **Dead Man's Curve**, Sunset Blvd west of Groverton Pl, near UCLA. The pop world's most notable road bend, which Jan and Dean sang about in their eponymous 1964 hit, and where a number of drivers died before the city regraded it.

▸▸ **Hollywood Bowl** (see p.263). One spot in town where you can enjoy any kind of music – from classical to jazz and rock – in a legendary setting that's hosted many famous concerts, none more so than the Beatles' second-to-last show on their 1965 farewell tour.

▸▸ **Landmark Hotel**, 7047 Franklin Ave, Hollywood. Now the Highland Gardens, a dreary spot where Janis Joplin overdosed on heroin, three years after her astonishing debut at the Monterey Pop Festival.

▸▸ **Laurel Canyon Country Store**, 2108 Laurel Canyon Blvd, Hollywood. The grocery-store epicentre of the late-1960s singer-songwriter movement, frequented by Joni Mitchell, Frank Zappa, Crosby, Stills and Nash, and many others.

▸▸ **Viper Room** (see p.258). Opened by Johnny Depp in 1993, a great showcase for indie music. Actor River Phoenix met his end on the sidewalk outside, a drug casualty on a Halloween morning.

diverse gay-male customers, along with a few bohemian straights. Amusements include go-go dancers, various crazy theme nights and copious dance music.

Hollywood

Arena 6655 Santa Monica Blvd ☎323/462-0714. Many clubs under one roof, large dancefloors throbbing to funk, house and hi-NRG grooves, and sometimes live bands and outrageous drag shows (also see p.253).

The Other Side 2538 Hyperion Ave ☎323/661-0618. Relaxed lounge atmosphere catering to older gay men with jazz music and nightly performances of Tin Pan Alley standards, Broadway favourites and adult contemporary.

Spotlight 1601 N Cahuenga Blvd ☎323/467-2425. The place to be if you want the feel of an old-time 1970s gay bar, with a mildly raunchy dive atmosphere, affordable drinks and a gently buzzing scene. The place has somehow endured since the 1960s.

West Hollywood

East/West Lounge 8851 Santa Monica Blvd ☎310/360-6186. Friendly spot in the hub of West Hollywood with somewhat pricey drinks, but a chic atmosphere, good range of cocktails and decent food. Sidewalk seating offers great people watching.

The Factory 652 N La Peer Drive ☎310/659-4551. DJs spin house, pop and retro-pop most nights of the week at what is one of West Hollywood's more popular clubs.

FUBAR 7994 Santa Monica Blvd ☎323/654-0396. If you recognize the acronym, you'll know what you're in for at this high-energy club, a popular scene that offers regular dance events, plus Friday-night drag shows and a Wednesday-night lesbian night – rare in LA.

Gold Coast 8228 Santa Monica Blvd ☎323/656-4879. A good approximation of a down-and-dirty 1970s-style gay dive bar, with the requisite grunge, but also a relaxed atmosphere and cheap drinks. A bit east of the main section of the WeHo scene.

Micky's 8857 Santa Monica Blvd ☎310/657-1176. Lively, pulsating scene with a full range of club nights, including retro-1970s and -80s dance-pop, thundering house beats and drag shows.

Mother Lode 8944 Santa Monica Blvd ☎310/659-9700. Strong drinks, wild dancing to house and hi-NRG music, karaoke and periodic drag antics make this one of the more colourful area clubs, with a full crush of customers on weekends.

The Palms 8572 Santa Monica Blvd ☎310/652-6188. Usually house and pop-music dance nights at West Hollywood's most established lesbian bar, which increasingly caters to a mixed crowd.

Rage 8911 Santa Monica Blvd ☎310/652-7055. Very flashy gay men's club and neighbourhood favourite, playing the latest house to a long-established crowd.

Ultra Suede 661 N Robertson Blvd ☎310/659-4551. Featuring various club nights where a mixed gay and straight crowd gyrates to techno-pop, house and retro-pop music. Neighbour to The Factory.

San Fernando Valley

Oil Can Harry's 11502 Ventura Blvd, Studio City ☎818/760-9749. Gay cowboy bar that plays high-stepping country music, as well as dance, pop and other genres, with line-dancing and a mildly cornpone atmosphere.

Sports and outdoor activities

Los Angeles has plenty of **sports** and **outdoor activities** to keep you occupied. Though Angelenos don't have the same feverish, die-hard enthusiasm for spectator sports as do, say, New Yorkers or Chicagoans, they still often make a good showing at basketball, baseball and hockey games, as well as college football contests. If you can't make it to a sporting event, there are always **sports bars** where you can catch local teams on television and knock back a few brews as well.

That said when most people think about LA sports, it's not team sports but participatory sports like **surfing**, along with more self-conscious pursuits like bodybuilding, that come to mind.

Water and **beach sports** are still the city's main claims to fame, be they swimming or surfing along the coast, snorkelling or scuba diving around Santa Catalina Island, or even kayaking and jet-skiing. If you'd rather not get wet, you can always try a bit of in-line skating, skateboarding, or bicycling along strips like the Venice Boardwalk, or simply suntanning at the beach. **Airborne activities** include ballooning above the LA basin, hang gliding off precarious seaside cliffs, or just taking a safe helicopter tour. If you want to sweat, there are ideal spots across the region for jogging, rock climbing and hiking – not to mention working out in a fitness club. Just as strenuous, **skiing** and **snowboarding** are both possible in the mountains east of LA, especially around the Big Bear region, a favourite weekend getaway for many locals. If all this sounds like too much work, there are plenty of other **leisure activities**, like horseriding, fishing and bowling, to keep you occupied.

Spectator sports

LA's **spectator sports** are just as exciting to watch as any in the country, though – with the notable exception of the Lakers – you can expect less enthusiasm here for the home squad than you'd find on the East Coast. For most LA locals, team sports are a diversion, not a way of life.

Baseball

LA has two area major-league **baseball teams**, playing from mid-April to early October: the **Dodgers** (T 323/224-1500, W www.dodgers.com), who play at the top-notch Dodger Stadium in Chavez Ravine, northwest of Downtown, and the clumsily named **Los Angeles Angels**

of Anaheim (Ⓣ1-888/796-4256, Ⓦwww.angelsbaseball.com), who play at drab, ugly Anaheim Stadium out in Orange County.

The Dodgers are historically the more beloved franchise, having relocated from Brooklyn in the late 1950s and pulled off a number of glory years in the 1970s and 80s – though they've taken some hits in recent years for being consistently overpaid and underachieving. Whereas the Dodgers last won a world championship back in 1988, the Angels had their best season in 2002, getting to and winning the World Series for the first time. And unlike the Dodgers, the Angels have made the playoffs regularly in recent years. Tickets for both teams are easy to get, with games generally running $8–75 for most seats.

Basketball

Basketball's flashy **LA Lakers** (Ⓣ213/480-3232, Ⓦwww.lakers.com) have boasted such luminaries as Kareem Abdul-Jabbar, Magic Johnson, Shaquille O'Neal and, currently, Kobe Bryant, and they've won a total of sixteen championships, the most recent coming in 2010. Needless to say, getting a game ticket is a matter of some cachet, and the closer you get to courtside, the bigger a player in town you must be; tickets run from $20 to more than $275. Home court is the Staples Center in Downtown LA.

The much lesser light in LA's basketball galaxy, the **LA Clippers** (Ⓣ213/742-7430, Ⓦwww.clippers.com), have a history of shocking ineptitude, and rarely make the playoffs; games are also held at the Staples Center, with seat prices $18–250, and you should have no problem getting a ticket – unless the Lakers are the opponent. The NBA **season** runs from November through late April, not including the playoffs.

The **Los Angeles Sparks** (Ⓣ1-877/44-SPARKS, Ⓦwww.wnba.com/sparks; tickets $10–55) is one of a dozen teams playing nationally in the WNBA women's basketball league. As with the other local basketball squads, the Sparks play their home games at the Staples Center, though on a summertime schedule (May–Aug).

Football

Los Angeles has had no professional **football** teams since 1994, and few locals seem to care. However, college ball is another story: Pasadena's 102,000-seat **Rose Bowl** (Ⓣ626/577-3101, Ⓦwww.rosebowlstadium.com) hosts one of the five Bowl Championship Series games to decide the national title, and is also the home field for UCLA's respectable football team (Ⓣ310/825-2101, Ⓦwww.uclabruins.com), who play there a half-dozen times during the autumn. The top-notch USC squad also plays in historic digs, at the LA Coliseum in South Central (Ⓣ213/740-GOSC, Ⓦwww.usctrojans.com), site of the 1932 and 1984 Olympics. Ticket prices for both schools can vary widely depending on the opponent (usually $40 and up for non-students). All games are played on Saturdays throughout fall.

Hockey

Hockey in LA didn't mean much until the late 1980s, when the **LA Kings** (Ⓣ1-888/KINGS-LA, Ⓦkings.nhl.com) traded for superstar Wayne Gretzky from the champion Edmonton Oilers. Gretzky's long gone from these parts, and the Kings have since moved from the Forum to the Staples Center; seats are $25–135. The **Anaheim Ducks**, in Orange County, play at Honda Center in Anaheim (Ⓣ714/704-2500, Ⓦducks.nhl.com) and won the Stanley Cup in 2007; tickets $20–175. The NHL season lasts throughout the winter and into early spring, when the playoffs take place.

Soccer

The **LA Galaxy** (Ⓣ1-877/3-GALAXY, Ⓦwww.lagalaxy.com) plays **soccer** in the MLS (Major League Soccer), featuring headliner David Beckham, and games take place at the Home Depot Center, in the city of Carson in the South Bay. Based at the same venue is another MLS team, **CD Chivas** ($15–100; Ⓣ1-877/CHIVAS-1, Ⓦwww.cdchivasusa), affiliated with its parent club, CD Guadalajara in Mexico. The soccer season runs much of the year, save winter; tickets $20–125.

Horse racing

Horse racing is a fairly popular spectator sport in the LA area, which has two main tracks. **Santa Anita**, in the San Gabriel Valley town of Arcadia at 285 W Huntington Drive, has an autumn and winter season (Ⓣ626/574-7223, Ⓦwww.santaanita.com); while **Hollywood Park**, 1050 S Prairie Ave in Inglewood, has a spring-to-autumn season (Ⓣ310/419-1500, Ⓦwww.hollywoodpark.com).

Water and beach sports

Many visitors to LA head straight for the ocean. Along the sands from Malibu to Orange County, you can find any number of options for **water** and **beach sports** to keep you busy. Among more passive pleasures at the seaside, **suntanning** with the crowds is always a popular option.

Swimming, snorkelling and scuba diving

Although you'd never believe it from watching TV, **swimming** in many LA coastal areas is definitely not recommended. As a rule, the further you go from most city piers, the better off you are. Piers, along with run-off pipes and channels, are sources of water-borne contamination, particular after heavy rains. (For more info, see Ⓦwww.healthebay.org, or the box, p.123.) The beaches closer to Malibu, Palos Verdes and Orange County are usually less crowded and safer than those around Santa Monica and Venice, though any spots near LA Harbor are to be avoided. **Parking** at major strips of sand will cost you upwards of $7–10, even for a short time, but you can usually find roadside spots where you can park if you want to take a dip along the rockier coves and crags. Similarly, **snorkelling** and **scuba diving** are better experienced well away from LA in places like Santa Catalina Island. Prices for excursions to see Catalina's astounding undersea life, kelp forest and shipwrecks can vary widely, but expect to pay at least $90–120 for any trip. Lover's Cove, a marine preserve just east of Avalon, is the best spot to view the local sea life close-up, though only snorkeling is allowed. For information on Santa Catalina Island see p.161.

Surfing, windsurfing, kayaking and jet-skiing

Since railroad magnate Henry Huntington first began importing Hawaiian talent in 1907 to publicize his Red Car route in the South Bay, **surfing** has been big business in LA and has made a major impact on the city's culture and image. If you want to give the sport a try, head to where the surfers are: along the Malibu section of the Pacific Coast Highway from Surfrider to Leo Carrillo beaches and around Point Dume; along the South Bay in towns like Manhattan Beach and Hermosa Beach; and at Orange County beaches from Huntington to San Clemente. Don't worry about buying equipment, though: **surfboards** are available for rent by the hour from rental shacks up and down the coast.

If you've never been **windsurfing**, a trip to LA might not be the ideal time to start, given the often challenging conditions. But for the confident, several coastal outlets in Long Beach rent windsurfers by the hour or day. **Kiteboarding** may be even more challenging: you hold onto a large kite while standing on a board, and let the wind pull you along the waves. Lessons can be very expensive. Somewhat easier is **kayaking**, and the ocean-going kayaks that you can rent are more basic and manageable than river kayaks; many are two-seaters. Finally, there's **jet-skiing**, a popular choice for those who'd rather get their thrills without too much labor. It will cost you around $100 to rent a machine for a half-day of splashing around Santa Monica Bay or elsewhere.

Alfredo's Beach Rentals five locations in Long Beach, info at ⓣ562/434-1542, ⓦwww.alfredosbeachclub.com. Rents kayaks for around $10–20 per hour, bikes and inline skates for $10 and hour, and pedal boats for $15 an hour.

Boat Rentals of America 13719 Fiji Way, Marina del Rey ⓣ310/574-2822, ⓦboats4rent.com. Rental outfit with several locations throughout LA, with kayak rentals for $15–25/hr, outboard motorboats for $65–125/hr, sailboats for $45–75, and wave runners for $75.

Kayaks on the Water 5411 E Ocean Blvd, Long Beach ⓣ562/434-0999, ⓦwww.kayakrentals.net. Good location for affordable kayak rentals, with singles at $8 per hour and doubles for $12–15. April–Sept only.

Long Beach Windsurf Center 3850 E Ocean Blvd, Long Beach ⓣ562/433-1014, ⓦwww.windsurfcenter.com. Located near the Belmont Pier, this operator rents in-line skates and kayaks for $10–20 per hour; windsurfers run upwards of $25–30 per hour.

Offshore Watersports 128 E Shoreline Drive, Long Beach ⓣ562/436-1996, ⓦwww.owsrentals.com. Has new jet skis, or wave runners, for $85–125 per hour, or fishing boat rental for $110 per hour.

Southwind Kayak Center E Coast Hwy at Bayside Drive, Newport Beach ⓣ1-800/SOUTHWIND, ⓦwww.southwindkayaks.com. Orange County operator with kayak rentals from $14–20 per hour for singles and doubles, or $50–65 per day. Excellent for access to beaches further south.

Zuma Jay Surfboards 22775 Pacific Coast Hwy, Malibu ⓣ310/456-8044, ⓦwww.zumajays.com. Solid choice for boards near some major waves. Expect to pay $20–25 per day, plus $10 for a wetsuit in winter months.

Rollerblading and bicycling

Inline skating, or **rollerblading**, is quite popular along the Venice Boardwalk and other beachside paths, and in certain parks and recreation zones. The famed **cycling path** from Santa Monica to Palos Verdes is a terrific route for exploring the seacoast of the metropolis. There are also myriad bike paths throughout the region, from the peaceful, leafy setting of the Arroyo Seco to the post-apocalyptic landscape of the LA River. You can rent a bike for as little as $6–8 per hour off the beaten trail, but the beachfront is the only place with a good selection of dealers, who may charge $10–15 an hour for skates or bikes, depending on the equipment.

Bikestation 222 E Broadway, Long Beach ⓣ562/436-BIKE, ⓦwww.bikestation.org. Offers bicycle rental, repair and storage, information on bike transit, and even valet bike-parking.

California Association of Bicycling Organizations ⓣ310/639-9348, ⓦwww.cabobike.org. Lobbyist group that's a good online source of maps and information, plus regular updates of California laws and municipal strategies affecting cyclists.

California Department of Transportation (CalTrans) LA office at 100 S Main St, Downtown ⓣ213/897-3656, ⓦwww.dot.ca.gov. Perhaps the most comprehensive source of guides and maps for the LA urban area and region, showing which commuter arterials are best for cycling, and which should be avoided.

Perry's Café and Rentals 100, 2500 & 3100 Ocean Front Walk, Venice ⓣ310/904-4849, ⓦwww.perryscafe.com; 930 Pacific Coast Hwy, Santa Monica ⓣ310/260-1114; 1200 PCH, Santa Monica ⓣ310/458-3975; and on the Santa Monica Pier ⓣ310/393-9778. A mini-chain of oceanside rental spots where the bikes and skates go for $20–25 per day or $8–10 per hour.

Sea Mist **1619 Ocean Front Walk, Venice ☎310/395-7076.** Located opposite the Venice Pier, with very affordable bike and skate rentals for $6 per hour, or $15 per day.

Segway LA **1660 Ocean Ave, Santa Monica ☎310/395-1395, ⓦwww.segway.la.** If you don't mind looking a bit goofy, you can rent one of these peculiar upright cycles ($79 per two hours) for tooling around the city or oceanfront.

Spokes 'n' Stuff **1700 Ocean Ave, Santa Monica ☎310/395-4748, ⓦspokes-n-stuff.com.** Among the better choices among many similar bike-rental agents along the sands; $6–8/hour or $18–35/day, or $18/day for inline skates. In Griffith Park, the outfit has a branch near the LA Zoo, at 4730 Crystal Springs Drive (☎323/662-6573), and in Marina del Rey at 4200 Admiralty Way (☎310/306-7666).

Airborne activities

For those who want to rise above the smog, LA has several thrilling **airborne activities**. The most affordable is **hang gliding**, in which you hang from a flexible or rigid-wing glider to drift down from a hill, mountain or cliff on air currents, and slowly come to a safe landing. Experienced hang gliders bring their gliders to the bluffs overlooking the Pacific near Point Fermin for a strikingly picturesque trip over the sea cliffs and toward the beach.

An appealing alternative is **soaring in enclosed gliders**, again using air currents to rise and fall. A ride in one of these simple craft can be memorable, if not quite as awe-inspiring as that of hang gliding. You'll doubtless spend most of your time watching from the back seat of the glider, while the pilot controls the flight.

A **helicopter ride** may provide all the airborne excitement you need, allowing you to view some of LA's premier sights, like the Hollywood sign, from several hundred to thousands of feet above the ground. There are a number of different packages and tours available, all at fairly steep prices. The most expensive, and most conventional, mode of flying is also available – an **airplane trip** in a single- or twin-engine craft flying from private or commercial airports.

Group 3 Aviation **16425 Hart St, Van Nuys Airport, San Fernando Valley ☎818/994-9376, ⓦwww.group3aviation.com.** Takes movie-oriented helicopter trips from the Valley to various points in Hollywood and along the coast (from $130–285).

LA Helicopters **Berth 75, Ports 'o Call Village, San Pedro ☎1-800/976-HELI, ⓦwww.lahelicopters.com.** Short, 20min helicopter excursions in the South Bay for $119 per person, and half-hour-long overhead tours of Long Beach's and San Pedro's top sights for $159, or trips to Santa Catalina Island and back for $389.

Southern California Soaring Academy **32810 165th St E, Llano, north of LA in the Antelope Valley ☎661/944-9449, ⓦwww.soaringacademy.org.** Provides gliders and lessons, at a cost of $295 for a basic two-hour lesson, or a minimum $86 (per one hour, plus tow) if you're already certified.

Windsports Hang Gliding Center **12623 Gridley St, Sylmar ☎818/367-2430, ⓦwww.windsports.com.** A well-known hang-gliding tour and rental outlet. For around $120, they will give you the basic experience, but for those who want a greater challenge, more expensive package deals are available for $200.

Fitness activities and extreme sports

LA's preoccupation with tanned, muscular and silicone-boosted physiques is most evident in the city's vigorous pursuit of **fitness activities**. For some, the goal is simply to keep their body in shape, while others zealously worship it or test its physical limits with **extreme sports**.

Fitness activities

For a dose of LA's health mania, try **working out** at a fitness club or along the beach. Whether you've come to pump iron or to watch the weightlifters go through their paces, there are few better spots than **Muscle Beach** near the Venice Boardwalk. Contact the Venice Beach Recreation Center, 1800 Ocean Front Walk (Ⓣ310/399-2775), for more information on bench-pressing with the local iron-pumpers. If you're not quite there yet, the exercise and training equipment just south of the **Santa Monica Pier** should start you on your way, but for less conspicuous bodybuilding and training, LA's numerous **health clubs** are everywhere.

If you want to go **jogging**, stick to the safer Westside. Although Hollywood would at first seem like a dubious choice for exercising, the steeply inclined paths and fine views of Runyon Canyon Park make for an excellent workout (enter off Mulholland Drive or Fuller Avenue), as does the circuit around Lake Hollywood. Elsewhere, the best options for joggers include the green median strip of San Vicente Boulevard from Brentwood to Santa Monica; the steep stairs between Santa Monica and Pacific Palisades (see p.127); Sunset Boulevard through Beverly Hills and Westwood (but not West Hollywood or Hollywood); the Arroyo Seco in Pasadena; and most stretches along the beach – except near the LA Harbor.

Also along the beach, you may be able to join a **volleyball** game at any of the sandy courts from Santa Monica to Marina del Rey. Hermosa Beach is another good choice for volleyball (the city famously hosts competitions throughout the year), as are Orange County's Huntington and Laguna beaches. There are **tennis** courts all over LA, with space available for visitors at city parks (notably Griffith Park) and universities. Call the city's Department of Recreation and Parks for more information on reserving a court (Ⓣ213/485-5555, Ⓦwww.laparks.org).

The best workout in town is also one of the cheapest: **hiking**. The Santa Monica Mountains – a huge natural preserve west of LA and north of Malibu – have many different trails and routes for exploration, most of which feature jaw-dropping scenery, copious wildlife and interesting rustic sights. Some of the best hiking parks are listed in the chapter "Malibu and the Santa Monica Mountains", p.183. Up in these mountains, the section of Mulholland Drive west of the 405 freeway is known as "Dirt Mulholland", and is closed to auto traffic for seven rutted, uneven miles, which are popular with hikers and bikers.

Audubon Society At Plummer Park, 7377 Santa Monica Blvd, West Hollywood Ⓣ323/876-0202, Ⓦlosangelesaudubon.org. Provides periodic guided hikes (event line Ⓣ323/874-1318) through the Santa Monica Mountains and other LA-area nature zones, as well as information on their various chirping and warbling denizens. Operates a bookstore and library at its headquarters.

California Department of Parks Ⓣ818/880-0350, Ⓦwww.parks.ca.gov. Good online source of information and maps, providing an overview of each state park and its resources.

LA Trails Ⓦwww.latrails.com. Good, all-around website for exploring the paths and trails of the region, from simple paved concourses to steep mountain scrambles.

Santa Monica Mountains Conservancy Ⓣ310/589-3200, Ⓦlamountains.com. The leader in efforts to preserve land in the mountains and ensure public access. Also a good source of information about the region at visitor centres in Franklin Canyon, Downtown at the LA River, Pacific Palisades and Ramirez Canyon.

Santa Monica Mountains Visitor Center 401 W Hillcrest Drive, Thousand Oaks Ⓣ805/370-2301, Ⓦwww.nps.gov/samo. Offers maps and information on hiking trails and parks in the area. Located in a suburb just north of LA.

Sierra Club 3435 Wilshire Blvd #320, Mid-Wilshire Ⓣ213/387-4287, Ⓦangeles.sierraclub.org. Major political and environmental advocacy group that offers information on local natural areas, and conducts hikes and tours of key ecological zones.

Extreme sports

Sports such as hang gliding or kayaking can be taken to death-defying limits, but LA also has a taste for some other daring **extreme sports**.

The original "extreme sport" was arguably **skateboarding**, and in the 1970s LA quickly became a trailblazer in the sport. Boards can be rented along the beach at spots like *Spokes n Stuff* (see p.278) for $7.50/hr or $18/day. Even more thrilling, **rock climbing** is offered in private rock "clubs" or "gyms" where you can scale vertical surfaces to your heart's content (rental equipment is available for an additional fee). For a closeup look at the sport without paying a dime, turn up at Stony Point near Chatsworth, in the San Fernando Valley, to watch crowds of hardcore rock enthusiasts dangling by their fingertips.

For sheer terror, **bungee jumping** is hard to beat, though it's lost a little lustre since its 1990s heyday, and there are far fewer operators in the business nowadays. Powering a **motocross** dirtbike around desert washes and boulder-strewn valleys can be a thrill if you've got excellent balance and aren't scared of taking a nasty spill.

Bungee America **Ⓣ310/322-8892, Ⓦwww.bungeeamerica.com.** Long-standing bungee operator that offers thrilling weekend jumps from the so-called "Bridge to Nowhere" in the Angeles National Forest, an abandoned span only accessible by a two-hour walk; package deals start from $79 for one leap to $199 for five (also available for night jumps).

MotoVentures **At Anza Riding Training Center (check for directions), Temecula Ⓣ951/767-0991, Ⓦwww.motoventures.com.** Motorcycle ranch two hours east of LA that offers instruction in motocross for novices and exhilarating two-wheel tours of the surrounding mountains and desert. If you have your own dirtbike, day-long tours start at $350; it's $300 more if you need a rental.

The Rock Gym **2599 E Willow St, north of Long Beach Ⓣ562/981-3200, Ⓦwww.therockgym.com.** One of LA's top climbing venues, with a 12,000-square-foot space for scaling. One climb is $16 ($13 for kids) and rental of a full climbing gear package is $6. Find other, similar operators around town by looking at listing for Los Angeles "Rock Gyms" or "Rock and Mountain Climbing Instruction" on Google or in the *Yellow Pages*.

RockReation **11866 La Grange Ave, West LA Ⓣ310/207-7199, Ⓦwww.rockreation.com.** Not the most thrilling spot, but good for its "bouldering cave" and 9000 square feet of rock-climbing surfaces. One-day pass $17, full equipment rental package $6.

Skateboard Parks **Ⓦskateboardparks.com.** Although you can certainly earn a daring reputation skateboarding illegally in city plazas and the like, to find a list of above-board skateboard parks in LA, visit this national website, which puts special emphasis on LA and Southern California.

Skiing and snowboarding

On the fringe of the LA region, the mountainside lake and hamlet of **Big Bear** is prime territory for **skiing** and **snowboarding** about two hours east of Downtown LA, north of San Bernardino near state highways 18 and 38. Along with Mount Baldy and other locations in or near the San Bernardino Mountains, Big Bear and its several appealing resorts are deservedly a top winter draw. Thousands of Angelenos drive out here (there are hardly any public transit options, except from San Bernardino itself) to experience the excellent ski and snowboard conditions from November through April. In summer, there is excellent hiking, boating, fishing and jet-skiing. Hotels and motels are plentiful, and the fine *Big Bear Hostel* (see p.216) provides cheap accommodation. Expect to pay around $40 for a full ski or snowboard package rental.

Bear Mountain 43101 Goldmine Drive, Big Bear Lake ⓣ909/585-2519, ⓦwww.bearmountain.com. Major ski area with twelve chairlifts, plus the added attraction of some of the country's top terrains parks, as well as all the summer activities. Lift tickets $53, kids $20; also good for use at Snow Summit.

Mount Baldy Off Mountain Avenue in the Angeles National Forest ⓣ909/981-3344, ⓦwww.mtbaldy.com. Located on the edge of LA County, with a nice assortment of straightforward skiing trails and routes, along with decent snowboarding. Lift tickets $54, kids $24.

Mountain High Near Wrightwood at 24512 Hwy-2 ⓣ888/754-7878, ⓦwww.mthigh.com. Caters to dedicated winter athletes with two high-speed chairlifts (out of twelve), plus night skiing every day of the week until 10pm. Also has terrain parks for snowboarders. Lift tickets $55, kids $25.

Snow Summit 880 Summit Blvd, Big Bear Lake ⓣ909/866-5766, ⓦwww.snowsummit.com. One of the best ski areas, with twelve chairlifts, one of which operates in summer for hikers and mountain bikers ($12 round trip rides). Thrilling terrain park for snowboarders, with a halfpipe and Superpipe. Winter lift tickets $53, kids $20; also good for use at Bear Mountain.

Snow Valley 35100 Hwy-18 near Running Springs ⓣ909/867-2751, ⓦwww.snow-valley.com. Located further from Big Bear Lake, a spot for the usual snow sports, with a terrain park and twelve chairlifts. Lift tickets $54, kids $24.

Leisure activities

You can enjoy LA's great outdoors without a lot of grunting and sweating, thanks to the city's diversity of **leisure activities**.

Fishing

Fishing is encouraged at a few locations, like the northern beaches around Malibu and the southern ones around Orange County. Elsewhere, however – especially near the Santa Monica and Venice piers – any fish you catch is likely to contain a bevy of nasty chemicals. A better, though more costly, alternative is to charter a **sport-fishing cruise** out to sea and cast your line there. Prices run from one to two thousand dollars for a six-hour trip on a winter weekday, to three thousand or more for an eight-hour cruise during a summer weekend.

A California state **fishing licence** is required for pier casting, ocean fishing and any other type of angling. It costs nonresidents $13, $21 or $42, for one, two, or ten days of fishing, with annual licences running $112 ($42 for residents). **Special permits** are required for salmon ($5.50 extra), steelhead ($6.30), abalone ($20) and spiny lobster ($8.40) fishing. Many cruise operators and fishing-supply dealers provide short-term fishing licences. For more information, check ⓦwww.dfg.ca.gov/licensing.

LA Harbor Sportfishing 1150 Nagoya Way, Berth 79, San Pedro ⓣ310/547-9916, ⓦwww.laharborsportfishing.com. Partial ($38 per person) or full-day ($50) trips to offshore waters, along with overnight trips ($120) and seasonal whale-watching cruises (2hr 30min; $20).

Long Beach Sportfishing 555 Pico Ave, Berth 55, Long Beach ⓣ562/432-8993, ⓦwww.longbeachsportfishing.com. Organizing full-day ($50) and half-day ($40) fishing expeditions to deep-sea waters, as well as whale-watching trips ($13–15).

Marina del Rey Sportfishing 13759 Fiji Way, Marina del Rey ⓣ310/822-3625, ⓦmarinadelreysportfishing.com. Somewhat more touristy than the other operators, though the tour prices and packages are much the same (rental equipment, licences, day or half-day trips for $50 and $38, whale watching for $20, etc).

Redondo Sportfishing 233 N Harbor Drive, Redondo Beach ⓣ310/372-2111, ⓦwww.redondosportfishing.com. Half- and full-day trips are offered ($40–60), sailing to waters near Palos Verdes all the way out to more distant islands off the California coast. Also offers whale-watching cruises ($15–22).

Bowling

Bowling in LA attracts a diehard crowd of local enthusiasts – still best exemplified by the crazy characters in the film *The Big Lebowski* (though that film's Hollywood Star Lanes is long since demolished). All around town you can find bowling alleys, from grungy old linoleum-and-formica lanes to newer bowl-o-ramas where flashy bowling nights feature glow-in-the-dark lanes and sparkly bowling balls. Costs start around $4–8 per game, with shoe rental a few bucks extra.

All Star Lanes 4459 Eagle Rock Blvd ⓣ323/254-2579, ⓦwww.allstarlanesbowling.com. Located between Glendale and Pasadena in little Eagle Rock, this retro-styled alley features a bar, dancefloor, video games and pool tables to keep you busy when you're not prowling the lanes.

Corbin Bowl 19616 Ventura Blvd, Tarzana ⓣ818/996-BOWL, ⓦwww.corbinbowl.net. Solid site in the San Fernando Valley for inspired rolling, with 26 lanes, video arcade, café, weekend music, lights and bar with karaoke.

Jewel City Bowl 135 S Glendale Ave, Glendale ⓣ818/243-1188, ⓦwww.jewelcitybowl.com. Clean and modern alleys with Friday and Saturday "extreme bowling", featuring a live DJ, and various weekday promotions featuring ultra-cheap rounds (bowling, as well as tequila).

Lucky Strike 6801 Hollywood Blvd ⓣ323/467-7776, ⓦwww.bowlluckystrike.com. Bowling Hollywood-style, with a smirky hipster atmosphere, higher prices than elsewhere, lounge atmosphere, karaoke, loud music and the usual rash of celebrity spottings.

Pickwick Bowling 1001 Riverside Drive, Burbank ⓣ818/845-5300, ⓦwww.pickwickgardens.com. With 24 lanes and a mixed crowd of young and old, this colorful Valley spot has gimmicks like Friday dance-music nights and Saturday bowling featuring copious amounts of dry ice and wild lighting.

Pinz Bowling Center 12655 Ventura Blvd, Studio City ⓣ818/769-7600, ⓦwww.pinzbowlingcenter.com. The place to be seen on the Valley bowling scene, with plenty of arcade games, light shows and a Rock 'n' Roll atmosphere. Don't be surprised to see a B-list TV actor or recent Hollywood has-been in the lane next to you.

Horseback riding

You can go **horseback riding** at several ranches and stables throughout the greater LA region, principally around the Santa Monica Mountains and the hills of Griffith Park. Most businesses give you a choice of packages that may include evening outings, individual or group rides, easy or difficult routes and various added amenities like dinners or barbecues. Costs can be anywhere from $15 to $50 per hour, depending on the location and package.

Circle K Stables 910 Mariposa St, Burbank ⓣ818/843-9890. Located near the LA Equestrian Center, these stables provide affordable rides for $25 per person per hour, giving you fine view of Griffith Park and the Hollywood Hills.

Diamond Bar Stables 1850 Riverside Drive, Glendale ⓣ818/242-8443, ⓦwww.diamondbarstables.com. A Griffith Park–area operator that provides guided equine tours during the daylight or evening hours, and occasionally under moonlight, starting at $20 per hour.

Dude's Ranch Tarzana, San Fernando Valley ⓣ661/269-2473, ⓦwww.dudesranch.com. Many tours through varying terrain around the Santa Monica Mountains – from hills and canyons to waterfalls and beaches – with most rides one to five hours long, at $55–65 per hour, per person. Rides at sunset and under moonlight are the same cost. Lessons $65 per hour.

LA Equestrian Center 480 Riverside Drive, Burbank ⓣ818/840-8401, ⓦwww.la-equestriancenter.com. Across the LA River from Griffith Park, this outfit presents various horse shows and offers rentals, through Griffith Park Horse Rentals, for $25 an hour or evening rides for $50–65.

Sunset Ranch 3400 N Beachwood Drive, Hollywood ⓣ323/469-5450, ⓦwww.sunsetranchhollywood.com. A Griffith Park operator providing evening horse rides through the surrounding area on a first-come first-served basis, sometimes with dinner; regular one- or two-hour rides $25 and $40.

Will Rogers State Historic Park 1501 Will Rogers State Park Rd, Pacific Palisades ⓣ310/662-3707, ⓦwww.willrogerstrailrides.com. Watch a polo match on the park's front lawn (April–Oct Sat 2–5pm, Sun 10am–1pm; free) before enjoying a guided horseback ride in the vicinity for $45.

18

Festivals and events

Los Angeles throws a lot of **parades** and **festivals**, from proud displays of ethnic culture to internationally famous spectacles to oddball street fairs and quirky bohemian gatherings. No matter when you come, you'll likely find some sort of event or celebration, especially in summer, when beach culture is in full bloom. This selective list concentrates on some of the more notable observances, along with smaller, local events that provide unusual or nontraditional festivities. Events especially worth checking out have been marked with a . For a list of national **public holidays**, see Basics, p.40.

January

Japanese New Year (1st) Art displays, ethnic cuisine, cultural exhibits and more at this annual Little Tokyo festival, centred around the Japanese American Community and Cultural Center. ⓣ213/628-2725, ⓦwww.jaccc.org.

Tournament of Roses Parade (1st) With more than a 120-year tradition, Pasadena's famous procession of floral floats and marching bands passes along a five-mile stretch of Colorado Boulevard, coinciding with the annual Rose Bowl football game. ⓣ626/795-9311 or 449-ROSE, ⓦwww.tournamentofroses.com.

Golden Globe Awards (mid) As the annual run-up to the Oscars, this awards show is held by the Hollywood Foreign Press Association, and attracts ever-increasing attention. Tourists are encouraged to watch the stars arrive, and gape accordingly. ⓣ310/657-1731, ⓦwww.hfpa.org.

Martin Luther King Parade and Celebration (mid) The civil-rights hero is honoured with activities at King Park, Baldwin Hills, Crenshaw and many other city locations. ⓣ323/290-4100.

February

Chinese New Year (early to mid) Three days of street parades, tasty food and cultural programmes, based in Alhambra, Monterey Park and Chinatown, where a spectacular Golden Dragon Parade heralds the event. ⓣ213/617-0396, ⓦwww.lachinesechamber.org, ⓦwww.lagoldendragonparade.com.

Mardi Gras (mid) Floats, parades, costumes and lots of singing and dancing at this Latin fun fest, with traditional ceremonies on Olvera Street Downtown (ⓣ213/625-7074) and campy antics in West Hollywood (ⓣ310/289-2525).

Queen Mary Scottish Festival (mid) All the haggis you can stand at this two-day Long Beach celebration, along with peppy Highland dancing and bagpipes. ⓣ562/499-1650, ⓦwww.queenmary.com.

Ragga Muffins Festival (mid) A two-day event that exalts reggae culture with food, music and plenty of spirit. At the Long Beach Arena. ⓣ310/515-3322, ⓦwww.raggamuffinsfestival.com.

March

The Academy Awards (early) The top movie awards, presented at the Kodak Theater at the Hollywood & Highland mall. Bleacher seats are available to watch the limousines draw up and the stars emerge for the ceremony. ⓣ310/247-3000, ⓦwww.oscars.org.

LA Marathon (mid) Cheer on the runners all around town, or sign up to participate in this 26.2-mile run, which covers a course from Dodger Stadium through Hollywood to the Westside and finishes by the sea in Santa Monica. ⓣ310/444-5544, ⓦwww.lamarathon.com.

PaleyFest (mid) If you love TV, this is one event you shouldn't miss, honouring shows from the past and present with clips, cast reunions, lectures and more. Presented by the Paley Center for Media. ⓣ310/786-1091, ⓦwww.paleycenter.org.

Spring Festival of Flowers (mid) A floral explosion of colour at Descanso Gardens, including different types of tulips, lilies and daffodils, among many others. Runs mid-March to June. ⓣ818/949-4200, ⓦwww.descansogardens.org.

St Patrick's Day (17th) Freely flowing green beer in the "Irish" bars along Fairfax Ave in Mid-Wilshire. Parade along Colorado Boulevard in Old Town Pasadena and another in Hermosa Beach. ⓣ213/689-8822, ⓦwww.discoverlosangeles.com.

April

Blessing of the Animals (early) A long-established Mexican ceremony in which locals come to Olvera Street to have their pets blessed, then watch a parade. ⓣ213/625-7074, ⓦolvera-street.com.

Renaissance Pleasure Faire (weekends, early April to late May) Dress up in your Tudor best for this celebration of olden times, which includes dancing, theatre, feasting and the inevitable jousting. Held in distant Irwindale near the Sante Fe Dam. ⓣ626/969-4750, ⓦrenfair.com/socal.

Songkran Festival (Thai New Year) (early) This prominent cultural event features spicy food and authentic music, and takes place in East Hollywood's "Thai Town" along a six-block stretch of Hollywood Boulevard. ⓣ213/689-8822, ⓦwww.discoverlosangeles.com.

Long Beach Grand Prix (mid) Some of auto-racing's best drivers and souped-up vehicles zoom around Shoreline Drive south of Downtown in the city's biggest annual event, which takes place over three days. ⓣ562/981-2600, ⓦwww.gplb.com.

California Poppy Festival (late) Although it's in a bleak northern valley, Lancaster's 1800-acre poppy reserve draws big crowds with its blinding orange colours each spring. To go with the blooms, the town throws a festival featuring local foodstuffs, folk art and crafts. ⓣ661/723-6075, ⓦwww.poppyfestival.com.

Cowboy Poetry and Music Festival (late) Folk music from the Old West and accompanying cowboy poems – some excellent, some cornpone – are the highlights of this three-day Santa Clarita celebration, just north of LA. ⓣ661/286-4021, ⓦwww.cowboyfestival.org.

Fiesta Broadway (late) Along Broadway in Downtown, this street fair presents lively Latino pop singers and delicious Mexican food. ⓣ310/914-0015, ⓦwww.fiestabroadway.la.

May

Doo-dah Parade (early) Absurdly costumed characters marching through East Pasadena are the main attraction at this immensely popular event, which began as a spoof of the Tournament of Roses parade. ⓣ626/590-1134, ⓦwww.pasadenadoodahparade.info.

Cinco de Mayo (5th) A day-long party to commemorate the 1862 Mexican victory at the Battle of Puebla. Besides a spirited parade along Olvera Street, several blocks of Downtown are blocked off for Latino music performances. There are also celebrations in LA parks. ⓣ213/628-1274, ⓦolvera-street.com.

Strawberry Festival (late) Garden Grove in Orange County is the setting for this huge, old-fashioned shindig of carnival rides, games, parades and other festivities – all in celebration of the humble strawberry. ⓣ714/638-0981, ⓦwww.strawberry festival.org.

Venice Art Walk (late) A great chance to peer into the private art studios in town, where you can see the work of both big-name local artists and lesser-known up-and-comers. Coordinated by the Venice Family Clinic. ⓣ310/392-9255, ⓦvenicefamilyclinic.org.

LA Modernism (end) This annual show, at Santa Monica Air Center, is a fine opportunity to see a wealth of modernist art and design from the twentieth century. ⓣ818/244-1126, ⓦwww.lamodernism.com.

UCLA Jazz and Reggae Festival (end) Two days of jazz and reggae concerts, plus heaps of food, on the UCLA campus. ⓣ310/825-9912, ⓦwww.jazzreggaefest.com.

June

Last Remaining Seats (Wednesdays throughout) An excellent film festival that draws huge crowds to the grand Los Angeles, Orpheum and Million Dollar movie palaces to watch revivals of classic Hollywood films. Tickets to each screening $20, often with live entertainment. ⓣ213/623-CITY, ⓦlaconservancy.org.

Irish Fair and Music Festival (mid) Sizable Irish music, food and culture celebration held in the Orange County town of Irvine ⓣ949/833-2770, ⓦwww.irishfair.org.

LA Pride (mid) Raucous parade along Santa Monica Blvd in West Hollywood, with hundreds of vendors, an all-male drag football-cheerleading team and a heady, carnival atmosphere. ⓣ323/969-8302, ⓦwww.lapride.org.

Playboy Jazz Festival (mid) Renowned event held at the Hollywood Bowl, with a line-up of traditional and not-so-traditional musicians. ⓣ213/450-1173, ⓦwww.playboyjazzfestival.com.

Los Angeles Film Festival (mid to late) Although Hollywood is better at making generic films than honouring good ones, this ten-day festival is an exception, screening notable independent and art-house films at a variety of Downtown venues. ⓣ1-866/FILMFEST, ⓦwww.lafilmfest.com.

Bayou Festival (late) Heaps of Creole food, wild parades and plenty of high-spirited Cajun and Zydeco music at this colourful Long Beach event in Rainbow Lagoon Park. ⓣ562/427-3713, ⓦwww.longbeach festival.com.

July

Festival of the Arts/Pageant of the Masters (early July to late Aug) Laguna Beach's signature street festival, featuring food, arts and dancing, but most memorable for its living tableaux, which re-create classic paintings (see box, p.201). ⓣ949/497-6582, ⓦwww.foapom.com.

Independence Day (4th) The *Queen Mary* in Long Beach hosts a particularly large fireworks display, as well as colourful entertainment (ⓣ562/435-3511). Other fireworks displays throughout LA, including West Hollywood's Plummer Park (ⓣ323/848-6530).

Lotus Festival (first weekend after 4th) An Echo Park celebration featuring pan-Pacific food, music and, of course, the resplendent lotus blooms around the lake. ⓣ213/413-1622, ⓦwww.laparks.org.

Jazzfest West (mid) West of Pasadena in the town of San Dimas' Bonelli Park, an event mixing mid- to big-name acts in mainstream jazz with appetizing foodstuffs and arts-and-crafts displays. ⓣ949/360-7800, ⓦwww.omegaevents.com.

South Bay Greek Festival (mid) Three days of food and music at St Katherine Greek Orthodox Church in Redondo Beach, with arts-and-crafts displays and energetic dancing adding to the festivities. ⓣ310/540-2434, ⓦwww.sbgreekfestival.com.

Central Avenue Jazz Festival (late) Jazz and blues concerts by big names and lesser-known performers, held on Central Avenue between 42nd and 43rd streets in South Central. ⓣ213/473-2309, ⓦwww.centralavejazz.org.

August

Festival of the Chariots (early) Giant decorated floats parade down Venice Boardwalk to the sound of lively music and the smell of vegetarian Indian food. Sponsored by the International Society for Krishna Consciousness. ⓣ310/836-2676, ⓦwww.festivalofchariots.com.

International Surf Festival (early) Newcomers and old-time fans party at this surfing tournament and festival in the South Bay. The exciting three-day spectacle also includes volleyball matches, lifeguard races, sand soccer and sandcastle design. ⓣ310/802-5413, ⓦwww.surffestival.org.

Long Beach Jazz Festival (mid) Relax and enjoy famous and local performers at the Rainbow Lagoon park in downtown Long Beach. ⓣ562/424-0013, ⓦwww.longbeachjazzfestival.com.

Nisei Week (mid to late) A celebration of Japanese America, with martial arts demonstrations, karaoke, Japanese brush painting, sake tasting and various performances. ⓣ213/687-7193, ⓦwww.niseiweek.org.

Sunset Junction Street Fair (late) A spirited neighbourhood party, and one of LA's most enjoyable fêtes, along Sunset Boulevard in Silver Lake. The live music, ethnic food and carnivalesque atmosphere draws a big crowd of locals in the know. ⓣ323/661-7771, ⓦwww.sunsetjunction.org.

September

Fiesta Hermosa (early) Labor Day weekend is a great time to visit this fun-loving beach town, which puts on a bash with food vendors, music, oceanside sports and other activities. ⓣ310/376-0951, ⓦwww.fiestahermosa.com.

Long Beach Blues Festival (early) Hear some of the country's top blues performers at this annual event at Cal State University at Long Beach. ⓣ562/985-7000, ⓦwww.kkjz.org/events.

Los Angeles County Fair (early Sept to early Oct) In the San Gabriel Valley, Pomona hosts the biggest county fair in the US, with livestock shows, horse races, pie-eating contests, rodeos and fairground rides. ⓣ909/623-3111, ⓦwww.lacountyfair.com.

LA's birthday (early) A civic ceremony and assorted street entertainment around El Pueblo de Los Angeles, to mark 230 years since the founding of the original pueblo in 1781. ⓣ213/625-5045, ⓦolvera-street.com.

Festival of Philippine Arts and Culture (second Sun) Good food, music, dancing, theatre and film at this annual Point Fermin event in San Pedro. ⓣ323/913-4663, ⓦfilamarts.org.

Oktoberfest (mid Sept to late Oct) Venture into Alpine Village, in the South Bay suburb of Torrance, to revel in Teutonic culture, from hearty German food to music and dancing. ⓣ310/327-4384, ⓦwww.alpinevillagecenter.com. Also a spirited event in Huntington Beach, Orange County. ⓣ714/895-8020, ⓦwww.oldworld.ws.

Watts Towers Day of the Drum/Jazz Festival (late) Two days of music and dancing – African, Asian, Cuban and Brazilian – with the towers as the striking backdrop. Taking place at the same time, and in the same location, the Jazz Festival is the oldest such event in LA. ⓣ213/487-4646.

LA Korean Festival (end) Dancing, parading and tae kwon do exhibitions are the main events at this Mid-Wilshire event held in Seoul International Park (ⓣ213/487-9696). A similar event takes place in Pasadena around the same time (ⓣ626/449-2742).

October

Catalina Island Jazz Trax (first three weekends) A huge line-up of major and rising jazz stars performs in the beautiful Art Deco ballroom of the historic Avalon Casino. ⓣ1-866/872-9849, ⓦwww.jazztrax.com.

Eagle Rock Music Festival (early) This funky district, due north of Downtown LA near Glendale, hosts a freewheeling festival of food, crafts and a widely eclectic assortment of music. ⓣ323/226-1617, ⓦwww.myspace.com/eaglerockmusicfestival.

Lithuanian Fair (early) Traditional music and food, and Easter egg painting, are some of the highlights of this Los Feliz fair, held at St

Casimir's Church. ⓣ323/664-4660, ⓦwww.lithuanianfair.com.

Los Angeles Bach Festival (mid to late) Revel in the Baroque master's music at the First Congregational Church, just north of Lafayette Park in Westlake. ⓣ213/385-1345, ⓦwww.fccla.org.

Halloween (31st) A wild procession in West Hollywood, featuring all manner of bizarre and splashy costumes and characters (ⓣ310/289-2525). Or you can opt for the Halloween-themed events on the *Queen Mary*. ⓣ562/435-3511.

November

Dia de Los Muertos (2nd) The "Day of the Dead", celebrated authentically throughout East LA and on Olvera Street and elsewhere. Mexican traditions, such as picnicking on the family burial spot and making skeleton puppets, are faithfully upheld. ⓣ213/625-5045, ⓦolvera-street.com.

AFI Film Festival (early) Arguably LA's most influential film festival, with a mix of engaging up-and-comers and Hollywood veterans testing the indie-film waters; showings can be popular and venues sell out early, so plan ahead. ⓣ323/856-7600, ⓦwww.afi.com/afifest.

Hollywood Christmas Parade (end) The biggest of LA's many Yuletide events begins the holiday season with a procession of elaborate floats, marching bands and famous and semi-famous names from film and TV. ⓣ323/469-2337, ⓦwww.thehollywoodchristmasparade.com.

December

Belmont Shore Christmas Parade (early) Homemade floats and marching bands kick off the holiday season at this East Long Beach event. ⓣ562/434-3066.

Griffith Park Light Festival (early to late) A huge favourite, this spectacle stretches a mile along Crystal Springs Road, complete with drive-through tunnels of light, thematic displays and representations of familiar LA sights like the Hollywood sign. ⓣ323/913-4688 ext. 9.

Marina del Rey Holiday Boat Parade (mid) The marina is the site for this annual, ocean-going procession of brightly lit water-craft, supposedly the largest of its kind on the West Coast. ⓣ310/670-7130, ⓦwww.mdrboatparade.org.

Las Posadas (mid to late) An Olvera Street re-enactment of the biblical tale of Mary and Joseph seeking a place to rest on Christmas Eve, culminating with a *piñata*-breaking. ⓣ213/625-5045, ⓦolvera-street.

LA County Holiday Celebration (Christmas Eve) Thousands of people pack the Dorothy Chandler Pavilion in Downtown LA to catch this juggernaut of multicultural entertainment, including everything from Japanese dance to Jamaican reggae. ⓣ213/974-1396, ⓦwww.lacountyarts.org/holiday.html.

19

Kids' LA

Although most of LA's attractions are geared for adults, the city does hold some appeal for **kids**, from popular **museums** and **aquariums** to the outdoor fun of the region's excellent **parks and beaches**. If these don't hold the kids' interest, treat them to a stop at one of the many worthwhile **toy shops** in town, where they can pick out something bright and shiny. Most, if not all, kids will doubtless want to go to major theme parks like **Disneyland, Knott's Berry Farm** and **Magic Mountain**, but the thrill fades after only a couple of days – or even hours – of being jostled by massive crowds, waiting in interminable lines, and eating crummy theme-park food. Some of the selections below are good alternatives.

Museums

Some LA **museums** feature kid-friendly exhibits and hands-on, interactive displays with lots of flashing lights and bright colours. **Exposition Park** (see p.139), south of Downtown, has the **California Science Center**, with lots of flashy displays and pressable buttons; the associated **Air and Space Gallery**, where aircraft hang from the ceiling; and the huge, all-encompassing nature films and 3-D extravaganzas of the **IMAX Theater**. Meanwhile, visitors of all ages enjoy the neighbouring **Natural History Museum of Los Angeles County** for its displays of dinosaur bones, sparkly gems and minerals, and pioneer history; its sister museum is the **George C. Page Discovery Center** in Mid-Wilshire (p.73), which is a fine place to view the colossal bones of extinct creatures, featuring mammoths, sloths, wolves and sabre-toothed cats dredged up from the adjacent **La Brea Tar Pits**.

For Western-tinged fun, **Will Rogers State Historic Park** (p.184) has a great ranch house loaded with lariats, cowboy gear and even the mounted head of a Texas Longhorn. Kids with a taste for roping and riding may also warm to the **William S. Hart Ranch and Museum** (p.181), for its wide range of Western duds, cowboy equipment and Tinseltown memorabilia, as well as the meatier exhibits at the **Museum of the American West** (p.86) in Griffith Park.

If all else fails, you can take older kids with a taste for the surreal to the **Museum of Jurassic Technology** (p.120), an institutional haunted house of sorts filled with all manner of bizarre displays, including creepy bugs.

Aquatic attractions

The region's biggest and most comprehensive collection of marine life is kept at the **Aquarium of the Pacific** (p.156) in Long Beach, where there are plenty of sharks, tide-pool creatures, jellyfish and other creatures to tantalize kids. Less crowded is the smaller **Cabrillo Marine Aquarium** (p.154) in San Pedro, while the Orange County coast is the home of the **Friends of the Sea Lion Marine Mammal Center** (p.201) – where kids can watch injured animals being nursed back to health.

Further north, along the rugged coastline of Palos Verdes, the **Point Vicente Interpretive Center** has simple exhibits on local marine life (p.151), but is best for its **whale watching** during the winter months. These massive creatures can also be spotted from other promontories along the Santa Monica Bay, and **whale-watching cruises** operate from Santa Catalina Island and Long Beach (see p.160 & p.156).

North of Point Vicente, Manhattan Beach's **Roundhouse and Aquarium** (p.149) offer an inexpensive look at the region's ocean flora and fauna, but for a much more in-depth view, the **Santa Monica Pier Aquarium** (p.124) is a good choice, where kids can eyeball sea creatures and learn about marine biology and ecology.

Parks

The most prominent of LA's outdoor recreation areas is **Griffith Park** (p.83), where you can find an excellent network of hiking, biking and horse-riding trails in the large, mountainous green space. The park has numerous attractions to pique children's interest, including a pleasant **Fern Dell**, as well as the imposing **Griffith Observatory** (p.85), chock full of astronomical and scientific exhibits that will entrance young and old alike. The observatory will probably appeal to older children more than the **LA Zoo** (p.85) on the other side of the park, where a standard array of animals is shown before the public in mostly outdated displays and cramped environments. Near the zoo, **Travel Town** (p.86) is geared to smaller tots who like funky old trains.

The **Santa Monica Mountains** are a good place to visit for the many hiking trails and buzzing wildlife. **Paramount Ranch** (p.191) is especially interesting for kids and adults as the filming site of numerous Hollywood Westerns. Not far away, **Malibu Creek State Park** (p.191) is a good choice for a half-day family outing into some of LA's more rugged, unspoiled terrain, while closer to the Westside, above Beverly Hills, **Franklin Canyon** (p.109) has pleasant nature walks and a nature centre.

Both parents and kids may enjoy spending time in the city's **ecological reserves**, which offer fine opportunities for hiking, birdwatching and sometimes horseriding and bicycling. The action on **Santa Catalina Island** (p.158) includes hiking, camping and bus tours around the island's unspoiled interior. Orange County, too, has several worthwhile options, including the striking **Crystal Cove State Park** (p.200) along the coast, and the **Bolsa Chica** (p.199) and **Upper Newport Bay** (p.200) ecological reserves, where kids can see nature in its sublime, undeveloped state.

Beaches and water parks

Of course, LA has a number of popular **beaches**. The best, and least polluted, are around **Malibu** and along the **Orange County coast**, while Santa **Catalina Island** is great for its many snorkelling sites. One beach is no good for swimming, but nevertheless caters to kids: the **Santa Monica Pier** is chock-full of cotton candy, video games and carnival rides (other city piers are mainly useful for fishing).

For freshwater amusement, the region's **water parks** are sure to delight kids with a yen for hydrotubes and splash pools. These include the excellent, often

Puppet shows

If the wee ones enjoy puppets, don't miss a visit to the **Bob Baker Marionette Theater**, 1345 W First St (shows Tues–Fri 10.30am, Sat & Sun 2.30pm; $20, toddlers free; by reservation only at ⓣ213/250-9995, ⓦwww.bobbakermarionettes.com), one of LA's best puppet shows for fifty years running, performed by a classic puppeteer. The only downside is the theatre's dicey location on the west side of the 110 freeway – don't linger after dark – though the marionettes make regular appearances around town, too (details at ⓣ818/487-0205).

expensive, rides at Magic Mountain's **Hurricane Harbor** (p.181), Knott's Berry Farm's **Soak City U.S.A.** (p.197) and **Wild Rivers** in the Orange County city of Irvine, at 8770 Irvine Center Drive (June–Aug hours vary, generally daily 10am–8pm; May & Sept Sat & Sun 10am–5pm; $33, kids $20; ⓣ949/788-0808, ⓦwww.wildrivers.com), loaded with water tubes, pools and flumes, and a short distance from the 405 freeway.

Toy and game shops

Dinosaur Farm 1510 Mission St, South Pasadena ⓣ1-888/658-2388, ⓦwww.dinosaurfarm.com. A paradise for little dino-lovers, bursting with games, puzzles, lunchboxes and models relating to the giant reptiles – not to mention clothing, masks and outfits for dressing like a T. Rex.

Giant Robot 2015 Sawtelle Blvd, West LA ⓣ310/478-1819, ⓦwww.giantrobot.com. If your kids have a flair for the surreal, this is the place to come, loaded with Asian-themed wind-up dolls, comic books, freakish dolls, miniatures and curiosities beyond description.

Hollywood Toys and Costumes 6600 Hollywood Blvd, Hollywood ⓣ323/464-4444, ⓦwww.hollywoodtoys.com. A classic, one-of-a-kind LA business, with not only an array of dolls and action figurines, but also dress-up treats – wigs, masks, Halloween outfits, costume jewellery and all kinds of colourful trinkets and eye-catching junk. As much for adults as kids.

Karen's Toys in the Encino Place mall, 16101 Ventura Blvd #135, Encino ⓣ818/906-2212. This San Fernando Valley retailer stocks a fine selection of dolls, puzzles, old-fashioned blocks, art supplies and more – all at prices lower than the big names.

Kip's Toyland in the Farmers Market, 6333 W Third St, Mid-Wilshire ⓣ323/939-8334. Venerable dealer in assorted toys, dolls, stuffed animals, puzzles and games – not always the flashiest items around, but the store maintains a loyal following in a central location.

San Marino Toy and Book Shoppe 2424 Huntington Drive, San Marino ⓣ626/309-0222, ⓦwww.toysandbooks.com. Excellent, pricey selection of puppets, dollhouses and building blocks, along with odd items like robot-explorer toys and magician training kits.

Wound & Wound Toy Company Universal CityWalk, Universal City ⓣ818/509-8129, ⓦwww.thewoundandwound.com. Packed with all kinds of wind-up toys, from goofy aliens and tin trucks to burgers with feet. The display cases full of rare collectibles – *Star Wars* dolls prominent among them – are worth a look.

20

Shopping

Shopping in LA is serious business. The level of disposable income in the wealthy parts of the city is astronomical, and an expedition to some of the ritzy **shopping districts** and outrageous stores can offer some insight into LA life – revealing who's the money and what they're capable of blowing it on. Besides the run-of-the-mill chain retailers you'll find anywhere, there are big **department stores** and mega-**malls** where most of the hard-core shopping goes on.

If you have bags of money to spend, you should feel right at home in LA's fashionable **art galleries**, where you can spot the latest works from the city's hottest artists offered at jaw-dropping prices.

Shopping districts

While you can find souvenirs and touristy merchandise in most retail zones, there are a few notable **shopping districts**. Downtown, the main shopping area is the **Fashion District**, where you can pick up a variety of fabrics and clothes, including designer knockoffs and markdowns, at some of the lowest prices on the West Coast.

Although its signature Miracle Mile has seen better days, Mid-Wilshire has no fewer than three major shopping areas: **La Brea Avenue**, just north of Wilshire, a stretch of clothing, furniture and antiques stores; **Third Street**, a strip of boutiques and restaurants east of the Beverly Center mall and west of the Grove mall; and **Larchmont Village**, a pocket of small retailers and chain stores on the edge of Hancock Park.

Just north in Hollywood, the irrepressible **Melrose Avenue** is LA's most conspicuously hip area, while further north, **Hollywood Boulevard** is one big cut-rate shopping zone, especially for movie memorabilia and discount T-shirts, with merchants thickest between La Brea Avenue and Gower Street, and the giant Hollywood & Highland mall anchoring the whole scene. To the east is the short **North Vermont Avenue** strip in Los Feliz, with its idiosyncratic boutiques and good restaurants. By contrast, West Hollywood is more self-consciously chic, and you can expect to find small boutiques along the western end of **Santa Monica Boulevard**, and numerous music and bookstores (and a few sex shops) along the **Sunset Strip**.

Beverly Hills is, of course, the pinnacle of high-end shopping, with stratospheric retailers concentrated in the downtown core known as the **Golden Triangle**, which includes **Rodeo Drive**. West LA retail is anchored by the colossal Westside Pavilion and Century City malls; Brentwood's **San Vicente Boulevard**, another ritzy zone; and **Westwood Village**, a student haven, full of inexpensive bookstores, clothing outlets and used-record stores.

Shopping categories

Out in Santa Monica, the **Third Street Promenade** is one of LA's busiest shopping strips, with a mix of small retailers and mega-chain stores; linked from the Promenade by a free bus (in summer), Santa Monica's **Main Street** is popular for its book dealers, clothing stores and gift shops. The same types of retailers, though of a funkier and more downmarket character, cluster further south, around Venice's **Windward Arcade**.

In the outlying areas, there are countless malls, minimalls and chain-store outlets, but only a few truly interesting places to shop or browse. **Downtown Long Beach**, especially around Pine Avenue, has some retail appeal; **Old Pasadena** – notably Colorado Boulevard – offers music stores, clothing boutiques and used-book sellers; **Ventura Boulevard**, running through Studio City in the San Fernando Valley, is a good place to buy new and used music, assorted souvenirs, colorful trinkets and cheap clothing; and along Newport Beach's **Balboa Peninsula**, on the Orange County coast, you can pick up expensive designer duds and similarly pricey outfits at numerous boutiques. The South Bay, San Fernando Valley and Orange County are also littered with malls. Oddly enough, the high-profile city of Malibu has relatively few unique shopping attractions open to the general public.

Department stores and shopping malls

You won't have to travel far to find LA's flagship **department stores**, located in **malls** throughout the region. For mall addresses see opposite.

Department stores

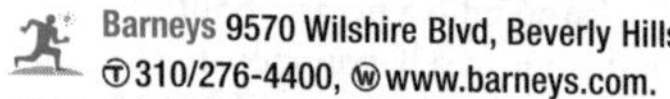

Barneys 9570 Wilshire Blvd, Beverly Hills ⓣ310/276-4400, ⓦwww.barneys.com. At the base of the Golden Triangle, this high-end retailer offers five levels of dapper shoes and clothing – and an exclusive restaurant, *Barney Greengrass* (see p.236) on the fifth floor; if you don't look like you belong there, expect the sales clerks to ignore you.

Bloomingdale's 10250 Santa Monica Blvd, in the Century City Marketplace, Century City ⓣ310/772-2100, ⓦwww.bloomingdales.com. This major chain features all the standard men's and women's apparel, kitchen items and assorted jewellery and kidswear. Also in Santa Monica Place, Beverly Center, Sherman Oaks Fashion Square and Newport Beach Fashion Island.

Macy's 8500 Beverly Blvd, in the Beverly Center mall ⓣ310/854-6655, ⓦwww.macys.com. One of the big boys on the US department store scene, at Century City Marketplace; 920 W Seventh St, Downtown; the Santa Monica Place mall; Westside Pavilion; Paseo

Colorado mall; 401 S Lake Ave, Pasadena; Del Amo Fashion Center; and various Orange County locations.

Neiman-Marcus 9700 Wilshire Blvd, Beverly Hills ☎310/550-5900, ⓦwww.neimanmarcus.com. Loaded with attitude and (overly) high prices, with three fancy restaurants, opulent displays of jewellery, and a plethora of fur coats, this store is quintessential Beverly Hills, located at the base of the Golden Triangle. Also in Orange County at Newport Beach Fashion Island ☎949/759-1900.

Nordstrom 10830 Pico Blvd, in the Westside Pavilion mall, West LA ☎310/470-6155, ⓦwww.nordstrom.com. Mostly clothing and accessories at this Westside department store. If you can't decide on the right party dress or power tie, a "personal shopper" can help you – for a price. Also at the Grove mall; Santa Monica Place; South Coast Plaza; and many other branches in the valleys and Orange County.

Saks Fifth Avenue 9600 Wilshire Blvd, Beverly Hills ☎310/275-4211, ⓦwww.saksfifthavenue.com. An upmarket chain with expensive perfume, eye-popping jewellery, and high fashion. Also at South Coast Plaza ☎714/540-3233.

Shopping malls

Beverly Center 8500 Beverly Blvd, between Mid-Wilshire and West Hollywood ☎310/854-0070. Seven acres of boutiques, plus Macy's and Bloomingdale's, all in one complex that resembles a giant brown concrete bunker – built over a parking garage, with active (off-limits) oil wells on its western side.

Burbank Town Center 201 E Magnolia Blvd at N San Fernando Rd, Burbank ☎818/566-8617. Branches of Sears, IKEA and Macy's occupy this complex of buildings just outside the heart of old Burbank, right beside the I-5 freeway.

Century City Marketplace 10250 Santa Monica Blvd, Century City ☎310/553-5300. An outdoor mall with one hundred upscale shops and one of the better food courts around. The place to come to see stars do their shopping, and a spot to catch a first-run movie in excellent surroundings at the AMC Century 15 Theaters (see p.269).

Del Amo Fashion Center Hawthorne Blvd at Carson St, Torrance ☎310/542-8525. The South Bay's own super-mall, one of the country's largest, with Sears, Macy's and JCPenney and a wealth of mid-level retailers and shoppers.

Glendale Galleria Central Ave at Colorado St, Glendale ☎818/240-9481. A sprawling downtown complex with Target, Nordstrom, JCPenney and Macy's, and a broad selection of clothiers.

The Grove 6301 W Third St, Mid-Wilshire ☎323/571-8830. A giant, open-air mega-structure by the farmers' market; has all the usual chain retailers and restaurants, movie theatres, and a more stylish design than the typical "dumb-box" construction found elsewhere.

Hollywood & Highland at the same intersection in Hollywood ☎323/960-2331. A mega-mall modelled after an elaborate silent-film set, but offering the usual corporate boutiques and trendy shops, and a multiplex connected to the Chinese Theatre.

Newport Beach Fashion Island 401 Newport Center Drive ☎949/721-2000. A reasonable alternative to Orange County's South Coast Plaza, though not as large, with an appealing outdoor setting. Anchored by Nordstrom, Bloomingdale's, Macy's and Neiman-Marcus.

Paseo Colorado E Colorado Blvd at S Los Robles Ave, Pasadena ☎626/795-8891. Two levels of (mostly chain) stores, including Macy's, beneath several levels of housing, with street-front entrances and an open-air design that invites strolling.

Santa Monica Place Broadway at Second St, Santa Monica ☎310/394-5451. Old Frank Gehry-designed mall that as of August 2010 was radically reconfigured into an open-air design. Sits at the south end of the Third Street Promenade, and is anchored by Bloomingdale's and Nordstrom.

Sherman Oaks Galleria 15301 Ventura Blvd, Sherman Oaks ☎818/382-4100. This former iconic mall has been reduced to a sliver of its former self – basically a branch of ArcLight Cinemas (see p.269), plus two dozen retailers and office space; only worthwhile if you're in the neighbourhood.

South Coast Plaza 3333 Bristol St, north of 405 freeway, Costa Mesa ☎714/435-2000. Orange County's self-described "shopping resort" and one of the most profitable malls in North America, with nearly three hundred shops and huge crowds of locals and tourists. Includes Macy's, Saks Fifth Avenue and Nordstrom and many top-name designer boutiques.

Third Street Promenade Third St between Broadway and Wilshire Blvd, Santa

Monica. Major outdoor mall, packed on weekend evenings with mobs scurrying about the fashion retailers, restaurants and cinemas. Throngs of musicians, homeless people and tourists round out the picture.

Westfield Fashion Square 14006 Riverside Drive, San Fernando Valley ⓣ818/783-0550. With the famed Galleria a fraction of its former self (see above), this is the Valley's major stab at mall respectability. Macy's and Bloomingdale's are the anchors, with a hundred other chain stores.

Westside Pavilion Pico and Westwood blvds, West LA ⓣ310/474-6255. The obligatory chain stores at this postmodern shopping complex centre around Nordstrom and Macy's. The formerly outdoor, western side of the mall has undergone a massive conversion into The Landmark theatres (see p.269).

Clothes and fashion

In LA's iconic **clothing** stores, you can reinvent yourself with a freshly bought Hermês bag, velvet cape or gold lamé dog collar. Apart from the usual chain-clothing stores, you'll find hordes of slick designer boutiques along Rodeo Drive, on the western side of West Hollywood, and along Melrose Avenue. Much more relaxed are the funky clothing stores for which LA is famous, many of them located along La Brea and north Vermont avenues and Santa Monica and Sunset boulevards. If you're just looking for cheap duds, however, LA has a good selection of secondhand and vintage clothiers to choose from.

Upscale chain stores

Chanel 400 N Rodeo Drive, Beverly Hills ⓣ310/278-5500. As you'd expect, a pricey selection of swanky clothes and perfumes from Paris. You'll get a healthy dose of attitude, too, if you've only come to browse. Also at 125 N Robertson Blvd, West LA ⓣ310/278-5505.

Christian Dior 309 N Rodeo Drive, Beverly Hills ⓣ310/859-4700. Top-flight high fashion for predictably high prices – but you knew that already.

Façonnable 9680 Wilshire Blvd, Beverly Hills ⓣ310/247-8277. An upper-bracket clothing merchant at the base of the Golden Triangle, selling sleek casual and dress wear, and an assortment of colognes and fragrances; a shade less pretentious than some of its bigger-name neighbours.

Fendi 355 N Rodeo Drive, Beverly Hills ⓣ310/276-8888. Ultra-chic designer shirts, sportswear and watches for Americans who want to look vaguely European, but not be too showy about it.

Giorgio Armani 436 N Rodeo Drive, Beverly Hills ⓣ310/271-5555 or Beverly Center ⓣ310/289-3610. One of LA's most elite fashion houses, featuring sleek, well-cut suits that are standard issue to movie agents, lawyers and other self-anointed big shots. For slightly cheaper clothing, try Emporio Armani at 9533 Brighton Way ⓣ310/271-7790.

Gucci 347 N Rodeo Drive, Beverly Hills ⓣ310/278-3451. Aside from the outlandishly priced shoes, wallets and accessories that you can find here, there's also a fair assortment of upscale men's and women's clothing. Also at Beverly Center ⓣ310/652-0375.

Hugo Boss 414 N Rodeo Drive, Beverly Hills ⓣ310/859-2888. The place to go if you're looking for a thousand-dollar suit. Also at the Beverly Center mall ⓣ310/657-0011.

Kenneth Cole Broadway at Second Street, in the Santa Monica Place mall ⓣ310/458-6633. Leather jackets, tapered boots, sleek earrings and hip-hugging pants – all in black – to help you get into the chic nightclubs in town. Also a branch at Beverly Center ⓣ310/659-2396 and Century City Marketplace ⓣ310/282-8535.

Louis Vuitton 295 N Rodeo Drive, Beverly Hills ⓣ310/859-0457. Designer wallets and luggage in plenty of expensive styles. Also at the Beverly Center mall ⓣ310/360-1506; Century City Mall ⓣ310/551-0090; and Hollywood & Highland mall ⓣ323/962-6216.

Prada 343 N Rodeo Drive, Beverly Hills ⓣ310/278-8661. Ultra-chic couturier attracting clients who don't bat an eyelash at paying thousands for a shirt.

Ralph Lauren 444 N Rodeo Drive, Beverly Hills ⓣ310/281-7200. The top place to get yourself outfitted to resemble a member of the English gentry. Pick up a gilded walking cane, finely tailored suit and a smart tweed cap, all for a small fortune. Also at 141 N Robertson Blvd ☎310/274-0171 and in Malibu at 3835 Cross Creek Rd ☎310/317-9414.

St. John 9536 Wilshire Blvd, Beverly Hills ☎310/858-1116. Chock full of elite women's power outfits for crushing the competition at a corporate meeting, or for dining in smart luxury at an exclusive restaurant. Several other area locations.

Designer boutiques

Betsey Johnson 8050 Melrose Ave, West Hollywood ☎323/852-1534. An upscale boutique where micro-miniskirts, flirty tops and girly handbags are all part of a funky look, for which you'll pay plenty. Other branches in the Sherman Oaks Fashion Square ☎818/986-9810 and in Canoga Park at 6600 Topanga Canyon Blvd ☎818/992-6190.

Diavolina 8471 W Third St, Mid-Wilshire ☎310/550-1341. Shoes in which you can really strike a "little devil" pose: killer stilettos, modest mules and funky boots, priced anywhere from around $100 to well over $500.

Fred Segal 8118 Melrose Ave, West Hollywood ☎323/651-1935. Melrose complex selling everything from stylish shoes and duds to cosmetics, which provides just the right mix of designer gloss and funky edge. Also with several other citywide branches.

Giselle 1306 Montana Ave, Santa Monica ☎310/451-2140. Well-made designer women's clothing in a variety of styles, but with a strong emphasis on wispy, pre-Raphaelite designs for size-2 waifs.

Jimmy Choo 240 N Rodeo Drive, Beverly Hills ☎310/860-9045. Even if you're just looking, and can't afford the exorbitant prices, there are enough strappy sandals and slender boots to give you warm memories on your trip home. Also in Canoga Park at 6600 Topanga Canyon Blvd ☎818/340-7221.

Lisa Kline 143 S Robertson Blvd ☎310/385-7113. If you want to dress on the leading edge of trendiness (in clothes that may be out of date by the time you fly home), this is the place to come, with an array of high-end denim jeans, among other women's garments. Also a branch for kidswear at 123 S Robertson Blvd ☎310/247-0488.

Maxfield 8825 Melrose Ave, West Hollywood ☎310/274-8800. One of LA's most exclusive boutiques, displaying pricey classic and modern antiques, expensive dresses and baubles, various books and an eye-popping array of jewellery. Also in Beverly Hills at 301 N Canon Drive ☎310/275-7007 and in Malibu at 3939 Cross Creek Rd ☎310/270-9009.

Paper Bag Princess 8818 Olympic Blvd, West LA ☎310/385-9036. A cross between an elite boutique and a secondhand store: an upscale dealer in gently worn vintage designer fashions. Some items on the racks are on consignment from celebrities (who allegedly frequent the place).

Veronica M 7122 Beverly Blvd, north of Mid-Wilshire ☎323/936-3802. Tasteful boutique with a smart selection of women's attire and jewellery, a bit more affordable than at comparable designer stores around town. Four other LA-area locations.

Funky clothing

Agent Provocateur 7961 Melrose Ave, West Hollywood ☎323/653-0229. If Victorian-style knickers and tasteful, yet racy, boudoir skimpies are what you're seeking, this is the spot. LA's own, quirkier spin on Victoria's Secret, with a lot more spark and imagination.

Frederick's of Hollywood 6751 Hollywood Blvd, Hollywood ☎323/957-5953. Offers a panoply of frilly, lacy and leathery lingerie (prices vary). Many other branches in and around LA; this one moved from its original, legendary location a block away.

Ipso Facto 517 N Harbor Blvd, Fullerton ☎714/525-7865. Piercing supplies for serious punks, ultra-black goth clothing and a full range of skull-emblazoned belts, rings and boots at this retailer in, of all places, Orange County.

Necromance 7220 Melrose Ave, north of Mid-Wilshire ☎323/934-8684. Try on the latest ghoulish clothing at this morbidly themed shop, which sells coffin ornaments, tarot cards and goth fashions that can make you look like a spooky spectre in no time.

Panty Raid 1953 Hillhurst Ave, Silver Lake ☎323/668-1888. One of LA's best spots for affordable and inventive styles of lingerie and, of course, underwear, with provocative g-strings, push-up bras and the like.

Trashy Lingerie 402 N La Cienega Blvd, West Hollywood ☎310/652-4543. Not only can you find the sort of undergarments you'd expect, you can also browse through a wide selection of more traditional satin and silk bras, teddies and bustiers. All of the revealing items are handmade, and you'll have to pay a $5 annual "membership fee" to get in.

Uncle Jer's 4459 Sunset Blvd, Silver Lake ☎323/662-6710. Quirky shop crammed with colourful and inexpensive garments, much of it handmade, along with soaps and fragrances, incense and "magic potions", and assorted trinkets.

Secondhand and vintage clothing

American Rag Cie 150 S La Brea Ave, Mid-Wilshire ☎323/935-3154. Not your typical secondhand clothing store; the beat-up denim jackets, floral-print dresses and retro shoes here are often high-end designer material, sometimes restyled into new forms. This is among the most prominent of LA's vintage dealers, so be prepared to shell out.

Decades 8214 Melrose Ave, West Hollywood ☎323/655-0223. Sells elegant designer wear, but also offers expensive retro-clothes from the 1960s, with occasional detours into stylish 1950s apparel and ungainly 1970s jumpsuits.

Golyester 136 S La Brea Ave, Mid-Wilshire ☎323/931-1339. Very vintage materials, with clothes dating as far back as the nineteenth century, in every sort of fabric imaginable. Also sells antiques.

It's a Wrap 1164 S Robertson Blvd, Mid-Wilshire ☎310/246-WRAP. Fascinating place to buy garments and wardrobes from recent movies and TV shows. The prices aren't too cheap, but if you can't go another minute without owning a jacket worn by one of the Desperate Housewives, this store is for you. Also at 3315 W Magnolia Blvd, Burbank ☎818/567-7366.

Jet Rag 825 N La Brea Ave, Hollywood ☎323/939-0528. Vintage dealer selling stylish club jackets from the old Hollywood days, as well as all kinds of bargains on dresses, hats, accessories and plenty more — sometimes for as little as $1 per item.

Ozzie Dots 4637 Hollywood Blvd, Los Feliz ☎323/663-2867. A vintage store that's best known for its costumes, but that also has colourful and eye-catching 1930s-through-1970s attire – plus props and accessories like feather boas, Tiki cuff links and soda-jerk hats.

Polkadots and Moonbeams 8367 W Third St, Mid-Wilshire ☎323/651-1746. Dresses, swimsuits and sweaters from the pre-1970s era, most in fine condition and some quite affordable. If it's more modern clothing you crave, drift down to the pricier contemporary outlet at 8381 W Third St ☎323/655-3880.

Re-Mix 7605 1/2 Beverly Blvd, Mid-Wilshire ☎323/936-6210. Stylish men's and women's shoes, from the dainty 1920s to the supper-club 1940s to the disco 1970s, many of them authentic (some reproduction) and none of them ever worn before.

SquaresVille 1800 N Vermont Ave, Los Feliz ☎323/669-8464. A bit off the beaten vintage path, but worth a trip for its cheap prices for mainly 1950s-through-1980s wear and colourful jewellery and accessories – plus a good selection of holiday (Halloween) wear during the season.

Wasteland 7428 Melrose Ave, north of Mid-Wilshire ☎323/653-3028. Solid vintage and used designer wear with a wide price range. Not the flashiest store on the block, but one of the more reliable vendors on this busy strip. Three other LA-area locations.

The Way We Wore 334 S La Brea Ave, Mid-Wilshire ☎323/937-0878. One of the best of the vintage clothiers in LA, stocking expensive dresses and shoes and other garments from the 1920s to the 80s, with classic shifts from Valentino and other name designers.

Spas and beauty services

As the capital of personal transformation, LA has a large array of **hair** and **make-up salons** where you can be teased, sprayed, plucked and painted. Cheap clip joints are everywhere, but if you're really looking to get a fancy makeover, or a massage, manicure or pedicure, head for one of the top-notch **spas** and salons around town, or to a more affordable but smart spot.

Ball Beauty Supply 416 N Fairfax Ave, north of Mid-Wilshire ☎323/655-2330. A great storehouse for inexpensive make-up, wigs and other adornments, where the clientele is a mix of youthful male and female club-hoppers and old-timers who've been coming here for ages.

Beauty Bar 1638 N Cahuenga Blvd, Hollywood ☎323/464-7676. A fun watering hole where you can pick from an array of beauty services at affordable prices – plus chill out with a neon-coloured alcoholic concoction. See also p.248.

Goodform 725 N Fairfax Ave, West Hollywood ☎323/658-8585. Whether you're primping for a night of clubbing or a power lunch, this colourful parlour will do the trick, using a variety of hair-styling and makeover techniques, along with more straightforward skin care and manicures.

Jessica's Nail Clinic 8627 Sunset Blvd, West Hollywood ☎310/659-9292. The place where the stars get their pedicures and manicures, and you can too. The occasional celebrity-peeping provides a small distraction.

Larchmont Beauty Center 208 N Larchmont Blvd, Mid-Wilshire ☎323/461-0162. Features a comprehensive – and pricey – assortment of bath products and beauty-care treatments, from hair styling, manicures and pedicures, makeovers and skin care to massage and aromatherapy.

Le Pink & Co. 3820 Sunset Blvd, Silver Lake ☎323/661-7465. Cosmetics and skin-care products as well as various lotions, creams and bath items are the draw at this vendor of fine beauty supplies.

Ona Spa 7373 Beverly Blvd, north of mid-Wilshire ☎323/931-4442. Chic spa with a trendy atmosphere and a vaguely Asian-inspired design, and such options as vitality and detox treatments for those in need of soul- as well as body-cleansing.

Robinson's Beautilities 12320 Venice Blvd, West LA ☎310/398-5757. Along with a good selection of hair-care products and cosmetics, this supply house stocks a fascinating assortment of designer and fright wigs, facial glitter and special-effects make-up for the movie biz.

Taka 2010 Sawtelle Blvd, West LA ☎310/575-6819. Hair styling with an Asian flair and a sharp modern edge that won't cost you a fortune (if it isn't entirely cheap, either), offering a full range of perms, cuts, weaves, straightenings, kinks and anything else you can dream up.

Umberto 416 N Canon Drive, Beverly Hills ☎310/274-6395. Another celebrity-friendly locale, with steep prices, but not quite as much pretension as some of its neighbours. While you wait, eat a sandwich, or sip a cappuccino from the in-house food service.

Vidal Sassoon 9403 Little Santa Monica Blvd, Beverly Hills ☎310/274-8791. While the full-price haircuts may seem out of reach, assistants in training charge roughly half – a very good deal considering the area. Cosmetology students can also tinker with your looks for much less at Vidal Sassoon's own "hair academy", located at 321 Santa Monica Blvd, Santa Monica ☎310/255-0011.

Food and drink

Since it's a matter of course to eat out in LA, you may never have to shop for **food** and **drink** at all. But if you're preparing a picnic, or want to indulge in a bit of home cooking, there are plenty of places to stock up. **Delis** and **groceries** can be found on many street corners. There are also a number of good **ethnic groceries** and **health-food stores**, as well as various fine **bakeries**, mainly clustered in West LA.

Delis and groceries

Art's Deli 12224 Ventura Blvd, Studio City ☎818/762-1221. Long-standing film-industry favourite, and the one deli that rarely provokes complaints among aficionados, providing a good range of sandwiches, soups and breads.

Brent's Deli 19565 Parthenia Ave, Northridge ☎818/886-5679. This New York-style deli, in a minimall in a remote corner of the San Fernando Valley, features a huge takeout selection of meat, fish, desserts, salads and sandwiches. The best of its kind in the Valley, or even in LA itself.

Bristol Farms 7880 W Sunset Blvd, Hollywood ☎323/874-6301. One of the region's best grocers, with delicious meats, cheeses, wine and caviar, but prices can be rather high. Still, a cut way above the standard gourmet supermarkets. Eight other citywide locations.

Canter's Deli 419 N Fairfax Ave, north of Mid-Wilshire ☎323/651-2030. An LA institution, next to its own unusual nightclub (see p.257), with tasty sandwiches, kosher soups, a good selection of meat and fish, and assorted sweets. Open 24 hrs.

Grand Central Market 317 S Broadway, Downtown ☎213/624-2378. One of the city's prime culinary destinations, with prime Mexican food, a warren of food stalls and vendors of all sorts of produce, meat, cheese, snacks and pastries from the region.

Izzy's Deli 1433 Wilshire Blvd, Santa Monica ☎310/394-1131. Long-standing favourite for straightforward deli fare, and one of the few good bets for authentic deli sandwiches along the coast. Open 24 hrs.

Jerry's Famous Deli 8701 Beverly Blvd, West Hollywood ☎310/289-1811. Not as good as other delis around town, but this local does sport a solid array of takeout soups, sandwiches and meats, as well as cakes and pies. Plus it's open 24 hrs, as is the one in Studio City at 12711 Ventura Blvd ☎818/980-4245. Many more (non-24hr) branches in LA.

Junior's 2379 Westwood Blvd, West LA ☎310/475-5771. This fine Westside deli and restaurant features a good bakery and deli counter that stocks all of the usual favourites – including lox, whitefish, matzo ball soup and various egg dishes.

Langer's 704 S Alvarado St, Mid-Wilshire ☎213/483-8050. One of LA's finest delis, with an excellent selection of takeout meats and baked goods, and twenty variations on LA's best (and most tender) pastrami sandwich. Closes at 4pm; curbside pickup available.

Nate 'n' Al's 414 N Beverly Drive, Beverly Hills ☎310/274-0101. This superior deli, in the middle of Beverly Hills' Golden Triangle, offers stargazing and a good array of meat and bread food stuffs – not to mention terrific blintzes, lox and matzo-ball soup. See also p.225.

Stan's Produce 9307 W Pico Blvd, West LA ☎310/274-1865. A popular neighbourhood grocer with a fine selection of fruits, vegetables and exotic produce. Just south of Beverly Hills.

Vicente Foods 12027 San Vicente Blvd, Brentwood ☎310/472-4613. If you're in this upscale neighbourhood, this is a good place to stop for a terrific selection of breads, cheeses and meats to suit your fancy; worth the high prices.

Ethnic groceries

Alpine Village 833 W Torrance Blvd, Torrance ☎310/327-4384. Though quite a hike from LA, and in a rather drab South Bay area, this place has all the bratwurst and schnitzel you'll ever need, and plays host to one of LA's more spirited Oktoberfest celebrations (see p.286).

American Armenian Grocery 1442 E Washington Blvd, Pasadena ☎626/794-9220. The place to come if you want to sample authentic food from the Caucasus region of Asia: scrumptious baked goods, cold cuts, pastries, nuts and spices, produce and chocolates.

Bang Luck Market 5170 Hollywood Blvd, Hollywood ☎323/660-8000. Located in "Thai Town", a Thai grocer in Los Feliz with super-cheap prices on meat, fish, sauces and noodles to help you make a Southeast Asian feast, or a simple snack.

Bay Cities Italian Deli 1517 Lincoln Blvd, Santa Monica ☎310/395-8279. An excellent, centrally located deli and retailer with an Italian focus. Offers piles of fresh pasta, meat, homemade pasta, spices and sauces, along with many imports, desserts, espresso and terrific lunchtime sandwiches.

Claro's Italian Market 1003 E Valley Blvd, San Gabriel ☎626/288-2026. This compact but well-stocked spot has everything from Italian wines, chocolate and crackers to frozen meals, plus a deli and a bakery offering many varieties of cookies. Five other citywide locations, mostly in the San Gabriel Valley.

Elat Meat Market 8730 Pico Blvd, West LA ☎310/659-7070. Mainly Persian and other Middle Eastern staples at cheap prices at this colourful kosher market, located near other ethnic grocers on Pico Blvd, just southeast of Beverly Hills.

Jeff's Gourmet Kosher Sausage Factory 8930 W Pico Blvd, West LA ☎310/858-8590. Despite the unassuming name, a top-notch vendor of well-crafted sausages, from merguez to jalapeno to Polish to veal bratwurst and Cajun chicken.

Marconda's in the Farmers Market, 6333 W Third St, Mid-Wilshire ☎323/938-5131. Longstanding favourite for its variety of excellent fresh-cut meats at affordable prices, including ribs, chops, steaks, lamb shanks and more daring items like oxtail and tripe.

Market World 3030 W Sepulveda Blvd, Torrance ☎310/539-8899. A good selection of prepared Korean and pan-Asian meats, vegetables and noodles at this South Bay grocery.

Nijiya Market 2130 Sawtelle Blvd, West LA ☎310/575-3300. Soups, sushi and bentos – rice-and-meat combos served in a bowl – are among the succulent takeout items available at this wide-ranging Japanese grocer. Part of a local chain, mainly based in the suburbs.

Olson's Deli 5560 Pico Blvd, Mid-Wilshire ☎323/938-0742. Herring, meatballs and assorted sausages at this solid Swedish grocer, one of the few Scandinavian food stores in LA and definitely worth a try.

Samosa House 11510 Washington Blvd, Culver City ☎310/398-6766. One of several excellent Indian grocers around this stretch of Culver City, providing some savory samosas and all the goods for making your own curries and vindaloo.

Thailand Plaza 5321 Hollywood Blvd, Hollywood ☎323/993-9000. This Thai supermarket and eatery has an impressive selection of Southeast Asian noodles, seafood, spices and other delicacies for very cheap prices.

Vallarta Supermarket 10950 Sherman Way, Burbank ☎818/846-1717. San Fernando Valley chain focusing on foodstuffs from Latin America, including special chilis and spices, with an on-site *taqueria* that doles out some delicious and inexpensive food.

Health-food stores

Beverly Hills Juice 8382 Beverly Blvd, north of Mid-Wilshire ☎323/655-8300. Raw foods are the focus of this vegan-oriented takeout vendor and grocery, which supplies fruit, veggies, meatless sushi, sprout rolls and, of course, ultra-healthy juices.

Co-Opportunity 1525 Broadway, Santa Monica ☎310/451-8902. A popular neighbourhood store selling bulk organic and vegetarian foods, with a coffee and juice bar, plenty of macrobiotic and other speciality foodstuffs and herbs, vitamins and oils meant to soothe the body and soul.

Erewhon 7660 Beverly Blvd, north of Mid-Wilshire ☎323/937-0777. Health-food supermarket that's the epitome of health-obsessed LA, selling pricey macrobiotic food, lots of vegetarian offerings and all the wheat grass you can stand.

Full o' Life 2515 W Magnolia Blvd, Burbank ☎818/845-8343. This mother of all health-food stores dates back to 1959 and offers an organic market, deli, dairy, restaurant and book department and there are nutritionists and a naturopath on the premises daily.

Mother's Market 225 E 17th St, Costa Mesa ☎949/631-4741. A large health-food retailer in Orange County, the perfect place to stock up on bulk juice, vitamins, veggie cuisine and even animal-friendly beauty supplies, with a nice deli and cafe on premises, too. Several other countywide locations.

Nature Mart 2080 Hillhurst Ave, Hollywood ☎323/660-0052. A Los Feliz storehouse for organic produce, non-sugary sweets, veggie options, hair and skin-care items and a wealth of vitamins and herbs. Somewhat cheaper than comparable Westside retailers.

One Life 3001 Main St, Santa Monica ☎310/392-4501. Healthy eating courtesy of this neighbourhood grocer that sells organic produce, bulk foods, herbs, brown rice and all the rest.

Simply Wholesome 4508 W Slauson Ave, South Central ☎323/294-2144. An agreeable health-food shop with juices, smoothies and nutritious products, with an on-site cafe for dining on soul food and veggie fare with a Caribbean flair.

VP Discount Health Food Mart 8001 Beverly Blvd, north of Mid-Wilshire ☎323/658-6506. A reliable chain retailer that has a following of hard-core vegans willing to pay a bit more for clean, sanctified food.

Bakeries

Beverlywood Bakery 9128 Pico Blvd, West LA ☎310/278-0122. Longstanding vendor of Old World desserts and baked goods, from dense strudels to chewy, thick-crusted breads, with premium prices that reflect the store's proximity to Beverly Hills, a block north.

Diamond Bakery 335 N Fairfax Ave, north of Mid-Wilshire ☎323/655-0534. In the heart of the Fairfax District, this grand old Jewish bakery makes traditional favourites, including great bagels, babka, challah, mandelbrot and rugelach, and a legendary pumpernickel bread.

Doughboys Café and Bakery 8136 W Third St, Mid-Wilshire ☎323/852-1020. Tasty pizzas, pancakes, scones and sandwiches are available for midday meals, but the real highlight of this Westside bakery is the bread: rich, hearty loaves with interesting ingredients like walnuts, olives and various cheeses.

Gourmet Cobbler Factory 33 N Catalina Ave, Pasadena ☎626/795-1005. Bakery selling a range of yummy, fruity cobblers, from blackberry and other berry flavours, to apple and peach, to pecan and sweet potato. Occupies a prime spot near Old Pasadena.

La Brea Bakery 624 S La Brea Ave, Mid-Wilshire ☎323/939-6813. This bakery (adjacent to the upscale *Campanile* restaurant; see p.231) is a serious treat for anyone with an interest in fine breads, from sourdough rolls to fancier olive- and raisin-laden loaves, as well as scrumptious cookies, tarts and cheeses.

Mäni's Bakery 519 S Fairfax Ave, Mid-Wilshire ☎323/938-8800. This vegetarian- and vegan-oriented bakery provides sugarless brownies and meatless sandwiches to local bohemians and wholefood-oriented yuppies.

Mousse Fantasy/Beard Papa's 2130 Sawtelle Blvd #110, West LA ☎310/479-6665. Pair of combined patisseries featuring a range of tasty tarts and pastries, highlighted by the eclairs, cream puffs and various mousses and cakes.

Portos Bakery 315 N Brand Blvd, Glendale ☎818/956-5996. In a town that used to be filled with Cuban immigrants, this great throwback to the old days offers tasty baked goods and desserts, along with flaky Cuban pastries, cheesecakes soaked in rum, muffins, Danishes, croissants and tortes.

Röckenwagner 12835 W Washington Blvd, Culver City ☎310/578-8171. A Westside culinary delight that offers chocolate desserts, rich pastries and scones, doughnuts, rolls and hearty breads like the signature pretzel bread. No credit cards. Also near the Third Street Promenade in Santa Monica at 311 Arizona Ave ☎310/394-4267.

Viktor Benes Continental Pastries 13455 Maxella Ave, Marina del Rey ☎310/578-6553. The place to go for freshly baked bread, coffee cakes, Danish pastries and chocolaty treats, and appreciative local fans know it. Many other area locations as well.

Ice cream and dairy

Al Gelato 806 S Robertson Blvd, West LA ☎310/659-8069. Delicious *gelato* flavours doled out in sizable helpings. The espresso *gelato* is particularly mouthwatering. Also offering Italian-styled soups and sandwiches.

The Cheese Store of Beverly Hills 419 N Beverly Drive, Beverly Hills ☎1-800/547-1515 or 310/278-2855. More than four hundred types of cheese from the US and all over the world – some suspended invitingly overhead; prices can be equally out of reach.

Fair Oaks Pharmacy and Soda Fountain 1526 Mission St, South Pasadena ☎626/799-1414. A fabulously restored soda fountain along the former Route 66, with many classic soda drinks, such as egg creams and old-fashioned ice-cream treats like sundaes and banana splits.

Fosselman's 1824 W Main St, Alhambra ☎626/282-6533. Reason alone to visit this San Gabriel Valley town: what many, many Angelenos regard as the region's best ice cream. The very long-standing (91 years) shop churns out rich, creamy concoctions, highlighted by a delicious macadamia crunch and burgundy cherry.

Say Cheese 2800 Hyperion Ave, Silver Lake ☎323/665-0545. A distinctive array of French and other international cheeses, priced from moderate to expensive. The delicious sandwiches may be your best bet.

Scoops 712 N Heliotrope Drive, north of Mid-Wilshire ☎323/906-2649. Located right off the freeway in a drab location, a terrific place to sample inventive, unexpected ice-cream flavours for cheap prices. Everything from pumpkin brandy to lychee to brown bread (!) may tempt your tongue if you let it.

Beer, wine and spirits

Greenblatt's Deli & Fine Wine 8017 Sunset Blvd, West Hollywood ☎323/656-0606. A Sunset Strip kosher deli and liquor mart that's a neighbourhood favourite, best known for its excellent sandwiches and wide assortment of wine, brandy, Champagne and Scotch. Open 'til 2am.

Hi-Time Wine Cellars 250 Ogle St, Costa Mesa ☎949/650-8463 or 1-800/331-3005. Despite the unimpressive name, this has been one of Southern California's finest purveyors of wine and spirits for fifty years, and perhaps its best overall choice for buying micro-brewed and European beers.

Red Carpet Wine 400 E Glenoaks Blvd, Glendale ⓣ818/247-5544 or 1-800/339-0609. Besides having a comfortable wine bar and a sizable stock of vino and beer, this store is also a fine, upscale spot to purchase spirits, cigars, Champagne and chocolates.

Silver Lake Wine 2395 Glendale Blvd ⓣ323/662-9024. Favourite Hollywood vino vendor that has a wealth of regional brands, including some obscure ones, which you can sample during regular Sunday wine tastings at 3pm, with other primo tastings on Mondays and Thursdays at 5pm.

Valley Beverage Company 14901 Ventura Blvd, Sherman Oaks ⓣ818/981-1566. Offering an excellent selection of California and international wines, many at discounted prices, with a special emphasis on kosher wines, Scotch, tequila and brandy.

Wally's 2107 Westwood Blvd, West LA ⓣ310/475-0606. A gourmet grocery that has a good assortment of international wines and beers, plus caviar, cheeses and other fancy treats; sells hard liquor and cigars, too.

Wine and Liquor Depot 16938 Saticoy St, Van Nuys ⓣ818/996-1414. Promising the lowest area prices on blended and single malt Scotch, this Valley dealer is also worth a look for its international wines, port, sherry, bourbon and beer.

Bookstores

Due to the rise of the internet and general declines in US readership, LA's **bookstores**, like those of other cities, have been in trouble in recent years. The chains stores and other major players in town (namely, Book Soup) have ridden out the lean years well, but others haven't done so well – going out of business in a matter of weeks, sometimes with little notice. What follows are the best of the surviving bookshops in LA.

General interest and new books

Book Soup 8818 W Sunset Blvd, West Hollywood ⓣ310/659-3110. Great selection, right on Sunset Strip. Narrow, winding aisles stuffed with books, strong in art, entertainment, travel, politics and photography. Celebs are sometimes known to drop by, attempting to look studious.

Bookstar 12136 Ventura Blvd, Studio City ⓣ818/505-9528. Connected to the Barnes & Noble chain, with countless other branches, this shop appeals for its setting in a converted old movie theatre and its discounts on new books and a slew of bargain volumes on a broad array of topics.

The Last Bookstore 400 S Main St, Downtown ⓣ213/617-0308. With a convenient location in the Old Bank District, this bookseller appeals for its broad selection and discounted prices on new books, many of them overstock, markdowns, etc, but consistently good and well chosen.

Metropolis Books 440 S Main St, Downtown ⓣ213/612-0174. A smallish shop that nonetheless has a smart selection of classics, nonfiction and contemporary fiction – some of it written by local authors, who appear regularly for readings and literary discussions.

Skylight Books 1818 N Vermont Ave, Hollywood ⓣ323/660-1175. Just north of Barnsdall Park in a trendy shopping zone, this Los Feliz bookseller has a broad range of mainstream and alternative literature, plus a fine selection of film books and regularly scheduled author readings.

Small World Books 1407 Ocean Front Walk, Venice ⓣ310/399-2360. A modest neighbourhood dealer by the beach that's strong on mystery novels and literature from local and national authors, including publications from small presses.

Vroman's 695 E Colorado Blvd, Pasadena ⓣ1-800/769-2665 or 626/449-5320. One of the San Gabriel Valley's major retailers, offering a good selection and a café. Although there are no real bargains here, smaller bookstores selling used and specialist books can be found within a few blocks.

Secondhand books

Alias Books 1650 Sawtelle Blvd, West LA ⓣ310/473-4442. Not the hugest or cheapest selection of used titles in town, but among the most carefully chosen, with strengths in scholarly titles, art, architecture, textbooks, comics and rare items.

Berkelouw Books 830 N Highland Ave, Hollywood ☎323/466-3321. An easy-to-miss dealer with voluminous stacks of titles in fiction, biography, entertainment and history – plus a knowledgeable owner who'll be glad to help you sift through his well-chosen collection.

Book Alley 1252 E Colorado Blvd, Pasadena ☎626/683-8083. A handsomely designed bookstore with a large stock of affordable used books on a wide variety of subjects.

Brand Book Shop 231 N Brand Blvd, Glendale ☎818/507-5943. Excellent Valley used-book seller with a huge range of liberal-arts titles and particular strengths in entertainment, history and politics. Located in the pulsing heart of downtown Glendale.

Cliff's Books 630 E Colorado Blvd, Pasadena ☎626/449-9541. This long-standing used-bookseller, with narrow aisles stacked with titles on a wide assortment of subjects, has a bigger selection than some other bookstores in the vicinity, with slightly higher prices as well.

Cosmopolitan Book Shop 7017 Melrose Ave, north of Mid-Wilshire ☎323/938-7119. Westside dealer loaded with thousands of titles stacked high in oversized bookcases, on a variety of subjects but especially strong on film and media.

Iliad Bookshop 5400 Cahuenga Blvd, San Fernando Valley ☎818/509-2665. Easily one of LA's best used booksellers, and meriting a trip out to North Hollywood. Features a broad selection of affordable titles, including some you probably won't find anywhere else.

Specialist bookstores

Arcana 1229 Third Street Promenade, Santa Monica ☎310/458-1499. Among the very last independent holdouts in the face of corporate chain store takeover of this strip, this is a fine place to choose from a nicely curated array of art books, with a particular strength in photography.

Circus of Books 4001 Sunset Blvd, Silver Lake ☎323/666-1304. Take a trip through LA's seamier side at this well-known (mainly magazine) dealer in weird murder tales, serial-killer exposés, S/M diaries and assorted pornography. Also a more gay-oriented branch at 8230 Santa Monica Blvd, West Hollywood ☎323/656-6533.

Distant Lands 56 S Raymond Ave, Pasadena ☎626/449-3220. Well-stocked travel bookstore in Old Pasadena, with some fairly hard to find titles, as well as maps and travel gear. Also hosts the occasional public speaker and globe-trotting slide show.

Geographia 4000 Riverside Drive, Burbank ☎818/848-1414. Solid San Fernando Valley choice for an array of travel titles, from the basic guides to detailed maps and other publications.

Hennessey and Ingalls 214 Wilshire Blvd, Santa Monica ☎310/458-9074. An impressive range of coffee-table art and architecture books makes this bookstore among the best of its kind in LA. Rare posters, catalogues and hard to find books are also in stock. Also in Hollywood at 1520 N Cahuenga Blvd ☎323/466-1256.

Hollywood Book and Poster Co. 6562 Hollywood Blvd, Hollywood ☎323/465-8764. A great place to stop if you're hunting for any kind of media memorabilia, including film stills of famous and obscure actors, books on "psychotronic" cinema and TV history, various screenplays and, of course, splashy old movie posters.

Larry Edmunds Book Shop 6644 Hollywood Blvd, Hollywood ☎323/463-3273. Many stacks of books, a large number of them out of print, are offered on every aspect of film and theatre, with movie stills and posters. Located at the centre of touristy Hollywood.

Norton Simon Museum Bookstore 411 W Colorado Blvd, Pasadena ☎626/449-6840. One of LA's better museum bookstores, with a superb stock of material – often with sizeable volumes on artists in the museum's collection.

Psychic Eye 13435 Ventura Blvd, Sherman Oaks ☎818/906-8263. Small chain of book shops focusing on New Age and occult topics, including astrology and Wicca, plus various candles, tools and oils for sale. Psychics give personal on-site readings ($20+).

Samuel French Theatre & Film Bookshop 7623 Sunset Blvd, Hollywood ☎323/876-0570. LA's broadest selection of theatre books is found in this local institution, along with a good collection of movie and media-related titles.

Taschen 354 N Beverly Drive, Beverly Hills ☎310/274-4300. Fun, edifying and weird titles that focus on everything from

Renaissance art to kitsch Americana to fetish photography. Cheap volumes on both familiar and obscure subjects, and even the coffee-table books are occasionally affordable. Also right outside the Farmers Market, 6333 W Third St, Mid-Wilshire ☎323/931-1168.

Traveler's Bookcase 8375 W Third St, Mid-Wilshire ☎323/655-0575. A bookseller with a limited but well-chosen selection of travel guides, maps and publications, along with a fine array of literary travel stories, novels, trip diaries and personal memoirs and essays.

Wacko 4633 Hollywood Blvd, Hollywood ☎323/663-0122. Although also great for its eclectic gift selection, this East Hollywood favourite stocks an excellent array of titles leaning toward the alternative: art and architecture, bizarre fetishes, alternative history, music guides and conspiracy theories and assorted rants.

Music stores

As elsewhere, many **record stores** have closed in LA in recent years due to competition from the internet and dysfunction in the music industry. While CDs are the dominant format, vinyl fans will be happy to find LPs here and there, thanks in equal parts to diehard collectors and club DJs. The selection below leans toward LA's better independent record stores.

Amoeba Music 6400 W Sunset Blvd, Hollywood ☎323/245-6400. Arguably the greatest record store in Southern California, featuring a vast selection of titles – supposedly numbering around half a million – on CD, tape and vinyl, which you can freely hear at listening carrels throughout the store. Also hosts occasional in-store live music.

Atomic Records 3812 W Magnolia Blvd, Burbank ☎818/848-7090. Retro-flavoured rock and a full complement of jazz are the focus at this primo dealer of CDs and vintage LPs and 45s, some of which are rare (and pricey) and others nicely affordable.

Backside Records 139 N San Fernando Rd, Burbank ☎818/559-7573. Though oriented toward DJs and the vinyl-minded, this store stocks both LPs and CDs with a broad range of electronica, plus some jazz, rap and soul. Also has a wide selection of apparel for young dudes and others.

Canterbury Records 805 E Colorado Blvd, Pasadena ☎626/792-7184. Classical and jazz of all stripes are the focus at this independent CD, DVD and vinyl seller of new and used music. Located near Vroman's Books.

Counterpoint 5911 Franklin Ave, Hollywood ☎323/957-7965. Although not the highest-profile dealer in town, it has a terrific smorgasbord of used vinyl, CDs, movies on cassette and DVD, books and even antique 78 records. Also connected to its own underground art gallery.

Fingerprints 4612 E Second St, Long Beach ☎562/433-4996. A formidable indie outfit in the South Bay, offering alternative-leaning CDs and vinyl, plus in-store performances from local rockers, and a mellow, soft-sell attitude. Located in the Belmont Shore district.

Freakbeat Records 13616 Ventura Blvd, Sherman Oaks ☎818/995-7603. One of the Valley's biggest dealers in CDs and vinyl. The store has plenty to browse over (and listen to), from vintage 1960s surf pioneers to latter-day punk nihilists, with cheap prices, too.

Headline Records 7706 Melrose Ave, Hollywood ☎323/655-2125. The last gasp of grungy old Melrose, this book, T-shirt and record joint is oriented toward all things punk, from proto-punk 1960s garage kings to latter-day thrashers and pogoers, with current CDs and hard to find vinyl rarities.

Origami 1816 W Sunset Blvd ☎213/413-3030. Small indie shop in Echo Park that appeals for its well-selected (if limited) selection of LPs, but mainly for getting a sense of the latest tunes from local LA talent, many of whom reside in the neighbourhood.

Orphaned CDs 8830 Reseda Blvd, Northridge ☎818/709-9100. Broad selection of all kinds of used CDs, good and bad, for some of the city's cheapest prices.

Poo-Bah Records 2636 E Colorado Blvd, Pasadena ☎626/449-3359. Plenty of American and imported sounds, along with 1980s technopop and many other genres.

Sometimes hosts in-store performances from local artists.

Record Surplus 11609 W Pico Blvd, West LA ☎310/478-4217. A massive LP collection of surf music, early Rock 'n' Roll, 1960s soundtracks, freakish spoken-word recordings and all manner of assorted junk you strangely want to own. Prices are excellent, with many items offered at very low prices. Anyone with an interest in classic, alternative or offbeat music knows this place.

Rockaway Records 2395 Glendale Blvd, Silver Lake ☎323/664-3232. Great place to come for used CDs and LPs, as well as DVDs. Also offers old magazines, posters and memorabilia. Located just east of the Silver Lake reservoir.

Speciality stores

Though you can find plenty of oddball merchants in places like Silver Lake, Echo Park and parts of the Westside, the **speciality stores** below are some of the more colourful you'll find in LA.

Cinema Secrets Beauty Supply 4400 W Riverside Drive, Burbank ☎818/846-0579. If you're disappointed that Halloween only comes one day of the year, come to this emporium crammed with over-the-top glam and glitz — stage make-up, fake eyelashes, wigs, masks and other accessories, including effects make-up such as fake blood and scars.

Family 436 N Fairfax Ave, north of Mid-Wilshire ☎323/782-9221. Offbeat name is appropriate to the many bizarre items here: limited-edition surrealist art books and artworks, weird and little-known CDs and movies, various comics and zines and many freaky T-shirts.

Munky King 7308 Melrose Ave, Hollywood ☎323/938-0091. Like a throwback to the old Melrose, this alternative adult toy shop has a full range of curiosities from Asia and from home-grown artists – angry robots, jumping brains, plush perversities and freaky action figures are but a few of the (often pricey) visual delights you'll encounter here.

Noisy Toys 8728 S Sepulveda Blvd, Westchester, just north of LAX ☎310/670-9957. A cacophonous shrine to percussion, loaded with drums and other instruments from around the world, including zithers, rain sticks, bongos, maracas, castanets, wooden whistles, tambourines and didgeridoos. You can play around with the instruments before you buy.

Off the Wall 7325 Melrose Ave, north of Mid-Wilshire ☎323/930-1185. Appealing mid-twentieth-century antiques cleaned up and sold as high-priced goods, from Bakelite jewellery to Fiestaware dishes, as well as Art Deco furniture and vintage road signs.

Plastica 8405 W Third St, Mid-Wilshire ☎323/655-1051. A one-of-a-kind shrine to all things plastic: shoes, boots, shirts, tank-tops, spectacles and accessories, along with toys, jewellery, furniture, handbags, pillows and countless other cheap knick-knacks.

Pulp 452 S La Brea Ave, Mid-Wilshire ☎323/937-3505. Innovative stock of mostly affordable, only-in-LA gifts – from handcrafted stationery to arty gift cards and eco-friendly goods – makes this vendor a good spot to grab a paper souvenir.

ReForm School 3902 Sunset Blvd ☎323/906-8660. Local artists get a chance to show off at this excellent vendor of oddments for the home – limited-edition cards, stationery and books; pencils with wacky messages; handmade jewellery and accessories; and colourful posters are but a few of the eye-catching items here.

Show 1722 N Vermont Ave, Los Feliz ☎323/644-1960. Loaded with all kinds of clever, if pricey, home furnishings, lights and oddments. Stop by for a look at antler sconces, quirky jewellery and salt shakers shaped like bones, as well as a few more conventional items.

Skeletons in the Closet 1104 N Mission Rd, Downtown ☎323/343-0760. Believe it or not, this is the LA County Coroner Gift Shop, selling everything from skeleton-adorned beach towels and T-shirts to toe-tag key chains – a great place to buy unique LA merchandise.

Soda Pop Stop 5702 York Blvd, Highland Park ☎323/255-7115. Soda lovers can't go wrong at this pop emporium, which stocks everything from old favourites like egg cream and chocolate soda to more bizarre items like green-tea and "extreme" ginger colas, and "microbrewed goji berry" energy drink. Also has copious amounts of beer, when you tire of the sweet stuff.

Vidiots 302 Pico Blvd, Santa Monica ⓣ310/392-8508. Easily one of LA's best video stores, providing an excellent selection of classics and current flicks, but also a good range of cult and bizarre films, strange government propaganda and experimental art movies.

Wacko 4633 Hollywood Blvd, Hollywood ⓣ323/663-0122. The name says it all – freakish alternative comic books, odd-smelling candles, funky posters and toys and various subversive trinkets. Part of a complex that includes the Soap Plant, where, along with soap, you can find body creams, fragrant oils and bubble baths, and La Luz de Jesus Gallery for eye-opening modern art.

Y-Que Trading Post 1770 N Vermont Ave, Los Feliz ⓣ323/664-0021. All kinds of cheap but essential junk at this clearinghouse for oddities, including toy action figures, weird stickers and books, "Fight Club" soap and T-shirts with the latest messages to capture the LA zeitgeist.

Galleries

The Westside is the province of LA's top art **galleries** for painting, mixed-media, sculpture and, especially, photography. Indeed, snapping pictures is what a city based on the movie industry does best, and you're likely to find terrific retrospectives of the greats among the breakout shows of up-and-coming local shutterbugs. Many of the establishments below are among LA's bigger art houses, but by wandering through the right parts of Venice, Silver Lake and Downtown's northeast fringe, you can often find art that's just as interesting and much cheaper – long before it reaches the walls of the top-name galleries.

Armory Center for the Arts 145 N Raymond Ave, Pasadena ⓣ626/792-5101. Shows by young artists and retrospectives of local painters and photographers at this enjoyable spot, which also offers creative training and instruction. Located just north of Old Pasadena.

Ben Maltz Gallery 9045 Lincoln Blvd, Westchester ⓣ310/665-6905. Perhaps the most renowned of LA's university galleries, overseen by the Otis College of Art and Design. Presents broad-ranging shows by established names and rising locals, incorporating media from traditional to multimedia and video.

Beyond Baroque 681 Venice Blvd, Venice ⓣ310/822-3006. A gallery and art centre that's interesting and unpredictable, with a wide spectrum of fiction and poetry readings, and selected artworks. Also offers classes and expensive tours of LA murals.

Center for Land Use Interpretation 9331 Venice Blvd, Culver City ⓣ310/839-5722, ⓦwww.clui.org. Narrowly focused but fascinating museum/gallery that looks at land use from various angles, notably time-lapse photography, satellite images and evocative exhibits on mudslide catch basins, aviation graveyards and windswept eastern deserts.

DiRT Gallery 7906 Santa Monica Blvd #218, West Hollywood ⓣ323/822-9359. One of the better places on the Westside to discover the most cutting-edge artworks in a variety of media. Some works are compelling, some aren't for the faint of heart.

Fahey-Klein 148 N La Brea Ave, Mid-Wilshire ⓣ323/934-2250. One of LA's heavyweight institutions, featuring much contemporary work, especially black-and-white photography.

Gagosian Gallery 456 N Camden Drive, Beverly Hills ⓣ310/271-9400. A major name in LA art that occasionally shows big names (with big names in attendance for openings), and is housed in a memorable modern shed designed by Richard Meier. Prices in the stratosphere.

Gallery 825 825 N La Cienega Blvd, West Hollywood ⓣ310/652-8272. Affiliated with the Los Angeles Art Association, this long-standing space is devoted to ground-breaking exhibits by emerging artists and thoughtful career retrospectives, in a variety of media, including photography, installation and multimedia.

Gallery of Functional Art 2525 Michigan Ave, Santa Monica ⓣ310/829-6990. Noise-emitting clocks, ornamental wooden furniture and funky, Space Age wall sconces are for sale at this Bergamot Station gallery, where form and function mix with intriguing results.

Jan Kesner Gallery 164 N La Brea Ave, north of Mid-Wilshire ☎323/938-6834. This excellent and well-respected gallery features retrospectives of noted artists – most of them photographers – as well as openings by up-and-comers. By appointment only.

Judson Studios 200 S Ave 66, Highland Park ☎1-800/445-8376. A good place for checking out what's going on in Downtown's artsy northeastern fringe, heavy on contemporary stained glass as well as exhibitions in a variety of media. Located in USC's former art and architecture school.

Koplin Del Rio 6031 Washington Blvd, Culver City ☎310/836-9055. Elite art dealer specializing in etchings, sculptures, paintings and drawings, with an eye toward contemporary art from LA and focusing strongly on representational pieces.

La Luz de Jesus 4633 Hollywood Blvd, Hollywood ☎323/666-7667. Connected to the Wacko strange-gift emporium (see above), and sharing its taste for the bizarre, perverse, experimental and quirky in a variety of media, with high-ticket items but many affordable prints and posters.

Los Angeles Contemporary Exhibitions 6522 Hollywood Blvd, Hollywood ☎323/957-1777. Also known as LACE, this esteemed institution hosts a wide-ranging selection of mixed-media, painting, drawing, installation and video work, while its community-outreach events and programmes bring art to the masses.

Margo Leavin Gallery 812 N Robertson Blvd, West Hollywood ☎310/273-0603. This eclectic gallery is worth a look for its exhibitions of modern and postmodern stalwarts, from David Smith to John Baldessari and Donald Judd, and other noteworthy figures.

Robert Berman Gallery 2525 Michigan Ave, Santa Monica ☎310/315-1937. A solid Bergamot Station dealer of artworks in a variety of media, often postmodern, focusing on multimedia, photo retrospectives, group shows and conceptual pieces.

Rosamund Felsen Gallery 2525 Michigan Ave, Santa Monica ☎310/828-8488. One of the bigger names in Bergamot Station, featuring established Southern California artists and more recent arrivals. The eclectic selection is often striking, but the prices are always sky-high.

Susanne Vielmetter/Los Angeles Projects 6006 W. Washington Blvd, Culver City ☎323/837-2117. Compelling gallery showing contemporary artists, particularly those working in nontraditional media, installations and conceptualism, with a strong Southern California bent.

Track 16 2525 Michigan Ave, Bergamot Station, Santa Monica ☎310/264-4678. Politically oriented and subversive artworks tending toward mixed-media and assemblage, though you can also find traditional painted and sculpted works.

Southern California

Southern California

San Diego

Set around a gracefully curving bay, **SAN DIEGO** is relatively free from the smog and byzantine freeways famously found in Los Angeles, with many of its residents being affluent, libertarian and easygoing. Despite being the site of the first Spanish mission in the state, the city – the second most populous in California – only really took off with the arrival of the Santa Fe Railroad in the 1880s, and it has long been in the shadow of Los Angeles. During World War II, however, the US Navy made San Diego its Pacific Command Center, and the military, along with tourism, continues to dominate the local economy. Ultimately, with its long white beaches, sunny weather and bronzed bodies – which have given rise to the city's nickname, "Sandy Ego" – San Diego is like LA in miniature, though with a more manageable size and transportation system, and a tamer and more family-oriented vibe.

Arrival, information and transportation

Amtrak **trains** on the Pacific Surfliner route from LA use the Santa Fe Railroad Depot, close to the western end of Broadway at 1050 Kettner Boulevard (ⓣ1-800/872-7245), while the Greyhound **bus** terminal is six blocks east at Broadway and First Avenue (ⓣ619/239-6737). Lindbergh Field **airport** (aka San Diego International; ⓣ619/400-2400, ⓦwww.san.org) is only two miles from Downtown, and is connected to it by buses #923 ($2.25) and #992 ($2.50). By car, San Diego is easily accessible via the I-5 freeway; the drive south from central Los Angeles takes about two hours.

Once you arrive, **getting around** without a car is comparatively easy, though travelling to the outlying areas requires more planning. The **bus** system within central San Diego County is called the Metropolitan Transit System (MTS; ⓣ1-619/595-4555, ⓦwww.sdmts.com), the most convenient and accessible means of public transport in the region. Typical one-way fares are $2.25–2.50, and $5–10 for the most lengthy journeys into rural terrain; the exact fare is required when boarding (dollar bills are accepted). The **Transit Store**, at First and Broadway (Mon–Sat 9am–5pm; ⓣ619/234-1060), has detailed timetables and sells a **Day Tripper Transit Pass** for one- to four-day visits ($5, $9, $12 and $15, respectively). The passes apply also to the tram-like **San Diego Trolley**, which has limited stops throughout the area (one-way tickets $2.50) and covers, among other routes, the sixteen miles from the Santa Fe Depot to the Mexican border-crossing at San Ysidro. North San Diego County is linked to Downtown via a commuter light-rail system called **The Coaster**. Fares are $5–6.50 (ⓣ760/966-6500,

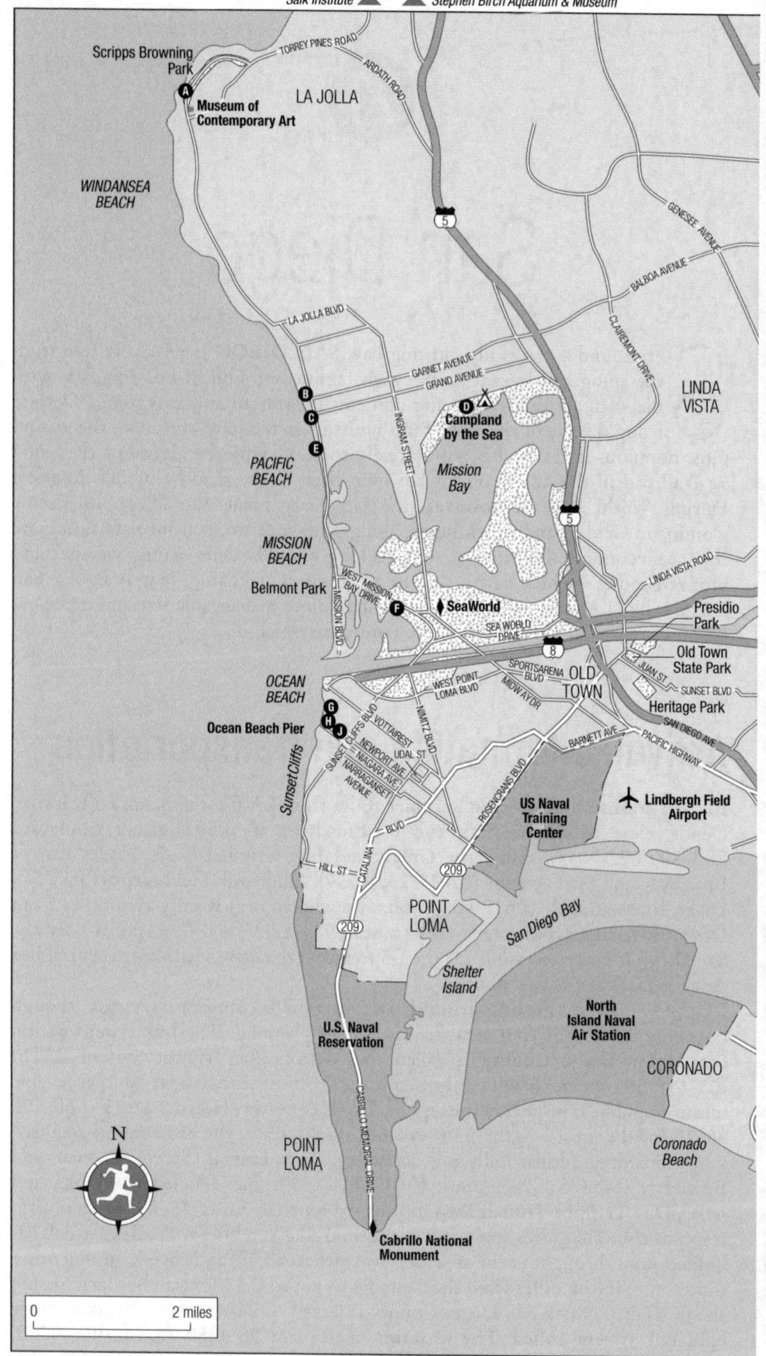
Salk Institute
Stephen Birch Aquarium & Museum
Scripps Browning Park
TORREY PINES ROAD
ARDATH ROAD
LA JOLLA
Museum of Contemporary Art
WINDANSEA BEACH
GENESEE AVENUE
BALBOA AVENUE
LA JOLLA BLVD
CLAIREMONT DRIVE
GARNET AVENUE
GRAND AVENUE
LINDA VISTA
Campland by the Sea
INGRAM STREET
PACIFIC BEACH
Mission Bay
MISSION BEACH
LINDA VISTA ROAD
Belmont Park
WEST MISSION BAY DRIVE
MISSION BLVD
SeaWorld
SEA WORLD DRIVE
Presidio Park
Old Town State Park
OCEAN BEACH
SPORTSARENA BLVD
OLD TOWN
WEST POINT LOMA BLVD
JUAN ST
SUNSET BLVD
MIDWAY DR
Heritage Park
Ocean Beach Pier
SUNSET CLIFFS BLVD
VOLTAIRE ST
NIMITZ BLVD
BARNETT AVE
SAN DIEGO AVE
PACIFIC HIGHWAY
UDAL ST
NEWPORT AVE
NIAGARA AVE
NARRAGANSET AVENUE
ROSECRANS BLVD
Sunset Cliffs
US Naval Training Center
Lindbergh Field Airport
BLVD
CATALINA
HILL ST
POINT LOMA
San Diego Bay
Shelter Island
North Island Naval Air Station
U.S. Naval Reservation
CORONADO
CABRILLO MEMORIAL DRIVE
N
POINT LOMA
Coronado Beach
Cabrillo National Monument
0
2 miles

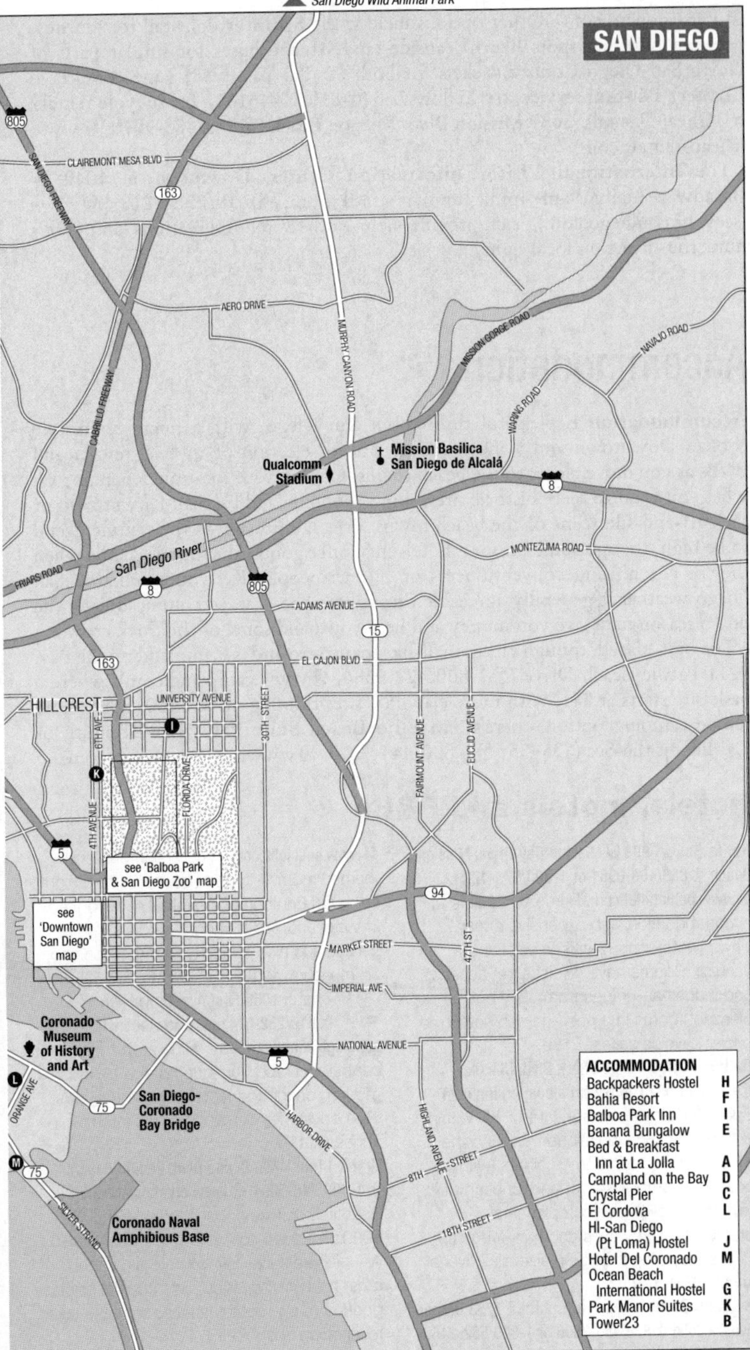
San Diego Wild Animal Park
SAN DIEGO
805
CLAIREMONT MESA BLVD
163
SAN DIEGO FREEWAY
AERO DRIVE
MURPHY CANYON ROAD
MISSION GORGE ROAD
NAVAJO ROAD
WARING ROAD
CABRILLO FREEWAY
Mission Basilica
San Diego de Alcalá
Qualcomm
Stadium
8
MONTEZUMA ROAD
FRIARS ROAD
San Diego River
8
805
ADAMS AVENUE
15
EL CAJON BLVD
163
HILLCREST
UNIVERSITY AVENUE
30TH STREET
6TH AVE
FLORIDA DRIVE
FAIRMOUNT AVENUE
EUCLID AVENUE
4TH AVENUE
5
see 'Balboa Park & San Diego Zoo' map
94
see 'Downtown San Diego' map
MARKET STREET
47TH ST
IMPERIAL AVE
Coronado Museum of History and Art
NATIONAL AVENUE
5
ORANGE AVE
75
San Diego-Coronado Bay Bridge
HARBOR DRIVE
HIGHLAND AVENUE
8TH STREET
75
SILVER STRAND
Coronado Naval Amphibious Base
18TH STREET
ACCOMMODATION
Backpackers Hostel H
Bahia Resort F
Balboa Park Inn I
Banana Bungalow E
Bed & Breakfast Inn at La Jolla A
Campland on the Bay D
Crystal Pier C
El Cordova L
HI-San Diego (Pt Loma) Hostel J
Hotel Del Coronado M
Ocean Beach International Hostel G
Park Manor Suites K
Tower23 B
Imperial Beach

Ⓦwww.gonctd.com). Other options include the **Sprinter** light rail for journeys between outlying spots like Oceanside, and **Breeze** buses for similar parts of North San Diego County (tickets for both $2, day passes $5; same contacts as Coaster). For **taxi** service, try Yellow Cab (Ⓣ619/234-6161); for **bicycle** rentals, try Cheap Rentals, 3689 Mission Blvd, Mission Beach (Ⓣ858/488-9070, Ⓦwww.cheap-rentals.com).

The **International Visitor Information Center,** Downtown at 1040 W Broadway (daily 9am–4pm, summer until 5pm; Ⓣ619/236-1212, Ⓦwww.seeyouinsandiego.com), can provide help with hotel reservations and offers numerous flyers on local sights.

Accommodation

Accommodation is plentiful throughout San Diego, with a range of upscale choices Downtown and a more widely priced selection of motels, resorts and B&Bs as you move closer to the beach towns. Choose your location depending on what you want to see – historic sites, ships, shopping and baseball Downtown, or the surf-and-sun scene of the beach towns. Prices, especially in the summer, tend to be high, though some business hotels may offer good value on weekends when they're not hosting conventioneers or businesspeople. Keep in mind that San Diego weather is generally agreeable throughout the year, so coming during the down season may save you money and help you avoid some of the thick crowds.

The best-placed, though rather mall-like, **campground** is Campland on the Bay, 2211 Pacific Beach Drive (Ⓣ1-800/422-9386, Ⓦwww.campland.com), where a basic site starts at $41, with more elaborate sites running up to $400. For a more serene camping option, there's **San Elijo Beach State Park**, Rte-21 south of Cardiff-by-the-Sea ($35–55; Ⓣ1-800/444-7275, Ⓦwww.reserveamerica.com).

Hotels, motels and B&Bs

Bahia Resort 998 W Mission Bay Drive, Mission Beach Ⓣ858/488-0551 or 1-800/576-4229, Ⓦwww.bahiahotel.com. Prime beachside accommodation with expansive ocean views, watersport rentals, a pool and a Jacuzzi. Rooms have wireless net access and fridges and range from cosy but pleasant rooms in a palm-garden setting to pricier bayside suites. $189.

Balboa Park Inn 3402 Park Blvd, Hillcrest Ⓣ619/298-0823, Ⓦwww.balboaparkinn.com. Spanish Colonial, gay-oriented B&B within walking distance of Balboa Park and the museums. The 26 themed suites (with oceanside, Impressionist and jungle motifs, to name a few) have complimentary breakfast, microwaves and mini-fridges. Prices vary, depending on size and level of kitsch. $99–149.

Bed and Breakfast Inn at La Jolla 7753 Draper Ave, La Jolla Ⓣ858/456-2066 or 1-800/582-2466, Ⓦwww.innlajolla.com. A collection of fifteen themed rooms – topped by the $425-a-night Irving Gill Penthouse, inexplicably decorated in Victoriana – with tranquil gardens, great service and nice proximity to the beach and art museum. $210

Bristol 1055 First Ave, Downtown Ⓣ619/232-6141, Ⓦwww.thebristolsandiego.com. Excellent value at this friendly, centrally located boutique hotel with stylish modern decor and tasteful amenities, plus iPod docks, flat-screen TVs and internet access. $139.

Crystal Pier 4500 Ocean Blvd, Pacific Beach Ⓣ1-800/748-5894, Ⓦwww.crystalpier.com. Beautiful, de luxe cottages built in the 1920s, situated right on Pacific Beach pier. All units are suites with private deck, and most have kitchenettes. This popular spot is booked many months ahead, so make your reservation soon. $299.

El Cordova 1351 Orange Ave, Coronado ⓣ1-800/229-2032, ⓦwww.elcordovahotel.com. One of the better deals in pricey Coronado, comprising Spanish Colonial buildings from 1902 arranged around lovely gardens. There's a pool, and many rooms have kitchenettes. Huge price spread, from cheap and basic units without a/c to grandly elegant suites. Starts around $179.

Horton Grand 311 Island Ave at Third Ave, Downtown ⓣ619/544-1886 or 1-800/542-1886, ⓦwww.hortongrand.com. Classy amalgam of two century-old hotels, with fireplaces in most of the rooms (some with balconies), an on-site restaurant and piano bar. Somewhat minimal amenities for such a historic spot, though. $179.

Hotel del Coronado 1500 Orange Ave, Coronado ⓣ19/522-8000 or 1-800/468-3533, ⓦwww.hoteldel.com. This luxurious spot put Coronado on the map and is still the area's major tourist sight (see p.316), thanks to its striking rooms and suites, expansive bay views and old-fashioned Victorian charm. $299

La Pensione 606 W Date St at India St ⓣ619/236-8000, ⓦwww.lapensionehotel.com. Good-value hotel within walking distance of the city centre. Rooms are small but equipped with wireless net access, microwaves, fridges and cable TVs, and there's an on-site laundry. $89

Manchester Grand Hyatt One Market Place, at Harbor Drive, Downtown ⓣ619/232-1234, ⓦwww.manchestergrand.hyatt.com. The most prominent hotel along the waterfront, a pair of gleaming white slabs of luxury with pool, spas, health club, several restaurants and lounges, and rooms with expansive views of the bay. Also ground zero for conventioneers. $169.

Park Manor Suites 525 Spruce St, near Balboa Park ⓣ1-800/874-2649, ⓦwww.parkmanorsuites.com. Stately old pile that's a hundred years old, now a tasteful hotel whose suites feature WiFi access, kitchens and nice sitting areas with sofas. Continental breakfast included. $159.

Solamar 435 6th Ave ⓣ619/531-8740, ⓦwww.hotelsolamar.com. Very tasteful and modern boutique hotel central to the Gaslamp District, whose rooms have net access, flatscreen TVs, CD and DVD players, and the site also offers spa and gym facilities, plus in-room yoga accessories. Suites with soaking and jetted tubs add to the hip appeal. $189.

Tower23 4551 Ocean Blvd, Pacific Beach ⓣ1-866/TOWER23, ⓦwww.tower23hotel.com. Despite being named for a lifeguard tower, this is among the most chic of the local boutique hotels, offering stylish rooms with flatscreen TVs, internet access and designer furnishings. The even more stylish suites variously come with balconies, cabanas and whirlpool tubs. $279.

US Grant 326 Broadway between Third and Fourth aves, Downtown ⓣ619/232-3121 or 1-800/237-5029, ⓦwww.usgrant.net. Downtown's poshest address since 1910, with a grand Neoclassical design, chandeliers, marble floors and cosy but comfortable guestrooms (with internet access) and more capacious suites. $255.

Hostels

Banana Bungalow 707 Reed Ave, Pacific Beach ⓣ858/273-3060 or 1-800/5-HOSTEL, ⓦwww.bananabungalow.com. Friendly if scruffy place with beach access, offering volleyball, BBQ cookouts and lively atmosphere. Free breakfast, internet access and a communal kitchen are included. Dorm beds $20–25, private rooms $65–105. Take bus #30, then it's a five-minute walk.

HI-Pt Loma 3790 Udall St, Ocean Beach ⓣ619/223-4778, ⓦwww.sandiegohostels.org. Well run and friendly, a couple of miles back from the beach and offering free breakfast, personal lockers, patio and weekly bonfires. Dorms for $20–31 and private rooms $45–63.

HI-San Diego Downtown 521 Market St at Fifth, Downtown ⓣ619/525-1531, ⓦwww.sandiegohostels.org. Handy for the Gaslamp District, with free breakfast and high-speed net access, plus a library, kitchen and various organized trips to Tijuana and other places. Dorm beds $28–31, private doubles $65–70.

Ocean Beach International Hostel 4961 Newport Ave, Ocean Beach ⓣ619/223-7873 or 1-800/339-7263, ⓦwww.californiahostel.com. Lively spot a block from the beach, offering barbecues, bike and surfboard rentals, airport transport and nightly movies. Dorm beds $16–24, with free WiFi, sheets, showers and continental breakfast.

USA Hostels – San Diego 726 Fifth Ave between F and G sts, Downtown ⓣ619/232-3100 or 1-800/438-8622, ⓦwww.usahostels.com/sandiego. Well-placed hostel on the edge of the Gaslamp District. Converted 1890s building, with six to eight beds per room, sheets and continental breakfast, for $28–31. Private rooms $62–74. Free breakfast, free WiFi and organized tours to Tijuana make this one of the city's best hostels.

The City

Bordered by the curve of San Diego Bay and the I-5 freeway, **Downtown** is, for those not headed straight to the beach, the inevitable nexus of San Diego and the best place to start a tour of the city. Many of the area's turn-of-the-century buildings have been stylishly renovated into modern clubs, restaurants and boutiques, while corporate towers left over from the boomtown 1980s and 90s showcase the city's trade with the Pacific Rim. Beyond Downtown, San Diego's lovely museum hub of **Balboa Park** and historic **Old Town** make for interesting cultural diversions. The sun-and-surf crowd will no doubt gravitate to the fun, hedonistic **beach cities**, where you can have a tropical drink while lounging by the sands, or perhaps play a game of volleyball or ride the surf.

Downtown

At the western end of Broadway, the tall Moorish archways of the **Santa Fe Railroad Depot**, built in 1915 for the Panama–California Exposition, still evoke a sense of grandeur. The depot is contiguous with the Downtown branch of the **Museum of Contemporary Art**, or MCA San Diego, 1001 Kettner Blvd (Thurs–Tues 11am–5pm; $10; ⓣ858/454-3541, ⓦwww.mcasd.org), a fine first stop for anyone interested in contemporary art with a California twist. Although its permanent collection focuses on American minimalism, pop art and the indigenous art of Mexico, the museum's temporary shows are the real appeal here, often involving irreverent imagery drawn from the intersection of pop-culture surrealism and daring agit-prop manifestos, among many other topics. Further west, **Broadway** slices through the middle of Downtown, becoming its most hectic between Fourth and Fifth avenues. Many visitors linger around the fountains on the square outside **Horton Plaza**, between First and Fourth avenues south of Broadway (Mon–Sat 10am–9pm, Sun 11am–7pm; ⓣ619/239-8180, ⓦwww.westfield.com/hortonplaza), a giant open-air mall and San Diego's de facto city centre. The complex's broad array of shops and eateries makes it a colossal tourist draw, but its whimsical postmodern style, loaded with quasi Art Deco and south-western motifs, also makes it worth a look.

A half-mile north of Broadway along India Street is the **Little Italy** district (ⓦwww.littleitalysd.com), one of the city's historic ethnic neighbourhoods, which today is mostly worth visiting for its restaurants and occasional festivals. These include the late-May Sicilian Festival (ⓦwww.sicilianfesta.com) and mid-October Festa among the highlights – both featuring the spicy, delicious food of the Old World.

The Gaslamp District

South of Broadway, a few blocks from Horton Plaza, lies the sixteen-block **Gaslamp District**, once the seedy heart of frontier San Diego but now filled with smart streets lined with cafés, antique stores, art galleries and, of course, "gas

lamps" – powered by electricity. Its late-nineteenth-century buildings are intriguing to examine, especially the grandiose **Louis Bank of Commerce**, 835 Fifth Ave, an eye-popping Victorian confection from 1888 replete with carved wooden and terracotta bay windows, a sheet-metal frieze across the front, and a pair of squat, colourful little towers on top. This classic building is best approached – and the area's general history gleaned – during a two-hour **walking tour** (Sat 11am; $10; ⓣ619/233-4692, ⓦwww.gaslampquarter.org/tours). Beginning at the small cobbled square at Fourth and Island avenues, the walk takes you through San Diego's original city centre, which in the 1880s became a notorious red-light district called the Stingaree. You'll hear about the exploits of the gunslinger Wyatt Earp, the more colourful of the town's Victorian-era whores, and other assorted miscreants who made the Stingaree the dynamic town it once was. The square where the walking tour starts is within the grounds of the **William Heath Davis House**, 410 Island Ave (Tues–Sat 10am–6pm, Sun 9am–3pm; $5; ⓣ619/233-4692), whose owner founded modern San Diego and built his saltbox-styled home here in 1850 – copious with photographs, with each room commemorating a different historical period.

Petco Park

The energetic hub of San Diego **nightlife**, especially on the weekend, is **Petco Park**, Seventh Ave at Harbor Drive (tickets $10–63; ⓣ619/795-5000, ⓦwww.sandiego.padres.mlb.com), which draws plenty of Padres baseball fans despite its limited options for parking. If you've come to play spectator, make an early trip on the Blue Line trolley (which passes alongside) – mass transit around game time resembles a rail-bound journey into deepest tourist hell.

The bayfront

Along San Diego's curving, enjoyable **bayfront**, the pathway of the **Embarcadero** runs a mile or so along the bay, curling around to the western end of Downtown; along this stretch, the expansive green lawn of **Embarcadero Marina Park South** provides some summertime amusement for its mainstream concerts. Beyond this, if you can't get enough of the US military on your TV set at home, clamber aboard for a tour of the **USS Midway**, 910 N Harbor Drive (daily 10am–5pm, last admission 4pm; $18; Ⓦwww.midway.org), which shows off its formidable collection of naval hardware and weapons to the public, along with flight simulators and various old-time planes. More vintage ships can be visited further north at the **Maritime Museum**, 1492 Harbor Drive (daily 9am–8pm; $12; Ⓣ619/234-9153, Ⓦwww.sdmaritime.com). Among the nine ships there, the highlights are the 1863 **Star of India**, the world's oldest iron sailing ship still afloat; the **Californian,** a modern replica of an 1847 cutter, which served as a federal lawboat patrolling the Pacific during the Gold Rush; the **HMS Surprise**, a replica of an eighteenth-century, 24-gun frigate, built for the film *Master and Commander*; and a creaky Soviet diesel submarine, the **B-39**, which was only decommissioned in the 1990s, well into the nuclear-sub era.

Coronado

Across San Diego Bay from Downtown, the isthmus of **Coronado** is a well-scrubbed resort community with a major naval station occupying its western end. It's reached by the majestically modern **Coronado Bay Bridge**, a curving 11,000-foot span that's one of the area's signature images, or on the **San Diego Bay ferry** (daily 9am–10pm; $3.50 each way; Ⓣ619/234-1111, Ⓦwww.sdhe.com), which leaves Broadway Pier on the hour, returning on the half-hour. The town of Coronado grew up around the **Hotel del Coronado** (see "Accommodation," p.313), a Victorian whirl of turrets and towers erected as a health resort in 1888. The "Del" is where Edward VIII (then Prince of Wales) first met Coronado housewife Wallis Warfield Simpson in 1920, and where *Some Like It Hot* was filmed in 1958, posing as a Miami Beach hotel. A less grandiose place to explore Coronado's past is the **Coronado Museum of History and Art**, 1100 Orange Ave (Mon–Fri 9am–5pm, Sat & Sun 10am–5pm; $4; Ⓣ619/435-7242, Ⓦwww.coronadohistory.org), which chronicles the town's early pioneers and first naval aviators, as well as its history of yachting and architecture. For a look at the historical importance of the various buildings in town, the museum offers hour-long **tours** (Wed 2pm; $10; reservations required).

Balboa Park

Northeast of Downtown, sumptuous **Balboa Park** contains one of the largest groups of **museums** in the US, as well as charming landscaping, traffic-free promenades and stately Spanish Colonial-style buildings. The park is large but easy to get around **on foot** – if you get tired, there's always the free tram. The **Balboa Park Passport**, a week-long pass that allows one-time admission to all fourteen of the park's museums and its Japanese garden (plus the San Diego Zoo, for an extra $25), is available for $45 from the **visitor information centre** (daily 9.30am–4.30pm; Ⓣ619/239-0512, Ⓦwww.balboapark.org), inside the on-site House of Hospitality. Near the centre, the **Spreckels Organ Pavilion** (concerts Sun 2pm; free; Ⓦwww.sosorgan.com) is worth a look as the home of one of the world's largest organs, with no fewer than 4500 pipes.

Most of the major museums flank **El Prado**, the pedestrian-oriented road that bisects the park. There's plenty to see, so plan on spending at least a full day or two here, especially if you bought a Passport. Highlights include the stirring collection of Russian icons and other Old World art at the **Timkin Museum of Art** (Tues–Sat 10am–4.30pm, Sun 1.30–4.30pm; closed Sept; free; ⓣ619/531-9640, ⓦwww.timkenmuseum.org). The **San Diego Museum of Art** (Tues–Sat 10am–5pm, Sun noon–5pm; $12; ⓣ619/232-7931, ⓦwww.sdmart.org) is the main venue for any big travelling shows – collections from Egypt, China and other places, which usually charge a $5–10 premium beyond museum admission. In the permanent collection, there's a solid stock of European paintings from the Renaissance to the nineteenth century, highlighted by Hals and Rembrandt. Straddling El Prado, the **Museum of Man** (daily 10am–4.30pm; $10; ⓣ619/239-2001, ⓦwww.museumofman.org), among other things, offers demonstrations of Mexican loom-weaving, replicas of huge Maya stones, interesting Native American artefacts and various Egyptian relics.

Close to the Park Boulevard end of El Prado, the **Reuben H. Fleet Science Center** (hours vary, often Mon–Thurs 9.30am–5pm, Fri & Sat 9.30am–8pm, Sun 9.30am–6pm; $10, kids $8.75, or $14.50 and $11.75 including an

IMAX film; Ⓦwww.rhfleet.org) presents an assortment of child-oriented exhibits of varying interest, focusing on the glitzier aspects of contemporary science, as well as the expected IMAX theatre and virtual-reality simulator. Across Plaza de Balboa, the **Natural History Museum** (daily 10am–5pm; $17; Ⓣ619/232-3821, Ⓦwww.sdnhm.org) features a great collection of fossils, a curious array of stuffed creatures, hands-on displays of minerals and entertaining exhibits on dinosaurs and crocodiles. South of El Prado, the **Casa de Balboa** houses three museums that are worth a look to enthusiasts of each subject. The **Museum of Photographic Arts** (Tues–Sun 10am–5pm, Thurs closes 9pm; $8; Ⓣ619/238-7559, Ⓦwww.mopa.org) offers a fine permanent collection that includes the work of Matthew Brady, Alfred Stieglitz, Paul Strand and other big names; rotating exhibits typically showcase the work of local and historical artists, with a bent toward popular culture. In the **San Diego Historical Society Museum** (Tues–Sun 10am–5pm; $5; Ⓣ619/232-6203, Ⓦwww.sandiegohistory.org), the main exhibit charts the booms that have elevated San Diego from scrubland into the seventh-largest city in the US within 150 years. Also in Casa de Balboa is the **Model Railroad Museum** (Tues–Fri 11am–4pm, Sat & Sun 11am–5pm; $5; Ⓣ619/696-0199, Ⓦwww.sdmodelrailroadm.com), which displays tiny, elaborate replicas of cityscapes, deserts and mountains, as well as the little trains that chug through them.

At the southern end of Pan American Plaza, the **Aerospace Museum** (daily 10am–4.30pm, summer closes 5.30pm; $16.50; Ⓣ619/234-8291, Ⓦwww.aerospacemuseum.org) recounts the history of aviation with its nearly seventy planes, including the *Spitfire*, the *Hellcat* and the mysterious spy plane *Blackbird*. Next door at the **Automotive Museum** (daily 10am–5pm; $8; Ⓣ619/231-2886, Ⓦwww.sdautomuseum.org) car enthusiasts will enjoy lingering over a host of classic cars and motorcycles, from Model Ts and Rolls Royces to more obscure models like the 1912 Flying Merkle cycle and the 1948 Tucker Torpedo – one of only fifty left.

On the northern border of Balboa Park, **Hillcrest** is a lively and artsy area at the centre of the city's **gay community**; the neighbourhood is about as close as San Diego gets to having a bohemian air away from the beach. Visit for something to eat – there's a selection of interesting cafés and restaurants around University and Fifth streets – or simply to stroll past the fine collection of Victorian homes.

The San Diego Zoo

Immediately north of the main museums of Balboa Park is the enormous **San Diego Zoo** (daily: mid-June to early Sept 9am–9pm; early Sept to mid-June 9am–5pm; Ⓣ619/231-1515, Ⓦwww.sandiegozoo.org), one of the world's most renowned. You can easily spend a full day here, taking in the major sections devoted to the likes of chimps and gorillas, sun and polar bears, lizards and lions, flamingos and pelicans, and habitats such as the rainforest and savanna. Take a **guided bus tour** early on to get a general idea of the layout, or survey the scene on the vertiginous **Skyfari**, an overhead tramway (both rides included with admission). Bear in mind, though, that many of the creatures get sleepy in the midday heat and retire behind bushes to take a nap. Moreover, the giant **pandas** Bai Yun and Gao Gao and four others spend a lot of time sleeping or being prodded by biologists in the park's Giant Panda Research Station. In addition to the main zoo facility, there's also a **children's zoo** in the park, with walk-through birdcages and an animal nursery. Regular **admission** ($37, kids $27) covers entry to the main zoo and children's zoo. A $70 ticket (kids $50) also admits you to the San Diego Zoo Safari Park near Escondido (hours vary, often daily 9am–4pm, summer closes 8pm; $37, $27 kids), a 2000-acre preserve for big cats, rhinos, giraffes and the like, which roam about outside your car's windows.

Presidio Hill and Old Town San Diego

In 1769, Spanish settlers chose **Presidio Hill** as the site of the first of California's missions. They soon began to build homes at the foot of the hill, which was dominated in turn by Mexican officials and then by early arrivals from the eastern US. **Old Town San Diego**, reachable from Downtown via the Trolley, is now a state historical park and the site of several original adobe dwellings – as well as the inevitable souvenir shops. The old buildings themselves are generally open 10am to 5pm and have free admission, but most things in the park that aren't historical – the shops and restaurants – open around 10am and close at 9 or 10pm. Highlights include the **Casa de Estudillo** on Mason Street, one of the poshest of the original adobes; it was built by the commander of the **presidio**, José Mariá de Estudillo, in 1827. Next door, the **Casa de Bandini** was the home of the politician and writer Juan Bandini and acted as the social centre of San Diego during the mid-nineteenth century. There's also a blacksmith shop, stables with antique wagons and an early school and print shop. Details on the many structures here are available from the **visitor centre**, inside the Robinson-Rose House, near Taylor and Congress streets (daily 10am–5pm; ⓣ619/220-5422, ⓦwww.oldtownsandiego.org).

The Spanish-style building now atop Presidio Hill is only a rough approximation of the original mission – moved in 1774 – but its **Junipero Serra Museum**, 10818 San Diego Mission Rd (Sat & Sun 10am–5pm; $5; ⓣ619/297-3258), offers an intriguing examination of Junípero Serra, the padre who led the aggressive Spanish colonization and Catholic conversion of California. The **Mission San Diego de Alcalá** itself was relocated six miles north to 10818 San Diego Mission Rd (daily 9am–4.45pm; donation; ⓣ619/283-7319, ⓦwww.missionsandiego.com), to be near a water source and fertile soils, and to be safer from attack. The present building is still a working parish church, with a small **museum**; among the objects and artefacts from the mission is the crucifix held by Serra at his death in 1834.

Ocean Beach and Point Loma

Ruled by the Hell's Angels in the 1960s, **OCEAN BEACH**, six miles northwest of Downtown, is a fun and relaxed beach town whose quaint, old-time streets and shops have preserved some of their funky character, though ongoing development has worn away some of their ramshackle appeal. The two big hangouts include **Newport Street**, where backpackers haunt snack bars, surf and skate rental shops, and **Voltaire Street**, which, in line with its name, has a good range of independent-minded local businesses. There is often good surf, and the beach itself can be quite fun – especially on weekends, when the local party scene gets cranking. South from the pier rise the dramatic **Sunset Cliffs**, a prime spot for twilight vistas.

South of Ocean Beach, at the southern end of the hilly green peninsula of **Point Loma**, the **Cabrillo National Monument** (daily 9am–5pm; seven-day pass $5 per vehicle, $3 per pedestrian or cyclist; ⓣ619/557-5450, ⓦwww.nps.gov/cabr) marks the spot where Juan Cabrillo and crew became the first Europeans to land in California, albeit briefly, in 1542. The startling views from this high spot easily repay a trip here. A platform atop the western cliffs of the park makes it easy to view the November-to-March **whale migration**, when scores of grey whales pass by en route to their breeding grounds off Baja California, Mexico. The nearby visitor centre (same hours as the park) contains information on the history and wildlife of the point, and lies near the **Old Point Loma Lighthouse** (daily 9am–5pm; free), which offers tours that lead past replica Victorian furnishings and equipment from the 1880s.

SeaWorld

North of Ocean Beach, **Mission Bay** is the site of San Diego's most popular tourist attraction: **SeaWorld** (hours vary, often mid-June to Labor Day 9am–dusk; rest of year 10am–dusk; $69, children $59; Ⓦwww.seaworld.com), the local branch of an entertainment colossus that stretches from Texas to Florida. SeaWorld has numerous exhibits and events, and for children it offers an undeniable, if very expensive, appeal. Along with various thrill rides, some of its spectacles include Shamu's SkySplash (orcas paired with music and fireworks); Forbidden Reef, stocked with moray eels and stingrays; the Wild Arctic, populated by walruses, beluga whales and polar bears; and the Shark Encounter, where sharks circle menacingly around visitors walking through a viewing tunnel.

Mission Beach and Pacific Beach

The biggest-name public beaches in San Diego are **Mission Beach**, the peninsula that separates Mission Bay from the ocean, and its northern extension, **Pacific Beach** – nightlife central for coastal San Diego. If you aren't up for bronzing on the sands, you can always nurse a beer at one of the many beachfront bars, or you can rollerblade or bike down **Ocean Front Walk**, the concrete boardwalk running the length of both beaches, and observe the toasty sands overrun with scantily clad babes and surfer dudes. A mile north of Pacific Beach's Crystal Pier, **Tourmaline Surfing Park**, or "Turmo", La Jolla Blvd at Tourmaline St, is reserved exclusively for surfing and windsurfing – no swimmers are allowed. If you don't have a board, **Windansea Beach**, a few miles north, is a good alternative. This favourite surfing hot spot is also fine for swimming as well as hiking alongside the oceanside rocks and reefs.

Near the southern end of Ocean Front Walk at 3146 Mission Blvd (hours vary, often Mon–Thurs 11am–8pm, Fri–Sun 11am–10pm; most rides $2–6, or full park pass for $20; Ⓦwww.belmontpark.com), once-derelict **Belmont Park** has been renovated with modern rides, though the two main attractions are both from 1925: the **Giant Dipper** roller coaster, one of the few of its era still around, and the **Plunge**, once the largest saltwater plunge in the world, and a regular film set for old-time Hollywood swim spectaculars.

La Jolla and around

A more pretentious air prevails in **La Jolla** (pronounced "La Hoya"), an elegant beach community just to the north. Stroll its immaculate, gallery-filled streets, fuel up on some California cuisine at one of the many sidewalk cafés, or visit the local outpost of the **Museum of Contemporary Art**, 700 Prospect St (Thurs–Tues 11am–5pm; $10; Ⓦwww.mcasandiego.org), which has a huge, regularly changing stock of paintings and sculptures from 1955 onwards, highlighted by California pop and minimalism. On the seaward side of the museum lies the small and tasteful **Ellen Scripps Browning Park**, named for the philanthropist whose Irving Gill-designed home now houses the museum. Where the park meets the coast is the popular **La Jolla Cove**, much of it an ecological reserve whose clear waters make it perfect for snorkelling (if you can find a parking space).

Just up the road, architecture fans won't want to miss a chance to tour one of the citadels of high modernism in the US, the **Salk Institute for Biological Studies**, 10010 N Torrey Pines Rd (Mon–Fri 8.30am–5pm; free tours Mon–Fri noon; reserve two days ahead at ⓣ858/453-4100 ext 1287, ⓦwww.salk.edu), a collection of rigid geometric concrete blocks and walls featuring stark vistas that look out over the Pacific Ocean, while further north, the **Stephen Birch Aquarium and Museum**, 2300 Expedition Way (daily 9am–5pm; $12, ⓦaquarium.ucsd.edu), has a wide range of highlights including the Hall of Fishes, a huge kelp forest home to countless sea creatures and the Shark Reef, displaying a nice range of fearsome creatures. Altogether, the museum is a much more edifying experience than anything at SeaWorld, and a lot cheaper, too.

Farther north, Torrey Pines Scenic Drive provides the main access (via a steep path) to **Black's Beach** (ⓦwww.blacksbeach.com) – the region's premier clothing-optional beach and one of the best and most daunting surfing beaches in Southern California, known for its huge barrelling waves during big swells. The beach lies within the southern part of the **Torrey Pines State Preserve** (daily 8am–sunset; ⓣ858/755-2063, ⓦwww.torreypine.org), which preserves the country's rarest species of pine, the Torrey Pine – one of two surviving stands. Thanks to salty conditions and stiff ocean breezes, the pines contort their ten-foot frames into a variety of tortured, twisted shapes.

Eating

Wherever you are in San Diego, you'll have few problems finding some place good to **eat** at reasonable prices. Everything, from crusty coffee shops to stylish ethnic restaurants, is in copious supply here, with seafood at its best around Mission Beach and the Gaslamp District, and the latter also home to the greatest concentration of restaurants.

Anthony's Fish Grotto 1360 Harbor Drive, Downtown ⓣ619/232-5103. Fish and chips and other reliable seafood favourites are the draw at this touristy bayside haunt, with mostly upper-end prices. Part of a local chain.

Bandar 825 4th Ave, Downtown ⓣ619/238-0101. Tasty Persian cuisine that tempts the palate with kebabs, lamb shank and stuffed grape leaves, as well as more inventive items like chicken tenderloin with barberry rice. Located near Horton Plaza.

Berta's 3928 Twiggs St, Old Town ⓣ619/295-2343. Solid south-of-the-border restaurant, offering well-priced, authentic cooking from all over Latin America. The affordable and savoury dishes include empanadas, seafood soups and paella.

Café 222 222 Island Ave, Downtown ⓣ619/236-9902. Hip café serving great breakfasts and lunches, with excellent pancakes, French toast and pumpkin and peanut-butter waffles. Also has inventive twists on traditional sandwiches and burgers (including vegetarian), all at reasonable prices.

Candelas 416 3rd Ave, Downtown ⓣ619/702-4455. Gaslamp District restaurant offering pricey Mexican fare with flavourful combinations of seafood and meat dishes with a California-cuisine influence. Try the ceviche, prawns with sashimi, or Serrano ham-stuffed chicken breast.

Chez Loma 1132 Loma Ave, Coronado ⓣ619/435-0661. Delicious upscale French cuisine; especially strong on old-line favourites, though with nouvelle influences too. Good for its roasted duck, sea scallops, lobster crepes and filet mignon tartare.

Chilango's Mexican Grill 142 University Ave, Hillcrest ⓣ619/294-8646. Regional, mid-priced Mexican food, highlighted by tasty shrimp, ceviche, enchiladas, tortilla soup and pork with tamarind sauce.

Cody's La Jolla 8030 Girard Ave ⓣ858/459-0040. Innovative California cuisine with good buttermilk pancakes, sage sausage, eggplant sandwiches and scrumptious burgers. A little more expensive than comparable breakfast and lunch spots, but worth it.

Confidential 901 4th Ave ⓣ619/696-8888. Curious Gaslamp choice for tapas in a trendy modern setting; the small plates are intriguing, if pricey, from lobster-bisque "shooters", to honey-rum-glazed duck, to "deconstructed" pizza broken down to its bare elements. Essential for adventurous eaters.

Croce's Restaurant and Jazz Bar 802 5th Ave, Gaslamp District ⓣ619/233-4355. Scrumptious choices such as rack of lamb, risotto and duck confit make this one of the pricier eateries in this area, and the Sunday jazz brunch is always a popular event.

de' Medici 815 5th Ave, Downtown ⓣ619/702-7228. Upscale Italian fare with the scampi Vesuvio, langostino lobster, king crab legs and saltimbocca rounding out a fine menu.

Dobson's 956 Broadway Circle, Downtown ⓣ619/231-6771. A chic restaurant in an old building, loaded with business types in power-ties. The cuisine leans toward Continental, and ranges from crab hash and oyster salad to flat-iron steak and rack of lamb.

Filippi's Pizza Grotto 1747 India St, Little Italy ⓣ619/232-5094. A good spot for devouring affordable favourites like thick, chewy pizzas and various pasta dishes, including a fine lasagna. Meals are served in a small room at the back of an Italian grocery.

Karinya 4475 Mission Blvd, Pacific Beach ⓣ858/270-5050. Hot and spicy soups, firecracker shrimp and volcano chicken to set your mouth ablaze, with a good range of Thai staples such as noodle dishes and satays as well. A tasty, inexpensive bet.

Kono's 704 Garnet Ave, Pacific Beach ⓣ858/483-1669. Crowded, touristy place for a cheap breakfast or lunch on the boardwalk, with hefty burritos, sandwiches, hamburgers and other favourites.

The Mission 3795 Mission Blvd, Mission Beach ⓣ858/488-9060. With all the delicious blackberry pancakes, roast-beef hash and steak quesadillas on the menu at this lunch-and-breakfast spot, your wallet won't end up busted, but your pant belt might.

Old Town Mexican Café 2489 San Diego Ave ⓣ619/297-4330. Among the better Mexican diners in Old Town, where the crowds

Exploring the North County coast

The towns of the **north coast of San Diego County** stretch 40 miles north from San Diego to the Camp Pendleton marine base, which divides the county from the outskirts of Los Angeles. The main attraction is, of course, the coast itself: miles of excellent beaches with great opportunities for swimming and surfing.

On the northern edge of the city of San Diego, the tall bluff that contains Torrey Pines State Preserve (see p.321) marks the southern boundary of **DEL MAR**, a town known mainly for its **Del Mar Racetrack**, which stages horse races between late July and early September (ⓣ858/755-1141, ⓦwww.dmtc.com), and has been going strong for seventy years, sited just a few blocks from the water's edge. Held throughout June until Independence Day at the San Diego County Fairgrounds, the **San Diego County Fair** (ⓣ858/755-1161, ⓦwww.sdfair.com) is an old-fashioned event with barbecues, kiddie games and face painting, and livestock shows. **SOLANA BEACH**, the next town north from Del Mar, was in 2003 the first US city to ban smoking from its coastline. It has some striking oceanside views from **Solana Beach County Park** (also known as "Pillbox" or "Fletcher Cove"), which offers good diving and surfing opportunities, and the town makes a reasonable place for a stop.

A short distance north, and 30 miles north of Downtown San Diego, the major flower-growing centre of **ENCINITAS** is at its best during the spring, when its blooms of floral colour are most radiant. The relaxing **San Diego Botanic Garden**, 230 Quail Gardens Drive (daily 9am–5pm; $12; ⓣ760/436-3036, ⓦwww.SDBGarden.org), hosts thirty different gardens, including some rich in bamboo, California endemics, palms and various selections of foliage from each continent. Also compelling is **San Elijo Lagoon Ecological Reserve**, 2710 Manchester Avenue (ⓣ760/436-3944, ⓦwww.sanelijo.org), one of the biggest remaining coastal wetlands in the state, a thousand queue up for the likes of pozole soup and carne asada tacos; only at breakfast are you unlikely to wait for a table.

Point Loma Seafoods 2805 Emerson St, Ocean Beach ⓣ619/223-1109. Fast, cheap counter serving up San Diego's freshest fish in a basket, along with a mean crab-cake sandwich.

Primavera 932 Orange Ave, Coronado ⓣ619/435-0454. Swank Italian cuisine that's among the best in town. There's pasta and risotto for those a little lighter in the wallet and fine osso buco, steak and lamb chops for the big spenders.

Sportsmen's Seafood 1617 Quivira Rd, Mission Beach ⓣ619/224-3551. A combo diner/market offering cheap and delicious fare – highlighted by great fish and chips, cioppino and fish sandwiches.

Taste of Thai 527 University Ave, Hillcrest ⓣ619/291-7525. Terrific Thai staples – spicy soups, curries, drunken noodles, pad thai and so on – for reasonable prices; expect a wait on weekends.

Nightlife

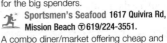

San Diego's upscale cultural focus is **classical music** and **opera**, the big names of which are Downtown: **San Diego Opera**, based at the Civic Theatre, 1200 Third Ave (ⓣ619/533-7000, ⓦwww.sdopera.com), and **San Diego Symphony**, Copley Symphony Hall, 750 B St (ⓣ619/235-0804, ⓦwww.sandiegosymphony.com). **Tickets** prices range widely at $20–210. Half-priced tickets and information are at the **Arts Tix** booth, Broadway at Third Avenue (Tues–Thurs 11am–6pm, Fri & Sat 10am–6pm, Sun 10am–5pm; ⓣ619/497-5000, ⓦwww.sdartstix.com). Elsewhere, the crowds flock to beachside **dance clubs** and boozy Gaslamp District **music venues** for evening amusement. For full listings, pick up the free **San Diego Reader** (ⓦwww.sandiegoreader.com), the Thursday

acres rich with endemic plants, fish and birds – and based around marshes, scrubland and chapparal – which you can explore on 7 miles of hiking trails.

Ten miles farther north, surfers are the main visitors to **South Carlsbad State Beach**, which also features swimming, fishing and scuba diving. The beach marks the edge of **CARLSBAD**, whose most popular attraction is the curious theme park of **Legoland California** (1 Lego Drive, exit Cannon Road off I-5; $67, kids $57, parking $12; ⓦwww.legoland.com), where kids can climb on larger-than-life Lego bricks, make their way through colourful mazes, experience pint-sized thrill rides, operate miniature cars and boats and view assorted cities built on a minuscule scale.

The most northerly town on the coast of San Diego County, **OCEANSIDE**, five miles north of Carlsbad, is dominated by the huge **Camp Pendleton** marine base, though its downtown is charming and its beaches are beautiful, decorated by the fetching town **pier** that extends nearly 2000 feet into the waves. Oceanside is also a major transit centre, and the town's prime attractions include the **Buena Vista Audubon Nature Center**, 2202 S Coast Highway (Tues–Sat 10am–4pm, Sun 1–4pm; free; ⓣ760/439-2473, ⓦwww.bvaudubon.org), which is adjacent to a lagoon that's especially good for spotting grebes, terns, coots and pelicans, and for relaxing walks. Engaging in a different way is the **California Surf Museum**, 312 Pier View Way (daily 10am–4pm; free; ⓦwww.surfmuseum.org), with displays on some of the top local surfers that tackled the most wicked breaks, and some of the most inventive board designers who gave shape to that quintessential California icon. Finally, the **Oceanside Museum of Art**, 704 Pier View Way (Tues–Sat 10am–4pm, Sun 1–4pm; $8; ⓣ760/435-3720, ⓦwww.oma-online.org), has a fine range of contemporary art from glassworks to photography to multimedia, shown in rotating exhibits during the year.

edition of the **San Diego Union-Tribune** (Ⓦ www.signonsandiego.com), or the youth-oriented **San Diego CityBeat** (Ⓦ www.sdcitybeat.com).

Bars, coffeeshops and clubs

Bitter End 770 5th Ave, Gaslamp District ⓣ619/338-9300. Three-storey venue in the Gaslamp, complete with dancefloor, Martini bar and, upstairs, a private VIP lounge for sophisticated poseurs.

Caffé Calabria 3933 30th St, Hillcrest ⓣ619/291-1759. Serious coffee drinks for serious coffee drinkers, serving up some fine espresso and French and Italian roasts from their own roasted beans, which you can also buy to take home. Also offers good pastries and panini.

Karl Strauss Brewery & Grill 1157 Columbia St, Downtown ⓣ619/234-2739. Part of a local chain with a reasonable selection of hearty ales and lagers brewed on the premises, and an adequate array of bar food.

Live Wire 2103 El Cajon Blvd, just east of Hillcrest ⓣ619/291-7450. A solid place to groove with the rocking jukebox and get hammered on imported and local beers. There's also pinball, pool and funky a sub-bohemian atmosphere to wet your whistle.

Onyx Room 852 5th Ave, Gaslamp District ⓣ619/235-6699. Groovy bar with lush decor, where you can knock back a few cocktails, then hit the back room for live jazz and dance tunes. The chic lounge upstairs has pricier drinks and bigger attitudes.

Ruby Room 1271 University Ave ⓣ619/299-7372. Good-time Hillcrest dive bar that serves up cheap brews and convivial company and presents the odd Rock 'n' Roll or burlesque show.

Thrusters Lounge 4633 Mission Blvd, Pacific Beach ⓣ858/483-6334. Sleek and narrow bar where the dance beats come hard and heavy, and jazz and rock make the odd appearance, too.

Upstart Crow 835 W Harbor Drive, Downtown ⓣ619/232-4855. This coffee bar fused with a bookstore offers a lively cross section of customers, primo java, well-chosen reading material and free Saturday-night jazz performances.

Whistle Stop Bar 2236 Fern St, South Park ⓣ619/284-6784. Sited on the east side of Balboa Park, this hip and lively bar presents a wide range of theme nights, from weekend DJs to Sunday "knitting jams" to movie matinees.

Live music venues

4th and B 345 B St, Downtown ⓣ619/231-4343. One of the city's more notable venues for metal, funk, hip hop and other music, with good sightlines if a barebones atmosphere, and a mix of local up-and-comers and old-timers.

Belly Up Tavern 143 S Cedros Ave, Solana Beach ⓣ858/481-9022. Mid-sized hall that plays host nightly to an eclectic range of live music – anything from grizzled rockers to salsa spectaculars and tub-thumping DJs.

Brick by Brick 1130 Buenos Ave, Mission Bay ⓣ619/275-5483. Lounge standby serving up a mix of indie rock, metal, hip hop and burlesque acts.

Casbah 2501 Kettner Blvd, Downtown ⓣ619/232-4355. A grungy joint that nevertheless has a solid reputation for its blues, funk, reggae, rock and indie bands. Local popularity contrasts with cramped environs.

Dizzy's at Harbor Club Towers, J St at 2nd, Downtown ⓣ858/270-7467. As the name suggests, this spot is devoted to straight-up jazz and little else – in a dark, intimate brick-walled environment.

Humphrey's by the Bay 2241 Shelter Island Drive, Point Loma ⓣ619/220-8497. Mainstream concert venue draws a range of mellow, agreeable pop, blues, jazz, country, folk and lite-rock acts, and its restaurant is a solid choice for seafood.

Kensington Club 4079 Adams Ave, Kensington District, north of Hillcrest ⓣ619/284-2848. Also called "The Ken" – a great divey joint for beer, wine and cocktails, but also for wide-ranging live music selections from thumping-dance DJs to head-banging rockers.

Winston's Beach Club 1921 Bacon St, Ocean Beach ⓣ619/222-6822. A former bowling alley turned semi-dive bar, this local club has rock bands most nights, with occasional reggae and comedy acts as well.

22

Palm Springs and the deserts

Amid lush farmland replete with golf courses, condos and millionaires, **Palm Springs** embodies a strange mix of Spanish Colonial and mid-twentieth-century modernism. Massive Mount San Jacinto looms over its low-slung buildings, casting a welcome shadow over the town in the boiling heat of the summer – the low season. Ever since Hollywood stars first came here in the 1930s, laying claim to ranch estates and holing up in elite hotels, the clean, dry air and sunshine, just 120 miles east of LA, have made Palm Springs irresistible to the masses. In recent years, the city has also become a major **gay and lesbian** resort (Ⓦwww.visitgaypalmsprings.com has a list of options). The town is more widely known for its **golf**, so if your handicap's well under 20, this should be one of your prime Southern California destinations.

If you tire of all the leisure activities, you can take a very different sort of jaunt into the deserts of Southern California. The highlight is seeing the fascinatingly gnarled trees and strange landscape of Joshua Tree National Park, which offers more than a thousand square miles of some of the best desert scenery Southern California has to offer.

Palm Springs

As most natives will tell you, the city of **PALM SPRINGS**, two hours east of downtown LA, is an oasis – a refuge not only from the desert's punishing conditions, but also for city dwellers from the smog, crime and chaos of the metropolis on the horizon. As a getaway it's quite convenient to Los Angeles, served well by public transit and freeways, and offering countless opportunities for swimming, sunning, golfing and partying under the dry, toasty skies. As with San Diego, it has an upscale libertarian vibe, but unlike that coastal city, a trip to Palm Springs has fewer options for those with limited means, so expect to open your wallet wide to really enjoy the place.

Arrival and information

Arriving by car, you drive into town on N Palm Canyon Drive, passing the **visitor centre** at no. 2901 (daily 9am–5pm, Sun closes 4pm; ⓣ1-800/347-7746, ⓦwww.visitpalmsprings.com), a classic piece of pop architecture with an upswept roof and boomerang design. Greyhound **buses** (4 daily from LA; 2hr 30min–3hr) pull in downtown at 311 N Indian Canyon Drive, while Amtrak

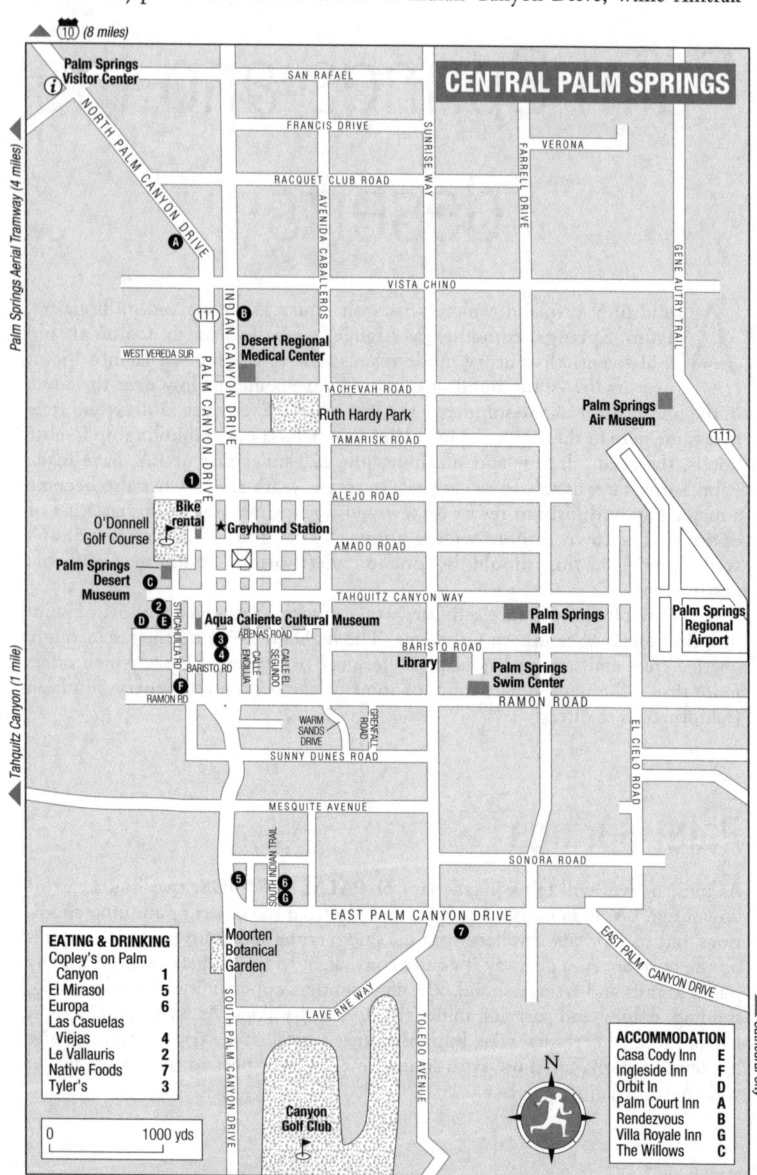

trains from LA (2 daily; 2hr 30min) stop just south of I-10 at N Indian Avenue, about ten minutes from downtown. The local operator SunBus (6am–10pm; tickets $1, day passes $3; ⓣ1-800/347-8628, ⓦwww.sunline.org) circulates in all the local resort towns. Guided **tours** of Palm Springs' stash of notable **modernist architecture**, among them designs by R.M. Schindler, Albert Frye and Richard Neutra, are organized by PS Modern Tours (2hr 30min; $75; ⓣ760/318-6118, ⓔpsmoderntours@aol.com).

Accommodation

Luxury **hotels** outnumber the cheaper variety in Palm Springs, but prices drop by as much as seventy percent as temperatures soar in the summer. The north end of town, along Hwy-111, holds many of the lower-priced places, including countless motels, virtually all of which have pools and air-conditioning. The prices below are **spring** and **autumn rates**; expect to pay about $20–50 more or less for winter and summer, respectively.

Casa Cody 175 S Cahuilla Rd ⓣ760/320-9346, ⓦwww.casacody.com. Built in the 1920s, this historic Southwestern-style B&B offers attractive rooms and a shady garden. A bit more comfortable than higher-priced retro-motels. $89

Ingleside Inn 200 W Ramon Rd ⓣ760/325-0046 or 1-800/772-6655, ⓦwww.inglesideinn.com. Compelling downtown option with a star-studded guest list and rooms with antiques, fireplaces, whirlpool tubs and patios (for double the price of a standard unit). Two-night minimum stay. $160

Orbit In 562 W Arenas Rd ⓣ1-877/996-7248, ⓦwww.orbitin.com. Old-style 1957 motel remade into a suave, yuppie-friendly hotel – where you can drink cutely named cocktails by the pool and enjoy plush amenities in stylish, arch-modern rooms. $199

Palm Court Inn 1983 N Palm Canyon Drive ⓣ760/416-2333, ⓦwww.palmcourt-inn.com. Decent motel with two pools, a Jacuzzi and gym, plus free continental breakfast and adequate rooms. $89

Rendezvous 1420 N Indian Canyon Drive ⓣ1-800/485-2808, ⓦwww.palmspringsrendezvous.com. Motel remodelled into a chic B&B with modern luxuries and retro-1950s designs in its themed rooms (Rat Pack, Marilyn, surfing, etc). $150

Villa Royale Inn 1620 S Indian Trail ⓣ1-800/245-2314, ⓦwww.villaroyale.com. Elegant inn with two pools, nicely furnished rooms and suites, as well as in-room Jacuzzis and a good restaurant. $129

The Willows 412 W Tahquitz Canyon ⓣ760/320-0771, ⓦwww.thewillowspalmsprings.com. The reason celebrities were first attracted to Palm Springs in the 1930s: a stunning hangout for the Hollywood elite that provides great views and opulent rooms. Rates begin at $450.

Downtown Palm Springs

For such a notable location, Palm Springs doesn't offer a great deal in the way of conventional attractions. You may begin at **Downtown Palm Springs**, which stretches for a mile along **Palm Canyon Drive** from Tamarisk to Ramon roads, much of it a wide, bright and modern strip of chain stores that has overrun the town's quaint Spanish Colonial–style buildings. In keeping with Hollywood tradition, a **Palm Springs Walk of Stars** extends along the Drive with some three hundred past and present bigwigs who frolicked in the city. Actually, few of them can actually be called celebrities, since the majority seem to be civic boosters and little-known millionaires of one stripe or another, but every once in a while you do come across a Mary Pickford, Bob Hope or Frank Sinatra (locations at ⓦwww.palmsprings.com/stars). Shops here run the gamut from upscale boutiques and art galleries to tacky T-shirt emporia and bookstores devoted to dead celebrities. In the vicinity you'll find the **Agua Caliente Cultural Museum**,

219 S Palm Canyon Dr (Wed–Sat 10am–5pm, Sun noon–5pm; summer Fri–Sun only; free; ⓣ760/323-0151, ⓦwww.accmuseum.org), with a fine selection of native baskets and pottery craftwork, as well as household objects from the local Cahuilla tribe, such as tools and utensils made from bone, reeds and stone.

The luxuriously housed **Palm Springs Desert Museum**, 101 Museum Drive (Tues, Wed, & Fri–Sun 10am–5pm, Thurs noon–8pm; summer Fri–Sun only, 10am–5pm; $12.50, children $5; ⓣ760/322-4800, ⓦwww.psmuseum.org), is strong on Native American and Southwestern art, as well as grand American landscape painting from the nineteenth century. There is a modern art gallery and some lovely sculpture courts on the grounds, and the museum hosts performances of music, theatre, comedy and dance in the 450-seat **Annenberg Theater** (tickets ⓣ760/325-4490).

There's an anarchic piece of landscape gardening at **Moorten Botanical Gardens**, 1701 S Palm Canyon Drive (Mon–Sat 9am–4.30pm, Sun 10am–4pm; $3; ⓣ760/327-6555, ⓦwww.palmsprings.com/moorten), an odd cornucopia of desert plants in settings designed to simulate their natural environments. Collections of flora include native agaves, barrel cacti and other succulents, as well as regional plants from as far away as South Africa and South America. Finally, near the airport, the **Palm Springs Air Museum**, 745 N Gene Autry Trail (daily 10am–4pm, Sun opens 11am; $12; ⓣ760/778-6262, ⓦwww.palmsprings airmuseum.org), has an impressive collection of World War II fighters and bombers, including Spitfires, Tomcats and a B-17 Flying Fortress.

Around Palm Springs

Most visitors to Palm Springs never leave poolside or the golf course, but desert enthusiasts still visit to hike and ride in the **Indian Canyons** (daily 8am–5pm, summer Fri–Sun only; $8; ⓦwww.indian-canyons.com), three miles southeast of downtown along S Palm Canyon Drive, where centuries ago, ancestors of the indigenous Cahuilla people developed extensive agricultural communities. The **Palm Canyon Trading Post**, 380 N Palm Canyon Drive (same hours as canyons; ⓣ760/323-6018), is a gift shop that serves as the de facto visitor centre, from which mile-long guided hikes (90min; $3) leave during regular canyon hours. The canyons can be toured by car, although it's worth walking at least a few miles; the easiest trails lead past the waterfalls, rocky gorges and copious palm trees of **Palm Canyon** (3 miles) and **Andreas Canyon** (1 mile). While you're here, you can take a jeep adventure around the mountains with Desert Adventures, 67555 E Palm Canyon Drive, Cathedral City (2hr 30min–5hr; $100–150; ⓣ760/340-2345, ⓦwww.red-jeep.com), which offers **guided tours** that focus on the various geological, cultural and historical aspects of the area.

If the desert heat becomes too much to bear, board one of the large cable cars that grind and sway over 8000 feet up the **Palm Springs Aerial Tramway**, Tramway Road, just off Hwy-111 north of Palm Springs (Mon–Fri 10am–8pm, Sat & Sun 8am–8pm; $23, children $16; ⓣ760/325-1391, ⓦwww .pstramway.com), heading to the striking 10,815ft summit of Mount San Jacinto–one of the area's signature sights. In the opposite direction from Palm Springs, a few miles east of town, **PALM DESERT** is, like the sun-baked towns further east, riddled with golf courses and elite resorts. It's also home to the **Living Desert**, a combination garden and zoo at 47900 Portola Ave, Palm Desert (daily: summer 8.30am–1pm; rest of year 9am–5pm; $12.50; ⓣ760/346-5694, ⓦwww.livingdesert.org), which is rich with cactus and palm gardens, and throws in an incongruous section devoted to African animals, such as giraffes, zebras, cheetahs and warthogs.

Eating and drinking

Although most of the better **restaurants** in Palm Springs are ultra-expensive, more reasonable options can be found with a little effort; the spots preferred by locals are, as ever, to be favoured over the mediocre cuisine served up by places catering to the tourist trade. Some of the better ones are listed below.

Copley's on Palm Canyon 621 N Palm Canyon Drive ⓣ760/327-9555. Hang out in Cary Grant's old digs while you sup on upscale California Cuisine, which may include Scottish salmon with Thai curry, lobster pot pie and ahi tacos.

El Mirasol 140 E Palm Canyon Drive ⓣ760/323-0721. Mid-priced Mexican dining that offers a mix of familiar staples, from tacos and tostadas to mole sauces, and more authentic fare from Zacatecas and other regions.

Europa 1620 S Indian Trail ⓣ1-800/245-2314. Located in the *Villa Royale Inn* (see p.327), a romantic, upscale French and Italian eatery, serving splendid dishes from duck confit to osso buco to escargots royale.

Las Casuelas Viejas 368 N Palm Canyon Drive ⓣ760/325-3213. Predictable, affordable Mexican favourite that's been around since 1958, and remains popular for its hefty portions and laid-back atmosphere.

Le Vallauris 385 W Tahquitz Canyon Way ⓣ760/325-5059. Fine California–Mediterranean cuisine in a gorgeous setting, with high prices for temptations such as Russian caviar, Dover sole and port-glazed squab. Reservations only.

Native Foods 1775 E Palm Canyon Drive ⓣ760/416-0070. One of the town's better choices for cheap vegetarian cuisine – with veggie chilli, chicken wings, pizzas, burgers and tacos, plus bean soups, rice bowls and tempeh burgers. Part of a regional chain.

Shame on the Moon 69950 Frank Sinatra Drive, Rancho Mirage ⓣ760/324-5515. Mid- to upper-end California cuisine is the draw here, highlighted by Long Island duck, sautéed calf's liver and ahi tuna steaks. Located eight miles east of downtown Palm Springs.

Tyler's 149 S Indian Canyon Drive ⓣ760/325-2990. The tasty burgers are what send residents tramping out here, but the potato salad, fries and sandwiches aren't bad, either.

Joshua Tree National Park

Where the low Colorado Desert meets the high Mojave a hundred miles northeast of Palm Springs, **JOSHUA TREE NATIONAL PARK** (ⓦwww.nps.gov/jotr) protects 1250 square miles of grotesquely gnarled plants, which aren't trees at all, but a type of **yucca**, an agave. Named by Mormons in the 1850s, who saw in their craggy branches the arms of Joshua pointing to the promised land, Joshua trees can rise up to 40 feet tall, and somehow manage to flourish despite the extreme aridity and rocky soil.

This unearthly landscape is ethereal at sunrise or sunset, when the desert floor is bathed in red light; at noon it can be a furnace, with temperatures topping 125°F in summer. Still, the park attracts campers, day-trippers and rock-climbers for its unspoiled beauty, gold-mine ruins, ancient petroglyphs, and striking rock formations. A half-mile guided tour of **Keys Ranch** (Oct–May Sat & Sun 10am & 1pm; $5; see park website for details) provides a testament to the difficulty of making a life in such a difficult environment, but if you'd rather wander around the national park by yourself, there are many options: one of the easiest hikes (three miles, foot-travel only) starts one-and-a-half miles from Canyon Road, six miles from the visitor centre at Twentynine Palms, at **Fortynine Palms Oasis**. West of the oasis, quartz boulders tower around the **Indian Cove** campground; a trail from the eastern branch of the campground road heads to **Rattlesnake Canyon**, where, after rainfall, the streams and waterfalls break an otherwise eerie silence among the monoliths.

Moving south into the main body of the park, the **Wonderland of Rocks** features rounded granite boulders that draw rock-climbers from around the world. One fascinating trail climbs four miles past abandoned mines to the antiquated foundations and equipment of **Lost Horse Mine** – which once produced around $20,000 in gold a week. You can find a brilliant desert panorama of badlands and mountains at the 5185ft **Keys View** nearby, from where Geology Tour Road leads down to the east through the best of Joshua Tree's **rock formations** and, further on, to the **Cholla Cactus Garden**.

Practicalities

Less than an hour's drive northeast from Palm Springs, Joshua Tree National Park (always open; $15 per vehicle for 7 days, $5 per cyclist or hiker) is best approached along Hwy-62, which branches off I-10. You can enter the park via the **west entrance**, on Park Boulevard in the town of Joshua Tree (daily 8am–5pm; ⓣ760/366-1855); the **north entrance** at Twentynine Palms, where you'll also find the **Oasis Visitor Center**, 74485 National Park Drive (daily 8am–5pm; ⓣ760/367-5500); or, if you're coming from the south, the **Cottonwood Visitor Center** (daily 9am–3pm; ⓣ760/367-5500), seven miles north of I-10.

The park has nine established **campgrounds**, all in the northwest except for one at Cottonwood. Only two have water – **Black Rock Canyon** ($15) and **Cottonwood** ($15–30) – and except for **Indian Cove** ($15), all the others are $10. You can reserve sites at **Black Rock** and **Indian Cove** by contacting the park reservation centre (ⓣ1-877/444-6777, ⓦwww.recreation.gov). The rest are operated on a first-come, first-served basis. Come prepared – gathering firewood is not allowed, and you should stock up on water. **TWENTYNINE PALMS**, a small desert town two minutes' drive from the park, has low-grade motels aplenty, but more pleasant is the historic **Twentynine Palms Inn**, 73950 Inn Ave (ⓣ760/367-3505, ⓦwww.29palmsinn.com; $110), with its nice wooden cabins and adobe bungalows, and fine **restaurant** where the bread is home-made and the vegetables are fresh from an on-site garden. Morongo Basin Transit Authority **buses** (ⓣ760/366-2395, ⓦwww.mbtabus.com) run between Palm Springs and Twentynine Palms (1hr 15min; $7–10 single, $11–15 roundtrip), but not into the park itself.

23

Santa Barbara

US-101 travels along the coast a hundred miles north of Los Angeles to **SANTA BARBARA**, a seaside resort beautifully situated on gently sloping hills above a curving bay. The town's low-rise Spanish Colonial Revival buildings feature red-tiled roofs and white stucco walls, a lovely background to the crescent of golden, palm-lined **beaches** below.

A weekend escape for much of the old money of Los Angeles and assorted celebrities, Santa Barbara has both a traditional conservative side, as well as a more relaxed libertarian character among the younger set. Still, it's a small city; local culture runs to playing volleyball, surfing, cycling, sipping coffee or cruising in expensive convertibles along the shore.

Arrival, information and transportation

From Los Angeles on the 101, Santa Barbara is less than an hour-and-a-half drive if you're lucky. Greyhound **buses** arrive from LA and San Francisco every few hours, stopping downtown at 34 W Carrillo Street, while Amtrak **trains** stop at 209 State Street, a block west of US-101. Santa Barbara Municipal **Airport** (Ⓣ805/683-4011, Ⓦwww.flysba.com), eight miles north of the town centre at 500 Fowler Road (near UC Santa Barbara), has a regular but often expensive scheduled service to other cities in the Western US.

For more information on Santa Barbara, or for help with finding a place to stay, contact the **visitor centre**, 1 Garden Street (Mon–Sat 9am–5pm, Sun 10am–5pm; Ⓣ805/965-3021, Ⓦwww.santabarbara.com). **Getting around** central Santa Barbara mainly involves walking, though there's a 25¢ **shuttle** that loops between downtown and the beach, and from the harbour to the zoo. Other areas are covered by **buses** of the Santa Barbara Metropolitan Transit District (SBMTD; fares $1.75; Ⓣ805/963-3366, Ⓦwww.sbmtd.gov).

Accommodation

Home to some of the West Coast's most de luxe resorts, Santa Barbara is among California's most expensive places to **stay**, with many rooms averaging over $250–300 a night. The less expensive places are usually booked throughout the summer, but if you get stuck, enlist the assistance of Hot Spots, a hotel-reservation site that offers specials on lodging (ⓣ1-800/793-7666, ⓦwww.hotspotsusa.com).

While there are no **campgrounds** in Santa Barbara proper, there are several spots along the coast to the north, including El Capitan and Refugio state beaches, and to the south, Carpinteria State Beach; all are accessible via Reserve America (ⓣ1-800/444-7275, ⓦwww.reserveamerica.com) and fees are $35 per car, or $10 if you come by bicycle or on foot.

Blue Sands Motel 421 S Milpas St ⓣ805/965-1624, ⓦwww.bluesandsmotel.com. A great bet for accommodation: clean rooms with gas fireplaces, free wireless internet, kitchenettes and flatscreen TVs – along with a heated pool. $119

Cheshire Cat 36 W Valerio St ⓣ805/569-1610, ⓦcheshirecat.com. Loaded with precious Victorian decor, this B&B has twelve rooms, three cottages and a coach house, and features a hot tub, bikes for guests' use, and an Alice in Wonderland theme. $159

Four Seasons 1260 Channel Drive ⓣ805/969-2261, ⓦwww.fourseasons.com. The apex of swank in the area, where the opulent rooms boast fireplaces and wrought-iron balconies, and the complex has a spa, pool and fitness centre. $475

Inn at East Beach 1029 Orilla del Mar ⓣ805/965-0546, ⓦwww.innateastbeach.com. Clean, modern rooms with free WiFi, microwaves and fridges and some suites with kitchens. $135

Inn of the Spanish Garden 915 Garden St ⓣ805/564-4700, ⓦwww.spanishgardeninn.com. Elegant boutique rooms in a chic Mediterranean complex with designer decor, fireplaces, high-speed internet connections, and on-site fitness centre. $349

Marina Beach Motel 21 Bath St t1-877/627-4621, ⓦwww.marinabeachmotel.com. Clean motel rooms with continental breakfast and options for bike rentals, kitchenettes and Jacuzzis. A pleasant getaway. $115, summer $184.

Montecito Inn 1295 Coast Village Rd ⓣ805/969-7854, ⓦwww.montecitoinn.com. Charming Spanish Revival inn with a wide range of rooms and rates, from quaint, basic units to elaborate suites, plus pool, sauna and Jacuzzi. Sometimes has midweek summer discounts of $100 or so. $265

Santa Barbara Tourist Hostel 134 Chapala St ⓣ805/963-0154, ⓦwww.sbhostel.com. Centrally located hostel near the beach and State St, with bicycle and surfboard rentals, complimentary breakfast and internet access. Dorm rooms go for $22–35, depending on the season, with private rooms also available ($59–95), some with private bath.

The Town

Somewhat ironically, Santa Barbara owes its current Mission-era atmosphere, with its attendant quaintness and historical "authenticity", to a devastating **earthquake** in 1925, after which the city authorities decided to rebuild virtually the entire town as an apocryphal Mission-era village – even the massive "historic" El Paseo shopping mall has a whitewashed adobe facade. The square-mile **historic centre**, squeezed between the south-facing **beaches** and the foothills of the Santa Ynez Mountains, has one of the region's liveliest street scenes. The main drag, **State Street**, is home to an assortment of restaurants, coffee bars and nightclubs catering as much to the needs of locals – among them twenty thousand UC Santa Barbara students – as to visitors.

The historic centre

The **historic centre** of Santa Barbara lies mostly along State Street a few blocks inland from the beach and the 101 freeway.

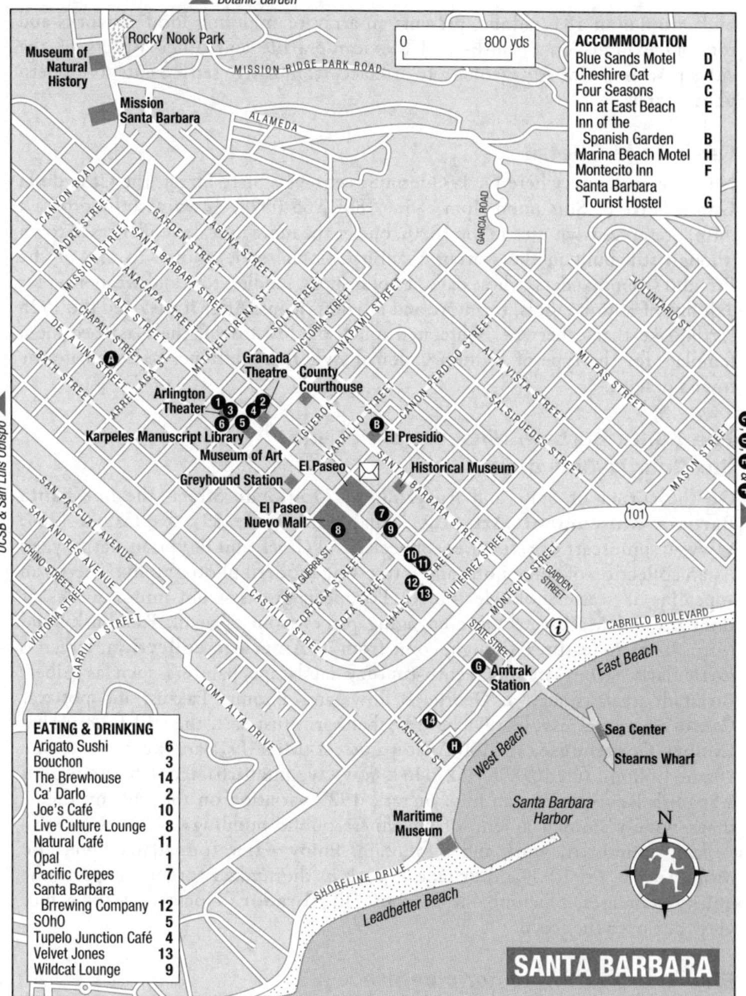

El Presidio de Santa Barbara

The town's few genuine Mission-era structures are preserved as **El Presidio de Santa Barbara**, a collection of whitewashed adobe buildings two blocks east of State Street at 123 E Canon Perdido St (daily 10.30am–4.30pm; $5; Ⓦwww.sbthp.org/presidio.htm), built around the fourth and last of the Spanish military garrisons in the region, though only the living quarters of the soldiers who once guarded the site remain. One of these structures, the modest **El Cuartel**, two blocks east of State Street at 123 Canon Perdido Street, is the second oldest building in California, dating from 1782, and now houses historical exhibits and a scale model of the small Spanish colony. A block away, at 136 E De la Guerra Street, the **Santa Barbara Historical Museum** (Tues–Sat 10am–5pm, Sun noon–5pm; free; Ⓣ805/966-1601, Ⓦwww.santabarbaramuseum.com), built around an 1817 adobe, presents an array of middling local artworks and rotating exhibits on Spanish- and Mexican-era life and other aspects of the city's past, from Ice Age geology to artefacts from native settlements to modern photographs.

Casa de la Guerra

Near the museum, where De la Guerra Street meets State Street, the **Casa de la Guerra** (Sat & Sun noon–4pm; $5; ⓣ805/965-0093, ⓦwww.sbthp.org/casa.htm) preserves what was, in the 1820s, one of the more upscale residences in town (though still built in the spartan Spanish Colonial style), home to one of the Presidio's commanders. These days, it holds spurs, saddles, toys and weapons, plus exhibits of antique tools, furniture and religious icons. After it survived the 1925 earthquake that otherwise obliterated much of downtown, the Casa became a template for the type of Spanish Colonial style that continues to dominate the town's design.

The Santa Barbara Museum of Art and the County Courthouse

On the corner of State and Anapamu, at 1130 State Street, the fine **Santa Barbara Museum of Art** (Tues–Sun 11am–5pm; $9; ⓣ805/963-4364, ⓦwww.sbmuseart.org) features some classical Greek and Egyptian statuary, an Asian collection of some note, and interesting modern photography. There's an appealing if scattershot selection of European greats, from minor works of Bonnard and Matisse to more engaging pieces from Chagall, Kandinsky and Miró. Its main features, though, come from its **American collection**, which is particularly strong in nineteenth-century landscape painters such as Albert Bierstadt, realists such as George Bellows and Thomas Eakins, and postwar California modernists like Richard Diebenkorn. Just east, the still-functioning **County Courthouse**, at 1100 Anacapa Street (Mon–Fri 8am–5pm, Sat & Sun 10am–4.30pm; free; ⓣ805/962-6464, ⓦwww.santabarbaracourthouse.org), is a Spanish Revival gem, an idiosyncratic 1929 variation on the Mission theme that's widely known as one of the finest public buildings in the US, with striking murals, tilework and a fountain. Enjoy a free tour (daily 2pm, also Mon, Tues & Fri 10.30am) or take a break in the sunken gardens, explore the quirky staircases, or climb the 70-foot **"El Mirador"** clocktower for a nice view out over the town.

Elsewhere in the historic centre

Two blocks up State Street, at no. 1317, the landmark 1930s **Arlington Theater** (ⓣ805/963-4408, ⓦwww.thearlingtontheatre.com) is an intact and functional movie palace and performance venue, with a trompe l'oeil interior modelled after an atmospheric Spanish village plaza. The respected Santa Barbara Symphony (tickets $30–75; ⓣ805/898-9386, ⓦwww.thesymphony.org) performs a block away to the 1924 Moorish-flavored **Granada Theatre**, 1216 State Street, gloriously renovated to serve as the town's main performing arts centre (information at ⓣ805/899-2222, ⓦwww.granadasb.org). Nearby, at 21 W Anapamu Street, the beautifully decorated **Karpeles Manuscript Library** (Wed–Sun 10am–4pm; free; ⓣ805/962-5322, ⓦwww.rain.org/~karpeles) is home to a diverse array of important documents, which display in rotating exhibitions, such as Napoleon's battle plans for his Russian invasion and manuscripts by figures such as Twain, Edison, Locke and Borges.

The beaches and around

Half a mile down State Street from the town centre, Cabrillo Boulevard runs along the south-facing shore, a long, clean strip stretching from the yacht and fishing harbour beyond palm-lined **West Beach** to the volleyball courts and golden sands of **East Beach**, where the touristy 1872 **Stearns Wharf** (Ⓦwww.stearnswharf.org) is the oldest wooden pier in the state. The victim of several earthquakes and fires, it has been restored to its former glory and is lined with knick-knack shops, seafood restaurants, ice-cream stands and the **Ty Warner Sea Center** (daily 10am–5pm; $8; Ⓣ805/962-2526), an annex of the Museum of Natural History (see below), offering a tot-friendly selection of touch tanks, interactive exhibits, whale bones and tide pools.

Just west, overlooking the marina, the **Santa Barbara Maritime Museum**, 113 Harbor Way, Suite 190 (Thurs–Tues 10am–6pm; $7; Ⓣ805/962-8404, Ⓦwww.sbmm.org), occupies the site of the old Naval Reserve Center and showcases old-fashioned ship models and exhibits on the whaling and tallow trade, seal hunting, native Chumash canoes, and the current nautical practices of recovering shipwrecks and communicating with shore.

Mission Santa Barbara and beyond

The mission from which the city takes its name, **Mission Santa Barbara** (daily 9am–4.30pm; $5; Ⓣ805/682-4713, Ⓦwww.sbmission.org), is located in the hills above town at 2201 Laguna Street. Known as the "Queen of the Missions", its imposing 1820 twin-towered facade – facing out over a perfectly manicured garden towards the sea – combines Romanesque and Mission styles, giving it a formidable character lacking in some of the prettier outposts. A small **museum** displays artefacts from the mission archives, and the cemetery contains the remains of some four thousand Native Americans. Many of them helped build the original complex, which includes aqueducts, waterworks, a grist mill and two reservoirs, with the old pottery kiln and tanning vats now in ruin.

Just beyond the mission at 2559 Puerta del Sol Road, the **Museum of Natural History** (daily 10am–5pm; $10; Ⓣ805/682-4711, Ⓦwww.sbnature.org) showcases intriguing artefacts from Chumash culture, various dioramas of mammals, birds, reptiles and insects, a planetarium, and actual skeletons of such extinct creatures as the pygmy mammoth, taken from Santa Rosa Island, off the Santa Barbara coast in Channel Islands National Park (see p.336). For a closer glimpse of nature, continue on into the hills from the mission until you come to the splendid **Botanic Garden**, 1212 Mission Canyon Road (daily 9am–6pm, Nov–Feb closes 5pm; $8; Ⓣ805/682-4726, Ⓦwww.sbbg.org), whose 65 acres feature pleasant hiking trails amid indigenous cacti, manzanita, trees and wildflowers – a relaxing respite among hillside meadows and glades.

Eating

Santa Barbara has a number of very good and very expensive **restaurants**, but it also has many more affordable options offering a range of cuisines. Since it's right on the Pacific, you'll find a lot of seafood and sushi, and Mexican places are numerous. Throughout, you'll also see local wine that comes from the vineyard-blanketed countryside northwest of the city.

Arigato Sushi 1225 State St ⓣ805/965-6074. The main draw for sushi in town, this boutique Japanese spot is a bit on the pricey side – with the requisite modernist chic and hipster diners – but the fresh, delicious raw fish tends to justify the expense.

Bouchon 9 W Victoria St ⓣ805/730-1160. Elite California cuisine favourite, presenting a rotating menu of scrumptious dishes such as escargot, rack of lamb, maple-glazed duck breast and a full selection of fresh seafood.

Ca' Darlo 37 E Victoria St ⓣ805/884-9419. Although there are a number of upscale Italian haunts in town, this is one of the few that lives up to its prices, with fine cheeses and pasta, and main dishes that include roasted quail, veal chops, crepes and fresh fish.

Joe's Café 536 State St ⓣ805/966-4638. Long-established bar and grill, still a great place to stop off for a burger, chowder, steak sandwich or pot roast. More or less midway between the beach and the downtown museums.

Natural Café 508 State St ⓣ805/962-9494. Good and cheap veggie meals – with pasta, sandwiches, salads, falafel and desserts – and meat entrees such as tacos and enchiladas, in a prime spot for people watching. Part of a regional chain.

Channel Islands National Park

Stretching north from Santa Catalina Island off the coast of Los Angeles, a chain of fascinating desert islands is preserved as the 250,000-acre **Channel Islands National Park**, offering excellent hiking trails and splendid views of marine life, as well as fishing and scuba and skin diving through the many caves, coves and shipwrecks in the crystal-clear Pacific waters. Five of the eight islands are accessible as part of the park, though the closest, Anacapa, some fourteen miles south of Ventura, has the most ecotourist traffic. The best time to visit is between February and April, when you can engage in whale watching. Inland hiking requires a permit (ⓣ805/658-5711, ⓦwww.nps.gov/chis) and divers can explore the two exposed wrecks on either side of the island.

Park practicalities

If you're considering visiting the Channel Islands, the best introduction to their **unique geology**, **flora** and **fauna** – endemic to the islands – can be found in Ventura, an hour north of Los Angeles, at the **park's visitor centre**, 1901 Spinnaker Drive (daily 8.30am–5pm; free; ⓣ805/658-5730), which also offers models, films and telescopes to view the islands at a distance. More information is available at the Outdoors Santa Barbara Visitor Center, in that town at 113 Harbor Way, 4th Floor (daily 10am–5pm; ⓣ805/884-1475, ⓦoutdoorsb.noaa.gov).

The Nature Conservancy acquired ninety percent of the islands in 1988 and has made them accessible to the public on **day-trip tours**; nearly the only way to visit the park is by boat, through operators that run from Ventura Harbor. Anacapa is served by several tours run by Island Packers, 1691 Spinnaker Drive, three miles west of US-101 and a mile south of Ventura (ⓣ805/642-7688 for 24-hour recorded information, ⓣ805/642-1393 for reservations 9am–5pm, ⓦwww.islandpackers.com). Packages include all-day trips with two to five hours on the given island ($45–75, depending on the island), two-day camping excursions ($58–108) and whale watching outings that last about three hours and start at $32. The trip over takes ninety minutes to three hours each way (or four to five hours for San Miguel), and boats don't run every day and often fill up, so reserve ahead. Truth Aquatics, 301 W Cabrillo Boulevard, Santa Barbara (ⓣ805/962-1127, ⓦwww.truthaquatics.com), has alternative itineraries to all the islands on smaller vessels at higher prices, including two-day hiking, diving and kayaking excursions.

Opal 1325 State St ☎805-966-9676. Fresh and inventive California cuisine that appeals for dishes such as crab cakes, tiger prawns and a range of pizzas and pastas. Mostly midpriced menu, though the duck and steak entrees are more toward the upper end.

Pacific Crêpes 705 Anacapa St ☎805/882-1123. About as close to a decent crepe as you're going to get here, prepared by real French cooks, who do an especially good job on the dessert crepes. Expect to wait for service.

Tupelo Junction Cafe 1218 State St ☎805/899-3100. One of the town's best spots for breakfast, focusing on such stick-to-your-ribs items like mushroom-and-truffle scrambles, crab cake and potato hash, vanilla French toast and Maine lobster chowder. Also serves lunch and dinner.

Bars and clubs

There are quite a few **bars** and **clubs** along State Street, especially downtown; for the most up-to-date **nightlife** listings, check out a copy of the free weekly *Santa Barbara Independent* (Ⓦwww.independent.com), available at area bookstores, record stores and convenience marts.

There are a number of free, primitive campgrounds (permits $15 per night; make reservations at ☎1-877/444-6777) on each island if you want to rough it. Bring plenty of food and especially water, as none is available on the island.

The Islands

Tiny **Anacapa** (Chumash for "mirage") is actually two islets: West Anacapa is largely a refuge for nesting brown pelicans, most of it off limits except Frenchy's Cove, a pristine beach and good base for scuba or snorkelling expeditions; East Anacapa has a small visitor centre and a 1.5-mile nature trail, and is known for its signature Arch Rock, encompassing a thin rocky bridge over the waves. There are no beaches here, but swimming in the cove where the boats dock is allowed. West of Anacapa, Santa Cruz is the largest and highest of the islands and is owned by the Nature Conservancy, which has recently managed the reintroduction of bald eagles to the terrain. Throughout the island, you can hike or even camp in the remote landscapes.

Almost as big as Santa Cruz, **Santa Rosa** has many grasslands, canyons and steep ravines, but overall contains gentler terrain — though it's still compelling for its hiking and kayaking opportunities. Especially interesting are its archeological sites, some of which date back 11,000 years and are still being investigated for their Chumash settlement relics. The most distant island – windswept **San Miguel**, fifty miles offshore – is alive with elephant seals and sea lions, and is thought to be the burial place of sixteenth-century Spanish explorer Juan Cabrillo. No grave has been found, but a monument has been erected at Cuyler Harbor on the island's eastern end. Seasoned hikers may also wish to make the rugged cross-island trip to Point Bennett to spy on the plentiful wildlife. Keep in mind, though, the island's perilous location — amid a low shelf riddled with hazardous rocks — can lead to regular cancellations of seagoing trips there. South of the main islands lies the smallest of the Channel group, **Santa Barbara**, named by Sebastian Vizcaíno, who dropped by on St Barbara's Day, December 4, 1602. The island's appeal these days is largely due to its sea lions, kestrels, larks and meadowlarks, which can be seen on land gradually recovering its native flora after years of destruction by now-extinct rabbits.

Of the three other islands in the full chain, San Clemente (the furthest south) and San Nicolas are controlled by the US Navy, while visiting the most urbanized, **Santa Catalina**, is a different sort of experience that constitutes its own weekend trip from LA (see p.158 for information).

The Brewhouse 229 W Montecito St ⓣ805/884-4664. Enjoyable brewpub with around ten handcrafted beers, including some savoury Belgian-style ales, plus decent comfort food (meatloaf, burgers, etc) and live music Wed–Sun.

Live Culture Lounge 11 W De La Guerra, in the Paseo Nuevo Mall ⓣ805/845-8800. Curious wine-bar-cafe-gallery that also presents handcrafted brews, eclectic live music, grilled sandwiches and frozen yogurt. The food is enjoyable and affordable and the cocktails strong and inventive.

Santa Barbara Brewing Company 501 State St ⓣ805/730-1040. Serviceable American fare – burgers, seafood and sandwiches – with solid microbrewed beers and live music on weekends. The Rincon Red and State Street Stout are both worth a swig.

Soho 1221 State St ⓣ805/962-7776, ⓦwww.sohosb.com. Favourite local place to catch a jazz show, with nightly performances and the occasional big name. Mixes the vibe with frequent rock, acoustic and world-beat artists and bands.

Velvet Jones 423 State St ⓣ805/965-8676, ⓦwww.velvet-jones.com. Among the few good places in town to catch a show, typically of the indie variety. Thurs–Sat, and the odd comedy and reggae show at other times.

Wildcat Lounge 15 W Ortega St ⓣ805/962-7970, ⓦwww.wildcatlounge.com. A good spot for seeing electronica DJs and various bands, in a chic atmosphere with a mix of locals, students and out-of-towners.

Contexts

Contexts

History

To casual observers, especially those on the East Coast, Los Angeles is a place with no sense of **history**, an ultramodern urban sprawl that lives up to its vapid stereotypes, nothing but sunny skies, surfer dudes and movie stars. In the 1990s a potent countermyth emerged of dystopic LA, in which earthquakes, riots and floods are commonplace, and lying beneath the city's sunny surface is a dark and dangerous underbelly. Neither one of these stereotypes is strictly accurate, though, for in a city as huge, eclectic and ever-changing as Los Angeles, no singular myth can ever hold sway, at least not for very long.

Prehistoric LA

Like other parts of the West Coast, the underlying **geology** that makes up the LA basin began as an **oceanic terrane**, basically a mobile chunk of land that pushed toward the North American landmass along the Pacific Plate. For 120 to 160 million years, the terrane came closer, drifting northward, and repeatedly rose above and sank below sea level, until it reached its current, above-ground position around five million years ago. By the time of the **Ice Age**, around 25,000 years ago, the LA region was literally an arcadia – a sylvan land of fertile, tree-covered plains, crystalline brooks and lakes, untamed rivers and a temperate climate. Despite the idyllic conditions, a natural peril awaited the region's creatures in the form of the **La Brea Tar Pits** (a redundancy: "The Tar" Tar Pits). These dark, boggy pools of natural asphalt – not tar – were visible evidence of the copious petroleum deposits in the region and spelled doom for any animals that wandered into them. Sinking into the murky ooze, they remained preserved in the muck until they were unearthed in the modern era by **William Orcutt**, giving a vivid picture of the rich ecology of the time, when prehistoric LA was populated with the likes of sabre-toothed tigers, giant ground sloths, mammoths, wolves, short-faced bears and even camels. The wide array of fauna and pristine environment would not last long, for as soon as humans began crossing into North America via the temporary land-bridge at the Bering Strait (about 18,000–25,000 years ago), such creatures were doomed to be prey for hunters or driven out of the area entirely, to become extinct.

Native peoples

For thousands of years prior to the arrival of Europeans, **native peoples** subsisted in different parts of the Los Angeles basin. The dominant groups in the area were **Tataviam**, **Chumash** and **Tongva** (whom the Spanish called Gabrieleño) peoples. Of these, the dominant tribes were the Chumash, who lived along the coast around modern-day Malibu and Ventura, and the Tongva, who occupied much of the central LA basin. Both tribes fished and traded by sea in pitch-blackened canoes, and were skilled enough navigators to meet explorer Juan Cabrillo before his 1542 landfall off San Pedro. Otherwise, these tribes had little in common, and were an easy target for later **Spanish** conquerors and missionaries – although it's also true that they were wiped out by European-borne epidemics as much as by Spanish military power.

Today, LA County is home to the greatest number of native peoples of any county in the US – up to two hundred thousand by some estimates, many migrating from other parts of the US. Indeed, most Native Americans in these parts are now Navajo, and little remains to mark the existence of the early tribes, aside from the faded remnants found at scattered archeological digs and the cultural treasures locked up behind glass in folk-art museums.

European discovery and colonization

After sighting San Diego harbor, Cabrillo continued north along the coast to Santa Catalina Island and the Channel Islands off Santa Barbara. He bestowed a number of other place names that survive, including, in the LA area, Santa Monica and San Pedro Bay, named for the first Bishop of Rome. Other European explorers followed, charting the California coast and naming more of the islands, bays and coastal towns, but it was the **Spanish**, moving up from their base in Mexico, who were to colonize Southern California and map out the future city of Los Angeles.

The Spanish occupation of California began in earnest in 1769 as a combination of military expediency (to prevent other powers from gaining a foothold) and missionary zeal (to convert Native Americans to Roman Catholicism). **Padre Junípero Serra** began the missions, setting off from Mexico and going all the way up to Monterey; assisting him was **Gaspar de Portola**, a soldier who led the expedition into LA.

The first mission sited in Los Angeles was **Mission San Gabriel**, in 1771; from that beginning, Spanish military garrisons served to hold the natives subject to the demands of Franciscan friars who ordered them to abandon their religious beliefs, cultural rituals and languages. The penalties for disobedience were stiff: flogging with twenty to forty lashes was standard practice. While the Spanish were trying to "convert the savages", they were also eradicating the native population, reducing their ranks by 95 percent over the course of 150 years. By World War I, less than 17,000 of them remained.

The Spanish era

Aside from abusing the natives, the Spanish who colonized Southern California effected the first designs for LA, which they established in 1781 at a site northwest of the current Plaza in Downtown. The city's original **pobladores**, or settlers, of which there were fewer than fifty, set a multicultural precedent for the region, as they were made up of a majority of black, mestizo, mixed-race and native peoples, with the white Spanish being a distinct, though powerful, minority. The early **pueblo** (town), designed by California's governor **Felipe de Neve**, grew in short spurts, aided by the creation of the *zanja madre*, or "mother ditch", which brought water into town. Despite half-hearted efforts by the Spanish to make the settlement grow, it took a devastating flood in 1815 for large-scale development to begin, starting with the construction of the current Plaza and its Plaza Church – La Placita – and the Avila Adobe.

As the town grew from remote outpost to regional centrepiece, the power of the Spanish Crown began to fade. While the military and missions exercised official power, the functional operation of the little burg was increasingly the province of a small group of mestizo families whose names are still reflected in major LA street names – Sepulveda, Pico and so on – along with a few white American expatriates who for various reasons found the region to their liking. By the early 1800s, the Spanish were playing only a *de jure* role in city administration; soon after, they would be forcibly removed from power.

Mexican rule

Mexico gained independence in 1821, calling itself the United States of Mexico, and over the next four years, the Mexican residents of Southern California evicted the Spanish and made the region into a territory of Mexico itself – Alta California.

The 24 subsequent years of Mexican rule upended the political and social order – causing the destruction and looting of many missions – but provided no end to the oppression of native peoples. The Tongva and others now found themselves at the bottom level of an oppressive new hierarchy, in which rich land barons controlled huge parcels of land known as **ranchos** and reduced the natives to a state of near-serfdom. (Despite the ugliness that took place there, the main estates of many ranchos survive in a well-preserved state, with lovely gardens and elegant architecture – though without the surrounding land holdings – making for an excellent starting point on any trip into LA history.)

Due to widespread social oppression and frequent clashes between the wealthy land bosses, the period was largely a chaotic one, well described by Richard Henry Dana Jr in his book *Two Years before the Mast*. By the time Governor **Pio Pico** successfully established his Alta California capital in Los Angeles (long his preferred spot for governance), the period of Mexican rule was almost at an end, its demise assured by the factional struggles and undisciplined ways of the rancho owners.

The Mexican–American War

From the 1830s onward, driven by the concept of **Manifest Destiny**, the popular, often religious, belief that Americans had a divine or moral charge to occupy the country from coast to coast, the US government's stated policy regarding California was to buy all of Mexico's land north of the Rio Grande, the river that now divides the US and Mexico. When militantly expansionist President James K. Polk annexed Texas – still claimed by Mexico – war broke out. Most of the fighting in the **Mexican–American War** took place in Texas, though a few skirmishes occurred in Southern California.

By the summer of 1846, after the American capture of Monterey and San Diego, Pico and his colleagues had difficulty even finding significant numbers of loyal Mexicans to defend LA against the US. A truce was signed to avoid bloodshed and American troops walked into the city virtually unopposed. However, despite this relatively pacific start, the military chieftains left local government in the hands of the incompetent **Archibald Gillespie**, who promptly instituted martial law and just as quickly turned the populace against the Americans. The situation further degenerated, with outbreaks of local hostilities, and by the time Mexican general Andreas Pico and American "pathfinder" John C. Fremont signed the final **peace treaty** in January 1847 at Campo de Cahuenga, after several battles and much bloodshed, the chasm between the Mexican residents and their new American conquerors had grown considerably.

Early American rule

California was admitted to the US as the 31st state in 1850, a move quickly followed by the **1851 Land Act**, through which the new white settlers targeted the rancho owners, forcing them to prove their legal right to the land they had been granted. The ensuing legal battles left many of the owners destitute, and while the rancho boundaries and some of their elemental chunks continued to linger for up to a century or more, the central goal of the new settlers had been accomplished: the old-line Mexicans were driven out and replaced by a gringo elite. However, even as this process was taking place, and the latest real-estate magnates were consolidating their power, the city's social structure continued its slide into chaos.

For many good reasons, LA was called **"Hell Town"** in the middle of the nineteenth century. The lives of the native peoples got even worse, as they were subject to all manner of mob aggression and legal disenfranchisement. Because the city had no effective municipal authority, and because it was crowded with hordes of aggressive fortune-hunters who had failed in the northern gold rush, it became a magnet for violent criminals and other miscreants, and was littered with gambling halls, saloons and brothels. The bellicose citizenry usually focused their rage against the groups at the bottom of the social hierarchy, tactics that eventually backfired when roving groups of Mexican bandidos, such as Tiburcio Vasquez, emerged to counter the threats.

The local situation got so bloody that "**vigilance committees**" were created to deal with the crime, which had reached the same levels as San Francisco even though LA only had a tenth as many people. The vigilantes summarily executed 32 people, and gave rise to even more extreme groups who would hunt down lawbreakers, real or imagined. The El Monte Rangers, an imported gang of Texas thugs, was perhaps the most notorious, though there were many others, and LA remained a city solidly under the thumb of mob rule until after the Civil War.

During the height of its social strife, the region managed to sketch the outlines of what would later become the metropolitan area. Post offices, banks, newspapers and churches were a few of the emblems of encroaching civilization, and the activity of such pioneering entrepreneurs as **Phineas Banning** – the developer of the Wilmington harbour plan – also brought early growth to the city.

In 1860, LA's citizens chose the wrong side in the **Civil War**, casting a meager eighteen percent of their ballots for Abraham Lincoln, and soon became possessed by secessionist rage and racial hatred. Adding to the rancour, many in the city and region were clamouring to split from northern California and create an autonomous enclave where they wouldn't be subject to state or federal power. Thirteen thousand soldiers were stationed in Wilmington's Drum Barracks to ensure domestic order, act against Southwest rebel activity, and, later, quash native uprisings. Just as tellingly, a crowd of revellers gathered in LA after hearing news of Lincoln's assassination. Their celebration was broken up – but only with the aid of the federal soldiers.

Late-nineteenth-century growth

The last three decades of the nineteenth century were an era of **rapid growth** and **technological change** in LA, principally because of three factors: periodic real-estate booms that led to the subdivision of the old ranchos into smaller, more profitable chunks; the building of railroad lines externally, to places like San Francisco, and internally, from Downtown to the port at San Pedro; and most importantly, the mass arrival of Midwesterners.

From the 1870s, LA gained a reputation as a bastion of healthy living. While eastern American cities were notorious for sooty air and water pollution, LA was touted as a sunny, clean-air paradise where the infirm could recover from their illnesses and everyone could enjoy the fruits of the invigorating desert lifestyle. The **orange** was the perfect symbol of this new arcadia, and trees and citrus groves were planted by the thousands, ultimately leading to towns being named for oranges and walnuts, and streets for magnolias and white oaks. Huge numbers of Iowans and Kansans moved to the city in the Victorian era, spurred on as well by cheap one-way railroad tickets: thanks to a price war between the Santa Fe and Southern Pacific railroads, fares from Kansas City to LA briefly dropped to a mere dollar; before long, the passenger cars were full of church-going Protestants seeking desert salvation.

The Midwesterners of the 1880s did much to displace lingering Hispanic influences, meanwhile exacerbating racial tensions, which flared up in such instances as the **anti-Chinese riot of 1871**. After a disagreement left a white man dead at the hands of a Chinese shopkeeper, a mob assembled and quickly set about attacking and murdering what Chinese residents it could get its hands on. While there were only about two hundred Chinese in LA at the time, the mob managed to strangle, shoot, stab and hang 22 of them. In an ominous portent of LA-style justice to come, few of the perpetrators faced jail time, and those that did only served a year or so.

Beyond its racial animus and Midwestern migrations, LA was becoming an attraction of sorts for a few of the nation's more colourful characters. **Charles Fletcher Lummis** was the first of these, a fervent supporter of the rights of native peoples, yet also an isolationist who saw a looming threat from foreign immigration. Aside from that, Lummis was a bit of a crank who was so committed to his own notion of healthy living that he created a boulder house, "El Alisal", which still stands in Highland Park, and he took the unusual step of coming to LA from Cincinnati **on foot** – a distance of nearly three thousand miles. Lummis would be just one of many individualists to inhabit the LA region, including others like the Pasadena artisans who created "**Arroyo culture**" just after the turn of the century (an Arts and Crafts philosophy that owed much to Lummis; see box, p.169), and left-wing political activists like **Job Harriman**, whose commune in the northern desert town of Llano del Rio was intended to be the blueprint for a socialist utopia.

While the dreamers and artists experimented with alternative living, the politicians and businessmen were busy expanding the city by every means possible: the **harbour** was developed at San Pedro, and **railway lines** were added throughout the region by Henry Huntington, through his electric Red Car transit system. Most importantly, entrepreneurs like Edward Doheny grew rich drilling for **oil** practically everywhere, and by 1900 the landscape of the city was peppered with oil derricks wide and far, as the commercial value of the black goo was realized first with kerosene, and later with a much more potent refinement – gasoline to power automobiles.

The early twentieth century: water and power

Around the turn of the century, LA's population reached one hundred thousand; perhaps more important to the city's development, however, **William Mulholland** was put in charge of the city's water department. Mulholland was the catalyst for a legendary water-stealing scheme, as various bankers, publishing magnates and railway bosses purchased large land holdings in the San Fernando

Valley, and shortly thereafter, a small cadre of city bankers secretly began buying up land in California's distant Owens Valley, 250 miles away. By the time the northern farmers realized what had happened, the bankers had consolidated control over the valley watershed and were making plans to bring the bulk of the region's water to the drought-stricken citizens of LA – or so it seemed. Modern evidence suggests that massive amounts of water were being deposited into the city sewers so area dams and reservoirs could drop precipitously, thus making it look as if the region was on the verge of a severe drought.

Following the land grab, Mulholland built a **giant canal system** – one of the country's biggest public-works projects (see box, p.174) – that carried the water to Southern California, but not LA proper. Instead, the aqueduct mysteriously ended in the San Fernando Valley and city politicians **annexed** the valley for housing, thus wiping out thousands of acres of fertile agricultural land and making the real-estate interests there – actually Downtown bankers and political powerbrokers who secretly bought up the land – wealthy beyond imagination. Learning how easily they'd been swindled, the Owens Valley farmers did not soon forget. In the 1920s, when Mulholland and company set about acquiring more property for the canal system, the farmers responded by destroying sections of the system with dynamite charges. This violence, coupled with the unrelated bursting of the St Francis dam north of LA – a catastrophe that killed more than four hundred people – destroyed Mulholland's reputation. However, by that time, his main work had already been accomplished: the aqueduct helped turn LA into a metropolis.

Accompanying the development of the modernizing city was the growth of **organized labour**. In 1910, a series of strikes at breweries and foundries crippled the city, and local labour was also responsible for nearly bringing socialist Job Harriman to power. However, when the main building of the *Los Angeles Times* – the right-wing organ of labour's archenemy **Harrison Gray Otis** – was bombed, a slow erosion of leftist support took place and ultimately led to defeat for Harriman, who then retreated to his northern desert commune.

World War I to the Great Depression

Metropolis or not, LA continued to display its regressive, provincial character in many ways, especially in its treatment of **minorities**. Chinese residents were still subject to all manner of exclusionary laws, as were the Japanese, and both were among the Asian immigrants targeted by the **1913 Alien Land Bill**, which kept them from purchasing further land tracts and limited their lease tenures. Finally, even though industrial production during World War I doubled the black population of the city, the total number of **African–Americans** was still fairly small (less than three percent of the population).

In the meantime the rapid growth continued, and after World War I, LA became quite a **tourist magnet** – long before the arrival of Disneyland. Sights like Abbot Kinney's pseudo-European Venice and the carnival midways in Santa Monica and Long Beach all drew good numbers of seasonal visitors, as did Santa Catalina Island and the Mount Lowe Railroad in the San Gabriel Mountains.

Soon, another great **wave of newcomers** began arriving, from all across America. By the 1920s, LA was gaining residents by one hundred thousand per year, most coming by car and flocking to **suburbs** such as Glendale, Long Beach and Pasadena. **Petroleum** was adding to the boom, from places like Signal Hill to Venice, with oil wells popping up all over the region, usually without regard to aesthetics or pollution. Naturally, the wells helped fuel the explosive growth of the local **car culture**, which even in the 1910s had become a potent force, and by the decade after made Los Angeles the nation's leader in paved roads for motoring – some thirty years before the development of modern freeways.

The quintessential symbol of the dynamic, forward-looking atmosphere of the time was **City Hall**, built in 1928 as a mix of classical and contemporary elements, and topped by none other than a small replica of one of the long-lost ancient wonders of the world – the Mausoleum at Halicarnassus. This was civic ego on a grand scale, a fitting reflection of the attitudes of the time, but also a symbolic portent of the 1930s.

Starting a decade into the twentieth century, the first **movie pioneers took root here**, many with Jewish backgrounds and origins in the Eastern garment industry, which led to scorn from the old Downtown elite. Because of exclusionary housing laws, film titans like Adolph Zukor and Samuel Goldwyn developed the Westside as their base of operations, an action that had long-lasting effects. Even today, West Hollywood, Beverly Hills and West LA remain the cultural focus of the city, despite the constant efforts of the current Downtown elite to remedy the situation.

The boom years ended with the onset of the **Great Depression**. Banks collapsed, businesses went bankrupt, and Midwestern drought brought a new round of immigrants to Southern California, much poorer and significantly more desperate than their forebears. By 1936 the LAPD – in its seemingly infinite powers – imposed a typically draconian solution: posting officers at the California state border to deter any more "damn Okies" from coming. Those that weren't sufficiently persuaded by the police department's strong-arm tactics faced six months in jail.

These hard times spawned a number of movements. Led by fiery evangelists like **Aimee Semple McPherson**, religious **cults** gained adherents by the thousands, Communist and Fascist organizations trawled for members among the city's more frustrated or simple-minded ranks, and the muckraker **Upton Sinclair** emerged as the greatest threat to LA's ruling hierarchy since Job Harriman. With his **End Poverty in California** (**EPIC**) campaign, Sinclair frightened the upper crust across the region, and was countered not only by the usual Downtown stalwarts, but also by their Westside adversaries, the Hollywood movie bosses, who rightly perceived a danger in Sinclair's message to their control over the film industry and film-crew labour. Fraudulent newsreel propaganda (showing hordes of homeless men and various halfwits testifying their allegiance to Sinclair) helped speed Sinclair's demise in the gubernatorial contest, but no one could stop the tide of reform, which brought down LA's ultra-corrupt mayor **Frank Shaw** and his henchmen. The entire political and social mess was reflected in the most famous literary works of the time: Nathanael West's *Day of the Locust* and Raymond Chandler's detective fiction, all of which portrayed a morally decayed society on the verge of collapse or conflagration.

World War II and after

By the time of **World War II**, LA was emerging as one of the top US sites for military hardware production and coastal defence. In San Pedro, Fort MacArthur, named after the father of one of the war's most famous generals, was the site of Battery Osgood, home to anti-aircraft guns on the watch for Japanese fighter planes. Similarly, at the man-made Terminal Island, the harbour area itself was a shipbuilding centre, still embodied by the presence of the hulking SS *Lane Victory*, one of the huge cargo ships that carried supplies for the Navy during the war.

The misery of the continuing Depression and the dark, paranoid atmosphere in the early part of the war exacerbated the underlying social tensions and unleashed yet more rounds of violence and oppression against the nation's perceived enemies. One of Franklin Roosevelt's executive orders gave the green light to mass deportations of Japanese–American citizens, who were forcibly relocated to bleak desert **internment camps** for the duration of the war. Minorities who hadn't been shipped away made for fat targets as well, especially Mexican–Americans.

The **Sleepy Lagoon Murder case** – in which seventeen Hispanics were rounded up and sent to jail for a single murder, only to be later released by a disgusted appellate court – was but a prelude to the turmoil that would come to be known as the **Zoot Suit Riots**, named for the popular apparel Hispanic youth wore at the time, with wide stripes, broad shoulders and accessories like dangling watch-chains and low-slung hats. Over the course of several days in early June 1943, two hundred sailors on leave attacked and beat up a large number of Mexican–Americans – with the handy assistance of local police, who made sure that the black-and-blue victims were promptly arrested on trumped-up charges. The violence continued until it became a federal issue, causing a rift in international relations between the US and Mexico. After the chaos ended, the LA City Council responded assertively to the ugly events – by banning the wearing of zoot suits.

Although anti-Asian and -Hispanic feelings still remained, the end of the war brought a shift in hostilities. A growing contingent of **black migrants** was drawn by the climate and defence-related jobs, and from 1940 to 1965, the number of blacks in LA increased from 75,000 to 600,000. The white elite kept blacks confined to eastern sections of town around Central Avenue and "redlined" them out of personal loans and business financing, but these tactics only served to heighten the hostility that would later erupt in mass violence.

In the meantime, LA was becoming one of the USA's largest cities, with the nonstop arrival of newcomers from across the country, the rebirth of the local economy, and the construction of a **vast freeway network** to replace the old Red Cars – due to great local enthusiasm for motoring, a decline in public-transit users, and active subversion by oil, gas and automotive interests. Defence industries, notably in aerospace, began a decades-long dominion over the local economy, superseding, most notably, the movie industry, which experienced a sharp decline in the 1950s because of television's impact and governmental antitrust actions (see "The Hollywood studio system," p.351). Not surprisingly, with the growth of the military-industrial complex, the LA region became a focus of Cold War defence as many hilltop sites, from San Pedro to the Santa Monica Mountains, were converted into command centres for launching missiles against nuclear bombers, and installations like the Jet Propulsion Laboratory and Edwards Air Force Base became the focus of a local economy still on a war footing. At the top of the military-industrial heap was the shadowy figure of **Howard Hughes**, who became well known for his dabbling in Hollywood B-flicks and flying the oversized "Spruce Goose", but whose real contribution to the economic growth of LA was as the head of Hughes Aircraft and Hughes Aerospace, which led the way in the development of air-to-air missiles to fight the presumed coming war against the Soviet foe.

Concurrently, suburbs like **Orange County** drew old-time residents from the heart of the city into expanding towns like Garden Grove, Huntington Beach and Anaheim – where **Disneyland** also acted as a pop-culture beacon. The northern valleys traded orange groves for subdivisions and asphalt, and before long, the entire LA basin was swelling with people in every conceivable direction. In contrast, much of the wealth in the Hollywood and Mid-Wilshire sections of town, areas that had first been developed by middle-class automotive travel in the 1920s and 1930s, left with the "white flight" of bourgeois residents to the outlying suburbs, and the old commuter suburbs west of Downtown increasingly became part of the inner city and the new home of working-poor minorities.

The 1960s to the 1980s

As elsewhere in the country, the face of Los Angeles began changing dramatically in the 1960s. Not only was the freeway system stitching the entire basin into an interconnected network of automobile suburbs, but LA's own classic Art Deco and Historic Revival buildings were quickly disappearing. Places like **Bunker Hill** changed from shambling Victorian neighbourhoods into auto-oriented corporate enclaves, poor Hispanic families were cleared out of Elysian Park to make way for Dodger Stadium, the old 20th-Century Fox movie lot was sold off to make way for the highrise towers of Century City, and the quaint homes of Playa del Rey were demolished to make way for expansion of LAX. However unpopular they were, many of these deals were, predictably, sealed behind closed doors, in the continuing atmosphere of secrecy and intrigue that pervaded city politics.

However, the type of leadership evident in LA's postwar politicians, such as the race-baiting mayor Sam Yorty, and the city's so-called **Committee of 25**, a business cabal that acted as a sort of shadow government from its California Club headquarters, got its comeuppance with 1965's **Watts Riots**. Starting with the arrest of one Marquette Frye for speeding, the riots lasted a week and ended with the arrival of 36,000 police and National Guard troops and $40 million worth of property damage (see p.142). Along with this, the late 1960s **protests** by student radicals, mostly against the involvement in Vietnam and the emergence of flower power and hippie counterculture caused a dramatic break between generations – the staid Orange County parents versus their rebellious, pot-smoking kids. The result was an explosion of psychedelic music, left-wing political diatribe, untamed sexuality and, occasionally, bursts of violence – evident with the Manson Family killings of 1969. These freewheeling attitudes were most evident in places like the Sunset Strip, then as now famed for its rock-music scene; Laurel Canyon in the Hollywood Hills, where the celebrities of that scene held sway; and Topanga Canyon, which became a hippie commune for wealthy musicians and producers.

After much effort, the progressive forces in LA politics finally began to undermine the power structure that had ruled LA for nearly a century. Eight years after the riots, LA's first black mayor, **Tom Bradley**, was elected by a coalition of black, Hispanic and Westside Jewish voters. The political success of these groups galvanized others into action on the LA political scene, notably women and gays. Accordingly, the *LA Times*, long a paragon of yellow journalism, underwent a historic change through the efforts of **Otis Chandler**, son of archconservative former publisher Harry Chandler, who turned the paper into a liberal icon with a range of world-class writers and critics.

Bradley's twenty-year tenure was also marked, less fortuitously, by the disappearance of LA's manufacturing base. South Central and Southeast LA ceased to be centres for oil, rubber and automotive production, San Fernando Valley car plants closed, and heavy industries like Kaiser's mammoth steel-making operation in Fontana shut down. Though this was somewhat tempered in the 1980s by the heavy investment of Japanese and Canadian money into Downtown real estate, the decade ended hard with the **demise of aerospace jobs**, which had been the region's military-industrial meal ticket since the early Cold War era. As one telling symbol of the change, the old Westside site of Hughes Aircraft is now occupied by a massive condo development.

Modern LA: 1990 to 2010

The early 1990s continued the hard times, which only got bleaker when black motorist **Rodney King** was videotaped being beaten by uniformed officers of the LA Police Department. The officers' subsequent acquittal by jurors in conservative Simi Valley sparked the April 1992 **riots**, which highlighted the economic disparities between rich and poor, along with the more obvious abuses of police power and privilege. Meanwhile, episodes like the **O.J. Simpson trial** only served to further confuse matters. In 1995, Simpson, a black former football star, was acquitted of killing his wife and her friend, in what was termed the "Trial of the Century", an ugly and protracted affair in which public opinion was split along racial lines.

All these factors combined to make the first five years of the 1990s the bleakest since the Great Depression, and **natural calamities** – regional flooding, Malibu fires and mudslides, and two dramatic earthquakes – only added to the general malaise.

The rest of the decade was not nearly as dramatic. **Richard Riordan**, a multimillionaire technocrat, was mayor for eight years in the mid- to late 1990s and presided over a major **revival** in the city's economic fortunes and a **restructuring** of its economic base – aerospace and automotive industries giving way to tourism, real estate and, as always, Hollywood. New property developments attempted to revitalize blighted sections of town, and even crime and violence tailed off. However, the city's old demons continued to stir. More than anything else, the allegations behind the **Rampart police scandal** – where a group of corrupt police officers acted worse than the gangs they were trying to shut down – made people realize what truly awful elements still lurked under LA's glossy surfaces.

The 2001 mayoral election of bland, uninspiring bureaucrat James Hahn didn't help matters, but his appointment of former New York police reformer **William Bratton** to head the LAPD surprised many, giving hope that an outsider with no connection to the department's entrenched ways might be just the person to reform it – and sure enough, since then Los Angeles has experienced a notable reduction in crime and violence, following national trends. After serving only a term, Hahn was defeated in his re-election bid by **Antonio Villaraigosa** – amazingly, LA's first Latino mayor since 1872. The new mayor had his share of controversies to be sure (namely a messy divorce), but soon became the emblem of the growing political power of Hispanics in the city, especially when part of a coalition joining blacks and progressive whites on the Westside.

In 2010, the metropolis is back on a much firmer footing than in the 1990s, even though it's suffered greatly in the ongoing national **recession** that began in 2007. Real-estate prices have dipped, jobs are hard to come by, and practically every municipal entity from the state itself down to the smallest city has grappled with deep budget cuts or unpopular tax-raising measures. However, things are on the upswing in a few areas. For one, the ugly character of much LA design from the 1960s into the 1990s – a mix of concrete Brutalism and corporate glass towers – is slowly changing with the arrival of a slew of innovative, high-profile **signature buildings**, including the Getty Center, Disney Hall and the CalTrans building. At the same time, the preservation of classic sections of town like Old Pasadena and Downtown's Spring Street and Broadway offers hope that the city may have finally learned from its mistakes in trying to demolish its past. And the once rigorous racial separatism that kept black, white, Latino and Asian Angelenos at each other's throats during the riot years is slowly subsiding. Perhaps the most symbolic image of this is the national rise of the **Korean taco**, a true melting-pot dish that combines bulgogi beef with tortillas to create a perfect culinary hybrid invented in LA itself – a fitting emblem for the kind of harmonious blend that's always been possible here, for anyone who can look past the darkness of history.

The Hollywood studio system

To this day, the word **Hollywood** remains synonymous with the motion picture industry, even if the reality of that association has not always held true. What follows is a brief history of the movie business in Los Angeles and how the **studio system** took root, from its genesis to the beginning of its decline.

Westward migration

While we now think of Hollywood's emergence as a simple matter of abundant sun, low taxes and cheap labour – all important factors, to be sure – the original reason the first filmmakers established themselves here was because of something much simpler: **fear**. But for the strong-arm tactics of Thomas Edison and company, the movie business might never have come to Southern California.

Edison and his competitors (companies like Biograph, Vitagraph and Pathé, among many others) had by 1909 consolidated their various patents on film technology and processing to form what was known as "**the Trust**": the Motion Picture Patents Company (the MPPC). Although it didn't even last a decade (thanks to bad business practices and a federal antitrust suit), the MPPC did manage to scare off many directors and producers in the first years of its existence, including producer William Selig and director Francis Boggs, both of whom wanted to get as far away from the MPPC's seat of power, New York City, as they possibly could. Southern California was their choice, and more prominent film-industry figures soon followed, finding the taxes, labour costs, weather and abundant shooting locations much to their liking.

Early Hollywood

Thomas Ince, **Mack Sennett** and **D.W. Griffith** were the early film legends who helped to establish Hollywood as the focus of the American movie business. Ince, with his studios in Culver City and Edendale, and his coastal "Inceville" north of Santa Monica, founded the elemental model of the studio system that was to hold sway for many decades: writers would prepare scripts in collaboration with directors and Ince himself, after which a tightly budgeted production would be filmed at prearranged locations, and a final cut of the movie would be edited. This sort of precise planning minimized the possibility of surprises during shooting, as well as inconsistent or off-kilter storytelling, and contributed to the **factory-like** character of Ince's operation.

By comparison, Sennett's **Keystone Film Company** in Edendale, in East Hollywood, produced Keystone Kops comedies in less rigorous fashion. However, with production needs mounting, Sennett adopted his former colleague's model (both had worked for Culver City's Triangle Films, on the lot that now houses Sony Studios) and went on to a two-decades-long career making his signature brand of wacky entertainment.

The largest creative presence in early Hollywood was, however, D.W. Griffith, who began as a theatrical actor and director of one-reel shorts and reached the peak of his fame with *Birth of a Nation*, a runaway hit in 1914 – despite its glamorization of the Ku Klux Klan, its epic length (2hr 40min), and its unprecedented $2 admission fee. Woodrow Wilson praised the film for "writing history with lightning", overlooking that its source was not actual history, but the bigoted ramblings of Southern preacher Thomas Dixon, on whose book, *The Clansman*, the movie had been based.

Generating a firestorm of controversy with the film, Griffith fired back at his critics with his next film, *Intolerance*, a bloated historical epic, but only succeeded at permanently damaging his career. With its preachy moralizing and colossal sets loaded with Babylonian columns and squatting elephants, *Intolerance* became a buzzword for box office failure and directorial narcissism. Griffith would make a slow slide into obscurity in the 1920s, but not before he perfected the essential aesthetic components he developed with *Birth of a Nation*: close-ups, flashbacks, cross-cutting and the like – essential elements of modern cinema storytelling to this day.

The birth of the big studios

In 1913, **Cecil B. DeMille**, an itinerant theatrical actor and director, came west to rent a horse barn for a movie. From this simple act, DeMille and his partners, glove-maker Sam Goldfish (soon to be renamed Goldwyn) and vaudeville producer Jesse Lasky, established the basis for the big studios that would follow. The film made in the barn (even as there were horses still in it) was *The Squaw Man*, which became a huge commercial triumph; DeMille became one of the early industry's most bankable directors of historical and biblical epics, and Lasky and Goldwyn later teamed with Adolph Zukor to create the colossus known as **Paramount Studios**.

Like other studios in the coming decades, Paramount used a number of underhand tactics to push its product, including "block booking" (in which film packages, rather than individual films, were sold to exhibitors, thus maximizing studio revenue) and buying up theatre chains across the country (to ensure exhibition spaces for its films). These influential practices served to consolidate the industry. By the end of World War I, three major studios had risen to dominance: Paramount, **Loew's** and **First National** – though only Paramount would survive in name during the height of the studio system.

The 1919 creation of **United Artists (UA)** looked promising for actors and directors. This studio, formed by Douglas Fairbanks Sr, Mary Pickford, D.W. Griffith and Charlie Chaplin, seemed to suggest a greater role might be in store for the creative individuals who actually made the films, instead of just the studio bosses and executive producers. Things didn't quite work out that way: the next decade saw UA in the role of bit player, along with Columbia and Universal, principally because it didn't own its own theatres and had to rely on one of the major studios for booking its films. The one major development UA prefigured was the dominance of the **star system**, by which big-name actors (such as Fairbanks and Pickford), rather than writers, directors or the story itself, would drive the production and marketing of studio product – a scheme that has barely changed in ninety years.

The golden age

The five largest studios from the 1920s to the 1940s were **Paramount**, the **Fox Film Corporation** (later 20th-Century Fox), **Warner Bros**, **Radio-Keith-Orpheum** (later RKO) and the biggest of them all, **Metro-Goldwyn-Mayer**, or MGM, which was controlled by the still-powerful Loew's corporation in New York. The majors used every method they could to rigidly control their operations, and they did much to industrialize the business, breaking down the stages of production and using specialists (editors, cinematographers and so on) to create the product, which was often exhibited in lavish, company-owned "**movie palaces**" that even today are regarded as the greatest spaces ever built for movie-watching. The arrival of **sound** in the late 1920s further specialized the industry, and the possibility of a lone professional with a camera shooting a nationally released film vanished.

Ince's original system had been perfected into rigorous, clinical efficiency. Even the content of the movies was controlled, in this case because of **Will Hays**, formerly postmaster general in the corrupt Harding administration, when a series of 1920s scandals (not least, Fatty Arbuckle's three trials for the rape and murder of actress Virginia Rappe) tarnished the industry and raised the spectre of government censorship. Hays' major claim to fame was as the developer of the 1930 "**Hays Code**", a series of official proscriptions and taboos that the studios were supposed to follow, involving intimations of sex, miscegenation, blasphemy and so on. Although Hays is often credited with enforcing movie-industry censorship, it was actually **Joseph Breen** who wielded the real censorial power starting in the mid-1930s, when the Code first began to be rigidly enforced. With Breen and the Catholic organization the **Legion of Decency** looking over its shoulder, Hollywood produced a brand of entertainment that was safe, fun and mostly noncontroversial. That filmmakers like John Ford, Orson Welles, Howard Hawks and Preston Sturges were able to make classic films in such a stifling environment says much about the degree of talent the studios were employing during this time – although the industry also produced many tepid, cloying melodramas and tiresome serials that followed the Code precisely and remain almost unwatchable.

Although Hollywood was, as an industrial system, unmatched by any other production complex in the world, it was, even at its height, something of an illusory power. For while the most visible and glamorous of the movie industry's stars and bosses smiled for the paparazzi in Hollywood, the real **financial muscle** continued to come from New York City. Companies like Loew's, which were based there, had the power – infrequently used until the 1950s – to command studios like MGM to change their policies and even films, simply by applying pressure in the corporate boardroom. It was only the financial discipline of the Southern California tycoons, their ability to turn a handsome profit and their fear of the Wall Street honchos that kept Hollywood with a reasonable degree of autonomy. And when times turned bad, New York took over – firing even the all-powerful Louis B. Mayer in 1951.

The demise of the studios

The emergence of the **film noir** style at the end of World War II should have sounded a warning to the old studio system. With bleak storylines, chiaroscuro photography, morally questionable antiheroes and dark endings, film noir was an abrupt departure from many of Hollywood's previous aesthetic conventions. This stylistic change, and the postwar disillusion it reflected, preceded several major transformations that permanently altered the way the studios did business.

The greatest threat to the system, the **federal government**, in its antitrust prosecution of Paramount, was beginning to dismantle the practices of block booking and theatrical ownership that had kept the majors in firm control over the exhibition of their films. The increasing power of independent producers, helped by this and other structural changes, also removed some of the majors' control over the industry, as did the increasing ability of actors to finally use the star system to their advantage by not allowing the studios to lock up their careers for interminable lengths of time (starting with Olivia de Havilland, who sued Warner Bros to get out of her contract and won in California's supreme court after a three-year legal battle). Along with these changes, **television** reduced film viewership by great numbers and the studio bosses had to resort to desperate devices like 3D, Cinemascope and Cinerama to try to lure back their audiences.

Furthermore, the institution that the Hays Code had censored, with the blessing of Congress, began to come under direct attack from McCarthyite politicians. The House Un-American Activities Committee (HUAC) dredged up information on the real and phantom presence of Communist and left-leaning groups in Hollywood, as well as supposed "hidden pro-Communist" messages in certain films, and many screenwriters, actors and directors were either humiliated into testifying or found themselves on an internal **blacklist** that kept them from working.

A case study: Hollywood's first and last major studio

Riding high on the heels of the success of their 1913 film *The Squaw Man*, Cecil B. DeMille, Sam Goldwyn and Jesse Lasky created **Paramount Studios** by merging their operation with **Adolph Zukor's Famous Players**, which owned property across Melrose Avenue at 650 N Bronson. By adopting the Paramount name and merging with twelve other movie companies three years later, the young company quickly became second in stature only to Culver City's MGM. It subsumed the facilities of **RKO Studios** when that company went under, and in its heyday, Paramount churned out more than a hundred films a year, and had biggies like the Marx Brothers, Cary Grant, D.W. Griffith, Marlon Brando and countless others under contract. Moreover, it even possessed a "**house style**" of glossy cinematography, sleek sets and smart dialogue, with impeccable directors like Ernst Lubitsch and Josef von Sternberg helping to define the very notion of the sophisticated, intelligent Paramount film.

Eventually, as with the other majors, Paramount's unique style would fade by the 1950s and the company found itself foundering. By 1967, the conglomerate **Gulf + Western** devoured the studio but later adopted its name to fully cash in on its snow-capped image and reputation. A surprising rebound was soon led by studio executive, and later independent producer **Robert Evans**, who with his freewheeling style and mountainous ego would do much to recall the glory days of the company's golden age, this time in the late 1960s and early 70s. With Evans bringing the studio back to prominence with a slew of commercially and/or critically successful films like *Rosemary's Baby*, *Love Story*, *The Godfather* and *Chinatown*, Paramount regained its stature as a major force in Hollywood. Today, as with its house style of old, Paramount's critical and commercial lustre faded, until its movies now resemble those of any other studio owned by a media conglomerate – faceless, sterile diversions. However, even though it's now owned by another giant corporation, Viacom, the nearly century-old Paramount continues to maintain one unique aspect that other studios have long since forsaken: its original Hollywood location.

After the HUAC proceedings, Hollywood was creatively damaged, but the government's activities didn't keep directors like Otto Preminger from challenging the Hays Code. Through a series of legendary battles, on films like *The Moon is Blue* and others, Preminger and other filmmakers succeeded in throwing off the yoke of the Code, which had been in place for more than thirty years. This change, combined with the diminishment of pressure groups like the Legion of Decency, further loosened the control of the studio bosses over movie content and later led to the late-1960s establishment of the **ratings system** in place today.

The aftermath

By the end of the 1950s, the studio system was finished, and it took many years for the majors to regain much of the ground they had lost. However, while the industry eventually **rebounded** – through greater international sales and the development of ancillary markets like cable TV and home video – and movie-making has become profitable once more to the studios, it's unlikely that the industry will see a return to Depression-era days, when each studio churned out hundreds of films per year and could afford to experiment occasionally with quirky low-budget projects or off-kilter genre pictures.

Currently, Hollywood only manages to pump out a few big-budget spectacles and a declining number of medium-budget flicks – often cumulatively less than fifteen annual films per studio. Modern American filmmaking, driven by exorbitant **talent costs**, is quite different from the old mechanized industry between the wars. With much of today's production budgets going into the wallets of the top actors, many of the formerly essential costs – elaborate sets, casts of thousands and so on – have been scaled back as expensive luxuries, especially on fantasy, sci-fi and historic pics that rely on expensive computer-enhanced **CGI** technology. Moreover, television–film studio mergers, DVD and Blu-ray sales and multimedia production have only served to highlight the differences from the old way of doing business. In one way, though, the studios have reasserted their dominance: by buying innovative independent companies like Miramax, or establishing their own "art-house" divisions such as Fox Searchlight, they have ensured that risky, lower-budget productions come under their direct control, to their direct benefit – just like the old days.

LA on film

Since its birth in the 1910s, Hollywood has often searched its own backyard for compelling scenes and interesting stories. While not always successful in conveying the truth of LA to a film audience, Hollywood **films** have nevertheless helped define the city for domestic and foreign audiences alike. The list below focuses on films that best use their LA backdrop as well as key works in Hollywood film history; films tagged with a ★ are particularly recommended.

Hollywood does Hollywood

Autofocus (Paul Schrader 2003). Memorably creepy portrait of mid-level actor Bob Crane, who played the sunny title character on TV's *Hogan's Heroes*, but was in reality a sex addict who ended up being murdered in a Scottsdale motel, in one of Tinseltown's still-unsolved mysteries.

The Bad and the Beautiful (Vincente Minnelli 1952). Kirk Douglas shines in one of his best roles, a megalomaniacal Hollywood producer whose machinations are described in retrospect by his associates and victims.

Barton Fink (Joel Coen 1991). Tinseltown in the 1940s is depicted by the Coen brothers as a dark world of greedy movie bosses, belligerent screenwriters and murderers disguised as travelling salesmen. Allegedly based on the experience of playwright Clifford Odets.

The Big Knife (Robert Aldrich 1955). An incisive portrayal of Hollywood politics, in which a weak-willed actor can't get free from the tentacles of a hack director, despite the pleas of his wife. Based on a play by Clifford Odets and filmed like one as well.

Ed Wood (Tim Burton 1994). The low-budget fringes of 1950s Hollywood are beautifully re-created in this loving tribute to the much-derided auteur of *Plan 9 from Outer Space* and *Glen or Glenda*. Gorgeously shot in black and white, with a magnificent performance by Martin Landau as an ailing but vivaciously vulgar Bela Lugosi.

Gods and Monsters (Bill Condon 1998). An interesting, fact-based tale of the final days of 1930s horror-film director James Whale, ignored by the moviemaking elite and slowly dying of malaise by his poolside in Hollywood. The title refers to a memorable Ernest Thesiger line from Whale's classic *Bride of Frankenstein*.

Good Morning, Babylon (Paolo and Vittorio Taviani 1987). Two restorers of European cathedrals find themselves in 1910s Hollywood, working to build the monstrous Babylonian set for D.W. Griffith's *Intolerance*, in this Italian story of the contribution of immigrants in early Tinseltown.

Hollywood on Trial (David Helpern Jr 1976). This interesting documentary examines the early 1950s witch-hunts in Hollywood and the blacklisted screenwriters, actors and directors.

★ **The Player** (Robert Altman 1992). Tim Robbins is a studio shark who thinks a disgruntled screenwriter is out to get him; he kills the writer (at South Pasadena's now-shuttered Rialto theatre), steals his girlfriend and waits for the cops to try to unravel it. A wickedly sharp satire about contemporary Hollywood, with some great celebrity cameos.

Singin' in the Rain (Stanley Donen/Gene Kelly 1952). A merry trip through Hollywood set during the birth of the sound era. Gene Kelly, Donald O'Connor and Debbie Reynolds sing and dance to many classic tunes, including *Good Morning*, *Moses* and *Broadway Melody*.

A Star Is Born (William Wellman 1937; George Cukor 1954). Based on the film *What Price Hollywood?*, these adaptations tell the story of the rise of a starlet mirroring the demise of her Svengali. Janet Gaynor and Fredric March star in the 1930s version, Judy Garland and James Mason in the later. (The 1977 remake with Barbra Streisand and Kris Kristofferson is worth avoiding, though.)

The State of Things (Wim Wenders 1982). A European filmmaker sees his financing disappear while stranded in LA and is beset by boredom in his mobile home. Essential if you're a fan of Wenders or of music by the punk band X – then near their peak.

Sullivan's Travels (Preston Sturges 1941). A high-spirited comedy about a director who wants to stop making schlock pictures and instead create gritty portrayals of what he thinks real life to be. The first two-thirds are great, though the film ends in mawkish fashion.

Sunset Boulevard (Billy Wilder 1950). Award-winning film about a screenwriter falling into the clutches of a long-faded silent-movie star. William Holden was near the beginning of his career, Gloria Swanson well past the end of hers. Erich von Stroheim fills in nicely as Swanson's butler, and even Cecil B. DeMille makes a cameo appearance.

What Price Hollywood? (George Cukor 1932). The template for the *A Star Is Born* movies that followed: Constance Bennett is the starlet, an ambitious waitress, and Lowell Sherman is the drunken director.

Whatever Happened to Baby Jane? (Robert Aldrich 1962). Bette Davis and Joan Crawford are former child stars who plot against one another in a rotting Malibu house. A fine slice of horror.

LA crime stories

Beverly Hills Cop (Martin Brest 1984). Still-amusing Eddie Murphy flick, in which the actor plays an unorthodox, fast-talking Detroit detective who takes LA by storm while trying to solve a murder case.

The Big Sleep (Howard Hawks 1946). One of the key film noirs of the 1940s, with Humphrey Bogart playing Philip Marlowe, and featuring a wildly confused plot – even screenwriter Raymond Chandler admitted he didn't know who killed a particular character. Still, there's crackling chemistry between Bogie and Lauren Bacall.

Chinatown (Roman Polanski 1974). One of the essential films about the city. Jack Nicholson hunts down corruption in this dark criticism of the forces that animate the town: venal politicians, black-hearted land barons, crooked cops and a morally bankrupt populace. Great use of locations, from Echo Park to the San Fernando Valley.

Devil in a Blue Dress (Carl Franklin 1995). Terrific modern noir, in which South Central detective Easy Rawlins (Denzel Washington) navigates the ethical squalor of elite 1940s white LA and uncovers a few ugly truths about the city's leaders.

Double Indemnity (Billy Wilder 1944). The prototypical noir. Greedy insurance salesman Fred MacMurray collaborates with harpy wife Barbara Stanwyck to murder her husband and cash in on the settlement. Edward G. Robinson observes on the sidelines as MacMurray's boss.

The Glass Shield (Charles Burnett 1995). Institutionalized racism in the LAPD is brought under the harsh glare of director Burnett, one of the great chroniclers of LA's black urban underclass.

The Grifters (Stephen Frears 1990). A memorable film with Annette Bening, John Cusack and Anjelica Huston playing the title characters – con artists hunting through the LA underworld for their next victims.

He Walked by Night (Alfred Werker 1948). This vérité-style crime story set in "the fastest growing city in the nation" starts with a random cop-killing in Santa Monica and ends with a manhunt through the seven hundred-mile subterranean city storm-drain system, stunningly shot by torch-light by peerless noir cinematographer John Alton.

Heat (Michael Mann 1995). Stars big names like De Niro and Pacino, but this crime drama, which does include some stunning set pieces (eg a Downtown LA shootout), is ultimately less than the sum of its parts, with a predictable ending.

In a Lonely Place (Nicholas Ray 1950). One of the all-time great noirs, and an unconventional one at that. Humphrey Bogart is a disturbed, violent screenwriter who causes trouble for those around him, particularly girlfriend Gloria Grahame – at the time, the director's real-life ex-wife.

Jackie Brown (Quentin Tarantino 1997). A glorious return to form for Pam Grier, who, as a tough airline stewardess, plays the perfect foil for Samuel L. Jackson's smooth gangster.

LA Confidential (Curtis Hanson 1997). Easily the best of the contemporary noir films, a perfectly realized adaptation of James Ellroy's novel about brutal cops, victimized prostitutes and scheming politicians in 1950s LA. Early, powerful roles for Russell Crowe and Guy Pearce.

The Long Goodbye (Robert Altman 1973). Altman intentionally mangles noir conventions in this Chandler adaptation. Elliott Gould plays Marlowe as a droning schlep who wanders across a sun-drenched landscape of casual corruption, encountering bizarre characters including future governor Arnold Schwarzenegger – in his underwear.

Murder My Sweet (Edward Dmytryk 1944). One-time Busby Berkeley crooner Dick Powell changed his tune and became a grim tough-guy detective in the best work from this director, who was briefly blacklisted for his former communist ties, then ratted on his colleagues once he was released.

One False Move (Carl Franklin 1991). A disturbing early role for Billy Bob Thornton, as a murderous hick who kills some people in an LA bungalow with his girlfriend and a psychotic, nerdy colleague, then gets pursued by the LAPD and a small-town Arkansas sheriff.

Point Blank (John Boorman 1967). Engaging, somewhat pretentious art-house flick with Lee Marvin as a hit man out for revenge. Begins and ends in Alcatraz, but in between successfully imagines LA as an impenetrable fortress of concrete and glass.

The Postman Always Rings Twice (Tay Garnett 1946). Lana Turner and John Garfield star in this seamy – and excellent – adaptation of the James M. Cain novel, first brought to the screen as *Ossessione*, an Italian adaptation by Luchino Visconti. Awkwardly remade by Bob Rafelson in 1981 with Jessica Lange and Jack Nicholson.

To Live & Die in LA (William Friedkin 1985). A violent cult film with a plot involving morally dubious characters and counterfeiting, but most remembered for its kinetic car chases and dark portrait of the sleek, cold LA of the 1980s.

Touch of Evil (Orson Welles 1958). Supposedly set at a Mexican border town, this *noir* classic was actually shot in a seedy, decrepit Venice. A bizarre, Baroque masterpiece with Charlton Heston playing a Mexican official, Janet Leigh as his beleaguered wife and Welles himself as a bloated, corrupt cop addicted to candy bars.

True Romance (Tony Scott 1993). With a Quentin Tarantino plot to guide them, Patricia Arquette and Christian Slater battle creeps and gangsters amid wonderful LA locations, from seedy motels to the classic *Rae's Diner* in Santa Monica.

Apocalyptic LA

Blade Runner (Ridley Scott 1982). The first theatrical version may have flopped, but the fully re-cut director's version confirms the film's stature as a sci-fi classic, in which dangerous "replicants" roam the streets of a dystopic future LA and soulless corporations rule from pyramidal towers.

Earthquake (Mark Robson 1974). Watch the Lake Hollywood dam collapse, people run for their lives and chaos hold sway in the City of Angels. Originally presented in "Sensurround!"

Falling Down (Joel Schumacher 1993). Fired defence-worker Michael Douglas tires of the traffic jams on the freeways and goes on a rampage through some of the city's less picturesque neighbourhoods, railing at injustice and wreaking havoc at every turn.

Kiss Me Deadly (Robert Aldrich 1955). Perhaps the bleakest of all noirs, starring Ralph Meeker as brutal detective Mike Hammer, who tramples on friends and enemies alike in his search for the great "whatsit" – a mysterious and deadly suitcase.

Lost Highway (David Lynch 1997). A lurid, frightening take on the city by director Lynch, using nonlinear storytelling and actors playing dual roles – essential viewing if you like Lynch.

Strange Days (Kathryn Bigelow 1995). In a chaotic, nightmarish vision of LA, Ralph Fiennes, Angela Bassett and Juliette Lewis run around the city screaming-in the new millennium. More interesting as a reflection of mid-1990s LA angst than as compelling cinema.

The Terminator (James Cameron 1984). Modern sci-fi classic, with Arnold Schwarzenegger as a robot from the future sent to kill the mother of an unborn rebel leader. Bravura special effects and amazing set pieces were followed up with the director's 1989 sequel, *T2: Judgment Day*, in which Arnold becomes a good robot, and the much less inspired sequels after that.

LA lifestyles

500 Days of Summer (Marc Webb 2009). Utterly charming tale of a romance between Joseph Gordon-Levitt and Zooey Deschanel that fails for the better. Many good LA locations (and discussions of those places), such as the Bradbury and Fine Arts buildings, make this movie a nice visual overview of the modern city.

Boyz N the Hood (John Singleton 1991). An excellent period piece that cemented the LA stereotype as a land of gangs and guns, starring Cuba Gooding Jr in his first big role, and Laurence Fishburne as his dad.

Clueless (Amy Heckerling 1995). Jane Austen's *Emma* transplanted to a rich Southern California high school, with a fine performance by Alicia Silverstone as a frustrated matchmaker.

The Cool School: The Story of the Ferus Art Gallery (Morgan Neville 2008). Striking portrait of the trail-blazing artists who in the 1960s made LA a vital node on the contemporary art scene. The phantasmic work of Ed Kienholz (notably in the DVD extras) is one of the highlights.

Crash (Paul Haggis 2005). An overly sentimental flick that somehow won a Best Picture Oscar, involving characters of various races and classes trying to rediscover their humanity.

Dogtown & Z-Boys (Stacy Peralta 2002). Even if you have no interest in skateboarding, this is a fun, high-spirited look at the glory days of the sport, when a daring group of LA kids took to using the empty swimming pools of the elite as their own private skate-parks.

Endless Summer (Bruce Brown 1966). Still the template for all surf films, a riveting portrait of the sport at its 1960s zenith, when catching a killer break could mean the world, and the waves teemed with legends. Good photography and portrait of the surfing world from one of its movie pioneers.

Faces (John Cassavetes 1968). A vivid, unforgettable portrait of middle-aged angst in upper-middle-class LA, in which a married couple breaks apart amid a nocturnal landscape of dive bars, dance clubs (the *Whisky-a-Go-Go*) and handsome estates – one of them the director's own home.

Ghost World (Terry Zwigoff 2001). Sardonic portrait of alienated high-schooler Thora Birch trying to find her place in a grim LA world of strip malls, pointless jobs and adult lies. Based on an equally effective and groundbreaking comic strip.

Go (Doug Liman 1999). A kinetic joyride through LA's rave subculture told from three perspectives, including Sarah Polley's botching of an aspirin-for-Ecstasy drug sale and Jay Mohr and Scott Wolf – as two secretly gay TV soap stars – stuck in a police sting operation.

Greenberg (Noah Baumbach 2010). Mordantly amusing, bleak tale of a socially inept, middle-aged carpenter trying to start a relationship with his brother's 20-something house-keeper. An incisive look at the lives and manners of the hipster class in contemporary Los Angeles.

The Limey (Steven Soderbergh 1999). Gangster Terence Stamp wanders into a morally adrift LA looking for his daughter's killer, and finds the burned-out husk of former hippie Peter Fonda.

The Loved One (Tony Richardson 1965). An effective adaptation of Evelyn Waugh's pointed satire about the dubious practices of the funeral industry, inspired by a trip to Forest Lawn.

Magnolia (Paul Thomas Anderson 1999). A dark travelogue of human misery starring Jason Robards and Tom Cruise, among many others. The San Fernando Valley serves as an emotional inferno of abusive parents, victimized children, haunted memories and a mysterious plague of frogs.

Mi Familia (Gregory Nava 1994). The saga of the Sanchez family, featuring fine performances by a range of Hollywood's best Hispanic actors, including Jimmy Smits, Edward James Olmos and Esai Morales. Overly earnest and sentimental in places, though.

Mi Vida Loca (Alison Anders 1993). Depressing ensemble piece about the hard lives of Latinas in Echo Park girl-gangs and the central reason the director won a prestigious MacArthur Fellowship.

Pulp Fiction (Quentin Tarantino 1994). A successful collection of underworld stories by cult director Tarantino. Set against a backdrop of downtrodden LA streets, bars, diners and makeshift torture chambers. Arguably the best American movie of the 1990s.

The Rapture (Michael Tolkin 1991). Mimi Rogers plays an LA telephone operator who abandons her hedonistic lifestyle after hearing a fundamentalist group talking about the impending "Rapture", and becomes born again, ultimately heading into the desert to await Armageddon.

Riding Giants (Stacy Peralta 2004). One of the best of the current batch of surfing documentaries, showing the glories of the sport (with modern, high-tech equipment), the life stories of some of its bigger names, and that perennial California backdrop of sun and waves.

Safe (Todd Haynes 1995). In Haynes' brilliant tale of millennial unease and corporeal paranoia, Julianne Moore plays a San Fernando Valley homemaker with seemingly little inner life and an opulent outer one, who is diagnosed with environmental sickness and finds refuge at a New Age desert retreat.

Short Cuts (Robert Altman 1993). Vaguely linked vignettes tracing the lives of LA suburbanites, from a trailer-park couple in Downey to an elite doctor in the Santa Monica Mountains. Strong ensemble cast bolsters the intentionally fractured narrative.

Slums of Beverly Hills (Tamara Jenkins 1998). Troubled teen Natasha Lyonne deals with growing pains in a less than glamorous section of town, where a pill-popping cousin, manic uncle, weird neighbours and her own expanding bustline are but a few of her worries.

Speed (Jan de Bont 1994). Ultimate LA action flick, in which a bus careens through the freeways and boulevards of the city – and will blow up if it slows below 50mph. The first major role for Sandra Bullock.

Star Maps (Miguel Arteta 1997). Melodrama of immigrant life on the fringes of Hollywood. Carlos, who has grandiose dreams of movie stardom, is doing time in his father's prostitution ring, standing on street corners ostensibly selling maps to stars' homes – in reality selling his body for cash.

Swingers (Doug Liman 1996). Cocktail culture gets skewered in this flick about a couple of dudes who flit from club to club to eye "beautiful babies" and shoot the breeze like Rat Pack-era Sinatras. Many LA locales shown, including the *Dresden Room* and *The Derby*.

Offbeat LA

Barfly (Barbet Schroeder 1987). Mickey Rourke channels slumming writing genius Charles Bukowski in this liquor-soaked romp through LA's seedy world of lowlifes, fistfights and general depravity.

Beach Blanket Bingo (William Asher 1965). A cult favourite – the epitome of sun-and-surf movies, with Frankie Avalon and Annette Funicello singing and cavorting amid hordes of wild-eyed teenagers.

The Big Lebowski (Joel Coen 1998). A bizarre Coen foray into LA, exploring the lower-class underbelly of the city – Jeff Bridges' "The Dude" and his pal John Goodman uncover mysteries, meet peculiar characters and do lots and lots of bowling.

Boogie Nights (Paul Thomas Anderson 1997). A suburban kid from Torrance hits the big time in LA – as a porn star. Mark Wahlberg, Julianne Moore and Burt Reynolds tread through a sex-drenched San Fernando Valley landscape of the disco years.

Escape from LA (John Carpenter 1996). In John Carpenter's alternative vision of the future, LA is cut off from the mainland by an earthquake and has been turned into a deportation zone for undesirables. Sent in to uproot insurrection, Kurt Russell battles psychotic plastic surgeons and surfs a tsunami to a showdown in a nether-world Disneyland.

Gidget (Paul Wendkos 1959). One of the most influential films about life in Southern California, for better or worse, establishing the emblematic LA images of teenagers playing in the sun, carefree romance and easy-as-pie surfing. The first of several in a series.

House on Haunted Hill (William Castle 1958). Not the clumsy remake, but the glorious Vincent Price original, with the King of Horror as master of ceremonies for a ghoulish party thrown at his Hollywood Hills estate – actually, Frank Lloyd Wright's Ennis House (see p.83).

Mayor of the Sunset Strip (George Hickenlooper 2003). Great, disturbing documentary about the title character, a former stand-in for one of the Monkees, legendary DJ, lounge denizen and apparent man-child who can't seem to get his life together, despite being pals with people like David Bowie.

Mulholland Drive (David Lynch 2001). Told in the director's inimitable style, a nightmarish tale of love, death, glamour and doom in LA – in which elfin cowboys mutter cryptic threats, elegant chanteuses lip-sync to phantom melodies and a blue key can unlock a shocking double identity.

Permanent Midnight (David Veloz 1998). A grim tour through the city's drug subculture, with Ben Stiller as your heroin-addicted guide. Based on the autobiographical novel by former sitcom writer Jerry Stahl, who was responsible for *Alf*.

Point Break (Kathryn Bigelow 1991). Cult pop favourite set in the surfer-dude world, with Keanu Reeves as a robbery-investigating FBI agent and Patrick Swayze as his rebel-surfer quarry.

Repo Man (Alex Cox 1984). Emilio Estevez is a surly young punk who repossesses cars for Harry Dean Stanton. Very imaginative and fun, and darkly comic.

Shampoo (Hal Ashby 1975). Using LA as his private playground, priapic hairdresser Warren Beatty freely acts on his formidable, though nonchalant, libido. A period piece memorable for its 1970s look.

They Live (John Carpenter 1988). Ludicrous but entertaining horror flick, in which a drifter living on the outskirts of LA discovers that aliens are subliminally encouraging the city's rampant consumerism.

Three Women (Robert Altman 1977). A fascinating, hypnotic, film in which Sissy Spacek and Shelley Duvall, co-workers at a geriatric centre in Desert Springs, mysteriously absorb each other's identity.

Valley Girl (Martha Coolidge 1983). Early Nicolas Cage flick, in which the actor winningly plays a new-wave freak trying to woo the title character (Debra Foreman) in a clash of LA cultures. Good soundtrack, too.

Who Framed Roger Rabbit? (Robert Zemeckis 1988). On the surface a lightweight live-action/cartoon hybrid, it's actually a revealing film about 1940s LA, where cartoon characters suffer abuse like everyone else and the big corporations seek to destroy the Red Car transit system.

Drama and history

The Aviator (Martin Scorsese 2004). In mid-century LA, aircraft pioneer Howard Hughes builds some of the world's fastest and biggest planes, dates Hollywood starlets and battles rival executives and politicians, all while obsessively washing his hands and collecting jars of his own urine.

The Doors (Oliver Stone 1991). Val Kilmer plays the great Jim Morrison at the height of his 1960s debauchery, under the frenetic direction of Oliver Stone.

The Killing of a Chinese Bookie (John Cassavetes 1976). Perfectly evoking the sleazy charms of the Sunset Strip, Cassavetes' behavioral crime story is about a club-owner (Ben Gazzara) in hock to the mob – just one of his many great LA character studies.

La Bamba (Luis Valdez 1987). The fictionalized story of Ritchie Valens, the LA rocker who died in an untimely plane crash with Buddy Holly. Lou Diamond Phillips gives a compelling performance, despite looking nothing like Valens.

Nixon (Oliver Stone 1996). A long, dark look at the first president from Southern California (played by Anthony Hopkins), and the old-time LA suburbs where he grew up.

Rebel Without a Cause (Nicholas Ray 1955). Troubled-youth film, starring, of course, James Dean. A Hollywood classic with many memorable images, notably the use of the Griffith Park Observatory as a shooting location.

Stand and Deliver (Ramon Menendez 1988). Inspired by the story of East LA's miracle-working teacher Jaime Escalante, played effectively by Edward James Olmos. A film better suited for TV than the big screen.

They Shoot Horses, Don't They? (Sydney Pollack 1969). Gloomy story set during the Depression, in which contestants desperately try to win money in an exhausting dance marathon. Aptly reflects the fatalistic attitudes of the late 1960s.

To Sleep with Anger (Charles Burnett 1990). An interesting view of LA's overlooked black middle class, directed with polish by a very underrated African–American filmmaker.

Tupac and Biggie (Nick Broomfield 2002). In-your-face documentary about the murders of rappers Tupac Shakur and Notorious B.I.G., implicating hip-hop producer Suge Knight and rogue elements of the LAPD.

Books

In the **book** reviews below, publishers are listed in the format UK/US, unless the title is available only in one country, in which case the country has been specified. Single listings mean the book is printed in both countries by the same publisher. Highly recommended titles are signified by ⭑. Out-of-print titles are indicated by o/p; books out of print that are available online through sites such as Amazon.com are noted as "e-books".

Travel and general

Mike Davis *Ecology of Fear* (Vintage US). Despite containing certain factual errors, a compelling read about LA's apocalyptic style, focusing on gloom and doom in movies and literary fiction, the danger of earthquakes and fires, mountain-lion attacks and even tornadoes.

Steve Grody *Graffiti LA* (Abrams). If you're inclined to probe LA's poorer neighbourhoods, you might discover many of the colourful pieces of home-grown art depicted here, which the author dissects according to their ethnic, cultural and (in places) gang affiliation. Includes CD-ROM.

Jim Heimann and Kevin Starr *Los Angeles: Portrait of a City* (Taschen). Nostalgic and evocative overview of LA history through a huge number of compelling photos, testimonials of anecdotes, in this coffee-table book that's essential reading (and viewing) for anyone with a taste for Southern California at its mid-century peak.

Robert Koenig *Mouse Tales* (Bonaventure Press). All the Disneyland dirt that's fit to print: a behind-the-scenes look at the ugly little secrets – from disenchanted workers to vermin infestations – that lurk behind the happy walls of the Magic Kingdom.

Anthony Lovett and Matt Maranian *LA Bizarro* (Chronicle US). Without a doubt the best alternative, off-kilter guide to the city: indispensable reading if you're touring LA's dingiest motels, grungiest bars, goofiest architecture and most infamous death sites. Recently updated.

Erin Mahoney *Walking L.A.: 38 Walking Tours…* (Wilderness Press US). A bevy of fascinating treks through the city, from the well-trod districts to obscure places off the radar of most locals and all tourists; well worth the journey.

⭑ **Leonard Pitt and Dale Pitt** *Los Angeles A to Z* (University of California Press US). Needs to be updated (publication date 2000), but if you're truly enthralled by the city, this is the tome for you: six hundred pages of encyclopedic references covering everything from conquistadors to movie stars.

Jerry Schad *Afoot and Afield Los Angeles County* (Wilderness Press US). Some two hundred excellent hikes are presented in this compendium of the long and short, steep and easy, gut-wrenching and easy-going trails that are laced around the city and its wild fringes.

Surfer Magazine Guide to Southern California Surf Spots (Chronicle US). A handy, comprehensive reference to the best places in the state to ride the pipeline and find a killer break – even better, the pages are waterproof.

John Waters *Crackpot* (Simon & Schuster; Scribner). The irreverent director of cult classics like *Pink Flamingos* and *Hairspray* takes you on a personalized tour of his native Baltimore, as well as the seamy underside of Los Angeles.

History and politics

Oscar Zeta Acosta *Revolt of the Cockroach People* (Vintage). The legendary model for Hunter S. Thompson's bloated "Dr. Gonzo", the author was in reality a trailblazing Hispanic lawyer who used colourful tactics to defend oppressed and indigent defendants. A striking, semi-autobiographical portrait of 1970s East LA, written just before the author's mysterious disappearance.

Vincent Bugliosi *Helter Skelter: The True Story of the Manson Murders* (WW Norton). The late 1960s wouldn't have been complete without the Manson Family, and here the prosecutor-author lays out the full story of the horrifying crimes carried out by the gang, inspired by their cult leader, formerly a Sunset Strip hippy and would-be pop songwriter.

John Buntin *L.A.. Noir: The Struggle for the Soul of America's Most Seductive City* (Harmony Press, 2009). A sweeping look at the intersection of governmental malfeasance, murder, organized crime and movieland vice in 1930s LA.

Erik Davis *Visionary State: A Journey Through California's Spiritual Landscape* (Chronicle Books US). A look at the various cults, New Agers and Zen philosophers that have illuminated LA and the state in recent decades, along with older shamans and showmen, all highlighted by evocative, tantalizing photographs.

Margaret Leslie Davis *Dark Side of Fortune: Triumph and Scandal in the Life of Oil Tycoon Edward L. Doheny* (University of California Press US). The best and most comprehensive volume available about a business giant of early twentieth-century LA, covering his rise to power via local petroleum fields, to his downfall in the Teapot Dome scandal.

Joan Didion *Slouching Towards Bethlehem* (Farrar Straus & Giroux US). One of California's best and most polarizing writers takes a critical look at 1960s California, from the acid culture of San Francisco to American tough guy John Wayne. In a similar style, *The White Album* (Farrar Straus & Giroux US) traces the West Coast characters and events that shaped the 1960s and 70s.

Robert Fogelson *The Fragmented Metropolis: Los Angeles 1850–1930* (University of California Press US). Deftly covers a hefty chunk of local history, with significant insight. A sweeping story from the early "Hell Town" to the go-go days of the 1920s.

Paul Greenstein et al *Bread and Hyacinths: The Rise and Fall of Utopian Los Angeles* (Boryanabooks e-book). A chronicle of the doomed efforts to create communal living by some city activists, particularly the socialist and near-mayor Job Harriman.

Lisa McGirr *Suburban Warriors: The Origins of the New American Right* (Princeton University Press US). The tale of how once-fringe right-wing activists in Southern California rose from the ashes of the 1960s to dominate state and, later, national politics, culminating with the presidency of Ronald Reagan and his various minions.

Carey McWilliams *Southern California: An Island on the Land* (Gibbs Smith). One of the most important books about the city ever written, detailing the social clashes and intrigues that rocked LA in the first half of the twentieth century. The author brings special insight as the lead defence attorney in LA's shameful prosecution of the Sleepy Lagoon Murder case.

Kevin Nelson *Wheels of Change: From Zero to 600 MPH, the Story of California and the Automobile* (Heyday US). If you love the glorious epoch of auto worship – and its street, salt-flat and drag racing, modified hot rods and car shows and other shrines to the mechanical beast – you'll love this sweeping overview of LA's seemingly indispensible icon.

Don Normark *Chavez Ravine, 1949* (Chronicle US). Black-and-white photographs and a compelling narrative provide a vivid look at life in a rural Hispanic community on the fringes of Downtown LA, just before the area was paved over to make way for Dodger Stadium.

Richard Rayner *A Bright and Guilty Place: Murder, Corruption, and L.A.'s Scandalous Coming of Age* (Anchor US). A probing history that shows how prostitution, mob violence and corruption developed in 1920s Los Angeles, leading to debacles such as the Teapot Dome and Owens River scandals and tainting the rise of the metropolis.

Mark Reisner *Cadillac Desert* (Penguin US). An essential guide to water problems in the American West, with special emphasis on LA's schemes to bring upstate California water to the metropolis. One of the best renderings of this sordid tale.

Kevin Roderick *The San Fernando Valley: America's Suburb* (Los Angeles Times Publishing US). A surprising and occasionally intriguing view of the history, geography and culture of "The Valley", provided by one of its former denizens. Also good is the author's *Wilshire Boulevard: Grand Concourse of Los Angeles* (Angel City Press US), analyzing and saluting the development of the nation's first "linear city".

Kevin Starr *Golden Dreams: California in an Age of Abundance, 1950–1963* (Oxford University Press). The latest round of Golden State history from the state's pre-eminent chronicler, one in a series of eight such volumes. Of those, the best overall is *Material Dreams: Southern California through the 1920s* (Oxford University Press), on the city's boom interwar years of celebrities and scandals.

Urban theory

Mike Davis *City of Quartz: Excavating the Future in Los Angeles* (Verso). A leftist counterpoint to Kevin Starr's mainstream history (see above). Written in the early 1990s, Davis's descriptions of racial hatred, security-system architecture, shifty politicians and industrial decay have dated somewhat, and his fact-finding methods have been questioned, but there's still plenty here worth reading.

Umberto Eco *Travels in Hyperreality* (Vintage; Harvest). A pointed examination of "simulacra", and a nice literary time-capsule of Southern California life several decades ago, discussing such things as a now-closed museum in Orange County that re-created the great works of art as wax figurines.

William Fulton *The Reluctant Metropolis: The Politics of Urban Growth in Los Angeles* (Johns Hopkins University Press US). A highly readable account of political and economic conflicts in contemporary LA, with notable sections on modern Chinatown and the aftermath of the 1992 riots.

Blake Gumprecht *The Los Angeles River: Its Life, Death and Possible Rebirth* (Johns Hopkins University Press US). The downhill history of the LA River, from its early days as a meandering stream to its final transformation into a bleak, lifeless flood-channel.

Architecture

Reyner Banham *Los Angeles: The Architecture of Four Ecologies* (University of California Press US). The book that made architectural historians take LA seriously, and still an enjoyable read. Valuable insights on the city's freeways, vernacular buildings and cultural attitudes.

Margaret Leslie Davis *Bullocks Wilshire* (Princeton Architectural Press o/p). A long-overdue tribute to the hallmark example of LA's stunning Zigzag Moderne architecture, a Mid-Wilshire department store that's now been reincarnated as a law-school library.

David Gebhard and Harriette Von Breton *Los Angeles in the Thirties: 1931–1941* (Hennessey & Ingalls US). Great old black-and-white photos documenting LA's Streamline Moderne architecture.

David Gebhard and Robert Winter *Los Angeles: An Architectural Guide* (Gibbs Smith US). For many years the essential guide to LA architecture, from historical treasures to contemporary quirks. Some of the quality has been lost with Gebhard's death, so try the 1994 edition (his last) for the best writing on modernist structures.

Jim Heimann *California Crazy and Beyond: Roadside Vernacular Architecture* (Chronicle Books o/p). This fun volume highlights the state's bizarre-chitecture, from diners shaped liked hot dogs to wigwam motels, and the influence it has had nationally.

Sam Hall Kaplan *LA Lost and Found* (Hennessey & Ingalls US). Of interest for the excellent pictures that accompany this former newspaper critic's lament for the good old days of local architecture.

Esther McCoy *Five California Architects* (Hennessey & Ingalls US). This core 1960s book was the first to draw attention to LA's Irving Gill, an early twentieth-century forerunner of the modern style, as well as Bernard Maybeck, R.M. Schindler and the Greene brothers.

Richard Meier *Building the Getty* (University of California Press US). Highly readable account of the conception and creation of the Getty Center, as told by its architect, the prince of modernism.

Charles Moore *The City Observed: Los Angeles* (Hennessey & Ingalls US). Classic volume that's still worth a look for its maps, pictures and anecdotes, plus recommendations to set you on your way to exploring the old-time nooks and crannies of LA.

Elizabeth A.T. Smith *Case Study Houses: the Complete CSH Program* (Taschen). An excellent compendium of essays, photos and articles about the built and unbuilt homes of the Case Study Program (see box, p.99). A huge, expensive ($200) book, but essential for modern architecture buffs.

Music

Clora Bryant et al *Central Avenue Sounds: Jazz in Los Angeles* (University of California Press US). Vividly re-creating the bouncy, kinetic scene on Central Avenue in the mid-twentieth century, and telling a long-overdue story in LA's, and the nation's, musical history.

Barney Hoskyns *Waiting for the Sun: Strange Days, Weird Scenes and the Sound of Los Angeles* (Backbeat US). Ironic, detached overview of pop and rock music history in LA, with well-written perspectives on such seminal figures as Brian Wilson and Arthur Lee, and a vivid account of how it all went wrong – thanks to drugs and violence – in the late 1960s and 70s. Also good is the author's *Hotel California* (Harper Perennial; Wiley), covering the rise of LA-style country rock pioneered by Jackson Browne, Linda Ronstadt, Gram Parsons et al.

Harvey Kubernik *Canyon of Dreams: The Magic and Music of Laurel Canyon* (Sterling). Evocative photos, stories and interviews about the golden years of "the Canyon" above the Sunset Strip, where mellow songsters like Joni Mitchell, Crosby Stills & Nash and the various Eagles would hang out, get high and deeply influence American music in the 1970s. A wistful journey into that famed era.

Don Snowden *Make the Music Go Bang: The Early LA Punk Scene* (St Martin's Press o/p). One of the few volumes on a critical stage in local music history, this book is most valuable for its striking pictures from the 1970s, highlighting such bands as Black Flag, the Germs and X.

Mark Spitz and Brendan Mullen *We Got the Neutron Bomb: The Untold Story of LA Punk* (Three Rivers Press). Long-overdue recollection of the frenzied glory days of the local punk and thrash scene in the 1970s.

Danny Sugarman *Wonderland Avenue* (Abacus; Little Brown). The former Doors' publicist gives a mind-bending tour of the local rock scene from the late 1960s on, providing lurid accounts of famous and infamous figures.

Hollywood and the movies

Kenneth Anger *Hollywood Babylon* (Dell US). Deliciously dark and lurid stories of sex scandals, bad behavior and murder in Tinseltown, written by the *enfant terrible* of 1960s experimental films. Not especially well written, but it holds your attention throughout.

Jeanine Basinger *Silent Stars* (Wesleyan University Press). Great ode to the still-famous and long-forgotten Hollywood figures of the silent era, with biographies that outline the careers of movie cowboys, vamps and sheiks. The author's *The Star Machine* (Vintage) is also good for exploring the way the studio system created movie icons out of unknowns, and how it kept them under tight rein.

Robert Berger *The Last Remaining Seats* (Hennessey & Ingalls US). An excellent photo guide to the extant movie palaces of Los Angeles, including many shots of theatres that are now closed to the public.

Peter Biskind *Easy Riders, Raging Bulls* (Bloomsbury; Simon & Schuster). Fascinating, gossipy account of the great wave of American filmmakers in the 1970s, among them Spielberg, Scorsese and Coppola, who redefined Hollywood cinema as a potential art form while indulging in lots of bad behaviour. The author's later *Down and Dirty Pictures* (Simon & Schuster US) artfully picks apart the indie film and festival scene.

Peter Bogdanovich *Who the Devil Made It* (Ballantine o/p). Acclaimed book of conversations with great old Hollywood filmmakers, including Alfred Hitchcock, Fritz Lang and Howard Hawks. A newer volume, *Who the Hell's in It* (Ballantine US), covers major actors of the Golden Age.

Kevin Brownlow *The Parade's Gone By* (Univ of California Press US). An intriguing look at the founders, stars and pioneers of American cinema in the silent era, as interviewed an esteemed filmmaker, historian and preservationist.

Robert Evans *The Kid Stays in the Picture* (Faber & Faber UK). Spellbinding insider's view of the machinations of Hollywood after the demise of the studio system, written with verve by one of LA's biggest egos and, it turns out, most compelling writers – the head of Paramount when that company was at its modern peak.

Otto Friedrich *City of Nets: A Portrait of Hollywood in the 1940s* (University of California Press US). Descriptions of the major actors, directors and studio bosses of the last good years of the studio system, before TV, antitrust actions and Joe McCarthy ruined it all.

Gerald Horne *Class Struggle in Hollywood: 1930–1950* (University of Texas Press US). Excellent exploration of a commonly overlooked aspect of Tinseltown – the ongoing strife between labour unions and the studios, which culminates here with strike and subsequent violence.

Ephraim Katz *The Film Encyclopedia* (Harper). The essential reference guide for anyone interested in the movies, providing valuable information on the old movie companies and countless studio-system bit players, along with more contemporary figures. The first, 1980, edition is the best – the original author died soon after.

Thomas Schatz *The Genius of the System* (Univ of Minnesota Press US). A laudatory account of the big studios and bosses of the golden age of movies, covering the structure of the industry and detailing the major and minor players. A bit overboard in its praise, but still a very worthwhile read.

Alain Silver and Julia Ward *Film Noir: An Encyclopedic Reference to the American Style* (Overlook). A large-format guide to the bleak films of the 1940s to the present, and an essential title that has gone through many editions. The best of author Silver's many excellent noir-related volumes.

Jerry Stahl *Permanent Midnight* (Process). When his employers on TV's *Alf* heard that star writer Stahl was spending more than his already-huge paycheck to support his heroin and other habits, they gave him a raise to cover the difference and keep him on the job. The result is another gritty descent into Tinseltown drug hell.

Gregory Paul Williams *The Story of Hollywood* (BL Press US). Perhaps the best modern take on the rise and international conquest of America's movie capital – well detailed but also very readable.

Fiction and literature

T.C. Boyle *Tortilla Curtain* (Bloomsbury; Penguin). Set in LA, this book boldly borrows its premise – a privileged white man running down a member of the city's ethnic underclass – from Tom Wolfe's *Bonfire of the Vanities*, but carries it off to great satiric effect.

James Brown *The Los Angeles Diaries* (Phoenix US). Difficult-to-stomach but strangely compelling memoir about life in the dark underbelly of drug abuse, child molestation, arson, suicide and Hollywood striving. A memorable self-view from a talented author and screenwriter.

Charles Bukowski *Post Office* (Virgin; Ecco). An alcohol- and sex-soaked romp through some of LA's festering back alleys, with a mailman surrogate for Bukowski as your guide. One of several books by the author exploring his encounters with the city's dark side.

James M. Cain *Double Indemnity, The Postman Always Rings Twice, Mildred Pierce* (Orion; Everyman's

Library). With Raymond Chandler, the ultimate writer of dark, tough-guy novels. His entire oeuvre is excellent reading, but these three are the best explorations of LA.

Raymond Chandler *Farewell, My Lovely*, *The Long Goodbye*, *The Lady in the Lake* (Penguin; Library of America). All of these books, and several more, have been adapted into movies, but Chandler's prose is inimitable: terse, pointed and vivid. More than just detective stories (centred on gumshoe detective Philip Marlowe), these are masterpieces of fiction.

Susan Compo *Life After Death and Other Stories* (Faber & Faber o/p). The club life of the black-clad members of the local goth-rock scene is the subject here, and the author's prose brings it to life in sordid detail.

Michael Connelly *Angels Flight* (Orion; Grand Central). A sixth volume of contemporary detective fiction featuring the LAPD investigator Harry Bosch, a keen observer of LA's blood-curdling mix of corruption, public scandals and violence.

Philip K. Dick *A Scanner Darkly* (Gollancz; Vintage). Erratic but brilliant author evokes the mid-1990s split between the Straights, the Dopers and the Narks – a dizzying study of identity, authority and drugs. Also key is *Do Androids Dream of Electric Sheep?* (Gollancz; Library of America), which gave rise to the film *Blade Runner*.

Joan Didion *Play It as It Lays* (Farrar, Straus & Giroux US). Hollywood rendered in booze-guzzling, pill-popping, sex-craving detail. Oddly, the author went on to write the uninspired script for a third adaptation of *A Star is Born*.

James Ellroy *The Black Dahlia*, *The Big Nowhere*, *LA Confidential*, *White Jazz* (Arrow; Vintage). The LA Quartet: an excellent saga of city cops from the postwar era to the 1960s, with each novel becoming progressively more complex and elliptical in style. The author's other LA-based works are also excellent – but start here.

Steve Erickson *Amnesiascope* and *Arc d'X* (Quartet Books UK). The two best of the author's wildly florid, postmodern novels about the city, featuring bizarre characters in surreal settings.

John Fante *Ask the Dust* (Canongate; Harper Perennial). The first and still the best of the author's stories of itinerant poet Arturo Bandini, whose wanderings during the Depression highlight the city's faded glory and struggling residents. Made into a subpar film.

Robert Ferrigno *The Horse Latitudes* (Arrow Books UK). A drug-dealer-turned-academic begins a descent into a bizarre LA world when he encounters a corpse at his home, possibly left by his missing ex-wife.

Carrie Fisher *Postcards from the Edge* (Pocket US). The real-life Princess Leia had serious problems: a mother from hell, the pressures of teenage stardom and the unstoppable Hollywood Movie Machine. After caving in to chemical comfort, she cleaned up her act, rebuilt her relationship with Mom, and wrote this thinly disguised novel – a *Heart of Darkness* for 1980s Hollywood.

F. Scott Fitzgerald *The Last Tycoon* (Penguin). The legendary author's unfinished final work, a major novel on the power and glory of Hollywood. Intriguing reading that gives a view of the studio system at its height. US edition features a reconstruction of what the finished version may have looked like.

Chester Himes *If He Hollers Let Him Go* (Serpent's Tail; Da Capo). A fine literary introduction to mid-twentieth-century racism in LA, narrated by one Bob Jones, whose struggles mirror those of author Himes, who eventually ended up living in Spain.

Aldous Huxley *Ape and Essence* (Vintage; Ivan R. Dee). Imaginative depiction of post-nuclear LA, in which books are burned in Pershing Square for warmth and the *Biltmore* hotel is the site of an annual orgy.

Helen Hunt Jackson *Ramona* (FQ Books US). Romanticized depiction of mission life that rightfully criticizes the American government's treatment of Indians while showing the natives to be noble savages and glorifying the Spanish exploiters. Not particularly good reading, but a valuable period piece – and perhaps the most influential piece of fiction ever written about LA.

Gavin Lambert *The Slide Area* (Serpents Tail UK). Seven short tales focusing on the dark side of Hollywood and LA's beachside towns, first published over forty years ago but still absorbing for its urban insights and lurid details.

Elmore Leonard *Get Shorty* (Phoenix; Harper). Ice-cool mobster Chili Palmer is a Miami debt collector who follows a client to Hollywood, and finds that the increasing intricacies of his own situation are translating themselves into a movie script.

Ross MacDonald *Black Money*, *The Blue Hammer*, *The Zebra-Striped Hearse*, *The Doomsters*, *The Instant Enemy* (most titles Vintage). Following in the footsteps of Spade and Marlowe, private detective Lew Archer looks behind the glitzy masks of Southern California life to reveal the underlying nastiness of creepy sexuality and manipulation.

Walter Mosley *Devil in a Blue Dress*, *A Red Death*, *White Butterfly*, *Black Betty*, *A Little Yellow Dog*, *Bad Boy Brawly Brown* (Mask Noir; Washington Square). Excellent modern noir novels featuring black private detective Easy Rawlins, who "does favors" from his South Central base. Mosley compellingly brings to life Watts and, later, Compton.

Kem Nunn *Tapping the Source* (No Exit Press; Thunder's Mouth). One of the most unexpected novels to emerge from California beach culture, this eerie murder-mystery is set amid the surfing scene of Orange County's Huntington Beach.

Thomas Pynchon *The Crying of Lot 49* (Vintage; Harper Perennial). The hilarious adventures of techno-freaks and potheads in 1960s California, revealing among other things the sexy side of stamp collecting.

Luis J Rodriguez *Republic of East LA* (Harper Perennial). Stark, memorable tales of life in the barrio, where struggling romantics and working-class strivers face the inequities of class and race, and gang crime looms ever-present.

Theodore Roszak *Flicker* (Chicago Review Press US). In an old LA movie house, Jonathan Gates discovers cinema and becomes obsessed by the director Max Castle – a genius of the silent era who disappeared under mysterious circumstances in the 1940s – leading Gates into a labyrinthine conspiracy rooted in medieval heresy.

Geoff Ryman *Was* (Gollancz UK). A pop-lit masterpiece that bizarrely updates and twists the *Wizard of Oz* for more contemporary times, creating a fascinating work of Southern Californian magical realism.

Danny Santiago *Famous All Over Town* (Plume US). A compelling portrayal of life in a struggling Hispanic community, set in the barrio of East LA, and featuring a cast of street gangs.

Budd Schulberg *What Makes Sammy Run?* (Vintage US). Classic anti-Hollywood vitriol by one of its insiders, a novelist and screenwriter whose acidic portrait of the movie business is unmatched.

Upton Sinclair *The Brass Check* (University of Illinois Press US). The failed California gubernatorial candidate and activist author's vigorous critique of LA's yellow journalism and the underhanded practices of its main figures. Sinclair also wrote *Oil!* (Frederick Ellis US), about the city's 1920s oil rush.

Terry Southern *Blue Movie* (Souvenir; Grove Press). Sordid, frequently hilarious take on the overlap between high-budget moviemaking and pornography, with the author's vulgar themes and characters cheerfully slashing through politically correct literary conventions.

Michael Tolkin *The Player* (Grove US). A convincing portrayal of the depravity and cut-throat dealings of the filmmaking community, with special scorn reserved for venal movie execs. Made into a classic flick by Robert Altman.

Gore Vidal *Hollywood* (Abacus; Vintage). The fifth volume in the author's "Empire" series about emerging US power on the world stage, this one focusing on the movie industry, its interaction with Washington bigwigs and boundless capacity for propaganda.

DJ Waldie *Holy Land* (WW Norton US). Strangely evocative memoir of growing up in the master-planned super-suburb of Lakewood in the 1950s, written in spare, haunting fragments by a poet who also happens to be the town's public information officer – though you'd never know it.

Evelyn Waugh *The Loved One* (Penguin; Back Bay). The essential literary companion to take with you on a trip to Forest Lawn – here rendered as Whispering Glades, the pinnacle of funerary pretension and a telling symbol of LA's status-obsessed ways.

Nathanael West *The Day of the Locust* (Penguin; Buccaneer). The best novel about LA not involving detectives; an apocalyptic story of the characters on the fringes of the film industry, culminating in a glorious riot and utter chaos.

Karen Tei Yamashita *Tropic of Orange* (Coffee House Press). Successful melding of the apocalyptic, noir and surreal styles that characterize LA, in the form of a vitriolic satire about the media, cultural dissonance and social disintegration.

Glossaries

Architectural terms

Art Deco Catch-all term for Zigzag Moderne, Streamline Moderne, governmental WPA and other styles, often identified by geometric motifs, sharp lines and sleek ornamentation. See the Miracle Mile, pp.71–73.

Beaux Arts Turn-of-the-century movement imported from New York and Europe emphasizing Neoclassical symmetry, imposing dimensions, grand columns and stairways and other features now associated with old-time banks. See the monumental Hall of Justice, p.53.

Brutalist Late-modern extreme architectural style first popularized in Britain and poorly executed in LA, emphasizing concrete, box-like construction and utter lack of ornament and aesthetic interest. See any parking garage or 1960s government building.

Bungalow Prototypical style of home design in the early twentieth century, originating in the Far East but finding popularity in LA for its use of shingles, porches and sloped roofs and compact design. Although it was most often linked to the Arts-and-Crafts movement, many varieties can be spotted with Spanish Colonial, Mission, Continental and even Moderne influences. See Bungalow Heaven in Pasadena, p.167.

Case Study Program Postwar design project initiated by *Arts and Architecture* magazine, which planned and sometimes constructed modern, affordable homes made principally of steel and glass. See box on p.99 for more details, or the Eames House in Pacific Palisades, p.184.

Corporate Modern Bland reduction of the original modern aesthetic, with glass curtain walls, boxy geometry and an inhuman scale. Usually found with towering office blocks Downtown or in Century City, though sometimes inventive, as with the Library Tower, p.62.

Craftsman Early twentieth-century style, using exposed wood beams, overhanging rooflines, large shingles, cobblestones and prominent fireplaces to create a rough-hewn look. See the Gamble House, p.168.

Deconstructivist Architecture that looks as if it's falling apart or incomplete, characterized by irregular shapes, aggressive asymmetry and lack of obvious coherence. See the work of Eric Owen Moss, p.119.

Folk Architecture Homemade structures created by untrained, self-taught builders, the Watts Towers being a glorious example, p.143.

Googie Free-spirited coffee-shop architecture, with bright colours, sharp curves and boomerang shapes, pitched roofs and neon trim. See *Pann's* in Inglewood, p.226, or *Bob's Big Boy* in Burbank, p.226.

High-Tech 1970s and 80s variant on the machine aesthetic, characterized by exposed pipes and ducts and industrial decor. Few good examples survive locally, although the post-industrial Carlson-Reges Residence, p.65, comes close.

Historic Revival The early twentieth-century use of various older architectural styles – notably Spanish Colonial in the 1920s. See box on the architectural firm of Morgan, Walls and Clements, p.73.

Mission Originally the unimposing, ranch-style buildings put up by the

Spanish in the eighteenth and early nineteenth centuries, such as Mission San Fernando, p.180. Later a period-revival style that reached its height with Union Station, p.51.

Modern Clean, geometric design aesthetic, beginning in the 1920s and 30s with houses built by R.M. Schindler, such as the architect's own home, p.102, and Richard Neutra, the Lovell House, p.83, and continuing on to today's Getty Center, p.115, and the more experimental CalTrans building, p.53.

Moderne A popular architectural style that used Art Deco ornamentation and sleek lines to convey quiet elegance. See Crossroads of the World, p.93.

Period Revival See "Historic Revival".

Postmodern Contemporary rehash/mishmash of Neoclassicism, often in pastel colours. See Charles Moore's Civic Center in Beverly Hills, p.107.

Pre-Columbian Quirky 1920s architecture, employing blocky sunbursts, abstract floral motifs and stylized faces to create an ancient look for the modern city. See the Ennis House, p.83, by Frank Lloyd Wright.

Programmatic Buildings taking a particular, nonarchitectural shape, such as dogs, boots, rockets and hats. See *Randy's Donuts*, p.226.

Ranch Quintessential style of Southern California design, typically found in suburban homes with low-slung, single-storey plans, open layouts with few interior walls and abundant windows. Best seen in its grandest form at the ranch at Will Rogers State Historic Park, p.184.

Sculptural Architecture as art, often "moulded" by the architect using computer-assisted design to create structures that would not be possible at a drafting table. Quite striking when successful, as in Frank Gehry's Disney Hall, p.60.

Spanish Colonial Perhaps the quintessential style for housing architecture in LA, especially in the period-revival 1920s, emphasizing tiled roofs, wrought ironwork, whitewashed walls and romantic landscaping. See Villa Aurora, p.185.

Streamline Moderne Buildings resembling ocean liners and sometimes airplanes, borne of a 1930s worship of all things mechanical. See the Coca-Cola Bottling Plant, p.141.

Victorian In America, a general term for late-1800s housing styles – Eastlake, Queen Anne, Stick – few of which remain in the city. See Angelino Heights, p.64, or Heritage Square, p.65.

Zigzag Moderne A late-1920s version of Art Deco that had particular popularity in LA, with strong verticality, narrow windows, geometric ornamentation and occasional use of pre-Columbian or Egyptian motifs. See Bullocks Wilshire, p.69.

Movie-industry terms

Above the line Budgeted costs for actors, writers, directors and producers.

Above the title Adjective or adverb referring to the placement of a major actor's film credit in studio advertising, often a contractual requirement.

Below the line Budgeted costs for camera, lighting and all other technical and behind-the-scenes costs.

Below the title Except for major actors, where everyone else – supporting players, writer, director and so on – gets named in studio advertising for a film, typically near the bottom in fine print.

Block booking Old studio-system practice of forcing exhibitors to carry whole "blocks" of studio films, including many awful titles they would otherwise reject. Since declared an illegal monopoly practice by the US Supreme Court.

Blockbuster Now the term for a big hit, its original meaning meant a film that appealed to all audiences and thus "busted" the "blocks" of disparate segments of viewers.

Box office The money generated by a particular film. Also called the "take".

Completion bond Finishing funds for a film project, given by a financial entity who in return gets some degree of control over the film.

Development The branch of a film company responsible for bringing projects into existence in pre-production, often through working with writers to re-craft their scripts for the big screen and getting notable actors and directors and sometimes producers on board.

Development hell The much-feared limbo during a film's pre-production, when the script suddenly requires multiple, contradictory revisions, prospective actors quit or the studio loses interest. Every screenwriter's nightmare.

Green light A verb meaning to approve the actual production of a given film.

Gross profit The raw financial returns of a film before costs are subtracted, published on Mondays in the trade press and watched eagerly by Hollywood players.

High concept A movie plot that can be summarized on a cocktail napkin, or more specifically, by a single, basic sentence, eg "A chimpanzee detective solves crimes in Hollywood."

In the can A finished film project, symbolically sitting in its reel or canister. However, the term does not mean the film is about to be released – projects can sit "in the can" for years, or never be released at all.

Independent Once applied to small companies operating outside the studio mainstream. Since such companies are now mostly controlled by the majors, the term currently refers to ultra-low-budget films and filmmakers. Also called "indie".

Lens Verb, mostly employed by the trade-industry press, meaning "to film". Possibly used this way only in Hollywood.

Lunch Verb meaning "to conduct business", and the place where business is conducted.

MPAA Acronym for the Motion Picture Association of America, the body that oversees the film-rating and classification board.

Oater Pejorative slang for Westerns – a nearly defunct genre.

Open Verb meaning "to begin playing" and, more importantly, "to draw an audience".

Player 1980s term for an important studio executive, film producer, or top director able to command financial respect throughout town and get a movie project "green lighted".

Points A percentage of profits taken from the gross earnings of a film, often as payment by actors and directors in lieu of salary.

Post Short for post-production: editing, adding sound effects, redubbing dialogue and the like.

Preview Outside LA, a short advertising clip, also known as a "trailer", preceding a film viewing. Within LA, an advance screening of a movie used to gauge an audience's response – positive or negative.

Scale Union-minimum wages that supporting players must accept to be involved with many productions, and that big-name actors will sometimes accept to be associated with a prestigious low-budget work or acclaimed director.

Sleeper A familiar term for an unheralded flick that manages to be a surprise hit.

Turnaround Occurs when a production company loses interest in a film project and either pawns it off on another company or shelves it for an indefinite period.

Vehicle Not an automobile, but a motion picture – often of limited creative value – that is used to forward the career of a major celebrity or rising actor. In the extreme, is known as a "vanity project".

Vertical integration The practice in the film world of owning the production, distribution and exhibition parts of the industry – studios controlling every step of the process. Declared an illegal practice by the US Supreme Court in the 1950s but since loosened by Congress with the rise of cable TV, videotape and digital filmmaking and their financial overlap.

Travel store

ROUGH
GUIDES

NOTES

Small print and Index

A Rough Guide to Rough Guides

Published in 1982, the first Rough Guide – to Greece – was a student scheme that became a publishing phenomenon. Mark Ellingham, a recent graduate in English from Bristol University, had been travelling in Greece the previous summer and couldn't find the right guidebook. With a small group of friends he wrote his own guide, combining a highly contemporary, journalistic style with a thoroughly practical approach to travellers' needs.

The immediate success of the book spawned a series that rapidly covered dozens of destinations. And, in addition to impecunious backpackers, Rough Guides soon acquired a much broader and older readership that relished the guides' wit and inquisitiveness as much as their enthusiastic, critical approach and value-for-money ethos.

These days, Rough Guides include recommendations from shoestring to luxury and cover more than 200 destinations around the globe, including almost every country in the Americas and Europe, more than half of Africa and most of Asia and Australasia. Our ever-growing team of authors and photographers is spread all over the world, particularly in Europe, the US and Australia.

In the early 1990s, Rough Guides branched out of travel, with the publication of Rough Guides to World Music, Classical Music and the Internet. All three have become benchmark titles in their fields, spearheading the publication of a wide range of books under the Rough Guide name.

Including the travel series, Rough Guides now number more than 350 titles, covering: phrasebooks, waterproof maps, music guides from Opera to Heavy Metal, reference works as diverse as Conspiracy Theories and Shakespeare, and popular culture books from iPods to Poker. Rough Guides also produce a series of more than 120 World Music CDs in partnership with World Music Network.

Visit www.roughguides.com to see our latest publications.

Rough Guide credits

Text editor: Steven Horak
Layout: Pradeep Thapliyal
Cartography: Jasbir Sandhu
Picture editor: Sarah Cummins
Production: Rebecca Short
Proofreader: Susannah Wight
Cover design: Nicole Newman, Dan May, Chloe Roberts
Photographers: Dan Bannister, Demetrio Carrasco
Editorial: **London** Andy Turner, Keith Drew, Edward Aves, Alice Park, Lucy White, Jo Kirby, James Smart, Natasha Foges, Róisín Cameron, James Rice, Emma Beatson, Emma Gibbs, Kathryn Lane, Monica Woods, Mani Ramaswamy, Harry Wilson, Lucy Cowie, Alison Roberts, Lara Kavanagh, Eleanor Aldridge, Ian Blenkinsop, Joe Staines, Matthew Milton, Tracy Hopkins; **Delhi** Madhavi Singh, Jalpreen Kaur Chhatwal, Jubbi Francis
Design & Pictures: **London** Scott Stickland, Dan May, Diana Jarvis, Mark Thomas, Nicole Newman, Emily Taylor; **Delhi** Umesh Aggarwal, Ajay Verma, Jessica Subramanian, Ankur Guha, Sachin Tanwar, Anita Singh, Nikhil Agarwal, Sachin Gupta
Production: Liz Cherry, Louise Daly, Erika Pepe
Cartography: **London** Ed Wright, Katie Lloyd-Jones; **Delhi** Rajesh Chhibber, Ashutosh Bharti, Rajesh Mishra, Animesh Pathak, Swati Handoo, Deshpal Dabas, Lokamata Sahu
Marketing, Publicity & roughguides.com: Liz Statham
Digital Travel Publisher: Peter Buckley
Reference Director: Andrew Lockett
Operations Coordinator: Becky Doyle
Publishing Director (Travel): Clare Currie
Commercial Manager: Gino Magnotta
Managing Director: John Duhigg

Publishing information

This second edition published April 2011 by
Rough Guides Ltd,
80 Strand, London WC2R 0RL
11, Community Centre, Panchsheel Park, New Delhi 110017, India

Distributed by the Penguin Group

Penguin Books Ltd,
80 Strand, London WC2R 0RL

Penguin Group (USA)
375 Hudson Street, NY 10014, USA

Penguin Group (Australia)
250 Camberwell Road, Camberwell, Victoria 3124, Australia

Penguin Group (NZ)
67 Apollo Drive, Mairangi Bay, Auckland 1310, New Zealand

Rough Guides is represented in Canada by Tourmaline Editions Inc. 662 King Street West, Suite 304, Toronto, Ontario M5V 1M7

Cover concept by Peter Dyer.

Typeset in Bembo and Helvetica to an original design by Henry Iles.

Printed in Singapore

400pp includes index
A catalogue record for this book is available from the British Library
ISBN: 978-1-84836-583-4

1 3 5 7 9 8 6 4 2

Help us update

We've gone to a lot of effort to ensure that the second edition of **The Rough Guide to Los Angeles & Southern California** is accurate and up-to-date. However, things change – places get "discovered", opening hours are notoriously fickle, restaurants and rooms raise prices or lower standards. If you feel we've got it wrong or left something out, we'd like to know, and if you can remember the address, the price, the hours, the phone number, so much the better.

Please send your comments with the subject line "**Rough Guide Los Angeles & Southern California Update**" to ©mail@uk.roughguides.com. We'll credit all contributions and send a copy of the next edition (or any other Rough Guide if you prefer) for the very best emails.

Find more travel information, connect with fellow travellers and book your trip on ⓦwww.roughguides.com

Acknowledgements

JD would like to thank his editor Steven Horak for expertly guiding the revision of this book and providing valuable input and improvements. Thanks also to all those who have provided current and ongoing help in the research of this book. Some of these names include Marcia Murphy, Allison Goldstein, Lisa Scarpelli, Leopoldo Marino, Aaron Wong, Eric Macey, Dennis Holifena, Kim Partlow, David Cohen, David Rodriguez, Doug Camp, and Michael Grochau. Also, the assistance of LACVB staff is much appreciated. Finally, thanks to everyone on the Rough Guide staff who have worked so assiduously, including Pradeep Thapliyal, Jasbir Sandhu, Sarah Cummins, Susannah Wright, Eleanor Aldridge and Katie Lloyd-Jones.

Photo credits

All photos © Rough Guides except the following:

Introduction

Los Angeles skyline © Ringo Chiu/ Zuma Press/Axoim

Pacific Park on the Santa Monica Pier © Jonathan Alcorn/Zuma Press/Axiom

Angelina Jolie greets fans © AP/Press Association Images

Lifegaurd station, Venice Beach © Naki Kouyioumtzis Ê/Axiom

Hollywood Boulevard © Naki Kouyioumtzis Ê/Axiom

Joshua Tree and granite outcrop © David Muench/Corbis

Disney Hall © Michael Tweed/Zuma Press/Axiom

Things not to miss

01 Sunset Strip © Superstock

03 The Getty Center © Chris Cheadle/Alamy

05 Pacific Coast Highway © Omni Photo Communications Inc./Index Stock/Corbis

06 Antiques shop 'Off the Wall' at Melrose Avenue © Werner Dieterich/Alamy

08 Busker on the boardwalk at Venice Beach © Pete Cutter/Alamy

10 Joshua Tree National Park © Nik Wheeler/Corbis

12 Griffith Observatory © Richard Cummins /Corbis

13 Installation at Broad Contemporary Art Museum at LACMA © Robert Landau/Corbis

14 Polar bear at San Diego Zoo © Jenny E. Ross/Corbis

Sun, sand and surf colour section

Sunset at San Clemente Beach © Design Pics Inc/Alamy

Santa Monica circa 1890 © American Stock/Getty

Endless Summer © Getty

Surfer at Malibu © David Puu/Corbis

Roller bladers, Venice Beach © Craig Lovell/Eagle Visions Photography/Alamy

Surfers, Santa Barbara © Aurora Photos/Alamy

Muscle Beach © David Zanzinger/Alamy

Crystal Cove © Richard Wong/Alamy

The Sounds of LA colour section

The Donnas at West Hollywood's Viper Room © Markus Cuff/Corbis

Couple Monterey Pop Festival © Ted Streshinsky/Corbis

The Doors © Henry Diltz/Corbis

The Beach Boys © Michael Ochs Archives/Corbis

Whisky-a-Go-Go © Wendy Connett/Alamy

Sunset Strip Music Festival © Paul Hebert/Icon SMI/Corbis

Dr Dre © Neal Preston/Corbis

Jane's Addiction © Neal Preston/Corbis

Silversun Pickups © David Atlas/Retna/Corbis

Index

Map entries are in colour.

C

INDEX

D

E

F

I

N

O

P

Q

R

S

T

U

V

W

Y

Z

Map symbols

maps are listed in the full index using coloured text

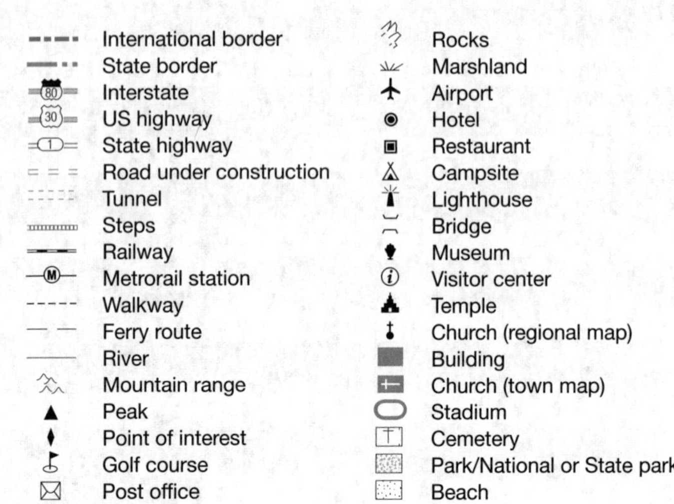

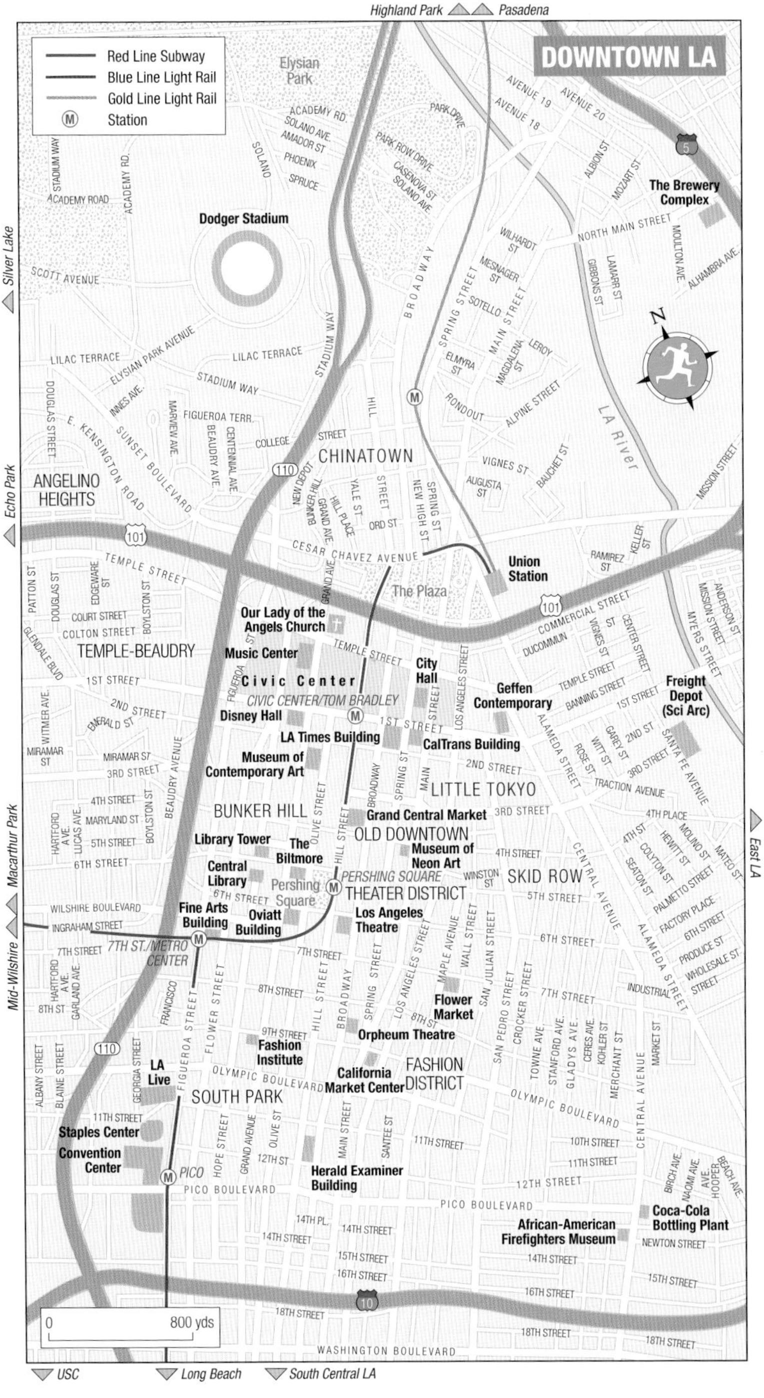

DOWNTOWN LA

- Red Line Subway
- Blue Line Light Rail
- Gold Line Light Rail
- (M) Station

Highland Park · Pasadena · Silver Lake · Echo Park · Macarthur Park · Mid-Wilshire · East LA · USC · Long Beach · South Central LA

Elysian Park
Dodger Stadium
The Brewery Complex
CHINATOWN
ANGELINO HEIGHTS
Union Station
The Plaza
Our Lady of the Angels Church
TEMPLE-BEAUDRY
Music Center
Civic Center
CIVIC CENTER/TOM BRADLEY
City Hall
Geffen Contemporary
Freight Depot (Sci Arc)
Disney Hall
LA Times Building
CalTrans Building
Museum of Contemporary Art
LITTLE TOKYO
BUNKER HILL
Grand Central Market
OLD DOWNTOWN
Library Tower
The Biltmore
Museum of Neon Art
Central Library
Pershing Square
PERSHING SQUARE
THEATER DISTRICT
SKID ROW
Fine Arts Building
Oviatt Building
Los Angeles Theatre
7TH ST./METRO CENTER
Flower Market
Fashion Institute
Orpheum Theatre
LA Live
California Market Center
FASHION DISTRICT
SOUTH PARK
Staples Center
Convention Center
PICO
Herald Examiner Building
Coca-Cola Bottling Plant
African-American Firefighters Museum
LA River

Academy Rd. · Solano Ave. · Amador St · Phoenix · Spruce · Solano · Park Drive · Park Row Drive · Casenova St · Solano Ave. · Avenue 19 · Avenue 20 · Avenue 18 · Albion St · Mozart St · North Main Street · Moulton Ave. · Alhambra Ave. · Lamarr St · Gibbons St · Wilhardt St · Mesnager St · Sotello · Main Street · Spring Street · Broadway · Leroy · Elmyra St · Magdalena St · Rondout · Alpine Street · Stadium Way · Academy Road · Academy Rd. · Scott Avenue · Lilac Terrace · Elysian Park Avenue · Innes Ave. · Douglas Street · E. Kensington Road · Sunset Boulevard · Marview Ave. · Figueroa Terr. · Beaudry Ave. · Centennial Ave. · College · Street · Hill · New Depot · Bunker Hill · Grand Ave. · Hill Place · Yale St · Street · Ord St · New High St · Spring St · Vignes St · Augusta St · Bauchet St · Mission Street · Cesar Chavez Avenue · Ramirez St · Keller St · Temple Street · Patton St · Douglas St · Edgeware St · Boylston St · Court Street · Colton Street · Glendale Blvd · Commercial Street · Ducommun · Vignes St · Center Street · Mission Street · Anderson St · Myers Street · Temple Street · Figueroa St · Los Angeles Street · Banning Street · 1st Street · 2nd Street · 3rd Street · Garey St · Witt St · Rose St · Alameda Street · Traction Avenue · Santa Fe Avenue · 1st Street · Witmer Ave. · 2nd Street · Emerald St · Miramar St · Beaudry Avenue · 3rd Street · 4th Street · Maryland St · Hartford Ave. · Lucas Ave. · 5th Street · 6th Street · Olive Street · Hill Street · Broadway · Spring St · Main · 2nd Street · 3rd Street · 4th Place · 4th St · Hewitt St · Molino St · Mateo St · Colyton St · Seaton St · Palmetto Street · Factory Place · 6th Street · Produce St · Wholesale St · Street · Industrial · Central Avenue · 4th Street · Winston St · 5th Street · 6th Street · 6th Street · Wilshire Boulevard · Ingraham Street · 7th Street · Hartford Ave. · Garland Ave. · 8th St · Francisco · Figueroa Street · Flower Street · 7th Street · 8th Street · Hill Street · Broadway · Spring Street · Los Angeles Street · Maple Avenue · Wall Street · San Julian Street · San Pedro Street · Crocker Street · 7th Street · 8th St · 9th Street · Towne Ave. · Stanford Ave. · Gladys Ave. · Ceres Ave. · Kohler St · Merchant St · Market St · Albany Street · Blaine Street · Georgia Street · Olympic Boulevard · Olympic Boulevard · Central Avenue · 11th Street · Hope Street · Grand Avenue · Olive St · Main Street · Santee St · 12th St · 11th Street · 10th Street · 11th Street · 12th Street · Pico Boulevard · Pico Boulevard · Birch Ave. · Naomi Ave. · Hooper Ave. · Beach Ave. · 14th Pl. · 14th Street · 14th Street · Newton Street · 14th Street · 15th Street · 16th Street · 15th Street · 16th Street · 18th Street · 18th Street · 18th Street · Washington Boulevard

5 · 101 · 110 · 10

0 800 yds

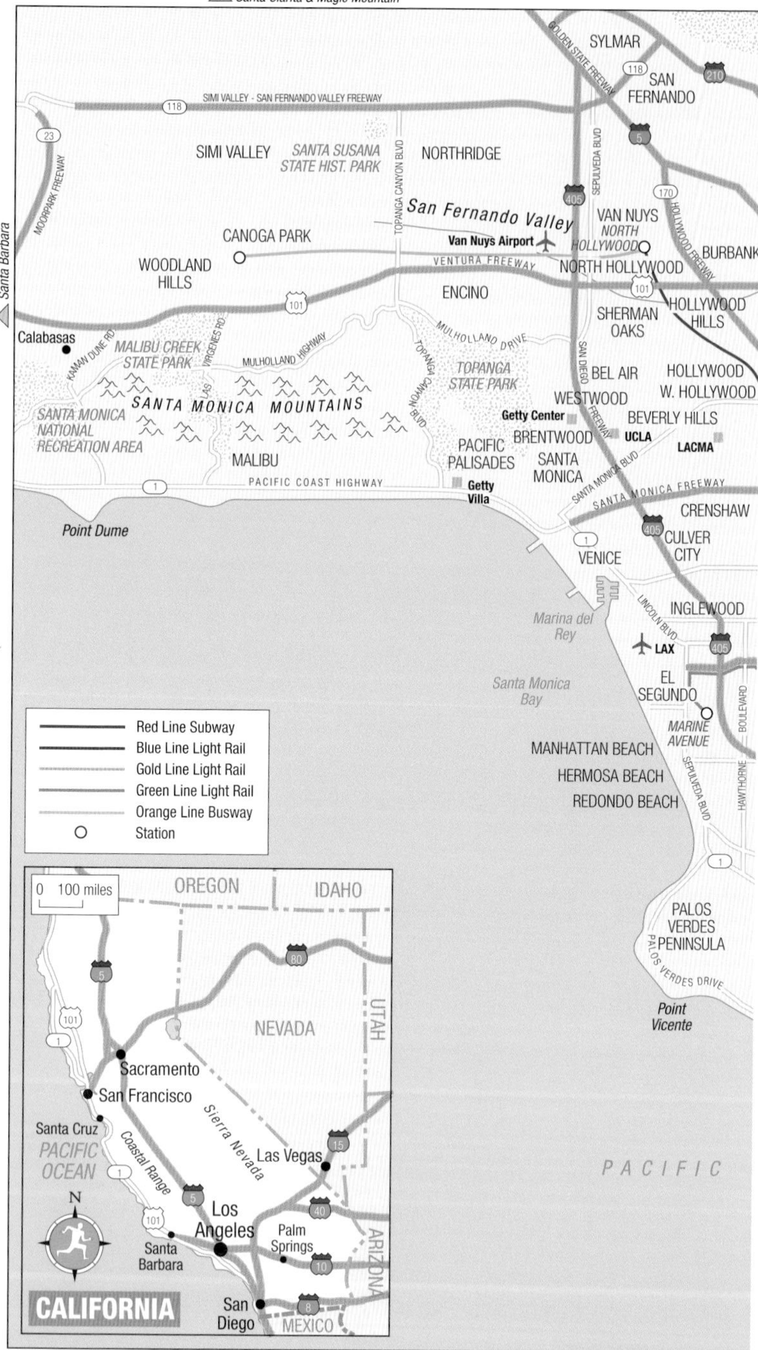

Santa Clarita & Magic Mountain
Santa Barbara
Santa Catalina Island
SYLMAR
SAN FERNANDO
SIMI VALLEY - SAN FERNANDO VALLEY FREEWAY
GOLDEN STATE FREEWAY
MOORPARK FREEWAY
SIMI VALLEY
SANTA SUSANA STATE HIST. PARK
NORTHRIDGE
TOPANGA CANYON BLVD
SEPULVEDA BLVD
HOLLYWOOD FREEWAY
San Fernando Valley
VAN NUYS
Van Nuys Airport
NORTH HOLLYWOOD
CANOGA PARK
WOODLAND HILLS
VENTURA FREEWAY
NORTH HOLLYWOOD
BURBANK
ENCINO
SHERMAN OAKS
HOLLYWOOD HILLS
Calabasas
KANAN DUNE RD
MALIBU CREEK STATE PARK
LAS VIRGENES RD
MULHOLLAND HIGHWAY
MULHOLLAND DRIVE
TOPANGA STATE PARK
SAN DIEGO FREEWAY
BEL AIR
HOLLYWOOD
W. HOLLYWOOD
SANTA MONICA MOUNTAINS
WESTWOOD
Getty Center
BEVERLY HILLS
SANTA MONICA NATIONAL RECREATION AREA
BRENTWOOD
UCLA
LACMA
PACIFIC PALISADES
SANTA MONICA
SANTA MONICA BLVD
MALIBU
PACIFIC COAST HIGHWAY
Getty Villa
SANTA MONICA FREEWAY
CRENSHAW
Point Dume
CULVER CITY
VENICE
LINCOLN BLVD
INGLEWOOD
Marina del Rey
LAX
EL SEGUNDO
Santa Monica Bay
MARINE AVENUE
BOULEVARD
HAWTHORNE
SEPULVEDA BLVD
MANHATTAN BEACH
HERMOSA BEACH
REDONDO BEACH
PALOS VERDES PENINSULA
PALOS VERDES DRIVE
Point Vicente
PACIFIC
Red Line Subway
Blue Line Light Rail
Gold Line Light Rail
Green Line Light Rail
Orange Line Busway
Station
0 100 miles
OREGON
IDAHO
NEVADA
UTAH
Sacramento
San Francisco
Sierra Nevada
Santa Cruz
PACIFIC OCEAN
Coastal Range
Las Vegas
Los Angeles
Palm Springs
ARIZONA
Santa Barbara
San Diego
MEXICO
N
CALIFORNIA

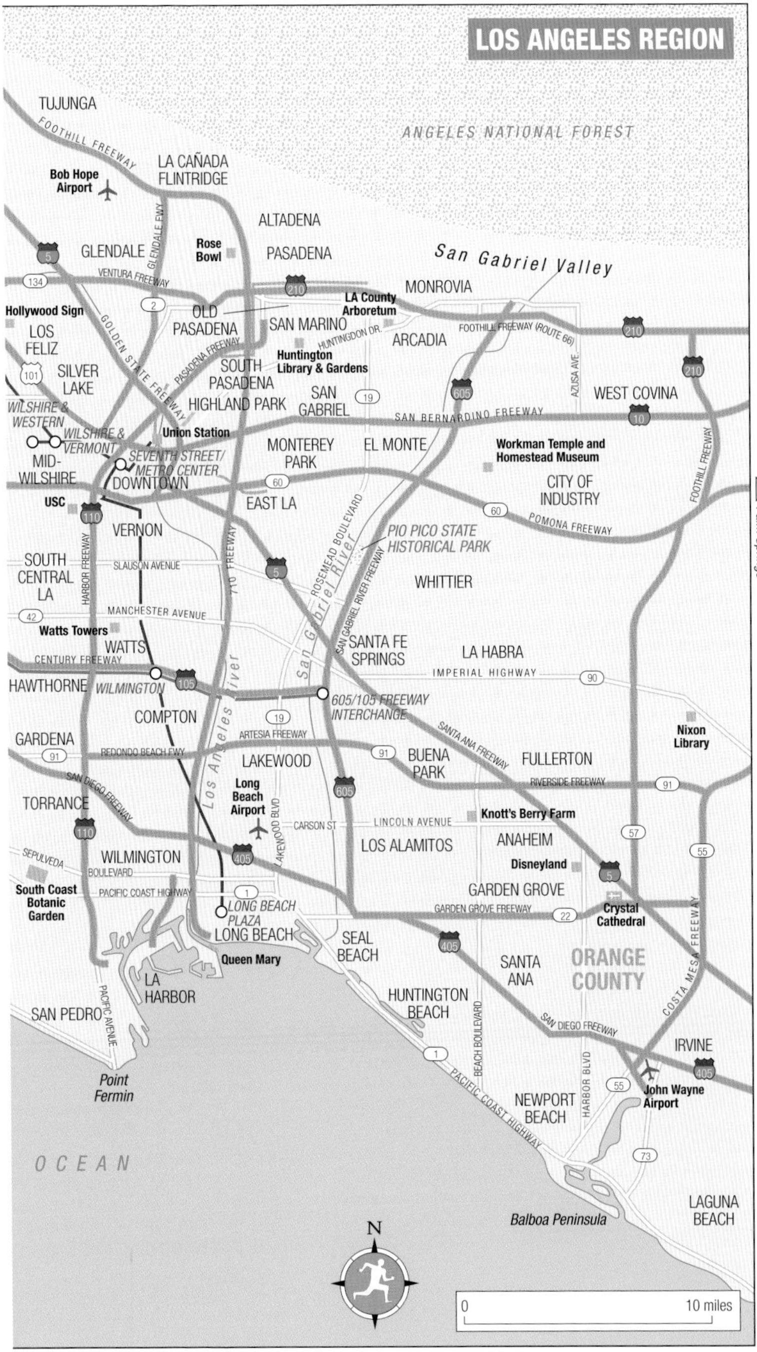

LOS ANGELES REGION

ANGELES NATIONAL FOREST
TUJUNGA
FOOTHILL FREEWAY
LA CAÑADA FLINTRIDGE
Bob Hope Airport
GLENDALE FWY
ALTADENA
5
GLENDALE
Rose Bowl
PASADENA
San Gabriel Valley
134
VENTURA FREEWAY
210
MONROVIA
2
LA County Arboretum
Hollywood Sign
OLD PASADENA
SAN MARINO
FOOTHILL FREEWAY (ROUTE 66)
210
LOS FELIZ
GOLDEN STATE FREEWAY
PASADENA FREEWAY
HUNTINGDON DR.
ARCADIA
101
SILVER LAKE
SOUTH PASADENA
Huntington Library & Gardens
AZUSA AVE.
210
605
WILSHIRE & WESTERN
HIGHLAND PARK
SAN GABRIEL
19
WEST COVINA
SAN BERNARDINO FREEWAY
10
WILSHIRE & VERMONT
Union Station
MONTEREY PARK
EL MONTE
Workman Temple and Homestead Museum
MID-WILSHIRE
SEVENTH STREET/METRO CENTER
DOWNTOWN
60
CITY OF INDUSTRY
FOOTHILL FREEWAY
USC
110
EAST LA
60
POMONA FREEWAY
Palm Springs
VERNON
ROSEMEAD BOULEVARD
PIO PICO STATE HISTORICAL PARK
SOUTH CENTRAL LA
HARBOR FREEWAY
SLAUSON AVENUE
710 FREEWAY
5
San Gabriel River
SAN GABRIEL RIVER FREEWAY
WHITTIER
42
MANCHESTER AVENUE
Watts Towers
WATTS
SANTA FE SPRINGS
LA HABRA
CENTURY FREEWAY
IMPERIAL HIGHWAY
90
HAWTHORNE
WILMINGTON
105
605/105 FREEWAY INTERCHANGE
COMPTON
19
Los Angeles River
Nixon Library
GARDENA
ARTESIA FREEWAY
SANTA ANA FREEWAY
91
REDONDO BEACH FWY
91
LAKEWOOD
BUENA PARK
FULLERTON
SAN DIEGO FREEWAY
Long Beach Airport
RIVERSIDE FREEWAY
91
TORRANCE
605
LAKEWOOD BLVD
CARSON ST
LINCOLN AVENUE
Knott's Berry Farm
110
57
SEPULVEDA BOULEVARD
WILMINGTON
405
LOS ALAMITOS
ANAHEIM
55
Disneyland
South Coast Botanic Garden
PACIFIC COAST HIGHWAY
1
5
GARDEN GROVE
LONG BEACH PLAZA
GARDEN GROVE FREEWAY
22
Crystal Cathedral
LONG BEACH
SEAL BEACH
405
Queen Mary
SANTA ANA
ORANGE COUNTY
COSTA MESA FREEWAY
LA HARBOR
PACIFIC AVENUE
HUNTINGTON BEACH
SAN PEDRO
SAN DIEGO FREEWAY
BEACH BOULEVARD
IRVINE
1
405
Point Fermin
55
John Wayne Airport
PACIFIC COAST HIGHWAY
NEWPORT BEACH
HARBOR BLVD
73
OCEAN
LAGUNA BEACH
Balboa Peninsula
N
0 10 miles

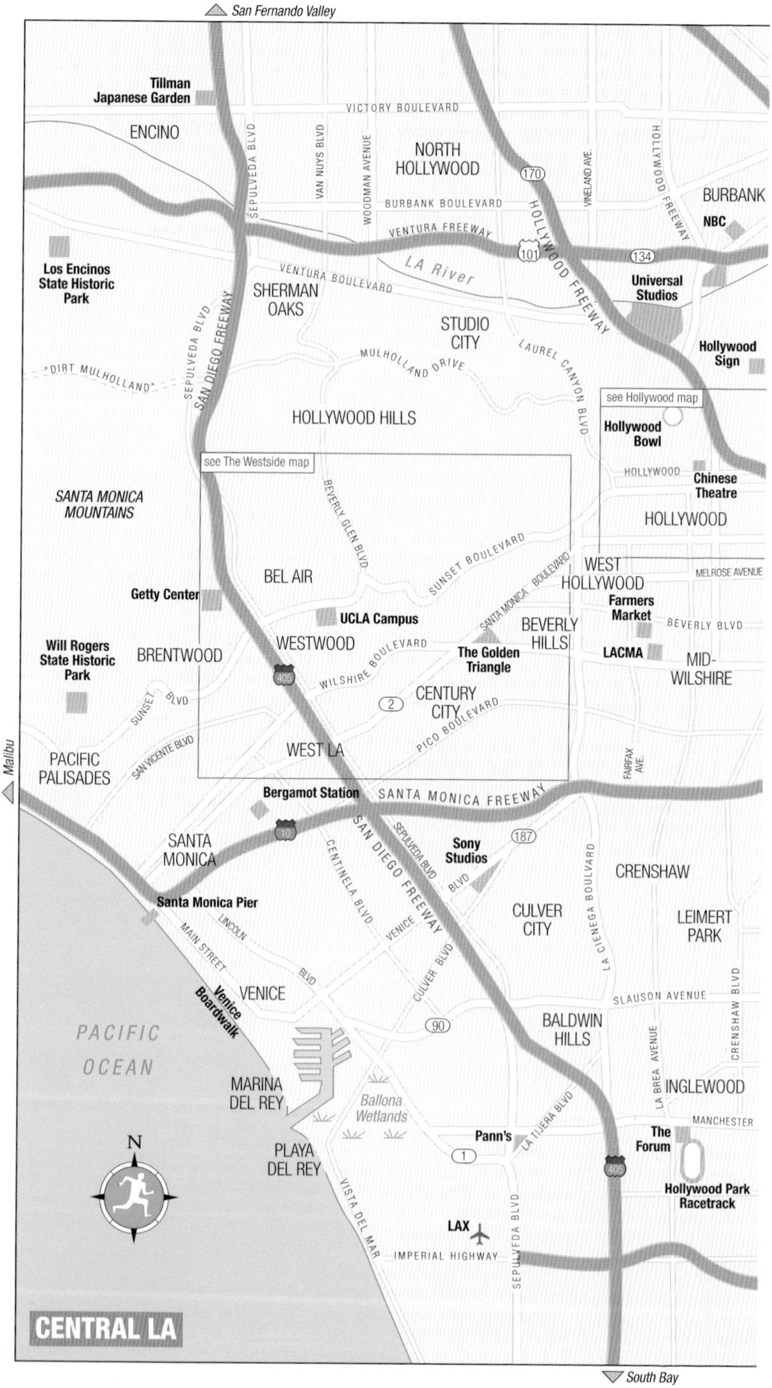

CENTRAL LA

San Fernando Valley

Tillman Japanese Garden
VICTORY BOULEVARD
ENCINO
SEPULVEDA BLVD
VAN NUYS BLVD
WOODMAN AVENUE
NORTH HOLLYWOOD
170
VINELAND AVE.
HOLLYWOOD FREEWAY
BURBANK
BURBANK BOULEVARD
HOLLYWOOD FREEWAY
NBC
VENTURA FREEWAY
101
134
Los Encinos State Historic Park
VENTURA BOULEVARD
LA River
Universal Studios
SHERMAN OAKS
SEPULVEDA BLVD
SAN DIEGO FREEWAY
STUDIO CITY
LAUREL CANYON BLVD
Hollywood Sign
"DIRT MULHOLLAND"
MULHOLLAND DRIVE
see Hollywood map
HOLLYWOOD HILLS
Hollywood Bowl
see The Westside map
HOLLYWOOD
Chinese Theatre
SANTA MONICA MOUNTAINS
BEVERLY GLEN BLVD
HOLLYWOOD
SUNSET BOULEVARD
SANTA MONICA BOULEVARD
WEST HOLLYWOOD
MELROSE AVENUE
BEL AIR
Getty Center
Farmers Market
UCLA Campus
BEVERLY HILLS
BEVERLY BLVD
Will Rogers State Historic Park
WESTWOOD
BRENTWOOD
WILSHIRE BOULEVARD
The Golden Triangle
LACMA
MID-WILSHIRE
405
SUNSET BLVD
2
CENTURY CITY
PICO BOULEVARD
Malibu
PACIFIC PALISADES
SAN VICENTE BLVD
WEST LA
FAIRFAX AVE.
Bergamot Station
SANTA MONICA FREEWAY
10
SAN DIEGO FREEWAY
SEPULVEDA BLVD
187
SANTA MONICA
CENTINELA BLVD
Sony Studios
BLVD
CRENSHAW
LA CIENEGA BOULVARD
Santa Monica Pier
LINCOLN
MAIN STREET
VENICE
CULVER CITY
LEIMERT PARK
BLVD
CULVER BLVD
VENICE
Venice Boardwalk
SLAUSON AVENUE
CRENSHAW BLVD
90
BALDWIN HILLS
PACIFIC OCEAN
LA BREA AVENUE
INGLEWOOD
MARINA DEL REY
Ballona Wetlands
LA TIJERA BLVD
MANCHESTER
The Forum
Pann's
1
PLAYA DEL REY
405
Hollywood Park Racetrack
VISTA DEL MAR
N
SEPULVEDA BLVD
LAX
IMPERIAL HIGHWAY
South Bay

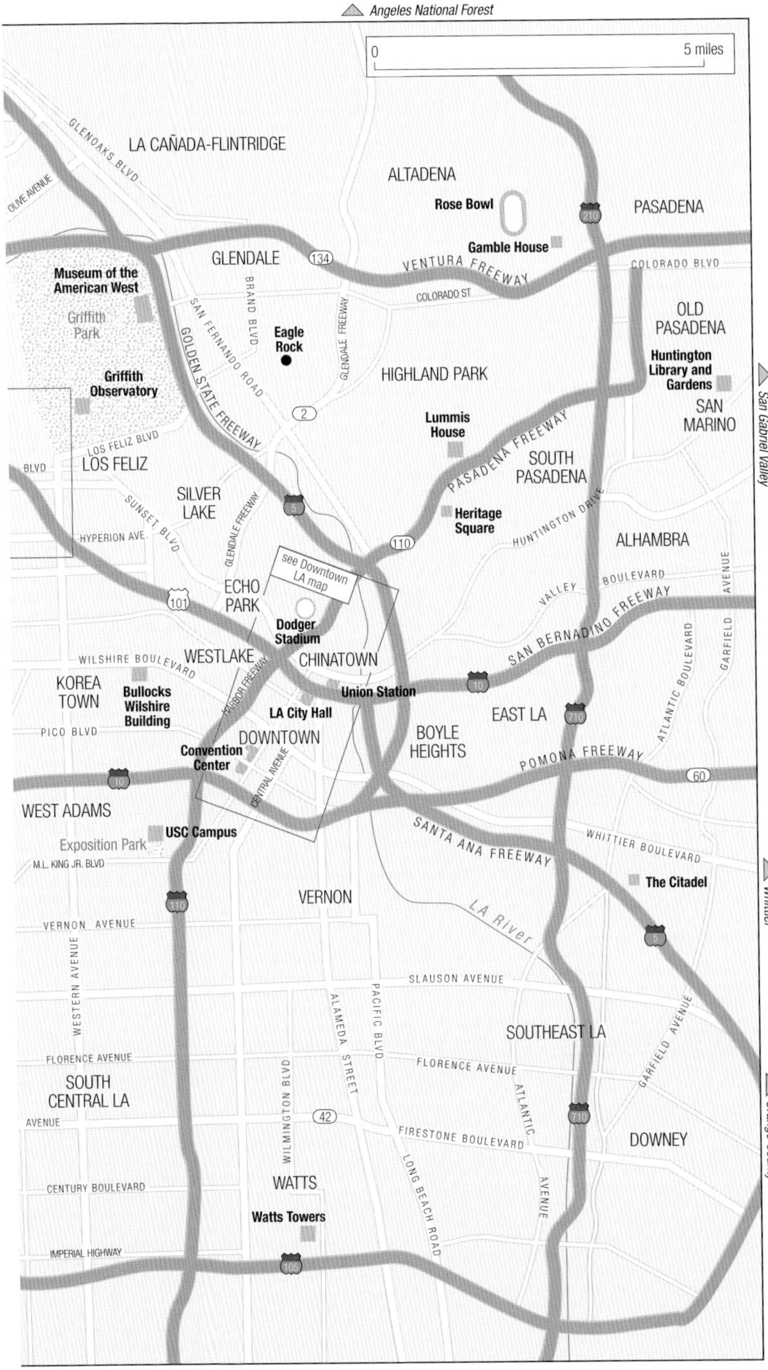

Angeles National Forest

0 5 miles

LA CAÑADA-FLINTRIDGE
GLENOAKS BLVD
OLIVE AVENUE
ALTADENA
Rose Bowl
210
PASADENA
Gamble House
GLENDALE
134
VENTURA FREEWAY
COLORADO BLVD
Museum of the American West
Griffith Park
BRAND BLVD
COLORADO ST
SAN FERNANDO ROAD
GOLDEN STATE FREEWAY
Eagle Rock
GLENDALE FREEWAY
OLD PASADENA
Huntington Library and Gardens
HIGHLAND PARK
Griffith Observatory
2
SAN MARINO
Lummis House
PASADENA FREEWAY
SOUTH PASADENA
San Gabriel Valley
LOS FELIZ BLVD
BLVD
LOS FELIZ
SILVER LAKE
SUNSET BLVD
GLENDALE FREEWAY
5
Heritage Square
HUNTINGTON DRIVE
HYPERION AVE.
110
ALHAMBRA
see Downtown LA map
ECHO PARK
101
VALLEY BOULEVARD
AVENUE
SAN BERNADINO FREEWAY
Dodger Stadium
WILSHIRE BOULEVARD
WESTLAKE
CHINATOWN
GARFIELD
ATLANTIC BOULEVARD
KOREA TOWN
Bullocks Wilshire Building
HARBOR FREEWAY
Union Station
10
EAST LA
710
LA City Hall
PICO BLVD
DOWNTOWN
BOYLE HEIGHTS
Convention Center
CENTRAL AVENUE
POMONA FREEWAY
60
10
WEST ADAMS
SANTA ANA FREEWAY
WHITTIER BOULEVARD
USC Campus
Exposition Park
M.L. KING JR. BLVD
The Citadel
Whittier
110
VERNON
LA River
VERNON AVENUE
5
WESTERN AVENUE
SLAUSON AVENUE
ALAMEDA STREET
PACIFIC BLVD
SOUTHEAST LA
GARFIELD AVENUE
FLORENCE AVENUE
FLORENCE AVENUE
ATLANTIC AVENUE
Orange County
SOUTH CENTRAL LA
WILMINGTON BLVD
AVENUE
42
710
FIRESTONE BOULEVARD
DOWNEY
LONG BEACH ROAD
CENTURY BOULEVARD
WATTS
Watts Towers
IMPERIAL HIGHWAY
105

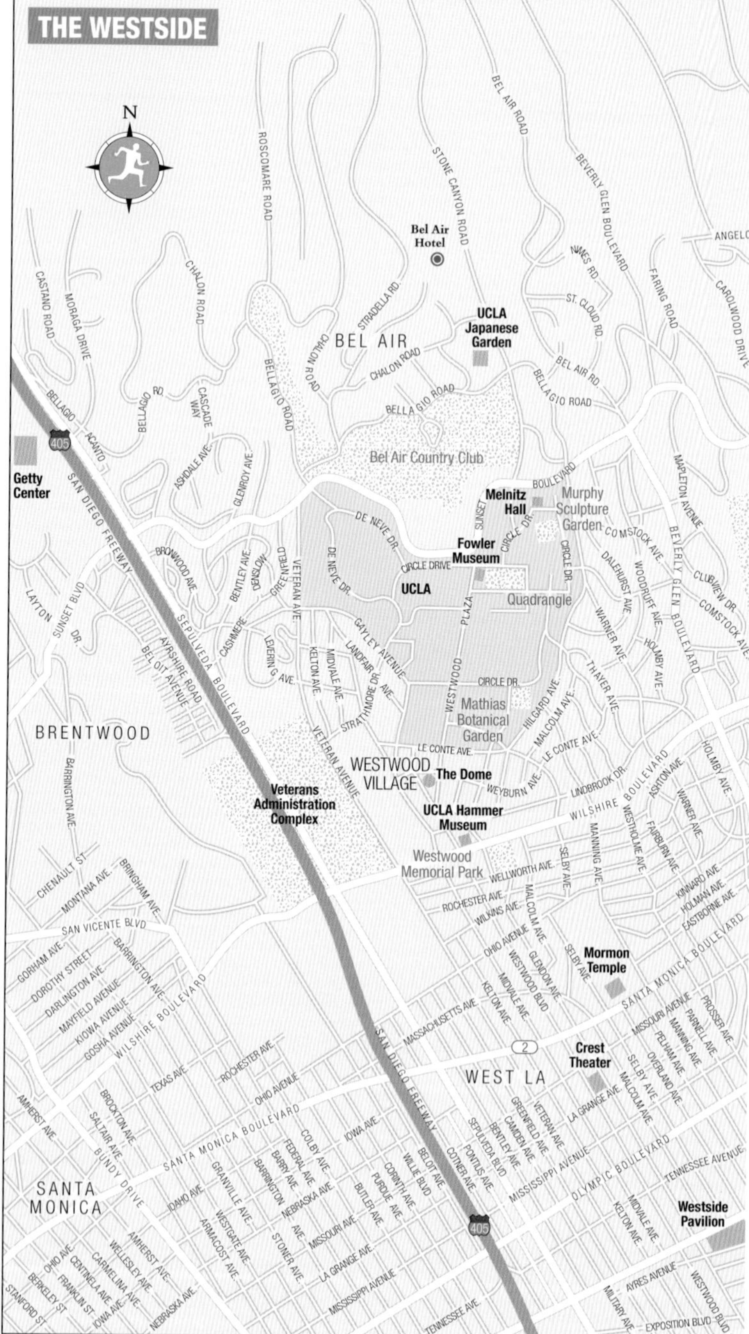
Sepulveda Pass
Mulholland Drive
THE WESTSIDE
N
Bel Air Hotel
UCLA Japanese Garden
BEL AIR
Bel Air Country Club
Getty Center
Melnitz Hall
Murphy Sculpture Garden
Fowler Museum
UCLA
Quadrangle
Mathias Botanical Garden
BRENTWOOD
WESTWOOD VILLAGE
The Dome
Veterans Administration Complex
UCLA Hammer Museum
Westwood Memorial Park
Mormon Temple
Crest Theater
WEST LA
SANTA MONICA
Westside Pavilion
SAN DIEGO FREEWAY
SEPULVEDA BOULEVARD
SUNSET BOULEVARD
WILSHIRE BOULEVARD
SANTA MONICA BOULEVARD
OLYMPIC BOULEVARD
SAN VICENTE BLVD
405
2
Venice
LAX

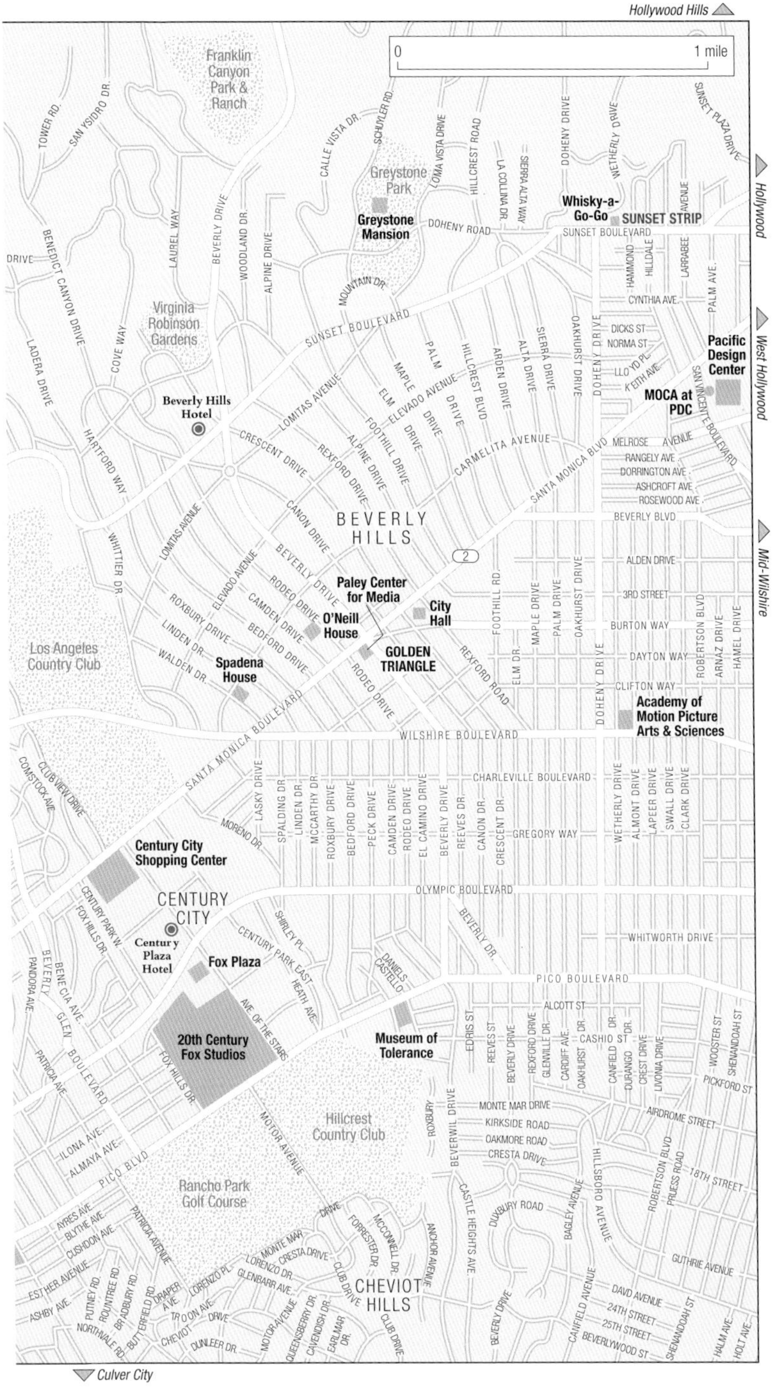

Hollywood Hills

0 1 mile

Franklin Canyon Park & Ranch
Greystone Park
Greystone Mansion
Whisky-a-Go-Go
SUNSET STRIP
Virginia Robinson Gardens
Beverly Hills Hotel
Pacific Design Center
MOCA at PDC
BEVERLY HILLS
Paley Center for Media
City Hall
O'Neill House
GOLDEN TRIANGLE
Spadena House
Los Angeles Country Club
Academy of Motion Picture Arts & Sciences
Century City Shopping Center
CENTURY CITY
Century Plaza Hotel
Fox Plaza
20th Century Fox Studios
Museum of Tolerance
Hillcrest Country Club
Rancho Park Golf Course
CHEVIOT HILLS

Hollywood
West Hollywood
Mid-Wilshire
Culver City

TOWER RD.
SAN YSIDRO DR.
CALLE VISTA DR.
SCHUYLER RD.
LOMA VISTA DRIVE
HILLCREST ROAD
LA COLINA DR.
SIERRA ALTA WAY
DOHENY DRIVE
WETHERLY DRIVE
SUNSET PLAZA DRIVE
BENEDICT CANYON DRIVE
LAUREL WAY
BEVERLY DRIVE
WOODLAND DR.
ALPINE DRIVE
DOHENY ROAD
SUNSET BOULEVARD
HAMMOND
HILLDALE
LARRABEE
AVENUE
PALM AVE.
MOUNTAIN DR.
CYNTHIA AVE.
LADERA DRIVE
COVE WAY
SUNSET BOULEVARD
PALM
MAPLE
ELM
HILLCREST BLVD
ARDEN DRIVE
ALTA DRIVE
SIERRA DRIVE
OAKHURST DRIVE
DOHENY DRIVE
DICKS ST
NORMA ST
LLOYD PL
KEITH AVE
LOMITAS AVENUE
ELEVADO AVENUE
DRIVE
FOOTHILL DRIVE
ALPINE DRIVE
HARTFORD WAY
CRESCENT DRIVE
REXFORD DRIVE
CARMELITA AVENUE
SANTA MONICA BLVD
SAN VICENTE BOULEVARD
MELROSE AVENUE
RANGELY AVE
DORRINGTON AVE
ASHCROFT AVE
ROSEWOOD AVE
BEVERLY BLVD
CANON DRIVE
WHITTIER DR.
LOMITAS AVENUE
2
ALDEN DRIVE
ELEVADO AVENUE
BEVERLY DRIVE
RODEO DRIVE
CAMDEN DRIVE
ROXBURY DRIVE
BEDFORD DRIVE
LINDEN DR.
WALDEN DR.
FOOTHILL RD.
MAPLE DRIVE
PALM DRIVE
OAKHURST DRIVE
3RD STREET
BURTON WAY
DAYTON WAY
CLIFTON WAY
ROBERTSON BLVD
ARNAZ DRIVE
HAMEL DRIVE
ELM DR.
REXFORD ROAD
RODEO DRIVE
DOHENY DRIVE
SANTA MONICA BOULEVARD
WILSHIRE BOULEVARD
COMSTOCK AVE
CLUBVIEW DRIVE
SANTA MONICA
LASKY DRIVE
SPALDING DR.
LINDEN DR.
MCCARTHY DR.
ROXBURY DRIVE
BEDFORD DRIVE
PECK DRIVE
CAMDEN DRIVE
RODEO DRIVE
EL CAMINO DRIVE
BEVERLY DRIVE
REEVES DR.
CANON DR.
CRESCENT DR.
CHARLEVILLE BOULEVARD
GREGORY WAY
WETHERLY DRIVE
ALMONT DRIVE
LAPEER DRIVE
SWALL DRIVE
CLARK DRIVE
MORENO DR.
OLYMPIC BOULEVARD
BEVERLY DR.
WHITWORTH DRIVE
CENTURY PARK W.
FOX HILLS DR.
SHIRLEY PL.
CENTURY PARK EAST
HEATH AVE.
DANIELS
CASTELLO
PICO BOULEVARD
PANDORA AVE.
BEVERLY
BENECIA AVE.
GLEN
BOULEVARD
AVE. OF THE STARS
ALCOTT ST
EDRIS ST
REEVES ST
BEVERLY DRIVE
REXFORD DRIVE
GLENVILLE DR.
CARDIFF AVE.
OAKHURST DR.
CASHIO ST
CANFIELD DR.
DURANGO DR.
CREST DRIVE
LIVONIA DRIVE
WOOSTER ST
SHENANDOAH ST
PICKFORD ST
PATRICIA AVE.
FOX HILLS DR.
MOTOR AVENUE
ROXBURY
BEVERWIL DRIVE
MONTE MAR DRIVE
KIRKSIDE ROAD
OAKMORE ROAD
CRESTA DRIVE
AIRDROME STREET
HILLSBORO AVENUE
ROBERTSON BLVD
PRUESS ROAD
18TH STREET
ILONA AVE.
ALMAYA AVE.
PICO BLVD
CASTLE HEIGHTS AVE.
DUXBURY ROAD
BAGLEY AVENUE
AYRES AVE.
BLYTHE AVE.
CUSHDON AVE.
PATRICIA AVENUE
DRIVE
FORRESTER DR.
MCCONNELL DR.
ANCHOR AVENUE
MONTE MAR
CRESTA DRIVE
LORENZO DR.
GLENBARR AVE.
GUTHRIE AVENUE
ESTHER AVENUE
ASHBY AVE.
PUTNEY RD.
ROUNTREE RD.
BRADBURY RD.
BUTTERFIELD RD.
DRAPER AVE.
LORENZO PL.
TROON AVE.
DRIVE
CHEVIOT
DUNLEER DR.
NORTHVALE RD.
MOTOR AVENUE
QUEENSBERRY DR.
CAVENDISH DR.
EARLMAR DR.
CLUB DRIVE
CLUB DRIVE
BEVERLY DRIVE
CANFIELD AVENUE
DAVID AVENUE
24TH STREET
25TH STREET
BEVERLYWOOD ST
SHENANDOAH ST
HALM AVE.
HOLT AVE.

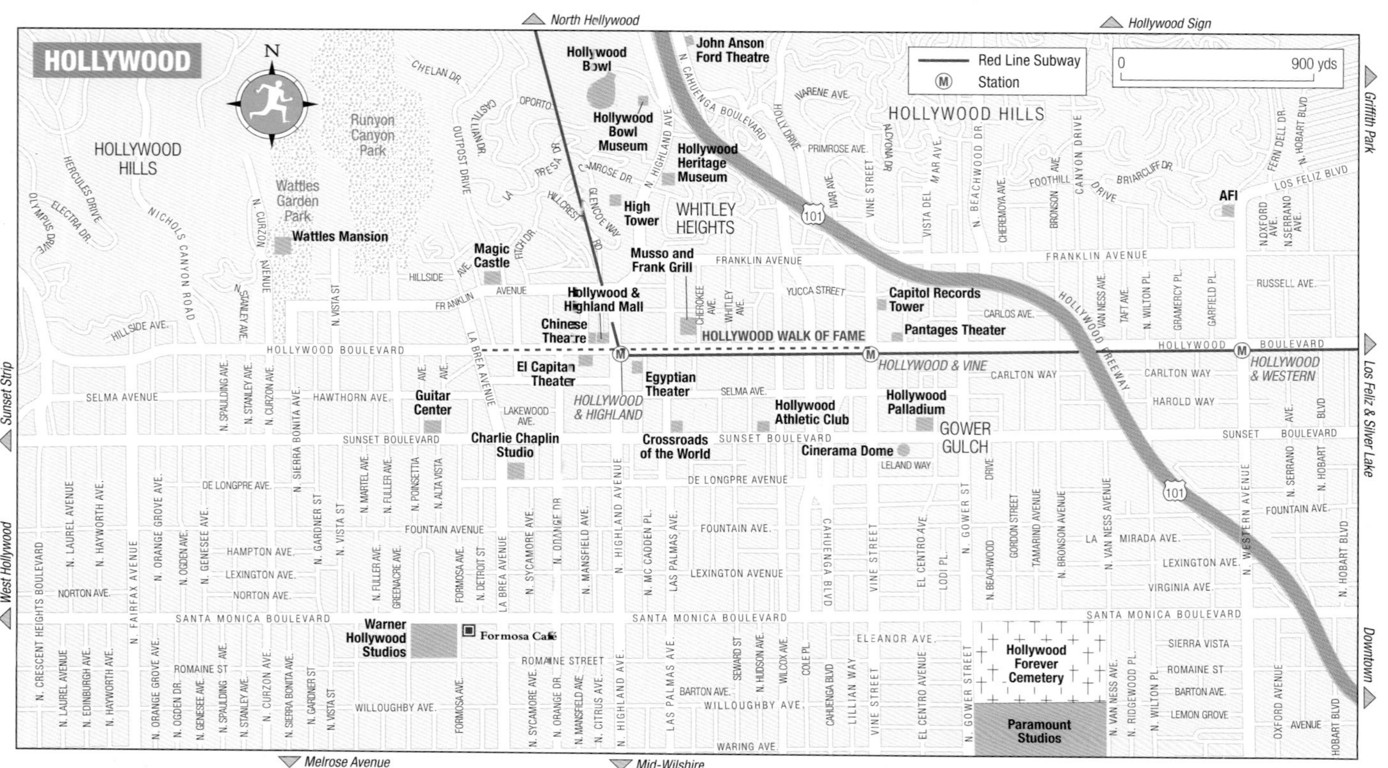
HOLLYWOOD
N
North Hollywood
Hollywood Sign
Griffith Park
Los Feliz & Silver Lake
Downtown
Sunset Strip
West Hollywood
Melrose Avenue
Mid-Wilshire
Red Line Subway
Station
0
900 yds
HOLLYWOOD HILLS
WHITLEY HEIGHTS
GOWER GULCH
Runyon Canyon Park
Wattles Garden Park
Wattles Mansion
Hollywood Bowl
Hollywood Bowl Museum
John Anson Ford Theatre
Hollywood Heritage Museum
High Tower
Magic Castle
Musso and Frank Grill
Hollywood & Highland Mall
Chinese Theatre
El Capitan Theater
Egyptian Theater
HOLLYWOOD WALK OF FAME
HOLLYWOOD & HIGHLAND
HOLLYWOOD & VINE
HOLLYWOOD & WESTERN
Capitol Records Tower
Pantages Theater
Hollywood Athletic Club
Hollywood Palladium
Cinerama Dome
Crossroads of the World
Charlie Chaplin Studio
Guitar Center
Warner Hollywood Studios
Formosa Café
Hollywood Forever Cemetery
Paramount Studios
AFI
HOLLYWOOD BOULEVARD
SUNSET BOULEVARD
SANTA MONICA BOULEVARD
FRANKLIN AVENUE
HOLLYWOOD FREEWAY
101
LA BREA AVENUE
N. HIGHLAND AVENUE
VINE STREET
CAHUENGA BLVD
N. GOWER STREET
N. WESTERN AVENUE
N. FAIRFAX AVENUE
FOUNTAIN AVENUE
DE LONGPRE AVENUE
SELMA AVENUE
LEXINGTON AVENUE
WILLOUGHBY AVE.
ROMAINE STREET
NICHOLS CANYON ROAD
OUTPOST DRIVE
N. CAHUENGA BOULEVARD
LOS FELIZ BLVD
CANYON DRIVE
N. BEACHWOOD DR.
YUCCA STREET
CARLTON WAY
HAROLD WAY
LELAND WAY
ELEANOR AVE.
WARING AVE.